Living Language™

COMMON USAGE DICTIONARY

JAPANESE-ENGLISH
ENGLISH-JAPANESE

D0752391

THE LIVING LANGUAGE COURSES®

Living Spanish
Living French
Living Italian
Living German
Living Japanese
Living Russian
Living Portuguese (South American)
Living Portuguese (Continental)
Living Hebrew
Living Swahili
Children's Living French
Children's Living Spanish
Advanced Living French
Advanced Living Spanish
Living English for Native Spanish Speakers
Living English for Native French Speakers
Living English for Native Italian Speakers
Living English for Native German Speakers
Living English for Native Portuguese Speakers
Living English for Native Chinese Speakers
Living Language™ Spanish Video
Living Language™ French Video
Living Language™ German Video

Additional Living Language™ conversation manuals and dictionaries may be purchased separately.

COMMON USAGE DICTIONARY

JAPANESE-ENGLISH
ENGLISH-JAPANESE

By Ichiro Shirato

BASED ON THE DICTIONARY DEVELOPED BY

Ralph Weiman

FORMERLY CHIEF OF LANGUAGE SECTION,
U.S. WAR DEPARTMENT

CONTAINING OVER 15,000 BASIC TERMS WITH
MEANINGS ILLUSTRATED BY PHRASES AND
SENTENCES, AND 1000 ESSENTIAL WORDS
SPECIALLY INDICATED

Crown Publishers, Inc., New York

THE LIVING LANGUAGE COURSE is a registered trademark, and
CROWN, and LIVING LANGUAGE and colophon are trademarks of
Crown Publishers, Inc., 225 Park Avenue South, New York, New York
10003

Manufactured in the United States of America

Library of Congress Catalog Card Number: 60-15399

ISBN: 0-517-55878-5

1985 Updated Edition   10   9   8   7   6   5

CONTENTS

INTRODUCTION

The Japanese Common Usage Dictionary lists the most frequently used spoken Japanese words, giving their most important meanings and illustrating their use.

1. The basic Japanese words are indicated by capitals.

2. Only the most important meanings in *spoken* Japanese are given.

3. These meanings are illustrated, wherever necessary, by means of everyday phrases and sentences. Where there is no close English equivalent for a Japanese word, or where the English equivalent has several different meanings, the context of the illustrative sentences helps to make the meaning clear.

4. Many important words are followed by the everyday expressions in which they most frequently occur. The Common Usage Dictionary serves accordingly as a phrase book or conversation guide since it contains innumerable everyday sentences which not only serve to illustrate the grammatical features of contemporary Japanese but which are of practical use. The Common Usage Dictionary should, therefore, prove helpful both to beginners who are building up their vocabulary and to advanced students who want to perfect their command of spoken Japanese.

5. In translating the Japanese phrases and sentences, an attempt has been made to give not a mere translation but an equivalent—that is, a phrase or sentence an English speaker would use in the same situation. However, translations have been added in some

places to illustrate more clearly how common Japanese expressions (particularly the very idiomatic and the very colloquial ones) can best be translated into English.

6. The English-Japanese section of the Common Usage Dictionary contains the most common English words and their Japanese equivalents. By consulting the sentences given under the Japanese word in the Japanese-English section, the reader can see various uses of the word.

EXPLANATORY NOTES

NOUNS, VERBS, AND ADJECTIVES. The designation of nouns (*n.*), verbs (*v.*), adjectives (*adj.*), and adverbs (*adv.*) given in this dictionary refers to the word-class (part of speech) of the English equivalent and *not* to the Japanese word.

Many nouns in Japanese can be converted into verbs simply by adding *suru*: (e.g. *benkyoo suru* = to study).

A verb which is translated in English in the infinitive form appears in the "plain present" form in Japanese. Beginners are reminded that when such a verb is used as a predicate verb in sentences, it should be changed to the appropriate -*masu* form -*masu*, -*mashita*, -*masen*, -*masen deshita*, -*mashoo*, etc.

Adjectives are listed in their "plain present" form. When they are used as predicate adjectives, an appropriate form of -*desu* (*desu, deshita, -kuarimasen, -ku ari-masen deshita,* etc.) should be added to them.

PERSON AND NUMBER. An arbitrary choice has been made for the person (i.e., I, you, he, she, it, we, you, they) and number (singular or plural) used in the English translation of a Japanese sentence in the Common Usage Dictionary. Usually a Japanese sentence can be translated in several other ways by changing the person or number, or both.

HOMONYM. In Japanese, there are many words which sound and are spelled alike but which have different meanings. In the traditional Japanese writing system, however, such words may be written with different symbols (ideographs).

COLLOQUIAL AND POLITE. Very colloquial words, phrases, and sentences are marked *colloq*. Very polite words, phrases, and sentences that can be used only in talking about someone else (and not about oneself) are marked *pol*.

JAPANESE-ENGLISH

A

a (*interj.*) O! oh! look! **a to iwaseru** to astonish, surprise. **A taihen.** Oh! heavens! Good Lord!

AA (*interj.*) O! oh! ah! alas! dear me! (*adv.*) in that way; like that; so; **aa suru** to do so (like that); **aa iu** to say so; like that; **aa iu hito** a man like that; **aa iu koto** a thing like that; **aa iu fúu na hito** that sort of man; **aa iu fúu ni** in that way; like that. **Aa kírei da!** Oh, how beautiful! **Aa omoshírokatta.** Oh, it was so interesting! **Aa sóo?** Really? Is it? Did you?

áachi arch; arch of green leaves.

aa iu = **aa yuu** that sort of; **aa iu koto** that sort of thing; **aa iu hanashi** that sort of story.

aakutoo arc light, arc lamp.

áasu ground wire.

abáku to disclose, to reveal (*a secret*); to expose; to bring to light.

abara ribs; side; **abara bone** rib, side of the chest.

abaráya crumbling house; poor hut.

abare- prefix denoting: rough; rowdy; unruly; **abareuma** runaway horse; **abaredásu** to get rowdy, riotous; to break loose; grow restive; to start to behave violently; **abarekko** unruly boy; naughty child; imp; **abarekómu** to force oneself into, burst into, break into; **abaremawáru** to rave, to run amuck; to riot; **heyá ni abarekómu** to force an entrance into a room; **ié ni abarekómu** to break into a house.

abaremono (*n.*) rowdy; hooligan.

abareru to act (behave) violently; to rage; to be riotous.

abekobe (*n.*) being topsy-turvy; **abekobe no** opposite; inverse; **abekobe ni** in a contrary manner; upside down.

abiru to pour on oneself; to bathe in; to be under fire; **hítofuro abiru** to have a bath; **chuumoku o abiru** to receive attention.

abisekakéru see **abiseru.**

abiseru = **abisekakéru** to pour on; to shower; to lay (something) on; to heap reproaches on.

ábu horsefly; gadfly.

abuku = **awa** bubble; froth, foam, suds.

abunage insecurity; unreliability.

ABUNAI dangerous, risky, precarious; critical; **abunai mé ni áu** to have a terrible experience. **Abunái!** Look out! Watch out!

abunakkashíi insecure, unsteady; unstable; unreliable; **abunakkashíi tétsuki de** in a clumsy manner,

ABUNAKU nearly; barely; **abunaku náru** to get dangerous. **Abunaku okureru tokoró deshita.** I almost missed the train.

abunasa danger, risk, peril; **abunasoo na** dangerous-looking.

ABURA oil; fat; **aburadárake** covered with grease; oil-stained; **abura de ageru** to fry in oil; **abura ga noru** to become interested in; **aburaáse** greasy sweat; **aburaáse o nagáshite** by the sweat of one's brow; **aburake no áru** oily, fatty, rich (food); **aburake no nái** lean; light; **aburakkéi** greasy, fatty, oily (food). **Aburakkói mono ga sukí desu.** I like greasy foods.

aburáe oil painting; **aburáe o káku** to paint in oils.

aburágami oiled paper (used for wrapping parcels, etc.).

aburáage = **age** bean curd fried in oil (popular food item).

aburagúsuri liniment; ointment.

aburámi fat; fatty part of meat.

aburámushi cockroach

abúru to place over a fire; to grill; to warm; to dry; **té o abúru** to warm one's hands at a fire.

achikóchi (*adv.*) = **achira kóchira** here and there; to and fro.

ACHIRA (*n.*) that direction; other side; over there; overseas; abroad; **achira no shuukan** customs of a foreign country. **Achira e ikimashóo.** Let's go that way.

ACHIRA KÓCHIRA (*n.*, *adv.*) here and there; various places; to and fro; up and down; **achira kóchira kara** from far and near; **achira kóchira o sagasu** to look for (something) here and there; **achira kóchira inaka o ryokoo suru** to travel about the country.

adá enemy; revenge; vengeance; resentment; harm.

ÁDAKAMO = **átakamo** just; just as if; so to speak; **ádakamo Nihonjín no yóo ni** just as if he were a Japanese.

adana nickname.

adokenái innocent, artless; naïve (*used when speaking of a child*); **adokenái yóosu** naïve manner; innocent air.

aegi pant; gasp; **aegi aegi** gaspingly; out of breath; **aégu** to pant; to gasp.

aen zinc.

AENAI untimely; sad; pitiful; **aenái saigo** pitiful end (death); **aenái saigo o togéru** to come to a sad end.

aénaku sadly; unexpectedly; flatly; **aénaku kotowáru** to refuse flatly; **aénaku naru** to die.

áete (*adv.*) boldly; without hesitation; by any means; **áete suru** to dare, venture; **áete iu** I presume; I venture to say.

afuréru to overflow, run over.

agáku to paw; to struggle; to worry.

agaméru to revere; to worship; to respect; to glorify.

aganai atonement; redemption; compensation.

AGANÁU to buy, purchase.

agaridaka proceeds; yield; produce.

agaridan staircase.

AGARIGUCHI entranceway in a Japanese-style house.

agaríori (*n.*) ascent and descent; **kaidan no agaríori** going up and down the staircase.

agarisagari rise and fall; fluctuation; **nedan no agarisagari** fluctuation of prices.

AGARU to go up, come up; to rise; to ascend, climb (up); to rise in rank; to improve; to come to an end; to visit; to go ashore; to eat, drink (honorific: used only for the second or third person); to become nervous; **chíi ga agaru** to be promoted. **udé ga agaru** to become more skillful. **áme ga agaru** to stop raining; **riku ni agaru** to go ashore. **Shigoto ga yatto deki agaru.** The work is completed at last. **Mata agaimashóo.** I will call again. **Okashi o oagari kudasái.** Help yourself to the sweet, please. **Pitchaa ga agaru.** The pitcher (*baseball*) is getting nervous.

age tuck (in Japanese clothes); = **aburáage** (fried bean curd).

ageashi fault-finding; hypercriticism.

AGEKU (*adv.*) = **ageku ni; ageku no hate ni** the end; finally, at last; on top of all this; to make matters worse. **Shigoto o nakushita ageku ni byooki ni natta.** He lost his job, and on top of that (to make matters worse), he became ill.

agemono fried food.

agenabe frying pan.

ageoroshi = **agésage** loading and unloading; raising and lowering; **hashi no ageoroshi ni mo kogoto o iu** to find fault with everything [to make comments even on how the chopsticks are handled].

AGERU to raise, elevate, lift (up); to give, present (honorific: used when the speaker gives something to someone else). **Okane o ageta.** I gave him some money.

agésage = **ageoroshi** raising and lowering; praise and blame; **háshi no agésage ni mo kogoto o iu** to be (too) particular about trifles.

ageshio flood (rising) tide.

AGÓ jaw; chin.

-agúmu suffix denoting: to grow tired of, get (become) weary; **machiagúmu** to grow tired of waiting.

agura o káku to sit cross-legged.

ahen opium

ahiru duck, drake; **ahiru no ko** duckling.

ahóo fool; idiot; blockhead; **ahóo na** foolish; stupid; **ahorashíi** foolish; silly; ridiculous; **ahóo na koto** foolish affair.

ÁI love; affection; attachment; **ai súru** to love; care for; **fukáku ai suru** to love tenderly (deeply).

ái indigo, blue; **ai-iro no** blue, bluish; **ai nézumi** bluish-gray.

ai- *prefix denoting*: mutually; with each other; **ai-mukatte** face to face; **ai-narande tátsu** to stand shoulder to shoulder.

aibiki secret meeting (of lovers); rendezvous.

aiboo partner; accomplice.

aibu caress; fondling; **aibu suru** to caress, fondle, pet.

aichaku deep attachment; passion;—**ni aichaku suru** to love passionately.

AIDA space (between); time (between); distance; interval; **sono aida** in the meanwhile; **nagai aida** for a long time; **hitotsuki no aida ni** in the course of a month; **watakushi ga ikite iru aida wa** as long as I live; **roppun no aida o oite** at intervals of six minutes.

aidagara relationship; terms; **shitashii aidagara de aru** to be on very friendly terms.

aidoku suru to read for pleasure; **aidokusha** subscriber; reader; reading public; **aidokusho** one's favorite book.

aifuku, aigi lightweight suit.

aijin lover, sweetheart; **aijoo** love, affection; **aijoo no aru hito** affectionate; warmhearted.

aikagi passkey.

AIKAWARAZU as usual; as always; **aikawarazu isogashii desu** as busy as ever.

aiko a tie, even game, draw; **aiko ni naru** to end in a tie. **Kore de aiko da.** This makes us even.

aikuchi dagger.

aikyóo charm; amiability; **aikyóo no áru hito** charming, amiable person; **aikyóo no nái hito** disagreeable person; **aikyóo o furimáku** to have a smile for everybody.

aima interval; leisure; **aima ni** at intervals; **shigoto no aima ni** in one's spare time.

aimai obscurity; ambiguity; **aimai na** obscure; ambiguous; vague.

AINIKU unluckily; unfortunately; **ainiku na** unfavorable; unfortunate. **Oainiku sama.** I am very sorry (that I do not have it). **Ainiku áme ga futte kimásiia.** Unfortunately, it started to rain.

ainoko (*n.*) hybrid; Eurasian.

Ainu Ainus (a minority tribe of northern Japan).

airashíi charming; amiable; sweet.

AIRON iron (for pressing), flatiron; **airon o kakéru** to iron.

áisatsu greeting, salutation; **áisatsu suru** to greet, salute.

aiso sociability, cordiality; **aiso no yói** sociable, cordial; **aiso no nái hito** cold, blunt person; **oaisó o iu** to flatter;—**ni aisó ga tsukiru** to be disgusted with. **Aiso yóku hanashimáshita.** He spoke very pleasantly.

aisukuriimu ice cream.

aita empty, vacant; opened; **té ga aita tóki** when he is free.

áitagai ni with each other.

AITE companion; partner; adversary;—**o aité**

ni suru to challenge, deal with;—**o aité ni shinai** to pay no attention to;—**no nái ni náru** to keep company with; to become a partner of.

aitsu that fellow; that rascal (derogatory).

áitsuide one after another; successively.

áizu signal; **áizu suru** to signal.

áji horse mackerel, tunny.

AJI taste, flavor; relish; **aji no áru** tasty; **aji no nái** tasteless;—**no aji ga suru** it tastes like; **aji ga kawaru** to become stale, turn sour; **aji o tsukéru** to flavor, season.

ÁJIA Asia; **Ájia no** (*adj.*) Asian, Asiatic; **Ajiájin** (*n.*) Asian, Asiatic.

ajikinái irksome, wearisome; lonely; **ajikináku kurasu** to lead a miserable life.

ajina dainty; clever; smart; **ajina kóto o suru** to act cleverly; **ajina kóto o iu** to say something clever.

ajisai hydrangea.

ajitsukénori seasoned seaweed (a popular food item).

ajiwáu to taste; to experience; to enjoy; to appreciate.

ÁKA (*n.*) red, crimson, scarlet; communism; communist; **akaku náru** to turn red, redden, blush; **áka no tanin** utter stranger.

aká dirt, filth; **aka dárake** dirty, filthy;—**ni aka ga tsuku** to become dirty; **aká o nagásu** to wash off dirt; to wash (oneself).

AKABOO redcap, porter (for luggage).

ÁKACHAN = **akago** baby, infant.

akaden redlight car (last trolley of the day).

akagétto "red blanket," country bumpkin; rustic sightseers (who formerly used red blankets as overcoats when in town).

akagire chap, crack (in the skin); **akagire ga kiréru** to become chapped.

akágo See **ákachan**.

akahádaka nakedness, nudity; **akahádaka no** nude, stark naked; **akahádaka ni náru** to strip naked; to become penniless; **akahádaka ni sareru** to be stripped naked; to be shorn of all possessions.

akahaji disgrace; open shame; **akahaji o kakasaréru** to be put to shame.

AKAI red, ruddy, flushed; **akai kao o suru** to blush.

akaji red figures, deficit; **akaji o dásu** to go into the red; to have a deficit.

akajímita soiled, dirty.

akaku ruddily; redly; **akaku náru** to redden; to flush; to glow; to join the Communist Party (colloq.).

akanboo baby, infant. (See also **ákachan**).

akami redness; tinge of red; lean meat.

Akamon Red Gate of Tokyo University; synonym for Tokyo University.

aka no góhan rice boiled with red beans (served on ceremonious occasions).

akanuke polish, gloss; refinement; **akanuke no shita hito** polished person; **akanuke no shinai hito** unpolished, uncouth person.

akarámu to turn red; to glow; to ripen (fruit).

akarasama na plain, clear; frank, candid; **akarasama ni** plainly; frankly; without reserve; **akarasama ni iéba** to be frank; to tell the truth in plain terms.

akari light, lamp; **akari o tsukéru** to light a lamp.

akarítori skylight.

AKARUI bright; light; knowing well; versed in; **akaruku náru** to grow light; **akarui heya** well-lighted room; **hooritsu ni akarui** to be familiar with the laws; **akarui uchi ni** while it is light; before it gets dark.

akarumi light place; light; **akarumi e dásu** to bring a thing to light; to expose (something).

akásu to spend the whole night; to sit up all night; to reveal the truth, to confess; to speak one's mind.

akásu to weary, tire; **kane ni akáshite** regardless of the expense; regardless of the cost.

akasúri washcloth, washrag.

akatsuchi red earth (clay).

akatsuki = **akegata** dawn, daybreak; **akatsuki chikáku** toward daybreak;—**no akatsuki ni wa** when; in the event of; in case of.

akazátoo brown sugar.

akegata See **akatsuki**.

akehanásu to throw open (a window).

akekure morning and evening; day and night; all the time.

AKERU to open; to turn over (pages); to make room (for); to evacuate (a house, premises); to empty (a box); to expire; **ie o akeru** to stay out; **aná o akeru** to make a hole; **mízu o akeru** to pour out water. **Yó ga akeru.** The day is breaking.

AKI room; space; vacancy; **aki o fusagu** to fill a gap.

ÁKI autumn, fall; tiredness, weariness; **akibare** a clear autumn day; **aki ga kúru** to get tired of, become sick of, become weary of.

aki- prefix denoting: vacant, unoccupied; spare; **akibin** empty bottle; **akichi** vacant lot; **akidaru** empty barrel; **akima** vacant room.

akihatéru to be quite tired of, be quite weary of.

akimékura illiterate (person).

akínai trade, business; **akínai suru** to do business; **akínai o shite iru** to be in business; to be engaged in a trade; **akinai jóozu** good at trade; **akinai beta** poor at trade.

akináu to deal in, trade in.

akíndo trader, merchant, dealer; shopkeeper.

AKÍRAKA brightness; clearness; **akíraka ni suru** to make clear; to account for; **akíraka ni** brightly; clearly; undoubtedly; no doubt. **Akíraka desu.** It is clear.

akirame resignation; relinquishment; **akiraméru** to give up; to resign oneself to; to submit to one's fate; to relinquish.

akireru to be amazed at; to be dumfounded; be disgusted with; **akirete** with astonishment; in amazement; **akirete monó ga ienai** to be dumfounded.

akíru to get tired of, be sick of; to have enough of; **akíru hodo kúu** to eat one's fill;—**ni akiyasúi** to be soon tired of; **akíru hodo asobu** to play to one's heart's content.

akisunérai sneakthief.

AKIYA vacant house; unoccupied house; house for rent.

akka suru to go from bad to worse.

akkan rascal, rogue.

akke (*n.*) being dumfounded when an event has happened; **akke nái** too soon; too brief; too sudden; **akké ni toraréru** to be taken aback; to be amazed. **Tsukihi ga akke náku tátte shimátta.** The days passed all too quickly. **Sore dé wa amari akke nái.** That's too abrupt.

akkoo abuse, insulting remarks; **akkoo suru** to abuse, insult.

akogare longing, yearning; desire; **akogareru** to long for, yearn for, yearn after.

áku evil, vice; wrong; wickedness; **áku ni mukuíru ni zén o motte suru** to return good for evil.

AKU (*n.*) lye; (*v.*) to open; to be opened; to become empty, become vacant; **té ga aku** to be free, be disengaged. **Makú ga aku.** The curtain rises.

akubi yawn; **ooákubi** great yawn; **akubi suru** to yawn.

akudói tedious; heavy (color or food); glaring.

akufuu evil practices; evil manners; evil habit.

akuheki bad habit; vice.

akuhitsu illegible handwriting; poor penmanship.

ÁKUI malice, ill will; malicious intent; **ákui de** from malice; purposely; **ákui no áru hito** malicious, evil-minded person.

ákuji evil thing; evil deed; criminal action.

AKUKÁNJOO ill feeling; ill will.

ákumade to the utmost; to the best of one's ability; persistently; **ákumade mo** to the last; stubbornly; to the end; **ákumade yaru** to do one's utmost.

akunin bad man, villain.

akuratsu na unscrupulous; sharp; crafty; wicked.

akurei bad precedent; bad example; **akurei o tsukúru** to set a bad precedent.

AKURU next, following (time); **akuru asa** the following morning; **akuru toshi** the following year.

ákuseku diligently, industriously; busily; restlessly; **ákuseku suru** to busy oneself; worry about;—**ni ákuseku to suru** to be busy with; **ákuseku to kaségu** to work hard (for a living).

ákusento accent, stress; pitch (of the voice), accent in Japanese.

ÁKUSHU handshake; **ákushu suru** to shake hands.

akushuu bad habit; evil practices; **akushuu ga tsuku** to develop a bad habit; **akushuu o dassúru** to get rid of a bad habit.

akutóo villain, scoundrel.

akuun ill luck; evil fate.

akuyoo misuse; improper use; abuse; **akuyoo suru** to misuse; abuse.

akuyuu bad friend; bad companion; **akuyuu to majiwaru** to keep bad company.

áma flax; fisherwoman; diving girl (professional pearl-diver); nun; **amádera** convent.

AMA- prefix denoting: rain; of rain, for rain; **amadare** raindrops; **amádo** rain door; **amagáitoo** raincoat; **amagása** umbrella; **amagoi** prayers for rain; **amágu** rain gear; **amagumo** rain cloud; **amámizu** rain water; **amágu o yooi shite déru** to go out prepared for rain; **amágu no yóoi o suru** to provide oneself with rain gear.

amádo rain door (sliding door); storm door; shutter; **amádo o kúru** to shut the rain door.

amaeru = amattareru to behave like a spoiled child; to coax; to be coquettish; to take advantage of; **amaeru yóo ni** coaxingly. **Okotoba ni amaemashóo.** I'll take advantage of your kind offer.

amaguri roast chestnuts.

AMAI sweet, sugary; not salted enough; indulgent; not strict; **amaku suru** to sweeten; **amai mono** sweets, candy; **amai kotoba** sweet (soft) words; **amaku míru** to have little regard for a person. **Kono sáke wa ama-jio da.** This salmon is not salted enough.

amajio slightly salted.

AMAI sweet flavor; sweetness; **amami no áru** sweetish; **amami o tsukéru** to sweeten. **Amami ga tarinai.** It is not sweet enough.

amami fondness for sweet things; sweet tooth; honeyed words. **Káre wa amakuchi da.** He has a sweet tooth.

amámori leak in the roof.

amamóyoi, amamóyoo signs of rain; **amamoyói no sóra** a threatening sky. **Amamóyoo desu.** It looks like rain.

AMANÉKU widely, universally; far and wide; **amanéku sékai ni shirarete iru** to be known all over the world; **amanéku zénkoku o jun'yuu suru** to travel all over the country.

AMANJÍRU, amanzúru to be content with, be satisfied with; to put up with; **amánjite** contentedly; willingly; **amánjite seisai o ukéru** to submit willingly to punishment. **Káre wa kore ni amánjite wa inai.** He is not content with this.

Amanógawa Milky Way; Galaxy.

amanzúru See **amanjíru.**

AMARI remainder, rest; surplus, excess; remnants; **AMÁRU** to remain, be left over; to be too much; to be in excess; to be beyond one's power; **mí ni amáru kooei** an undeserved honor; **chikará ni amáru** beyond one's power. **Anó hito wa koko ni juunen ámari súnde imásu.** He has lived here more than ten years. **Konogoro wa amari aimasén.** I haven't seen much of him (her). **Hitótsu amaru.** There is one too many.

amásu to leave over; to save; **kane o amasázu tsukau** to spend all one's money. **Hitotsu mo amasánakatta.** I didn't leave even one.

ÁMATA (a great) many; many a; a number of; numerous.

AMATSUSAE besides; moreover; what is more; into the bargain; to make matters worse.

amattareru See **amaeru.**

amattarui sweetish; sugary; **amattarui kotoba** honeyed words; **amattarui shibai** sentimental play (drama).

amayádori suru to take shelter from the rain.

amayakasu to pet; to indulge (a child) too much; to spoil.

amayoke shelter from the rain; protection against rain.

amazake sweet drink made from fermented rice.

amazarashi exposure to rain.

ÁME rain; **áme no** rainy; wet; **ame tsúzuki** spell of rainy weather; **áme ni náru** to change to rain; to begin to rain; **áme ni áu** to be caught in the rain. **Ame ga furisóo desu.** It looks like rain.

AME candy; wheat gluten; **ame o kuwásu** to deceive with honeyed words.

AMEFÚRI rain; rainy weather; rainy day; **amefúri ni sóto o arúku** to walk in the rain.

ameiro no light brown.

AMERIKA America; **Amerika no** (*adj.*) American; **AMERIKÁJIN** (*n.*) American; **Amerika Gasshúukoku** United States of America; **Amerika námari** Americanism (in speech).

ami net; seine; **ami no me** meshes (of a net).

amiagé gutsu laced boots.

amibári, amíboo knitting needles.

amidana rack (in a train or bus).

amímono (*n.*) knitting; crocheting; **amímono o suru** to knit.

aminome mesh.

amizáiku network; crocheting.

ámu to knit; to braid. **Kutsúshita o ámu.** To knit socks.

án bean paste, bean jam; proposal; bill; draft; plan; opinion; idea; **án o dásu** to make a proposal; **án o tatéru** to make a plan; **án o tsukúru** to make a draft; **án ni sooi shite** contrary to expectation; **án no gótoku** as was expected.

ANÁ hole; aperture; den, cave; pit; loss; shortage; fault; **aná o akeru** to make a hole, perforate; **záisan ni ána o akeru** to cut into one's assets; **aná o fusagu** to fill up a hole; stop a gap.

anadori contempt; disdain; **anadóru** to despise; to slight; to make light of; to look down upon; **anadori o ukéru** to be despised; to be scorned; **anadorigatái** formidable. **Shooteki o anadóru na.** Don't despise a weak enemy.

anago sea eel.

an'ánri ni tacitly; by tacit agreement; secretly; **an'ánri ni shoodaku suru** to give tacit consent. **An'ánri ni itchi shita.** It was tacitly agreed.

anaságashi o suru to find fault (with).

ANÁTA you, sweetheart.

ANATAGATA you (*pl.* formal).

ANÁTATACHI you (*pl.* formal).

anaúnsaa announcer.

ANBÁI seasoning; taste; state of health; condition; **anbái suru** to season; to arrange; **yói anbái ni** fortunately; **anbái ga warúi** to feel ill; to be unwell. **Anbái wa ikága desu ka?** How does it taste? How do you feel? **Kyóo wa anbái ga íi desu.** I'm well today. **Bánji anbái yoku itte iru.** Everything is going on all right.

anchaku safe arrival; **anchaku suru** to arrive safely.

ANCHOKU NA cheap, low-priced, inexpensive; **anchoku ni** cheaply, inexpensively.

anchuu mosaku suru to grope in the dark.

ANE elder sister, older sister.

anemúko husband of an older sister.

ANGAI NA unexpected; unforeseen; surprising; **angai ni** unexpectedly; **angai muzukashii** more difficult than imagined.

ÁNI elder brother.

aníyome elder brother's wife.

anji hint; suggestion; **anji suru** to hint; to suggest; **anji o ataéru** to give a hint; **anji ni tónda** suggestive; full of suggestions.

ANJÍRU to be anxious, be concerned; to worry.

ÁNKA cheapness; low price; **ánka na** cheap; inexpensive; **ánka ni** cheaply; at a low price; **ánka na seikatsu** cheap living; **ánka na káiraku** cheap pleasure.

anka foot warmer; warming pan.

anki suru to learn by heart, memorize.

ANMARI, amari too much; excessively; too hard; cruel; unreasonable. **Sore wa anmarí desu.** That's too hard. That's too cruel. **Anmari omoshíroku nái.** It's not too interesting.

anma masseur; massage; **anma suru** to massage.

ANMIN quiet sleep; sound sleep; **anmin suru** to sleep well; **anmin o boogai suru** to disturb someone else's sleep.

anmoku tacit consent, tacit understanding; **anmoku no uchi ni** by tacit consent.

anna that sort of; like that; such; **anna ni** like that; in that way; **anna utsukushii musume** such a pretty girl; a girl as pretty as that; **anna hito** a man like that; that sort of man.

ANNÁI guidance; conduct; invitation; **annái suru** to usher, guide; to invite; **annáijoo** letter or card of invitation; **ANNÁIKI** guidebook; **annáisha** guide; usher; pilot; **annaisho** guidebook, handbook; **annái náshi ni** unannounced; without knowing; without a guide; **annái o kóu** to ask to see. **Anná náshi ni háitte kita.** He entered the room without knocking.

annei public peace; public welfare.

án ni by hints; tacitly; in secret; implicitly; **án ni shiraseru** to hint; suggest; insinuate.

ANO that; those; over there; **ano yóo na** like that; of that sort; that sort of; **ano kata** he; she; that person. **Ano ne.** You see! I say. Listen!

ano yo other world; next world; **ano yo de** in the world to come.

anpan bean-jam bun; bun.

anpera bulrush mat.

ÁNPI safety; welfare; health; **ánpi o tazunéru** to inquire after (someone's) health.

anpoo fomentation; compress.

ÁNRAKU comfort, ease; **ánraku na** comfortable, easy; happy; **anrakú isu** easy chair; **ánraku na seikatsu o suru** to lead a life of ease; **ánraku ni kurasu** to live comfortably.

ANSEI quietness; rest; **ansei ni** quietly; in quiet; **ansei o tamótsu** to keep quiet; to lie quietly.

ANSHIN peace of mind, freedom from anxiety; confidence; **anshin suru** to feel at ease; to feel relieved; **anshin saseru** to set (someone) at ease; **anshin no dekíru hito** reliable person; **anshin no dekinai** unreliable person; **anshin shite** with confidence; with peace of mind.

anshutsu invention; contrivance; **anshutsu suru** to think out; to contrive, devise, invent.

ansoku rest, repose **ansoku suru** to rest; to take a rest.

ANSOKÚJITSU Sunday, Sabbath.

ÁNTA = **anáta** (*colloq.*) you.

antei stability; equilibrium; **antei suru** to be stabilized; to be settled; **antei o tamótsu** to keep one's balance; **antei o ushináu** to lose one's balance.

antena antenna.

ANZEN safety, security; **anzen na** safe; secure; **anzen ni** safely; securely; **anzen chitái** safety zone; **anzen kámisori** safety razor.

ANZU apricot.

anzúru to be anxious about, worry about. **Watakushi no kotó o anjínaide kudasái.** Don't worry about me.

ÁO blue; green; **aoáo shita** verdant; freshly green; **áoba** green leaves, foliage.

aobúkure no pale and swollen.

aodake green bamboo; **aodake iro** bluish-green.

aodátami new or freshly renovated mat.

aógu to fan; to raise one's eyes; to ask for; to depend upon; **hójo o aógu** to ask for aid. **Sóra o aóida.** He looked up at the sky.

aoi hollyhock.

AÓI blue; green; pale; unripe; inexperienced; **áoku náru** to become blue (pale); **áoku someru** to dye (something) blue. **Aói kao o shite iru.** He looks pale. **Sóra ga áoku hárete iru.** The sky is clear.

aoíki gasp; **aoíki o tsuku** to gasp; to heave a deep sigh; **aoíki tóiki de** gaspingly; with greatest effort. **Aoiki tóiki desu.** I am in great distress.

aojáshin blueprint.

aojirói pale, pallid; sickly.

aomi blueness; blue tint; greenness; **aomi gakátta** bluish; greenish.

aómono vegetables; **aomono íchiba** vegetable market; **aomonoya** greengrocer; vegetable seller.

aomuki ni on one's back. **aomuki ni taoréru** to fall on one's back; **aomúku** to look up, turn one's face up.

aonisai greenhorn; raw youth; stripling.

aónori seaweed processed for food.

aori flapping; bump; **aori o kurau** to feel the influence of; to be hit by; **aóru** to fan; to flap; to stir up, incite; **kaze ni aorárete iru** to flap in the wind. **Kaze ga kaen o aótta.** The strong wind fanned the flames.

aoténjoo (azure) heaven; vault of heaven; open sky.

aounábara blue expanse of water; ocean.

aozaméru to turn pale. **Aozámeta kao o shite iru.** His face is white as a sheet.

aozóra blue sky.

APÁATO apartment house.

appaku pressure; stress; oppression; **appaku suru** to oppress; bear down upon.

ap'páre (*n.*) being splendid; bravo!; well

done! **appáre na** splendid! admirable;
appáre no hataraki splendid
achievement; **appáre na jinbutsu** man
of fine (admirable) character.

ára ah! oh! good gracious! oh, my! (used by
women)

ará defect, fault, blemish; bony parts (of
fish); **ará o sagasu** to look for defects
(in others); find fault with others.

ARA new, brand-new; fresh; **ara no** new.

ara- prefix denoting: coarse, rough, harsh;
araarashíi violent; harsh; rough;
aráshiku violently; harshly; roughly;
arashígoto a rough work.

Arabia Arabia; **Arabia no** (*adj.*) Arabic;
Arabian; **Arabiago** Arabic language;
Arabiájin (*n.*) Arab; Arabian; **Arabia
súuji** Arabic numerals.

aradatéru to excite; to agitate; to exasperate;
to inflame; to complicate; **kotó o
aradatéru** to complicate matters; to
aggravate the matter.

aragane ore; unwrought metal.

aragyoo asceticism.

ARÁI rough; coarse; rude; wild; violent; **arai
shimá** a rough pattern; **araku** harshly;
roughly. **Úmi ga arai.** The sea is
rough.

arai wash; washing; raw fish slices; **araigami**
newly washed and untied hair; **araitate**
just washed; **araitate no** newly
washed; **arai ga kiku** to wash well; to
be washable; **arai ga kikanai** not
washable.

arakajime previously; in anticipation;
arakajime tsuuchi suru to inform
beforehand; **arakajime yóoi suru** to
prepare beforehand.

ARAKATA for the most part; mostly; most
of. **Shigoto wa arakata dekiagari
máshita.** The work is nearly
completed.

arakezuri no roughly planned; rough-hewn.

arakure ótoko (*n.*) rough; rowdy.

aramashi roughly; nearly; almost; practically;
all but; briefly.

aramónoya kitchenware dealer.

ARANKÁGIRI as much as possible;
arankágiri ni every; all; utmost;
arankágiri no chikará o dáshite with
the utmost exertion; **arankagiri no kóe
de** at the top of one's voice; as loudly
as possible.

arappói rough; rough-mannered; violent.

arare hail; hailstone; salty rice cracker
(seasoned with soy sauce). **Arare ga
fútte iru.** It is hailing.

araryóoji drastic treatment, drastic remedy;
drastic measures.

araságashi (*n.*) fault-finding.

ÁRASHI storm; **árashi no** stormy.

arashígoto rough work; rough labor.

ARASOI quarrel; contention; **arasoi o okósu**
to start a dispute; **uchiwa no arasoi**
family quarrel; internal troubles;
ARASÓU to quarrel; to dispute; to

struggle, compete, vie; **saki o arasóu**
to scramble for a seat; **arasóu koto no
dekínai** indisputable.

arasuji outline, brief summary.

arátaka na efficacious; miraculous;
marvelous.

ARATAMÁRU to be changed, be altered; to
be improved, be reformed; to take a
turn for the worse (in illness); to stand
on ceremony; **arataméru** to renew; to
renovate, alter, change, revise; to
improve; to examine. **Yámai ga
aratamarimáshita.** He took a turn for
the worse. **Soo aratamaránaide
kudasái.** Don't stand on ceremony.

aratámete anew; another time; **aratámete
tazunéru** to ask again. **Aratámete
mairimásu.** I'll come another time. I'll
come again.

árata na new, fresh, novel; **árata na súmai** a
new house; **árata ni hajimeru** to begin
anew; **arate** fresh force; new hand.

ARAU to wash; to purify; to cleanse; to dash
on, dash against; **ashí o arau** to wash
one's hands of a matter; to quit.

araúmi rough sea, stormy sea.

arawaréru to come out; to make an
appearance, turn up, show oneself.
Kao ni arawárete iru. It is written on
your face.

ARAWÁSU to show, display; to bring to
light, lay bare; to write (a book, novel,
etc.); to publish; to make known;
udemáe o arawásu to show ability;
tookaku o arawásu to stand head and
shoulders above others; **ikarí o kao ni
arawásu** to show anger (in one's face);
na o arawásu to win fame; to
distinguish oneself.

ARAYÚRU all; every possible; all sorts of;
arayúru shúrui no hito all sorts of
men; **arayúru shudan o kokoromíru**
to try every known method.

ARE that; it; roughness, coarseness; **ARE!**
listen! look! **are hodo** like that; that
(so) much; that degree; **are hodo ittá
noni** in spite of all that I have said; **are
hodo kane ga átte mo** with all his
riches; **are ka kore ka** this or that; **are
ya kóre ya** this and that; with one
thing or another; **are ya kóre ya de ki
o momu** to worry oneself with one
thing or another. **Are! Nán daroo?**
Listen! What can that be?

arebíyori stormy weather.

arechi wasteland; uncultivated land.

arehatéru to be dilapidated; to be utterly
ruined; **areháteta** dilapidated; ruined.

arekkiri since then; any more; all; last.
Arekkiri otosata ga arimasén. I
haven't heard from him since then.
Arekkiri yoshimáshita. After that I
left off completely.

aremawáru to rush about furiously.

aremóyoo threatening sky; signs of
approaching storm.

areno wildness; wilds; wild tract of land.

areru to fall into decay; to lie waste; to rush about furiously; to be rough. **Ûmi wa arete ita.** The sea was rough.

ari ant; **arízuka** an anthill.

ariamáru (*prenoun*) ample; abundant; **ariamáru hodo kane ga áru** to have money to spare.

ariári to vividly; distinctly; plainly.

ariawase potluck; **ariawase no** ready; on hand; **misé ni ariawase no shinamono** articles in stock; **ariawase no mono o tabéru** to take potluck; eat what is available.

aribai alibi.

arifureru to be found everywhere; **arifureta** common; ordinary.

arigáchi frequent occurrence; **arigáchi no** common; frequent. **Konna kotó wa arigáchi desu.** Such things are apt to happen.

arigane cash on hand.

arigatagáru to be thankful, feel grateful; **arigata méiwaku** unappreciated favor; misplaced kindness; **arigata námida** tears of gratitude. **Anó hito wa watashi no okurimono o arigatagarimáshita.** He was thankful for my gift.

arigatái thankful; **arigatái kotó ni wa** fortunately; **arigátaku** with thanks.

arigatámi gratefulness, sense of gratitude.

ARIGÁTOO many thanks; I am much obliged to you. **Arigátoo gozaimasu.** Thank you.

arika whereabouts; place where a thing is.

arikitari common, commonplace, ordinary, usual; **arikitari no** customary; conventional; **arikitari no hoohoo** the customary method.

arimásu (*form of* **aru**) there is.

ari no mama exact fact; plain fact; **ari no mamá o iu** to tell the exact truth; **ari no mamá ni** just as it is; frankly.

arísama circumstances; state; condition. **Soo iu arísama desu.** That's the situation.

arisóo na seemingly possible; **arisóo mo nái** unlikely; improbable. **Arisóo na kotó desu.** It's likely to happen.

aritei as it is; frankly (*colloq.*); **aritei ni iu** to speak the truth; state frankly.

aritsúku to come by, come upon; to find; to get, obtain; **shigoto ni aritsúku** to get work.

arittake all that there is; all that one has; **arittake no chikará o dásu** to put forth all one's efforts.

ARIUBEKARAZÁRU impossible; improbable; **ARIUBÉKI** possible; probable. **Sore wa ariubekarazáru kotó desu.** That's impossible. That could never happen.

ÁRU certain; some; a; an; **áru tokoro de** at a certain place; **áru hi** one day; once; **áru hito** a certain man; a man; somebody; **áru toki** on a certain occasion; once upon a time.

ÁRU to be at; to exist, live; to be situated, to lie; to have; to take place; to experience; to find; to get. **Hón ga tsukue no úe ni arimásu.** The book is on the desk. **Oomori wa Tookyoo to Yokohama no aida ni áru.** Omori lies between Tokyo and Yokohama. **Tookyoo ni ítta kotó ga arimásu ka?** Have you ever been to Tokyo? **Kono hón wa dóko ni arimáshita ka?** Where did you find this book? **Taihen na kotó ga átta no desu.** A dreadful thing happened.

arufabétto alphabet.

ARÚIWA or else; perhaps; probably; maybe. **Arúiwa sóo ka mo shirenai.** It may be so. It is not impossible.

áruji master; host; head of the family.

arukaséru to make walk, let walk (said of a child, horse, etc.).

arukikáta one's manner of walking.

arukimawáru to walk about; to wander about, go round, go around.

arukooru alcohol.

ARÚKU to walk, go on foot. **Arúku no wa karada ni taihen íi desu.** Walking is very good for your health.

arumájiki improper; unbecoming; improbable.

arumi, aruminyuumu aluminum.

áruto alto.

ÁSA morning; in the morning; **ása háyaku** early in the morning; **ása no aida** all morning; **ása kara ban máde** from morning till evening; **ásaban** every morning and evening.

asa hemp; flax; linen; **asaito** hemp yarn; **asanawa** hempen cord, rope.

asa- prefix denoting: light; shallow; **asamídori** light green.

aságao morning glory.

asagi (*n.*) light green.

asagurói dark; dark-skinned; brown.

asáhaka na shallow (of mind); superficial; half-witted.

ASAHAN = **asameshi** breakfast. **Asahan wa hachíji desu.** Breakfast is at eight.

ásahi morning sun; rising sun.

ASAI shallow; superficial; short, brief; **asai kawa** shallow river; **asai kangáe** shallow thought; **hi ga asai . . .** it is a short time (since).

asakusá nori dried seaweed (food).

asamashíi mean, miserable; wretched; **asamashíi yonónaka** the wretched world; **asamashíi kokoro no otoko** a mean-spirited man.

asameshi See **asahan.**

asamídori (*n.*) light green, light blue.

asanagi morning calm.

asáne o suru to lie in bed late; to sleep late; **asanéboo** late-riser, sleepyhead; **asanéboo o suru** to oversleep; to get up late.

asariarúku to prowl; **asarimawáru** to prowl about.

8

asáru to fish for; to search for; to hunt for; **iró o asáru** to philander.

asase shoal; shallows; **asase ni noriagéru** to run aground.

asatsuyu morning dew.

ASÁTTE day after tomorrow. **Asátte ome ni kakarimásu.** I will see you the day after tomorrow.

asayake morning glow; sky at dawn.

ÁSE, ásemizu sweat; perspiration; **asebámu** to become sweaty; to be wet with sweat; **asékaki** one who perspires profusely; **áse ga déru** to perspire; **áse o káku** to perspire; to become sweaty; **asemídoro ni nátte** in a sweat; soaked with sweat; **ásemizu o nagáshite hataraku** to sweat with hard work; work by the sweat of one's brow.

asebo = **asemo** prickly heat.

asejúban undershirt (for native costume).

asemo See **asebo.**

aséru to hurry; to get impatient; to be hasty; to fade, discolor. **Iró ga aséta.** The color has faded.

aseshírazu prickly-heat powder.

ASHÍ foot; leg; paw; step; pace; **ashi no kóo** instep; **ashi nó ura** sole; **ashiáto** footprint; **ashí ni makásete iku** to go without knowing where; **ashí ga tsuku** to be traced; leave a clue.

áshi reed; rush.

ashiba scaffolding; foothold.

ashibumi step; **ashibumi suru** to step; stamp one's feet.

ashibyóoshi keeping time with the feet.

ashida high clogs (for walking on muddy roads).

ashidamari stand; footing; **ashidamari o éru** to get a footing.

ashidome confinement; **ashidome o suru** to keep (someone) indoors.

ashidori gait; manner of walking; tread.

ashikake foothold; pedal. **Kite kara ashikake gonen ni náru.** It is five [calendar] years since I came here.

ashikárazu not amiss; not bad. **Dóozo ashikárazu.** Please don't take it amiss.

ASHÍKUBI ankle.

ashimóto place where one stands; **ashimóto ni** at (near) one's feet; **ashimóto no akarui uchi ni** before it gets dark; before getting caught; **ashimóto o míru** to take advantage of (someone else's) weakness.

ashinami pace; **ashinami o soróete** with measured steps; keeping pace with; **ashinami o soróete arúku** to walk in step.

ashioto footfall, sound of a footstep.

ashirai treatment; reception; **ashiráu** to treat, entertain; to receive; to handle, deal with; to harmonize; to add.

ashi shígeku often, frequently (refers to visits); **ashi shigeku kayou** to visit frequently.

ASHITA = **asú** tomorrow. **Ashita mata.** See you again tomorrow.

ashitemátoi encumbrance, burden, nuisance; **ashitemátoi ni náru** to become a nuisance; to get in the way.

asobaseru to leave (something) idle; **kane o asobasete oku** to let money lie idle.

ASOBI play; sport; amusement; pleasure; recreation; sensual pleasure; dissipation; **ASOBU** to play; to be idle; to go on a spree; to amuse; **asobi ni iku** to go out to play; to seek recreation; **asobi gátera** for amusement; half in play.

ASOKO that place; there; **asoko ni** over there; yonder.

assaku pressure; compression; **assaku suru** to press.

ASSÁRI simply; lightly; moderately; briefly; **assári shita** simple; light; plain; **assári katazukéru** to make short work of.

assen help, assistance; **assen suru** to help; mediate; arbitrate; **assénsha** mediator, arbitrator.

ASÚ See **ashita.**

asupírin aspirin.

ataéru to give; to let have; to present, award; **shigoto o ataéru** to give work;—**ni songai o ataéru** to inflict damage on; **ataeráreta shigoto** work assigned.

átafuta to hurriedly; helter-skelter.

atai price; value; **atai suru** to be worth; cost; deserve.

átakamo See **ádakamo.**

ATAMÁ head; top; brains; **atamá o sagéru** to bow respectfully; **atamá ga yói** a clear head; **atamá ga warúi** stupid; **atama gónashi ni** unsparingly; cruelly; **atamá kara ashi no saki máde** from head to foot; **atamákabu** leader; leading member.

atamakázu number of persons.

atama wari equal division; **atama wari ni suru** to divide equally, allot equal shares.

ATARASHÍI new, fresh, novel; recent; latest; **atarashíi sakana** fresh fish; **ataráshiku** newly; anew; afresh; **ataráshiku suru** to renovate; freshen; **ataráshiku hajimeru** to begin anew.

átari neighborhood; vicinity; near;—**no átari ni** in the neighborhood of; near; about; **átari kamáwazu** regardless of the people present.

atari success.

atari doshi fruitful (successful) year; **atari fuda** prize-number ticket; **atari hazure** hit or miss; success or failure; **atari o tóru** to make a hit.

ATARIMAE NO right, proper, reasonable; deserving; natural; usual; **atarimae no kotó** a matter of course. **Okóru no wa atarimae désu.** He has good reason to get angry.

atarisawari consequence; **atarisawari no nái** neutral, noncommittal; **atarisawari no**

nái koto o iu to talk so as not to hurt someone's feelings.

ataru to strike; to come true; to be exposed; to disagree with; to warm oneself; to succeed; to try; **soozoo ga ataru** to guess right; **ataru bekarazáru** irresistible; overwhelming; overpowering. **Keikaku ga atatta.** The plan succeeded. **Tónikaku atatte kudakéro da.** Try anyhow.

ATATAKÁI warm; genial; mild; **atatakái hito** warm-hearted, genial person; **atatakai fuyu** warm winter; **atatákaku náru** to become warm; **atatakami** mildness; warmth; geniality; **atatakami no áru** warm, warmhearted.

atatakasóo ni snugly.

atatamáru to get warm; to warm oneself; **atataméru** to warm up, heat; **kyuukoo o atataméru** to renew an old friendship; **té o atataméru** to warm one's hands (over a brazier). **Yatto kore de atatamarimáshita.** Now I'm warm.

ate aim, object; **ate ni naránai** unreliable; **ate náshi ni** aimlessly; at random; **atedo náku** aimlessly, without an aim, at random; **ate ni suru** to depend on; **ate ga nái** to find no clue.

ategai appointment; allotment; **ategaibuchi** rations; stipend (*colloq.*); **ategáu** to apportion; to allow; to give rations; to supply.

atehamáru to apply to; to hold good for; to conform to; **atehaméru** to apply; to fit; to conform.

atekkosuri, atekosuri sly hint; insinuating remark; **atekosúru** to make an insinuating remark; to satirize.

atekkura guess.

atekomi anticipation; expectation; **atekómu** to expect; to hope; **atekónde** in expectation of.

atena address (place); **atena no hito** addressee; **atena o káku** to address.

aterareru to be hit; to be affected by (weather); to disagree with; **ateru** to hit; to touch; to guess; to expose to; to address to; **mató ni ateru** to hit the mark. **Sukkári ateraremáshita.** You have hit it exactly. **Tábeta sakana ni ateraremáshita.** The fish I ate didn't agree with me. **Anó hito ni atete tegami o dashimáshita.** I sent a letter to his attention. **Hí ni atenáide kudasai.** Do not expose it to the sun.

atezuiryoo conjecture, random guess; **atezuíryoo o suru** to hazard a guess.

atezuppoo guess; guesswork; **atezuppoo ni** at random; **atezuppoo o iu** to hazard a guess.

ÁTO back, rear; results; **áto ni** behind; **áto de** later; **áto ni nokóru** to stay behind; **áto o ou** to chase after. **Áto ga warúi daroo.** The results won't be good.

atogama successor; **atogama ni suwaru** to succeed (someone).

átokara átokara one after another; in rapid succession.

atokata trace, vestige; proof, evidence; **atokata mo nái** unfounded, groundless.

atokatázuke clearing up; **atokatázuke o suru** to put things in order after a work is completed.

atomáwashi postponement, deferment; **atomáwashi ni suru** to defer, postpone.

atomódori relapse; setback; **atomódori suru** to go back; to degenerate.

atóoshi o suru to push from behind; to back up; to support; to abet.

atosaki fore and aft; first and last; both ends; **átosaki ni náru** to be mixed up; to be in wrong order; **átosaki no kangáe naku** regardless of the consequences; thoughtlessly.

atoshímatsu settlement (of an affair); **atoshímatsu o suru** to put in order.

atótori inheritor; successor.

atsugami pasteboard, cardboard.

atsugáru to be very sensitive to the heat. **Watashi wa atsugári desu.** I feel the heat.

atsugéshoo heavy make-up; **atsugéshoo shita** thickly made up; heavily powdered.

atsugi many layers of clothing; **atsugi suru** to be warmly dressed.

ATSUI very warm; hot; **átsuku naru** to become hotter; **átsuku suru** to warm; heat; **onná ni átsuku naru** to run madly after a woman.

ATSUI thick; heavy; **atsui kimono** heavy clothes; **atsui hón** bulky book.

atsukai management; handling, treatment; reception. **Shínsetsu na atsukai o ukemáshita.** I received kind treatment.

atsukamashíi impudent, brazen, shameless; **atsukamáshiku suru** to act shamelessly; **atsukamáshisa** impudence, shamelessness.

atsukau to handle, manage; to transact; **jímu o atsukau** to transact business; **kázoku to shite atsukau** to treat as a member of the family.

atsukurushíi close; sultry; sweltering.

ATSUMARI meeting, assembly; crowd, group; **atsumáru** to meet, assemble; **atsuméru** to gather, collect; to call together; **hitai o atsuméru** to put two heads together; to talk over something. **Kúji ni atsumarimashóo.** Let's meet at nine. **Atsumáre!** Line up!

atsurae order (purchase); **atsurae no custom** made; **atsuráeru** to order from; to place an order; **atsurae muki no** just the thing; the very thing (person) for . . .

atsúryoku pressure; stress; **atsúryoku o kuwaeru** to pressure.

átsusa heat, warmth; **atsusa átari** heat

prostration; sunstroke; **átsusa ni ataru** to suffer from the (summer) heat.

atsusa thickness. **Atsusa wa íkura arimásu ka?** How thick is that?

attooteki overwhelming; **attooteki daitassuu** overwhelming majority.

ÁU to meet; to see; to have an interview with, meet with; to agree with; to fit; to be in tune; to keep good time; **hito ni áu** to meet someone; **hidói me ni áu** to have a terrible time; **áme ni áu** to be caught in the rain; **pittári aú** to fit perfectly. **Kono tabemóno wa watakushi ni wa aimasén.** This food doesn't agree with me.

áuto out; out of play (in baseball).

awá bubbles, foam, lather; **awá ga tátsu** to bubble, foam; to ferment; **awá o kúu** to be flustered.

áwa millet.

áwabi abalone.

áware pity; sadness; **áware na** pitiful, poor, sad, miserable; **awaremi** pity, compassion, mercy; **awarému** to pity; **awaremubéki** poor, pitiable, miserable, wretched; **awareppói** pitiful, poor, sad, miserable; **áware ni omoú** to feel pity; **awaremi o kakéru** to treat with tenderness or compassion; **awaremi no fukái hito** person of great compassion.

awase lined lightweight garment.

awaseme joint; seam.

awaséru to put together, unite; **chikará o awaséru** to combine efforts; **hanashi no chooshi o awaséru** to chime in; **tokei o awaséru** to set a watch by; **genbun to awaséru** to compare with the original.

awatadashíi restless; busy; hurried.

awatemono giddy (flighty) person.

AWATERU to be confused; to lose one's head; to hurry.

áwaya exclamation of alarm, agitation, or surprise; **áwaya to míru ma ni** in an instant; in the twinkling of an eye.

awayókuba if things go well.

ayá figure, design; twill; damask; figure of speech.

ayabúmu to fear; to doubt; to hesitate; to have misgivings.

ayadóru to interweave; to embellish; to make designs.

ayamachi fault; mistake; blunder.

ayamári mistake, error; apology; **ayamáru** to apologize; to err. **Sentaku o ayamarimáshita.** He made a mistake in his choice.

ayame iris.

AYASHII suspicious; uncertain; **ayashii ningen** suspicious (shady) person; **ayashii eigo** poor English; **ayashimu** to suspect; to doubt; to wonder at.

ayásu to amuse; to humor; to caress (an infant).

ayatsuri níngyoo puppet, marionette;

ayatsúru to handle; to control; to pull the wires; **hito o ayatsúru** to play on a man's weakness.

ayáui dangerous; very near; **ayauku** barely; narrowly; on the point of; **ayauku nogaréru** to have a narrow escape; **ayauku suru** to imperil, jeopardize, endanger.

áyu sweetfish (fresh-water game fish).

azá birthmark.

azami thistle.

azamúku to deceive; to cheat; to impose upon; **azamúki yasui** gullible; **haná o azamúku bijin** a beautiful woman.

azawarai derisive laughter; contempt; ridicule; **azawaráu** to laugh at, ridicule; to sneer at.

azáyaka na clear; splendid; vivid; **azáyaka ni** clearly; splendidly.

aze footpaths between rice fields; low dikes separating rice fields.

azukari taking charge (custody) of; draw, tie (in a game); **azukarimono, azukemono** something left in one's charge; **azukáru** to take part in, participate; to share; to be concerned with; to keep; to be trusted with; **azukéru** to leave in someone's charge; to make a deposit (of money); **azukénushi** depositor; **soodan ni azukáru** to be consulted; **azukátte chikará ga áru** to contribute greatly to; **okane o ginkoo ni azukéru** to deposit money in a bank. **Sore o oazukari itashimashóo.** I will keep it for you. **Tomodachi ni kodomo o azúkete Nihón e ikimásu.** I am going to Japan, leaving my child with a friend of mine.

azuki red bean.

azusa catalpa tree.

B

BAAI occasion; time; moment; case; circumstances; **—no baai ni wa** when; in case; in the event that; on the occasion of; **baai ni yotté wa** according to circumstances; **hitsuyoo no baai ní wa** in case of need.

báaya wet nurse; old-woman servant.

báchirusu bacillus; parasite.

BAI double; twice (as large, as many, as much); **bai ni suru** to make twice as large; to double; times; -fold (a counter); **ni bai** twice; two times; **ni bai ni suru** to double.

báibai (n.) buying and selling; **báibai suru** to trade in; **baibai kéiyaku** bargain; contract of sale.

baidoku syphilis.

báika selling price; **baikyaku** disposal by sale; sale.

baikai mediation; matchmaking; **baikai suru** to mediate; to convey; **baikáibutsu** medium; agent; **baikáisha** go-between.

baikin bacillus.
baimei no to publicity-seeker.
baiorin violin.
baishaku (*n.*) matchmaking; **baishaku suru** to arrange marriages; **baishakunin** go-between; matchmaker.
baishoo compensation, indemnity, reparation; **baishoo suru** to indemnify, make reparation for a loss; **baishookin** money for reparations, damages.
baishuu purchase; bribe; **baishuu suru** to bribe, buy off.
baiten stand, stall, booth; store.
baiyaku contract of sale; patent medicine. **Baiyakuzumi!** Sold!
báji toofuu utter indifference; **báji toofuu to kikinagásu** to turn a deaf ear to.
BÁKA fool, blockhead, idiot, folly, nonsense, absurdity; **báka o iu** to talk nonsense; **báka o miru** to be fooled; **báka o suru** to make a fool of oneself; **baka ni suru** to make fun of; make a fool of; **báka na hito** foolish person; **báka ni** awfully. **BAKABAKASHÍI** foolish, silly; **bakabakashíi koto** foolish matter. **Baka yároo** You fool! Idiot!
BÁKARI about; some; just; only; almost; on the point of;—**bákari de náku** not only ... but. **Íma kita bákari desu.** I've just come. **Nakan bákari de átta.** She was ready to cry.
bakashóojiki stubborn honesty; simpleness. **Ano otoko wa bakashóojiki da.** That man is too honest.
bakawárai boisterous laughter; horse laugh.
bakazu experience; **bakazu o fumu** to gain experience; **bakazu o funda** experienced; veteran.
bakemóno ghost; goblin.
baken pool ticket; pari mutuel ticket; **bakenjoo** grandstand at a racetrack.
bake no kawá dissemblance; disguise; **bake no kawá ga arawaréru** to reveal one's true colors.
BAKETSU bucket.
bakkin fine, penalty; **bakkin o kasúru** to levy a fine.
bákku back; background; backer; **bákku suru** to back up (a vehicle); **bakku míraa** rearview mirror (in a car).
bakuchi gambling; **bakuchi o útsu** to gamble; **bakuchiba** gambling place; **bakuchiuchi** gambler; **bakuchiyádo** gambling house.
bakudai na enormous, vast; immense, tremendous.
bakudan bomb; **bakudan tóoka** (*n.*) bombing; **bakudan o tóoka suru** to bomb.
bakuhatsu explosion, detonation; **bakuhatsu suru** to explode, blow up, burst.
bakuon explosive sound; roaring of an engine; buzzing.
bákuro exposure; disclosure; **bákuro suru** to expose; lay bare.

bakushin rush; dash; **bakushin suru** to rush; to dash forward.
báku to shita vague, uncertain; ambiguous, indefinite; **bakuzen** vaguely; **Ími ga báku to shite iru.** The meaning is vague.
BAN evening; night; **ban ni** in the evening; **Nichiyoo no ban ni** on Sunday evening.
bán watch, guard, lookout; number; order; turn; time; round; game; **bán o suru** to keep watch.
BAN- prefix denoting: numerous; innumerable; all; every; **bánji** everything.
BANANA banana.
BANBAN probably, possibly; certainly; entirely; very well; **banban shoochi shite iru** to know very well. **Bánban sonna kotó wa arumái to omóu.** I don't think it's true.
bánbutsu all things (under the sun); creation; entire universe.
bancha coarse tea; green tea of poor quality. **bancha mo dehana** everything is in its season.
banchi lot number; address.
bandai all ages; eternity; **bandai ni** through all ages; forever; **bandai fueki no** immutable, eternal.
bangai (*n.*) extra; additional turn; **bangai no** (*adj.*) extra; additional.
bangása coarse oilpaper umbrella.
bangata evening; nightfall; **bangata ni** in the evening; toward evening.
bangóo number; **bangóo o útsu** to number.
BANGUMI program; list.
bánji everything; all things. **Bánji kootsúgoo ni ítte iru.** Everything is going well.
bankara Bohemianism; bohemian; **bankara no** unconventional; uncouth; rough and coarse.
banken watchdog.
bankókushi world history.
bankurúwase surprise; expected result; **bankurúwase no** unexpected.
-BANME suffix denoting: ordinal number; **kádo kura sanbanmé no ie** the third house from the corner.
BANMESHI supper; **banmeshi o suru** to eat supper.
bannen in one's old age.
bannín watchman; caretaker.
bánpaa bumper.
banpei sentry, sentinel, guard.
BANSAN supper; dinner; **bansánkai** dinner party.
banshaku evening drink; **banshaku o yaru** to have a drink with supper.
bansoo accompaniment; **bansoo suru** to accompany; **bansóosha** accompanist.
bansookoo adhesive plaster; bandage strip.
bantoo clerk; bathhouse attendant.
banzái cheers: "long live"; **"banzai"**; "viva"; **banzái o sanshoo suru** to give three cheers.
banzuke list; program, schedule; playbill.

bara rose; rosebush.

barabara (*n.*) being in pieces, drops; **barabara ni** in bits or pieces; **barabara ni suru** to break up.

barákku barracks; shack.

baramáku to scatter; **kane o baramáku** to spend money recklessly.

barásu to break into pieces; to lay bare (a secret); to dispose of; to kill.

báree ballet.

barikan hair clippers.

bariki horsepower; **bariki o kakéru** to get up steam; to make an effort.

básha carriage; coach; bus; cab; cart.

basho space, place; seat; location; situation; room.

bashogara character (of a place); locality; neighborhood.

bassui extract; selection; **bassui suru** to extract; select.

bassúru to punish; to bring to justice.

BÁSU bus; **yuuran básu** sight-seeing bus; **básu de** by bus.

basue outskirts, suburbs.

basuketto bóoru basketball.

BÁTA butter; **batakusái** exotic, alien (lit.: having the smell of butter). **Ano hito wa batakusái.** He acts like a Westerner.

bátabata with a clatter (onomatopoetic); one after another; noisily; to flap. **Kaze de to ga bátabata suru.** The wind makes the doors rattle (clatter).

batoo abuse; denunciation; **batoo suru** to abuse; denounce.

bátsu punishment, penalty; clique; faction; clan; **batsu suru, bassuru** to punish; **bátsu o ukéru** to be punished.

batsugun no distinguished; conspicuous.

batta grasshopper.

báttaa batter (in baseball); **battaajun** batting order.

BATTARI suddenly; unexpectedly; with a thud. **battári yukiáu** to come across, fall in with (a person); **battári butsukaru** to run against, bump into; **battári taoréru** to fall down with a thud; **battári tomaru** to come to an abrupt stop.

batteki suru to select; to single out; to promote.

battén demerit; black mark.

bátto bat.

bázaa bazaar.

Beekoku See **Beikoku.**

béeru veil.

beesubóoru baseball.

béi- prefix denoting: of rice, pertaining to rice; **béika** the price of rice.

Bei = prefix denoting: U.S.A.

Beigun American Army; **Beijin, Beikokújin** (*n.*) American; **béika** American currency; **beikan** American warship; **BEIKOKU = Beekoku** America (U.S.A.).

bekkoo tortoise shell; **bekkoo no kushí** tortoise-shell comb; **bekkoo buchi** tortoise-shell rims; **bekkoo buchi no mégane** tortoise-shell glasses; **bekkoo iro** amber color; **bekkoo záiku** tortoise-shell work.

bekkyo separation; **bekkyo suru** to be separated.

bén flower petal; valve; reed; eloquence; dialect; convenience; facilities; feces; **bén ga tátsu** to speak fluently; **Oosakaben** Osaka dialect;—**no bén hakátte** for the convenience of. **Noriai jidóosha no bén ga áru.** Buses are available.

bénchi bench.

béngi convenience; facilities; **béngi o ataéru** to provide facilities; to give aid to; **bengijoo** for the sake of convenience.

béngo defense; **béngo suru** to plead; to defend; **bengonin** counsel (for the defense); lawyer; **bengóshi** lawyer; public attorney.

BÉNI red, crimson; rouge; lipstick; **béni o tsukéru** to put on lipstick.

benímasu red trout.

BENJÓ privy; toilet; **benjó ni iku** to go to the toilet; to wash one's hands. **Benjó wa dóko desu ka?** Where is the toilet?

benkai explanation; apology; **benkai suru** to explain; to apologize.

benkeijima checks, plaid (pattern).

bénki chamber pot; bedpan.

BENKYOO study; diligence; industry; selling at a small profit; **benkyoo suru** to study; to work hard; **benkyoo suru misé** a shop where prices are cheap; **benkyooka** studious person; hard worker.

benpi constipation.

BÉNRI convenience; facilities; handiness; **bénri na** convenient; handy; useful; **bénri ni** conveniently; **bénri na tokoró ni súnde iru** to live in a very convenient location.

bénshi orator, speaker.

benshoo reparation, compensation.

bensúu fraction (math).

BENTÓO box lunch; **bentóo o tabéru** to eat a box lunch; **bentóobako** lunchbox; **bentóodai** lunch money; cost of lunch.

bentsuu bowel movement.

bénzetsu eloquence; tongue; **bénzetsu sawáyaka na** eloquent; fluent; **bénzetsu sawáyaka ni** eloquently, fluently; **benzúru** to talk eloquently. **Bénzetsu ga takumi da.** He speaks fluently.

beppin (somewhat vulgar word) pretty girl; good-looking woman; beauty.

beppuu separate cover; **beppuu no tegami** a letter under separate cover.

bérabera continually; volubly; **bérabera shabéru** to chatter unceasingly; to talk volubly.

beraboo (slang) blockhead; fool; **beraboo ni**

awfully; **beraboo ni samúi** awfully cold. **Beraboo me!** Confound it, you fool you!

béru bell; doorbell; **béru o narasu** to ring a bell.

béso wry face; **béso o káku** to be ready to cry.

BÉSUTO best; **bésuto o tsukúsu** to do one's best.

bétabeta all over; thickly; sticky (referring to paint or powder); **bétabeta oshiroi o nuru** to powder one's face thickly.

BETSU difference; discrimination; **betsu no** different; another; **betsu no** different; another; **betsu na hito** another man; **betsu náku** without discrimination; alike; **dánjo no betsu náku** regardless of sex.

betsu átsurae special order; **betsu átsurae no** made to order; **betsu átsurae no kutsu** custom-made shoes.

BETSUBETSU NA separate; **betsubetsu ni** separately; **betsubetsu ni náru** to become separate; to be separated; **betsubetsu ni suru** to keep separate.

betsudan special; specially; particularly; in particular; **betsujítate** (n.) being specially made or equipped; **betsujítate no tsukai** special messenger.

bí beauty; prettiness; grace; **bíjin** beautiful woman; beautiful girl; **bidan** beautiful story; fine anecdote.

BIFUTEKI beefsteak.

bigánjutsu facial (beauty treatment); **biganjutsúshi** beautician.

bíiru beer; ale; **bíiru** draught beer; **chozoo bíiru** lager beer.

bíjutsu fine arts; **bijutsu gákkoo** art school; **bijutsu tenránkai** art exhibition; **bijutsúhin** object (work) of art; **bijutsuka** artist; **bijutsúkan** art museum; **bijutsuteki** artistic; **bijutsuteki ni** artistically.

bíkko lameness; lame person; **bíkko no** lame; crippled; wrongly paired; unsymmetrical; **bíkko o hiku** to limp. **Kono tsukue no ashí wa bíkko da.** The legs of this table are uneven.

BIKKÚRI SURU to start (with surprise); to be surprised; **bikkúri saseru** to startle; **bikkúri gyooten** astonishment, amazement; **bikkúri gyooten suru** to be frightened out of one's wits. **Áa bikkúri shita!** How you startled me!

bikoo incognito; **bikoo suru** to go incognito; to go in disguise.

bíkubiku suru to tremble with fear, be afraid; to feel nervous.

bíku to mo shinai to remain unmoved (calm, composed); to be unflinching; to be unperturbed.

bimyoo na delicate; nice; fine; **hijoo ni bimyoo na ten** a very delicate point.

BÍN opportunity, occasíon; message; news; mail; bottle, jar, decanter; **momo no binzume** a jar of peaches; **tsugí no bin de** by the next mail; **kishabin de** by railway express.

BÍNBOO NA poor, destitute; **binboonin** poor man; poor (people).

biníiru vinyl.

BINJOO SURU to travel on board, take passage on (a ship); to take advantage of;—**binjoo shite** on board ship.

binkan sensitiveness; susceptibility; **binkan na** susceptible; sensitive.

binkatsu quickness; promptness; **binkatsu na** quick; alert; prompt; **binkatsu na shóchi o tóru** to take prompt measures; **binkatsu ni hataraku** to work rapidly.

BINSEN letter paper; pad of letter paper.

binsen boat, steamer **tsugí no binsen de** by the next boat.

binshoo quickness, alertness, sharpness, smartness, shrewdness; **binshoo na** quick, sharp, smart, shrewd; **binshoo ni** quickly, etc.; **koodoo ga binshoo da** quick in action.

binsoku quickness, promptness; **binsoku na** quick, prompt; **binsoku ni** quickly, promptly; **binsoku ni haitatsu suru** to deliver promptly.

binzume no bottled; in a jar; **binzume no sake** bottled sake.

bíri (n.) last; bottom (of the class).

biroodo velvet.

BÍRU, BÍRUDINGU building.

biryoku slight ability; humble effort; **biryoku o tsukúsu** to do one's best.

bíshibishi rigorously; severely.

bíshobisho thoroughly drenched, soaked to the skin; drizzling. **Áme ga bishobisho fúru.** It is drizzling.

bishonure no dripping, drenched; **bishonure ni náru** to get wet through.

bishoo smile; **bishoo suru** to smile; **bishoo shite** with a smile.

bishóonen handsome youth; Adonis.

bisshóri thoroughly; (wet) to the skin; **bisshóri áse o káku** to be soaked with sweat.

BISUKÉTTO cookies; tea biscuits.

bitámin vitamin.

biten, bitoku virtue; good quality.

bíwa loquat (plumlike fruit); Japanese musical instrument with four strings; **bíwa o hiku** to play the biwa.

bóchi graveyard, cemetery.

bodáiju linden tree.

bohyoo gravestone; tomb.

boikótto boycott.

boin vowel (sound).

bokashí gradation; shading, shade (of color); **bokásu** to shade, soften, blend colors.

boke Japanese quince.

bokéru to be senile; to be in one's dotage; to be weak-minded; to fade; to grow faint. **Kón ga bóketa.** The indigo has faded. **Anó hito wa atamá ga bókete iru.** He is senile.

boki bookkeeping; **bokichoo** account book.

bokkoo sudden rise; **bokkoo suru** to rise suddenly (in power); to spring into existence; **kóogyoo no bokkoo** the growth of industry.

bokkui See **boogui.**

bókkusu box.

bókoku mother country, homeland; **bokokugo** mother tongue.

bókoo alma mater.

BÓKU I (used in men's talk).

bokuchiku stock farming; **bokuchikuka** stock farmer; **bokujoo** stock farm; pasture.

bokumetsu destruction, extermination; **bokumetsu suru** to destroy; stamp out.

bokushi pastor, minister.

bókushingu boxing.

bokutotsu honesty, artlessness, simplicity; **bokutotsu na** artless; simple; plain-spoken.

bon tray.

Bón Feast of Lanterns; Buddhist All Souls' Day in July.

bonchi basin; valley.

bonjín ordinary man; mediocre person.

bonnoo passion; lust.

bonsai dwarf tree; miniature garden set in a pot.

bonseki miniature landscape (on a tray).

bon'yári stupid person, blockhead; absentmindedly; vacantly; distractedly; **bon'yári kangaekómu** to be lost in reverie; **bon'yári ichinichí o kurasu** to idle away a whole day; **bon'yarimono** dull-witted, absent-minded person; **bon'yárishita** dull-witted, stupid; absent-minded; vacant; dim. **Imi ga bon'yari shite iru.** The meaning is vague. **Késa wa atamá ga bon'yári shite iru.** My head is not clear this morning.

BOO staff, club, rod, stick; **boo de útsu** to strike with a stick; **shíndai o boo ni furu** to squander one's fortune; **ichinichí o boo ni furu** to waste a whole day.

bóo- prefix denoting: one; certain (one); **boosho** (a certain) place; **bóoshi** (a certain) person.

boobaku táru vast, boundless, limitless; vague; obscure; **boobaku táru úmi** a vast expanse of sea. **Zénto wa boobaku táru monó da.** The prospects are very dim.

bóobi defense; defensive preparations.

booboo táru extensive; boundless, vast; **bóoboo to** shaggily; thickly; **booboo to hige o nobáshita otoko** a man with a shaggy beard.

boochoo attendance; sitting in conference; **boochóoken** admission ticket (for a visitor to the Diet, a conference, etc.); **boochóoryoo** admission fee.

boodoo disturbance; riot, insurrection.

BOOEKI trade; commerce; **booeki suru** to trade, carry on commerce; **booekifuu** trade wind; **booekíshoo** merchant trader (importer or exporter); **booeki shóokai** trading firm.

booenkyoo telescope; binoculars.

boofúu storm; stormy weather; typhoon; **boofuu kéihoo** storm warning; **boofúu no** stormy; **boofúu no chuushin** storm center.

boofuzai antiseptic; preservative.

boogai disturbance; obstruction, hindrance, obstacle; **boogai suru** to disturb, etc.

boogen violent language; **boogen a háku** to use violent (abusive) language.

boogui = **bokkui** post, pile, stake.

bóogyo defense; **bóogyo no** defensive; **bóogyo suru** to defend; **boogyosen** line of defense.

boohatei breakwater.

bóoi tyranny, despotism.

booka (n.) fireproof; fire prevention; **booka no** (adj.) fireproof; fire-resisting; **booka sétsubi** fire protection; **bookáheki** fireproof walls.

bookan (n.) bully; rough; rowdy.

bookán sha spectator; onlooker; **bookan suru** to remain a spectator.

booken adventure; risk, hazard; **booken suru** to venture, hazard, run a risk; **bookéndan** tale of adventure; adventure; **bookenka** adventurer; **bookenteki** risky; hazardous; adventurous.

bookoo bladder; violence, violent conduct; outrage; **bookoo suru** to use violence; **bookoo o kuwaeru** to assault.

bóokun tyrant, despot.

bóokyo violence; violent conduct.

boomei flight; **boomei suru** to flee, take flight, seek refuge; **booméisha** refugee; fugitive; exile.

bóonasu bonus.

boonénkai social gathering at the end of the year.

boorei ghost.

bóori excessive profit; **bóori o musabóru** to profiteer, make excessive profit; **bóori torishimari rei** ordinance to control excessive profits.

booru bowl; ball.

boorubako pasteboard box, carton.

boorugami cardboard, pasteboard.

bóoryoku brute force, violence; **booryokúdan** gang of roughs.

boosatsu sareru to be hard-pressed with business.

booseki spinning; **booseki gáisha** fabric (spinning) company; **booseki kóojoo** fabric mill.

BOOSHI hat, cap; bonnet; **booshi o kabúru** to put on one's hat; **booshi o kabútte míru** to try on a hat; **booshi o núgu** to take off one's hat; **booshíkake** hat rack, hat peg; **booshiya** hatter; milliner; hat store.

booshi prevention; arrest.

booshokúzai antiseptic; anti-corrosive.

boosui waterproof; protection against floods; **boosuífu** waterproof cloth.

bóoto mob; insurgents; rioters.

bóoto rowboat; **bóoto o kógu** to row a boat.

bootoo abnormal rise; boom. **Satóo ga bootoo shita.** The price of sugar has gone up enormously.

bóoya (diminutive) my child; my darling (said of an infant).

bóozu (derogatory) monk.

bora gray mullet.

bóro rags, tatters; hidden fault; **bóro no** ragged, threadbare; **bóro o kíta in** rags; **bóro o dásu** to betray a weakness; show one's true colors; **boroboro no** tattered, ragged; **boroboro ni náru** to crumble, fall to pieces; **borogímono** old (threadbare) clothes; rags; **borókai** ragman; junkman.

bóru to charge exorbitant prices; to profiteer.

bosei motherhood, maternity; **boséiai** maternal love.

boseki tombstone.

boshuu levy; recruiting; **boshuu suru** to collect; recruit; raise.

bosshuu confiscation, forfeiture; **bosshuu suru** to confiscate, forfeit, seize.

bossúru to sink; to hide.

bótan tree peony.

BOTAN button; stud; knob; **botan o kakéru** to button; **botan o hazusu** to unbutton; **botan o osu** to push a button.

bótchan boy (someone else's son); green youth; young master.

botsukóoshoo (n.) being independent;—**tó wa botsukóoshoo de aru** to have no relation with; to have no connection (between).

botsuraku ruin; downfall; **botsuraku suru** to be ruined.

bottoo suru to be absorbed in; to devote oneself to; to be engrossed with; **shigoto ni bottoo suru** to bury oneself in work.

bóya small fire.

bu rate, percentage; part, portion, section, division; department; copy (a "counter" for newspapers, pamphlets, etc.); **buai** rate, commission, royalty; **buai o dásu** to give (someone) a percentage. **Ríshi wa sán bu desu.** The interest rate is 3 per cent.

buáikyoo surliness; curtness; bluntness; **buáikyoo na** surly; blunt; unobliging.

buáisoo inhospitableness; curtness, unsociability; **buáisoo na** unsociable, curt, inhospitable; **buáisoo na henji** a curt reply; **hito ni buáisoo o suru** to be surly.

bubátta warlike, martial, soldierly.

búbun part, portion, section; **bubunhin** parts (of machines); **bubunteki** partial; sectional; local; **bubunteki ni** partially; locally.

búchi spots, specks; patches; **búchi no** spotted, speckled; **buchi neko** tabby cat.

buchoo chief (head) of a section (or department).

budoo grape; grapevine; **budoo no fusa** a bunch of grapes; **budooen** vineyard; **budóoshu** wine; claret; **shiro budóoshu** white wine; **aka budóoshu** red wine.

buénryo rudeness; boldness; **buénryo na** unreserved; rude; bold; **buénryo ni** without reserve, boldly.

buji peace; safety; good health; **buji na** safe, sound; peaceful; **buji ni** safely; peacefully; **búji ni kurushímu** to be tired of a quiet life.

bujoku insult, affront; disgrace; **bujoku suru** to insult, disgrace; **bujoku o ukéru** to be insulted.

búka (n.) subordinate; under-officer.

bukákkoo clumsiness, awkwardness (in appearance); **bukákkoo na** clumsy, awkward; **bukákkoo ni** clumsily, bunglingly.

búki arms, weapons.

bukíyoo lack of skill, clumsiness.

bukka prices; **bukka o toosei suru** to control prices; **bukka chóosetsu** price control. **Bukka ga geraku suru.** Prices are falling. **Bukka ga tooki suru.** Prices are rising.

bukkaku Buddhist temple.

bukkiráboo abruptness; curtness; **bukkiráboo na kotáe o suru** to make a curt reply; **bukkiráboo ni kotowáru** to refuse curtly.

Bukkyoo Buddhism; **Bukkyóoto** Buddhist.

bukotsu bluntness; roughness; rusticity; **bukotsu na** blunt; rustic; clumsy.

búkubuku bubbling; baggy; bulging; **búkubuku futóru** to become very fat; **búkubuku awadátsu** to bubble up.

bumon class; branch; department; **bumon ni wakéru** to classify.

bún portion, share; social position, lot in life; state of affairs; writing, composition; **bún ni yasunzúru** to be contented with one's lot. **Kore wa watakshi no bún desu.** This is my share. **Bún wa bú yori mo chikará ga áru.** The pen is mightier than the sword.

bun- prefix denoting: writing, literature; civil life; **bundan** literary circles; **búngaku** literature; **búngaku no** literary; **bungei** literature; **bungo** literary expression; written language; classical Japanese; **bungoo** great writer.

búna beech tree.

bunan na safe, secure; **bunan ni** safely; tolerably well.

bun'an draft, sketch; **bun'an o tsukúru** to make a draft; draw up (a deed, etc.).

bunchoo rice (paddy) bird.

bundori capture, seizure; spoil, plunder; **bundoríhin** trophy, booty, spoils.

16

bunjoo division; distribution; **bunjoo suru** to divide, distribute; **bunjóochi** land for sale in lots.

búnka culture, civilization; **bunkateki** cultural.

bunkai analysis; decomposition; **bunkai suru** to analyze; to resolve; to decompose; to break up; to pull to pieces.

bunkan civil official.

bunke branch of a family.

bunken literature; documents, records.

bunko handbox; bookcase; library; collection of works.

bunkóojoo branch factory.

bunmei civilization; **bunmei no** civilized; **bunméikoku** civilized country.

bunpai division, distribution; **bunpai suru** to divide, share; **ríeki no bunpai** a division of profits.

bunpoo grammar. **Bunpoo o machigáeta.** I made a mistake in grammar.

bunpóogu stationery; **bunpooguya** stationer, one who sells paper, etc.

bunpu distribution (geographical).

bunretsu split, rupture; **bunretsu suru** to break up; split.

bunri separation; isolation; **bunri suru** to separate; to isolate.

bunrui classification, assortment.

bunryóo quantity.

bunseki analysis, assay.

búnshi writer; numerator; molecule.

búnshoo composition, writing; **bunshooka** good (clear) writer.

bunsúirei watershed.

buntan allotment, share; **buntánkin** share of expenses.

buntsuu correspondence; **buntsuu suru** to write to.

buppin article; goods, commodities.

búrabura idly, aimlessly; leisurely; **búrabura arúku** to walk leisurely, take a stroll; **búrabura suru** to loaf, be idle; **búrabura shite hi o okuru** to while away one's time.

burakku rísuto black list.

búraku community; village.

búranko swing.

búrashi brush; **búrashi o kakéru** to brush up; to brush.

buratsuku to wander about, walk aimlessly; **machí o buratsuku** to window-shop.

buráusu blouse.

buréeki, buréiki brake. **Buréiki ga kikanai.** The brake does not work.

buréi breach of etiquette; incivility, rudeness; **buréi na** rude, insolent; **buréi na kotó o iu** to speak insultingly; **buréi na kotó o suru** to behave impolitely; to act insultingly.

búri yellowtail, yellowfish.

-buri suffix denoting: way, manner; after (a time); **gonenburi de** after a lapse of five years; **hanashiburi** way of talking.

burikáesu to relapse, have a relapse.

burikikan tin can.

burikki, buriki tin plate.

buróochi brooch.

-búru suffix denoting: to give oneself airs.

búruburu suru to shiver, shudder.

burui class, order, sort, group; **burui o wakéru** to sort, classify; **burui wake** classification; **burui wake o suru** to catalogue.

burujoa (*n.*) bourgeois.

búryoku military power, armed force.

busahoo mono ill-mannered person, boor.

busata long silence; **gobusata suru** to neglect to write (or visit) for a long time.

búshi warrior, samurai.

búsho appointed post; place of duty.

bushóo laziness, sloth, indolence; **bushóo na** lazy; **bushoo mono** lazy man; lazy-bones.

busoo arms, armaments; **busoo káijo** disarmament.

bussan products; produce.

bússhi goods, commodities, raw materials, resources; **bússhi no yútaka na** rich in natural resources; **busshitsu** matter, substance; **busshitsuteki** material, physical; worldly; **busshitsuteki ni** materially, physically.

bussóo unsafe, dangerous; suspicious; **bussóo na yonónaka** restless times (days).

busui na unfashionable; in poor taste; inelegant.

BUTA pig, swine; pork; **buta no abura** lard; **butagoya** pigsty; **BUTANIKU** pork; **tonkatsu** pork cutlet.

bútai stage (theatre); footlights; scene; sphere; **bútai ni tátsu** to go on the stage; **butáigeki** theatrical drama.

butchigai ni crosswise, across.

bútoo dance; dancing; **bútoo suru** to dance; **butóokai** ball, dance (party).

butsubutsu rash; **kao ni butsubutsu ga dekíru** to get a rash on the face.

bútsubutsu murmuring; grumbling; **bútsubutsu iu** to grumble; to murmur.

butsubutsu kóokan barter.

Butsudan (household) Buddhist shrine.

Butsudoo Buddhist teachings.

bútsugi discussion; public censure.

butsukaru to collide with; to clash; to knock (run) against; to fall on; **kónnan ni butsukaru** to encounter difficulties. **Saijitsu ga Nichiyóobi ni butsukaru.** The national holiday falls on Sunday.

butsukeru to throw at; to knock against. **Atamá o hashira ni butsuketa.** I knocked my head against a post.

bútsuri natural laws, physical laws, physics; **butsuriteki** physical.

butsurígaku physics; **butsurigákusha** physicist.

butsuyoku worldly desires.

buttooshi ni throughout; all through; without a break; **tooká kan buttooshi ni** for ten days running.

buttsuke ni directly; personally; outright.
búyo gnat; sandfly.
buyoo ballet; dance; **buyóogeki** dance drama.
buyóojin na insecure, unsafe (from burglary).
buyúuden heroic story.
búzama na ungainly; uncouth; clumsy.
BYÓO second (of time); tack; rivet; ancestral
  shrine; mausoleum; **byoo o kizamu** to
  tick away the time; **byóo de tomeru** to
  tack down.
byoo- prefix denoting: disease, illness;
  byoodoku virus; disease germs;
  byoogen cause of a disease;
  byoogénkin germs; **byóogo**
  convalescence; **byóogo no hito** a
  convalescent; **BYOOIN** hospital;
  byooin ni háiru to be hospitalized;
  byooki illness; **byooki ni kakáru** to
  fall ill; **byooki no** sick, ill; **atama no
  byooki** mental illness; **BYOONIN** sick
  person; **byoosei** condition (of a
  disease); **byóoshin no** weak, sickly,
  delicate, in poor health; **byooshitsu**
  sick room; ward; **byooshoo** sickbed.
  Byoosei ga aratamárimashita. He
  took a turn for the worse.
-byoo suffix denoting: disease, illness;
  haibyoo (lung) tuberculosis; **ganbyoo**
  eye disease.
byoobu folding screen; **byoobu o tateru** to set
  up a screen.
byoodoo equality; **byoodoo no** equal;
  byoodoo ni equally; without
  discrimination; **byoodoo ni suru** to
  make equal; **byoodoo no kenri** an
  equal right.
byoosha depiction; description,
  representation; **byoosha suru** to
  sketch, describe.

CH

CHA = OCHA tea; **cha o ireru** to prepare
  tea; **cha o irekáeru** to make fresh tea;
  cha o dásu to serve (offer) a cup of
  tea; **cha o tsugu** to pour tea; **cha no yu**
  tea ceremony; art of tea-making;
  chabánashi tea-talk, gossip, chat (over
  a bowl of tea); **chabashira** tea stalk
  floating erect in one's cup (foretelling
  something good, according to
  superstition); **chadansu** tea cabinet;
  chadóogu tea-things, tea set; **chagama**
  teakettle; **chagara** used tea leaves;
  chagáshi cake, sweets (served with
  tea); **CHAKA = saka** tea and cake;
  light refreshment; **chamise** tea stall;
  refreshment house; **chaseki** place
  where the tea ceremony is held; **chasen**
  (bamboo) tea whisk; tea stirrer for
  powdered tea (used in the tea
  ceremony); **chashaku** tea ladle; tea
  scoop; **chataku** tea saucer; **chawákai**
  social tea party; **CHAWAN** teacup;
  rice bowl; **CHAYA** teahouse; roadside

snack bar. **Chabashira ga tatte imasu.**
  A tea stalk is floating erect in his cup.
chabudai low eating-table.
chadai tip, gratuity.
CHAIRO (*n.*) light brown; **chairo no** (*adj.*)
  light brown; brownish.
chakásshoku light-brown color.
chakásu to laugh, banter; to make fun of.
-chaku suffix denoting a "counter" for a suit
  of clothes; **yoofuku itchaku** a suit of
  Western clothes.
chaku arrival; **chaku súru** to arrive at, reach;
  to receive; **chaku shídai** upon arrival;
  rokúji cháku arriving at six o'clock.
chakuchaku (*adv.*) steadily; step by step;
  chakuchaku shinchoku suru to make
  steady progress.
chakugánten point aimed at; viewpoint.
chakujitsu sincerity; steadiness and honesty;
  chakujitsu na honestly; faithfully.
chakuriku suru to land, alight.
chakurikuba, chakurikujoo landing field;
  airstrip.
chakushoku sháshin artificially colored
  photograph.
chákushu commencement, start; **chakushu
  suru** to commence, set about, start,
  begin.
cháme playfulness, sportiness; playful fellow;
  urchin; **cháme o hakki suru** to be
  jovial (jolly).
chánpon mixture; **chánpon ni** alternately.
chanoma sitting room; living room; tearoom.
CHAN TO (*adv.*) in good order, neatly;
  properly; thoroughly; fully, exactly,
  precisely, correctly; **chan to shita
  fukusoo** proper dress; **kimono o chan
  to kiru** to dress properly.
Cháppurin (Charlie) Chaplin (the actor).
  chappurin shiki no comical.
CHASAJI teaspoon.
chazuke rice steeped in hot tea (eaten as a
  simple meal or after rich food);
  chazuke o kakikómu to eat a hasty
  meal.
chékki luggage receipt, baggage check;
  chékki suru to check one's baggage.
CHI blood; blood relation; **chi ga déru** to
  bleed; **chi o tomeru** to stop bleeding;
  chi no meguri no yói quick-witted;
  sensible; **chi no meguri no warúi**
  dull-witted; not sensible; **chi o wákete**
  related by blood; **chibashiru** to
  become bloodshot; **chibashitta me**
  bloodshot eyes; **chidarake no** bloody.
chí intellect; **chiteki** intellectual.
chíbi dwarf, pygmy.
chíbusa breast.
chíbusu typhoid fever; typhus.
CHICHÍ father; **chichikata no** paternal.
  Chichikata no shinseki ga áru. I have
  relatives on my father's side.
CHICHÍ milk; **chichíya** milkman; dairy.
chichuu ground, earth; **chichuu ni** in the
  ground; underground.
Chichúukai Mediterranean Sea.

chié wisdom, intelligence; sense; advice, counsel; **chie no áru** wise; **chie no nai** unwise; **chié o kasu** to advise; **chié o shibóru** to rack one's brains; **chié o tsukéru** to suggest.

chieba wisdom tooth.

chigaeru to change, alter; to make a mistake; to dislocate, put out of joint; **yakusoku o chigaeru** to break a promise.

CHIGAI difference, disparity; distinction; mistake, error; **CHIGAI NÁKU** certainly, surely; without doubt;—**ni chigai nái** there is no mistake about it (that); **. . . undei no chigai ga áru** to be as different as heaven and earth; **CHIGAU** to be different, differ (from); to be unlike; to disagree, not be in accordance with, to be wrong, be mistaken. **Chigai ga áru.** There is a difference. **Kimi wa káre ni átta ni chigai nái.** You must have seen him. **Anó hito wa chótto hito to chigau.** He is a little different from other people.

chigiréru to be torn off; to come off; **chigíru** (constant verb) to tear off; to pluck; to pick; to pledge oneself; to vow, promise; **eikyuu no majiwári o chigíru** to swear eternal friendship. **Sode ga chigíreta.** A sleeve was torn off.

chíguhagu no odd, uneven, unequal.

chiheisen horizon; **chiheisen joo ni** above (on) the horizon.

chihóo locality; country (rural area); **chihóo no** local; provincial; **chihóoshoku** local color.

chíi rank, social status, position.

chiichái See **chiisái.**

chíiki tract of land; area.

chíimu team.

CHIISÁI = chiichai small, trifling; **chiisáku náru** to dwindle; to cringe, shrink.

CHÍIZU cheese.

chijimaru to shrink; to become shortened; **chijimeru** to shorten; to reduce; to draw in; **kimono o chijimeru** to cut a dress short; **chijimiagáru** to shrink (tremble) with fear; to cringe; to feel small; **chijimu** to shrink, contract; to shorten. **Keorímono wa nettoo ni ireréba chijimimásu.** Woolen cloth shrinks in hot water.

chijimi cotton crepe.

chijin acquaintance; friend.

chijireke frizzled, wavy hair; **chijireru** to be wavy; to become curly.

chijoku disgrace, dishonor, shame.

CHIJOO surface of the earth; earth; world; **chijoo no** earthly, terrestrial; on the earth; **chijoo ni** on the ground, on the earth.

chiká subterranean, underground; **chiká ni** under the ground; **chikadoo** underground passage.

CHIKÁGORO recently, lately; nowadays, in these days, **chikágoro made** till recent times; until lately.

chikai oath, vow; **chikai o tatéru** to make a vow, swear an oath, give a pledge; **chikai o mamóru** to keep an oath; **chikai o yabúru** to break an oath (vow). See also **chikau.**

CHIKÁI near; intimate; verging on; akin to; **chikái miyori** a near relation; **chikái uchi ni** before long; one of these days; **kanzen ni chikái.** It is nearly perfect. It is close to perfection.

CHIKÁKU nearby place; nearly; in the neighborhood of; shortly; in a short time; **shóogo chikáku káeru** to go home close to noon. **Sugu kono chikáku ni súnde imásu.** I live near here.

chikáme nearsightedness; nearsighted person; **chikáme no** nearsighted.

chikámichi short cut; **chikámichi o suru** to take a short cut.

CHIKARA strength, might, power, force; spirit; vigor; efforts, exertions; ability, talent; authority; **chikará ga yowái** weak; **chikará ga tsuyoi** strong; **chikara no áru** strong, powerful; **chikara no nái** powerless, incapable; **chikará ga tsukíru** to get exhausted; **chikará ni oyobanai** to be beyond one's power; **chikará o otósu** to be discouraged; **chikará o tsukéru** to cheer up, encourage; **chikarazúku** to recover one's strength or health; to be cheered up.

chikashíi close, intimate; familiar; **chikashii aida de** between friends.

chikáshitsu basement, cellar.

CHIKATETSU = chikatétsudoo subway.

chikatte upon my word, upon my honor.

chikau to swear, vow, pledge one's word.

chikayoru to draw near, approach.

chikazukéru to keep company with; to allow to come close to; to allow; **chikazúki** acquaintance; **chikazuki ni náru** to get acquainted with; **chikazúku** to draw near, approach; **chikazukánai yóoni suru** to keep away from.

chikazukigatái to be inaccessible, be difficult of access.

chikazukiyasúi to be accessible.

chikei topography; lay of the land.

chíki acquaintance; friend.

chíkkyo confinement in one's house; **chíkkyo suru** to stay indoors.

chikoku suru to be late.

chíkubi teat; nipple.

chikúchiku prickle; tingle; sharp pain.

chikudénchi storage battery.

chikuónki = puréeyaa record player; **chikuonki o kakéru** to play a phonograph record.

chikushoo birds and beasts; beast; brute (of a man). **Chikushoo!** Damn it! Hang it! **Kon chikushoo me!** You brute!

chikyuu earth; **chikyúugi** globe.

chimayóu to go mad, be crazed.

chimei place name.

chimei no well-known, noted, celebrated; **chimei no shi** man of distinction; celebrity.

chimidoro ni nátte strenuously; desperately.

chín Japanese spaniel.

-chin suffix denoting: charge, price; **kisháchin** train fare; **yáshin** house rent.

chinámu to be associated with; to call (or name) after.

chínba lameness; odd pair.

chinbotsu sinking; floundering; shipwreck.

chíngin wages; fare; **chingin seikátsusha** wage-earner.

chinka sinking, submersion; subsidence; **chinka suru** to sink to the bottom; to be put out, to be brought under control, to be extinguished.

chinkyaku rare guest; welcome visitor.

chinmári little, but well arranged; **chinmári shita** snug, comfortable. **Kono ié wa chinmari to shite sumi gokochi ga yói.** This house is snug and comfortable to live in.

chínmi dainty (thing); delicacy.

chinmoku silence, reticence; **chinmoku suru** to be silent; to hold one's tongue; **chinmoku saseru** to silence.

chinomígo suckling, infant.

chínpu na stale; old-fashioned commonplace; hackneyed; **chínpu na share** a stale joke.

chinretsu exhibition, display, arrangement; **chinretsu suru** to exhibit, display, show; **chinretsúbako** showcase; **chinretsúkan** museum; gallery; exhibition; **chinretsumádo** show window; **chinretsúshitsu** showroom. Sore wa chinretsu shite áru. It is on view.

chínsen wages; fare; charge.

chin shígoto piecework; **chin shígoto o suru** to do piecework.

CHÍPPU tip; **chíppu o yaru** to tip (a waiter, etc.).

chirabaru to be scattered, be in disorder; **chirakaru** (v. i.) to be scattered. **chirakasu** to scatter; to disarrange. **Hón ga chirabatte ita.** Books were scattered about.

chírachira flutteringly; flickeringly; gleamingly. **Yuki ga chírachira fútte ita.** The snow flakes were falling lightly. **Ki no aida kara hikarí ga chírachira shite ita.** The light gleamed through the trees. **Hikarí de mé ga chírachira suru.** The light dazzles my eyes.

chírahora here and there. **Sakura ga chírahora sakidáshita.** The cherry trees have started to bloom here and there.

chirari to at a glance; by accident; **chirarí to kikikómu** to hear by accident; **chirarí**

to míru to catch a glimpse of; glance at (a thing).

chirashi handbill, leaflet.

chirasu to scatter, disperse; **ki o chirasu** to distract (someone's) attention; to divert. (See also **chirabaru**.)

chíri geography; topography.

chirí dust; **chirihárai** duster; **chiritóri** dustpan. **chiri hodo mo nai.** There isn't a bit.

chiriakuta rubbish; garbage.

chiribaméru to inlay; to set; **shinju o chiribámeta yubiwa** a ring set with pearls.

CHIRIGAMI toilet paper; facial tissue.

chirijiri ni in all directions; separately; **chirijiri ni náru** to disperse in all directions, scatter; **chirijiri ni nátte iru** to be scattered about, be dispersed.

chirimen crepe; **chirimengami** crepe paper.

chirin chirin tingling; jingle-jangle; **chirín chirin naru** to ring.

CHIRU (chitte) to fall; to disperse; to be scattered; to be distracted; **ki ga chiru** to be distracted (mentally). **Kúmo ga chitte iru.** The clouds are dispersing.

chiryoo medical treatment; cure; **chiryoo suru** to treat; to cure; **chiryoo o ukéru** to receive treatment.

chisei geographical features; topography.

chishiki knowledge, information, learning; **chishik(j)in** learned man; intellectual.

chissoku suffocation.

chisuji blood; lineage, descent.

chitchái = **chiizai** small.

chitsújo order; **chitsújo no áru** orderly; **chitsújo no nái** disorderly; **chitsújo ga midárete iru** to be out of order; **chitsújo tadashíi** to be in good order; **chitsujo tadáshiku** in an orderly manner; systematically.

CHITTÓ MO = **chotto mo** (used with a negative) not at all; not a bit. **Góhan ga chittó mo oishikunái.** I don't have any appetite at all. **Chittó mo kamawánai.** He doesn't care a bit.

chízu map; topographical chart; atlas.

chochiku savings; **chochiku suru** to save up, store, lay by; **chochiku gínkoo** savings bank; **chochikúshin (chokushin) no áru** thrifty; **chochikúshin no nái** extravagant, prodigal.

chokin savings; **chokin suru** to save money.

chokkaku right angle; **chokkaku ni** at right angles.

chokkei diameter.

chokkoo through train; nonstop trip; direct voyage; **chokkoo suru** to go direct to.

chokkyuu straight ball; line drive.

chóko sake cup.

chókochoko at a trot; with short, mincing steps; **chókochoko komata ni arúku** to walk with short steps; to mince along.

CHOKORÉETO chocolate.

chókuchoku now and then. **Chókuchoku hanáshi ni kúru.** He comes to see us now and then.

chokumen suru to face, confront.

chokuritsu suru to stand up.

chokusen straight line.

chisoo entertainment, treat; feast; **gochisoo o suru** to treat someone; to entertain. **Goochisoo sama.** Thank you for the fine meal.

chokusetsu kóodoo direct action; **chokusetsu no** direct; immediate; personal; **chokusetsu ni** directly; personally; **chokutsuu** direct communication; through traffic; **chokutsuu réssha** through train.

chokuyaku literal translation.

chomei na well-known, famous, noted.

chóo intestines, bowels; **chóo** chief, head; **chóochoo** town headman; mayor.

CHOO- prefix denoting: town; street; **chóonai de** in the town.

-choo suffix denoting: government office; **Kikákuchoo** Planning Board.

chooba counter for Japanese style establishment (hotel, etc.).

choobatsu discipline; punishment.

choobo account book; register; **choobo o tsukéru** to keep accounts.

choochín paper lantern;—**no choochín o mótsu** to sing someone's praises; boast; **choochín ni tsurigane** an ill-assorted couple (in a marriage); an ill-matched pair.

CHÓOCHOO butterfly; **Chóochoo san** Madame Butterfly.

choodai suru (humble form) to receive; to drink; to eat. **Koohíi no kawari ni ocha o choodai itashimashóo.** I will take tea instead of coffee.

CHOODO just; right; exactly; **choodo góji ni** exactly at five o'clock; **choodo yói tokí ni** just at the right time; **choodo mannaka ni** right in the middle.

chooetsu superiority, excellence; **chooetsu suru** to surpass; to be superior to.

choogoo (n.) compounding, mixing, preparation; **choogoo suru** to mix, concoct, prepare; **choogóozai** compound, mixture.

choohatsu suru to requisition.

choohónnin ringleader; leader.

choohoogáru to find a thing useful; **chóohoo na** convenient; handy, useful; **chóohoo na** convenient; handy, useful; **chóohoo na hito** handy man. **Kuchi wa chóohoo na monó da.** The mouth is a convenient thing (You can say what you please).

choohóokei rectangle; **choohóokei no** rectangular, oblong.

chooji words of condolence; funeral address, eulogy.

choojin superman; **choojinteki** superhuman.

chóojo eldest daughter.

CHOOJÓO top, summit; **choojoo káigi** summit conference.

chooka excess; **chooka suru** to exceed.

chookan morning edition (of a newspaper).

chookeshi cancellation; writing off; **chookeshi ni suru** to square accounts. **Kore de chookeshi da.** Now we're quits.

chookoku, chookokúbutsu engraving; sculpture; **chookókushi** engraver; sculptor.

chookoo sign(s); symptom; attendance at a lecture; **jidai no chookoo** a sign of the times; **chookóoken** admission ticket; **chookóoryoo** lecture fee; admission fee.

chookyori long distance; **chookyóri dénwa** long-distance telephone; **chookyori hikóo** long-distance flight.

-CHOOME suffix denoting: street (employed when an ordinal number is used to name a thoroughfare or section of town). **Itchoome** First Street; **Nichoome** Second Street.

chóomei long life; longevity; **chóomei no** long-lived; **choomei suru** to enjoy a long life.

CHOOMÉN notebook.

chóomi seasoning, flavor; **choomíryoo** seasoning, condiments, spices.

choomúsubi rosette; bow.

chóonan eldest son.

chóoryoku (power of) hearing.

chooryuu tidal current, tide; tendency, trend.

chóosa examination, investigation, inquiry; **chóosa suru** to investigate, examine.

choosei regulation; adjustment; preparation, drafting, drawing up; **choosei suru** to regulate; to put in order; to prepare, draft, draw up.

choosen challenge; defiance; **choosen suru** to challenge; **choosen ni oozúru** to accept a challenge; **choosenteki** challenging; aggressive; defiant.

CHOOSÉN Korea; **Choosenjín** Korean people; **Choosengo** Korean language. (See also **Kánkoku**.)

choosetsu regulation, control; adjustment; **choosetsu suru** to regulate, control; **bukka o choosetsu suru** to regulate prices.

chooshi tune; pitch; key; rate of stroke; **chooshi ga átte iru** to be in tune; **chooshi ga átte inai** out of tune; **chooshi no yói** harmonious; melodious.

chooshínki stethoscope.

chóosho strong point; one's forte; merit.

chóoshu suru to hear; to listen in.

chooshuu audience; (people in) attendance. **Chooshuu ga óoi.** There is a large audience.

chooshuu collection; levy, assessment;

chooshuu suru to collect; levy; **zéi o chooshuu suru** to collect taxes.

chootéisha arbitrator, mediator.

chóoten highest point, apex, zenith.

chóoto long distance; long journey. **Chóoto no ryokoo ni tsúita.** He started on a long journey.

chootsúgai hinge.

choowa harmony, accord, agreement; **choowa suru** to harmonize; to agree with; **iro no choowa** harmony of colors.

choozen to aloof; above the world.

choozoo sculpture; statue.

chórochoro trickling (of a brook).

chosaku literary work; **chosakuken** copyright; **chosákusha, chósha** writer, author; **chósho** work (literary); production; publication.

chosúichi reservoir.

CHÓTTO just for a moment; a few minutes; a little; a bit; **chotto no ma ni** in a moment; in no time. **Chótto mátte kudasái.** Just a moment, please. Wait a bit, please. **Chótto dekinai.** It's no easy thing. **Chotto shita kotó de kenka shita.** They quarreled over a trifle. **Chotto shita ié ga aru.** There's a nice-looking house.

Chotto mo See **chittó mo.**

chozoomai stored rice.

chuu comment; annotation; footnote.

chúubu central part; center; **Chuubu chíhoo** Central Japan.

chúucho hesitation; indecision; **chúucho suru** to hesitate, waver; **chúucho shite** hesitatingly.

chuudan interruption; break; **chuudan suru** to cut in two; break in the middle.

chúudoku (n.) poisoning; ptomaine; **chuudokusei no** poisonous, toxic.

chuugáeri somersault.

chuugákkoo junior high school.

chuugata medium size; **chuugata no** medium-sized; medium.

chuugen last day of the Lantern Festival; midyear; presents exchanged at **chuugen.**

CHÚUGOKU China; **Chuukyoo** Communist China; Chinese Communist Party; **Chuugokújin** Chinese people; **Chuugokugo** Chinese language. (See also **Shina.**)

chúui attention, care; warning, caution; advice; hint; **chúui suru** to pay attention to; to attend to; to warn, etc.; **chúui shite** with care; **hito no chúui o hiku** to attract someone's attention; **chúui o ukéru** to be warned; **chúui o unagasu** to call attention to; **chuuibukaí** cautious, careful; attentive; **chuuí jínbutsu** marked man; suspicious character; **chuuí ryoku** attentiveness; **chúuisubeki** noteworthy, worthy of notice.

chuujitsu faithfulness; honesty; **chuujitsu na** faithful; honest; **chuujitsu ni** faithfully; honestly.

chuujun middle ten days of a month; **Gógatsu no chuujun ni** about (in) the middle of May.

CHÚUKA Middle Kingdom (China); **chuuka ryóori** Chinese food; **Chuuka Mínkoku** Chinese Republic (Nationalist China); **Chúuka Jínmin Kyoowá koku** Peoples' Republic of China (Communist China).

chuukan (n.) the middle; midway; **chuukan no** middle, intermediate;—**no chuukan ni** halfway between.

chuuken main body; backbone; center field (in baseball).

chuukoku advice, counsel; warning; **chuukoku suru** to advise; to warn; **chuukoku o ireru** to follow advice; **chuukoku ni somúku** to act against advice.

chuumoku notice, observation; attention; **chuumoku suru** to pay attention to; to watch, keep an eye on.

CHUUMON order; command(s); request; **chuumon suru** to order; **chuumon o tóru** to take an order.

chuumón tori traveling salesman; canvasser.

chuunen middle age; **chuunen no** middleaged.

chuuniku chuuzei medium build.

chuunyuu injection; pouring into; cramming.

chuuoo center, middle; **chuuoo shíjoo** central market.

chuuritsu neutrality; **chuuritsu chitái** neutral zone.

chúuryaku omission; ellipsis.

chuuryuu midstream; middle class; **chuuryuu kaíkyuu** middle class.

chuusai mediation, arbitration; **chuusai nin** mediator, peacemaker; **chuusai suru** to mediate, arbitrate.

chuusan moderate means (wealth); **chuusan káíkyuu** middle class.

chuusei neuter gender.

chúusei Middle Ages; **chúusei no** medieval.

chuusen lottery, drawing; **chuusen suru** to draw lots; **chuusen de sadaméru** to decide by lots; **chuusénken** lottery ticket.

chuushi suspension, stoppage; steady gaze; close observation; **chuushi suru** to stop, suspend, discontinue; to gaze steadily at; to watch closely; **jígyoo no chuushi** work stoppage; **shiai o chuushi suru** to call off a game.

chuushin center, core, heart; balance; **chuushin o tóru** to balance; **machi no chuushin ni** in the center of the city; **chuushin jínbutsu** central figure; leader.

chuusho defamation, slander.

CHUUTO midway, halfway; in the middle; unfinished; **chuuto de yameru** to stop in the middle of; to drop out of; **chuuto hánpa** (n.) halfway; **chuuto**

hánpa no (*adj.*) unfinished; **chuuto hánpa ni** (*adv.*) halfway; **chuuto hánpa na kotó o suru** to do things by halves.

chuutóngun army of occupation.

chuutoo (*n.*) second grade (class); medium quality; **chuutoo no middle grade**; medium; **chuutoo no shinamono** goods of medium quality.

chúuya day and night; **chúuya yasumázu hataraku** to work day and night without rest.

chuuyoo moderation; **chuuyoo o mamóru** to take the middle course; **chuuyoo o éta** moderate; **chuuyoo o énai** immoderate; one-sided.

chuuzai residence; **chuuzai no** resident; **chuuzai suru** to reside.

chuuzaisho police station.

chuuzetsu interruption; suspension; **chuuzetsu suru** to be interrupted; to be suspended; discontinued. **Shigoto wa chuuzetsu shita.** The work has been held up. **Chuuzetsu shite iru.** It is in abeyance.

D

DA plain present of **desu**, it is. **Kore wa nán da?** What is this? **Fude da.** It is a writing brush. **Are wa dáre da?** Who is he? **Bóku wa yuku nó wa iyá da.** I don't want to go.

DÁASU dozen; **ichi dáasu** one dozen; **dáasu de uru** to sell by the dozen.

dábi cremation.

dabókushoo bruise.

dabora (*colloq.*) big talk; **dabora o fuku** to boast.

dabudabu loose; baggy; **dabudabu no zubón** baggy trousers.

dachin reward; tip; small consideration; **dachin ni** in payment for. **Kore wa otsukai no dachin da.** This is your reward for doing the errand.

dadákko spoiled child; cross, fretful child.

daden suru to telegraph, wire.

daeki saliva, spittle.

DÁGA = DÉSU GA but; for all that; all the same; at the same time; on the other hand. (See also **dakedo**.).

dagashi coarse (cheap) confectionery (candy).

dageki blow; hit; shock; hitting, batting (in baseball); **dageki o kuwaeru** to deal a blow; **dageki o ukéru** to receive a blow.

dáha (*n.*) overthrow; **dáha suru** to break down; to overthrow; to frustrate.

dai money given in exchange for anything; cost; price; **dai o haráu** to pay off the cost.

DÁI time, period, age, generation; title, heading, theme; subject, topic; question, problem; reign, dynasty; (one's) lifetime; pedestal, block; stand; rest; table; bench; **dai o dasu** to put a question to.

d'ai- prefix which makes an ordinal from a cardinal number; counter for vehicles; **d'aiichi** the first; **d'aini** the second.

dái- prefix denoting: big, large, great; grand, high; colossal; **daitókai** a big city.

DAIBU, DAIBUN greatly, considerably, remarkably, rather, much, many; **daibúbun** greater part; best part; bulk; for the most part, mostly. **Daibu atsúi.** It is pretty hot. **Késa wa daibu yói.** I am much better this morning. **Daibu són o shita.** He suffered a big loss. **Daibu kane ga kakaru.** It takes a lot of money.

dáichi earth; ground.

dáichoo large intestines; colon.

daidai bitter orange.

dáidai successive generations; from generation to generation; **dáidai no** successive; hereditary.

daidaiteki na big, grand; splendid; wholesale; **daidaiteki ni** on a large (grand) scale; splendidly; **daidaiteki ni kookoku suru** to advertise extensively.

DAIDOKORO kitchen; **daidokoro dóogu** kitchen utensils.

daidoo énzetsu soap-box oration; street speaker.

daidoo shóoi general similarity; **daidoo shóoi de aru** to be nearly the same. **Yoo súru ni daidoo shóoi de aru.** In short, there is no choice between them.

daidoo shóonin street stall-keeper; pushcart peddler.

daigaku university, college; **daigákusei** college student.

daigíshi member of the House of Representatives.

daihon text of a play; libretto.

daihyoo representation; type; **daihyóosha** (*n.*) representative, deputy, delegate; **daihyooteki** (*adj.*) representative, typical.

DÁIICHI NI in the first place, first of all, firstly; **dáiichi no** first, foremost, primary.

daiji preface.

DÁIJI great enterprise; great thing; serious affair; emergency; **daiji na** important; serious; precious; **daiji na yooji** an important matter; **daiji ni suru** to take care of; **daiji o tóru** to be cautious; **daijígyoo** great enterprise; **daijínbutsu** great man (man of great character). **Kimi wa daiji o torisugíru.** You are overcautious. **Odaiji ni.** Take care of yourself.

DAIJÓOBU safe, secure, certain; strong; certainly, undoubtedly, without fail; I am sure; I assure you. **Sono hako wa daijóobu desu ka?** Is that box safe? **Moo daijóobu desu.** I am quite out of danger now. **Daijóobu naorimásu.** You will surely get well.

DAIKA = daikin price, charge; purchase money; **daikin hikikae** cash on delivery; C.O.D.; **daikin hikikae yúubin** C.O.D. **Daika wa íkura desu ka?** What is the price?

daikágeki grand opera.

daikin See **daika.**

dáikirai hateful, loathsome; abominable, detestable; **dáikirai da** to hate, loathe, have an antipathy to, have a strong aversion to. **Watakushi wa hébi ga dáikirai desu.** I loathe snakes.

daikon white radish; **daikon óroshi** radish grater; grated radish; **daikon óroshi** radish actors.

dáiku carpenter; carpentry.

daiméishi pronoun.

daimoku title (of a book); heading.

dainamáito dynamite.

dainashi spoiled, ruined; dirty; **dainashi ni suru** to spoil, ruin; to soil; **dainashi ní náru** to become spoiled, ruined. **Kimono ga dainashi ni nátta.** The garment is ruined. **Booshi o dainashi ni shita.** You've ruined your hat.

daióojoo peaceful death.

dairi deputation; agency; **dairi o suru** to act for, take the place of; **dairi no** acting; deputy; **dairinin** proxy; representative, agent; **dairíten** agency.

dajriseki marble.

DÁIROKU sixth; **dáirokujúu** sixtieth; **dáirokkan** sixth sense.

DÁISAN third; **DÁISÁNJUU** thirtieth; **DÁISÁNSHA** third person; bystander; **dáisánsha no tachibá kara kangáeru** to put oneself in a third person's position.

daishárin big wheel; giant swing (gymnastics); strenuous efforts; utmost exertion; **daishárin ni náru** to exert oneself to the utmost; **daishárin de hataraku** to work with all one's might; to work feverishly.

daishi pasteboard; board-mounting; **shashin o daishi ni haru** to mount a photograph.

DÁISHI fourth; **DÁISHIJÚU** fortieth.

DAISHICHI seventh; **DAISHICHIJÚU** the seventeenth.

daishin doctor's assistant.

daishonin scribe; notary.

daishoo compensation; recompense;—**no daishoo to shite** in compensation for; in recompense for.

daisóreta audacious, bold, insolent; atrocious; **daisóreta mane o suru** to behave atrociously.

dáisuki (adj.) favorite, pet; **dáisuki de aru** to have a great liking (for), be extremely fond of; **watakushi no dáisuki na hón** my favorite book.

daisúu, daisuugaku algebra.

DAITAI (n., adv.) main points, gist; outline, mainly; on the whole; **daitai ni óite** on the whole; in general; taking all things together; **daitai no mitsumori** rough estimate; **jíken no daitai o hanásu** to give an outline of the case.

daitán bravery; boldness, audacity; **daitán na** brave, fearless; bold, daring; **daitán ni** fearlessly; boldly, audaciously.

daitóoryoo president (of a republic); **daitooryoo kánsha** the White House.

daiyamóndo diamond.

daiyaru dial.

daiyoo substitution; **daiyoo suru** to substitute for, use in place of; to serve as, serve the purpose of;—**no daiyoo ni náru** to be used as a substitute; to serve the purpose of; **daiyóobutsu** substitute.

daizai subject matter, theme.

daizáinin great (criminal) offender.

DAIZU soya bean.

dajare poor joke; cheap jest; **dajare o íu** to crack a joke.

dákara = désukara.

DÁKARA accordingly, therefore, so; and so. **Dákara sonna kóto o shité wa ikenai.** That's why you must not do such a thing.

DAKE only; alone; by; as much (many) as; as . . . as; worth; **ni ínchi dake nagái** to be two inches too long; **dekiru dake háyaku** as fast (soon) as one can. **Onegai wa sore dake.** That's all I ask. **Bóku hitori daké de atta.** I was all by myself.

DÁKEDO = dákeredomo, dága but; for all that; all the same; on the other hand.

dákedomo, dákeredomo See **dakedo.**

dakiagéru to lift up in one's arms.

dakiáu to embrace (each other).

dakikómu to bring over to one's side, win over; to buy off; to entice.

dakishiméru to embrace closely, hug.

dakitoméru to stop by throwing one's arms round another; to hold (a person) back.

dakitsúku to fly into (someone's) arms; to cling to, embrace affectionately.

dakiyoséru to draw (someone) close to one's breast.

daku to embrace, to hug; to hatch (eggs).

dákudaku in stream; **dákudaku déru** to gush out, spout forth.

dákuhi answer (in the affirmative or negative); yes or no.

dakuon voiced consonant (such as **b, d, g,** or **z**).

dakuryuu, dakusui muddy stream or river; turbid water.

dakyoo compromise; agreement; **dakyoo suru** to compromise; to come to an agreement.

dakyuu polo.

damáru to be silent. **Damátte kudasái.** Please stop talking.

damásu to deceive, cheat, defraud; to impose upon; to bewitch; to soothe, humor (a crying child).

damátte silently, in silence; without telling; without leave; **damátte kiite iru** to be listening in silence; **damátte hito no monó o tsukau** to use someone else's things without permission.

DAMÉ na fruitless; hopeless; futile; **damé de**

aru to be useless; to be hopeless; to be futile; to be all over (with someone); **damé ni náru** to fail; **damé ni suru** to render useless; spoil.

dámu dam.

dán platform, rostrum, dais; steps, stairs; flight of stairs; grade, class; act; scene; **saidan** altar.

-dan suffix denoting; talk, conversation; story, tale; group, body, party, team; **ryokóodan** account of one's travels; **ichidan o náshite** in a group; **jitsugyóodan** party of businessmen.

dan'an decision; conclusion; **dan'an o kudasu** to make a decision.

dan'atsu suppression; oppression.

danboo sóochi heating apparatus.

danchígai de aru to be no match for; to outclass.

danchoo leader of a party.

DANDAN gradually, little by little; by and by. **Dandan kuraku nátte kimáshita.** By and by it became dark.

dandori plan, program, design.

dangai precipice, cliff.

dangan bullet, shot; shell.

dangén assertion; affirmation.

dango dumpling.

dangoo consultation, conference; **dangoo suru** to consult, confer with.

dangoku warm country; warm climate.

DANJITE absolutely; decidedly, on my word; never; by no means. **Danjite ikenai!** Positively no!

dánjo man and woman; both sexes; **dánjo kyoogaku** coeducation.

dankai steps, grade, gradation.

dankoo suru to take decisive steps, act resolutely.

dánko taru decisive, resolute, determined, positive; **dánko to shite** decisively, positively.

danmari dumb show; silence; reticence; man of few words.

danna (colloq.) master; husband; sir; gentlemen; **dannasáma** master (of the house).

dannén suru to abandon (an idea, hope, desire).

dánpan negotiation; parley. **Dánpan ga haretsu suru.** There is a breakdown in the negotiations.

danpatsu bobbed hair.

danpen fragment, piece; odds and ends; **danpenteki** fragmentary.

danran circle; harmony; **danran suru** to sit (around) together.

dánro heating stove; fireplace.

danryoku elasticity; **danryoku áru** elastic, springy.

dánsaa dancer; taxi dancer.

DANSEI male; man; masculinity; **danseiteki** masculine, manly.

dansen disconnection (of a wire).

DÁNSHI boy; man; **danshirashíi** manly; **danshiráshikunái** unmanly. **Dánshi.** Men's Room.

dánsu dance, dancing (occidental style).

dantai party, body; group.

dantei decision; conclusion; **dantei suru** to decide; to conclude.

danwa conversation, talk; **danwa suru** to talk, chat; **danwatai** colloquial, conversational style.

danzetsu suru to be cut off; to become extinct, be disconnected.

danzoku intermission; **danzokuteki no** intermittent; **danzokuteki ni** intermittently, on and off.

dáradara in drops, lazily, sluggishly; leisurely; sloppily; **dáradara suru** to work sloppily; **asé ga dáradara nageréru** to sweat profusely; **daradará zaka** a gentle slope.

-dárake suffix denoting: full of; covered with; **asedárake no** covered with sweat.

darakéru to feel dull, languid.

daraku depravity, corruption.

dararí to loosely; languidly.

darashi nái loose; careless, untidy; **darashi nái fúu o suru** to dress sloppily.

DÁRE = **TÁRE, dónata** who; **dáre no** whose; **dáre de mo** anyone, anybody; whoever; **dáre de mo mína** everyone, everybody; **dáre ka** someone, somebody; anyone, anybody. **Dáre ga shimashita ka?** Who did it? **Kore wa dáre no desu ka?** Whose is this? **Dáre ni agemashóo ka?** Who should I give it to? **Dáre ka anáta o yonde iru.** Someone is calling you.

daréru to grow listless; to get bored; to relax; to be dull. **Hanashí ga dáreta.** The conversation lagged.

daróo See **da.**

DARÚI to be dull; to feel languid, feel heavy. **Ashi ga darui desu.** My legs feel heavy.

daruma Dharma; toy image of Dharma.

daryoku See **dasei.**

dasan calculation; **dasan suru** to calculate, count; **dasanteki no** calculating, mercenary.

dasei = **daryoku** inertia; **ima máde no dasei** by force of habit.

dashimóno program; repertoire.

dashin suru to tap, sound.

DASHINUKE suddenness, abruptness; **dashinuke ni** suddenly; abruptly; unexpectedly; without warning; **dashinuke o kurau** to be taken by surprise.

dashinúku to forestall; to get ahead of.

dashishibúru to begrudge.

dassen suru to digress; to deviate.

dasshímen absorbent cotton.

dassoo desertion; flight; escape; **dassoo suru** to desert, run away; **dassóosha** fugitive, runaway.

dassúru to get out; to escape from; to omit, leave out; to get rid of; **akushuu o dassúru** to get rid of a bad habit.

DÁSU to put forth; to take out; to produce; to turn on; to turn away; to lay bare; to serve (a meal, tea, etc.); **tegami o dásu** to mail a letter; **shigoto ni té o dásu** to throw oneself into the job.

datai abortion.

datchoo hernia, rupture.

dátta -ta form (past) of **da**.

dátte (*colloq.*) but, still; because; for. **Náze gakkoo e ikanái no desu ka? Dátte atamá ga itái n desu mono.** Why don't you go to school? Because I have a headache.

DE in; at; flow; going out; rise; birth; origin; outset; start; in the matter of; **mikka de** in three days; **jikan de** by the hour; **de ga yói** to flow easily. **Tookyoo dé wa ichiban íi misé desu.** In Tokyo, it's the best store. **Amerika de kaimáshita.** I bought it in America. **Mizu de arau.** I wash it in water. **Kyoo wa hito no de ga yói.** There is a large turnout today.

de áru = desu.

dearúku to go out; to gad about.

DEÁU to meet, come across; to happen to meet.

déba debaboocho big kitchen knife.

débudebu no fat, plump.

debúshoo one who prefers to stay at home.

dedokoro source; origin.

degara tea leaves; coffee grounds.

DÉGUCHI exit.

deiri entrance and exit; **deiri suru** to go in and out; to frequent, visit regularly; **deiríguchi** entrance; doorway.

deisui intoxication; **deisui suru** to be dead drunk; **deisúisha** drunkard.

DEKAKERU to go out; to start, set out; **degake ni** on the point of going, on one's way; **ryokoo ní dekakeru** to start on a trip. **Degake ni denwa ga kakátta.** Just as I was on the point of going out, I received a phone call.

dekasegi emigration; working in another country; **dekasegi suru** to emigrate; to work away from home; **dekaseginin** emigrant.

dekáta attitude; move.

deki workmanship; make; tailoring; cut; result, effect; crop, yield; **deki no yói** of fine workmanship; **deki no warúi** of poor workmanship; **Amerika deki no** American made; **deki fúdeki** success and failure. **Deki fúdeki ga arimásu.** It is not always successful.

dekiagáru to be finished, be completed, be ready.

dekiai no ready made.

dekibáe effect, result; manner of execution. **Rippa na dekibáe deshita.** It was a fine performance.

dekigókoro sudden impulse; passing fancy; **dekigókoro de** on the spur of the moment.

dekígoto event, incident; **híbi no dekígoto** daily occurrence; everyday event; **saikin no dekígoto** recent event.

dekimóno boil; sore; tumor; ulcer.

dekínai cannot do; poor. **Nihongo ga yóku dekímasen.** I can't speak Japanese well.

DEKÍRU can, may; to be able; to be possible, to be capable of; be done, be completed; **dekíru kotó nara** if possible [it is a thing that I can do]. **Shokuji ga dékita.** Dinner is ready.

dekiru dake to the best of one's ability; as . . . as possible; **dekiru dake háyaku** as soon as possible; as early as possible; **dekiru dake no kotó o suru** to do what one can; to do everything one can.

dekishi drowning; **dekishi suru** to drown; **dekishísha** a drowned person.

dekisokonai failure; **dekisokonai no** defective; bungled; half-baked; clumsy; deformed; **dekisokonáu** to fail; to be a failure; to be badly done, be botched, be bungled. **Shigoto wa dekisokonátta.** The job was bungled.

dekitate brand-new; just made; fresh.

dékki deck.

dekoboko unevenness; **dekoboko no** uneven, bumpy; rough; jagged.

demado bay window.

demae catering. **Demae o suru.** They do catering.

déme protruding eyes; **déme no** goggle-eyed.

demise branch (store); **demise o dásu** to open a branch.

-DÉMO even, though; even if; as well, also; but, still. **Watakushi démo dekimásu.** Even I can do it. **Dónna pén démo íi desu.** Any pen will do.

demodori divorcée.

demukae meeting; reception; **demukae o ukéru** to be met (by someone); **DEMUKÁERU** to go to meet (on arrival).

denaósu to come again; to go again; to call again.

den'atsu voltage.

denbun telegram.

dénchi electric cell; battery.

denchuu telegraph or telephone pole; electric-light pole.

dendoo missionary work; **dendóoshi** evangelist, missionary.

den'en country, farms; rural districts; **den'en no** rural, countrified.

denji farmland; rice fields.

denka electrification; **denka suru** to put in electricity; to operate by electricity; **DÉNKI** electricity; **dénki no** electric(al); **denkidókei** electric clock; **denkijíkake no** operated by electricity; **DENKYUU** electric bulb; **dennétsuki** electric heater; **dénryoku** electric power; electricity; **denryuu** electric current. (See also **dentoo**.)

denki biography.

DENPOO telegram; cable; **denpoo de**

wire, by cable; **denpoo o útsu** to send a telegram (wire, cable); **denpóoryoo** telegraph fee. (See also **denshin**.)

densen telegraph wire, electric wire; infection, contagion; **densen suru** to be infectious; to be infected with; **densenbyoo** infectious, contagious disease; epidemic.

densetsu tradition; legend; **densetsuteki** traditional, legendary.

DÉNSHA streetcar, electric, trolley; **dénsha de iku** to go by streetcar; **dénsha ni noru** to take a streetcar; **densháchin** streetcar fare; **denshadóori** street with a trolley line.

denshin telegram; **denshin báshira** telegraph pole; **denshínkyoku** telegraph office. (See also **denpoo**.)

dentoo tradition; convention; **dentooteki** conventional; traditional.

DENTOO electric light; **dentoo gáisha** electric company; **dentoo o hiku** to have electricity installed; **dentoo o tsukéru** to turn on the lights; **dentoo o kesu** to turn off the lights. (See also **denka**.)

DENWA telephone; **denwa choo** telephone directory; **denwa de** by telephone; **denwá shitsu** telephone booth; **kooshuu dénwa** public telephone; **denwa o kakéru** to call, make a phone call; **denwa o kíru** to hang up; **denwa o hiku** to have a phone installed.

DEPÁATO department store.

DÉRU to come out; to appear; to rise; to be up; to go out; to attend; to flow out; to break out (inside); **sóto e déru** to go out (outside); **uchi o déru** to leave the house; **shikí ni déru** to attend a ceremony. **Mizu ga déru.** There is a flood.

desakari rush hour; height of the season.

desaki place to which someone has gone. **Desakí ga wakaránai.** I don't know where he has gone.

deshabáru to meddle, interfere.

deshí pupil, disciple, apprentice.

déshita See **desu**.

deshóo See **desu**.

desoróu to come out fully; to be all out.

—DESU = **de aru** = **da** be; it is; equals. **Watakushi wa gakusei desu.** I am a student. **Amerikasei déshita.** It was an American make (product). **Eikokújin deshóo.** Probably he is British.

desu ga = **dá ga.**

desugiru to protrude (stick out) too much; to be too far out; to be too strong.

DÉSUKARA = **dákara** that is why; therefore. **Desukara mínna ni sukarémasu.** That is why he is liked by everyone.

detarame irresponsible remark; nonsense; **detarame o iu** to speak nonsense.

DÉWA then, in that case, if so. **Déwa sayoonára.** Good-by now. **Déwa**

mata. I'll be seeing you. **Déwa soo shite kudasai.** If that is the case, please do so.

DEZÁATO desert.

dezáin design.

do degree, measure, extent; times; **ichi ni do** once or twice; **do o sugósu** to go to extremes.

DÓA door (Western style).

dobin earthen teapot.

doboku public works; engineering; **doboku gíshi** civil engineer.

dobu ditch.

dobunézumi water rat.

doburoku raw (unrefined) sake.

DÓCHIRA which way; which (of the two); where; what place; **dóchira e?** where?; **dóchira démo** whichever; either; both.

dodai foundation, basis.

dógimagi in confusion; **dógimagi suru** to act confused, act flustered.

dohyoo sandbag; Japanese wrestling ring, arena. **dohyoo giwa de** at the last possible moment; at the eleventh hour.

DÓITSU Germany; **Dóitsu no** (*adj.*) German; **Doitsújin** (*n.*) German; **Doitsugo** German language; **Nishi Dóitsu** Western Germany.

dojoo earth, soil.

dókadoka in rapid succession; in crowds; **dókadoka háitte kúru** to come in crowds, to rush in.

dokán to See **dokkari.**

dokata laborer; coolie.

dokeru to remove; to get out of the way.

dóki earthenware; anger; resentment; **dóki o obite** in anger.

dókidoki suru to throb violently. **Muné ga dókidoki shimásu.** My heart is beating rapidly.

dokítto suru to be startled, get a shock.

dokkári to = **dokán to** heavily; with a thud.

dókku dock; **dókku ni háiru** to dock (as a ship).

DÓKO where, what place; **dóko e itté mo** wherever you go; **dóko ka** somewhere; **dóko kara** from where; **dóko made** how far; **dóko mo** everywhere.

dókoro ka far from; to say nothing of; anything but. **Hikooki dókoro ka jidoosha mo mótte imásen.** He doesn't even own a car, let alone an airplane.

dokú poison; harm; **doku no áru** poisonous; **dokú ni náru** to be bad for; **doku súru** to harm; to poison. **Oki no doku sama.** I'm sorry for you.

doku to get out of the way; to move aside. **Doite kure.** Clear the way! Get out of my way (rough)!

dokudan arbitrary decision; **dokudanteki** dogmatic, arbitrary.

dokudokushíi malicious, spiteful; poisonous-looking; **dokudokushíi kotó o iu** to say malicious things.

dokuen solo performance, recital.

dokugaku studying by oneself, without a teacher.

dokuhitsu suru to libel.

dókuja poisonous snake.

dókuji no original; personal; individual; **dokujisei** originality; **dókuji no kangáe** personal opinion.

dokukeshi antidote.

dokuritsu independence; self-support; **dokuritsu suru** to be independent, stand on one's own feet; **dokuritsu no** independent; **dokuritsu de** independently; **dokurítsukoku** independent state; **dokurítsushin** independent spirit. **Dokurítsusai** Independence Day (Fourth of July).

dokuro skull.

dokuryoku de on one's own, by oneself, singlehanded; **dokuryoku de yaru** to do something on one's own.

dokusai dictatorship; **dokusai séiji** dictatorship; **dokusaika** dictator.

dokusatsu suru to poison.

dokusen monopoly; **dokusen jígyoo** monopolistic enterprise, monopoly; **dokusenteki** monopolistic, exclusive.

dókusha reader; subscriber; reading public; **dókusho** reading; **dókusho suru** to read (books); **dokushoka** book-lover; great reader.

dokushoo vocal solo.

dokushuu = **dokugaku** studying without a teacher; **dokushuusho** book for self-teaching; "do-it-yourself" book.

dokusoo originality; **dokusooteki no** original; creative; **dokusoo no sái** creative ability; talent.

dokuyaku poison.

dókyoo spirit; courage; **dókyoo no áru** daring, courageous; **dókyoo no nái** timid; cowardly.

domá earthen floor.

donabe earthen pot.

donáru to shout, thunder at.

DÓNATA who (polite); **dónata de mo** anybody. **Dónata desu ka?** Who are you? **Dónata ka ome ni kakaritái soo desu.** Someone wishes to see you.

donburi deep bowl; **donburi meshi** boiled rice served in a deep bowl; **oyako dónburi** chicken and rice in a deep bowl.

dóndon rub-a-dub; rat-a-rat; **dóndon susumu** to advance rapidly; **dóndon mookéru** to make money rapidly.

DÓNNA what; what sort of, kind of; **dónna ni** how much; however. **Dónna hón desu ka?** What kind of a book is it?

DÓNO which; what; **dono kurai** to what degree?; how long?; how far?; **dóno hito** which person?

donzoko nédan rock-bottom price.

DÓO how; what; copper; torso, body; frame; hull; **dóo atte mo** in any case. **Doo itashimáshite.** Don't mention it! Not

at all! **Sore wa dóo ni mo narimasen.** It can't be helped.

doo (can also be prefix) the same; the said (aforementioned); corresponding; equal; **doo bánchi** the same street number; **doodan** same, ditto; **dooyoo** the same, ditto; **doo mikka** the third day of the same month; (*n.*) temple; shrine; hall; **doo ní íru** to attain proficiency, become an expert at.

DOOBUTSU animal; living creature; **doobútsuen** zoo; **doobutsúgaku** zoology.

DOO DE MÓ in any way; **doo de mo kóo de mo** by any means, at any cost; **doo de mo íi koto** a trivial matter. **Doo de mo ii desu.** It doesn't matter one way or the other.

doodoo suru to go with, accompany.

doofuu enclosure(s); **doofuu no tegami** the enclosed letter.

dóogi morality, morals, principles, ethics; motion made during a meeting.

DOOGU tools, implements, utensils; sets; property; household goods; **doogúbako** toolbox; **dooguya** secondhand dealer; curio shop; furniture shop.

doohai equal colleague.

doohan suru to accompany.

dooi consent, approval, agreement; **dooi suru** to consent jo, approve.

DOO ITASHIMASHITE! Don't mention it. Not at all. The pleasure is mine.

dooitsu equality; **dooitsu no** same, identical, equal.

dooji same time; **dooji no** simultaneous, concurrent; **dooji ni** at the same time; **doojidai** same age; **doojídai no** contemporary; **dóojitsu** same (very) day; **doojoo** exercise hall (for Judo, fencing, etc.); arena; Buddhist seminary.

doojoo sympathy, compassion; **doojoo áru** sympathetic, warm-hearted; **doojoo no nái** unsympathetic.

DÓOKA = **dóozo** please; somehow or other; **DOOKA KÓOKA** somehow or other; some way or other; barely; with difficulty; **dóoka shite** somehow, one way or another.

dooka assimilation.

dóoka copper coin.

dookaku same rank, status, etc.

dookan same sentiment, same feeling; same opinion; **dookan de áru** to be of the same opinion; **dookan suru** to feel the same way.

dooke (*n.*) clowning; **dooke shíbai** farce; **dooke yákusha** clown; **dookéta** comic, foolish; **dookéru** to clown.

dookei aspiration, longing; worship.

dooki motive, incentive; throbbing; palpitation; **dooki ga suru** to throb, palpitate.

dóoki same period; same class; **dóoki no** of the same year; **dookísei, dookyúusei** classmate.

28

dookokújin fellow countryman.

dookoo pupil of the eye.

dookoo suru to go together; **dookóosha** traveling companion.

doomeí alliance; league; **doomei hígyoo** strike; walkout.

DÓOMO very; much; rather; quite. **Dóomo arígatoo gozaimasu.** I'm much obliged.

doonen same year; same age; **doonen de aru** to be the same age.

DÓO NI KA somehow or other; **dóo ni ka suru** To manage somehow, try one's best.

DÓORO road.

dooryoku motor power; power.

DOOSE anyway; after all; at best; of course; at all. **Doose yaraneba naránai desu.** I must do it anyway.

DÓO SHITE why; how; **DÓO SHITE MO** in any case; by any means; whatever may happen. **Dóo shite sore o gozonji desu ka?** How do you know that? **Dóo shite mo ikanákereba narimasen.** Whatever may happen (in any case, no matter what happens) I have to go.

dootoo equality; parity; **dootoo no** equal, equivalent; **dootoo ní** equally; **dootoo ni suru** to make equal, equalize.

DÓOZO please; if you please. **Dóozo moo ichido itte kudasái.** Please say it again.

doozoo bronze statue.

dóra gong.

dórama drama

dorámu drum (musical); **dorámu kan** drum (for storage).

DÓRE which one? **Dóre ga ichiban yói desu ka?** Which is the best?

doró mud; **doro dárake no** muddy; **dorómizu** muddy water.

doroboo thief.

DÓRU dollar; **doru sóoba** exchange rate of the dollar.

dóryoku effort, exertion; **dóryoku suru** to exert oneself; to endeavor.

dosakusa confusion; tumult; trouble.

dóshidoshi in large numbers; rapidly; in rapid succession.

DOSSÁRI in great quantity or numbers. **Tegami ga dossári kita.** Many letters came.

DOTTO all of a sudden; suddenly; with a rush.

DOYÓOBI Saturday.

dozoo storehouse with earthen walls.

E

E particle denoting: to, toward, in the direction of; —(n.) handle, crank, haft, shaft; bait, feed, food (for fish, for birds); **tsuribari ni e o tsukéru** to bait a fishhook. **Kyóoto e ikimásu.** I'm going to Kyoto.

É picture, painting; drawing, illustration; sketch; **é o káku** to make (draw, paint) a picture; **é no yoo na** like a picture; picturesque.

ebi lobster; shrimp; prawn.

ebicha maroon; brownish red.

eda branch, bough; twig; **edaburi** spread of branches; **edaha** branches; ramifications; digressions; **hanashí ga edaha ni háiru** to digress; **edaha no gíron** side issue; digression.

ÉE = HAI yes. **Ée, sóo desu.** Yes, that is so. Correct.

eeteru ether.

ee to let me see; well (used when stalling for time). **Ee to, sore wa nán deshita ka?** Let me see, what was it?

égao smiling face; smile; **égao o suru** to smile; **égao de** with a smile.

egataí hard to get; not easily obtainable; **matá to egataí kikái** a rare opportunity.

EHÁGAKI picture post card.

ehón picture book for children; illustrated book.

Ei- prefix denoting: Anglo-, English, British; **Ei-taishí kan** British Embassy.

Éi-Bei England and America; **Éi-Bei no** Anglo-American; **Ei-Béijin** the English and the Americans.

eibin na keen, sharp, smart, clever, quickwitted; **eibin na kansatsu** keen observation; **eibin na mímí** sharp ears.

EIBUN English; English sentence; English composition; English-language text; **Eibúngaku** English literature; **Eibun wáyaku** translation from English into Japanese.

eien eternity; permanence; **eien no** eternal; permanent; everlasting; **eien ni** forever, perpetually.

ÉIGA movie; motion pictures; **eiga káisha** film-producing company; **eigákai no meiyuu** movie star; **EIGÁKAN** movie theatre.

EIGO English language; English; **Eigo no** English; written in English; **Eigo ga dekíru, Eigo de hanásu** to speak in English; **Eigo ga wakáru** to understand English.

EIGYOO business, trade; trading; **eigyoo suru** to engage in business, trade in; **eigyóohi** business expenses; **eigyoo jíkan** business (office) hours; **eigyóozei** business tax.

eijuu permanent residence; **eijuu no** settled; resident; **eijuu suru** to reside permanently.

Éika English currency; sterling; British-made goods.

eikan crown of glory; laurels.

éiki high spirits; vigor; energy. **Éiki o sógu.** To dampen one's enthusiasm.

EIKOKU England, Great Britain; **Eikoku no** English; **Eikokújin** Englishman. (See also **Eigo.**)

EIKYOO influence; effect; **eikyoo suru** to

influence; to affect; **eikyoo o ukéru** to be influenced, be affected.

eikyuu, eikyuusei permanence; eternity; **eikyuuteki** permanent; perpetual, eternal; **eikyuu ni** permanently, forever.

eimin death (human only); **eimin suru** to die.

éiri gain, profit; **eiriteki no** money-making; commercial; **eiri jígyoo** commercial undertaking; **eiri gáisha** commercial concern.

éiri na sharp, keen; sharp-edged.

Eiryoo British dominion.

eisei hygiene, sanitation; health; satellite; **eisei ni yói** healthful; wholesome; **eisei ni waruí** bad for the health; **eiséikoku** satellite nations; **eiseiteki no** hygienic; sanitary; **jinkoo eisei** man-made satellite.

eisháki film projector.

eisháshitsu operating room.

eiten promotion; transfer on promotion.

EI-WA JÍSHO English-Japanese dictionary.

Eiyaku English translation.

éiyo honor; glory.

eiyoo nutrition, nourishment; **eiyoo áru** nutritious, nourishing; **eiyoo fúryoo** malnutrition; **eiyóobutsu** nutritious food.

eizoku permanence; continuation; **eizokuteki** lasting, permanent; **eizoku suru** to last long, remain permanently.

eizúru to be reflected (as in a mirror; in water); to impress.

ÉKI use; good; benefit, advantage, profit, gain; war; battle; juice, sap; liquid, fluid; **éki no áru** beneficial, profitable; **éki no nái** useless; unprofitable; **eki súru** to benefit, do good to.

ÉKI = **teishajoo** railway station; **ekichoo** stationmaster; **ekifu** railway porter; station employee; **Tokyooeki** Tokyo Station.

ekibyoo epidemic, pestilence, plague.

ekiri dysentery; children's summer diarrhea.

ékisu extract, essence; **gyuuniku ékisu** beef bouillon.

ekitai liquid, fluid.

ekkisu kóosen X rays.

ekohíiki partiality, favoritism; **ekohíiki no** partial, unfair; **ekohíiki no nái** impartial, fair; **ekohíiki suru** to show partiality to; be partial to.

ekoji na stubborn, perverse, obstinate; **ekoji ni nátte** in spite; out of spite.

ékubo dimple.

emono game, a catch; trophy; prize, spoils.

ÉN yen (Japanese money); affinity; fate; blood relation; connection; feast, banquet; dinner party; **hyaku en** 100 yen (about 28c); **hyaku én satsu** 100-yen note; **én o kíru** to sever relations; to divorce; **én o musubu** to marry; **én o haru** to give a dinner party.

enban disk, discus.

enbífuku (male) evening dress.

enboo vista; distant view.

enchaku suru to arrive late; to be delayed.

enchoo continuation, extension; **enchoo suru** to extend, prolong, lengthen.

endan proposal (of marriage); rostrum, platform; **endóo pea**; **endóo mame** peas.

endoo route; road; **endoo ni** enroute; along the road.

en'en in a blaze; **en'en táru** blazing, flaming; **en'en to shite** in (fierce) flames.

enérugii energy.

engan coast; **engan no** on the shore along the coast.

engan = **enshi** farsightednesss.

ENGAWA veranda, porch.

engei dramatic performance; entertainment; **engéisha** performer, artist; **engeijoo** variety theatre; an entertainment hall; **engéikai** variety show; **engei mókuroku** program; repertoire.

engeki play; theatrical performance.

engi luck; omen; history; legend; acting; performance; **engi no yói** lucky, auspicious; **engi no waruí** unlucky, ominous, ill-omened.

éngo support; backing.

engumi marriage; alliance; adoption (of a son); **engumi suru** to marry; to adopt.

énja relative, kinsman.

énjo assistance, help, aid; **enjo suru** to assist, help; to support.

enjuku maturity; mellowness; perfection; **enjuku suru** to grow ripe, mature; to mellow; **enjuku shita** mature; mellow; perfect.

énka exchange rate, value, of the yen.

enkai social gathering; feast, banquet; dinner party; coast; sea (near land); **enkai no** inshore; **enkai o híraku** to give a dinner party; **enkáishuu** Maritime Provinces.

enkei distant view; perspective; circle; **enkei no** round, circular.

enki postponement; adjournment; **enki suru** to postpone, put off.

enkin distance; far and near; **enkin kara** from far and near.

énko connection; relation; affinity.

enkyóri far distance, great distance; **enkyori de** at a great distance.

enmachoo black list; teacher's record book.

enman perfection; harmony; **enman na** perfect; harmonious; peaceful; **enman ni** harmoniously, smoothly; peacefully; **enman na katei** happy home; **enman ni kotó o osaméru** to settle the matter smoothly.

ennetsu burning (scorching) heat; heat of the sun.

énnichi fete day (of a local deity); fair; festival.

en nó shita ground or space under the veranda or floor in a Japanese house; **en nó shita no chikarámochi o suru** to be engaged in a thankless task; to labor in the background.

enogu paints, oils; colors, pigments; **enogúzara** dish for blending colors.

ENPITSU pencil; **iro-énpitsu** colored pencils; **enpitsu kézuri** a pencil sharpener.

enpoo great distance; distant place.

enrai no kyaku visitor (guest) from a distant place.

énro long way; great distance; long journey. **Énro go-sokúroo o wazurawashimáshite aisumimasén.** I thank you for coming all the way.

ENRYO reserve; modesty; respect; **enryo suru** to be reserved; to refrain from; to withhold; **enryo náku** without reserve, freely; **enryo bukái** reserved; shy;—**ni enryo shite** out of respect for (someone); **enryo éshaku mo náku** without the least reserve.

ensaki edge of a veranda.

ensei, enséikan pessimism; **enseiteki** pessimistic; **enseika** pessimist.

enshoo inflammation; spread of a fire; **enshoo suru** to catch fire.

enshutsu performance (of a play, an opera, a film); **enshutsu suru** to play, perform; to execute.

ensoku excursion (on foot); hike; picnic; **ensoku ni iku** to go on a hike; to take a long walk.

ensoo musical performance; recital; **ensóosha** performer; player; **ensóokai** concert, recital.

entaku round table. (See also **tákushii**.)

enten blazing (burning) sun; heat of the day.

ENTOTSU chimney; chimney stack; funnel.

en'yoo gyógyoo deep-sea fishing.

en'yoo kóokai ocean voyage.

en'yúukai garden party.

enzetsu speech, address; **enzetsu suru** to make a speech; **enzetsúkai** lecture.

enzúku to be married.

episóodo episode.

ERÁBU to choose, select, elect, single out; to sort; **hón o erábu** to select a book. **Íi no daké o erabimashoo.** Let's choose only a good one.

ERÁI great; extraordinary; worthy; eminent; wonderful; serious; heavy. **Erái kotó ni nátta.** It looks bad.

EREBÉETAA elevator.

ERÍ neck; neckband; collar; **eríkubi** nape of the neck; **erímaki** muffler, scarf; **erí o tadásu** to adjust one's dress; to sit up straight.

eridome brooch; breastpin.

éru to gain; to get.

éshaku greeting, salutation; **éshaku suru** to greet; to bow slightly.

esukaréetaa escalator.

etai form, shape; nature; **etai no shirenu** unfamiliar, strange; nondescript; **etai no shirenu hito** a perfect stranger.

eté skill; specialty, one's forte; **ete ni ho o ageru** to sail before the wind; to give

scope to one's skill;—**ga eté da** to be a good hand at;—**wa eté de nái** to be a poor hand at.

etoku understanding, comprehension; **stoku suru** to understand, grasp; **etoku shiyói** easy to understand; **etoku shinikúi** difficult to understand.

F

FÁAMASHII pharmacy.

faindaa finder.

fán fan, enthusiast; **eiga fan** movie fan.

fássho fascist.

fáuru foul ball (in baseball).

feruto See **fueruto.**

ffíto = fuííto feet (a measure).

Firíppin Philippine Islands; **Firíppinjin** Filipino.

fírumu = fuirumu film.

fírutaa filter.

fóoku fork.

-fú suffix denoting: urban prefecture (used only with Kyoto and Osaka); **Kyooto fu** Kyoto prefecture.

fuan insecurity; anxiety; **fuan na** unsafe; insecure; anxious; **fuánshin** uneasiness, anxiety.

fuan ni omóu to feel insecure (uncertain, anxious) about. **Fuánshin de átta.** I felt uneasy.

fuánnai unfamiliarity; ignorance; **fuánnai na** unfamiliar; ignorant; **fuánnai na tochi** strange place; **tochi ni fuánnai na hito** stranger, person who is not familiar with a place. **Watakushi wa koko wa fuánnai desu.** I am pretty much of a stranger here.

fuántei instability; **fuántei na** unstable; unsteady; insecure.

FÚBEN inconvenience; **fúben na** inconvenient; **fúben o shoozuru** to cause inconvenience; **fúben o shinóbu** to put up with inconvenience; **fúben o kanzuru** to be put to inconvenience.

fúbi deficiency; defect, imperfection; **fúbi na** defective; incomplete; imperfect; **fúbi no ten** defects; imperfections.

fúbin na pitiful; poor; **fúbin ni omóu** to pity, take pity on.

FÚBO parents.

fúbuki snowstorm, blizzard.

fuchakuriku hikóo non-stop flight.

fuchaku suru to stick to; to attach.

fuchí edge, brink, rim; margin, border; **fuchí o tóru** to hem; to fringe, etc.; **fuchí o tsukéru** to frame, border.

fuchi deep pool, deep water; abyss.

fuchin ups and downs; rise and fall; **isshoo no fuchin ni kansuru dáiji** a matter affecting one's whole life.

fuchoo sign; mark; price tag; disagreement; rupture; failure; **fuchoo ni owaru** to end in failure.

fuchóowa discord; incongruity; **fuchóowa na**

31

unharmonious, discordant; **fuchóowa de aru** to clash.

fuchúui carelessness; inattention; **fuchúui na** careless; inattentive; **fuchúui ni** carelessly.

fuchúujitsu unfaithfulness, disloyalty; **fuchúujitsu na** unfaithful, disloyal.

FUDA card; label, tag; placard; **fuda o tsukéru** to attach a card (or label); to tag.

FÚDAN usually, ordinarily; habitually; **fúdan no** usual; habitual; common; **fúdan no tóori** as usual.

fudángi everyday clothes.

fude writing brush.

fúdeki failure; poor work; **fudeki na** badly made (done); clumsy. **Kono hako wa fúdeki desu.** This box is badly made. **Íne ga fúdeki desu.** The rice crop is poor.

fudoo difference, diversity, dissimilarity; inequality; **fudoo de aru** to be unequal; to differ; to be irregular.

fudóoi disagreement, difference of opinion.

fudóosan immovable property; real estate.

fudóotoku immorality; **fudóotoku na** immoral, unprincipled.

fue flute.

fuéisei no unsanitary; unhealthy.

FUÉRU to increase (in number or quantity), multiply. **Mizu ga fúerte kita.** The river is rising. **Okane ga fúeta.** His income has increased.

fueruto = feruto felt.

fúete weak point; unskillfulness; **fúete na** unskillful, inexpert. **Sono hóo wa fúete desu.** I'm a poor hand at it. It's not in my line.

fufuku dissatisfaction, discontent; disapproval; objection; **fufuku ga áru** to be dissatisfied, etc.; **fufuku o iu** to express dissatisfaction.

fugai nái unmanly, effeminate; poor-spirited; cowardly.

fugen natural resources; sources of wealth.

fúgi immorality; injustice; adultery; **fúgi no** immoral; improper.

fúgiri ingratitude; dishonesty; **fúgiri no** unjust; dishonest; ungrateful; **fúgiri ga áru** to owe a debt.

fugoo wealthy man, millionaire; mark, sign, symbol; cipher.

fugóokaku failure; elimination; rejection; **fugóokaku to náru** to fail.

fugóori absurdity; **fugóori na** absurd; irrational, illogical.

fúgu deformity; **fúgu no** deformed, disfigured, crippled; **fúgu ni náru** to become disfigured; **fugúsha** cripple.

fuguu misfortune, adversity; **fuguu no** unfortunate.

fugyóoseki loose conduct; dissipation.

fuhai decomposition; decay; **fuhai suru** to rot; to be corrupted.

fuhei discontent; dissatisfaction; **fuhei o iu** to grumble, complain; **fuhei de áru** to be discontented; **fuhei o mótte iru** to have a complaint; **fuheika** grumbler, malcontent.

fuhéikin inequality, disproportion; **fuhéikin no** unequal; disproportionate.

fuhen unchangeability; **fuhen no** unchangeable, constant; invariable.

fuhínkoo immoral conduct; dissipation; **fuhínkoo na** loose, immoral.

fuhitsúyoo na needless, unnecessary.

fuhón'i unwillingness, reluctance; **fuhón'i no** unwilling, reluctant; **fuhon'i nágara** against one's will.

fuhoo na unlawful, violent; illegal.

fui unexpectedness; suddenness; **fui no** unexpected; sudden; unlooked for; **fui o útsu** to take by surprise; **fui o kurau** to be taken by surprise.

fuichoo announcement; advertisement; recommendation; **fuichoo suru** to announce; to advertise; to make known.

fuíito See **fíito.**

fuirumu film.

fuiuchi unexpected blow, surprise attack.

fujichaku, fujichakuriku forced landing, emergency landing.

FUJÌN woman; lady; **fujinrashíi** womanly; ladylike.

fúji no incurable; fatal.

fujitsu insincerity; faithlessness; lack of feeling; **fujitsu no** faithless; insincere; unfeeling.

fújiyuu inconvenience; want; discomfort; **fújiyuu na** uncomfortable; inconvenient; **fújiyuu o suru** to be short (wanting).

fújo assistance, aid; support; **fújo suru** to assist, aid.

fujóori unreasonableness, irrationality; **fujóori na** unreasonable, irrational.

fujun impurity; unseasonableness; irregularity; **fujun no** impure; unseasonable; irregular; **fujúubun** insufficiency; **fujúubun na** insufficient; incomplete.

fuka addition, supplement; **fuka suru** to add, supplement.

fukágen slight illness, indisposition; unsavoriness; **fukágen na** unsavory; indisposed, unwell.

FUKÁI deep, profound; thick, dense; illness; displeasure; **fukai na, fukai no** unpleasant; displeased; unwell; **fukái ni omóu** to be displeased; **fukái kangáe** deep thought; **fukái kiri** dense fog; **fukái náka ni náru** to form a close relationship.

fukairi (n.) going too far; addiction; **fukairi suru** to go deeply into; to be taken up too much with.

fukákai mystery; **fukákai na** mysterious; insoluble; **fukákai na kotó** mystery, mysterious affair.

fukakóoryoku no unavoidable; inevitable; irresistible.

fukaku negligence, fault; **fukaku o tóru** to be beaten. **Sore wa watakushi no fukaku déshita.** It was my fault.

fukákujitsu uncertainty; unreliability; **fukákujitsu no** uncertain; unreliable.

fukami depth; deep place; **fukami no áru** deep, profound; **fukami ni háiru** to get beyond one's depth.

fukánoo impossibility; **fukánoo no** impossible; impractical. **Hotóndo fukánoo de áru.** It is almost impossible.

fukánzen imperfection; incompleteness; **fukánzen na** defective; incomplete.

fukkáppatsu inactivity; stagnation; dullness; **fukáppatsu na** dull; inactive; stagnant.

fukása depth. **Fukása ga go fíito desu.** It is five feet deep.

fukásu to keep late hours.

fukéiki depression; dullness; hard times; **fukéiki na** dull; depressed, gloomy, dismal.

fukéizai na uneconomical; wasteful.

fukékka failure; bad result; **fukékka ni owaru** to be unsuccessful.

fukénkoo unhealthiness; poor health; **fukénkoo na** unhealthy, unwholesome.

fukénshiki lack of proper judgment; **fukénshiki na** disgraceful, shameful.

fukénzen na morbid, unwholesome.

FUKÉRU to grow old, age; to grow late, advance; **yó ga fukéru made hataraku** to work late into the night. **Yó wa dandan fukéta.** The night wore away. It grew late.

fuketsu dirtiness; **fuketsu na** dirty, filthy; **fuketsúbutsu** dirt, filth.

fukí appendix; **fuki súru** to add.

fukiagéru to blow up; to spout; to throw up.

fukichirásu to scatter about; to blow away.

fukidásu to spout, gush out; to burst out laughing.

fukidemono (body) rash.

fukikakéru to pick (a quarrel); to breathe on. **Kimi wa bóku ni kenka o fukikakéru no ka?** Do you want to pick a fight with me?

fukikésu to blow out a light.

fukikómu to blow into (a house, room, etc.); to inspire; to instill in one's mind; to record (make a sound recording); to polish, rub bright.

fukimakúru to blow about; to sweep along.

fukín neighborhood; **fukín ni** in the neighborhood; **fukín no** neighboring, adjacent.

FUKÍN a napkin; dish towel, dishcloth.

fukinshin na indiscreet; immodest.

fukiorósu to blow down.

fukíritsu lack of discipline; irregularity; **fukíritsu na** disorderly; undisciplined; irregular.

fukísoku irregularity; **fukísoku na** unsystematic; irregular.

fukisóoji housework; wiping; cleaning; **fukisóoji o suru** to do housework.

fukisusámu to blow furiously.

fukitóru to wipe; to wipe out.

fukitsu ill omen; ill luck; **fukitsu na** unlucky, ill-omened; ominous.

fukitsukéru to blow against; to beat against. **Áme ga mádo ni fukitsukéru.** The rain beats against the window.

fukiyoséru to drift; to blow together.

fukkatsu revival; **fukkatsu suru** to revive.

FUKKÁTSUSAI, FUKKÁTSUSETSU Easter.

fukkoo revival, renaissance; restoration; **fukkoo suru** to revive, be restored.

fukkyuu restoration; **fukkyuu suru** to restore to the original state; be restored to normalcy.

fukókoroe indiscretion; misconduct; **fukókoroe na** unwise, indiscreet; **fukókoroe na kotó o suru** to behave badly; to act indiscreetly.

fukoku decree, proclamation; notification; **fukoku suru** to notify; to decree, proclaim.

fukóo misery; unhappiness; disaster; mishap; disobedience to parents; **fukóo na** unhappy; unfortunate; miserable; undutiful, unfilial; **fukóo ni mo** unfortunately; **fukóo ni áu** to have a misfortune.

fukóohei unfairness, partiality; **fukóohei na** unfair, partial, unjust; **fukóohei ni** unjustly, unfairly.

FUKU to wipe; to dry; to mop; to rub off; to blow; to breathe; to emit; to sound; to whistle; to talk big (*colloq.*); to spout, spurt out, gush out; to roof; **hora o fuku** to boast; **fue o fuku** to play a flute; **me o fuku** to send out new shoots; **tenugui de té o fuku** to wipe the hands with a towel. **Hidoku fuite iru.** It is blowing hard.

fuku- prefix denoting: assistant, vice-, sub-; double; composite; **fukugíchoo** vice-chairman; **Fukudaitóoryoo** Vice-President (of the U.S.A.); **fukúri** compound interest.

-fuku Suffix denoting: clothes, dress; garment; **yoofuku** European clothes; **fujínfuku** women's clothes.

fukuan plan, idea; scheme. **Watakushi ni fukuan ga arimásu.** I have a good plan.

fukubiki lottery; distribution of prizes.

fukubukushíi happy-looking; radiant.

fukugyoo subsidiary business; side job.

fukúmu to have (hold) in the mouth; to bear in mind; to include; to imply. **Dóozo kono kóto o ofukumioki kudasái.** Please keep this in mind.

fukurahagi calf (of the leg).

fukuramasu to swell, expasnd, puff out; **fukurami** bulge, swelling.

fukureru to swell, puff out; to be sulky; to become sore.

fukurettsura (*colloq.*) sulky, sullen look.

FUKURO bag, sack, pouch.
fukurodátaki sound thrashing, drubbing.
fukuryóoji vice-consul.
fukusánbutsu by-product.
fukusáyoo ill effect; secondary reaction;
   harmful side-effects; **fukusáyoo no
   nái** harmless.
fukusei reproduction; duplication; **fukusha**
   copying; **fukusha suru** to copy,
   reproduce; **fukusháki** duplicator.
fukusháchoo vice-president (of a company).
fukushi adverb.
fukushin devotion; confidence; **fukushin no**
   devoted; confidential; faithful;
   fukushin no tómo devoted friend.
fukushoku reappointment; **fukushoku suru**
   to resume office.
fukushuu reappointment; **fukushoku suru** to
   resume office.
fukushuu review; revenge; vengeance;
   fukushuu suru to review, go over; to
   revenge, be revenged.
fukusúu (n.) plural (number); **fukusúu no**
   (adj.) plural.
fukutsu no inflexible; indomitable.
fukutsuu stomach-ache; bellyache.
fukuyoo suru to take a dose of medicine.
fukuzatsu na complex, complicated, intricate;
   fukuzatsu suru to be complicated.
fukuzoo reserve; **fukuzoo náku** without
   reserve, frankly; **fukuzoo no nái**
   frank, candid, unreserved; **fukuzoo
   náku iéba** to be frank with you;
   fukuzoo náku íken o nobéru to
   express one's views freely, without
   reserve.
fukyoo business depression, slump, inactivity,
   slackness; displeasure; ill-humor;
   disfavor; **fukyoo no** inactive;
   depressed; weak; in a slump.
fukyuu diffusion, propagation, spread;
   immortality; eternity; **fukyuu suru** to
   diffuse, propagate, spread; **fukyuu no**
   eternal; immortal; undying.
fuman, fumanzoku discontent,
   dissatisfaction; **fuman na**
   discontented, dissatisfied; **fuman ni
   omóu** to be displeased with,
   dissatisfied with.
fumei obscurity; uncertainty; ignorance;
   fumei no obscure, indistinct, vague;
   fuméiryoo not clear, indistinct.
   Yukusaki wa fumei da. His
   destination is unknown.
fuméiyo disgrace, dishonor; discredit;
   fuméiyo na disgraceful, dishonorable.
fumetsu immortality; indestructibility.
fumidai step; footstool; **fumidan** step; steps,
   stairs; **fumidásu** to step forward.
fumihazúsu to miss (lose) one's footing.
fumikataméru to tread; to stamp down.
fumikiri railway crossing; grade crossing.
fumikoéru to step over (a thing); **fumikómi**
   to step into; to make a raid; to rush in;
   to trespass; to force an entrance.
fumikudáku to trample.
fumímochi dissipation; immoral conduct.

fuminarásu to stamp (one's feet) noisily; to
   tread; to level by treading.
fumin fukyuu without sleep or rest;
   fumínshoo insomnia, sleeplessness.
fuminijíru to trample, crush with the feet.
fumataósu to kick down; to evade payment;
   to bargain.
fumitodomáru to stand one's ground, remain.
fumitsukéru to trample; to treat with
   contempt; **hito o fumitsuke ni shita
   kotó o iu** to make an insulting remark.
fumoto foot of a hill or mountain.
fumu to step; to tread on; to go through; to
   value at; **jitchi o fumu** to experience;
   tetsúzuki o fumu to go through the
   formalities; **shinamono no ne o fumu**
   to put a price on something.
fúmuki unfit for, unsuitable for.
FÚN = **pún** minute; **íppun** one minute;
   gofún kan for five minutes.
funaashi speed, draft, headway (of a ship);
   funaashi no hayái fúne fast boat;
   funaásobi boat excursion; **funaásobi
   ni yuku** to go boating.
funáchin passage fare; shipping freight;
   freightage.
funade ship departure; sailing; **funade suru**
   to set sail.
funani shóoken bill of lading.
funánori sailor, seaman.
fúnare unfamiliarity; inexperience; **fúnare na**
   unfamiliar; inexperienced; **roodoo ni
   fúnare de aru** to be unaccustomed to
   labor.
funáyoi seasickness.
funbáru to stretch one's legs; to straddle; to
   make an effort; to persevere; **sáigo
   made funbáru** to hold fast to the end.
fúnbetsu discretion, good sense; discernment;
   fúnbetsu no áru discreet, prudent;
   thoughtful; **fúnbetsu no nái** indiscreet,
   etc.; **funbetsu zákari no hito** mature
   man.
fundan in plenty, fully. **Tabemóno ga
   fundan ni áru.** There is plenty to eat.
FÚNE ship, boat, vessel; **fúne ni noru** to
   board a ship; to go to sea; **fúne ni yóu**
   to get seasick.
funésshin indifference; **funésshin na**
   half-hearted, indifferent, lukewarm.
fungai resentment, indignation; **fungai shite**
   indignantly; **fungai suru** to be
   indignant, resent.
funíai unbecoming (to), unsuitable;
   ill-matched; **funíai no fúufu**
   ill-matched couple.
fun'íki atmosphere.
funínjoo na unfeeling, cold-hearted.
funka eruption, volcanic activity; **funkázan**
   volcano.
fúnki suru to be stirred up, be inspired by; to
   rouse oneself to action.
funmatsu powder; **funmatsu ni suru** to
   pulverize.
funoo impossibility; incompetency;
   impotency; **funoo no** impossible.

funpatsu exertion, endeavor(s); **funpatsu suru** to exert oneself; to rouse; to make a great effort.

funrei strenuous effort.

funsai suru to shatter (smash) to pieces.

funshitsu loss; **funshitsu suru** to lose; to miss; to be missing; **funshitsú butsu** lost article.

funshutsu spout, gush, jet; **funshutsu suru** to gush out.

funsoo trouble; dispute; difficulties; impersonation; **funsoo suru = fun suru** to disguise; to impersonate.

funsui fountain; jet.

fun súru See **funsoo suru.**

funtoo hard struggle, desperate fight; **funtoo suru** to struggle, fight desperately.

funzen resolutely; plucking up one's courage; indignantly; in a fit of anger.

fuon unrest disquiet; **fuon na** threatening; disquieting; improper; riotous; **fuon na fuusetsu** unsettling news. **Keisei ga fuon de áru.** The situation is quite disturbing.

fuóntoo impropriety, inappropriateness; **fuontoo no, fuóntoo na** improper, inappropriate; unjust.

fúrachi outrageousness; insolence; misconduct; **fúrachi na** outrageous, insolent; vicious; **fúrachi na kotó o suru** to misconduct oneself; to act viciously.

fúrafura to dizzy, unsteady; **fúrafura suru** to feel dizzy; to reel, stagger. **Atamá ga fúrafura suru.** My head is swimming.

furai fried; **sakana no furai** fried fish; **furaipan** frying pan.

furanneru flannel.

FURANSU France; **Furansugo** French language; **Furansújin** Frenchman.

furareru to be jilted.

furasshu ránpu flashlight.

furekomi announcement, proclamation; **furekómu** to announce; to represent oneself as.

furemawásu to broadcast, to spread news.

fureru to touch; to strike against; to refer to; to conflict with; **hooritsu ni fureru** to be contrary to the law; **mondai ni fureru** to refer to the question.

fúri disadvantage, drawback; **fúri na** disadvantageous, unfavorable; unprofitable.

furí appearance; air; pretension; **shiranai furí o suru** to pretend ignorance.

furi- prefix denoting: to shake; to brandish, wave, flourish.

furidashi drawing; start, starting point; issue.

furidásu to begin to fall (as rain or snow). **Áme ga furidáshita.** It began to rain.

furíeki disadvantage; handicap.

furigana Kana (Japanese syllabic sign) attached to ideographs to show the pronunciation.

furihanásu to shake free from; to break away.

furiharáu to shake from.

furikae change; transfer.

furikáeru = furimúku to turn around; to look back over one's shoulder.

furikakáru to fall on; to befall, happen; **furikakéru** to sprinkle over.

furikazásu to hold aloft; to brandish.

furikíru break away from.

furiko pendulum.

furimawásu to brandish, flourish.

furimúku See **furikáeru.**

furiotósu to shake off.

furishikíru to rain or snow incessantly.

furisutéru to leave, abandon, to shake off.

furitatéru to shake; to toss; to raise one's voice.

furitsuke dance composition; choreography.

furitsuzuku to rain continuously.

FÚRO bath, hot bath; **fúro ni háiru** to take a bath; **furoba** bathroom; **furóya** bathhouse.

furoku supplement, appendix.

furoonin wanderer; tramp.

FUROSHIKI wrapping cloth (square piece of cotton or silk used to wrap and carry something); **furoshiki de tsutsúmu** to wrap in a wrapping cloth.

FÚRU to fall; to come down (rain, etc.). **Hídoku áme ga fútte iru.** Rain is falling heavily. **Yukí ga fútta.** There was a snowfall.

furu to shake; to wave, wag; **kubi o táte ni furu** to nod, assent to.

furu- prefix denoting: old; **furuhon** old book; **furuhonya** secondhand book store; **furubíru** to be worn out; to be aged; **furúbita** old, worn-out; **furumono** secondhand goods; **furudóogu** old furniture; secondhand household utensils; **furudooguya** secondhand dealer; curio shop; **furugi** old clothes; secondhand clothes; **furugi ya** secondhand-clothes dealer.

furue (*n.*) shaking, trembling, shivering; **furueagáru** to tremble with fear; **furuegóe** trembling voice; timid voice; **furueru** to shake, shudder, tremble.

furui sieve; **furui ni kakéru** to sift (out), sieve.

furúi old (used when speaking of things); ancient; antique.

furuiokósu to stir up, rouse, awaken; **Yúuki o furuiokosu** to summon up courage.

furuitátsu to stir up; to be roused to action.

furukizu old wound; scar; former misdeed.

furukusái stale; old-fashioned; hackneyed.

furumái behavior, conduct, action; **furumáu** to behave, act; to treat, behave toward (a person).

furutte energetically; voluntarily; willingly. **Furutte goshusseki kudasái.** Please make every effort to attend.

furúuto flute (Western style).

fúryo no unexpected, accidental; **fúryo no dekígoto** accident; unforeseen event, an emergency.

furyoo bad; poor; unsatisfactory; delinquent; **furyoo shóonen** bad boy(s); **furyoohin** inferior goods; **furyóoken** indiscretion; rash act; **furyóoken na** rash; ill-advised.

fusá tassel; tuft; fringe; bunch; cluster.

fusagaru to get blocked; to become choked; to be occupied, engaged; to be filled. **Kono michi wa saki ga fusagatte iru.** This road is blocked. **Sono ié wa fusagatte iru.** That house is occupied. **Kono séki wa fusagatte iru.** This seat is taken. **Íma té ga fusagatte imásu.** I am tied up just now. I am busy now.

fusagikómu to be in low spirits; to mope.

fusagu to close, shut up; to stand in the way; to be dejected, depressed; **basho o fusagu** to take up room; **jikan o fusagu** to fill up the time; **michi o fusagu** to stand in the way.

fusái debt; loan.

fusánesi disapproval; dissent; **fusánsei de aru** to dissent; disapprove; **fusánsei o tonaéru** to raise objections to; to express disapproval. **Kimi wa sansei ka fusánsei ka?** Are you for or against it?

FUSAWASHÍI suitable, becoming.

fuségu to defend, protect, guard against; to prevent; to resist.

fusei dishonesty; injustice; unlawfulness; **fusei na** dishonest; wrong; corrupt; unlawful; etc.; **fuseihin** sham (fraudulent article); **fuséijitsu** insincerity, dishonesty; **fuséijitsu na** dishonest, false.

fuséikaku uncertainty; inaccuracy.

fuséikoo failure; fiasco; miscarriage; **fuséikoo no** unsuccessful, abortive; **fuséiseki** poor (unsatisfactory) result; bad record; poor performance; failure; **fuséiseki de áru** to be unsuccessful, be a failure; **fuséiseki ni owaru** to end in failure.

fusen tag, label; slip.

fuséru to put upside down; to turn over; to lie down; to take cover.

fussési na intemperate, immoderate.

fushi joint; knuckle; knot; **fushi ana** knothole.

fushiáwase unhappiness; misfortune; **fushiáwase na** unhappy; unfortunate; unlucky; **fushiáwase ni mo** unfortunately.

fushídara untidiness; looseness, laxity; **fushídara na** untidy; sloppy; irregular; loose; dissipated.

FUSHIGI wonder, miracle; **fushigi na** wonderful, marvelous; mysterious; miraculous; strange; **fushigi ni** wonderfully, miraculously.

fushímatsu mismanagement; carelessness; misconduct; prodigality; **fushímatsu na** lax; wasteful; irregular.

fushin doubt, suspicion; question; **fushin no** doubtful, suspicious; questionable;

construction; **fushin ni omóu** to wonder; to think strange; **fushin suru** to build; to repair; **fushínjin** unbelief; impiety; **fushínjin na** unbelieving, irreligious; **fushínjitsu** insincerity; faithlessness; **fushínjitsu na** faithless, insincere; **fushínkoo** unbelief; **fushínkoo no** unbelieving; freethinking.

fushínsetsu unkindness; **fushínsetsu na** unkind; unobliging.

fushín'yoo distrust, lack of confidence.

fushízen unnatural, artificial; affected.

fushoo injury, wound; **fushoo suru** to be injured, get hurt; **fushóo sha** injured person.

fushoo búshoo ni reluctantly, unwillingly.

fushóochi dissent; disapproval; **fushóochi o iu** to dissent; to disapprove.

fushóojiki dishonesty; **fushóojiki na** dishonest.

fushóoka indigestion.

fushóbi failure, fiasco; displeasure; **fushúbi ni náru** to fall into disfavor; **fushúbi ni owaru** to end in failure.

fusoku shortage, deficiency; dissatisfaction; **fusoku suru** to want, lack, be short; **fusoku o iu** to grumble, complain; **fusokú gaku** shortage, deficit.

fusóooo na unsuitable, unfitting, unbecoming; undue; **míbun fusóooo na seikatsu o suru** to live above one's means.

FUSUMA sliding screen door covered with paper.

FUTA lid, cover; **futatsuki no** covered; **futa o suru, futa o shimeru** to cover, put on a lid; **futa o tóru** to lift the lid.

futáe double, twofold.

futago twins.

futaoya one's parents.

FUTARI couple, two persons.

futáshika uncertainty; **futáshika na** uncertain; doubtful.

FUTATABI again.

FUTATSU two; **futatsu hénji de** ready enough; most willingly; **futatsu to nái** matchless, unique; **futatsu tomo** both; **futatsú ni wakéru** to divide in two.

futei na uncertain, indefinite; inconstant.

futéisai na unseemly, indecent; unsightly; clumsy.

futeki na bold, daring, fearless.

futékinin unfitness, incompetency; **futékinin de aru** to be unfit (for a task), be unsuitable for, be unqualified for; **futekinínsha** a misfit.

futéttei imperfect; inconsistent; unconvincing; not thoroughgoing.

FUTO suddenly; by chance, by accident; **futo omoidásu** to remember in a flash.

futódoki na insolent, rude.

FUTÓI big; thick; deep; sonorous.

futokoro bosom; purse; pocket; **futokoro ga sabishíi** to be short (of money); **futokoro ni suru** to put in one's pocket.

futókusaku poor plan; unwise course; disadvantage; **futókusaku na** unwise, inadvisable, inexpedient.

futomomo thigh.

FUTON mattress; quilt; cushion; bedding. **futon o shiku** to make a bed.

futoo wharf, pier; injustice; **futoo na** unjust, unfair; unreasonable; **futoo rítoku** unreasonable profits.

futóppara generosity; broad-mindedness; **futóppara no** generous; broad-minded.

futoraséru to fatten; **FUTÓRU** to grow fat; **shíndai ga futóru** to prosper.

futósa thickness; bulk.

FUTÓTTA fat; plump; **futótta hito** fat man.

futsúgoo inconvenience; misconduct; **futsúgoo na** wrong, improper, objectionable; inconvenient; **futsúgoo na kotó o suru** to behave wrongly.

FUTSUKA two days; second day (of the month); **Sángatsu futsuka** March 2.

futsukayoi hang-over; **futsukayoi o suru** to have a hang-over.

futsúriai incongruity; imbalance, disproportion; **futsúriai no** disproportionate; ill-matched.

FUTSUU usually, normally.

futsuu ni náru to be suspended, cut off, interrupted.

futtei scarcity, shortage; **futtei de áru** to be scarce; **futtei suru** to run short.

futtémo téttemo rain or shine; no matter what the weather.

futtoo boiling; bubbling; agitation; **futtoo suru** to boil up; to bubble; **futtóo ten** boiling point. **Gíron ga futtoo shita.** The discussion became heated.

FUTTSÚRI utterly, entirely. **Íto ga futtsúri kíreta.** The string snapped.

fúu appearance; customs; manners; way; seal; closing; **fúu suru** to seal; to fasten.

fuubun rumor.

fuubutsu scenery; nature; landscape.

fúuchi taste; beauty; elegance; **fúuchi no yói** tasteful; elegant; artistic; charming.

fuuchoo trend of the times; fashion, tendency.

FÚUFU man and wife; married couple; **fúufu ni náru** to marry; **fuufu wákare** divorce; **fuufunáka** married life.

fúuga elegance; refinement; **fúuga na** elegant; refined.

fúugetsu scenery; (beauties of) nature.

fúugi manners; customs; **fúugi no yói** well-mannered; well-bred; **fuugi no warúi** ill-mannered; ill-bred.

fúuha wind and waves; storm; heavy sea; discord; trouble.

fuuhyoo current rumor; report.

fúukei landscape; scenery; **fuukeiga** landscape; seascape (painting); **fuukeigá ka** landscape painter.

fuukiri release; **fuukiri suru** to break a seal; to release (a film, etc.).

fúumi flavor; taste; **fúumi no yói** tasty, delicious.

fuurin wind bell (tiny bell that tinkles in the wind).

fúuryuu elegance; taste; **fúuryuu no** elegant.

fuusa blockade.

fuusen balloon.

fuusetsu snowstorm, blizzard; rumor, hearsay.

fuushuu manners; custom, usage, practice.

fuusoku wind velocity.

fúutei appearance, looks; dress.

FUUTOO envelope. **Fuutoo ni irete kudasai.** Please put it in an envelope.

fúun misfortune; ill-luck; **fúun na** unfortunate, unlucky.

fúuu wind and rain; rainstorm; **fúuu ni sarasareta** weather-beaten; **fúuu ni sarasu** to expose to the weather; **fúuu o okashite iku** go in spite of the storm.

fúuzoku customs; manners; public morals.

fúwa discord; strife; **fúwa de áru** to be on bad terms; **fúwa ni náru** to become estranged.

fúwafuwa light; thin; soft; spongy; lightly; softly.

fuwarí lightly; softly; buoyantly.

fuyakásu to steep, soak.

fuyakéru to swell up; to get soaked; to be saturated.

fuyásu to increase; to add to; to raise.

fuyoo ni náru to be out of use; to fall into disuse.

fuyóoi na unprepared; careless; thoughtless.

fuyóojoo neglect of health; intemperance; **fuyóojoo na** careless of one's health.

FUYÚ winter; **fuyu no** wintry; winter; **fuyufuku, fuyu no mo** no winter clothes; **fuyuyásumi** winter vacation.

fuyúkai unpleasantness; discomfort; **fuyúkai na** unpleasant; uncomfortable; **fuyúkai ni** unpleasantly, uncomfortably.

fuyukitódoki carelessness; neglect; **fuyukitódoki na** careless, negligent.

fuzai absence; **fuzai de áru** to be absent.

fuzoku attached to; belonging to; **fuzoku suru** to be attached to; to belong to; **fuzokúhin** accessories.

G

GA particle marking an emphatic subject; (n.) self; ego; self-will; selfishness; (conj.) but; and yet; however; although; **ga o óru** to give in; to yield; **ga o tóosu** to have one's way; **ga no tsuyói** self-willed; obstinate. **Súmisu san e denwa o kakemáshita ga rúsu deshita.** I phoned Mr. Smith, but he was not in.

gaarusukáuto girl scout.

gáaze cheesecloth; surgical gauze.

gába to all of a sudden; **gába to okiagáru** to spring out of bed; to spring to one's feet.

gábugabu nómu to take long draughts; to swill.

gaburí to used only with nomu, kuitsuku; **gaburí to nómu** to drain at one gulp;

to gulp down; **gaburí to kuitsuku** to
bite (snap) at.
gáchagacha clattering, rattling; **gáchagacha
saseru** to clatter, rattle.
-GÁCHI suffix denoting: apt to, prone to;
prevailing; of frequent occurrence;
okotarigáchi no prone to neglect;
byookigáchi prone to illness; ill most
of the time; **kumorigachi no** cloudy;
gloomy.
gáhaku painter, artist.
gái injury, harm, damage; **gai súru** to injure,
harm, hurt; **gái ni náru** to be injurious
or harmful.
gáibu outside, exterior; **gáibu no** external,
outer; **gáibu no hito** outsiders.
gaibun reputation; honor.
gaichuu harmful insect; blight; vermin.
GÁIDO tourist guide.
gaihaku suru to stay out, stay away from
home (at night).
gaihoo foreign news; foreign telegram.
gaijin foreigner.
gaikai outside world; **gaikan** external
appearance; outside view; general
view; outline; **gaikei** external form;
gaiken outward appearance.
GAIKOKU foreign country; **gaikoku no**
foreign; exotic; alien; **gaikoku e iku** to
go abroad; **gaikoku sei no** foreign
(product); **gaikoku bóoeki** foreign
trade; **gaikoku káwase** foreign
exchange (rate); **gaikoku shíjoo**
foreign market; **gaikokusen** foreign
ships; **GAIKOKUGO** foreign
language; **GAIKOKÚJIN** foreigner;
gaikokujín machi section where many
foreigners live.
gaikoo diplomacy; **gaikooka, gaikóokan**
diplomat; **gaikooteki** diplomatic;
gaikóodan diplomatic corps.
gaikóoin canvasser.
gáikotsu skeleton; bones.
gaimai rice grown outside of Japan.
gaimen (n.) outside; surface; **gaimen no**
exterior, external; outside.
gáimu foreign affairs.
gáinen concept, general idea; conception.
gairai foreign; exotic; imported.
GÁISHITE in general; generally speaking; on
the whole.
gaishutsu suru to go out; **gaishutsúgi** street
dress.
GAITOO overcoat; street lamp; street; **gaitoo
enzetsu** soapbox oratory; **gaitoo ni
tatsu** to go out (in the street); **gaitoo
suru** to fall under; to correspond to.
gaiyuu suru to travel abroad.
gaka painter; artist.
gake cliff, precipice; **gakekúzure** landslide.
-gake suffix denoting: being on the way to;
toorigake ni in passing; **negake ni** just
before going to bed.
gakka lesson; course of study, subject.
GAKKÁRI SURU to be disappointed; to lose
heart; to be tired out, be exhausted.
   Kabuki ni ikenákute gakkári shita. I

was disappointed because I could not
get to the Kabuki theatre.
gakki musical instrument; school term;
semester.
GAKKOO school; college; **gakkoo e yuku** to
go to school; **gakkoo tómodachi**
schoolmate.
gakkyoku tune, musical piece.
gakkyuu class, grade.
gáku learning, studies; science; amount, sum;
denomination.
gaku framed picture; **gaku buchi** picture
frame.
gakuha school; academic group.
gakujin musician.
gakumen face value; par; **gakumen íka ni
sagáru** to fall below par.
gakúmon learning; study; **gakúmon suru** to
study.
GAKUSEI student; schoolboy (-girl); **gakusei
jídai** schooldays.
gakusetsu theory; doctrine.
gakusha learned man; scholar; **gakushiki**
scholarship; learning; **gakushuu** study;
gakushuu suru to study.
gakutai (musical) band.
gákuto students; scholars.
gakuya dressing room; **gakuyá guchi** stage
door.
gakuyuu fellow student; classmate.
gakuzen in amazement; amazed; aghast;
gakuzen to suru to strike with horror;
to shock.
gamaguchi purse; pouch.
GÁMAN patience, endurance; pardon;
gaman zuyói patient; having great
endurance; **gáman suru** to bear,
endure. **Káre ni wa gáman ga
dekínai.** I'm out of patience with him.
gan invocation, prayer; cancer.
gan- prefix denoting: pertaining to the eye;
ganbyoo eye disease; sore eyes.
ganbáru to persist in; to stand firm, refuse to
give in.
gánchuu ni in one's eyes; **gánchuu ni nái**
beneath one's notice; **gánchuu ni
okanai** to take no notice of; to ignore;
to think nothing of.
gángan dingdong; clang; **gángan naru** to
clang, ring noisily. **Mimí ga gángan
suru.** My ears are ringing. **Atamá ga
gángan suru.** My head aches.
GANJITSU New Year's Day.
ganjoo na solid; robust; strongly built.
gánko stubbornness, obstinacy; **gánko na**
stubborn, obstinate.
gankyoo stubbornness; persistence; **gankyoo
na** obstinate, stubborn; persistent;
gankyoo ni stubbornly, obstinately.
ganmoo desire, wish.
ganpeki quay, wharf, pier.
gánrai originally; from the first; by nature.
gánseki rock; crag; stones.
ganshiki discernment, insight; critical eye.
gánsho written application.
gánso originator, founder, father of.

GANTAN New Year's Day; morning of New Year's Day.

gan'yaku pill; pellet.

ganze nái innocent, artless; helpless.

ganzoo forgery.

gappei union; combination; amalgamation; **gappei suru** to amalgamate; incorporate.

GARA pattern, design; build; nature (character); **iegara** the family standing.

gáragara clattering; rattling; rattle (toy).

garakuta rubbish; worn-out articles.

garandoo empty, vacant; hollow **garánto suru** to appear empty; to seem deserted.

gararí to completely; with a clatter; suddenly; **gararí to kawaru** to change completely.

GARASU (*n.*) glass; **garasu no** (*adj.*) glass; glazed; **garasu íta** (glass) pane; plate glass; **garasu kóoba** glass factory.

GARÉEJI garage.

GÁRIGARI noisily, with noise; **gárigari kajíru** to munch; **gárigari hikkáku** to scrape; to scratch.

gáron gallon.

-gáru suffix denoting: to wish, want; to be inclined to; **mitagáru** to want to see; **ikitagáru** to want to go; **ureshigáru** to feel glad.

garyoo generosity; tolerance; **garyoo no áru** tolerant; generous; broad-minded; **garyoo no nái** intolerant; ungenerous.

garyuu de in one's own way.

gásagasa suru to rustle; **gasagasa no** rough; loose.

gasatsu na rude, rough, unmannerly; **gasatsu na otoko** unmannerly (rude) person.

gáshi suru to starve to death.

gashitsu studio

GASORIN gasoline; **gasorin sutándo** gas station.

gassaku collaboration; **gassaku suru** to collaborate, work jointly; **gassáku sha** a collaborator.

gasshíri to tightly; closely; **gasshíri shita** massive; well built; sturdy; **gasshíri shite iru** to be massive, etc.

gasshoo chorus; **gasshoo suru** to sing together; **gasshootai** chorus; choir.

Gasshúukoku United States.

gasshukusho dormitory; boarding house.

gassoo playing music together; **nibu gássoo** duet.

gassúru to add (join) together; to unite.

GÁSU gas; **gásu o tsukéru** to light the gas; **gásu o tomeru** to turn down the gas; **gasu sutóobu** gas heater; **gasugáisha** gas company.

gátagata rattling (clattering) sound; **gátagata furueru** to shake, shiver, tremble; **gátagata iu** to rattle, to shake.

-gatái suffix denoting: cannot; hard, difficult; impossible; **egatái** hard to get; unobtainable; **shinjigatái** difficult to believe; incredible.

gátapishi noisily; roughly; with a bang.

gatén comprehension, understanding; consent, agreement; **gatén suru** to understand, grasp the meaning; to be convinced of; to agree, consent; **gatén no ikanai** puzzling; doubtful.

-GATSU suffix denoting; month of; **Ichigatsu** January.

gátsugatsu greedily; ravenously; **gátsugatsu kúu** to eat greedily.

gawa outside; side; **soto gawa** outside; **uchi gawa** inside; **minami gawa** south side.

gáyagaya noisily; **gáyagaya sawágu** to make noise, clamor.

gébita vulgar; low; mean.

géemu game; **géemu o yaru** to play a game.

gehín meanness; vulgarity; **gehín na** mean; vulgar; low.

géi arts; accomplishments; feats; tricks; performance; **géi no áru hito** accomplished person.

geijutsu art; fine arts; **geijutsuteki** artistic; **geijutsuka** artist.

geinin professional entertainer.

GEISHA geisha (girl).

GEJUN latter part of a month; last ten days of a month.

geka surgery; **gekái** surgeon.

gekai this world; earth.

géki play, drama; **gekiteki** dramatic; **gekidan** theatrical world; dramatic company; **gekihyoo** theatrical criticism; **gekihyooka** theatre critic; **GEKIJOO** theatre, playhouse; **gekisakuka** dramatist; playwright. (See also **gikyoku.**)

gékiha suru to defeat, rout.

gekirei encouragement; **gekirei suru** to encourage.

gekiron heated discussion; **gekiron suru** to argue hotly.

gekiryuu rapid stream; swift current.

gekishin severe earthquake. **Sakúban gekishin ga átta.** There was a severe earthquake last night.

gekiyaku powerful medicine; violent poison.

gekízoo sudden increase.

gekkan monthly publication; **gekkan zásshi** monthly magazine.

gekkei menstruation.

gekken fencing (Japanese style).

GEKKOO moonlight; moonbeams.

GEKKYUU monthly salary; **gekkyúu bi** payday; **gekkyuu búkuro** pay envelope; **gekkyúu tori** a salaried man.

gén words; speech; **gén o sáyuu ni takúshite** on one pretext or another.

gen- prefix denoting: original; primary; fundamental; **genbun** original text; **genba** the actual place, scene; **genba de** on the spot; **genga** original picture.

génan manservant.

genbatsu severe punishment.

GÉNDAI present time; modern times; **gendaiteki no** modern; **gendaika suru** to modernize.

géngai unexpressed; between the lines; **géngai**

no ími o toru to read between the lines.

gengákki stringed instrument.

gengaku reduction, discount; **gengaku suru** to reduce, cut down, curtail.

GÉNGO language, speech; words; **géngo ni zessúru** to be unspeakable; to be beyond description.

gen'in cause; origin;—**ni gen'in suru** to be due to, attributable to; **gen'in fumei** unaccountable; unknown.

genjitsu reality, actuality; **genjitsu no** real, actual; **genjitsu bákuro** disillusionment; **genjitsu shúgi** realism.

genjoo status quo, existing state of things; actual place, scene (of the action); **genjoo de** on the spot; in the very act; then and there; **genjoo íji** maintenance of the status quo.

genjuu severity, strictness; **genjuu na** severe, strict; **genjuu ni** severely.

genkai limit, boundary.

genkaku strictness; sternness; **genkaku na** strict; rigorous; stern; **genkaku ni** rigorously.

GÉNKAN, genkanguchi entrance hall.

GÉNKI spirits; courage; vigor; energy; **génki no yói** cheerful; healthy; **génki yóku** in high spirits; cheerfully; **génki no nai** in poor (low) spritis; **génki o dásu** to brace up; **génki o tsukéru** to encourage; to cheer up.

genkin strict prohibition, ban; **genkin suru** to ban.

GENKÍN cash; **genkín de kau** to buy for cash; **genkin bárai** cash payment; **genkin gákari** cashier; **genkin tórihiki** cash transaction.

GENKO first; **genko o katameru** to clench a fist.

genkoo manuscript; draft; words and deeds; speech and action; existing; **genkóo roku** memoirs; **genkoo yóoshi** copy paper; writing pad; **genkoo itchí suru** to live up to one's word; **genkoohan** flagrant offense; **genkoo chuu ni torawaréru** to be caught red-handed. **Genkóohan de káre wa táihosareta.** He was caught red-handed.

genkoku plaintiff; accuser.

GÉNKON at present; nowadays.

génmai unpolished rice, unhulled rice (eaten for high nutritive value).

genmei declaration, statement; announcement; **genmei suru** to make a statement.

genmetsu disillusionment.

genmitsu strictness; precision; **genmitsu na** strict; precise; exact; **genmitsu ni** strictly; closely; **genmitsu ni iéba** strictly speaking.

gén ni actually; before one's eyes. **Watakushi wa gén ni sore o míta no desu.** I saw it with my own eyes.

génpin goods; thing.

génri See **gensoku.**

genryóo raw materials.

gensánchi country of origin; habitat; home. **genseki** home address; **genséki chi** permanent home.

génshi atom; beginning; origin; **génshi no** atomic; **genshi bákudan** atomic bomb.

gensho original (work); **Eigo no gensho de yómu** to read in the original English.

genshoo phenomenon; decrease; **genshoo suru** to decrease, diminish.

genshoku primary color(s); **genshoku sháshin** color photograph.

génshu strict observance; **génshu suru** to observe strictly; **jikan o génshuu suru** to be punctual.

genshuku gravity, solemnity; **genshuku na** solemn, grave.

genshutsu appearance; disclosure; **genshutsu suru** to appear; to be disclosed.

génso element (chem.).

gensoku = genri principle; fundamental law; **gensoku to shite** as a general rule.

genson no existing, in existence.

gentoo lantern slide.

GÉNZAI (*n., adv.*) present time; at present; actually; at the present moment.

genzei tax reduction.

genzoo suru to develop (photography).

geppoo monthly salary.

geppu monthly installment; **geppu de** by monthly payments.

géragera warau to cackle; to give a horselaugh.

geraku fall; decline; depreciation; **geraku suru** to fall; decline; depreciate.

geri diarrhea.

gésha stopover; **gésha suru** to stop over.

GESHUKU (*n.*) lodging; boarding; lodging-house; **geshuku suru** to lodge; to board; **geshukunin** lodger; **geshukuya** lodging-house; **geshukúryoo** lodging charge (rate).

geshunin murderer; criminal.

gessha monthly fee; tuition fee.

gesui sewer; drain; sewage.

GETA wooden clogs; **geta o haku** to put on clogs; **geta o núgu** to take off clogs; **getaya** clog shop.

getsugaku monthly sum (amount).

getsumatsu end of a month; **getsumatsu kánjoo** end-of-the-month payment.

GETSUYÓOBI Monday.

gezai laxative.

gíchoo chairman.

gidai subject for discussion.

gidayuu ballad drama.

gigochinái stiff-mannered; awkward.

gihitsu forgery (handwriting or picture).

gíin House, Diet; member of assembly or Diet.

gíji proceedings.

gijoo assembly hall; chamber; conference site.

gíjutsu art; useful art; technique; skill; **gijutsujoo no** technical.

gíkai Diet; assembly.

gíkan chief engineer; technical official.

gikei brother-in-law (elder sister's husband).

giketsu decision; resolution.

gikoo artistic excellence; technical skill.

gikyoku drama; **gikyoku sákusha** dramatist, playwright. (See also **géki**.)

gikyóodai brother-in-law.

gimei assumed name, false name.

GIMON question; doubt; **gimónfu** question mark.

gímu duty; obligation; **gímu o hatásu** to perform one's duty.

GÍN silver; **gín no** silvered; silver; **gin iro no** silvery; **gíngami** silver paper; tin foil; **gínka** silver coin; **ginkónshiki** silver wedding anniversary; **ginmékki no** (adj.) silver-plated; **ginpai** silver medal; cup; **ginzan** silver mine.

GINKOO bank; **ginkooka** banker; **ginkóo'in** bank employees.

ginmí examination, trial.

ginnán fruit of the gingko; gingko nut.

gínoo ability, capacity; skill; **gínoo no áru** able; skillful; talented.

gin zúru to recite; to sing.

gíragira glittering; dazzling; **giragira suru** to glitter; to dazzle; to glare.

girí obligation; duty; honor; courtesy; **giri no** adoptive; step—;—in-law; **giri no kyóodai** brother-in-law; **girí o kaku** to fail to do one's duty; **girigatái** having a high sense of duty.

Gírisha Greece; **Girishájin** (n.) Greek; **Girishago** Greek language.

gíron argument; discussion; debate; dispute; **gíron suru** to argue, etc.; **gironzúki na** argumentative.

gíryoo ability; talent, skill; **gíryoo no áru** talented.

gisei sacrifice; victim; scapegoat.

gíshi engineer; technical expert; **gíshi choo** chief engineer.

gíshiki ceremony, rite; **gíshiki no** ritual.

gíshu artificial arm; assistant engineer.

gishu artificial leg.

gisshíri closely; compactly; **gisshíri tsumekomu** to pack, jam, cram.

gítaa guitar.

gitei brother-in-law (younger sister's husband); agreement; enactment.

gizagiza notches.

gizen hypocrisy; **gizénsha** hypocrite; **gizenteki** hypocritical.

gizoo forgery. (See also **gihitsu**.)

go game resembling checkers; **go o útsu** to play "go"; **goban** "go" board; checkerboard; **goban gata no** checkered; **goishi** pieces used in playing "go."

GO five; word; term; language; **DAIGO** fifth; **Eigo** (an) English word; English language; **gó o tsuyómete iu** to speak emphatically; **góbi** ending (of a word); end (of a sentence); **gobi hénka** inflection; **góbu** 5 per cent; **GOJÚU** fifty; **dái gójuu** fiftieth; **gojuu no too** five-story pagoda.

-go suffix denoting: after; **sonogo** after that; since then; **sensoogo** postwar.

gobugari short haircut, crew cut.

gobugobu equally well matched; equal; **gobugobu ni náru** to end in a draw (tie); **gobugobu no tachiba de** on equal terms.

GOBUSATA SURU to neglect to write or call. **Gobusata itashimáshita.** I am sorry I didn't write you. I am sorry I didn't call you earlier.

gochagocha no mixed-up, confused; **góchagocha suru** to mix up, jumble; **gochagocha ni náru** to be confused.

GOCHISOO treat; feast. **Kyóo wa watashi ga gochisoo shimashóo.** Let me treat you to dinner today. Be my guest at dinner today. **Gochisoosama.** Thanks for the fine dinner.

gochoo tone of voice; accent.

goei guard; escort; **goei suru** to guard; to escort; **goéi hei** bodyguard.

gofuku dry goods; **gofukuya** dry-goods dealer.

gogaku study of languages.

GÓGATSU May.

GÓGO afternoon; **gógo níji** two p.m.

GÓHAN boiled rice; meal; **góhan o tabéru** to eat a meal; **góhan o taku** to cook rice.

gohoo false report.

gójitsu some other day; in the future.

gojuunénsai semi-centennial; jubilee.

gojuúon Japanese syllabary.

gokai misunderstanding; **gokai suru** to misunderstand; to take amiss.

goke widow; widowhood.

góki tone; manner of speaking; **góki surudóku** sharply, in a sharp tone; **góki o tsuyómete hanásu** to speak emphatically.

gókoo halo; glory.

GÓKU very; extremely; **góku mezurashíi** extremely rare; **góku chiisái** very small, tiny.

gókui secret; secret principles.

gokuin stamp; hallmark.

gokujoo (n.) first-rate; best quality; **gokujoo no** (adj.) best; first-rate; first-class.

gokuraku paradise; Eden.

goma sesame seed; **goma o súru** to grind sesame seed; to flatter; to fawn upon; **gomaábura** sesame oil.

gomakashi trickery; hocus-pocus; deception; **gomakashi no** fraudulent, sham; **gomakásu** to deceive; to cheat; to cover up; to tamper with.

GOMEN pardon, permission; **GOMEN NASÁI.** Pardon me. Excuse me. **Chótto gomen kudasái.** Excuse me a minute.

GOMÍ rubbish, refuse; dirt; **gomitóri** dustpan; **gomíbaku** garbage (rubbish) can.

GÓMU gum; rubber; **gumbándo** rubber band; **gomúgutsu** rubber boots; **gomúhimo** elastic tape; **gomúmari** rubber ball; **gomúnori** mucilage; **gomuwa** rubber tire.

góngo doodan unspeakable; outrageous; absurd.

góo village, country, district; number; issue; pen name; title; fate, destiny; inevitable retribution; **dái sán goo** issue no. 3; **sono zasshi no Gogátsugoo** the May issue of the magazine; **góo no fukái** sinful; **góo o niyasu** to be greatly disturbed; to be mortified. **Góo ni itte wa góo ni shitagáe.** When in Rome, do as the Romans do.

goodatsu seizure; extortion; plunder.

goodoo combination; union; **goodoo suru** to amalgamate; to incorporate; **goodoo no** united; incorporated.

googai "extra": special issue of a newspaper.

gooi agreement; mutual understanding; **gooi de** by mutual agreement.

goojoo obstinacy, stubbornness; **goojoo na** stubborn, obstinate; **goojoo o haru** to be obstinate.

gookaban deluxe edition; **gookasen** luxury liner.

gookaku eligibility; success; **gookaku suru** to be eligible for; to pass; to be successful in.

gookan rape; assault.

GOOKEI sum total, total amount; **gookei suru** to sum up; **gookei . . . ni náru** to amount to . . . in all; to add up to.

gooketsu hero; great man.

gookin metallic compound; alloy.

gooman haughtiness, arrogance.

goomon torture; **goomon ni kakéru** to torture.

goorei command, order; **goorei suru** to command, order; to rule; **goorei o kakéru** to give a command or order.

gooriki great strength; mountain guide.

góoru goal.

góosha luxury; magnificence; **góosha na** luxurious; magnificent; **góosha o kiwameru** to live in magnificent style.

gootán fearlessness; boldness; **gootán na** fearless; daring; bold.

gootoo burglar, thief.

góou heavy rain.

gooyoku avarice, greed.

gooyuu extravagant pleasures; spree; **gooyuu suru** to go on a spree.

goozen haughtily, arrogantly; proudly.

goraku pleasure; pastime; amusement; recreation; **gorakuyoo no** for amusement; **gorakúshitsu** recreation room.

goran (*n.*) seeing, viewing (used only in reference to the second or third person); **goran ni ireru** to present something for inspection. **Goran kudasái.** Please take a look. **Goran no tóori.** As you see. **Chótto kore o goran nasai.** Just look at this. **Máa kangáete goran nasai.** Think it over, anyway.

górira gorilla.

-GÓRO suffix denoting: about (in point of time); around; toward; **nijigóro** about two o'clock; **yoakegóro** toward dawn.

goro sound.

góro grounder (in baseball).

górogoro rumbling; rolling; gurgling; lying idle; **górogoro korobu** to roll about; **mé ga gorogoro suru** to have a sore (an irritated) eye. **Káre wa máinichi górogoro shite iru.** He idles away his time every day. **Néko ga nódo o górogoro narasu.** The cat purrs.

górufu golf; **górufu o suru** to play golf; **gorufujoo** golf links.

gosai second wife; **gosai o mukaeru** to marry again.

gosan miscalculation; **gosan suru** to miscalculate.

goshin suru to diagnose wrongly.

Gósho Imperial Palace.

góshoo daijí ni with the greatest possible care; most carefully; **góshoo daijí ni suru** to take care of; **góshoo daijí ni tsutoméru** to serve most faithfully.

gosoo escort; convoy.

gotagota trouble; difficulties; confusion; disorder; **gótagota suru** to be in confusion; to be disordered. **Gotagota ga okorikákete iru.** Trouble is brewing.

gotamaze jumble; muddle.

gotatsuku to quarrel; to be agitated; to be in disorder.

gotcha in confusion.

GÓTO NI every; every time; at intervals of; **ni mairu góto ni** every two miles; **hi goto ni** every day; **mikka góto ni** every three days.

gótsugotsu rough; rugged; harsh; stiff; **gótsugotsu iu** to speak harshly; **gótsugotsu shite iru** to be stiff; to be rough.

gozá mat; matting; **gozá o shiku** to spread a mat (on the floor).

GOZAIMASU = ARIMASU there is, there are.

GÓZEN forenoon; **gózen ni** in the morning.

guai condition; fitness; manner; working order; **guai ga warúi** to feel indisposed, be unwell; to be out of order. **Kono hikidashi wa guai ga warúi.** This drawer does not work smoothly. **Bánji guai yóku itta.** Everything went very well.

guchi idle complaints; **guchi o kobósu** to grumble; complain; **guchippói** grumbling; complaining.

gumi company, firm; gang; **Fujita gumi** Fujita Company.

gun district; county.

gún crowd; army; forces; troops; **gún o násu** to crowd; to flock; **gún o núku** to be far above the crowd (to distinguish oneself); **gúnbi** arms, **gúnbi shukushoo** disarmament; **gunshuu** crowd of people, multitude; **gunshuu**

suru to crowd together; to throng; **gúntai** army, military.
guntoo archipelago, group of islands.
gúnyagunya flabby; limp.
gúragura suru to be shaky; to totter, waver; to be rickety; **guratsuku** to totter; to be shaky.
-GÚRAI = kurai suffix denoting: about; almost; some; something like; or so. **Anó hito wa sanjuu-gúrai deshoo.** He must be about 30 years old.
gúramu gram.
guretsu na stupid; ridiculous; absurd; silly; foolish.
guron foolish argument; absurd opinion.
gúru conspiracy, collusion; accomplice, conspirator; **gúru ni náru** to conspire with, plot together; **—to gúru ni nátte** in collusion with (someone).
GÚRUGURU round and round; **gúruguru mawaru** to whirl; spin round and round.
gururí circumference; surroundings; **gururí ni** about, around; **gururí to** round; **ie no gururí ni** around the house.
-gurushíi suffix denoting: to be unpleasant to, repulsive to; **negurushíi** to be sleepless; to sleep badly.
gurúupu group.
guusúu even number; **guusúu no** even-numbered.
gutto considerably; firmly; with great strength; **gutto nómu** to gulp down; **gutto fuéru** to increase markedly.
GUUZEN by chance; accidentally; **guuzen no** accidental; unexpected; casual; **guuzen no dekígoto** an accident; **guuzen desu** to come across, meet by chance.
guuzoo image, idol, statue.
gúzu imbecile; weak-minded person.
gúzuguzu lazily; idly; tardily; **gúzuguzu suru** to hesitate; to loiter; **gúzuguzu iu** to complain; to murmur.
guzúru to be peevish; to be fretful.
gyakkoo retrogression; **gyakkoo suru** to move back; to run counter to; to retrogress; **gyaku** opposite, contrary, reverse. **gyaku ni** contrarily, conversely; **gyaku ni suru** to reverse; to invert; **gyaku ni mawasu** to turn (something) the other way; **gyakumódori** retrogression; reversal; **gyakumódori suru** to go (turn) backward); to have a relapse; to lapse into; **gyakuten** sudden change; reversal; **gyakuten suru** to retrogress.
gyakusatsu slaughter; massacre.
gyakutai ill-treatment.
gyangu gang.
gyogyoo fishery; fishing industry.
gyokuro sweet green tea (the best and most expensive type).
gyóo line; verse.
gyoogi behavior; manners; **gyoogi no yói** well behaved; well mannered; **gyoogi no warui** poorly behaved; **gyoogi sáhoo** etiquette.
gyóoja devotee; pilgrim; ascetic.

gyooji observances; functions; proceedings; referee (of Japanese wrestling).
gyoojoo behavior, conduct.
gyooketsu coagulation, congealing.
gyóomu business; affairs; duties.
gyooretsu procession, parade; **gyooretsu o náshite** in procession.
gyoosei administration; **gyooséikan** administrator.
gyooshoo peddling; peddler.
gyooten suru to be surprised, amazed, astounded.
gyoozui (*n.*) taking a shower (Japanese style: pouring water over the body from a small tub); bathing; **gyoozui suru** to take a Japanese-style shower.
gyosen fishing boat.
gyoson fishing village.
gyotto suru to be startled, alarmed.
gyúuba oxen and horses; horses and cattle.
GYUUNIKU beef; **gyuunikuya** butcher shop.
GYUUNYUU cow's milk; **gyuunyuu ya** milkman; **gyuunyúu bin** milk bottle.
gyuutto hard; violently; firmly; **gyuutto osu** to push violently (with force); **gyuutto hiku** to pull with a jerk.

H

HÁ tooth; cog; support; cutting edge; sect; party, faction; school; **há no áru** toothed; cogged; **há no nái** toothless; blunt; **há no tsúita** sharp-edged; **há ga uku** to set the teeth on edge; **há o migaku** to brush the teeth; **há ga itámu** to have a toothache; **há o tsukéru** to sharpen.
ha leaf (of a plant).
háapu harp.
háato heart (in a card game).
HABA width, breadth; **haba ga kiku** to have great influence over; **haba o kikasu** to exert great influence; **haba go ínchi áru** five inches wide.
habakiki influential person.
habátaki suru to flutter, flap wings.
habikóru to spread; to grow thick; to become powerful.
habúku to curtail; to save; to leave out; **jikan o habúku** to save time; **híyoo o habúku** to cut expenses.
HABÚRASHI toothbrush.
haburi influence; power; **haburi ga yói** to be influential.
hábutae glossy silk.
HACHI eight; **dái hachí** eighth.
hachi bee; **hachi no su** beehive; **hachimitsu** honey.
HACHI bowl, basin; pot.
hachiáwase suru to be brought face to face (bump heads together).
HACHIGATSU August.
HACHIJÚU eighty; **dái hachijuu** eightieth.
hachímaki headband; hand towel tied around the head (worn by laborers).
hachiue potted plant.
háda skin; body; disposition; character; **shirói**

háda fair skin; **háda ga áu** to get on well (with); **hadaka** nakedness, nudity; **hadaka no** naked, nude, bare; **hadaka ni náru** to strip off one's clothes; **hadámi** body; one's person.

HADAGI underwear.

hadashi bare feet; **hadashi de arúku** to walk barefoot; **kuróoto hadashi da** to put even a professional to shame.

hadazáwari touch. **Biroodo wa hadazáwari ga yói.** Velvet feels soft [is agreeable to touch].

HADÉ gaiety; flashiness; display; **hadé na** gay; bright; flashy; **hadé na iro** bright (gay) color; **hade zúki de áru** to be fond of display.

HAE fly.

haegiwa hairline.

haéru to grow; to sprout; to spring up. **Hana no táne ga háeta.** The flower seeds sprouted.

HAGAKI post card; **hagaki o dásu** to drop (send) a card.

hagami suru to gnash one's teeth.

hagane steel.

hagásu to strip; to tear off.

hagayúi to feel impatient; to feel irritated. **Káre no gúzuguzu shite irú no ga hagayúkatta.** I was irritated by his dawdling.

háge bald spot; bald head; **hageátama** bald head; **hagéru** to grow bald; to come off; to fade; **iro no hágeta** discolored; faded.

hagemásu to encourage; to cheer up; to stimulate; **hagemí** stimulation; encouragement; diligence; **hagemí ga tsuku** to be stimulated; to be encouraged; **hagemí o tsukéru** to encourage; **HAGÉMU** to endeavor; to exert oneself; to be diligent.

hageshíi violent, severe, intense; furious; **hageshíku** violently; **hageshíi seishitsu** violent nature (referring to a person); **hageshíi átsusa** intensely hot weather.

hagíshiri suru to grit one's teeth.

hagitóru to strip off; to deprive; to tear off; **hágu** to strip; to strip off clothes; **kí no kawá o hágu** to strip the bark off a tree.

háguki gums (of the mouth).

haguréru to stray; to be separated from (one's companions).

hagúruma cog, gear (of a wheel); toothed wheel.

HÁHA, HAHAOYA mother; motherhood; **haha rashíi** motherly; maternal; **Háha no hi** Mother's Day; **hahakata** maternal (side); **hahakata no shinseki** maternal relative.

HÁI yes; yes, sir.

hai ashes; cinder; **hai ni náru** to be reduced to ashes; lungs; **haibyoo** lung disease; consumption.

haiagáru to creep (crawl) up; to climb up.

haichi arrangement; **haichi suru** to dispose; to arrange; to station.

haidásu to crawl out, creep out.

haien pneumonia.

haigamai rice with embryo buds, whole rice.

háigo rear; back (of a person);—**no háigo ni** at the rear of; behind. **Káre no háigo ni shisanka ga hikáete iru.** He has a wealthy supporter behind him.

haigoo harmony; combination; arrangement; **haigoo suru** to harmonize; to combine; to match. **Iro no haigoo ga warúi.** These colors do not match.

haigyoo suru to close up shop; to give up one's practice; to quit business.

haihíiru high heel.

haiiro ash-gray (color).

haikan suru to discontinue publication.

haikara na stylish; foppish; fashionable. **Haikara na yoofuku o kite imashita.** He was wearing a high-styled suit.

haikei background; background scenery.

háikei Dear Sir (as used in a formal letter).

HAIKEN (*n.*) looking at; inspection (pol.: used for first person only); **haiken suru** to see; to look at. **Chótto haiken.** Please let me see it. **Haiken shimáshita.** I saw it.

háikingu hiking.

haikómu to crawl (creep) in.

haiku See **hokku.**

haikyuu distribution; supply; **haikyuu suru** to distribute; supply.

hainichi anti-Japanese.

hairetsu arrangement; distribution; **hairetsu suru** to arrange in order.

hairikómu to get in; to force one's way in.

HÁIRU to enter; to go in; to break into; to join; to hold; to accommodate; **kúrabu ni háiru** to join a club; **oyu ni háiru** to take a bath. **O hairi.** Come in! Walk in! **Hí ga nishi ni háiru.** The sun sets in the west.

haiseki expulsion; exclusion; **haiseki suru** to exclude; to ostracize.

HÁISHA dentist.

haishaku suru to borrow (pol.). **Haishaku itashimásu.** I'll borrow it.

haishi suru to abolish, discontinue.

haishutsu to discharge; to exhaust; **haishutsúguchi** outlet; issue; **haishutsukan** exhaust pipe.

haisui drainage; sewerage; supply of water; **haisui suru** to drain; to pump out; **haisuíike** a reservoir.

haitáki fly-swatter.

HAITATSU delivery; distribution; **haitatsu suru** to deliver; to distribute; **haitatsú ryoo** delivery charge; **haitatsunin** distributor; carrier; **haitatsusaki** receiver; destination (of a delivery).

haitoo allotment; dividend; **haitoo suru** to pay a dividend; to allot to; **haitóokin** dividend.

haitori flytrap.

haiyuu actor; actress.

haizara ash tray.

haji edge, border; end; **haji kara haji máde** from end to end; **dóoro no haji no hóo o tóoru** to keep to the side of the road.

hají shame; disgrace; dishonor; **hají o káku** to be put to shame; **hají o kakaséru** to put to shame; **hají shírazu** without a sense of shame; shameless.

hajikéru to split open; to pop.

hajíku to flip; to snap; to repeal; to repel; **yubi o hajíku** to snap one's fingers.

HAJIME commencement, beginning; outset; origin; **hajime no** first; original; initial; **hajime kara owari máde** from beginning to end; **hajime wa** at first; **HAJIMÁRU** to begin, commence; to be opened; to originate from; **HAJIMÉRU** to begin; commence; to open; **shóobai o hajimeru** to open a business; **benkyoo o hajimeru** to begin studying; **HAJÍMETE** first; for the first time; for once. **Hajímete ome ni kakarimásu.** How do you do. Glad to meet you [I meet you for the first time]. **Hajímete ikimáshita.** I went there for the first time.

hajíru to be ashamed of.

haká grave, tomb; **hakaba** graveyard, cemetery.

hakadóru to progress rapidly; to make good progress.

hakai destruction; demolition; **hakai suru** to destroy, demolish, wreck; **hakaiteki** destructive; **hakáiryoku** destructive power.

hakaku no exceptional; unprecedented; special.

hakamá loose Japanese trousers; pleated skirt.

hakanái transient, passing; uncertain; vain; hopeless; **hakanái sáigo o togéru** to meet with an untimely death; **hakanái nozomi** vain hope.

hakarai management; arrangement; disposal; **hakaráu** to manage; to arrange; to take measures; **Kono hen wa anáta no ohakarai ni omakaseshimásu.** I'll leave the matter to your discretion. **Sore ni tsúite wa anáta ga yói yóo ni hakarátte ii desu.** You can do about it as you think best.

HAKARÁZU MO unexpectedly; by chance.

hakari balance, scales; **hakari ni kakéru** to weigh on a scale.

hakarigoto stratagem, ruse; artifice; plan, scheme; **hakarigoto ni ochíru** to fall for a trick; **hakarigoto o megurásu** to devise a stratagem; to form plans.

HAKÁRU to measure; to weigh; to survey; to sound; to judge (a person's mind); **mekata o hakáru** to check a weight; **nágasa o hakáru** to measure a length. **Anó hito no kimochi o hakáru kotó wa muzukashíi.** It is hard to understand his mind.

hákase See **hakushi**.

haké drainage; flow; sale; demand; brush;

haké ga yói to flow freely; to sell well; **hakéru** to drain off; to sell.

haken dispatch; **haken suru** to dispatch, send; **hakéngun** expeditionary force.

háki breach; annulment; **háki suru** to break and throw away; to annul.

hakichigaéru to wear someone else's clogs (shoes) by mistake; to mistake; to misunderstand.

hakidame rubbish heap.

hakidasu to sweep out; to spit out; to emit; to breathe out.

hakiké nausea; **hakiké o moyoósu** to feel sick; to be nauseous.

HAKIMONO footgear; clogs.

hakiyoseru to sweep up, gather up with a broom.

hakka peppermint; mint; firing; ignition; **hakka suru** to catch fire, ignite.

hakken discovery; **hakken suru** to discover; **hakkén sha** discover.

hakkin platinum.

HAKKÍRI clearly; distinctly; positively; definitely; exactly; **hakkíri shita** clear, distinct, positive, etc.; **hakkíri shita kóe** clear voice; **hakkíri shita henji** definite answer. **Hakkiri zonjimasén.** I don't know exactly.

hakkoo publication; issue; fermentation; **hakkoo suru** to publish; to issue; to float (a loan); to ferment.

hakkotsu skeleton; bleached bones.

hakkutsu excavation.

hakkyuu low (small) salary.

HAKO box; case; chest. **Hako ni irete kudasái.** Please put it in the box.

hakobi progress; arrangement; **ashi no hakobi** walking pace; **HAKOBU** to carry, convey, transport; to go on; to progress; **nimotsu o hakobu** to carry the baggage; **shíbashiba ashí o hakobu** to make frequent calls. **Shigoto ga umaku hakobimashita.** Everything went all right. Everything turned out all right.

hakoiri packed in a box; boxed; **hakozume ni suru** to pack in a box.

hakoniwa miniature garden.

HAKU to put on (on the feet or legs: clogs, sandals, shoes, socks, etc.); **kutsú o haku** to put on shoes.

háku to sweep; to vomit, throw up; to express; to utter; **heyá o háku** to sweep the room; **tsúba o háku** to spit.

hakuboku chalk; piece of chalk.

hakubútsukan museum.

hakuchi idiot; imbecile.

hakuchoo swan.

hakuchuu broad daylight.

hakugai persecution; **hakugai suru** to persecute.

hakugaku erudition, learning; **hakugaku no** erudite; learned.

hakuhatsu white hair; gray hair; **hakuhatsu no roojin** white-haired old man.

hakujaku feebleness, weakness; **hakujaku na**

feeble, weak; fragile; **seishin
hakujaku jídoo** mentally handicapped
child.

hakujin white man; white race; foreigner
(Occidental).

hákujoo confession; cold-heartedness;
hakujoo suru to confess, make a clean
breast of; **hakujoo na** unfeeling;
cold-hearted; heartless. **Ano hitó wa
hakujoo na hito desu.** He is a
cold-hearted man.

hakúmai hulled (cleaned) rice.

hakumei misfortune; sad fate; **hakumei na**
unfortunate; ill-fated.

hakurai imported; **hakuráihin** imported
merchandise. **Hakuraihin wa takái
kara kaemasen.** I can't buy imported
goods because they are expensive.

hakuránkai exposition; fair; **hakurankaijoo**
fair grounds.

hákushi = **hákase** doctor; doctorate degree,
Ph.D.; **hakushígoo** doctorate degree;
Yamada Hakushi Dr. Yamada.

hakushi blank sheet of paper; white paper;
clean slate.

hakushiki wide knowledge, erudition.

hákushu applause; **hákushu suru** to clap
hands, applaud; to cheer; **hákushu
kássai** applause and cheers.

hakyuu propagation, spread; **hakyuu suru** to
extend, spread, propagate; to
influence; to effect; **zénkoku ni
hakyuu suru** to extend over the whole
country.

hama seashore, beach; **hama zútai ni** along
the beach; **hamabe** seashore; beach.

hamáguri clam.

hamaki cigar.

hamarikómu to fall (sink) into; to become
infatuated with; to be addicted to;
onná ni hamarikómu to be infatuated
with a girl.

hamaru to be fixed; to fit; to fall into.

hameru to put in, insert; to fix in; to set; to
have (wear) on (one's finger).

hametsu ruin, destruction; **hametsu suru** to
be ruined, destroyed.

hamidásu to protrude, stick out.

HAMÍGAKI tooth powder, tooth paste;
hamigákiko tooth powder; **neri
hamígaki** tooth paste; **hamigaki yóoji**
toothbrush.

hamon suru to excommunicate; to expel.

hamonika harmonica.

hámono edged tool; cutlery.

HÁMU ham; **hamu salada** ham salad.

HÁN stamp; personal seal (used in place of a
signature); printing; edition; **hán o osu**
to stamp; to seal; **hán de oshita yóo na**
stereotyped, cut-and-dried; **hán o
kasaneru** to go through many editions;
shohan first edition.

HAN- prefix denoting: half, pan-; **hantoshi**
half a year; **hantsuki** half a month;
Han-Ámerika shúgi

Pan-Americanism; **Han Taiheiyoo
káigi** Pan-Pacific Conference.

HANÁ flower, blossom; essence, spirit; belle;
hana no floral; **haná o kíru** to cut
flowers; **haná o ikéru** to arrange
flowers; **hanabásami** flower scissors;
pruning shears; **hanaiké** flower vase;
hanatába bunch of flowers, bouquet;
hanauri flowerseller, flower girl;
hanawa wreath, garland; **hanáya**
florist, flower shop; **hanáyaka na**
flowery; showy; gay. **Wakái uchi ga
haná.** Youth is the springtime of life.
Gíron.ni haná ga saite kita. The
discussion is becoming heated.
Hanayáka na kai deshita. It was a gay
party.

HANA nose, nasal mucus; **hana o susuru** to
sniff; **hana o kamu** to blow one's
nose; **hana o tarásu** to have a runny
nose; **hana ga kiku** to have a good
sense of smell; **hana ni kakéru** to be
vain; **hana o akasu** to take the conceit
out of someone; **hana o tákaku suru**
to be proud; **hanasaki ni** under one's
very nose; **hanagoe** nasal sound;
twang; **hanaiki** (*n.*) breathing through
the nose; snoring; **hanaiki ga arai** to
be arrogant; to swagger; **hito no
hanaiki o ukagau** to curry favor with
someone; **hanaji** nosebleed; **hanaji o
dásu** to have a nosebleed; **hanakaze**
head cold. **Hanakaze o hiita.** I have a
cold in the head.

hanamégane pince-nez; **hanabáshira,
hanappashira, hanasuji** bridge of the
nose. **Hanabáshira ga tsuyói desu.**
He is haughty.

hanabanashii brilliant; splendid; glorious;
hanabanáshiku brilliantly; splendidly.

hánabi fireworks display; **hánabi o ageru** to
set off fireworks.

hanágata floral pattern; star; **eiga no
hanagata yákusha** screen star;
hanagata sénshu star player.

hanagumori springtime cloudy weather.

hanahadashíi excessive, extreme, exceeding.

hanamí (*n.*) flower-viewing; **hanamí ni iku**
to visit places well known for their
flower displays (such as cherry
blossoms).

hanamúko bridegroom.

HANAO clog thong; straps.

hanare, hanaréya detached room, detached
house.

hanarebánare separated, loose;
hanarebánare ni separately, apart
from each other; **hanarebánare ni
náru** to become separated.

HANARÉRU to separate, part from; to come
off; **hanáreta** separated, detached,
isolated, distant, far off; **hanáreta
tokoró kara míru** to watch from a
distance; **hanáreta tochi** distant place;
hanárete iru be distant, live apart

from; **hanarezashiki** detached
guestroom. **Ima shoku o hanárete
iru.** He is now out of work.
HANASHÍ talk, conversation, chat; gossip,
story; **hanashi jóozu** good speaker;
hanashibeta poor speaker; **hanashi
áite** companion to talk with; **hanashí o
suru** to talk, chat; **hanashiburi** way
(manner) of speaking; **hanashichuu**
busy signal (telephone); **hanashiai**
conference, consultation; **hanashiáu** to
talk with, consult with; **hanashigóe**
voices (in conversation); **hanashí no
táne** topic for conversation; **hanashí
ga tsuku** to arrive at an understanding;
hanashí o soraseru to change the
subject; **hanashika** professional
storyteller; **hanashikómu** to chat for
hours; **hanashizúki na** talkative.
HANÁSU to speak, talk, converse; to tell,
state, relate; to separate, part, set free,
loose; **te o hanasu** to loose one's hold,
let go of (someone's) hand. **Eigo de
hanáshite kudasái.** Please speak
English. **Anáta ni hanashitái koto ga
aru.** I have something I'd like to tell
you.
hanauta humming; **hanauta o utau** to hum a
song or tune.
hanáyome bride.
hanazákari full bloom.
hanazono flower garden.
hanbai sale; **hanbai suru** to sell, deal in;
hanbainin dealer, **hanbaigákari**
salesman, saleswoman; **hanbáiten**
distributor.
HANBÚN half; **hanbún ni suru** to divide into
halves.
hándan judgment, interpretation.
handobággu handbag.
handoo reaction; **handoo suru** to react upon;
handooteki reactionary.
handon half-holiday.
handoru handle; steering wheel.
hane feather; plumage; wing; shuttlecock;
hane búton feather quilt.
hané (*n.*) splashes of mud; to close; to break
up; **hané ga agatte iru** to be splashed
with mud; **hanekásu** to splash, spatter.
Shibai no hané wa júuji desu. The
theatre closes at ten.
hanekáeru to rebound, spring back.
hanemawáru to bounce about, leap about; to
romp.
han'enkei semicircle; **han'enkei no**
semi-circular.
han'eri ornamental neckband for women.
hanéru to reject; to throw out; to set aside; to
exclude; to leap, spring, bound; to
splash, splatter. **Sooba ga hanéta.**
Prices jumped. **Abura ga hánete
yakedo o sita.** The cooking oil
splashed and I got burnt.
hanetsukéru to refuse; to reject; to repel.
hangaku half (amount); half the sum (price,
fare, etc.); **hangaku de** at half-price,

half-fare. **Kodomo no jooshácḥiṇ wa
hangaku desu.** Children can travel for
half-price. **Kodomo no nyuujóo ryoo
wa hangaku desu.** Children are
admitted for half-price.
hangen reduction by half; **hangen suru** to
reduce by half.
hangutsu low laced shoes.
hán'i scope, sphere; limit, bounds.
hanikámu to be shy, bashful.
hánji judge.
HANJIKAN half an hour.
hánjoo good business; prosperity; **hánjoo
suru** to prosper, flourish, do a good
business.
hanjuku half-cooked; soft-boiled; half-ripe;
hanjuku no tamágo soft-boiled egg.
hankáchi See **hankéchi.**
hankan antipathy, ill-feeling; **hankan o idáku**
to provoke ill-feeling.
HANKÉCHI = hankáchi handkerchief.
hánkei radius.
hanko seal.
hankoo resistance, opposition; defiance;
hankooteki defiant, rebellious.
hankyoo echo; response; anti-communism;
hankyoo suru. To echo, resound.
hankyuu half-holiday.
hanmen profile, silhouette; one side; **hanmen
no shínri** half truth; **kao no hanmen**
one side of the face; **hanménzoo**
profile.
hanmoku hostility, antagonism.
hanmon interrogation; **hanmon** anguish;
agony; mortification; **hanmon suru** to
be in agony; to feel anguish; to be
mortified.
hanne half the price; **hanne de uru** to sell at
half the price.
hannichi half a day.
hánnin offender, criminal.
hannoo reaction, response; **hannoo suru** to
react, respond; to act upon.
hanpa odds; odds and ends; fragments; **hanpa
no odd;** half-done; incomplete; **hanpa
mono** a broken set. **Ano hito wa
hanpa no sigeto sika dekimasen.** He
never finishes his tasks.
hanran rebellion, revolt.
hantai opposition; contradiction; **hantai suru**
to oppose; to object to; **hantai na**
opposite; opposed; **hantai ni** on the
contrary; in the opposite direction;
hantai úndoo opposition movement,
counter movement; **hantáisha**
opponent; objector; **hantaitoo**
opposition party.
hantei judgment, decision.
hantén short coat; workman's coat.
hantoo peninsula.
hantoshi half a year.
hantsuki half a month.
hantsukimai half-hulled rice (processed to
retain rice germ; often preferred for its
nutritive value).

han'yake partly burned; half-roasted, half-baked.

hanzai crime, offense; **hanzai nin** criminal, culprit; **hanzai kóoi** criminal act.

hanzatsu complication; **hanzatsu na** complex, complicated.

hanzen clearly, distinctly; definitely; **hanzen to shita** clear, distinct; definite. **Sono hanashi o kiite hanzen to simashita.** Now that I've heard that explanation, the whole story has become clear.

haori Japanese coat.

happóo all directions; all sides; **happóo ni** in all directions; on all sides; all around; **happóo bíjin** everybody's friend.

happun suru to be roused to action.

happyoo announcement; publication; **happyoo suru** to announce; to publish; to make known.

hára field; plain; moor; prairie; wild region.

hará (colloq.) belly; bowels; abdomen; stomach; **hará ga itámu** to have a stomach-ache; **hará no ookíi** magnanimous; **hará ni suwatta** resolute, firm; **hará ga heru** to feel hungry; **hará ga tátsu** to be offended; **hará o kakaete warau** to split with laughter; **harabai ni náru** to lie on one's stomach; **haramaki** belt.

harachígai half-brother, half-sister.

hárahara unrestrained; **hárahara suru** to feel uneasy; to be in suspense. **Námida o hárahara to nagáshita.** The tears fell in big drops. **Míte ite mo hárahara shita.** I felt nervous just looking at it.

haraí payment; account **haraikomi** payment; installment payment; **haraikómu** to pay in, pay up; **haraimodoshi** repayment; refund; **haraimodósu** to pay back, repay.

haraisage government surplus sale.

harásu to clear away; to divert; **uramí o harásu** to pay off old scores.

HARÁU to pay (a bill, etc.); to brush off; to clear away; **shakkín o haráu** to pay off a debt. **Námida o harátte shigoto o tsuzuketa.** She brushed away her tears and resumed her task.

harawáta (colloq.) intestines; bowels; heart; character; **harawáta o tátsu** to break (someone's) heart.

hare (n.) swelling; **hareru** to swell; **haremono** swelling, boil.

háre fine (fair) weather; **háre no kimono** holiday (Sunday) clothes; **haregi** holiday clothes.

HARÉRU to clear up (weather); to clear away; to be dispelled; **kéngi ga haréru** to be cleared of a charge. **Sora ga haréta.** The sky has cleared.

haretsu explosion; eruption; **haretsu suru** to explode, burst, blow up; to be broken off.

HÁRI needle; pin; hand (of a watch); fish-hook; sting (of a bee); beam; crossbeam; **hári no médo** eye of a needle; **haribako** needlecase; lady's workbox; **harisáshi** pincushion; **harishígoto** needlework; **harishígoto o suru** to sew.

haridásu to post (on a bulletin board); **keiji o haridásu** to post a notice.

harifuda bill; poster; **harifuda o suru** to put up a poster.

harigami label; poster.

harigane wire.

haritsukéru to stick on, paste on; to paste over.

HÁRU spring (season). **Haru ni Amerika e kaerimasu.** I am returning to the United States in the spring.

haru to stretch, spread; to stick; **kitte o haru** to paste on a stamp.

hasamáru to get in between; to lie between. **Niku ga há no aida ni hasamarimashita.** A piece of meat got stuck between his teeth.

HASAMÍ scissors, shears; **niwaki ni hasamí o ireru** to prune bushes.

hasámu to place; to hold between; to pinch; to pick up; **híbashi de monó o hasámu** to pick up something with tongs.

HASHÍ pair of chopsticks; **háshi o tsukéru** to start eating.

HASHÍ bridge; **hashí o wataru** to cross a bridge.

hashi edge, border; end.

hashigo ladder; flight of stairs; **hashigodan** staircase.

hashika measles.

hashikkói smart, shrewd, sharp.

HASHIRA pillar, post, column; pole; prop; **hashira dókei** wall clock; **daikoku háshira** main pillar; main support (a person).

hashirí (n.) running; movement; first (of something); **hashiri mawáru** to run about; **cha no hashirí** the first supply of tea; **hashirígaki suru** to write hurriedly; to scribble; **hashiriyomi o suru** to read hurriedly; to skim; **hashirizúkai** errand boy; running an errand. **Kono to no hashirí ga yói.** This sliding door moves easily.

HASHÍRU to run; to sail; to move fast. **Káre wa yá no yóo ni hashítte itta.** He was off like a shot.

hashita fraction; fragment; odds and ends.

hashutsúfu daily houseworker (female).

hashutsusho branch station; police box.

hassha starting (of a train, bus, etc.); **hassha suru** to start; to depart.

hasshin suru to dispatch a message; to send a letter.

hassoo suru to send off; to forward (a letter or package).

hassúru to emit; to radiate; to fire; to discharge (a gun); to issue.

hatá flag, banner, standard; **hatazao** flagstaff.

hata side; neighborhood; **hata de** nearby; beside; **hata no móno** bystanders; outsiders.

48

hátabi national holiday.
HÁTACHI twenty years old (said of a person). **Watakushi wa hátachi desu.** I am twenty years old.
hatairo outlook, circumstances; **hatairo o míru** to see how things go.
hatake field; kitchen garden; farm.
hatakí duster (made of pieces of cloth attached to a stick); **hatáku** to dust; to beat; to slap; to empty; to use up; **saifu no soko o hatáku** to spend every penny one has.
hatankyoo almond.
hataori weaver; weaving; **hataori kikái** power loom; **hataori kóoba** mill.
HATARAKI action; motion; work, labor; ability, talent; merits; **hataraki no áru hito** an able man; **hataraki mono** a hard worker; **HATARAKU** to work, toil, labor; to commit; to do. **Ichinichi juu sóto de hatarakimáshita.** I worked outside all day long.
HATÁSHITE sure enough; just as I expected.
hatásu to accomplish, achieve; to fulfill; **yakusoku o hatásu** to fulfill one's promise; **mokuteki o hatásu** to achieve one's purpose; **gímu o hatásu** to do one's duty.
háta to suddenly; completely.
HATE end, termination; consequence; result; limit; failure; **hate ni** finally; in the end; **hate ga nái** limitless, endless; **haténkoo** record-breaking; unprecedented; unheard of.
hateshi end; limits; **hateshi nái** endless, boundless; **hateshi nái gíron** an endless argument.
háto dove, pigeon.
hatoba wharf, dock, pier.
hatsú first, beginning; **hatsú no** first; initial; new.
hatsuan suggestion, proposal; **hatsuan suru** to suggest, propose.
hatsubai for sale; **hatsubai suru** to offer for sale, put on sale.
hatsubútai debut; first public performance.
hatsubyoo suru to fall ill.
hatsudóoki engine; motor; **hatsudookisen** motorboat.
hatsufuyu early winter.
hatsugen speech; **hatsugen suru** to open one's mouth; to speak (at a conference); **hatsugénsha** speaker.
hátsugi proposal, motion.
hátsui suggestion; instance; proposal; original idea; **jibun no hátsui de** on one's own initiative.
HATSUKA the twentieth (of the month); (for) twenty days.
hatsukóokai maiden voyage.
hatsumei invention; **hatsuméisha** inventor.
hatsumimi news (to a person). **Kore wa hatsumimi da.** This is news to me.
hatsunetsu suru to have a fever.
HATSUON pronunciation; **hatsuon suru** to pronounce. **Ano hito no Nihongo no hatsuon wa taihen ii desu.** His

pronunciation of Japanese words is very good.
hatsuratsu to shita lively; keen; animated.
hattatsu development, progress, growth; **hattatsu suru** to develop, make progress, grow.
hatten development, expansion, growth; **hatten suru** to develop, expand, extend.
háu to crawl, creep.
hayá- prefix denoting: quick; fast; swift; early; **hayáashi** quick steps; trot; **hayagátten** hasty conclusion; **hayagátten suru** to jump to a conclusion; **hayagáwari** quick change (of costume); **hayagáwari suru** to make a quick change.
HAYÁI quick, fast, rapid, swift; early; **háyaku** quickly, promptly, early, etc.; **ki no hayái** excitable (person).
hayaku breach of contract; **hayaku suru** to break a contract.
hayákuchi rapid speech; **hayákuchi de hanásu** to jabber; to speak rapidly; **hayákuchi no** glib-tongued.
hayamáru to be overhasty, be rash; to act hastily; **hayamátta** rash; hasty; **hayamátta kotó o suru** to act rashly; **hayaméru** to quicken, hasten, accelerate; **ashí o hayameru** to quicken one's steps. **Sonna ni hayamátte wa ikemasén.** Don't be so hasty. **Nán to iu hayamátta kotó o shite kureta.** What a rash thing you've done!
hayame ni somewhat early, before time; **uchi o hayame ni déru** to leave home a little early.
hayáne o suru to go to bed early; **hayáne hayáoki** early to bed and early to rise.
hayanómikomi o suru to jump to a conclusion.
hayáoki suru to get up early.
hayari fashion, mode, vogue; **hayari no** fashionable, popular; **hayari no shingata** new style.
hayaríuta popular song.
HAYÁRU to be in fashion; to prevail; to rage; to prosper; to be hasty; to be impetuous; **hayaránaku náru** to go out of fashion; to lose popularity. **Ano misé wa yóku hayátte iru.** That store is doing a good business.
háyasa quickness, swiftness, rapidity, speed, velocity.
hayashi forest, wood, grove.
hayásu to cut into small fragments; to slice up; to hash; to grow; to let grow; **hige o hayásu** to grow a beard; to grow a mustache.
hayawákari quick understanding; **hayawákari no suru** to be quick of understanding; to be intelligent; to be easy to understand.
hayawaza clever trick; sleight of hand.

HAZU ought to; is to be; (*n.*) notch (of a bow);—**hazu wa nái** cannot be; must not be; there is no reason to believe that . . . **Káre wa késa shuppatsu suru hazu deshita.** He was to start this morning. **Anó hito wa kyoo kúru hazu desu.** He is expected here today. **Anó hito ga kyoo kuru hazu wa nái.** There is no reason to believe that he would come here today.

hazukashigáru to be shy, be bashful; **HAZUKASHII** to be ashamed; to be shameful; to be dishonorable; to be bashful, shy; **ohazukashii kotó desu ga** . . . to my shame I must confess that . . . ; **hazukashime** shame, disgrace; insult; **hito kara hazukashime o ukéru** to be humiliated by someone; **hazukashiméru** to put to shame; to outrage.

hazumi momentum, impetus; **hazumi o tsukéru** to give impetus to; **hazumi ga tsuku** to be encouraged; to be stimulated; **toki no hazumi de** on the spur of the moment; **hazumu** to bounce; to rebound; to get lively; to treat oneself to; **íki ga hazumu** to be out of breath; to pant.

hazure end, edge; outskirts; miss; disappointment; failure (of crops); poor harvest; **machi no hazure** the end of a street.

hazureru to be disconnected, be dislocated; to come off; to be out of joint; to fail; to miss; **ate ga hazureru** to be disappointed in one's expectations.

hazusu to remove; to unfasten; to lose; to avoid; **mégane o hazusu** to take off one's glasses; **kikái o hazusu** to lose an opportunity; **séki o hazusu** to slip out of the room; to leave the table.

hébi snake, serpent.

hedatari distance; difference; gap; **hedatáru** to be distant; to become estranged.

hedate distinction; discrimination; reserve; estrangement; barrier; **hedate no áru** distant; discriminating; **hedate no nái** candid; open-hearted; **hedate náku hanásu** to speak without reserve; **hedatéru** to part from; separate by; to intervene, come between; to alienate; **hedátete** apart; at a distance; at intervals of; **júunen o hedátete** after an interval of ten years.

heddoráito headlight.

héi vice; evil; abuses; evil practice; **heigai** evils; evil influence, evil effect.

hei wall; fence; **hei o megurásu** to surround with a wall.

heian peace, tranquility; **heian ni** peacefully, in peace.

heibon commonness; mediocrity; **heibon na** commonplace, mediocre; tame; uneventful; **heibon na tsuki** an uneventful month.

heihei bonbon commonplace, mediocre.

Héika His (Her) Majesty.

heikai closing, adjournment; **heikai suru** to adjourn.

heiki coolness, calmness, composure; **heiki na** cool, calm, composed; indifferent; unconcerned; **heiki de** calmly; with composure. **Heiki na kao o shite imashita.** He looked unconcerned.

heikin average; balance; equilibrium; **heikin shite** on the average.

heikoo suru to be defeated; to be silenced; to be annoyed; to be embarrassed.

heion tranquility; peace and quiet; **heion no, heion na** quiet; tranquil; **heion ni náru** to become quiet.

heisei composure; **kokoro no heisei o tamótsu** to keep one's presence of mind.

heitai soldier.

heiten (*n.*) closing of a shop or business; **heiten suru** to close up shop.

heiwa peace; **heiwa no, heiwa na** peaceful, peaceable; **heiwa ni** peacefully; **heiwarónsha** pacifist.

heiya plain; moor; prairie.

HEIZEI at ordinary times; usually. **Heizei wa yoru uchi ni imasu.** I am usually at home at night.

heizen, heizen to shite calmly, composedly.

hekieki suru to shrink from; to flinch; to be nonplused.

hekomasu to hollow, to depress; to defeat; to silence; **hekomu** to become hollow; to become depressed; to be humiliated; to give in, yield.

hekotareru to be discouraged; to be exhausted.

hen neighborhood; region; side; **kono hen ni** in this neighborhood.

hén chapter; book, volume.

henbutsu = **henjín** eccentric person, odd fish.

henden telegram (in reply); **henden suru** to reply by telegram.

hendoo change, alteration; fluctuations; **hendoo suru** to change; to fluctuate.

HENJÍ = **hentóo** reply, answer; **henjí suru** to reply, answer; **tegami no henjí o dásu** to answer a letter.

henjín See **henbutsu.**

hénka change, variation; **hénka suru** to change, alter.

henken prejudice; prejudiced view.

henkin repayment; refund; **henkin suru** to pay back, repay.

henkoo alteration, making changes.

hénkutsu eccentricity; obstinacy; narrow-mindedness; **hénkutsu na** eccentric; narrow-minded; cranky; obstinate. **Ano hito wa henkutsu na hito desu.** He is an eccentric person.

HÉN NA odd, strange, queer; **hén na mé ni áu** to have an odd experience; **hén na kokochi ga suru** to have a strange sensation; **hén ni omóu** to think (something) to be strange.

hennyuu admission; assignment.

hénrei return (of a present or call);—**no hénrei ni** in return for.

hensai repayment; **hensai suru** to repay.

hensan compilation; editing.

hensei organization; formation.

hensen change; vicissitudes; **hensen suru** to change, undergo a change.

henshi unnatural death.

henshin change of mind; unfaithfulness; **henshin suru** to change one's mind.

henshoku partiality (weakness) for a particular kind of food.

hensoo disguise.

hentai abnormality.

hentóo See **henji.**

hentoosen tonsils; **hentoosén en** tonsillitis.

herí border, edge, brim, brink; **herí o tóru** to hem, border.

herikóputaa helicopter.

herikudáru to be modest; to humble oneself; **herikudátte** modestly, humbly.

heríkutsu o iu to quibble; to argue for the sake of arguing.

HERU to decrease, lessen; to be reduced; **herasu** to decrease, lessen, reduce. **Áme de hitode ga hetta.** Because of the rain, the crowds have thinned out.

héru to pass; to elapse; to pass through; to go by way of.

herumétto helmet.

hesokurigane secret savings; pin money.

HETÁ unskillfulness, awkwardness; stem; calyx; **hetá na** unskillful, awkward, clumsy. **Watakushi wa Nihongo ga hetá desu.** My Japanese is poor.

héte after; through; by way of; **ichínen o héte** after a year; **yuujin no té o héte** through a friend; **Róndon o héte** by way of London.

hetoheto ni náru to be reduced to a pulp; to be tired out; to be exhausted.

hetsurai flattery; **hetsurai mono** flatterer; **hetsuráu** to flatter; to fawn on.

hétto fat.

HEYÁ room, chamber; apartment.

HI sun; day; time; date; **hi no de** sunrise; **hi no iri** sunset; **hi no me** sun, sunlight; **áru hi** one day; **hiatari** exposure to sun; **hiatari ga yoi** to be sunny, have plenty of sunshine; **hiatari ga warui** to be dark and gloomy; **hi ni yakeru** to be sunburnt; **hi ni sarasu** to expose to the sun; **hi no me o miru** to see the light of day; **hi no me o mínai** to lack sun. **Hi ga nagaku nátte kita.** The days are getting longer. **Hi wa rokuzi ni deta.** The sun rose at six.

HÍ fire, flame; spark; light; wrong; defect, fault, error; tombstone, monument; **hí ga tsuku** to catch fire; **hí ni ataru** to warm oneself by a fire; **hí no ko** flying sparks; **hí no mi** fire lookout; **hí no te** flames; blaze; **hí no te ga agaru** to burst into flames; **hí no yoo na** fiery, blazing; **hí o narasu** to attack; to declaim against; **hi no uchidokoro ga**

nái unimpeachable; **híbana** sparks; **híbana o tobasu** to shoot out sparks; **híbashi** fire tongs; **hikeshi** fireman (see also **kasai**).

hi- prefix denoting: un-; anti-; non-; **hikínzoku** non-metal.

hiagáru to dry up; to be parched; to starve to death.

hiai sadness; sorrow.

hiashi sun; day; spread of fire; **hiashi ga mijikai** the days are short. **Hiashi ga háyakatta.** The fire spread very swiftly. (See also **hi, hí.**)

HIBACHI brazier; charcoal brazier; **hibachi ni ataru** to warm oneself at a brazier.

híban off duty; **híban de aru** to be off duty.

hibí crack; fissure; flaw; **hibí ga iru** to be cracked; to have a flaw; **hibí ga kiréru** to be chapped.

hibikí sound; echo, reverberation; **hibiki watáru** to resound, reverberate; **hibíku** to sound; to echo; to affect; to influence; **myóo ni hibíku** to sound strange.

hibon na, hibon no out of the ordinary, extraordinary; uncommon.

hiboshi drying in the sun.

hibúkure blister caused by a burn.

hibúnmei uncivilized; uncultured.

hída fold; tuck; plait; **hída o tóru** to tuck; to fold; crease.

hidachi growth; recovery; convalescence.

HIDARI left; **hidari no** left; left side; **hidari ni** to the left; on the left; **hidarí kiki** left-handedness; left-handed person; winelover, a heavy drinker; **hidarí kiki no** left-handed.

hidarímae adversity; downward course. **Shínshoo ga hidarímae ni náru.** His luck is failing. Luck is deserting him.

hidátsu to do well; to get on well.

hiden secret; trade secret.

hideri drought, dry weather.

HIDÓI severe; excessive; intense; violent; awful; terrible; **hidói mé ni áu** to have a bad time of it.

hídoku severely; intensely; violently; hard.

hidori o kimeru to fix a date, fix on a day; to name a day.

hiéru to grow cold, get chilly.

HÍFU skin.

higaeri return trip made in one day; **higaeri suru, higaeri ni suru** to go and return in one day.

hígai damage, injury; **higáisha** sufferer; victim.

higamí jaundice; warp; **higámu** to be jealous; to be prejudiced.

higan other shore (side); goal.

HIGASHI east. **Táiyoo wa higashi kara déru.** The sun rises in the east.

higáshi confectionery.

hige mustache; beard; whiskers; humility; self-depreciation; **híge suru** to humble oneself; **hige o hayásu** to raise a mustache (or beard); **hige moja no** heavily bearded.

hígeki tragedy, tragic event.

HIGORO always; for a long time; **higoro no** usual; long-cherished. **Káre wa higoro kara kinben da.** He has always been industrious. **Higoro no negái ga kanátta.** My long-cherished dream has been fulfilled.

higoto ni everyday; day by day.

HIGURE twilight; nightfall; **higure ni** toward evening; at dusk.

hihan comment; criticism; **hihan suru** to criticize; to censure.

hihoo sad news.

hihyoo critique; comment; **hihyoo suru** to criticize, comment, review; **hihyooteki** critical; **hihyooka** critic, reviewer.

híiki favor; patronage; partiality; **híiki o suru** to favor, be partial to; **híiki no** favorite; **hiikíkyaku** patron.

HIJÍ elbow; **hijikaké isu** armchair.

hijidéppoo rebuff; cold shoulder; **hijidéppoo o kuwaséru** to give (someone) the cold shoulder.

HIJOO extraordinary occasion; emergency; **hijoo na** extraordinary; uncommon; **HIJOO NI** extraordinarily; exceedingly; **hijoo no sái ni wa** in case of emergency; **hijóoguchi** emergency exit; **hijóoji** emergency, crisis; **hijooshúdan** exceptional measures.

hijóoshiki lack of common sense; **hijóoshiki na** eccentric; nonsensical. **Hijóoshiki na hito desu.** He lacks common sense.

hikae note, memorandum; duplicate; **hikáeru** to jot down, note down; to wait; to be moderate; to stop.

hikaeme moderation; modesty; temperance; **hikaeme ni** moderately; with reserve; **hikaeme ni suru** to be moderate; **bánji hikaeme ni suru** to do all things with moderation.

hikage shade; shadow; shady spot.

hikaku comparison; **hikaku suru** to compare; **hikakuteki** comparatively.

hikan pessimism; **hikan suru** to be pessimistic; **hikan rónsha** pessimist.

hikarabiru to dry up, shrivel, wither.

HIKARI light; brightness, brilliancy; glimmer; twinkle; luster, gloss; **hikaraséru** to brighten; to polish; to cause to shine; to glimmer, etc.; **hikáru** to shine; to be bright, sparkle; etc.

hikazu number of days; **hikazu ga kakáru** to take many days.

hike weak point; **hike o tóru** to be defeated, be inferior to; **hikedoki** closing hour.

hikeru to be closed; to close; to lose courage; to feel small. **Yakushó ga goji ni hikeru.** The office closes at five. **Watakushi wa sore o kangáeru to ki ga hikeru.** I feel small when I think of it.

hiketsu secret; **seikoo no hiketsu** secret of success.

hikí joy and sorrow; **hikí komógomo itáru** to have a mixed feeling of joy and sorrow.

hiki (*n.*) pulling; help; backing; influence. **Anó hito wa yói hiki ga áru.** He has good connections.

hiki- prefix denoting: pulling; drawing; **hikishio** ebb tide; low tide.

-HIKI counter head denoting: (for four-legged animals); **ippikí no ushi** one head of cattle; **nĩhiki no ushi** two head of cattle.

hikiage pulling up; evacuation; withdrawal; **hikiagéru** to pull up, draw up; to evacuate; to withdraw.

hikiai witness; instance; example; **hikiai ni dásu** to use as an example.

hikiáu to pay (off) well; to make a good return. **Sono shigoto wa hikiawánai.** The work does not pay.

hikiawase introduction; bringing together; comparison; **hikiawaséru** to introduce; to compare with; to check up.

hikicha powdered tea.

hikichigíru to pull off; to tear off.

hikidashi drawer; **hikidashi o akeru** to open a drawer.

hikidásu to draw out; to pull out; **yokin o hikidásu** to draw money from a bank.

hikifune towboat; tugboat.

hikígeki tragicomedy.

hikiharáu to vacate; to remove; **ié o hikiharáu** to move from a house.

hikiiréru to draw into; to pull into; to win over; **mikata ni hikiiréru** to win a person (over) to one's side; **hikiíru** to lead; to head; to control; to manage.

hikikae exchange; conversion;—**to hikikae ni** in exchange for; **hikikáeru** to exchange; to convert; **sore ni hikikáete** on the contrary; on the other hand.

hikikáesu to come back; to turn back; to return.

hikikomisen railway siding; service wire.

hikikomóru to shut oneself in; to be confined.

hikikómu to retire.

hikimodósu to bring back; to revert to; to restore.

HIKINIKU chopped meat; **hikinikúki** meat grinder.

hikin na familiar; common; popular; **hikin na réi** familiar example.

hikinobásu to stretch; to draw out; to enlarge (a photo); to postpone; to put off. **hikinobashi sháshin** photographic enlargement.

hikiokósu to raise up; to lift up; to cause; to give rise to; to awaken.

hikiorósu to pull down.

hikisagáru to withdraw; to retire.

hikisáku to tear up, tear to pieces.

hikishimáru to tighten; to tie harder; to brace; to be tightened up; to grow tight; to be braced up; **hikishimátta** firm; tight; tense; **fukuro no himo o hikishiméru** to draw the strings of a bag together.

hikitaósu to pull down.
hikitate favor; patronage; **hikitatéru** to favor; to patronize; to set off (beauty); to set off to advantage; **ki o hikitatéru** to encourage.
hikitátsu to look well (better); to improve; to become active; **ki ga hikitátsu** to cheer up; to be inspired with hope.
hikite catch; knob.
hikitoméru to detain; to stop.
hikitóru to withdraw; to take back; to take over.
hikitsúgu to succeed in; to take over.
hikitsuke convulsion.
hikitsukéru to draw toward one; to attract.
HIKITSUZÚITE continually; successively; **gonen hikitsuzúite** for five years running; **hikitsuzuki** continuation; succession; sequel; **hikitsuzúku** to continue; to last.
hikiuke undertaking; **hikiukéru** to undertake; to accept; to take over; to assume; to shoulder the responsibility for. **Ano ginkoo wa kono tegate no hikiuke o kobanda.** That bank didn't honor this check.
hikiwake draw, tie; **hikiwake ni náru** to end in a draw.
hikiwakéru to part; to pull apart; to separate.
hikiwatashi delivery; transfer; surrender; **hikiwatásu** to deliver; to hand over; to surrender. **Shoohin no hikiwatashi wa yokka ni súnda.** The delivery of merchandise was completed on the fourth.
hikiyoséru to draw near; to bring close; to pull near.
hikízan subtraction.
hikizuru to drag, pull along; **ashí o hikizutte arúku** to drag one's feet; **hikizuridásu** to pull out, drag out; **hikizurikómu** to drag in; to bring in.
hikkabúru to pull (draw) over one's head.
hikkakáru to be caught (on a nail, tree, etc.); to be hooked; to be entangled; to be cheated; **hikkakéru** to hook; to hang on; to cheat; to seduce; to evade payment; **íppai hikkakéru** to have a drink.
hikkáku to scratch; to claw.
hikki suru to write down; to copy; to take notes; **hikkísha** stenographer; **hikkíchoo** notebook.
hikkishikén written examination.
hikkomeru to pull (draw) in; to draw back; to move back.
hikkómu to retire, withdraw; to disappear; **hikkomigachi** (n.), **hikkomijían no** retiring (in disposition); **inaka e hikkómu** to retire to the country. **Ié wa dóoro kara hikkónde iru.** The house stands back from the road.
hikkónda secluded; sunken; hollow; **hikkónda basho** secluded place.
HIKKÓSU to move (into another house); **hikkoshi no torráku** moving van.

Tookyoo e hikkoshimásu. I am going to move to Tokyo.
hikkurikáeru to tumble down; to be upset; to tip over; to be overturned.
hikkurikaeshi topsy-turvy; upside down; wrong side up; inside out. **Uchi no náka wa hikkurikaeshi ni natte imasu.** The house is upside down.
hikkurikáesu to overturn; upset; to topple over; to knock down.
hikkuruméru to bundle (together); to include.
hikoku defendant; prisoner.
HIKOO flight; aviation; **hikoo suru** to fly; **HIKOOJOO** airport; **HIKÓOKI** airplane; **hikoosen** blimp; dirigible.
hikóoshiki no informal, not official; **hikóoshiki ni** unofficially; informally.
HIKU to draw; to attract; to lead; to install; to quote; to consult; to subtract; to play (an instrument); to saw; to grind; to resign, retire from service; to abate, subside; to recede, ebb; to fall; **Kúji o hiku** to draw lots; **sode o hiku** to pull (someone) by the sleeve; **kuruma o hiku** to draw a cart; **chúui o hiku** to attract attention; **doojoo o hiku** to win sympathy; **kaze o hiku** to catch a cold; **denwa o hiku** to install a telephone; **jísho o hiku** to refer to a dictionary; **nedan o hiku** to cut the price; **chisuji o hiku** to descend from; **piano o hiku** to play the piano; **múgi o kó ni hiku** to grind wheat into flour. **Hare ga hikimáshita.** The swelling has gone down. **Netsú ga hikimáshita.** The fever has dropped.
HIKÚI low; humble; mena; short; flat; **hikúi hana** a flat nose; **hikúi kóe** a low voice. **Séi ga hikúi.** He is short (in stature).
hikutsu meanness; servility; **hikutsu na** servile; mean.
hikyóo cowardice; **hikyóo na** cowardly; **hikyoo mono** coward.
HIMA leisure; (spare) time; dismissal; leave; interval; recess; **hima de áru** to be free, be at leisure; **hima ga iru** to require (more) time; **hima ga nái** to have no time; **hima o dásu** to dismiss (a servant); **hima o tóru** to resign; **himadóru** to take (much) time; to delay; **himajin** leisured or unemployed person. **Shóobai ga hima de áru.** Business is slack.
himashi ni more and more each day; **himashi ni byooki ga yóku naru** to get better day by day.
himei cry of distress; shriek; **himei o ageru** to utter a groan.
himitsu secret; secrecy; **himitsu no** secret, confidential, private; **himitsu ni** secretly, privately; **himitsu ni suru** to keep secret; **himitsu o abáku** to divulge a secret.
HIMO string, cord; braid; tape; ribbon; thong; **himo o musubu** to tie a string.

himo de musubu to tie (something) with string.

himojii to be hungry. **Taihen himojii omoi o shimashita.** I was very hungry.

himono dried fish.

hín poverty; **hin súru** to be poor;

hin elegance; grace; refinement; article; piece; item; **hin ga tsuku** to be refined; **hin no yói** refined; elegant; **hin no warúi** vulgar; uncouth; coarse; **hin o sagéru** to disgrace oneself.

HINAKA broad daylight; daytime.

hínan refuge, shelter; blame, censure, reproach; **hínan suru** to blame; **hinánsha** refugee; **hinan sho** refuge; shelter.

hinata sunny place; sunshine; **hinata ni hósu** to dry in the sun; **hinata bókko o suru** to take a sun bath.

hinekúreta twisted; crooked; distorted; perverse; **hinekúreta onna** perverse woman; **hinekúreta kangáe** distorted view; **hinekuréru** to become crooked; **hinekúru** to twirl; to finger; to toy with.

hinéru to twirl; to turn on (or off); **gásu o hinéru** to turn on the gas (in a stove).

hiniku sarcasm; caustic remark; **hiniku na** sarcastic; cynical; ironic; **hiniku o iu** to speak sarcastically or ironically.

hinjaku meagerness; poverty.

hinketsu anemia.

hinkoo behavior, conduct; **hinkoo no yói** well-behaved.

hinmínkutsu slums.

hinobe postponement; extension of time; reprieve; **hinobe suru** to postpone, etc.

hinoki bútai (theatre) stage (of cypress).

hi no kuruma extreme poverty; **hi no kuruma de áru** to be in great financial difficulty.

hi no maru national flag of Japan; disk of the sun; red circle.

HINOSHI iron; flatiron;—**ni honoshí o kakéru** to iron (clothes).

hinpan frequency; **hinpan na** frequent; incessant; **hinpan ni, hinpin** frequently; incessantly.

hínshi dying; **hínshi no jootai ni áru** to be on the verge of death.

hinshitsu quality.

hínsoo poor appearance; **hínsoo na narí o shite iru** to be poorly dressed.

hippaku pressure (for money); tightness (of money). **Ano hito wa shikin ni hippaku site iru.** He is pressed for funds.

hipparidáko de áru to be sought for eagerly; to be in great demand.

HIPPÁRU to pull, draw, drag, tug; to stretch; to entice; to solicit; **mikata ni hippáru** to win over to our side.

hira- prefix denoting: flat, level; plain, simple; common; **hiraya** one-story house; **hirachi** level land, flat ground.

HIRAGÁNA phonetic symbols used in Japanese writing system.

hírahira fluttering; flapping. **Kí no ha ga hírahira to chitta.** The leaves fluttered down.

hiráishin lightning rod.

hirakéru to become civilized; to become modernized; to be cultivated; to develop; to grow; **hiráketa** modernized; up-to-date; civilized; **hiráketa hito** man of the world.

hirakí opening; closet; difference; distance; gap; **HIRÁKU** to open; to lift (a lid); to unfold; to commence; to set up; to cultivate; to bloom; **tenránkai o hiráku** to open an exhibit. **Haná ga hiraite iru.** The flower is blooming.

hiramekásu to flash; to brandish; **hirameki** flash; flashing; gleam; **hirameku** to flash; to gleam; to wave.

híra ni humbly; earnestly; intently. **Híra ni goyóosha o kóu.** I sincerely hope you will pardon me (used in letters).

hirarí to nimbly; lightly.

hiratai, hirrattái flat, level; simple, plain; **hirataku** flatly; evenly; easily; simply, plainly; **hirataku suru** to flatten; **hirataku iéba** to speak plainly.

HIRATE palm of the hand; open hand; **hirate de útsu** to slap.

hiraya one-story house.

hiré fin.

HÍREE steak; filet mignon.

hiretsu meanness; baseness.

híríhiri suru to be pungent; to have a burning taste; to smart.

hiroba open space; square (of a town).

hirobíro spaciously; **hirobíro to shita** spacious; roomy; open; extensive.

hirogari extension; expansion; spread; **hirogaru** to extend; to spread; **HIROGERU** to spread; to extend; to widen; to open; to unfold; to unroll. **Michi o hirogemashita.** They widened the road. **Mise o hirogeru tsumori desu.** I intend to expand (enlarge) the store.

HIRÓI wide, broad; extensive; roomy; **hirói heya** spacious (big) room.

hiroiagéru to pick up.

hiroiatsuméru to gather, collect; to select.

hiroimono piece of good luck; find; **hiroimono o suru** to find (pick up) (something); to make a rare find.

hiroiyomi o suru to read here and there; to skim; to skip over (details); to pick up the chief points.

híroku widely, extensively; generally; universally; **híroku suru** to widen; to enlarge.

híroma spacious room; hall.

hiromáru to circulate; to be circulated; to be diffused; **hiroméru** to spread, propagate.

hirome announcement; debut.

hiroo fatigue; exhaustion; **hiroo suru** to get weary, to be exhausted.

híroo announcement; introduction; **híroo suru** to announce; to introduce.

hírosa width, breadth; area; dimension. **Kono kooen no hírosa wa dore hodo arimásu ka?** How large is this park?

HIROU to pick up; to find; to gather; **ará o hirou** to find fault with. **Michi de sen én satsu o hirotta.** I found a thousand-yen bill on the road.

HIRU daytime; noon, midday; **hiru hínaka** in broad daylight.

HIRUGÓHAN See hiruhan.

hirugáeru to wave; to fly; to float; to flap; **hirugáesu** to wave; to fly; to change; **zensetsu o hirugáesu** to change one's opinion.

HIRUHÁN = HIRUMESHI, HIRUGÓHAN lunch, midday meal; **hiruhan o tabéru** to have lunch.

HIRUMÁ daytime; **hirumá ni** in the daytime.

hirumáe forenoon; **hirumáe ni** in the morning.

HIRUMESHI See hiruhan.

hirúmu to flinch; to shrink.

hirune midday nap; siesta; **hirune o suru** to take a nap.

hirusúgi shortly after noon.

HIRUYÁSUMI midday recess; lunch hour.

híryoo manure; fertilizer.

hisan misery; distress; **hisan na** tragic; miserable, wretched.

hisashi visor (of a cap); eaves; canopy.

HISASHIBURI DE after a long time; for the first time in many days (weeks, years, etc.); **hisashiburi de áu** to see after a long interval. **Hisashiburi desu née!** It's a long time since I last saw you.

hisashíi long; long continued; of long standing; **hisashíi aida** for a long time.

HISÁSHIKU for a long time. **Káre ni wa hisáshiku awánai.** I haven't seen him for a long time.

hisénron pacifism; **hisenrónsha** pacifist.

hishaku ladle; dipper.

hishíhishi to firmly; tightly; densely; deeply.

hishiméku to clamor, make a noise.

hishóchi summer resort.

hisóhiso in whispers; secretly; **hisohiso bánashi** whispered conversation.

hisoméru to raise or knit (one's) brows; **máyu o hisómeta** with a frown.

hisoo touching, pathetic.

hísshi desperation; **hísshi no** desperate; **hísshi ni** desperately; **hísshi to nátte** in desperation; **hísshi no dóryoku o suru** to make desperate efforts.

hisutérii hysteria, hysterics; **hisutérii o okósu** to go into hysterics.

HITÁI forehead; brow.

hitasu to steep; to dip; to soak.

HITO man; person; mankind; people; others; nature; disposition; **hito no yói** good-natured; **hito no warúi** ill-natured; **hito no desakaru jíkoku** rush hour.

hitó- prefix denoting: one; **hitóban** one night (evening); all night; whole night; **hitóhako** one box.

HITÓBITO people.

hitochígai mistaken identity.

hitodánomi o suru to depend on someone else.

hitode helping hand; help; **hitode ga tarinai** short of hands; short of help; **hitode o kariru** to ask for help; **hitode ni wataru** to change hands.

hitode = hitogomi crowd; throng. **Taihen na hitode de átta.** There was a large crowd.

hitodenashi inhuman wretch; ungrateful person.

hitodoori pedestrian traffic; **hitodoori no óoi machí** a busy street. **Koko wa hitodoori ga óoi.** It is very crowded here.

hitoemono summer clothes.

hitófude line; stroke; **hitófude de** with one stroke of the brush.

hitogara personal character; personal appearance.

hitogoe voice.

hitogomi (See also **hitode**.) **hitogomi no náka o oshiwákete iku** to push through a crowd of people.

hitogoroshi murder; murderer.

hitogoto other people's affairs. **Hitogoto tó wa omoénai.** I feel as if it were my own concern.

hitóhada núgu to lend a helping hand; to give every assistance possible.

hitóiki breath; **hitóiki tsúite** after a pause; **hitóiki de** in one breath; at a stretch.

hitókasane suit of clothes.

hitokata naránu unusual, uncommon; great, immense.

HITOKATA NÁRAZU not a little; extremely, immensely.

HITÓKIWA especially, particularly; conspicuously; in a high degree; still more.

hitókoto single word; **hitokoto mo iwanai** to be silent; not to say a single word.

hitókuchi mouthful; bite; morsel; **hitókuchi ni kúu** to eat in one bite.

hitókuse peculiarity; uncommon trait.

hitomae de in public.

hitómaku act; scene; **hitómaku mono** one-act play.

hitomane imitation; mimicry.

hitómatome ni in a lump; in a bunch; **hitómatome ni suru** to put together.

hitómawari turn; round; **hitómawari suru** to go on one's rounds; **kooen o hitómawari sanpo suru** to take a walk through the park.

HITÓMAZU for the present; for the time being; for a while; anyhow.

hitome notice; attention; **hitome o shinóbu** to avoid the public eye; **hitome o shinónde** in secret; secretly; **hitome o hiku** to attract attention.

hitóme look; glance; **hitóme de** at a glance; **hitóme míru** to glance at.

hitomishiri suru to be afraid of strangers; to be bashful.

hitómukashi age; decade.

hitonaka crowd of people; **hitonaka de** in the presence of others.

hitonami no average; common; ordinary; **hitonami ni** like other people; **hitonami hazureta** uncommon; eccentric.

hitónemuri nap; short sleep.

hitónigiri handful; **hitónigiri no kome** handful of rice.

hitóomoi ni without further hesitation; instantly; at once; without further ado.

HITÓRI (single) person; **hitóri de** alone; unaided; **hitorimono** bachelor. **Hitóri de shimáshita.** I did it myself.

hitoriánnai guidebook.

hitori bítori = **hitori hitori** one by one; one after another (person). **Hitori bítori de kangae ga chigau.** Each person has his own opinion.

hitoride ni spontaneously.

hitorigáten one's own judgment; hasty conclusion.

hitorígo only child.

hitorigoto soliloquy; **hitorigoto o iu** to talk to oneself.

hitorigúrashi living alone; bachelorhood.

hitori hitóri (See hitori bítori.) one by one; one at a time. **Hitori hitóri no kangáe o itte kudasái.** Will each of you express your opinion?

hitorimúsuko only son; **hitorimúsume** only daughter.

hitori nokórazu everyone; to a man; to the last man.

hitorítabi (n.) traveling alone.

hitoríténgu self-sufficient person; conceited person.

hitoriyógari self-satisfaction; self-complacency; **hitoriyógari no** self-satisfied.

hitosárai abduction, kidnaping; kidnaper.

HITOSASHÍYUBI forefinger.

hitosáwagase scare; false alarm.

hitoshíi equal to; equivalent to.

hitósoroi set; suit; **hitósoroi no chadóogu** tea set; **fuyugí hitósoroi** winter suit.

hitósuji line; **hitósuji michi** straight road; **hitósuji ni** straight; in a straight line; intently.

HITOTONARI personality; character.

hitotoori in a general way; **hitotoori no** general; common; **hitotoori naránu** unusual, uncommon; **hitotoori hanáshite kikaseru** to give a short account.

HITÓTSU one; same; identical; **hitótsu no** one; single; **hitótsu ni suru** to unite, join, combine; **hitotsu bítotsu** one by one; separately; **hitotsu óki ni** alternately.

hitótsubu grain; **hitótsubu no kome** grain of rice.

hitótsukami handful; fistful.

hitóuchi blow; stroke; **hitóuchi ni** at one blow.

hitozuki attractiveness; amiability; **hitozuki no suru** attractive; pleasing; amiable; charming; **hitozuki no shinai** unprepossessing; unattractive.

hitozute hearsay; **hitozute ni** secondhand; by hearsay. **Hitozute ni kiite shitte imasu.** I know it through hearsay. **Sore wa hitozute ni kiitá no desu.** It came to me secondhand.

HITSUYOO necessity; need; **HITSUYOO NA** necessary, requisite, required; **hitsuyoo no sái wa** in case of need. **Ano hón ga zéhi hitsuyoo desu.** I must have that book.

hittakúru to snatch, take by force.

hiwari daily rate; schedule; program; **hiwari de harau** to pay by the day; **hiwari o kimeru** to fix the dates.

hiyáase o káku to be in a cold sweat.

híyahiya suru to be chilly; to be in great fear.

hiyakashi banter; jeering; ridicule; (mere) inspection; **hiyakásu** to make fun of; just to look at. **Chótto hiyakáshi ni iku daké desu.** I'll just go and look at the things. **Anó hito wa anáta o hiyakáshite irú no da.** He is making fun of you.

hiyarí to suru to feel chilled; to be startled, be alarmed at.

hiyásu to cool; to refrigerate; **hiyáshite oku** to keep (something) cool.

hiyáyaka coldness; cold-heartedness. **hiyáyaka ni** cold-heartedly; coolly; **hiyáyaka na hito** cold-hearted person; **hiyáyaka na kaze** chilly wind.

hiyoke screen (against sun); awning; **hiyoke o suru** to screen from the sun.

HÍYOO cost, expense, expenditure; **hiyoo ga kakáru** to be expensive. **Dore hodo híyoo ga kakarimashita ka?** How much did it cost you?

HIYORI weather; fine weather; condition; state of affairs; **hiyori o míru** to watch which way the wind blows; to sit on the fence. **Hiyori ga kawatta.** The weather has changed.

HIZA knee; lap; **hiza o tsuku** to kneel; **hizagáshira** kneecap; **hizakake** lap robe (rug); **hizamazúku** to kneel; to fall on one's knees.

hizoo treasure, valuable possession; **hizoo no** treasured, valued; dearest; **hizoo suru** to treasure, cherish, keep with great care; **hizóo hin** valued possession.

hizuke date; **tegami ni hízuke o suru** to date a letter.

hobáshira mast.

HÓBO (adv.) almost, nearly; about; (n.) nurse; kindergarten teacher.

hochoo pace, step; **hochoo o soroéru** to keep pace with.

HODO degree; limit; moderation; some; about; the more . . . the more; as; **hodo héte** some time after; after a time; **hodo yóku** moderately; properly; modestly; **kore hodo** this much; so much; **sore hodo** that much. **Joodán ni mo hodo ga áru.** There is a limit even to a joke. **Háyakereba hayai hodo yói desu.** The sooner the better.

hodoai moderation; golden mean.

hodokoshi alms, charity; **hodokósu** to give; to give alms; to practice; to try; **arayúru shudan o hodokósu** to try every means.

HODÓKU to untie, unfasten; to loosen; to disentangle; **hodokéru** to come loose; to get untied; **nímotsu o hodóku** to unpack (luggage); **himo o hodóku** to untie a knot.

HODO NAKU shortly; before long; by and by.

hodoo footpath; sidewalk; pavement; paved road.

hoéru to bark; to howl; to roar. **Ano inú wa yóku hoéru.** That dog is noisy.

hogáraka melodiousness; cheerfulness; **hogáraka na** sonorous; cheerful; bright; **hogáraka na kóe** in a clear voice; **hogáraka ni** cheerfully.

hógo protection; wastepaper; **hógo suru** to protect; **hogósha** protector, guardian. (See also **hógu.**)

hogósu to unfasten, untie; to disentangle; to unravel.

hógu, hógo wastepaper; **hógu ni suru** to annul, invalidate.

hojíru, hojikúru to pick; to dig; to ferret out.

hójo assistance, aid, subsidy; **hójo no** subsidiary, auxiliary; **hójo suru** to aid, subsidize; **hójo o ukéru** to be subsidized; **hojókin** subsidy, grant in aid.

hojuu suru to supplement; to replenish.

HÓKA others; rest; besides; another phase; **hoka ni** besides; **hoka no** another; the other;—**no hoka wa** except; **hoka no tokoro** another place; elsewhere; **hoka no hitótachi** other people.

hokan suru to take custody of; to take in charge; **hokannin** custodian.

hoken insurance; **hoken suru** to insure, guarantee; **hoken o tsukéru** to insure (against accidents); **seimei hóken** life insurance; **kasai hóken** fire insurance.

hoketsu suru to fill a vacancy; to make up for.

hokidasu to spit out; disgorge.

hokki promotion; proposal, suggestion.

hókku hook; nail.

HOKORI dust; pride; **hokori dárake** dusty; **hokori ga tátsu** to be dusty; **hokori o haráu** to dust. **Kodomo o hokori ni site imasu.** He takes pride in his children.

hokoróbi rip; run (ravel); **hokorobíru** to get ripped; to be torn open; to unravel, run.

hokóru to boast of; to be proud.

hokuro mole (body).

hokyuu supply; replenishment; **hokyuu suru** to supply; to make up the lack.

HOMÉRU to praise, commend; to admire. **Mina anáta o hómete imásu.** Everybody speaks well of you.

HÓN book, volume; **hón'ya** bookstore; bookdealer; **hónbako** bookcase; **hóndana** bookshelf.

HON- prefix denoting: original; natural; proper; main; head; chief; true; real; regular; genuine; this; present; our; **hónbun** body (of a letter); text; **hóndo** mainland; **honkan** main building; **hónke** head (main) family; originator; original manufacturer; head house.

-hon counter denoting: things which have length, such as pencils, sticks, and poles; **enpitsu níhon** two pencils.

honba home; best place for.

hónbu home office; headquarters.

honburi downpour. **Áme ga iyóiyo honburi ni narimashita.** The rain was coming down in earnest. There was a sudden downpour.

honé bone; frame (of a sliding door); spirit; **honé to kawá bakari** to be (only) skin and bones; **honé o óru** to take the trouble to; **honé ga oréru** to be troublesome; to require great effort; **hone no áru otoko** man of courage; **honedárake na** bony; full of bones; **honegumi** build; physique; framework.

honeóri exertion; labor; foil; **honeorizón** (*n.*) working for nothing. **Honeorizón no kutabire móoke.** It was so much useless labor.

honeóshimi laziness; **honeóshimi suru** to spare oneself.

honki seriousness, earnestness; **honki no** serious, earnest; **honki de** seriously, in earnest. **Anáta wa honki désu ka?** Are you serious?

honkyoku head (main) office.

honmono real thing; genuine article; original article; **honmono no** real, genuine.

hónnin person in question.

HON NO mere; just; little; few; **hon no sukóshi** just a little. **Máda hon no kodomo desu.** He is a mere child.

honomekásu to allude, hint, suggest.

hónnoo instinct.

hónoo flame.

hónpoo principal salary.

HONSAI (legal) wife.

hónseki permanent residence.

honshiki regular (orthodox) way; **honshiki no** regular; formal; orthodox.

honshoku one's regular occupation; **honshoku no** professional.

honsoo suru to run about (in pursuit of something); to busy oneself about.

hóntate bookstand; bookrest.

HONTOO truth; reality; fact; **hontoo no** true, real, genuine; regular; **hontoo ni** truly, really; **hontoo ni suru** to accept as fact; to take seriously.

hon'yaku translation; **hon'yaku suru** to translate; **hon'yákusha** translator.

HÓO direction; quarter; side; **migi no hóo ni** on the right side. **Kono hóo ga ii desu.**

This is better. **Iku hóo ga ii desu.** It's
better to go.
hoo law; method, way; measures.
HÓO cheek; **hoobone** cheekbone; **hoobeni**
rouge; **hoohige** whiskers.
hoobáru to stuff one's mouth; to eat in one
mouthful.
hoobi prize; reward; **hoobi o morau** to be
around. **Hóoboo anata o
sagashimáshita.** I looked all over for
you.
hoochiku dismissal; banishment. **hoochiku
suru** to expel, dismiss; to banish; to
turn out.
HOOCHOO kitchen knife.
-hóodai suffix denoting: as one pleases; to
one's heart's content; **iitaihóodai o iu**
to talk as one likes; **shitaihóodai o
suru** to act as one pleases.
hoodoo information; report.
hoofu abundance; **hoofu na** rich; abundant.
hóofu ambition, aspiration.
hoofuku zettoo suru to be convulsed with
laughter, be doubled up with laughter.
hoogai na exorbitant; **hoogai no takáne**
exorbitant price.
hoogaku direction; bearings; **hoogaku ga
wakaránaku náru** to lose one's
bearings; to be unable to find one's way.
hoogén dialect; provincialism.
hoohoo no téi de precipitately, hurriedly;
sneakingly; **hoohoo no téi de nigedasu**
to beat a hasty retreat.
hooka arson.
HÓOKI broom; **hóoki no e** broomstick.
hookoku report; information; direction;
course; **hookoku suru** to report; to
inform.
hóokoo public duty; service; apprenticeship;
hookoonin servant; domestic;
hookooguchi domestic position;
hóokoo suru to enter (domestic)
service.
hookyuu salary; **hookyúubi** payday; **hookyuu
seikátsusha** salaried person.
hooman laxity, looseness; **hooman na** lax,
loose; reckless; wild.
hoomen release; acquittal; direction; quarter;
district; **hoomen suru** to release,
liberate, release from custody; to
acquit; **Shizuoka hóomen** the
Shizuoka district.
HOOMON call; visit; **hoomon suru** to call
on, visit; **hoomón kyaku** visitor;
hoomon o ukéru to receive a visit.
hoomotsu treasure; heirloom.
hoomúran home run (in baseball).
hoomushíkku homesick.
hooriagéru to furl up; to throw up.
hooridásu to throw away, cast away, cast out.
hoorikómu to throw in, into.
hooritsukéru to throw at, against.
hooritsu law. **Sore wa hooritsu íhan da.** It's
against the law.
hooroku baking pan; earthen pan used for
parching tea, etc., at high
temperatures.

hooru to throw, fling.
hooshin course, aim; plan; principle; policy;
hooshin o sadaméru to shape one's
course; to decide on a policy.
hóosoo = **shutoo** vaccination.
hoosoo (radio) broadcasting; **hoosóokyoku**
broadcasting station.
hóosu hose.
hootai bandage.
hóra boast; brag; tall (big) talk; **hóra o fuku**
to blow one's own horn; to boast;
horáfuki braggart.
horaana cave, cavern; natural cavity.
horebóre suru to be charmed; to be
fascinated.
horéru (*colloq.*) to fall in love; to be
enamored of.
horidásu to dig out; to unearth, excavate.
horikáesu to dig (turn over the soil).
hóru to dig; to excavate; to burrow; to scoop
out; to sink (a well).
HOSHI star. **Sóra ni hoshi ga kagayaite iru.**
Stars are glittering in the sky. **Kotoshi
wa hoshimáwari ga yói.** I am lucky
this year.
hoshigáru to wish for; to long for; to crave; to
covet.
HOSHÍI to be desirous of having (something);
to want. **Ano hón ga hoshíi.** I want
that book.
hoshímóno laundered clothes.
hoshoo guarantee; **hoshóo nin** guarantor;
certifier.
hosobíki cord, rope.
HOSÓI slender; fine; narrow; thin; **hosome**
narrowness; fineness; **hosome ni**
slightly; narrowly; **hosome ni kíru** to
cut fine; **hosómichi** narrow path; lane;
hosonagai long and slender; lanky.
hósu to dry (in the air); to sun; to empty a
liquid; to draw off; to pump dry;
sakazuki o hósu to drink up.
HOTÉRU to feel hot; to burn. **Kao ga
hotéru.** My face burns.
hotoke Buddha; deceased (person); departed
soul.
HOTÓNDO almost, very nearly, all but;
approximately; hardly, scarcely. **Ano
bíru wa hotóndo kanseishite iru.**
That building is near completion.
hotsuréru to become loose; to be frayed.
hotto suru to sigh with relief; **hotto íki o
tsuku** to heave a deep sigh.
hoyoo preservation of health; recreation;
relaxation; **hoyoo suru** to take care of
oneself; to recuperate; to relax.
HYAKÚ (*n.*) hundred; **hyakú mo
shoochishite iru** to know too well; to
be well aware of.
hyakushóo peasant, farmer, rustic,
countryman.
hyoo table, chart; **jikanhyoo** timetable.
hyooban reputation; fame; popularity; report;
rumor; **hyooban no** famed; notorious;
hyooban no yói popular; of good
reputation; **hyooban no warúi**

unpopular; **hyooban ni náru** to be
much talked about.

hyoomén (*n.*) surface; outside; **hyoomén no**
(*adj.*) outside, external.

hyoosatsu doorplate; name plate.

HYOOSHI time; tact; chance; rhythm; cover;
binding; **kami hyóoshi** paper cover,
paper binding; **hyooshi o tóru** to beat
time.

hyórohyoro staggeringly; slimly; **hyórohyoro
shita** staggering, reeling; slim; lanky.

HYOTTO by chance, by accident; **hyotto
shitára** possibly, maybe.

hyúuhyuu whistling; whizzing. **Kaze ga
hyúuhyuu fuku.** The wind whistles.

I

I stomach.

iawaséru to happen to be present.

ibáru to be haughty; to brag; to give oneself
airs.

ibikí snoring; **ibikí o káku** to snore.

ibúru to smolder, smoke. **Kono sumí wa
ibúru.** This charcoal smokes.

ibúsu to smoke; to fumigate.

ICHI one; **tsuitachí** first day of the month;
ichijitsu one day; **ICHÍBAN** first;
number one; game, round; **ichiban áto
de** last of all; at the very end; **ichiban
saki no** first, foremost; **ichiban osoi**
slowest.

íchi position; situation; location.

ÍCHIBA market place, market; **aomono
íchiba** vegetable market; **uo íchiba**
fish market.

ichíbu part, portion; some part; **ichibu shíjuu**
the whole, all the details; from
beginning to end; **ichidáiji** serious
affair.

ICHIDO once, one time.

ICHIDÓO all; all (the persons) present;
kánai ichidóo all the members of the
family.

ICHIGATSÚ January.

ICHIÍCHI in every single case; in detail.
Ichíichi mónku o iwanáide kudasái.
Please don't complain all the time.

ichíji one o'clock; for the present; for a while;
ichijiteki no temporary.

ICHIJITSU day; particular day (of the past);
first day of the month.

ichímai sheet; leaf of a tree.

ICHIMEN entire area, whole surface; one
side; other hand; first page (of a
newspaper); **ichimenkíji** front-page
news; **—no ichimen ni wa . . . on the
other hand . . . Ichimen ni haná ga
saite iru.** Everything is in bloom.

ichimoku glance, look; **ichimoku ryoozen** to
be clear at a glance; **ichimókusan ni** at
full speed.

ICHÍNEN one year; **ichinen juu** all year
round.

ICHINICHI one day; whole day through; all
day; **ichinichi óki ni** every other day.

ICHIOO once; for the time being; in the first
place; first; in outline. **Ichioo soo shite
okimashóo.** We will leave it that way,
at least for the time being.

ICHIRYÓOJITSU day or two; **ichiryoojitsu
chuu ni** in a day or two.

ichiryuu first class; **ichiryuu no** first rate.

ichíyaku at a single bound.

iden heredity.

ído well (for water); **idobata** side of a well.
idobata káigi gossiping.

IDOKORO address; residence; whereabouts.

IÉ house; dwelling; cottage; home, family; **ié
o tatéru** to build a house; **ié ni káeru**
to go home.

iegara birth, lineage.

igai na unexpected; unlooked for; **igai ni**
unexpectedly.

igen dignity; prestige; **igen áru fuusai**
dignified appearance.

IGIRISU = Eikoku England; **Igirisu no**
English.

igokochi comfortableness; **igokochi ga yói**
snug; comfortable; **igokochi ga warúi**
uncomfortable.

ihan violation; infringement; **ihan suru** to act
against; to infringe upon.

IÍ = yói good; pretty; likable; **ií hito** nice
person. **Ií kimi da.** It serves you right.

iiarasóu to dispute, quarrel.

iiatéru to guess correctly.

IIE no. **Iie, moo takusán desu.** No, thank
you. (I've had enough.)

iifurásu to spread a story, circulate a tale.

iiháru to insist on; to persist in; to assert
positively.

iihirakí vindication.

iikáeru to express in another word; **iikáereba**
that is to say.

iikanéru to hesitate to say; to be unable to
speak out.

iikata way of speaking; expression.

iikíru to speak positively; to assert.

iimorásu to neglect to tell; to forget to tell.

íin committee; committee member.

iinazuke fiancé; fiancée; betrothal,
engagement.

iine de at the price asked.

iinuke excuse; evasive answer.

iisokonai slip of the tongue; misstatement.

iisugi exaggeration; **iisugíru** to say too much;
to exaggerate.

iitsuke order, command; instruction; **iitsukéru**
to order, command; to bid.

iitsutae tradition; legend; hearsay.

IIWAKE apology; excuse; pretext; **iiwake o
suru** to apologize; **iiwake ga tatánai**
to be inexcusable.

iiwatásu to tell; to pass judgment; to sentence.

ijí temper; disposition; **ijí o haru** to be
obstinate, be stubborn; **soko iji ga áru**
strong-willed.

ijikéru to cower.

ijikitaní greedy.

ijimeru to tease; to treat badly; to torment.

ijippáru to persist in; to be obstinate.

ijirashíi pitiable; pathetic; touching.

ijíru to finger; to play with.

IJIWÁRU ill-natured person; **ijiwáru na** nasty, mean; **ijiwarúi** ill-natured, ill-tempered; **ijiwáruku** spitefully.

ÍJOO more than; above-mentioned; above; upward of, beyond; since, now that; **yottsu íjoo** more than four.

IJOO something unusual; abnormal symptoms; deformity; **ijoo na** unusual, abnormal. **Betsu ni íjoo wa arimasén.** That is nothing unusual.

ijuu suru to move to; to migrate.

IKA (*n.*) following; less than, under. **Juunisai íka wa táda desu.** There is no charge for children under twelve. **Sore wa gosen en ika desu.** It costs less than 5000 yen.

IKÁGA how; what (*pol.*). **Kyóo wa okagen wa ikága desu ka?** How do you feel today? **Goíken wa ikaga desu ka?** What is your opinion?

ikagawashíi questionable; doubtful.

IKÁHODO how much; how many.

ikameshíi solemn, grave; stern; authoritative.

IKÁNIMO very; truly; indeed.

ikásu to make good use of; to spare one's life; to keep alive; **kane o ikáshite tsukau** to make good use of money.

iké pond.

ikedoru to capture.

íken opinion; view; **iken o nobéru** to give an opinion; **íken suru** to admonish; to give advice.

IKENAI be of no use; will not do. **Kore wa ikenai.** This will not do. **Ame ga fúru to ikenái kara.** Lest it rain. **Ikanákereba ikenai.** I must go. [It won't do if I don't go.]

ikéru to bury (in the ground); to bank (a fire); to arrange flowers.

íki breath; spirit; **íki ga kiréru** to be out of breath; **íki o tsuku** to breathe; to heave a sigh of relief; **íki yoo yóo to** triumphantly.

iki smartness, stylishness; **iki na** smart, stylish, fashionable.

ikidóoru to be angry, be enraged; to be indignant.

ikigomi eagerness; ardor, zeal; **ikigómu** to set one's heart on.

ikigurushíi suffocating, stifling, choking.

iki íki shita lively; active; spirited; vivid; fresh; **iki íki shita sakana** fresh-looking fish.

ikímono living thing; creature; animal.

IKINARI suddenly; all at once.

ikinokóru to survive; to outlive.

ikíoi power, force, energy; **ikiói no nái** spiritless, lifeless; **ikiói no yói** lively; vigorous; **ikiói yoku** vigorously.

IKÍRU to live.

ikiutsushi exact copy; **ikiutsushi no** lifelike, true to life.

íkka whole family.

IKKAI first floor; one floor, one story; **ikkai date no uchi** one-story house. **Kutsú wa ikkai de utte imásu.** Shoes are sold on the first floor.

ikkén affair; matter.

ikkoku moment; second; **ikkoku mo háyaku** as soon as possible.

ikkoo party (of tourists); suite.

ikoo intention; ikoo o sagúru to sound; to speak one's mind.

IKU = YUKU to go; **machí e iku** to go to town. **Háyaku itte kudasai.** Please go quickly.

ÍKU- prefix denoting: how many; **ÍKUDO** how often; how many times; **íkudo to náku** countless times; **íkue** manyfold; **íkue ní mo** many times over; repeatedly; earnestly; on bended knee; **ikunichi** how many days; **IKURA** how many; how much; **ikura ka** somewhat; to some extent; **ikura demo** as many (much) as one pleases; any amount; **ÍKUTSU** how many; how old. **Íkura desu ka?** How much? **Kyóo wa ikura ka kíbun ga yói.** I feel a little better today. **Nihongo ga ikura ka hanasemásu.** I can speak Japanese to some extent. **Íkutsu desu ka?** How old are you? **Íkutsu arimásu ka?** How many are there?

IKUBUN partly; somewhat. **Anata mo ikubun ka sekinin ga aru.** You, too, are responsible for it.

íku dooon ni unanimously.

íkuji spirit; backbone; **íkuji no nái** spiritless; weak.

ÍMA now; **ima mótte** as yet. **Íma ni kimásu.** He will soon come.

ímada yet (used only with a negative verb). **Imada ní kónai.** It hasn't come yet.

IMADOKI now; nowadays; these days.

IMAGORO about this time. **Imagoro náni o shite irú daroo.** What would he be doing at this time?

imaimashíi provoking; mortifying; disgusting.

ímani very soon; before long; by and by. **Ímani kuru deshoo.** He will probably come very soon.

imasara now; at this time (in a negative sense). **Imasara sonna kotó mo iemasén.** How can you say such a thing now!

imashime instruction; warning, admonition, rebuke, reprimand; **imashiméru** to instruct; to caution, admonish; to warn against; to reprimand, rebuke.

imásu See **iru.**

imawashíi offensive; abominable.

ÍMI meaning, sense, significance; **imi aríge na** significant, meaningful; **ími shinchoo** profound meaning. **Sore wa dóo iu ími desu ka?** What do you mean by that?

IMOOTO younger sister.

-in suffix denoting: one who; member of; **jimúin** clerk; **kaisháin** businessman.

inagara without any effort; without stirring.

ÍNAI within; less than; not exceeding. **Gofun**

ínai ni ome ni kakarimásu. I will see you within five minutes.

inaka countryside, country; **inaka no** rural, rustic. **Inaka ni súnde imasu.** I live in the country.

inbai prostitution; **inbáifu** prostitute.

ínchi inch.

inchiki na fraudulent; sham; feigned.

Índo India; **Indoyoo** Indian Ocean; **Indójin** Indian; Hindu.

íne rice plant.

inemúri nap; **inemúri suru** to nap; to doze.

infure inflation.

infuruénza influenza.

ínga cause and effect; misfortune; **ínga na** unlucky; **ínga to akiraméru** to resign oneself to fate.

ingin politeness, courtesy; **ingin na** polite, courteous.

ingoo na stubborn; merciless.

inki gloominess; melancholy; **inki na** cheerless, gloomy, dismal.

ÍNKU, INKI ink.

innen affinity; relation; fate; objection.

ÍNOCHI life; **inochi bíroi o suru** to have a narrow escape.

inokóru to remain behind; stay behind.

inóru to pray; **seikoo o inóru** to wish someone every success.

insatsu (*n.*) printing; **insatsubutsu** printed matter; **insatsujo** printing house; press.

inseki relative by marriage.

inshoo impression; **inshoo o ataéru** to impress; to make an impression.

insotsu suru to lead, conduct, command.

intai retirement; **intai suru** to retire; to resign.

interi intelligentsia; intellectuals.

INÚ dog; **inugoya** kennel.

in'utsu gloom, gloominess; **in'utsu na** gloomy.

inwai obscenity; indecency; **inwai na** obscene, lewd, indecent.

inzei royalty (on a literary work).

ioo sulphur.

íppa religious sect; school; party; faction.

ÍPPAI cupful, bowlful; full of. **Mizu o íppai kudasái.** May I have a glass of water?

ippaku night's lodging; **ippaku suru** to put up for the night.

IPPAN generality; outline; **ippan no** general; common; **ippan ni** generally.

IPPEN once.

ippen suru to change completely, to undergo a complete change.

ippon chóoshi monotone; **ippon chóoshi no** monotonous; simple-minded.

ippondachi independence; **ippondachi de** independently.

ippóo one side; one party; **ippóo ni oité wa** on the one hand.

ippuu kawatta curious; funny; queer.

iradátsu to be irritated; to be excited.

irai dependence; reliance; request; **irai suru** to rely on; to request; **irai ni oozúru** to comply with a request.

ÍRAI since; since then.

íra ira suru to be irritated; to be fretful.

IRASSHÁRU to come, go, be at (*pol.*). **Yamada-san wa Tookyoo ni irasshaimásu.** Mr. Yamada is in Tokyo. **Tanaka-san wa Kyooto e irasshaimáshita.** Mr. Tanaka went to Kyoto.

ireba artificial tooth.

irechigaéru to misplace, put in the wrong place.

irechigáu to come just as someone else leaves; to leave just as someone else comes in. **Yamada-san wa Tanaka-san to irechigai ni déte itta.** Mr. Yamada had just gone out when Mr. Tanaka came in.

irekáeru to replace; to change; to make (tea, coffee) afresh.

iremono receptacle; vessel; case.

IRERU to put in; to let in; to hold; to comply with; to listen to; **hito no sétsu o ireru** to take advice; **ocha o ireru** to make tea.

irezumi tattoo.

iri attendance, audience; contents; **ooiri** full house.

IRIAI twilight; sunset.

iribitáru to be a constant guest; to stay all the time.

irichigáu to pass each other; to arrive just as someone else leaves.

irie inlet; creek.

IRIGUCHI entrance; door.

irikawari tachikawari in rapid succession; one after another; **irikawáru** to change places; **séki o irikawáru** to change seats with someone else.

irikómu to enter; to force an entrance.

irikúmu to be complicated.

irimidaréru to be mixed up; to be in confusion.

iritsukéru to parch; to sizzle.

IRÓ color, tint, hue; lover (*colloq.*); **iro age** (*n.*) redying; restoring a color; **iro ótoko** lover; **iro onna** mistress; **iroke** coloring; shade; tone; sexual passion; tender passion; **irozuri** color print; **iroke no áru** seductive; amorous; **iroke no nái** unromantic; innocent; **kaoiro** complexion (facial); **iro age suru** to redye; **iró o nasu** to turn red with anger; **irodóru** to color; to paint.

iróha 47-syllable poem containing all of the 47 syllables in the traditional table of Japanese syllabaries. **Iróha mo shiranai.** He doesn't know even the simplest things (not even the A B C's).

IROIRO NA various; many; diverse; (all) kinds of. **Iroiro shitsumon sareta.** I was asked several questions.

iroméku to be alive; to be stirred; to show signs of uneasiness; to become animated.

irori hearth; fireplace.

irótsuya gloss; luster; complexion; **irótsuya no yói** ruddy; healthy.

irozúku to color; to be tinged; to turn red (as foliage).

IRU to require, want, need. **Watakushi wa kore ga irimásu.** I need this. **Soko e háiru ní wa okane ga irimásu.** You have to pay [money] to enter. **Sore wa iranai deshóo.** It would not be necessary.

IRU = IMÁSU to be at, exist; to be present; to live; to stay. Following a *-te* form verb, it makes a progressive or stative form (describing a state resulting from an action that has taken place). **Sonó hito wa heyá ni imásu.** He is in the room. **Áme ga fútte imásu.** It is raining. **Yamada-san wa kité imásu.** Yamada is here (as a result of having come). **Tookyoo ni imásu.** He is in Tokyo. **Kyóoto ni mikka imáshita.** I was in Kyoto for three days. **Nihongo o benkyoo shite imásu.** I'm studying Japanese. **Tegami ga kité imásu.** There is [has come and is here] a letter for you.

íru to toast; to parch; to shoot; to hit; to cast (a statue in bronze); to mint money; **= hairu** to go in; to get in; to go down.

írui clothes, garments.

íryoo medical treatment.

iryúuhin lost article; (thing) left behind.

isagiyói clean; pure; upright; brave; manly.

ísai particulars, details.

isakai quarrel.

isamashíi courageous, brave.

isamé admonition; advice, counsel.

isámu to be encouraged; to be in high spirits; to take heart.

isan legacy, inheritance; **isan soozokunin** heir, heiress.

isásaka little; bit; slightly; rather. **Isásaka odorokimáshita.** I was a bit surprised.

iseebi lobster.

isei power; influence; other (opposite) sex. **Ano hito wa isei no aida ni koosai ga hiroi desu.** He has a large acquaintance among the opposite sex.

iséisha statesman.

iseki ruins, remains; relics.

isetsu different view(s); conflicting opinion.

ISHA doctor; physician; M.D. **isha ni kakáru** to go to a doctor; **isba ni míte morau** to consult a doctor. **Isha ni kakáru to nakanaka kane ga irimasu.** Medical expenses are very high these days.

ísha comfort, consolation; **ísha suru** to console.

íshi stone; rock; will; intention; one's dying wishes; **ishi dóoroo** stone lantern (in front of a shrine); **íshi no tsuyói hito** man of strong will; **ishidan** stone steps; **ishigaki** stone wall; **ishiya** stonecutter; **íshi ga sotsuu suru** to come to an understanding.

íshiki consciousness; **ishikiteki ni** consciously; **íshiki suru** to be conscious of.

íshin restoration; renovation; **íshin denshin** tacit understanding; telepathy.

ishiwata asbestos.

ishízue foundation; basis; groundwork.

ísho will, testament.

íshoku food and clothing; means of support; **ishokújuu** food, clothes, and shelter.

ishoku commission; request; charge.

ishoo design; idea.

íshoo clothes, dress, garments.

ishugáeshi revenge, retaliation.

isobe beach, shore.

isogaséru to hurry up, urge on.

ISOGASHÍI busy, occupied, engaged. **Shikén de taihen isogashíi desu.** I am very busy with my exams.

ISOGI hurry, haste; **isogi no** hasty; urgent, pressing; **ISÓGU** to hurry, hasten; to be in a hurry. **Isógu hitsuyoo wa arimasén.** There is no rush.

ísoiso to cheerfully; lightheartedly.

isooróo parasite; hanger-on;

íssai all; altogether, every; wholly.

issakúban evening before last.

issakújitsu day before yesterday.

issakunen year before last.

issaku sakújitsu three days ago.

issaku sakunen three years ago.

issakúya night before last.

issei ni simultaneously; all at once.

íssha sénri rush; **íssha sénri ni** in a rush; in a hurry; at full speed.

isshiki complete set (of).

isshinfuran whole mind; single heart; **isshinfuran ni** wholeheartedly; intently; with undivided attention.

ISSHO together; at the same time; all at once; **ISSHO NI** together with; simultaneously. **Issho ni ikimashóo.** Let's go together.

isshoo laugh; smile; lifetime; all through one's life; **isshoo shite** with a laugh; with a smile; **isshoo ni fúsu** to dismiss with a laugh; to laugh one's troubles away; **isshoo no nozomi** lifelong desire.

ISSHOOKÉNMEI as hard as one can; with all one's might (efforts); with one's whole heart. **Isshookénmei benkyoo shite imásu.** He is studying hard.

ísshu kind, type, variety.

isshuu one round, lap; **isshuu suru** to go round; to make a tour; **sékai isshuu ryókoo** round-the-world trip.

ISSHÚUKAN one week.

isso rather; sooner; preferably.

issoku pair (of shoes or other footgear).

ISSÓO much more; all the more.

ISSÚN one *sun* (Japanese unit of length, one tenth of a *shaku*); **issun saki mo miénai** pitch dark.

issúru to miss; to lose; **kóoki o issúru** to miss a good opportunity.

ISU chair; sofa; couch; **isu ni kakéru** to take a seat.

isuwáru to remain in the same position (in office); to remain in power.

íta board; plank; plate; sheet; **itábei** wooden wall; board fence.

itabásami fix; predicament; **itabásami ni náru** to be in a fix.

itachi weasel.

itadaku to receive; to be presented with; to be given; to accept with gratitude (*pol.*). **Juubun itadakimáshita.** I've had enough, thank you.

itade hard blow; severe wound.

itagane sheet metal.

itagárasu plate glass.

ITÁI painful; sore. **Atamá ga itái desu.** I have a headache. **Onaka ga itái desu.** I have a stomach-ache.

itaitashíi pathetic, sad, pitiful.

itamashíi miserable; touching, sad, pathetic.

itaméru to hurt, injure; to worry; **kokoró o itaméru** to be worried about (something).

itami pain, ache; sore, bruise; **itámu** to ache, feel a pain; to mourn (for the dead).

itami íru to be greatly obliged; to feel grateful. **Dóomo itamiirimasu.** I'm much obliged to you.

ITÁRI = ITARIYA Italy.

itáru to arrive, reach; to result in; to come to; **itáru tokoro** everywhere; throughout; **háru kara áki ni itáru máde** from spring to autumn.

ítasa pain.

itashikata nái it can't be helped; **itashikata náku** necessarily; of necessity.

ITÁSU to do, make (*pol.*). **Soo itashimashóo.** Let's do so. **Dóo itashimáshite.** Don't mention it.

itátte exceedingly, extremely, very.

itawáru to pity, sympathize with, console.

itazura mischief; prank; **itazura hánbun** for fun; **itazura na** naughty; mischievous; **itazura ni** needlessly; to no purpose.

itchaku first (in a race); one suit of clothes.

itchi agreement; harmony; **itchi suru** to agree with; harmonize.

itchoo once; one day (*literary usage*); **itchoo isseki ni** in a single day; in a short space of time.

itchókusen straight line; **itchókusen ni** in a straight line.

iten transfer, removal; **iten suru** to transfer; to move. **Inakara machí e iten shimashita.** We moved from the country to the city.

ÍTO thread; yarn; twine; string; **momen ito** cotton thread; **kinu ito** silk thread.

itóguchi clue; beginning; **itóguchi o hiráku** to make a start.

itogúruma spinning wheel.

ITÓKO cousin.

itomá leisure; time to spare; leave of absence; **yasúmu itomá mo nái** to have no time to rest.

itomaki spool, bobbin, reel.

itonámu to carry on; to conduct (business); to run, operate; **seikei o itonámu** to earn a living.

itóosu to shoot through; to pierce.

ÍTSU when; at what time; how soon; **ítsu demo** at any time; at a moment's notice; **ítsu kara** how long; since when; **ítsu made** how long; till when; **ítsu ka** some day; **ítsu mo** always; **ítsu ni** solely, entirely.

itsukushími love; affection; compassion (*literary usage*); **itsukushímu** to love; to treat with tenderness.

ITSÚTSU five.

itsuwa anecdote.

itsuwari lie; **itsuwari no** false, untrue; **itsuwáru** to lie, tell a lie.

ittai zentai on earth; in the world. **Ittai zéntai dáre daroo.** I wonder who in the world it can be.

ittán part; outline; one end.

ittan once, if. **Ittan kankyuu áreba . . .** Should an emergency arise . . .

itte hánbai sole agency; monopoly; **itte hanbainin** sole agent; sole distributor.

ittei no fixed, immovable, set; definite; regular.

ittén point; dot; spot.

ittenbari persistency; **ittenbari de** sticking to; solely by.

ITTÓO first class; **ittóo ni noru** to travel first class; **ittoo gíppu, ittoo kippu** first class ticket; **nitóo sha** second-class car. **Ittoo íi mono désu.** It is the best.

ittsuu copy; letter.

IU = YUU to say, speak, tell, relate, mention; to fasten; to tie; to bind; **ookíku iu** to exaggerate; **iu máde mo náku** of course, naturally. **Iu máde mo nái.** It goes without saying.

iwa rock; **iwa no óoi** rocky.

íwaba in a word; so-to-speak.

iwai celebration; feast; festival.

iwakú reason; **iwakú ga átte** for certain reasons; **iwakú o tsukéru** to find fault with.

iware reason, cause; origin; **iware mo naku** without any cause; **iware no nái** unreasonable; unwarranted.

iwashi sardine.

iwáu to congratulate; to celebrate.

IWAYÚRU so-called; what you call. **Káre wa iwayúru jiyuu shugísha desu.** He is a so-called liberal.

IYÁ dislike, aversion; distaste; **iyá na** disagreeable; unpleasant; distasteful; disgusting; offensive; **iyagáru** to dislike; to hate; **iyami** offensiveness; bad taste; cutting remark; sarcasm; **iyami no áru** offensive, disagreeable; **iyashímu** to despise; to look down on; to scorn; **iyá na kao o suru** to frown. **Iyá na yátsu da.** What a disgusting fellow.

ÍYA = IIE no.

iyahóon earphone.

iya iya reluctantly; **iya iya nágara** unwillingly; with reluctance.

íyaku medicine; physic.

iyashíí low; humble; vulgar.
iyáshikumo at all; in the least.
iyóiyo still more; all the more; certainly; positively; no doubt.
íza come now; now then; **íza to náreba** at the last moment; when the time comes; at a pinch. **Íza saraba.** Farewell.
izakaya tavern, saloon, bar.
ízen ago; before; prior to; formerly. **Tooka ízen ni kite kudasai.** Please come before the tenth.
izen as before; as it was.
izon objection; **izon nái** to have no objection; **izon ga áru** to have an objection.
izumi spring; fountain.
IZURE which; someday; sometime; sooner or later; **izure mo** any; all; either; every; both; **izure ni shité mo** in either case; **izure sono uchi ni** one of these days.

J

JA, JÁA well; then; in that case. **Ja, sayonara.** Well, so long.
jaanarisuto journalist.
JAGAIMO potato.
jaguchi faucet, tap; spout.
jáken meanness, unkindness; **jáken na** cruel, unkind.
jáketsu sweater.
jakkan some; little; number of.
-jáku suffix denoting: little less than, little short of. **Yokohama máde wa nijuu máirujaku desu.** It is a little less than twenty miles to Yokohama.
JAMA obstruction, obstacle, hindrance; **jama suru** to obstruct, hinder; **jama ni náru** to stand (be) in the way; **jama o nozoku** to remove an obstacle. **Ojama shimáshita.** Excuse me for disturbing you. **Ojama dé wa arimasén ka.** I hope I'm not disturbing you.
jámu jam, jelly.
janen vicious mind; evil thought.
ján jan jingle jingle; dingdong; profusely; a lot (slang).
janken Japanese equivalent of tossup. **Janken de kimemashoo.** Let's toss for it.
jaratsuku to flirt with.
jaréru to be playful.
jari gravel; pebbles.
jasui distrust; groundless suspicion; **jasui suru** to distrust; suspect without reason; **jasui bukái** suspicious, distrustful.
jázu jazz.
ji piles, hemorrhoids.
JI character, letter, ideograph; ground, earth, soil; texture, weave; **jí o káku** to write; **jí o oboéru** to learn how to read and write (characters); **kanji** Chinese characters (used in Japanese writing system); **jí no mono** local people.
ji- prefix denoting: next; second; vice-; **jibin** the next mail.

-JI suffix denoting: o'clock; hour; time; **ichíji** one o'clock. **Ichíji wa soo omoimashita.** Once I thought that way but now I have a different opinion.
jiban base, foundation.
jibara o kíru to pay out of one's own pocket.
JIBIKÍ dictionary; lexicon; **jibikí o hiku** to look something up in the dictionary; to use a dictionary.
jiboojíki desperation; despair; **jiboojíki ni náru** to become desperate.
JIBUN oneself; **jibun no** my own, your own, mine; personal; **jibun hitóri de** by oneself; **jibun to shite wa** for my part.
jíbyoo chronic disease.
jíchi self-government.
jichoo self-respect; self-love; caution; **jichóoshin** self-respect. **Jichoo shite kudasai.** Take good care of yourself.
jidai time, period, epoch, era; **jidai sákugo** anachronism; **jidaimono** old-fashioned article (furniture, etc.); historical drama; **jidaiókure** one who is old-fashioned; **jidaiókure no** old-fashioned, antiquated.
jídan private settlement; compromise.
jidaraku sloppiness, untidiness; **jidaraku na** sloppy, untidy.
jiden autobiography.
jídoo child; boys and girls; **jídoo no** juvenile.
jidoo automatic action; **jidoo no** automatic; **JIDOO DÉNWA** public telephone; **jidoo hanbáiki** slot machine; **jidoo jiténsha** motorcycle.
JIDÓOSHA automobile, car; **jidóosha ni noru** to ride in a car.
jiei self-defense.
jifúshin pride; self-confidence.
jigane metal, ore; bullion; true character.
jigoku hell.
jígyoo enterprise, undertaking; achievement; deed; work; **jigyóokai** the business (industrial) world.
jihaku confession; **jihaku suru** to confess.
jihatsuteki voluntary; spontaneous; **jihatsuteki ni** voluntarily.
jíhen emergency; disaster; incident.
jihi mercy; benevolence; pity; (one's own) expense; **jihi bukái** benevolent; charitable; **jihi de** at one's own expense.
jihitsu handwriting; autograph.
jihoo time signal; current news.
jíi intention to resign.
jíin Buddhist temple.
jíji current events.
jíjíi (colloq.) grandfather; old man (derogatory).
jíjitsu time; date; fact; truth; **jijitsujóo** practically, virtually; in reality, actually.
jijoo circumstances; reasons; state of affairs; **koo iu jijoo dá kara** under these circumstances.
jíka current price.

jikaku self-consciousness; **jikaku suru** to be conscious, aware of; to realize.

JIKAN time; hour; **jikan ni ma ni áu** to be on time; **jikan ni ma ni awánai** to be late. **Máda daibu jikan ga áru.** There is still plenty of time.

jikanhyoo = jikokuhyoo timetable; schedule.

jíkani personally; at firsthand; directly.

jikatsu suru to support oneself.

jken affair; matter; scandal.

jiketsu self-determination; resignation; suicide.

JÍKI time; period; season.

jiki- prefix denoting: direct; **jikiyúnyuu** direct importation.

JIKI NI immediately; at once; presently; **jiki sóba ni** very near by; close by.

jikken experiment; test.

jikkoo practice; action; execution; **jikkoo suru** to carry out; to put into practice; **jikkoo shigatái** impractical; difficult to put into practice.

jíko self; ego; obstacle; accident; incident; **jiko chúushin no** egocentric; **kootsuu jíko** traffic accident.

jíkoku time; hour; **jikokuhyoo** timetable; schedule.

JIKOO season; weather; current fashion; latest style, vogue; **jikoo házure no** unseasonable.

jíku phraseology; expressions; wording.

jikú axis; axle; pivot; shaft; stem; stalk.

jíkyoku situation, state of affairs; political crisis.

jikyuu self-support; independence.

jiman pride, boast; **jiman suru** to boast; to be conceited.

jíme jime shita damp; wet; moist; humid.

jímen ground; surface of the earth; plot of land; **jímen o kau** to buy a lot of land.

jimí na simple; modest; unpretentious; **jimí na hito** unpretentious person; quiet person.

jímu business; duties; **jimúin** clerk; office worker; **jimúsho** office; **jimúchoo** chief clerk; head official; purser (of a ship).

-JIN suffix denoting: people; men; **Nihonjín** Japanese; **Amerikájin** American.

jínan second son.

jinboo popularity; **jinboo áru hito** idol (of the people).

jínbutsu person; man of character; portrait.

jinchóoge sweet-smelling daphne (common garden plant in Japan).

jindai na extraordinary; enormous, huge, great. **Songai wa jindai na monó deshita.** The damage was very great.

jindoo humanity; morality; sidewalk, pavement; **jindoo o arúku** to walk on the pavement.

jingúu Shinto shrine.

jínja Shinto shrine (a national monument).

jínji fusei unconsciousness; **jínji fusei ni náru** to faint; **jínji fusei no** unconscious.

jinjoo commonness; **jinjoo no** common, ordinary; **jinjoo ni** commonly.

jinkaku personality, character.

jinken artificial silk; rayon.

jinken juurin infringement of personal rights.

jinkoo population; artificiality; **jinkoo chuumitsu na** thickly populated; **jinkoo no** artificial; **jinkoo kókyuu** artificial respiration.

jinmei human life; **jinméibo** list of names of persons; directory; **jinmeijísho** biographical dictionary.

jinmín people; public.

jinmon inquiry; examination.

jinrin moral law; human relations.

jínrui mankind, man.

jinryoku human power, human strength; effort, endeavor; help; **jinryoku suru** to make an effort; to work on someone's behalf.

jínsei human existence; life.

jinshu (human) race; **jinshuteki henken** racial prejudice.

jinsoku swiftness, rapidity; **jinsoku na** swift, rapid, quick.

jíntai human body.

jinushi landlord.

jinzoo (*n.*) kidney; (*adj.*) aritificial, synthetic; **jinzoo gómu** synthetic rubber.

jíppa hitókarage ni in a wholesale way; sweepingly.

jippi actual expenses; cost of production; **jippi de** at cost.

jippu one's natural father.

jirásu to provoke, irritate; to tease.

jirei government order; written order; manner of speaking.

jirénma dilemma.

jiréru to be irritated; to fret and fume; to become impatient.

jirettái irritating, provoking; irritated.

JÍRIJIRI slowly; gradually, little by little. **Jirijiri tsume yosemashita.** He edged up to me.

jiriki to be by oneself.

jiritsu independence; self-supprt; **jiritsu suru** to stand on one's own feet.

jíro jiro míru to stare at; **jirorí to** with a glance; **jirorí to míru** to glance at.

jiron personal opinion; pet theory.

jíryoku magnetism.

jisan (*n.*) bringing; carrying; **jisan suru** to bring; to carry along.

jisatsu suicide (the act); **jisatsú sha** suicide (person).

jisei times; mood of the times; **jisei ni okureru** to fall behind the times.

jisei self-control; **jisei suru** to control oneself.

jísetsu season; times; age; **jisetsu házure no** out of season; **jísetsu toorai** the time has come.

jíshaku magnet; compass.

JISHIN earthquake. **Nihón wa jishin ga óoi.** Earthquakes occur frequently in Japan.

JÍSHO land, plot of ground, estate; dictionary.

jishoku resignation.

jison self-respect; pride; **jisón shin o kizutsukéru** to hurt one's pride.

jishoo self-styled, would-be; **jishoo shíjin.** A would-be poet.

jissai truth; reality; **jissai wa** in reality; in fact; **jissai no** actual; practical.

jisshi enforcement; one's natural child; **jisshi suru** to put into effect; to enforce.

jisshín hoo decimal system.

jisshitsu substance, essence.

jisúberi landslide.

jisui suru to cook one's meals.

jisúru to decline; to refuse; to resign.

jítai situation; state of affairs.

jitaku house, residence; **jitaku e káeru** to go home.

jiten = **jíshoo** dictionary.

jiténsha bicycle; **jiténsha ni noru** to ride a bicycle.

JITSÚ truth; reality; **JITSÚ NI** really; truly; very, exceedingly; in fact; surely; exceedingly; **jitsú no** true; real; **jitsú wa** in reality; to tell the truth.

jítsubo one's natural mother.

jitsubutsu real thing; actual object; **jitsubutsú dai no** life-size.

jitsugen realization; **jitsugen suru** to realize; to materialize.

jitsugyoo business, industry; **jitsugyoo no** commercial, industrial; **jitsugyóokai** business world.

jitsujoo actual condition; true state of affairs. **Jitsujoo wa kóo desu.** The fact is this.

jitsuyoo utility; practical use; **jitsuyoo ni tekisúru** to be of practical use; **jitsuyoo muki no** serviceable; practical; **jitsuyóohin** necessity; article having practical use.

jitsúzuki adjoining land.

jitto fixedly; firmly; steadily; **jitto mitsuméru** to stare at, look fixedly at; **jittó shite iru** to keep still.

jiyoo nourishment; **jiyóo butsu** nourishing food; **jiyoo áru** nourishing, nutritious.

jiyúu liberty, freedom; **jiyuu bóoeki** free trade; **jiyuu kyóosoo** open (free) competition; **jiyúu na** free; **jiyúu ni suru** to do as one pleases. **Gojiyuu ni.** Help yourself.

jizen jígyoo philanthropic work; **jizen ka** philanthropist.

jobun preface, foreword, introduction.

jochoo promotion; advancement; **jochoo suru** to promote, foster, encourage.

jochuu maid, housemaid.

jodóoshi auxiliary verb; inflected particle, i.e. -(r)areru (passive) and -(s)aseru (causative).

jogai exception; **jogai suru** to make an exception of; to exclude; to exempt from.

jogákkoo girls' school; **jogákusei** girl student.

jogon advice, counsel; suggeston, hint; **jogon suru** to give advice; to suggest.

joi female doctor.

jójo ni slowly; gradually.

jojóoshi lyrical poem, ballad.

jojutsu description; **jojutsu no** descriptive; **jojutsu suru** to describe; to narrate; **jojutsúbun** description.

jokoo slow pace; **jokoo suru** to go slowly. **Jokoo.** Go slow. Drive slowly.

jokyuu waitress.

joo feeling, emotion, sentiment; affection, love; sympathy; article, item; line; stripe; lock, padlock; standard-size floor mat, about 3' X 6' (Japanese rooms are measured by the number of joo mats they contain); **joo ga fukái** affectionate; warm-hearted; **joo ga nái** cold, heartless; **joo ni moroi** emotional, sentimental; **joo o orósu** to lock; **joo o hazusu** to unlock **juujoo no ma** a 10-mat room.

jóo girl, young lady; measure of length equal to 9.9 feet or 10 Japanese feet (a *shaku*); quire (unit used in selling writing paper, consisting of 20 or 48 sheets); **ojóo-san** your (his) daughter.

-joo suffix denoting: letter; **shookáijoo** letter of introduction; **annáijoo** (letter of) invitation; **shookánjoo** warrant.

jooai affection, love; **jooai no fukái** loving, affectionate.

jooba horseback riding.

jóobu top, upper part, upper surface.

JOOBU good health; soundness of body; **joobu na** durable; robust, strong; **joobu soo na** strong-looking, healthy-looking; **joobu ni náru** to grow strong.

joobúkuro envelope.

joochoo mood; atmosphere.

joodán joke, prank; fun; **joodán o iu** to joke; **joodán ni** to take as a joke.

joodeki good performance; success; good work; **joodeki no** well-done; excellent. **Joodeki!** Well done! Bravo!

jooen suru to put on, perform (a play); to put on the stage.

jóoge top and bottom, upper and lower.

joogi ruler; square; standard; norm.

jóogo funnel; drinker, sake-lover.

joohatsu evaporation; **joohatsu suru** to evaporate.

joohín elegance; refinement; **joohín na** refined; elegant; graceful.

jóoho concession, compromise.

joohoo report; information.

joojitsu personal feelings (considerations).

jóoju accomplishment, achievement; **jóoju suru** to achieve, realize, accomplish.

JOOJUN first ten days of the month; **Ichigatsu joojun** early in January.

jooken condition, term; **jooken zuki** conditional; qualified.

jóoki regular (normal) course; steam, vapor; **jooki kikán** steam engine; **jookisen** steamship; **jóoki o issúru** to deviate, depart from the normal course.

jookígen good humor; **jookígen de** in a good humor.

jookyaku passenger.

jookyoo state of affairs; conditions.

joomae lock.

joomúin trainman; train crew.

jóomu torishimari managing director.

joomyaku vein.

joonetsu passion.

jooó queen.

jooriku suru to disembark, go ashore; **jooriku chitén** point of embarkation.

jóoro watering can.

jooruri Japanese ballad-drama.

jooryokúju evergreen (tree or shrub).

joosei state of affairs; **génka no joosei dé wa** under the present circumstances.

joosha (n.) taking a train, bus, etc.; **joosha suru** to take a train; to board a train; **jooshátchin** carfare, train fare; **joosháken** ticket (for a train, streetcar, or bus).

jooshiki common sense; **jooshiki o kaku** to lack common sense; **jooshikiteki na** sensible; practical.

jooshúbi success; happy result; **jooshúbi no** successful. **Jooshúbi da.** It's all right.

joosoo upper layer; upper stories (of a buildng); (top) social class.

jootai condition, state; circumstances; **mókka no jootai dé wa** as matters now stand.

jootatsu suru to improve; advance; progress.

jooténki fine (splendid) weather.

JOOTOO (n.) best; first class; **jootóo hin** first-class article; (adj.) **jootoo no** best, superior.

jootoogo hackneyed expression, trite saying.

jooyaku treaty, pact, agreement.

jóoyoku lust.

joozai tablet (medicinal).

JOOZÚ skill, dexterity, proficiency; **JOOZÚ NA** skillful, expert, proficient. **Joozú desu.** He is skillful. **Anó hito wa hanashí ga joozú desu.** He is a good speaker.

joozúru to multiply; to take advantage of.

jóryoku aid, assistance; **jóryoku suru** to aid, help.

joryuu sákka female author.

josainái shrewd, clever, smart.

josánpu midwife.

josei aid, assistance; womanhood, femininity; fair sex; weaker sex. **josei suru** to aid, assist (financially); to subsidize; **joséikin** subsidy; **joseiteki** feminine.

joshi particle (gram), e.g., **wa, ga, o,** etc. (used in postposition).

jóshi woman; girl; daughter; female.

JÓYA New Year's Eve.

joyaku assistant official.

joyuu actress.

júgaku = **júkyoo** Confucianism.

júgyoo teaching, instruction; **júgyoo o suru** to teach; **júgyoo o ukéru** to take lessons.

jukkoo reflection; careful consideration; **jukkoo suru** to consider carefully; to reflect; to deliberate. **Sono mondai wa jukkoo chuu desu.** That matter is receiving careful consideration.

júkuchi suru to have full knowledge of; to be familiar with. **Watakushi wa sono kotó o júkuchi shite imásu.** I'm fully aware of that.

jukuren skill, dexterity; **jukuren suru** to become skilled; **jukuren o kaku** to lack skill.

jukusui suru to sleep soundly.

juku súru to ripen, mature, become ripe.

júkyoo See **júgaku.**

júmoku trees. **Sono kooen ni wa jumoku ga óoi desu.** There are many trees in that park.

jumyoo life; life span.

jún pureness, purity; **jún na** pure; genuine; innocent.

jun, junban regular order; turn; **jun ni, junban ni** in regular order; in turn; **jun ni naraberu** to arrange in order. **Junban o matte kudasai.** Please wait your turn.

júnbi preparations, arrangements; **júnbi suru** to prepare, arrange; to get ready for; **júnbi ga dékite iru** to be prepared.

junchoo favorable, satisfactory condition; **junchoo ni** smoothly; favorably, without a hitch; **junchoo ni iku** to go well; **junchoo ni mukau** to improve.

jun'eki net profit; **jun'eki o éru** to earn a net profit, to clear.

júnjo order, sequence; **júnjo tadáshiku** in good order.

junkan suru to circulate; recur.

junkésshoo semi-finals.

junketsu purity; cleanliness; **junketsu na** pure, chaste; clean; **junkin** pure gold.

junrei pilgrim; pilgrimage.

JÚNSA policeman; **junsa hashutsujo** police box; **junsa búchoo** police sergeant. **Keisatsusho de júnsa ni hanashimashita.** I told it to a policeman at the police station.

junshi inspection tour; **junshi suru** to make the rounds.

junshin pureness; genuineness; **junshin na** pure; unsophisticated.

junsui purity, genuineness. **Kore wa junsui no Nihon no kínu desu.** This is genuine Japanese silk.

juntoo natural; regular; appropriate; normal. **Juntoo ni ikéba tooka ni dekimásu.** If all goes well, it will be done on the tenth.

jusanjo employment agency (office).

jushin suru to receive a letter or message.

jutai suru to conceive, become pregnant.

jutsu art; technique; means; way; trick.

JÚU ten, tenth; **júu ga júu made** in every case.

-JUU suffix denoting: all through the course of; during; all over; throughout. **Tookyoojuu** throughout Tokyo.

Uchijuu de dekakemasu. The entire family goes out together.

juubako pile (nest) of lacquered boxes used as picnic boxes or as containers for foods at festivals.

juban undergarment worn with Japanese clothing.

JUUBÚN plenty; enough; **juubún na** full; sufficient, enough; **juubún ni tabéru** to eat enough.

juubyoo serious illness.

juudai importance; seriousness; **juudai na** important; **juudaishi suru** to take seriously.

JUUGATSU October.

JÚUGO fifteen; **juugoya no tsukí** harvest moon.

JUUHACHÍ eighteen; **juuhachíban** one's forte; hobby; favorite trick.

JUUICHI eleven.

JUUICHIGATSU November.

juuji = **juujika** (n.) cross; **juuji ni** crosswise. **juuji no** cross-shaped; **juujígun** crusade.

juujika (See also **juuji.**) **juujiká zoo** crucifix.

júuji suru to engage in, practice, pursue.

juujitsu perfection; enrichment; fullness.

juujun gentleness; obedience; **juujun na** gentle, meek; obedient.

juuketsu congestion (medical). **Mé ga juuketsu shite imasu.** His eyes are bloodshot.

JÚUKU nineteen; **dái juuku** nineteenth.

júukyo dwelling, residence; **juukyonin** resident.

juuman suru to be filled with; to be replete with.

juumin residents, inhabitants.

juumonji cross; **juumonji ni** crosswise. (See also **juuji.**)

júunen decade.

JUUNÍ twelve, dozen; **juunibun ni** more than enough.

JUUNIGATSU December.

júunin ten persons; **juunin nami ni** ordinary, average, normal; mediocre.

júurai heretofore; so far; up to now; **júurai no** old; traditional; **júurai no tóori** as in the past.

júurui beast; animals.

juuryóo weight; **juuryoo fusoku** short weight.

juuryoo hunting (with a gun); **juuryooka** sportsman.

JUUSHÍ fourteen.

JUUSHICHÍ seventeen.

juushímatsu lovebird.

juushoku high office; responsible position.

JÚUSHO dwelling, residence; address; **júusho séimei** name and address. **Gojúusho wa dochira desu ka?** What's your address?

juushoo serious wound, injury.

juusoo bicarbonate of soda.

JÚUSU juice; **orenji juusu** orange juice.

juutai critical stage; serious condition.

juutaku house, residence; **juutákuchi** residential section.

juuyaku director; board of directors.

juuyoo importance; **juuyoo na** important; **juuyoo de nái** unimportant.

juuzai felony; capital offense.

juuzei heavy taxation; heavy tax.

juwáki telephone receiver.

júyo suru to award (a prize); to confer (a degree).

juyoo demand; **juyoo suru** to be in demand; **juyoo o mitásu** to meet the demand.

juzu rosary (mainly Buddhist).

K

kabu turnip.

kabu stock, share; **kabúnushi** shareholder.

kabuki classic Japanese play.

kabun superfluous; **kabun no** excessive; undue.

kabureru to be poisoned; to be influenced.

KABÚRU to put on or over one's head; to be covered with; to take upon oneself; **booshi o kabúru** to put on a hat.

kabusáru to get covered; to overlap.

kabuséru to cover with; to put a thing on.

kábuto helmet; **kábuto o núgu** to admit defeat; to throw in the sponge; **kabutó mushi** beetle.

kachí victory, conquest; success; **kachí o seisuru** to get the upper hand; to gain a victory; to win a battle.

káchi value, worth, merit; **káchi aru** valuable.

kachiáu to clash with; to knock against; to collide with.

kachikí na unyielding; strong-minded; resolute.

kachiku domestic animals; livestock.

kadai subject, theme; (n.) being too big; **kadai no** too big; exaggerated; too much; too heavy.

kádan garden; flower bed.

KÁDO corner; turn; angle; excess; immoderateness; the reason; charge; suspicion; grounds; **kádo no misé** corner store; gate; entrance;—**no kádo de** on the grounds of; on account of; for the reason that. **Soo iu to kádo ga tátsu.** That sounds harsh.

kadode departure; **kadode suru** to set out; to leave home.

kadowák:u to kidnap.

kaede maple tree.

kaerigake ni on the way back; upon one's return.

kaeri michi return road; way home.

kaerimíru to look back; to reflect upon; to think of.

KÁERU to return, come back; to go back; to be hatched. **Okaeri nasái.** Welcome back!

KAERU (n.) frog; (v.) to change, alter; to exchange; to replace; to convert; **sétsu o kaeru** to change one's opinion;

michi o kaeru to take another road;
kane o kaeru to change money.

KÁESU to give back, restore, return; to pay
back; to hatch (eggs); **okane o káesu**
to repay money.

KÁETTE on the contrary; instead; on the
other hand; all the more.

káfu stoker; fireman.

káfuu family customs (tradition).

kafun pollen.

káfusu cuff(s).

kagáisha assailant.

kágaku chemistry; science; **kágaku no**
scientific; **kagakujoo no** chemical;
kagákusha scientist.

kagameru to bend; to bow; **koshi o
kagameru** to stoop, bend down;
kagamu to bend, bow; to crouch.

KAGAMI mirror; **kagamí o míru** to look in a
mirror.

kagaríbi campfire; bonfire.

kagashi scarecrow.

kagayakasu to light up; to make shine; to
brighten.

kagayaki luster; brilliance; glitter; **kagayaku**
to shine, glitter, sparkle, glisten.

káge shadow; silhouette; image; reflection;
shade; **káge ni náru** to be shaded;
káge ni in the shade; **káge ga sásu** to
cast a shadow; **kagéru** to become
shady; to get dark; to darken.

kagéguchi malicious gossip; **kagéguchi o iu**
to gossip maliciously.

kágehinata two-faced; faithless; **kágehinata
no nái** faithful; conscientious.

kágeki opera; operetta; **kagekí dan** opera
company; **kagekijoo** opera house.

kageki excessive; extreme; violent; radical;
kagekiha radicals (political); **kageki
shisoo** radical ideas; dangerous
thoughts. **Kageki na undoo o shite wa
ikemasen.** You must not engage in
strenuous physical exercise.

kagemúsha man who pulls strings or exerts
influence behind the scenes.

kagen degree, proportion, extent.

kagéroo fly living only one day; **kagéroo no
yóo na** short-lived, ephemeral.

-KÁGETSU suffix denoting: (one) month's
duration; **ikkágetsu** one month;
nikágetsu two months; **sankágetsu**
three months.

KAGÍ key; hook; **kagi ana** keyhole; **kagigata
no** hook-shaped; **kagí de akeru** to
unlock; **kagí o kakéru** to lock; **kagí ni**
kakéru to hang on a hook.

kagirí limit, bounds; **kagirí no áru** limited,
restricted; **kagíru** to limit, restrict.
Watakushi no shiru kágiri. As far as
I know.

kago basket; cage; sedan chair; **kago ni noru**
to ride in a sedan chair.

kagoo suru to combine.

KÁGU furniture, furnishings; **kagúya**
furniture store.

kagu to smell; to scent; to sniff; **kagitsukéru**
to get wind of.

kágura sacred music and dancing in front of a
shrine (Shinto).

káhei money; currency.

káhi right or wrong; good or bad; propriety.
**Sono káhi wa toohyoo de
kimemasyoo.** Let's decide the matter
by vote.

kahoo ancestral treasure; heirloom.

káhoo luck; good fortune; **káhoo na** lucky.

kai avail, effect, use; **kai ga nai** of no effect;
kai náku without avail; **kai no nái**
useless; fruitless.

kái meeting, assembly; association; society;
times; cycle; oar, paddle; shellfish;
shell; **nikái** two times, twice; **kaiin**
(society) member; **kái o tsukau** to
row; **kai hi** membership fee;
subscription; admission fee.

-kai suffix denoting: stairs; story (of a
building); sea; **ikkai** first floor;
nikai-date two-story house; **Nihónkai**
Japan Sea.

kaiagéru to purchase, buy; to requisition.

kaibatsu above sea level.

kaiboo autopsy; dissection; analysis.

kaibutsu monster.

kaichiku rebuilding, reconstruction.

kaichuu pocket; **kaichuu mono** purse;
kaichuudókei pocket watch.

kaidaku willing consent; **kaidaku suru** to
give ready consent; to consent readily.

KAIDAN stairway, staircase; flight of steps;
ghost story; **kaidan suru** to have an
interview with. **Heya wa kaidan o
agatte hidari no hoo desu.** My room
is to the left of the stairway.

kaidashi marketing, shopping; daily needs.

kaidásu to drain off; to ladle; to scoop out.

kaifuku recovery; restoration;
re-establishment; **kaifuku suru** to
recover; restore, etc.

kaifuu suru to open a letter; break a seal.

káiga pictures; painting(s); **kaiga
chinrétsukan** art gallery; **kaiga
tenránkai** art exhibition.

kaigai (n.) abroad; foreign country; **kaigai
kara** from abroad; **káigai ni iku** to go
abroad.

kaigaishíi prompt; brisk; faithful; **kaigáishiku**
promptly; briskly; willingly.

kaigan seashore, coast; **kaigansen** coast line.

káigi council; conference; convention.

kaigoo meeting, assembly.

káigun navy; **káigun no** naval.

kaigyoo suru to open a shop; to open a
business.

kaihan revised edition.

kaihatsu suru to develop; to exploit; to
cultivate; to open up.

kaihen seashore, seaside, beach.

kaihi suru to avoid, shun, evade.

kaihoo liberation, release; good news;
opening; **kaihoo suru** to set free; to
open to the public.

káihoo suru to nurse (tend) a sick person.

kaihyoo suru to count votes.

kaiín shiki opening ceremony of the Diet (Japanese Parliament).

kaijin ashes; **kaijin ni kisúru** to be reduced to ashes.

káijo cancellation; release, discharge; **káijo suru** to cancel, rescind, etc.

kaijoo sea; circular (letter); **kaijoo no** marine, maritime; **kaijoo o mawasu** to send out a circular.

kaijoo ni upstairs; **kaijoo e iku** to go upstairs.

kaikabúru to pay too much; to overestimate, overrate.

kaikaku reformation; reorganization; **kaikaku suru** to reform; reorganize; innovate.

kaikan hall; assembly hall.

kaikata buyer; bull (on the stock market).

kaikatsu cheerfulness; **kaikatsu na** cheerful; gay; jovial.

kaikei accounts; **kaikéibo** account book; **kaikei gákari** accountant; cashier; **kaikei hóokoku** financial report.

kaiken interview, audience; **kaiken o mooshikómu** to ask for an interview; **kaiken suru** to interview.

kaiketsu settlement; solution; **kaiketsu suru** to settle; to solve; to fix up; **kaiketsu ga tsuku** to come to a settlement; to arrive at a solution.

káiko silkworm; discharge, dismissal; retrospection; reflection; review; **káiko suru** to discharge, dismiss; to look back; to reflect.

kaikómu to hold (carry) under one's arm.

kaikon development; clearing.

kaikoojoo open port.

kaikyoo strait; sound.

kaikyuu class; rank; order; grade.

kaimaki quilt; sleeved coverlet.

kaimen surface of the sea.

kaimetsu destruction, ruin.

kaimodósu to buy back, repurchase.

KAIMOKU entirely, utterly, altogether (used with a negative). **Kaimoku wakarimasen.** I don't understand it at all.

KAIMONO shopping; marketing; purchase; **kaimono o suru** to buy, shop; **kaimono ni iku** to go shopping.

káimu (*n.*) having nothing; having none at all; nil. **Okane wa káimu desu.** I have no money at all.

káin Lower House of the Diet.

kainarásu to tame, domesticate.

káinushi owner of an animal; keeper; master.

kainushi buyer; purchaser. **Watakushi no ie no kainushi ga mitsukarimashita.** We found a buyer for our house.

káiri nautical mile.

kairiki superhuman strength.

káiro sea route; pocket warmer; body heater; circuit; **káiro o iku** to go by sea.

kairoo corridor; passageway; gallery.

kairyoo improvement; reform; **kairyoo suru** to reform; to imporove.

kairyuu tide; tidal current; trend.

kaisaku adaptation.

kaisan dispersion; liquidation; breakup; **kaisan suru** to break up; to dissolve; to liquidate.

kaisánbutsu marine products; **kaisángyoo** marine-products industry (processing and selling fish, lobsters, oysters, clams and edible seaweeds).

kaisatsúguchi ticket gate.

kaisei fine weather; clear sky.

kaisetsu explanation; interpretation; **kaisetsu suru** to explain; to interpret; to comment on.

KAISHA company; corporation; firm; **kaisháin** employee of a business firm. **Ano kaisha ni tsutómete imásu.** I am working for that firm.

káishaku interpretation; construction; explanation.

kaishiméru to buy up; to corner (the market).

kaishi suru to begin.

kaishoo dissolution; extinction; cancellation.

kaishuu withdrawal; collection; **kaishuu suru** to withdraw; to call in.

kaisoku regulations, rules of an organization.

kaisoo seaweed; shipping; (marine) forwarding; recollection; reminiscence; **kaisoo suru** to recollect; reminisce; to forward; to transport; **kaisoogyóosha** shipping agency.

kaisui sea water; salt water; **kaisuiyóku joo** seaside resort; beach; **kaisuíyoku o suru** to go bathing in the sea.

kaisúu frequency; **kaisúu o kasaneru** to repeat many times.

kaitai dissection; dismemberment.

kaite buyer, purchaser.

kaiten revolution, rotation; **kaiten suru** to revolve, rotate; **kaiténgi** gyroscope.

kaitoo solution; reply; answer; president (of an organization); **kaitoo suru** to solve; to reply, answer.

kaitsumande to make a long story short; in a word. **Kaitsumande ohanashi shimashoo.** I will tell you briefly.

kaiúngyoo marine shipping. (See also **kaisoo**.)

KAIWA conversation.

káiwai neighborhood; **káiwai ni** in the neighborhood.

kaizoku pirate.

KÁJI fire; blacksmith; domestic affairs; domestic duties; housework; rudder; helm; **káji o tóru** to steer (a ship); **kajítori** helmsman. **Watakushi wa kyónen káji ni aimáshita.** I had (suffered from) a fire last year.

kajikamu to be numb with cold; to be numbed.

kajiritsúku to hold onto; to clutch.

kajíru to gnaw; to nibble; to bite; to get a smattering of.

kájitsu fruit; berry; nut.

kajoo excess; superfluity, surplus; article; item; clause; **kajoo o ageru** to itemize.

kajuu overweight; too fat; obese.

kakae embrace; employ; **kakaeru** to hold in

or under one's arms; to embrace; to employ; to hire.

kakageru to hold up; to raise, hoist; to insert (an advertisement in a newspaper).

KAKAKU price; value; **kakaku o tsukéru** to set a price; to fix the value of.

KÁKARI charge(s); duty; expenses; **kakaríin** official in charge; head clerk. **Kongetsu wa kákari ga óokatta desu.** We had heavy expenses this month. [We had to pay a lot for expenses this month.]

kakariai implication; involvement; **kakariai ni náru** to be involved in.

KAKÁRU to hang; to stand; to rest (against); to set about; to be dependent on; to concern; to catch; to be caught; to begin, start; to take; to need; **byooki ni kakáru** to become ill; **isha ni kakáru** to consult a doctor. **Soko e ikú no ni ichijíkan kakárimasu.** It takes an hour to get there. **Íkura kakarimásu ka?** How much does it cost?

kakasazu regularly, consistently; without missing; constantly.

KAKATO heel.

KAKAWÁRAZU in spite of, despite; no matter (how, what); regardless of; **áme ni mo kakawárazu** in spite of the rain.

kakawáru to take part, participate in; to concern; to affect; to be at stake.

kaké betting; credit; trust; **kaké o suru** gambling; **kaké o suru** to make a bet, wager; **kaké de kau** to buy on credit.

kakeai negotiation; consultation; **kakeai o suru** to negotiate (with); **kakeáu** to negotiate; to bargain with.

kakéashi run; double time; gallop; **kakéashi de** on the double; at a run; **kakéashi ni náru** to break into a run; to gallop.

kakebúton quilt; bed-coverlet.

kakedasu to start running; to run out.

kakegae substitute; spare; **kakegae no nái** irreplaceable (most precious) thing.

kakegóe yell, shout; **kakegóe o kakéru** to yell, shout.

kakehi waterpipe, drainpipe.

kakéhiki bargaining; tactics; tact, diplomacy; **kakéhiki o suru** to bargain (with a person).

kakei lineage, genealogy.

kakejaya teahouse along the wayside.

kakékin installment; premium; **kakékin o suru** to pay in installments.

kakékkura race; **kakékkura o suru** to run a race.

kakemochi part-time job; working at two or more jobs at one time.

kakémono hanging picture-scroll.

kakené overcharge; high price; **kakené o iu** to overcharge.

kakeochi elopement.

KAKÉRU to sit, take a seat; to spend; to invest; to gallop; to run; to hang; to suspend; to cover; to spread on; to put on; to pour on; **isu ni kakéru** to sit on a chair; **kane o kakéru** to spend money; **koshi o kakéru** to sit down; **kugi ni kakéru** to hang (something) on a peg; **mégane o kakéru** to wear glasses; **yomikakéru** to begin to read. **Kono uchi ni wa okane ga kakátte iru.** He spent a great deal of money on this house.

kakeru to be broken; to be cracked; to be short of.

kaketsu approval; adoption; passage; **kaketsu suru** to pass, be approved.

kakézu map, chart.

káki oyster; **kaki fúrai** fried oysters.

kakiarawásu to put in writing.

kakiatsuméru to collect; to rake together; to gather up.

kakiawaséru to adjust, arrange.

kakiire entry; notes; insertion; **kakiireru** to insert; to write in, to mortgage.

kakikae rewriting; transfer; **kakikaeru** to rewrite; to transfer.

kakimawasu to stir (coffee, etc.); to beat; to rummage; to ransack.

kakimidásu to confuse, throw into confusion; to disturb.

kakímochi dried ricecake.

kakimóno written document; writing.

kakimushíru to tear; to scratch off.

kakíne hedge.

kakinokéru to push aside.

kakinuki extract; abstract.

kakioki will; posthumous letter.

kakiorósu to write down.

kakiotósu to scrape off.

kakisoeru to add a postscript.

kakitatéru to play up; to write up; to make a big story of.

kakitome = **kakitome yuubin** registered mail. **Kono tegami o kakitome ni shite kudasái.** Please register this letter.

kakitomeru to make notes of; to make a memo.

kakitome yúubin See **kakitome.**

kakitorásu to dictate.

kakitsuke document; bill.

kakiwakéru to push (elbow) aside, to force oneself through.

kákka Your (His) Excellency.

kakké beriberi.

kakki animation; spirit; **kakki no áru** animated; **kakki no nái** lifeless; dull.

kákko parentheses, brackets.

kakkoo shape, form; appearance; style; **kakoo na** suitable; moderate; **kakkoo no yói** well-formed; stylish.

káko (n.) past; bygone days; previous existence; **káko ní oite** in the past.

kakoi enclosure; fence; **kakoi o suru** to enclose; to fence in.

kakomi siege; **kakomu** to surround; to enclose; to close in on.

kakotsuke pretense, pretext; **kakotsukeru** to

make a pretense of; **kakotsukete** under the pretext (pretense) of.

kakou to keep; to store; to preserve.

KÁKU (*v.*) to write; to draw; to paint; to rake; to scratch; **tegami o káku** to write a letter; **é o káku** to draw (paint) a picture; **yukí o káku** to clear away snow; **hají o káku** to be put to shame; (*adj.*) each; every; várious; (*n.*) angle; square; **chokkaku** right angle.

KAKUBETSU especially, particularly; **kakubetsu no** particular; special.

kakuchoo suru to extend, expand, enlarge.

kakudai suru to magnify; **kakudai kyoo** magnifying glass.

kakugén maxim, saying.

kakugetsu every other month.

kakúgo preparedness; resolution; resignation; **kakúgo suru** to be prepared; to be resolved.

kakuhoo authentic news, definite report.

kákuhoomen in every direction; in all directions.

kakujitsu reliability; authenticity; certainty; every other day; every second day; **kakujitsu na** reliable; sure; authentic; **kakujitsu ni** certainly.

kakumáu to shelter; to protect.

kakumei revolution; **kakumeiteki** revolutionary.

kakunin confirmation; **kakunin suru** to confirm, affirm.

kakunóoko airplane hangar.

kakuran disturbance.

kakuréga hiding place; den.

KAKURERU to hide oneself; to take shelter; to disappear. **Tsukí ga kúmo ni kakúreta.** The moon disappeared in the cloud.

kákuri isolation; **kakurishitsu** isolation ward.

kakuritsu suru to establish; to fix; to settle.

kakusaku plan, scheme; project; **kakusaku suru** to plan, scheme.

kakusei disillusionment; **kakusei suru** to awake, be awakened; to be disillusioned.

kakuseiki loud-speaker.

kakushí pocket.

kakushidate concealment; **kakushidate o suru** to conceal a fact.

kakushiki social status.

kakushin reform; renovation; firm belief, strong conviction. **kakushin suru** to reform; to innovate; to believe strongly; to be confident of.

kákusho every place; various places; **kákusho ni** everywhere; in several places.

kakushoo conclusive evidence; proof.

KÁKUSHU every kind; **kákushu no** of every kind.

KAKÚSU to hide, conceal.

kakutei decision; settlement; **kakutei suru** to decide; to settle.

kákuteru cocktail.

kakutoku acquisition; possession; **kakutoku suru** to acquire, obtain, secure.

kakutoo suru to give a definite answer.

kakuu no imaginary; fanciful.

KAKUYASU NA cheap; **kakuyasu ni** cheaply; at a moderate price.

kakuzátoo lump (cube) sugar.

kakuzuke classification, grading; **kakuzuke suru** to classify, grade.

kákyoku melody, tune.

kakyuu no petty; low-grade; low-class; inferior; subordinate; pressing; urgent; imminent.

KAMA kettle; iron pot; kiln; **kamado** oven, range.

káma scythe.

kamáe structure; appearance; **kamáeru** to build, construct; to set up house; to take an attitude.

KAMÁU to care, mind, be concerned about; to trouble oneself about; to give attention to; **kamawázu** regardless of. **Kamawánaide kudasái.** Please don't trouble yourself on my account. Don't bother me.

káme turtle.

kamé jar; jug; vase; urn.

kamei family name; family honor; alliance; affiliation.

kamen mask; disguise.

KÁMERA camera.

kámí god, deity; **kami dana** family shrine (a shelf in a Japanese house for Shinto tablets).

KAMÍ hair; paper; **kamí o suku** to comb one's hair; **kami byóoshi** paper cover; **kami kúzu** wastepaper; scraps of paper; **kamibásami** paper clip; **kamiyásuri** sandpaper.

kami- prefix denoting: biting; gnawing; chewing; **kamikíru** to bite off; **kamikonásu** to chew; **kamitsuku** to bite. (See also **kámu**.)

KAMINÁRI thunder. **Kaminári ga natte imasu.** It is thundering.

KAMISÓRI razor; **kamisóri o ateru** to shave.

kamite upstage (in a theatre).

kamoku course, subject, lesson.

kamósu to stir up, arouse.

kámotsu freight, cargo; merchandise; **kamotsusen** freighter (ship).

KÁMU = **kami-** to chew; to bite; to gnaw. **Kánde fukúméru yóo ni setsumei shimáshita.** He explained it, taking great pains to make it clear.

kamufúráaji camouflage, disguise.

KÁN tin can; coffin; pipe; tube; volume; reel (motion picture); large building; hotel; perception; feeling, sentiment, emotion; **kán kiwamáru** to be filled with emotion; to be deeply moved. **KANZUME** canned goods; **ikkan** volume.

kan temper; irritability; **kan o okosu** to become impatient; **kan ga tsuyói** to be hot-tempered; **kan o osaéru** to control one's temper.

-kan suffix denoting: duration or space between; **isshuukan** one week; **Tookyoo Oosaká kan** between Tokyo and Osaka; **ikkagetsúkan** during one month.

kana Japanese syllabary.

kanaboo crowbar; metal rod; horizontal bar.

kanadárai metal basin; washbowl.

kanaéru to grant; to comply with; **negai o kanáeru** to grant one's wishes; to answer one's prayers.

kanagu metal ornaments or fittings.

KÁNAI family; household; wife; **kanaijuu** the whole family. (See also **sai.**)

kanakirigóe shrill, voice; **kanakirigóe o dásu** to scream.

kanamono hardware; ironware; **kanamonoya** hardware store or dealer.

KANARAZU certainly; no doubt, by all means; without fail; invariably. **Kanarazu kité kudasai.** Please be sure to come. Please come without fail.

KÁNARI fairly; pretty; considerably; **kánari no** considerable; **kánari yói** fairly well.

kanariya canary.

KANASHII sad, sorrowful; **kanashími** sorrow, grief; **kanashímu** to lament; to mourn; to regret.

kanáu to suit; to be suitable; to conform to; to accomplish; to agree with. **Mokuteki ni kanáu.** It answers the purpose.

kanazúchi iron hammer.

kanban signboard, billboard.

kanbashíi sweet; fragrant.

kanbashítta shrill, piercing; sharp.

kanbatsu drought.

kanben na handy; convenient; **kanben ni** simply; easily.

kánben suru to pardon, forgive. **Kánben shite kudasái.** Please excuse me.

kánbi completion; perfection.

kanboo cold; flu.

kanbotsu suru to sink, subside; to cave in.

kánbu staff; management.

kanbutsuya grocery specializing in dried vegetables and fruits.

kánbyoo = kángo (*n.*) nursing; **kanbyoonin** nurse.

kanchoo spy.

kánchoo government office.

kandai generosity; leniency; tolerance; **kandai na** generous; lenient; tolerant.

kandánkei thermometer.

kandan nái continual, incessant, endless; **kandan náku** continually.

kandoo emotion; impression; excitement; disinheritance; **kandoo suru** to be moved, be affected; to disown, disinherit; **kandoo saseru** to move; to impress; to inspire; to appeal to.

kane money; metal; bell; **kane ga nái** to have no money; **kaneíre** money box; purse; **kanekáshi** moneylender; **kanebako** money box; till; **kanemóchi** rich man; **kanetsukidoo** bell tower; **kanezúkai** manner of spending money; **kane**

banare no yói generous with money; **kane ga kakáru** to be costly; **kane o narasu** to ring a bell; **kanekáshi suru** to lend money; **ookanémochi** very rich man; **kanezúkai no arai hito** a free spender.

kanegane previously; beforehand.

kánete already; previously; lately; some time ago.

kangáe thought, idea, opinion; **KANGÁERU** to think, consider, deliberate, believe, be of the opinion; **kangae bukái** thoughtful; **kangaenaósu** to reconsider. **Sore wa kangáeru no mo iyá desu.** I dislike the very thought of it.

kangaechígai misunderstanding; mistake; mistaken ideal; **kangaechígai suru** to misunderstand.

kangei welcome; reception; **kangei suru** to welcome; **kangei o ukéru** to be received warmly.

kangeki (*n.*) theatre-going; **kangeki ni dekakeru** to go to the theatre; **kangekíkai** theatre party.

kangeki emotion; excitement; inspiration. **Sono hanashi o kiite kangeki shimashita.** I was very much moved when I heard the story.

kángo See **kánbyoo; kangófu** nurse.

kani crab.

kán'i simplicity; **kán'i na** simple; **kán'i ni** simply.

kan'in adultery.

kanja (*n.*) patient.

kánji manager; staff secretary; executive committee.

kanji Chinese character (ideograph) used in the Japanese writing system; sense, feeling; **kanji no hayái** sensitive; **kanji no nibúi** insensitive; **kanjiyasúi** sensitive; sentimental.

kanjin na important; essential, vital.

KANJIRU = KANZURU to feel; **átsusa o kanjiru** to feel the heat; **kónnan o kanjiru** to find difficulty.

kanjoo feeling, sentiment, passion; **kanjooteki** emotional.

KANJÓO calculation, counting; **kanjóo ni ireru** to take into account; **kanjoogaki** check, bill. **Háyaku kanjóo shite kudasái.** Please count it quickly. **Kanjóo o machigáeta.** I miscalculated.

kanjusei susceptibility; receptivity.

kánka influence.

kankaku sensation, sense; space, distance; interval.

kankei relation, connection; concern, interest; relationship;—**to kankei ga áru** to have a relation to, be connected with, etc.

KÁNKOKU South Korea.

kankoo publication; sight-seeing; **kankóo kyaku** sight-seer; **kankoo ni iku** to go sight-seeing; **kankoo suru** to publish; **kankóobutsu** publication; **kankóodan**

tourist party; **Kankookyoku** Tourist Bureau; **teiki kankoobutsu** periodical.

kankyoo environment, surroundings.

kankyuu emergency; **kankyuu suru** to be moved to tears.

kanmei terseness; deep impression; **kanmei na** terse, concise, simple and brief; **kanmei suru** to impress deeply; to be deeply impressed; to be deeply moved.

kanmuri crown.

kánnen idea, sense, concept, notion.

kánnin patience; forgiveness.

kannukí bolt, bar (of a gate or door); **kannuki o kakéru** to bolt; **kannuki o hazusu** to unbolt.

kanoo possibility; suppuration; infection; **kanoo na** possible; **kanoo suru** to be infected.

kanpai toast; **kanpai suru** to drink a toast.

kanpan deck; **jookánpan** upper deck; **chuukánpan** main deck.

kanraku fall; cave in; **kanraku suru** to fall; to sink; to collapse; to cave in.

kánri management, administration, control; **kanrísha** superintendent; manager.

kanryaku simplicity; brevity; **kanryaku na** simple; brief; **kanryaku ni** simply; briefly. **Kanryaku ni shite kudasai.** Please make it very brief.

kanryoo completion; conclusion.

kansatsu observation.

kansen infection; contagion.

kansen trunk line; main line.

kansetsu joint; indirectness; **kansetsu o kujíku** to dislocate (a joint); **kansetsu no** roundabout, indirect; **kansetsu ni** at second hand, indirectly.

kánsha thanks, gratitude; official residence. **Kánsha no kotobá mo arimasén.** I can't thank you enough.

kanshaku passion; temper; impatience; **kanshaku no tsuyói** hot-tempered; irritable; **kanshaku o okósu** to lose one's temper.

kanshi watch, lookout, vigil; **kanshi suru** to watch, keep an eye on.

kanshin concern, interest; **kanshin na** admirable, praiseworthy; **kanshin ni** admirably; **kanshin o mótsu** to be concerned about, be interested in; **kanshin suru** to admire; to wonder at.

kanshoku suru to eat between meals.

kanshoo appreciation; sentimentality; interference, meddling; **kanshoo shúgi** sentimentalism; **kanshoo suru** to appreciate; to meddle, interfere; **kanshooteki** appreciative; sentimental; pathetic.

kanshuu spectators.

kansoku observation; survey; **kansokusho** observatory (weather, etc.).

kansoo aridity; impression(s); thoughts; **kansoo suru** to dry; **kansoo o nobéru** to give one's impression.

kansoo dénpoo deferred telegram.

kan súru to be concerned with; to relate to,

bear on; to be connected with;—**ni kán shite** in regard to.

KANTAN brevity; simplicity; **KANTAN NA** simple, brief; **kantan ni** briefly; in a few words; simply, easily. **Soko e wa kantan ni ikemasu.** You can go there very easily.

kantan suru to admire.

kantei judgment; expert opinion; appraisal; official residence.

kantoku supervision; control; superintendent; inspector; **kantoku suru** to supervise; control.

kantsuu penetration; **kantsuu suru** to penetrate, pierce.

KAN'YOO NA important; necessary.

kanyuu entry; joining; admission; **kanyuu suru** to join; to subscribe; to enter; **kanyúusha** member; subscriber.

kanzei customs (duty); **kanzei no kakáru** dutiable; **kanzei no kakáranai** duty free.

KANZEN perfection; completeness; **kanzen na** perfect; complete; integral; **kanzen ni** perfectly.

kanzúku to get wind of; to have an inkling of; to suspect.

KANZURU = KANJIRU to feel; to be sensitive to; to be moved; to be conscious of.

KAO face; looks; complexion; **kao ga urete iru** to be well known.

kaoru to smell; to be fragrant.

kappa old-fashioned raincoat; oilskin.

kapparai shoplifter; pilfering, thieving.

kappatsu activity; briskness; **kappatsu na** active, lively; brisk.

káppu cup (trophy). (See also **koppu**.)

KARA (n.) being empty; vacant; husks, hulls, shells; (adj.) **kara no** empty; **kara ni suru** to empty. **Kara desu.** It is empty.

KARA from; out of; since; on; in; and so; because; as; entirely, altogether, utterly; for (following a sentence-ending form of a verb or adjective); **kore kara nochi** from now on; **Tookyoo kara Oosaka máde** from Tokyo to Osaka. **Byooki déshita kara ikimasén deshita.** I was sick so I didn't go.

KARADA body; **karada no** physical; bodily; **karada no tamé ni náru** to be good for one's health. **Karada ga warúi.** He is sick. I am sick.

karagéru to tie up, bind; to tuck in.

KARAÍ hot; acrid; salty; pungent. **Kono otsúyu wa karái desu.** This soup is too salty.

karaíbari bluff; empty boast.

karakáu to tease; to make fun of; to play a joke on.

karákaze dry wind.

karamáru, karámu to twine around; to coil; to be entangled.

KARARÍ TO completely, fully, entirely. **Sóra ga kararí to háremashita.** The sky has cleared.

kara sáwagi much ado about nothing; **kara sáwagi suru** to make a big fuss about nothing.

karasu to let wither; to dry up. (See also **KARERU**.)

karátto carat.

karazeki dry (hacking) cough.

KARE he; **káre no** his; **kare ni** to him; **káre o** him; **kárera** they, their, them.

kare- prefix denoting: dry; withered; hoarse; **karegóe** hoarse voice.

káree curry; **raisu káree** curried rice; **kareiko** curry powder.

KÁREKORE this and that; one thing and another; some; about; **kárekore ninen bákari** two years or so.

karéndaa calendar.

KARERU to wither, dry up; to die; to get hoarse. **Kóe ga karete kimashita.** My voice is hoarse. **Ído ga karemashita.** The well has dried up. **Ki ga karemashita.** The tree has died. (See also **karasu**.)

kári hunting.

KARI (n.) loan; debt; borrowing; (adj.) temporary; tentative; **kari no** temporary; **kari ni** temporarily; tentatively.

kariru to borrow; **karikata** debtor; **kariukenin** borrower. **Yamada-san ni okane o karimáshita.** I borrowed some money from Mr. Yamada.

kariatsuméru to gather together, muster.

karidásu to hunt out; to round up.

kariréru to harvest, gather in.

karikomi (n.) cutting, pruning; **karikómu** to cut, trim, prune.

karikoshi outstanding debt; overdraft.

karinui (n.) basting, sewing loosely; **karinui suru** to baste.

KARÓOJITE with much difficulty; barely, hardly.

karu to reap; to cut; to trim; to hunt; to chase; **kusá o karu** to cut grass; **íne o karu** to harvest rice.

karuhazumi rashness; hastiness; **karuhazumi na** rash; hasty; thoughtless.

KARUI light, not heavy, slight, trifling; not serious; simple; insignificant; **karui shigoto** light work; **karui nimotsu** light baggage; **karuku** lightly; slightly; minor, etc.; **karuku suru** to lighten, ease; **karuku útsu** to tap; to pat.

káryoku heating power.

karyuu downstream.

KÁSA umbrella; parasol.

kasa bulk, volume; size; quantity; **kasabátta** bulky.

kasabuta scab.

kasai fire, blaze; **kasai o okósu** to start a fire; **kasai hoochíki** fire alarm; **kasai hóken** fire insurance. (See also **hí**.)

kasamu to swell, increase in volume.

kasanaru to be piled up; to lie one on top of another; **kasaneru** to pile up, put one on top of the other; to repeat; **kasanete** in layers, one on the other; repeatedly.

kasanegásane repeatedly, again and again, over and over.

kasei (n.) keeping house; **kaseí o osaméru** to manage a household.

Kasei Mars.

kasetsu construction; hypothesis; **kasetsu suru** to construct, erect; to lay; **kasetsu no** temporary, provisional; **denwa o kasetsu suru** to have a telephone installed; **kasetsuchuu de áru** to be under construction.

kásha freight car; truck.

kashi riverbank, riverside; lending; **kashikata** creditor; **kashikín** loan.

káshi cake; confectionery; sweets; candy; **kashíya** confectionery store.

kashigéru to incline; **kubi o kashigéru** to tilt one's head.

Kashi kandánkei Fahrenheit thermometer.

kashikíru to make reservations.

KASHIKÓI wise, clever, intelligent.

kashikomáru to obey; to assent to; to sit straight. **Kashikomarimashita.** Yes, sir, I'll follow your instructions.

KASHIMA room to let; apartment; **kashiya** house for rent.

kashimashíi noisy; boisterous.

kashirá (n.) head, chief; ringleader; (adj.) **kashira dátta** chief, leading, principal.

káshu singer.

kassai ovation.

kásu refuse, dregs, scum; sediment.

KASU to lend; **kane o kasu** to lend money.

KÁSUKA NA faint, dim, vague, indistinct; **kásuka ni** faintly, etc.; **kásuka ni kioku suru** to have a faint recollection.

kasumi haze; mist; **kasumi no kakátta** hazy; misty; **kasumu** to grow hazy, grow dim.

kasuréru to get hoarse.

kasuríkizu scratch; bruise; **kasúru** to graze, scrape, scratch.

KÁTA shoulder; **katákake** shawl; **káta o mótsu** to take sides. **Káta ga kóru.** I have a stiff neck.

kata form, shape; pattern, model, figure; design, mold; **KATACHI** form, shape; figure; personal appearance; **mime katachi no íi** handsome; shapely. **Sore wa dónna katachi o shite imásu ka?** What kind of shape does it have?

kata- prefix denoting: single; **katáhoo** one of a pair; **kataashi de tátsu** to stand on one leg.

-kata suffix denoting: person (pol.); **kono káta** this person; **ano káta** that person.

katachínba cripple.

katágata by way of; at the same time; partly; combined with. **Sanpo katagata ikimashita.** I went there both to take a walk and [at the same time] pay a visit.

katagawa one side; **katagawa michi** one-way street.

katagi honest; honorable; decent.

KATAI hard; tough; stiff; upright; strong;

firm; conscientious; **kataku** strongly;
firmly; tightly; strictly; resolutely;
stubbornly; **katakurushíi** strict;
stiff-mannered; formal; **kataku suru**
to harden; stiffen. **Anó hito wa katai
hitó desu.** He is a conscientious
person. **Kono nikú wa taihen katái
desu.** This meat is very tough.

KATAKÁNA one of the two sets of Japanese
phonetic symbols called **kana** symbols.
Sore wa katakána de káite kudasái.
Please write it in **katakana**.

katamari lump; clod; mass; **katamaru** to
coagulate; congeal; to group together;
katameru to harden; to solidify; to
stiffen; to consolidate.

kátami honor; **kátami ga hirói** to feel proud.

katami memento, souvenir; **kátami to suru**
to keep as a memento.

KATAMICHI one way; one trip; **katamichi
joosháken** one-way ticket.

katamukéru to incline, bend, tilt; **katamuki**
trend; slant; slope;—**no kkéiko ga
áru** to be apt to, to be inclined to;
katamúku to incline, lean; to decline.

katana sword.

katan íto cotton thread.

katappáshi (*colloq.*) one by one; one and all;
wholesale.

katasa hardness; toughness; solidity.

katasúmi corner; nook; **heya no katasúmi ni**
in a corner of the room.

kataware fragment, piece.

katazukéru to put in order; to clear; to put
away; to dispose of; to settle;
katazúku to be put in order; to be
settled; to come to an end.

KATEI home; family; household;
assumption, supposition; **katei no**
domestic; household; house; **katei
suru** to assume, suppose.

katoo inferiority; **katoo no** low; coarse;
vulgar.

kátsu to conquer, be victorious, win.

katsudoo = katsuyaku activity;
katsudooteki active; energetic;
katsudooka active man;
katsudóoryoku vitality; energy.

katsúgu to shoulder, carry; to carry on the
shoulder.

katsuyaku = katsuyaku activity; action;
boom (rapid, expanding growth);
katsuyaku suru to be active in; to play
an active part.

KATTE one's own way; selfishness;
condition; circumstances; **KATTE NA**
selfish; willful; **temae kátte ni**
selfishly; **katte ni furumáu** to have
one's own way; **katte no yói** handy,
convenient.

KAU to buy, purchase; to incur; to provoke;
kenka o kau to pick a quarrel. **Kono
hón o hyakuen de kaimáshita.** I
bought this book for one hundred yen.

KÁU to keep, raise (an animal or bird).

Watakushi wa inú o kátte imasu. I
have a dog.

KAWÁ skin, hide; leather; bark; peel; etc.;
river; stream; **kawá o hágu** to peel off
(skin or bark); **kawazuki no** unpeeled;
kawabata riverside, riverbank.

KAWAIGÁRU to love; to pet, fondle, caress.
**Káre wa muyámi to néko o
kawaigátta.** He made a great pet of a
cat.

KAWAII dear; darling; loving; tiny; **kawaii
akanboo** precious baby; **kawaii kóe**
sweet voice; **kawairashíi** sweet;
lovely; pretty; charming; amiable;
KAWAISÓO NA poor; pitiful;
pathetic. **Ano hito ni wa kawairashii
akanboo ga arimasu.** She has a cute
baby. **Kawaisóo na kotó o shita.** That
was a pity.

KAWAKÁSU to dry; **KAWÁKU** to dry; to
get dry; to feel thirsty; **nódo ga
kawáku** to be thirsty; **kimono o
kawakásu** to dry clothes. **Kuchi ga
kawáita.** My mouth felt dry.

KAWAKI thirst.

kawara tile; **kawarabuki no** tiled.

KAWARI substitute, proxy; compensation;
change, variation; **kawari ni** on behalf
of; in place of; **kawari o suru** to
substitute, take someone's place;
kawarime turning point; transitional
period; **kawariyasúi** changeable;
unsettled; **kawaru** to change; to shift;
to take the place of, replace; **yóku
kawaru** changeable; **kawarugáwaru**
in turn; by turns. **Kawari ga nái.**
Nothing is the matter. **Áme ga yukí ni
kawarimashíta.** The rain changed to
snow.

KAWASE money order; exchange; **kawase
sóoba** rate of exchange. **Kawase de
gosénen okutta.** I sent a money order
for 50,000 yen.

KAYÓOBI Tuesday.

kayou to pass to and fro; to frequent; to go
regularly; **gakkoo e kayou** to attend
school.

kayowái weak; tender; delicate, fragile.

kayúi itchy.

KÁZARU to adorn, decorate, embellish; to
display; **kikazáru** dress up.

KAZE wind; breeze; cold; **kaze o hiku** to
catch a cold; **kásuka na kaze** breath of
air; light breeze. **Kaze ga fuite imasu.**
The wind is blowing.

kazei taxation; **kazéihin** taxable item;
kazéiritsu tax rate.

KAZOÉRU to count, calculate; to number; **hi
o kazoéru** to count the days.

KÁZOKU family; household.

KÁZU number; **kázu kagiri nái** innumerable,
countless; **kázu no** many; numerous.

KE hair; house; family; **ke darake no** hairy;
ke no nái bald, hairless; **Fujiwara ke**
Fujiwara family; the Fujiwaras.

-KE suffix denoting: temper, feeling; nature;
hínoke signs of fire.

kebakebashíi gaudy, showy.
kéchi fault; stinginess; poor quality; **kéchi na** stingy, miserly; **kéchi o tsukéru** to find fault with.
kechirásu to kick about.
kedakái dignified; noble.
kedamono beast.
KEGÁ wound, injury; accident; **KEGÁ O SURU** to get hurt; **kegá o saseru** to injure, hurt; **kega no kóomyoo** lucky mistake; lucky hit.
kegare pollution, contamination; stain; **kegareru** to be polluted; **kegasu** to stain; to soil; to pollute; to disgrace.
kegírai prejudice; **kegírai suru** to be prejudiced against.
kéi plan, scheme, plot, stratagem; sum, total.
keiba horse race; **keibajoo** race track.
keibetsu contempt; slight; insult; **keibetsu suru** to despise; to sneer at.
keiei management, conduct.
keifuku suru to respect; to admire; to look up to.
keiji notice, notification; **keijiban** bulletin board.
keika progress; development; course; **jíken no keika** the course of an event.
keikai watch; guard; **keikai shingoo** warning signal; **keikai suru** to watch for; guard against.
keikaku plan, project, scheme; **keikaku suru** to plan, etc.
KEIKEN experience; **keiken áru** experienced; **keiken na** pious, devout; **keiken no nái** inexperienced; **keiken suru** to experience; **keikénsha** man of experience.
keiki condition, state; times; **kookéiki** business boom. **Keiki ga yói desu.** Trade is brisk.
kéiko exercise, practice, drill; study; **kéiko suru** to practice; to take lessons.
keikoku warning; advice; **keikoku suru** to warn, admonish.
keikoo tendency, inclination; trend.
keimusho prison.
KEINIKU chicken (as food).
KEIRAN (chicken) egg.
keirei salute, salutation.
keiren convulsions; spasm.
keiryaku stratagem, artifice.
keisan calculation, reckoning; estimation; **keisankata** accountant; **keisánki** adding machine.
KEISATSU police station; **keisatsúkan** police officer.
keisha slant, incline, slope.
keishiki forms, formality; **keishikiteki** formal; conventional; **keishikiteki ni** formally.
keiteki foghorn; police whistle; alarm whistle.
keito worsted; woolen yarn.
keitoo system; lineage; **keitoo tatéru** to systematize; **keitooteki** systematic.
keitoo suru to exhaust; to concentrate.
keiyaku contract; agreement; promise;

keiyaku suru to make a contract; **keiyakúsho** written contract.
kéizai economy; finance; **keizaiteki** economical; **keizaijoo** financially.
KEKKA result, outcome, consequence, effect; **sono kekka** consequently.
kekkan blood vessel.
KEKKIN absence (from work); **kekkin suru** to be absent; **kekkínsha** absentee.
kekkon marriage; wedding; **KEKKON SURU** to marry; **kekkónshiki** marriage ceremony.
kekkoo structure, framework; **kékkoo na** splendid; fine; good; beautiful; **kékkoo na nikú** delicious meat; **kekkoo suru** to take decisive action; to carry out (something) decisively.
KEKKYOKU eventually, finally, ultimately, in the end; **kekkyoku no** final, ultimate.
kemono beast, brute.
kemui smoky; **KEMURI** smoke; fumes; **kemuru** to smoke, smolder; **kemutai** smoky; feel awkward; be shy. **Heyá ga kemui.** The room is smoky. **Kemuri ga tatsu.** Smoke rises.
KÉN Japanese measure, equals 1.98 yds.; house (used as a counter); prefecture; sword, saber; hand of a clock; needle of a compass; **níken** two houses; **kénchoo** prefectural office; **kenchíji** prefectural governor; **Chibáken** Chiba prefecture. **Kádo kara sangenmé no ié desu.** It is the third house from the corner. (In **sangenme**, *k* becomes *g*.)
kenage na brave, heroic; manly; **kenage ni** bravely; heroically; nobly.
ken'aku na dangerous; serious; stormy; rough; **ken'aku na sóra** stormy (threatening) sky.
kenasu to abuse, slander.
KENBUTSU sight-seeing; **kenbutsunin** sight-seer; visitor; **kenbutsu suru** to see, look at; to pay a visit to; **kenbutsu ni iku** to go sight-seeing.
kenchiku construction, erection; building; architecture; **kenchiku yóoshiki** architectural style; **kenchiku suru** to build.
kengaku observation; inspection; **kengaku suru** to visit (a factory, etc.) for study.
kéngi suspicion; **kéngi o kakéru** to suspect; **kéngi ga kakáru** to be under suspicion.
kéngo na strong; stable, firm, solid; **kéngo ni** firmly; strongly.
kenka quarrel, dispute, brawl; **kenka suru** to quarrel, fight; **kenka o shikakéru** to pick a fight, quarrel.
KENKOO health; **kenkoo na** healthy.
KENKYUU research, study, investigation; **kénkyuu suru** to study; to do research; **kenkyúukai** learned society; society for scientific research; **kenkyuujo** laboratory; research institute.
kén mo hororo no áisatsu curt, blunt, or brusque reply; rebuff.

kénpoo constitution; constitutional law.

kénpu silk cloth.

kénri right, privilege; **kénri o shuchoo suru** to insist on one's rights.

kénryoku power, authority, influence; **kénryoku no áru** powerful, influential.

kénsa inspection; investigation; **kénsa suru** to inspect, examine.

kensetsu construction; establishment; building; **kensetsu suru** to construct; to found; to establish.

kensoku arrest, restraint; surveillance. **kensoku suru** to restrain, check.

kenson modesty, humility; **kenson na** modest, humble; **kenson suru** to be modest.

kentoo boxing. **kentoo suru** to box; **kentooka** boxer, fighter.

kentóo aim; anticipation; **kentóo o tsukéru** to anticipate; to take aim at; **kentóo ga hazureru** to miss one's aim.

ken'yaku economy; thrift; **ken'yaku suru** to economize; **ken'yaku no** economical, thrifty.

keorímono woolen fabric.

keppaku purity, innocence; **keppaku na** pure, innocent, spotless, clean.

KÉREMODO but, however, although, yet. **Kyóo wa hídoku atsúi keremodo ikimashóo.** It is hot today, but let's go anyway.

KÉRU to kick.

KÉSA this morning. **Késa wa ikága desu ka?** How are you feeling this morning?

keshikáran outrageous; rude; insulting; insolent.

KÉSHIKI view, sight; scenery, landscape. **Taihen késhiki ga yói.** The scenery is very good.

keshitoméru to put out (a fire).

kessaku masterpiece.

kesseki absence (from school or a meeting); **mukésseki** regular attendance.

késshin resolution, determination; **késshin suru** to be resolute; to make up one's mind.

KESSHITE never; by no means; not at all; not in the least; **Kesshite sonna kotó wa itashimasén.** I wouldn't do it for anything. **Kesshite sawatte wa ikemasen.** Don't touch it under any circumstances.

KESU to put out, extinguish; to blow out; to switch off; to erase; to cancel; **súgata o kesu** to vanish; to disappear; **akari o kesu** to switch off the light; to put out the light.

ketatamashíi noisy, loud; piercing; alarming; **ketatamáshiku** frantically; noisily, loudly.

ketsuron conclusion; **ketsuron suru** to conclude; **ketsuron to shite** in conclusion.

kettei determination; decision; conclusion; **ketteiteki** decisive; conclusive; **kettei suru** to decide upon; to be decided.

kettén flaw, defect, blemish; **kettén áru** defective, imperfect; **kettén no nái** flawless; perfect.

ketto blanket.

kewashíi steep, precipitous.

KEZURU to shave; to sharpen; **enpitsu o kezuru** to sharpen a pencil; **namae o kezuru** to remove a name from a list. **Honemí o kezutte shigoto ni hagénda.** He worked hard without sparing himself.

ki- prefix denoting: air; vapor; atmosphere; **kiatsu** atmospheric pressure; **kion** temperature (of the air).

kibarashi diversion, pastime; **kibarashi o suru** to amuse oneself.

kibaru to exert oneself; to bear down.

kibatsu na original; extraordinary; novel; unusual.

kíbikibi shita vivacious, full of life.

kibin smartness; **kibin na** smart, clever. quick-witted; **kibini ni** cleverly.

kibishíi severe, strict, stern; **kibishíku** severely, strictly.

kibone care, worry; **kibone no oréru** to be troublesome.

KIBOO wish, desire, hope; **kiboo suru** to hope, wish, desire.

KÍBUN feeling, frame of mind, mood; **kibun ga yói desu** to feel better. **Kibun ga warui desu.** I feel sick.

kichí dangerous situation; **kichí o dassúru** to have a close shave; to have a narrow escape.

kichigái madness, insanity; madman, insane person; **kichigai ni náru** to go mad.

kichín to precisely; neatly; **kichín to shita** orderly, tidy; **kichín to shite iru** to be in good order.

kichoomen na orderly; precise; **kichoomen na hito** one who works in an orderly manner.

kidate disposition, temper; **kidate no yói** good-tempered.

kidoru to assume airs, be conceited; **kidotte** affectedly.

kien tall talk; **kien o ageru** to talk big; to boast.

KIERU to go out; to be put out, be extinguished; **súgata ga kieru** to disappear. **Hí ga kieta.** The fire has gone out.

kífu contribution, donation; subscription; **kífu suru** to contribute; to subscribe. **kifúsha** contributor; subscriber.

kigae change of clothes.

kigakari anxiety, worry; misgivings.

KIGARU NA cheerful, light-hearted; pleasant, agreeable.

KIGEN state of health; temper; mood; **kigen no yói** good-humored; cheerful; **kigen o sokonáu** to offend.

KÍGEN term, period, time; **kígen ga kúru** to come due; **kigen ga keikasuru** to overdue.

kigoo sign, symbol, mark, emblem.

kigurai pride; **kigurai no takái** proud.

kihon foundation, basis; standard; **kihonteki** fundamental, basic.

KIIROI yellow; **kiiroi booshi** yellow cap; **kiiroi kóe** shrill voice.

kíji description; account (in a newspaper or magazine).

kíji grain (of wood), color (of wood).

kíjitsu appointed date; fixed date.

KIKÁI machine; implement; apparatus; machinery; opportunity, chance; **kikaiteki** mechanical; **kikáigaku** mechanics; **kikáishi** mechanic, machinist; **kikái no arishídai** at the first chance; **kikái o toraéru** to seize the opportunity.

KIKIAWASÉRU to inquire, make inquiries.

KIKIDÁSU to hear; to find out; to get wind of.

kikiíréru to comply with, assent to, consent to.

kikiíru to listen to.

kikikajiri smattering (of information).

kikikajíru to get a smattering of.

kikikómu to be informed of, get wind of.

kikime effect; efficacy; benefit; **kikime no áru** effective; **kikime no nái** ineffective.

KIKIMORÁSU to fail to hear; not to hear (catch) what is said.

kikín famine.

kikinagásu to pay no heed (to what is said).

kikinaósu to ask someone to repeat (something).

kikinaréru to get used to hearing, be accustomed to hearing.

kikinikúi difficult to hear.

kikioboe recollection (feeling) that one has heard (something) before.

kikisokonai mishearing; misunderstanding.

kikitadásu to ascertain, confirm.

kikitagáru to be inquisitive, be curious.

kikitóru to hear; to get wind of.

kikitsutae hearsay; **kikitsutaéru** to hear from others, hear second hand.

KIKKÁRI punctually; exactly, precisely.

KIKOERU to hear; to be able to hear; to be audible; **KIKU** to hear, listen to; to ask; to accept; **kiku tokoró ni yoréba** ... I hear that, ... it is said that ... **Watakushi wa mimí ga yóku kikoemasén.** I'm hard of hearing. **Utá ga kikoemásu.** I hear a song.

KIKOO climate, season; weather; **onwa na kikoo** mild climate.

kimae generosity; **kimae no yói** generous; openhanded; **kimae yóku kane o tsukau** to be generous with one's money.

kimagure caprice; **kimagure na** capricious, whimsical; **kimagure ni** capriciously.

kimama waywardness; **kimama na** selfish, etc.

kimari settlement; conclusion; rule; custom; **kimari o tsukéru** to settle, arrange; **kimatta** regular, fixed, routine;

kimaru to be settled, come to an agreement; to be fixed; **KIMERU** to settle, decide; to arrange; to determine; **hi o kimeru** to set the day; **kimeta jikan ní** at the appointed time; **hará o kimeru** to make up one's mind. **Hanashí ga kimaru.** The matter is settled.

kimazui disagreeable, unpleasant.

kimetsukéru to scold, reprimand.

kimi = anata you (used colloq. by men).

kimí egg yolk.

kimijika na short-tempered, touchy.

kimochi feeling, sensation; **kimochi no yói** pleasant; refreshing; **kimochi ga warúi** to feel uncomfortable.

KIMONO Japanese clothing, garment; **kimono o kiru** to get dressed; **kimono o núgu** to get undressed; **kimono o kikaéru** to change one's clothes.

kimuzukashíi hard to please; moody.

KÍN gold; money; **kin'iro no** golden; **kinpatsu** blond hair.

kinchoku conscientiousness; **kinchoku na** conscientious; scrupulous; discreet; honest.

kinchoo tension, strain; **kinchoo suru** to strain; to become tense.

kíndai modern times; **kindai shísoo** modern ideas; **kindaika suru** to modernize.

kin'en prohibition against smoking; **kin'énsha** non-smoker.

kinen commemoration, remembrance; memory; **kinen suru** to commemorate; **kinen no táme ni** in memory of; **kinénhi** monument.

kingan nearsightedness; **kinankyoo** eye-glasses for a near-sighted person. (See also **kinshigan.**)

KÍNJO neighborhood; **kínjo no** neighboring; **kínjo no hitó** neighbor.

kinkán kumquat.

kínko safe; cashbox.

kínniku muscles; **kínniku róodoo** physical labor; **kínniku no** muscular.

kínomi kinomama de in the clothes one is wearing; without changing clothes; **kínomi kinomama de neru** to go to sleep without changing into pajamas.

KINOO = sakújitsu yesterday; **kinoo no híru** yesterday at noon. **Kinoo gakkoo o yasumimáshita.** I was absent from school yesterday.

kinshi prohibition, ban, embargo; **kinshi suru** to prohibit, forbid; **kinshi o tóku** to lift an embargo. **Kitsuen kinshi.** No smoking.

kinshigan = kingan nearsightedness; **kinshigan no** nearsighted.

kinshu abstinence, teetotalism; **kinshu suru** to abstain from drinking alcoholic beverages.

KÍNU silk; **kinu ito** silk thread; **kinu orímono** silk fabric; **kinu ura** silk lining.

kinuke (*n.*) being dejected; **kinuke no shita** dejected, spiritless; absent-minded; **kinuke suru** to be dejected.

KIN'YÓOBI Friday.

kínzoku metal; **kínzoku no** metallic; **kinzoku séihin** metal goods; hardware.

kin zúru to forbid, prohibit; to suppress.

kioku memory, recollection; **kioku suru** to remember, recollect; **kioku subéki** memorable, noteworthy; **kioku ga yói** to have a good memory; **kioku ga warúi** to have a poor memory.

kippári to explicitly, distinctly; definitely, decidedly; **kippári to kotowáru** to refuse flatly.

KIPPU ticket, pass; **kippu o kíru** to punch a ticket; **kippu úriba** ticket window.

KIRAI dislike, distaste, aversion; **kirai na** distasteful; abominable. **Kirai desu.** I dislike it. I don't like it.

kírakira brilliantly; glitteringly; **kírakira suru** to glitter; to dazzle.

KIRAKU NA easy-going, easy, carefree, happy-go-lucky; **kiraku na monó** easygoing person; **kiraku ni kurasu** to take things easy; to lead a relaxed life. **Dóozo okiraku ni.** Make yourself comfortable!

kiraméku to glitter, sparkle.

kirásu to run out of, be short of; **íki o kirásu** to be short of breath.

kirau to dislike; to hate, detest.

KIRÉ piece, bit, scrap, fragment; slice; dress goods, cloth; **momen no kiré** cotton cloth. **Pán o hitókire kudasái.** Please give me a piece of bread.

KÍREI NA beautiful, lovely, pretty; handsome, good-looking; clean; clear; **kírei na onna no hito** a beautiful (good-looking) woman; **kírei na mizu** clear water; **kírei ni suru** to clean; to tidy up; to put in order.

kiremé gap, break; pause, intermission; **kiremé o tsunagu** to close a gap.

kiremono cutlery, knives.

kiréru to cut (well); to be sharp; to run out; to be worn out; to wear out. **Kimono ga kiréta.** The clothes have worn out. **Náifu ga yóku kiréru.** The knife cuts well. **Kígen ga kiréta.** The term has expired.

kiri fog, mist; **kiri ame** drizzle; **kiribue** foghorn. **Kiri ga fukái.** Is is foggy.

kirí end; limit; **kirí ga nái** unlimited.

-kiri suffix denoting: all (there is); only; sole; no more. **Korekkiri désu.** This is all I have.

kiriagéru to stop; to close; to cut short; to wind up; **hanashí o kiriagéru** to end a talk; cut a conversation short.

kiridásu to quarry; to cut down (timber); to break ice; **hanashí o kiridásu** to broach a subject; to break the ice (conversationally).

kirihanásu to cut off; to separate.

kiriharáu to cut and clear away; prune.

kirihiráku to cut open; to clear (land).

kirikabu tree stump.

kiríkuchi cut end; opening; slit; section.

kirikuzúsu to cut down; to demolish.

kirimí fish slices, fillets.

kirinukéru to cut one's way through; to find the way out of (a difficulty); to struggle through; **kirinuki** cutting, clipping, scrap; excerpt; **kirinuku** to cut out, clip, etc.

KIRISUTO Christ.

KIRISUTOKYOO Christianity; **Kirisutokyoo Seinénkai** Y.W.C.A., **Kirisuto kyóokai** Christian church.

kiritsu order, discipline; rule, regulations; (*n.*) standing up; **kiritsu áru** orderly, disciplined; **kiritsu o mamóru** to obey the rules; **kiritsu suru** to stand up, to get to one's feet; **kiritsu o yabúru** to break the rules.

kiritsuméru to shorten, reduce, curtail; **híyoo o kiritsuméru** to cut down on expenses.

-KÍRO suffix denoting: kilometer; kilogram; kiloliter; kilowatt.

kiroku annals; archives; minutes, record; **kiroku suru** to record, write down, keep records.

KÍRU to cut; to chop; to carve; to break off (relations); **yubí o kíru** to cut one's finger; **denwa o kíru** to hang up (the telephone receiver). **Káre to wa té o kítta.** I am through with him.

KIRU to wear; to put on; **kimono o kíru** to put on clothes, dress; **kite iru** to be dressed in; to have on. **Náni o kite ikóo ka?** What shall I wear (in going there)?

kiryoku energy, vigor; virility; **kiryoku ga nái** to be languid, lacking in energy; **kiryoku ga otoroéru** to lose one's vigor; to have less energy.

kíryoo personal appearance, looks, features (usually used when speaking of women); **kíryoo no yói** pretty, beautiful, handsome, etc.

KISEN steamship, steamer; **kisen de** by ship; **kisen de íku** to go by ship; **kisen káisha** steamship company.

kiseru to dress, clothe; to plate, gild, coat; to impute; **tsúmi o hito ni kiseru** to put the blame on someone else.

KISÉTSU season; **kisétsu no** in season, seasonal; **kisetsu házure no** out of season; **kisetsu fuu** monsoon season; **sakura no kisétsu** cherry blossom season.

KISHÁ railroad train; writer, journalist; **kishá ni noru** to get on a train; **kishá de iku** to go by train; **kishá o oríru** to get off a train; **KISHÁCHIN** train fare; **yógisha** night train; **tsuushin kisha** correspondent; **kisháseki** press gallery.

KISHÍ shore, coast; bank; **mukoo gishi** other side of the river.

kishitsu disposition, temperament; **yói kishitsu no hitó** man of good disposition.

kishoku mood, feeling; **kishoku ga yói** to be in a good mood; to feel well; **kishoku ga warúi** to be in a bad mood.

kishoo weather; weather conditions; **kishoodai** weather bureau.

kishú horseman, jockey, rider.

kishuku lodging; room and board; **kishukunin** a boarder; **kishuku suru** to board at; **kishukúsha** dormitory.

KISÓKU rule, regulations; **kisoku tadashíi** regular; systematic, orderly; **kisoku tadáshiku** regularly, systematically; **kisóku o mamóru** to observe the rules.

KISSÁTEN tearoom; coffee shop.

kissui no pure; genuine.

kisúu odd number.

KITÁ north; **kitá no** northerly; northern.

kitaéru to forge; to drill, train; to discipline; to harden.

kitai expectation, anticipation. **kitai suru** to expect, hope for; to look forward to; to count on; **kitai ni sóu** to meet expectations.

kitaku suru to go home; to come home.

KITANÁI dirty; filthy; nasty; shabby; **kitanáku suru** to soil, make dirty.

kitchíri punctually, sharp; exactly; **kitchíri niji ni** at two o'clock sharp; at two on the dot.

kiteki siren; steam whistle; **kiteki o narasu** to blow a whistle; to sound a siren.

kiten ready wit; tact; **kiten no kiíta** tactful; quick-witted; **kiten o kikasu** to be on the alert.

kitoku serious, critical. **Seimei kitoku desu.** He is seriously ill.

kitsuen smoking; **kitsuen suru** to smoke; **kitsuénshitsu** smoking room; **kitsuénsha** smoking car (on a train).

kitsui brave; strong; intense; severe.

KITTE postage stamp; **kitte o haru** to put a stamp on (a letter). **Kono tegami ni wa íkura no kitte o harú n desu ka?** How much is the postage for this letter?

KITTO certainly, without fail; undoubtedly, surely. **Kitto kité kudasai.** Please be sure to come. **Kitto mairimásu.** Certainly I'll come.

kiwadátsu to stand out, be conspicuous; to be in contrast with.

kiwadói critical; dangerous, risky; **kiwadói shóobu** a close game (match); **kiwadói tokoró de** in the nick of time; at the last minute.

kiwaméru to exhaust; to get to the bottom of; to carry to an extreme; **shinsoo o kiwaméru** to get at the truth.

kiwámete extremely, exceedingly; excessively.

kíyoo na clever, skillful; ingenious; **kíyoo na hitó** jack-of-all-trades; handy man.

kiyowai timid, shy.

kíza na offensive; conceited.

kizetsu (*n.*) fainting; **kizetsu suru** to faint.

KIZU wound, injury, bruise; flaw, defect; **kizuato** scar; **kizugúsuri** ointment for a bruise or wound; **kizutsukéru** to hurt, injure, wound; **kizutsúku** to be wounded, hurt.

kizúkai fear; anxiety; **kizukare** worry; mental fatigue; **kizukare ga suru** to be worried.

kizutsúku to stick fast, cling.

kizúku to become aware of.

kizuyoi resolute; brave; **kizuyóku omóu** to be reassured; to be confident.

KO child; infant, baby; cub of an animal.

ko- prefix denoting: little, small; **koburi** light rain; light fall of snow; **koneko** kitten; **kojima** small island.

-ko suffix denoting: lake; **Biwako** Lake Biwa.

kobiritsúku to stick fast, cling.

kobore overflow; droppings; **kobore záiwai** windfall; godsend; **KOBORÉRU** to run over, overflow; to drop; to spill; to be scattered; **kobósu** to spill; to drop; to pour out; **námida o kobósu** to shed tears; **mizu o kobósu** to spill water.

kobú bump, swelling, protuberance.

KOCHIRA this place, here; this one; **KOCHIRAGAWA** this side. **Dóozo kochira e.** This way, please. **Tabakoya wa toori no kochiragawa désu.** The cigar store is on this side of the street.

kódachi grove, clump of trees.

KODOMO child; **kodomo rashíi** childish; **kodomoppói** childlike; childish. **Watakushi wa kodomo ga sannin arimásu.** I have three children. **Kodomoátsukai ni suru na.** Don't treat me like a child.

KÓE voice; **koedaka ni** in a loud voice; **kóe o kágiri ni** at the top of one's voice; **chiisái kóe de** in a low voice; softly; **kogoe** low voice; whisper; **kogoe de** in a low voice; in a whisper.

koeda twig, sprig, small branch.

koéru to cross, go across; to pass; to go beyond, exceed.

kogásu to burn; to scorch, singe.

kogatána small knife; pocketknife.

kogáwase postal money order.

kogechairo dark brown, umber.

kogéru to get scorched, to get burned.

KOGÍTTE (bank) check; **kogítte o kíru** to issue a check; **kogítte de shiharáu** to pay by check.

kogoeru to be frozen; to be chilled to the bone, be numb with cold.

kogoto scolding; blame; **kogoto o iu** to scold; **kogoto o kúu** to be scolded; to be blamed.

kógu to row; **kogiwatáru** to row across.

kohaku amber.

kói evil intention; evil will; **kói no** intentional, deliberate; **kói ni** on purpose, intentionally. **Koi no koto de wa arimasen.** It isn't anything that was done intentionally.

KÓI (*n.*) love; (*adj.*) dark; deep; thick; strong (as tea); **kói suru** to love; to fall in love; **koibito** lover; **koishíi** dear; beloved; **koishigáru** to yearn for.

koishi pebble.

koitsu this man (vulgar). **Koitsu!** You rat!

kojikí beggar.

kójin individual; private citizen; **kojinteki** personal, private individual; **kojinsei** individuality.

kojinmári to cozily; **kojinmári to shita** snug, cozy.

kojiréru to go wrong; to get complicated.

kojíru to wrench; **kojiakeru** to wrench open.

kojitsuke distortion; forced meaning; **kojitsuke no** distorted; farfetched; **kojitsukéru** to distort, (twist) the meaning.

kokage shade of a tree.

kokiorósu to disparage; to abuse.

kokitsukáu to work like a horse; to drive (someone) hard.

kókka state, country, nation; **kokkágaku** political science; **kokka shúgi** nationalism.

kokkai parliament, national assembly, Diet.

kokkan severe cold, intense cold.

kokkei na comical; **kokkei na hanashi** funny (comical) story.

kokki (national) flag.

kokkoo diplomatic relations.

kokkyoo frontier, border; boundaries.

KOKO this place; here; **koko ni** here, in this place; **koko kara** from here; **koko shibáraku** for the present; for some time to come. **Koko da, koko da.** Here we are. This is the place.

kókoku one's native land.

KOKONOKA ninth day of the month.

KOKÓNOTSU nine.

KOKORÓ heart; mind; spirit; **kokoro áru hito** thoughtful person; **kokoro yukú made** as one pleases; to one's heart's content; **kokoró ni kakáru** to be anxious; **kokoró ni ukabu** to occur to one; **kokoró ni tomeru** to bear in mind; **kokoró ga kawaru** to change one's mind; **kokoro yásuku náru** to become intimate; **kokoro no ookíi** broadminded; **kokoro átari** clue; **kokoro átari ga nái** to have no idea of; **KOKORO BOSÓI** helpless; uneasy; **kokoro bósoku omóu** to feel helpless; **kokoroe** understanding; knowledge; **kokoroe chigai** misunderstanding, misapprehension; **KOKOROÉRU** to know; to think; to consider.

kokorogákari care; anxiety; concern; **kokorogákari ni náru** to feel uneasy; to be anxious; **kokorogake** purpose, intention, aim; attention; **kokorogake no yói** careful; conscientious; **kokorogakéru** to keep in mind; to think about; **kokorogámae** preparedness; **kokorogáwari** change of

mind; caprice; **kokorogáwari no suru** fickle; faithless; capricious.

kokorogumi design; intention.

kokorogurushíi to be uneasy.

kokoromi trial; experiment; attempt; **kokoromi ni** tentatively; **kokoromíru** to try, attempt, make an attempt.

kokoromochi feeling, sensation; mood; idea; shade; **íi kokoromochi ga suru** to feel comfortable; **kokoromochi yóku** willingly; **kokoromochi o wáruku suru** to hurt (someone's) feelings; to displease.

kokoromotonái insecure; apprehensive.

kokoronáki thoughtless; heartless.

kokorone feelings; heart.

kokoroyasúi intimate, friendly.

kokoroyói pleasant, agreeable, nice; delightful.

kokorozashi will; intention; motive; **kokorozásu** to intend; to aim at, aspire to.

kokorozúkai worry, anxiety, concern.

KOKOROZUKE tip, gratuity.

kokorozuyói assuring.

koku- prefix denoting: pertaining to a country, nation, or state; **kokuboo** national defense; **kokufu** national wealth; **kokuhoo** law of the land; **kokúgai** abroad; overseas; outside the country; **kokugo** (national) language; Japanese language; **KOKUMIN** nation; people; **kokumin kéizai** national economy; **kokumin séikatsu** national life; **kokuseki** nationality, citizenship.

kokuban blackboard; **kokubán fuki** blackboard eraser.

kokubyaku black and white; right and wrong; **kokubyaku o tsukéru** to tell right from wrong; to discriminate between good and bad; **kokubyaku o arasóu** to argue the merits (of something).

kokuhatsu prosecution; indictment; accusation.

Kokujin Negro; **Kokujínshu** Negro race.

kokúmotsu cereals, grain, corn; **kokumotsugura** granary.

kokúnai (*n.*) interior; **kokúnai no** domestic; internal; home; **kokunai shoogyoo** domestic commerce.

kokyuu breath; breathing; **kokyuu suru** to breathe.

KOMÁKA NA = KOMAKÁI small, minute; fine, detailed; delicate; thrifty; **komáka na koto** trifling matter; **komakáku chúui suru** to pay close attention.

komaraseru to annoy; to trouble; to muzzle; **KOMÁRU** to be distressed; to be embarrassed; to be in trouble; to have a hard time, be hard up.

KOMÉ rice; **komé o tsukúru** to grow (cultivate) rice.

komiáu to be crowded; to be full; to swarm; **KÓMU** to be crowded; to be jammed;

to be full up. **Kono kishá wa kómu deshoo.** This train will probably be crowded.

kómichi path, lane.

komiíru to be complicated; to get entangled.

komogómo alternately, by turns; reciprocally.

komugi wheat; corn; **komugiko** wheat flour.

kon- prefix denoting: present, current; **KÓNBAN** this evening; tonight; **konchoo** this morning; **KONGETSU** this month; **kongetsu tooka** on the tenth of this month; **KÓNNICHI** today; nowadays; the present time; **kónnichi ígo** from now on; from today on. **KONBAN WA.** Good evening. **KONNICHI WA!** Good morning! Good day!

koná flour; powder; **konagona ni kudáku** to break into pieces; pulverize; **konasu** to grind, reduce to powder; to digest; to handle; **joozú ni konasu** to handle with skill.

konboo club, cudgel.

KONDATE menu.

KÓNDO now; this time; next time; new; **kóndo no** this; next; coming; **kóndo iku tóki** the next time I go. **Kóndo no kisha de ikimashoo.** Let's take the next train. **Kóndo wa yurúshite agemásu.** I'll forgive you this time.

kongarakáru to get entangled, become involved; to get confused.

kón'i acquaintance; friendship; **kón'i na** intimate, familiar; **kón'i ni shite iru** to be on friendly terms.

KONÍMOTSU baggage, luggage.

konki energy; perseverance; patience; **konki no yói** energetic.

konmóri densely; thickly; **konmori shigétta** densely wooded.

KONNA such; this sort of; **konna fúu ni** in this manner; **konna tóki ni** at a time like this.

kónnan difficulty; difficulties; troubles; **kónnan na** difficult; troublesome; **kónnan suru** to be in difficulty, be in trouble.

KONO this; these; **konogoro** lately; **kono hen ni** in this neighborhood; **kono tsúgi** next time; **kono máe** before this; the last time; **kono saki** hereafter; in the future; **kono yo** this world; this life; **kono yo no** worldly, mundane; **kono yóo na** such; of this sort.

KONOAIDA the other day; recently; not too long ago. **konoaida no ban** the other evening.

KONOGORO these days. **Konogoro wa ikága desu ka?** How have you been lately?

KONOKÁTA since; **júnnen konokáta** these ten years; in the past ten years.

konomí liking, preference, choice; **konómu** to like, be fond of; to prefer.

konran commotion, confusion, disorder;

konran suru to be confused, be in confusion.

KONSHUU this week. **Konshuu no Kin'yóobi ni kité kudasái.** Please come to see me this week on Friday.

konton chaos; **konton táru** chaotic.

kon'yaku (marriage) engagement, betrothal; **kon'yaku suru** to be engaged; **kon'yaku o háki suru** to break an engagement.

kónzatsu disorder; complication; **kónzatsu suru** to be in disorder, be confused; to be complicated.

KOO this way. **Koo shite kudasái.** Please do it this way. **Koo nátte wa shikata ga nái.** We can't do much when things go this way.

kooan design, plan; **kooan suru** to design, scheme, plan.

KOOBÁ factory, mill. **Watakushi wa ano koobá de hataraite imásu.** I am working at that factory.

koobashíi fragrant; savory; favorable.

KOOCHA Western black tea.

koochoo school principal; high tide; climax.

koodan platform, pulpit, rostrum.

koodoo action, movement; conduct, behavior; lecture hall; auditorium; **koodoo suru** to act, conduct oneself; to move.

KOOEN park, public gardens; support, aid, backing; lecture; address; **kooen suru** to back up, support; **kooénsha** lecturer; supporter.

kóofu workman.

koofuku happiness; well-being; bliss; good fortune; **koofuku na** happy; fortunate; **koofuku ni kurasu** to live a happy life.

koofun stimulation; excitement; **koofun suru** to be stimulated; to be excited.

KÓOGAI suburbs.

koogen plateau.

koogi lecture, discourse.

koogyoo industry; manufacturing; **koogyóochi** manufacturing district; **koogyooka** manufacturer; **kóogyoo no** industrial.

koohei impartiality; fair play; **koohei na** fair, just, impartial.

KOOHII coffee.

koohyoo favorable criticism; **koohyoo de áru** to be popular, win popularity; to receive favorable criticism.

kóoi kind intentions; kindness.

KOO IU such; this sort of; **koo iu fúu ni** this way; **koo iu kotó** such a thing as this.

kooji construction; works; alley, lane, narrow street; **kooji chuu** under construction; **hirokooji** boulevard, avenue.

koojíru to grow worse, change for the worse.

koojitsu excuse, pretext.

koojóo works, factory, mill.

kóoka effect, result, fruits; **kóoka ga nái** not to take effect; to have no result or effect; **kóoka ga áru** to be effective.

kóokai voyage, crossing; **kóokai suru** to sail; navigate.

KOOKAN favorable impression, good impression; exchange; **íken kookan** exchange of views; **kookan kákaku** exchange value; **kookándai** telephone switchboard; **kookánshu** telephone operator.

kookei spectacle, sight; scene.

kooken suru to contribute, make a contribution toward; to be conducive to; to go far toward.

kookíshin curiosity; **kookishin no tsuyoi** curious.

KOOKOKU advertisement; notice, announcement; **kookoku bíra** poster, placard; **kookoku suru** to advertise.

kóokoo (*n.*) filial piety; obedience to parents; (*adv.*) so and so; such and such; **kóokoo iu wáke de** under such (these) circumstances.

kookotsu rapture, ecstasy; **kookotsu to suru** to be in ecstasy; to be enraptured; to be enchanted.

kookuubin airmail.

kookúuki aircraft.

kookyoo (*n.*) public; society; prosperity; business boom; **kookyoo no** public; common; booming, prosperous; **kookyóoshin no áru** community-minded.

kookyóogaku symphony; **kookyoogakudan** symphony orchestra.

KOONOO = **kóoryoku** effect, efficacy; virture; **koonoo no nái** ineffective; **koonoo no áru** effective; useful; **koonoo ga áru** to be good for; to be effective; be useful.

KOORI ice; **koori no hatta** frozen; covered with ice; **koorízume no** refrigerated; iced; **kooru** to freeze.

kooroo merits; meritorious deed; **kooroo áru** meritorious.

kooron public opinion; dispute; **kooron suru** to dispute, quarrel.

kóoryoku = **KOONOO** effect, efficacy; **kóoryoku no áru** valid; effective.

koosa intersection, crossing; **koosa suru** to interesect, cross **koosáten** intersection, crossroad.

koosai intercourse; association; society; company; fellowship; **koosaika** sociable person; good mixer.

koosan surrender, capitulation; **koosan suru** to surrender, submit; **koosan saseru** to make someone surrender.

koosatsu consideration; contemplation; **koosatsu suru** to consider, weigh; to examine; to contemplate.

kooseki distinguished service.

koosen light; beam (ray) of light; **koosen o ireru** to let in the light.

koosetsu public; municipal; **koosetsu shíjoo** public market.

kóoshi lecturer; minister (diplomatic service);

kooshíkan legation; **kooshikán'in** attaché; legation personnel.

kooshiki formula; formality; **kooshiki no** formal; state; official; **kooshiki de arawásu** to formulate.

kooshoo negotiation; **kooshoo chuu** under negotiation; **kooshoo suru** to negotiate; **nánra no kooshoo mo nái** to have nothing to do with.

kooshuu (*n.*) public; **kooshuu bénjo** comfort station, public lavatory; **kooshuu yókujoo** public bath; **kooshuu no** public; common.

koosoku confinement; restraint; detention; **koosoku suru** to confine, detain, etc.; **koosoku o úkete inái** to be free from restraint.

koosókudo high speed; rapid transit.

koosui perfume, cologne, scent; **koosui o tsukéru** to use perfume.

kootai relief; substitution; **kootai ni** alternately; in turn; **kootai suru** to relieve; take turns.

Kootáishi Crown Prince.

kootei fluctuation; high and low; unevenness; undulations; affirmation; **kootei áru** fluctuating; undulating; **kootei suru** to affirm; to acknowledge; **kooteiteki** affirmative.

kootoo oral, verbal; **kootoo de** orally, verbally; **kootoo gákkoo** senior high school.

KOOTSUU communication; traffic; **kootsuu kikán** means of communication; **kootsuu o séiri suru** to control traffic; **kootsuu no bén o hakáru** to facilitate communications.

kootsúgoo favorable circumstances; **kootsúgoo no** convenient; **kootsúgoo na** favorable; fortunate; **kootsúgoo ni** conveniently, etc.; **kootsúgoo de áru** to suit one's convenience.

kooun good luck, stroke of luck; **kooun na** lucky, fortunate; **kooun ní mo** fortunately; luckily.

kooza (university) chair, professorship; university course.

kóozan mine; **koozan gíshi** mining engineer; **koozángyoo** mining industry.

koozen openly; in public; **koozen no** open; public; official.

koozoo construction; structure; formation.

kóozui flood, inundation.

KOPPU glass (for drinking). **Koppu ni mizu o íppai kudasái.** May I have a glass of water? (See also **káppu.**)

koraéru to bear, endure; to control; to restrain; **itása o koraéru** to endure the pain.

KORE this; these; **kore hodo** this much; so much, so many; **kore kágiri** this is all; once and for all.

korikatamáru to coagulate; to be absorbed in; to be bigoted.

korikóri suru to learn from experience; **koríru** to take warning from; to learn by experience.

-KÓRO suffix denoting: about (said only of a point of time); **konogoro** these days, nowadays; **juuji kóro** about ten o'clock.

koroai suitable; adequate, handy; **koroai o hakátte** just in time.

korobu to roll over; to tumble down; **korogaru** to roll to; to tumble; to fall; to lie down; **korogasu** to roll; to tumble down.

korosu to kill, put to death; **íki o koroshite** with bated breath, breathlessly.

kóru to be absorbed in; to be devoted to; to get stiff; **kenkyuu ni kóru** to be absorbed in one's studies; **tabemóno ni kóru** to be fussy about eating.

kosame light rain, drizzle.

kósei individuality; personality; idiosyncracy.

KOSHI hip(s); waist; loin. **KOSHI O KAKÉRU** to sit, take a seat (on a chair); **koshi o suéru** to settle down; **koshi byóobu** low folding-screen; **koshikáke** seat, stool, etc.; **KOSHIKAKÉRU** to sit on a chair.

KOSHIRAERU to make, manufacture; to prepare; to build; to raise; **hako o koshiraeru** to make a box; **kane o koshiraeru** to raise funds; to make a fortune.

koshoo obstacle, hitch; defect; accident; protest, objection; mechanical trouble; **koshoo náku** without a hitch; without any trouble. **Koshoo ga nái.** Nothing is wrong. Nothing is the matter.

KOSHÓO pepper.

kósokoso stealthily, secretly, sneakingly; **kósokoso déte iku** to sneak out.

kosu to go over, go across; to outrun; to move; to pass; **yamá o kosu** to go over the top; to pass the most difficult point.

kosui lake; **kosui no sóba** lakeside.

kosúru to rub; to scrub; to scrape; **mé o kosúru** to rub one's eyes.

kotáe answer, reply, response; solution; **KOTAÉRU** to answer, reply, respond; to come home; to strike home; to have an effect on; to be a strain on;—**ni kotáete** in reply (answer) to; **sóo da to kotaéru** to answer in the affirmative; **shitsumon ni kotaéru** to answer a question. **Ano hito no kotoba wa mi ni kotaemashita.** His words came home to me.

KOTE iron (for clothes); soldering iron; trowel; **kote o ateru** to iron clothes; to solder; to curl with tongs.

KOTÓ thing; matter; affair; account; event, occurrence; duty, task; **kotó naku** without a hitch; uneventfully, peacefully. **Sore wa nán no kotó desu ka?** What does it mean? What do you mean? **Sore wa kotó to baai ni yoru.** That depends on the circumstances.

kotoyósete on the pretense that; under the guise of. **Byooki ni kotoyósete jishoku shimashita.** He resigned his post on the pretext of ill health.

KOTOBÁ language; word; term; speech; expression; **kotobá o kakéru** to speak; to call to; **kotobá o kawasu** to exchange words with; **kotobá o nigósu** to give a vague answer; **kotoba tákumi ni** persuasively, convincingly. **Kono kotoba no imi wa nán desu ka?** What is the meaning of this word?

KOTOGÓTOKU wholly, entirely; completely; without exception, in every case. **Koko ni aru hón wa kotogotoku yomimashita.** I have read all the books here.

KÓTO NI especially; above all, moreover. **koto no hoka** remarkably, extremely, unusually.

kotosara ni intentionally, on purpose, purposely.

KOTOSHI this year; present year. **Kotoshi no natsú wa taihen atsúi desu.** It is very hot this summer.

kotowári excuse; denial; refusal; warning; notice; **kotowári mo náku** without permission, without one's knowledge; **KOTOWÁRU** to make excuses; to refuse, decline; to ask permission; **téi yoku kotowáru** to decline politely.

kotowaza saying, maxim, proverb.

kótsukotsu to untiringly; laboriously; **kótsukotsu to arúku** to plod; **kótsukotsu to shigoto o suru** to work untiringly.

kowabáru to stiffen; to get stiff.

kowagáru to fear, be afraid of; to be frightened; **kowagowa** timidly, fearfully. **Nani mo kowagaru kotó wa nái.** You have nothing to be afraid of.

kowái fearful, frightful, terrible, horrible; **kowái kao** angry look; grim face; **kowái mé ni áu** to have a terrible experience.

koware breakage; fragment; **kowaremono** fragile thing; **KOWARÉRU** to break; to be broken; to be ruined; **kowareyasúi** fragile; **KOWASÚ** to break down; to destroy, demolish, smash, wreck; **ié o kowásu** to pull down a house; **karada o kowásu** to ruin one's health. **Mádo ga kowárete imasu.** The window is broken.

koyá hut, shed, cabin; pen.

koyashí manure; fertilizer.

koyomi calendar; almanac.

KÓZÚTSUMI parcel; small package; **kozutsumi yúubin de** by parcel post.

KU = KYUU nine; pain; suffering; bitterness; **dáiku** ninth; **kú ni náru** become worried about; bother; to cause anxiety; **kú ni suru** take seriously; be concerned about, be worried about. **Áme wa sukoshi mo kú ni narimasén.** The rain doesn't bother me at all. **Sonna kotó o kú ni surú na.** Don't trouble yourself about such a matter.

kubáru to distribute; to deal out; to dispose

(of); **shíhoo ni mé o kubáru** to deliver a newspaper.

kúbetsu distinction; classification, division; **kúbetsu suru** to distribute; to differentiate (between good and bad); **kúbetsu o tsukéru** to make a distinction.

KUBI neck; head; **kubi ni suru** to dismiss; discharge; **kubi ni náru** to be dismissed; **kubi o nágaku shite matsu** to wait impatiently; **kubimaki** scarf, muffler; **kubíwa** necklace; (dog) collar.

kubomi cavity; hollow; dent; **kubomu** to become hollow; to be depressed; to sink.

KUBU DOORI nearly; in all probability; ten to one. **Kubu doori dekimashita.** It is nearly done.

kubun division; **kubun suru** to divide, partition.

KUCHI mouth; door; aperture; hole; post; kind; share; **kuchi no tassha na** fluent; **kuchi no karui** talkative; **kuchi ga aku** to open; burst open; **kuchi o kíru** to break a seal; to open the mouth; **KUCHIBIRU** lips; **kuchibue** whistle; **kuchibue o fúku** to whistle.

kuchidashi meddling, interference; **kuchidashi suru** to meddle; to poke one's nose in someone else's business.

kuchidome suru to hush up (a matter); to stop (someone) from speaking.

kuchigótae retort; **kuchigótae suru** to answer back.

kuchiurusái nagging; critical.

kuchiyakamashíi = **kuchiurusai** nagging; critical.

KUDÁMONO fruit; **kudamónoya** fruit-seller. **Kudamono ga hoshii desu.** I want some fruit.

KUDARANAI stupid; foolish; absurd; useless; insignificant; **kudaranai kotó o iu** to talk foolishly.

kudari (n.) going down; down; **kudarizaka** downgrade; downhill.

KUDASAI please give me. **Sore o kudasái.** Please give it to me.

kudasáru to offer; to give. **Kore o watakushi ni kudasáru no desu ka?** Is this for me? **Hitótsu kudasaru wáke ni wa ikimasén ka?** Can't you spare me one of these?

kudói tedious; long-winded.

kudóku to make love to; to attempt to seduce; to entreat; to solicit.

KÚGATSU September.

kugi nail; **kugi o útsu** to nail; **kugi o sásu** to remind someone of what he must do.

kugirí full stop; pause; period; **kugirí o tsukéru** to settle; to put an end to.

kugúru to pass through; **món o kugúru** to go through a gate.

kui post; stake; pile.

kúiki limit; boundary; **kúiki no** inside the boundary.

kuikomi loss; deficit; **kuikómu** to eat into; to encroach upon; to leave a deficit; to go into one's capital **Sengetsu wa ichi man en kuikomimashita.** Last month there was a deficit of ten thousand yen.

kuíru to regret; be sorry for.

kuitomeru to check; hold in check; arrest.

kuitsuku to bite; to snap; to take the bait. **Inu ni ashi o kuitsukaremashita.** I was bitten by a dog.

kuitsuméru to have no means of subsistence.

kujikéru to be disheartened; to lose heart.

kujíku to sprain; wrench; break; crush; discourage; **udé o kujíku** to break an arm; **ashíkubi o kujíku** to sprain an ankle.

KUJÚU = KYÚUJUU ninety.

KUKKÍRI clearly; distinctly; plainly; strikingly.

kukyoo adversity; awkward situation; **kukyoo ni ochíiru** to be put in an awkward situation.

kumen contrivance; makeshift; **kumen suru** to devise; to contrive; to manage.

KUMÍ class; gang; band; company; team; crew; set, pack, etc.; **kumigáshira** head of a group; boss; **kumiawaséru** to combine, join together; to match; **kúmiai** association; guild; partnership; **kumiáiin** member (of an association); **kumiai kéisan** joint account; **kumiawaséru** to combine; to group together.

kumidásu to dip out; to bail out.

kumitate structure, framework; system, organization.

KÚMO cloud(s); **kúmo o tsuku yóo na** lofty; towering; **kúmo o tsukámu yóo na** vague; visionary; **kumogire** break in the clouds; **kumo yuki o míru** to see how the wind blows; to wait for the results; **kumori** cloudy, overcast; **kumori náki** clean; clear; cloudless; spotless; **kumoríbi** cloudy day; **kumori gárasu** frosted glass; **KUMÓRU** to get cloudy. **Sóra ga kumotte kimashita.** The sky is getting cloudy. **Káre wa kao ga kumorimashita.** His face became clouded.

kúmu to unite; to associate with; to be in a partnership with; to braid; to fit together; to pair with; **híza o kúmu** to cross one's legs; **udé o kúmu** to fold one's arms.

-kun suffix denoting: Mr. (same as **san** but used only for and by men); **Yamada-kun** Mr. Yamada.

KUNI country, land, state, nation; province; territory; **kunimoto** native (home) province; **kuni námari** dialect. **Dóno kuni kara irasshaimashita ka?** From which country have you come?

kurá warehouse; storehouse; granary; **kurabárai** clearance sale.

KURABERU to compare; to contrast; to match; **ookisa o kuraberu** to compare the size.

kuragari darkness; dark place; **kuragari de** in the dark.

KURAI (n.) grade, rank; (adj.) dark, dim, gloomy; obscure; **kurai suru** to stand; to be situated, to be located; to lie; **kurai ga tsuku** to gain in dignity; **kuraku náru** to get (become) dark. **Anmari kurai desu.** It's too dark.

-KURAI about; some; no more than; how much (how far, etc.); **kore kurai** this much; so much. **Dono kurai kakari máshita ka?** How much did it cost (you)?

kurashi living, livelihood; **kurashikata** one's manner of living; **kurashi o tatéru** to make one's living; **KURASU** to live; to make a living; **rippa ni kurasu** to live well.

kurayami dark, darkness; **kurayami de** in the dark.

kuregure repeatedly; earnestly.

KURERU to give; to grant. **Anó hito ga watakushi ni sore o kureta.** He gave it to me.

kureru to grow dark. **Hi ga kurete kimashita.** The day is growing dark.

kuréyon crayon.

kuriagéru to move up; advance; **kíjitsu o kuriagéru** to move up a date.

kuriawase arrangement.

kuriawaséru, kuriawásu to make time; to arrange the time.

kuriiréru to transfer; to carry forward.

KURIKÁESU to repeat; reiterate. **Moo ichido kurikáeshite kudasái.** Please repeat it.

kurikómu to carry over; to carry into.

kurikósu to transfer; to carry forward; to bring over.

KURISÚMASU Christmas.

KÚRO black; **kuro nuri no** black-lacquered; painted black; **kuro kumo** dark clouds; **KURÓI** tanned; dusky; **kurói kamí** black hair. **Anó hito wa iró ga kurói.** He has a dark complexion.

kúroo hardship; suffering; care, concern; **kuróo shoo no** nervous; worrisome; **kúroo suru** to work hard.

kuróoto expert; professional; specialist; connoisseur.

KÚRU to come; to come over; to arrive. **Háru ga kimáshita.** Spring has come. **Otégami ga kimáshita.** Here is a letter for you. **Ashita kuru deshoo.** It will probably come tomorrow.

kuruí disorder, confusion; madness; **kuruí ga kúru** to get out of order.

KURUMA car, vehicle, carriage, cart, wagon; wheel; ricksha; **kuruma de iku** to go by car.

kurumáru to be wrapped up in; to tuck oneself into or wrap oneself in; **kúrumu** to wrap up; to cover up; to coat, gild.

KURUSHII painful; hard; trying; distressing; **kurushíi mé ni áu** to undergo great suffering; **kurushíi tachíba ni iru** to be in an awkward position; **kurushiméru** to torment, torture; to persecute; **kokoró o kurushiméru** to worry; **doobutsu o kurushiméru** to be cruel to (an) animal (s); **kurushimi** pain, suffering; hardship; agony; torture; **KURUSHÍMU** to feel pain; to suffer from; to be worried; **hín ni kurushímu** to be poverty-stricken. **Náni o sonna ni kurushínde irú no desu ka?** What are you suffering so much from? What makes you suffer so?

kurúu to go mad; to get out of order; to go wrong; to fluctuate. **Kono tokei wa dóko ka kurútte iru.** There is something wrong with this watch.

kusá grass; herb; weed; **kusá o karu** to mow grass; **niwa no kusá o tóru** to weed a garden.

kusái stinking, bad-smelling; **kusamí** stink, offensive odor.

kusarásu to corrupt; to cause to decay; to spoil; **kusáru** to rot, decay; to turn sour; to corrode; **kusátta** rotten; sour. **ki ga kusáru** to feel low.

kusari chain; tether.

kusé habit, way; characteristic, peculiarity; **kusé ga tsuku** to get into a habit; **kusé o tsukéru** to form a habit; **kusé o naósu** to break a habit.

kushakusha na creased; wrinkled.

kushami sneezing; sneeze; **kushami ga déru** to sneeze.

KUSHÍ comb; **kushí** skewer, spit; **kushí de kamí o tóku** to comb hair.

kushín care; anxiety; struggle; **kushín suru** to take pains; to do one's best.

kushoo bitter smile; forced smile.

kusubúru to smoke, smolder; **uchi ni kusubútte iru** to remain indoors.

KUSURI medicine, drug; remedy; cure; physic; **kusuri o kau** to buy a medicine; **kusuri o nómu** to take a medicine; **kusuriya** pharmacist; druggist; drugstore.

KUTABIRÉRU = TSUKARERU to get tired; to be exhausted; **machikutabiréru** to be tired of waiting.

KUTSU shoes; boots; **kutsu zure ga dekíru** to have one's feet hurt from one's shoes; **kutsu bake** shoebrush; **kutsu himo** shoelace; **kutsúzumi** shoe polish; **KUTSÚYA** shoe store; shoe-repair shop.

kutsurógu to be at ease; to relax; to make oneself comfortable; **kutsuróide hanásu** to have a heart-to-heart talk.

KUTSÚSHITA socks; stockings; **kutsushitadome** garters.

kuttsukéru to join; to attach; to glue; to stick.

KÚUKI air; atmosphere; **shinsen na kúuki** fresh air; **kuuki no ryuutsuu** the ventilation of air.

kuusoo fancy; vision; fantasy; **kuusooka** dreamer; **kuusooteki** visionary; imaginary; **kuusoo o egáku** to build castles in the sky.

kuwadate plan, scheme; attempt, undertaking; **kuwadatéru** to plan, scheme; to devise; to attempt, undertake.

kuwaéru to add (up); to give; to deliver; to offer; **bujoku o kuwaeru** to insult someone; **Ní ni ní o kuwaeru to yón desu.** Two and two are four.

kuwaeru to hold in the mouth; to bite; **yubí o kuwaete** looking wistfully [with finger in the mouth].

KUWASHÍI to be well versed; detailed; minute; particular; familiar with; **kuwáshiku** minutely; in detail; at length; particularly; **kuwáshiku nobéru** to explain in detail; to give full particulars. **Kuwashíi hanashí wa áto de hanashimashóo.** Later we shall talk about it in detail. **Ano hito wa rekishi ni kuwashíi desu.** He is well versed in history.

KUWAWARU to join; to enter; to participate, take part in; **ikkoo ni kuwawaru** to join the party; **kyóogi ni kuwawaru** to take part in the same.

kuyamí condolence; repentance; regret; **kuyamíjoo** letter of condolence; **kuyami o nobéru** to offer one's condolences; **kuyámu** to regret; to repent of; to lament; **kuyashíi** regrettable; vexing; **kuyáshisa** regret.

kúyokuyo suru to worry about; to worry (oneself); to take to heart; to brood over.

kuuzen no unprecedented; unequaled; record-breaking. **Sore wa kuuzen no dekigoto desu.** That is an unprecedented event.

kúzu waste, refuse, trash; **kuzúkago** wastepaper basket; **kuzutetsu** scrap iron.

kuzuréru to go to pieces, collapse, give way; to get out of shape.

KUZÚSU to pull down; to break down; to destroy; to change. **Kono sen en satsu o kuzushite kudasai.** Please break this one-thousand-yen bill.

KYAKU visitor; guest; customer; patron; passenger; **kyakusha** passenger train; **kyakusen** passenger boat; **okyaku sama** personal guest (*pol.*).

kyakuhon script, scenario; **kyakuhon sákusha** playwright; **kyakushoku** dramatization; adaptation; plot.

kyóhi suru to deny, refuse; to reject.

kyóka permission; leave; admission; license;

kyóka suru to permit, allow; to admit; to authorize.

kyóku office; department; bureau; **kyóku ni ataru** to take charge; to face a situation; **kyokuin** office staff.

KYOKUTOO Far East.

KYÓNEN last year; **kyónen no Ichigatsu** January of last year.

kyoo interest; amusement; **kyoo o samásu** to spoil the fun; **kyoo o soéru** to add to the fun; **kyoo ga áru** to be interested.

KYÓO today. **Kyóo wa nan'yóobi desu ka?** What day of the week is today?

kyooboo collusion, complicity; **kyooboo suru** to conspire; plot together; **kyoobóosha** accomplice.

kyoochoo co-operation; **kyoochoo suru** to co-operate; to act harmoniously.

KYÓODAI brothers (and sisters). **Kyóodai wa nánn in arimasu ka?** How many brothers and sisters do you have?

kyoodan teacher's platform; pulpit.

kyoodoo co-operation; collaboration; partnership; association; union; **kyoodoo dóosa** united action; **kyoodoo kánri** joint control; **kyoodoo no** common, joint; **kyoodoo bénjo** public toilet.

kyoofu fear, fright, dread; **kyoofu suru** to fear, etc.

kyoogaku coeducation.

kyóogi game, match; **kyoogijoo** arena; **kyoogíkai** tournament, meet; **kyoogísha** contestant.

kyóogi conference; discussion; **kyóogi suru** to consult; to confer with.

kyooguu condition; situation; circumstance.

kyoohaku compulsion; threat, menace; **kyoohaku suru** to compel; to threaten, intimidate.

kyoohan complicity; **kyoohánasha** accomplice.

kyóoi astonishment, wonder; **kyooiteki** surprising; wonderful.

kyooiku education; training; **kyooiku suru** to educate; to train; to bring up; **kyooin = kyóoshi** teacher; **kyooju** teaching; instruction; professor; faculty; **kyoojuhoo** methods of teaching.

kyookai association.

kyookai church; religious association; **kyookaidoo** church building; cathedral.

kyookai border, boundary.

kyoomei resonance; sympathy; response; **kyoomei suru** to sympathize with; to echo; respond to.

kyóomi interest, appeal; **kyóomi no áru** interesting; attractive; **kyóomi no nái** dull, uninteresting; lacking in appeal.

kyóoshi teacher, tutor; professor; master (See also **kyooiku**); **kyóoshitsu** schoolroom; classroom.

kyooshuku obligation; humiliation; **kyooshuku suru** to be much obliged, be grateful to, appreciate deeply; to be sorry for, regret. **Osokunátte kyooshuku desu.** I am sorry to be late.

kyoosoo competition, rivalry; foot race; sprint; **kyoosoo shikén** competitive examination; **kyoosoo suru** to compete, contest; to run a race.

kyoosóosha rival, competitor.

kyootei agreement, pact; **kyootei suru** to agree; to agree upon; **kyootei nédan** stipulated price.

kyootsuu no common; **kyootsúuten** common feature; thing in common.

kyooyaku agreement, pact.

kyooyoo extortion; exaction; **kyooyoo no** for common use; **kyooyoo suru** to extort; to use something in common.

kyooyuu co-ownership; **kyooyuu suru** to hold jointly; **kyooyúusha** co-owner, joint owner; **kyooyuuzáisan** common property.

kyoozai teaching materials.

kyóri distance; range; radius; **kyóri ga áru** to be far, distant.

kyozetsu refusal; rejection; **kyozetsu suru** to refuse; reject.

KYÚU = KU, KOKONOTSU nine.

kyúu class; grade (in a school); **ikkyuu** first grade; **nikyuu** second grade.

kyuu- prefix denoting: quick, sudden, abrupt; steep; **kyuubyoo** sudden illness; **kyuuhen** sudden change.

KYUU urgency; emergency; **kyuu ni** suddenly; **kyuu ni sonaéru** to provide for an emergency; **kyuu o tsugeru** to be urgent; to become critical; **kyuu o yoosúru** urgent; **kyuuba** critical moment; **kyuuba no shóchi** emergency measure.

kyúuchi difficult situation; fix.

kyuuen rescue; help; **kyuuen suru** to relieve; rescue; to reinforce.

kyuugyoo vacation; suspension of operation; **kyuugyoo suru** to close; to take a holiday; to suspend one's business.

KYUUJI waiter; office boy; cabin boy. **Kyuuji-san!** Waiter!

kyúujo relief, help; **kyúujo suru** to rescue, save; to help; **kyuujoami** safety net; **kyuujosen** lifeboat.

kyuuka holidays, vacation; leave of absence.

kyuukai adjournment; **kyuukai suru** to adjourn.

KYUUKOO express (train); **kyuukoo suru** to rush; to dash; to go like an express; **kyuukooréssha** express train; **tokubetsu kyuukooréssha** special express train; **kyuukooryóokin** express charges.

M

ma space; room; apartment; time, interval, spare moments; truth; **ma ga áru** to have time; **ma mó naku** before long, in a little while; **magashi suru** to rent out a room; **ma ga wáruku**

unfortunately; **ma ni ukéru** to accept as the truth; to believe what one hears.

MÁA come! do! indeed!; women-talk: well! I should say! **Máa dóoshita no?** Dear me! What happened? **Máa omachi nasái.** Just wait, please.

maatarashíi brand-new.

mabara sparse, thin; scattered; **mabara ni** sparsely, thinly; here and there.

mabátaki wink, blink; **mabátaki suru** to wink, blink; **mabátaki suru ma ni** in the twinkling of an eye.

mabayúi dazzling, glaring.

mabíku to thin out; to eliminate.

maboroshi phantom; apparition; vision; illusion.

mabúsu to cover with, sprinkle with.

MÁBUTA eyelid.

MACHI town, city; street; **machi házure** outskirts of town; **machí e iku** to go to town.

MACHIAISHITSU waiting room.

machiawaséru to meet, rendezvous (with); to wait for.

machibooke waiting in vain; **machibooke o kúu** to wait for someone in vain; **machibooke o kuwásu** to keep someone waiting in vain.

machidooshíi to be impatient; to be long in coming. **Omachidoo sama.** I'm sorry to have kept you waiting.

MACHIGAÉRU to mistake, err, make a mistake, blunder; **hatsuon o machigaéru** to pronounce incorrectly; **michi o machigaéru** to take the wrong road; **machigáete** by mistake, in error. **MACHIGAI** mistake, error; fault; accident; **machigái naku** without fail; certainly; **machigái o shoozúru** to cause an accident; **machigáu** to make a mistake. **Futatsu machigáemashita.** I made two mistakes.

machikamaéru to await eagerly; to wait anxiously; **machikanéru** to wait impatiently for. **Omachikane no nimotsu ga todokimashita.** The baggage that you have been waiting for so long has arrived.

machimachi diversity; variety; **machimachi no** diverse, various; divergent, conflicting.

MÁDA as yet; not yet (when used with a negative); still; so far. **Anó ko wa máda honno kodomo désu.** She (he) is still a mere child. **Máda futatsu arimasu.** We still have two.

MÁDE till, until, up to; to; as far as; **Tookyoo máde** as far as Tokyo; **ása kara ban máde** from morning till night.

MÁDO window; **mado gárasu** window pane; **mádo o akeru** to open a window. **Mádo o shiméru** to close a window.

MÁE time before; past; front; since; **máe no** previous, former; **máe ni** formerly, prior; **mae mótte** beforehand; **máe kara** previously; from the front.

máeba front tooth; front prop (support).

maebárai prepayment; **maebárai no** prepaid; **maebárai suru** to pay in advance.

maebure announcement; preliminary notice.

maekake apron.

maekóojoo prologue; preamble.

maeoki preliminary statement, introduction.

magari crook, bend, turn; **MAGARU** to bend; to yield; to turn; to wind; **magatta** bent, crooked, etc.; **magarikunétta michi** winding (rambling) road; **MAGERU** to bend, curve. **Soko o magete onegai itashimásu.** Please say yes. [Please bring yourself to consent (against your will).]

magirásu to turn away, divert; **ki o magirásu** to divert (someone's) attention.

magirawashíí confusing; ambiguous; misleading; **magire** confusion; **magire mo nái** evident, unmistakable; **magire mo náku** undoubtedly; **magirekómu** to get mixed with; lost among; **gunshuu ni magirekómu** to get lost in the crowd; to be hidden in the crowd; **magiréru** to be mistaken for; to become confused.

mágiwa verge, brink; **mágiwa ni** on the verge of; **mágiwa ni nátte** at the last minute.

MAGÓ grandchild.

magókoro sincerity; devotion; **magókoro no áru** sincere.

mágomago suru to be at a loss; to be bewildered.

magureátari lucky hit, lucky shot; fluke (*colloq.*).

MAGURO tuna fish.

mahi paralysis; numbness; **mahi suru** to be paralyzed; **mahi shíta** paralyzed.

MAI- prefix denoting: every, each; **maido** every time, each time; **maigetsu** every month; **mainen** every year; **máiasa** every morning; **máiban** every evening.

-MAI suffix denoting: sheet; piece; page; leaf (a counter); **kami sánmai** three sheets of paper.

majiwari association; relations; **majiwáru** to associate with; to mingle with. **Ano hito wa hito to majiwaru koto o kiraimasu.** He dislikes mingling with people.

makaséru to entrust (something to someone); to leave a person with some matter or business; **nariyuki ni makaséru** to let the matter take its course. **Bánji kimi ni makasemásu.** I leave everything to you.

makasu to beat; to overpower; to beat down (a price); to bargain; **hyaku yen ni makasu** to beat down the price to 100 yen. **Káre o iimakásu kotó ga dekínai.** I can't beat him in an argument.

make defeat; loss; lost game; **makeru** to lose, be defeated; to concede, yield; to be outdone; to reduce (the price); **makezu otórazu** closely matched. **Makete kuremasen ka?** Can't you make it cheaper?

makijaku tape measure.

makikómu to roll up; to wrap up, enfold in.

MAKITÁBAKO = SHIGARÉTTO cigarette; **makitábako ikko** pack of cigarettes; **makitabakóire** cigarette case.

MAKKÁ NA crimson, deep red; **makká na úso** outright lie; **makká ni náru** to turn red, blush deeply.

makkúra pitch darkness; **makkúra na** pitch dark.

MAKKÚRO NA deep black, ebony; **makkúro na kami nó ke** jet-black hair.

MAKOTO truth; sincerity; honesty; faithfulness; **makoto no** genuine; real; sincere; **MAKOTO NI** truthfully; sincerely; really; greatly, exceedingly.

makú curtain, hanging screen, drapery; act; **shomaku** opening act, first act; **makú o hikishibóru** to pull a curtain aside. **Makú ga aku.** The curtain rises.

MAKU to wind, roll, coil, reel; **tokei no neji o maku** to wind up a clock.

MÁKU to scatter, strew, sprinkle; to sow; **shibafu ni mizu o máku** to sprinkle the lawn with water.

MÁKURA pillow, cushion; **mákura o suru** to rest one's head on a pillow.

makuru to turn (roll, tuck) up; **udé o makuru.** To roll up one's sleeves.

makushitatéru to argue furiously.

MAMA as; as is; as it stands; intact; **sono mama** just as it is; **sono mama ni shite oku** to leave (something, or someone) as is. **Mamá yo.** I don't care. Never mind.

mamé beans; peas; soybeans; midget; tinny. **mame jidóosha** midget car.

mame na healthy, robust; brisk, active; faithful; **mame ni hataraku** to work briskly.

mamiréru to be covered, stained with; **doró ni mamiréru** to be covered with mud.

MAMÓRU to protect, defend, guard; to obey; **hoo o mamóru** to obey the laws; **yakusoku o mamóru** to keep a promise.

MAMÚKOO just opposite; just in front of; **mamúkoo no** just opposite; **mamúkoo ni** right (just) in front of.

MÁN ten thousand; myriad; **mán ni hitótsu** one in ten thousand.

manabu to learn, study.

manben náku without exception; equally; uniformly.

mane imitation, mimicry; **maneru** to imitate, copy, mimic, simulate; **manete** in imitation of.

manekí invitation; beckoning; **MANÉKU** to invite; to call in; to bring upon oneself.

maniawase (*n.*) makeshift, expedient; **maniawase no** temporary;

maniawaséru to manage with, make do, serve the purpose.

MÁN'ICHI by any chance; by any possibility; even though; **mán'ichi no baai ní wa** if anything should happen; in case of emergency.

MAN'IN no vacancy; full house; crowded; **man'ín fuda** "sold out" notice; "SRO" notice.

manjoo whole house, hall, assembly; **manjoo ittchi de** unanimously; with one accord.

manki expiration (of a contract); maturity; **manki ni náru** to fall due; to expire; to serve a full term.

manmaru na spherical; **manmarui** perfectly round.

MANNAKA center, middle; heart; **mannaka ni** in the center; right in the middle.

MANNÉNHITSU fountain pen.

mansei no chronic, confirmed.

manukaréru to escape; to get rid of, be freed from; to be exempt; **ayauku manukaréru** to have a narrow escape.

manuke (*colloq.*) stupid person, ass; half wit; **manuke na** stupid, foolish.

manzara not wholly; not altogether. **Manzara báka de wa nái.** He is not a complete fool.

manzen at random, aimlessly; vaguely.

MÁNZOKU satisfaction, gratification; **mánzoku na** satisfactory; complete; **mánzoku ni** satisfactorily; **mánzoku shite** contentedly; **mánzoku suru** to be satisfied. **Mánzoku shimashita.** I am satisfied.

mappádaka nakedness, nudity; **mappádaka ni** stark naked.

mappíra not by any means; not for anything. **Sonna kotó wa mappíra desu.** I wouldn't do it for anything. **Mappíra gomen nasai.** Please excuse me.

mapputátsu ni right in two; **mapputátsu ni suru** to cut right in two.

marason marathon (race).

MARE NA rare, unusual, uncommon; **mare ni** rarely, seldom.

marí ball; **marí o tsuku** to play (with a) ball.

maru circle, ring; **marui** circular, round, spherical; **MARUI** round; **marui kao (marugao)** round face; **MARUKU** round; in a circle; peacefully; smoothly; **mé o maruku shite** wide-eyed; with the eyes wide open; **maruku osameru** to smooth over (a quarrel); to patch up; **marumeru** to make round.

MARUDE quite; thoroughly; almost like. **Marude nátte inai.** It's quite hopeless. **Marude Nihonjin no yoo ni hanashimasu.** He speaks almost like a Japanese.

marukiri = **marukkiri** completely, entirely.

marumóoke clear profit; cleanup; **marumóoke o suru** make a clear profit.

MÁSAKA by no means, on no account; surely not; you don't say; **másaka no tokí ni** in time of need; in an emergency. **Másaka sonna kotó wa arumái.** It's not at all likely.

mása ni just, exactly; **Mása ni rokuji desu.** It's exactly six o'clock.

masáru to surpass, excel.

masáshiku certainly, no doubt. **Masashiku ano hito no yatta koto desu.** There is no question that he has done it.

masatsu rubbing, chafing, friction; **masatsu suru** to rub (against or with), chafe.

máseta kodomo precocious child; **másete iru** to be precocious.

mashi increase; addition; extra; **mashi jikan** overtime; extra time; **ichi warí mashi** a 10 per cent increase.

-MÁSHITA verb ending; past of **masu** (marks ordinary pol. verbs). **Kinoo gakkoo e ikimáshita.** I went to school yesterday. **Tsukue no ué ni hón ga arimáshita.** There was a book on the table.

MASHITÁNI right under, directly below; **mádo no mashitá ni** right beneath the window.

MÁSHITE much more; how much more. **Hawai ní itta kotó mo nái no desu. Máshite Nihón ni wa ichido mo ikimasen.** I haven't been to Hawaii, let alone Japan.

massáichuu in the midst of; at the height of; **massákari** height; prime; full bloom; **massákari de áru** to be at the height of; to be in full bloom.

massákasama ni headfirst; headlong; head over heels; **massáki** (*n.*) foremost; head. **massaki no** first; foremost; **massáki ni** at the very beginning; first of all.

massáo na deep blue; deadly pale; white as a sheet; **massáo ni náru** to turn as white as a sheet.

masshígura ni impetuously; at full speed; full tilt.

masshiro (*n.*) pure white; snow white; **masshiro na kímono** pure white clothes.

MASSHÓOMEN direct front; **masshóomen ni** directly in front of; directly opposite; full in the face; **masshóomen no tatemóno** the building directly opposite.

MASSÚGU NA straight; direct; upright; **massúgu ni** directly; in a straight line.

MASU to increase; to swell; to raise; to rise. **Jinkoo ga kyónen yóri níwari mashimashita.** The population increased by 20 per cent over last year. **MASUMASU** more and more; still more; increasingly. **Masumasu muzukashiku náru deshoo.** It will probably get increasingly difficult.

MATA and; besides; again; too; also; indirect; another: **MATÁ WA** or else; **mata áru toki wa** on another occasion; **matagiki** indirect information; hearsay; **mata**

tanomisuru to ask something (of someone) indirectly (through someone else). **Watakushi mo mata mótte iru.** I have it, too. So have I. **Mata dekakeru n desu ka?** Are you going out again?

matagáru to mount (a horse); to extend over, stretch over, span; **umá ni matagáru** to ride horseback; **sannen ni matagáru** extending over three years; **matágu** to step over; to straddle.

mataséru to keep a person waiting.

matatáku to wink, blink.

MÁTCHI match; matches; **matchíbako** matchbox; **mátchi o súru** to light a match; **matchíbako no yóo na ie** tiny house (like a matchbox).

mato target, mark; point; **mato ga hazurete iru** to be wide of the mark; miss the point.

matomari conclusion; settlement; unity; coherence; **matomaru** to be settled, decided; to come to a conclusion; to be completed; **matomeru** to adjust, settle; to decide; to finish.

matomo ni right in front.

MÁTSU to wait; to await; to watch for, be on the lookout for; to expect; **máte!** wait!; hold on!; **nezu ni mátsu** to sit up and wait for (someone); (*n.*) pine (tree); **matsukása** pine cone; **matsubáyashi** pine forest, grove.

matsubazúe crutches.

matsuri festival; memorial services for one's ancestors.

matsúru to deify; to worship; to enshrine.

MATTAKU completely, entirely, totally; quite; perfectly, etc.; **mattakú no** entire, complete, etc. **Mattaku sóo desu!** You're quite right! **Mattaku fushigi desu!** How strange! **Mattaku wakarimasen.** I don't get it at all.

mattoo suru to accomplish; to fulfill; to complete.

máu to dance.

maue just above, right above; **atama no maué ni** directly overhead. **Ano hito no heya wa kono maué ni arimasu.** His room is right over this room.

MAWARI circumference; surroundings; neighborhood; **mawaridóoi** roundabout; **mawarimichi** detour; roundabout road, roundabout way; **MAWARU** to turn (around); to go round, to come around, revolve, rotate; to spin. **Ichinen ni nido mawatte kimasu.** He comes around twice a year. **Ie no mawari wa hatake desu.** The farmland surrounds my house. **Mawari wa roku mairu arimasu.** The circumference is six miles.

mawari awase luck; chance.

MAWASU to turn; to revolve, rotate; to roll; to whirl; to forward; to pass around; **kuruma o mawasu** to turn a wheel; to dispatch a car; **tsugí e mawasu** to pass on to the next.

mayoi delusion; superstition; illusion; infatuation.

mayónaka dead of night.

mayóu to be puzzled; to waver, hesitate; to go astray; to lose one's way; **mayowásu** to puzzle, bewilder; to mislead, misguide; to fascinate, captivate; to seduce.

MÁYU eyebrows; **máyu o hisoméru** to frown; **mayúzumi** eyebrow pencil.

mazamáza to clearly, distinctly, vividly.

mazarimono mixture; compound; **mazáru** to mingle; **mazéru** to mix, adulterate.

mazekáesu to interrupt, butt in; to ridicule, sneer at.

MÁZU first; in the first place; to begin with; about; almost; nearly; anyway; anyhow. **Mázu!** Well! **Mázu joodeki da.** It is fairly successful.

MAZÚI tasteless, untasty, insipid; plain homely; poor; awkward, clumsy; **mazusóo na** unappetizing. **Góhan ga mazúi desu.** I don't enjoy eating.

MÉ eye; sight, look, glance; eyesight, vision; notice, observation; point of view; discrimination; insight; bud, sprout, shoot; **mé no todóku kágiri** as far as one can see; as far as the eye can see; **mé ga tsubureru** to lose one's sight; to become blind; **mé ni amáru** to be innumerable; to be too much for; to be unpardonable; **mé ni miénai** to be invisible, be unseen; **mé ni tsuku** to attract (someone's) attention; to catch the eye; **mé ga warúi** to have poor eyesight; **mé ga saméru** to wake up; to be awakened; to have one's eyes opened; **mé o ageru** to lift one's eyes, look up; **mé o maruku shite odoróku** to stare in wonder; **mé o muku** to stare; to glare at; **mé to mé o miawásu** to exchange glances; **mé ni háiru** to come into sight; to come into view; **mé ni tátsu** to be conspicuous; **mé ga kiku** to have an eye for; to be a good judge of; **mé ga déru** to bud, sprout; **mé o tsumu** to nip (anything) in the bud. **Nagái mé de míte ite kudasái.** Time will tell.

-me suffix denoting: order in which things are arranged; **sandome** the third time.

méate aim, object, end; **méate ni suru** to aim at, aim for.

méboshi objective, aim.

mebúnryoo rough estimation (done by the eye).

mechamecha ni in disorder, in confusion. **mechamecha ni suru** to make a mess of, upset; to ruin, wreck; **mechamecha ni náru** to go to pieces; to be spoiled; to get mixed up.

medátsu to be conspicuous; to stand out; **medátsu iro** a loud, gay color; **medátta** striking, remarkable.

medetái happy; auspicious; successful; **medetái koto** happy event; matter for congratulations; **medetáku** happily,

auspiciously; **medetáku owaru** to end
happily. **Omedetoo!** Congratulations!

meetoru meter (measure); gauge;
meetoruhoo metric system.

MÉGANE eyeglasses; insight;
discrimination; judgment; **meganeya**
optician. **Mégane náshi de
yomemasén.** I can't read without
glasses.

megurásu to enclose with; surround; **meguri**
circumference, a tour; round;
circulation; flow; **meisho méguri o
suru** to make a tour of famous places;
megúru to go round; circulate.

meguriáu to come across; to happen to meet.

MÉI niece.

meian good idea, good suggestion; bright
(brilliant) plan.

meibo register, roll of names, roster.

méibutsu specialty; noted product; attraction;
feature. **Koko no méibutsu wa nán
desu ka?** What is this place noted for?

meichuu hit; **meichuu suru** to hit the mark; to
tell; **meichuu shinai** to miss, go wide
(of the mark).

méigetsu full moon; **chuushuu no méigetsu**
harvest moon.

MEIGI name; **meigijoo no** nominal, titular;
meigijoo wa nominally; ostensibly.

meihaku na clear, distinct, explicit.

méi famous physician.

meijín expert; master.

meikaku na clear; definite; distinct; clear-cut;
méiki suru to state clearly; to specify.

meimei christening, naming; **meiméishiki**
christening ceremony; **meimei suru** to
christen, name.

meirei command, order, injunction;
meireiteki na imperative, peremptory;
meirei ni yotte by order of; **meirei
suru** to order, command, decree; to
give orders to.

meisai particulars, details; **meisai na** detailed,
minute. **meisai ni** minutely, in detail;
fully; **meisaigaki** detailed description,
statement, account.

meisaku masterpiece; fine piece of work.

meisan noted product.

meisei fame, reputation; **meisei áru** noted,
renowned.

meishi calling card, visiting card; business
card.

meishin superstition; **meishinteki na**
superstitous.

meisho famous place; famous sight; **meisho o
mawaru** to see the sights.

meishoo place of scenic beauty.

meisoo meditation, contemplation; dream,
illusion; fallacy, erroneous idea;
meisoo suru to meditate.

meitei drunkenness; **meitéisha** drunkard;
meitei suru to get drunk.

MÉIWAKU trouble; bother; nuisance;
méiwaku na troublesome, annoying;
méiwaku suru to be troubled; to have
trouble; to get into trouble; **méiwaku o
kakéru** to bother, annoy. **Gomeiwaku**

de wa arimasen ka? (Are you sure)
I'm not bothering you?

méiyo honor; glory; fame; **méiyo o hakusúru**
to attain an honor; to attain a
reputation; **méiyo o omonzúru** to have
a sense of honor; **meiyóshin** ambition;
desire for fame.

meizúru to command, give orders.

méjiri corner of the eye.

mejírushi mark; landmark; sign; guide.

mekákushi blindfold; screen; blind.

mekásu to primp; deck oneself out; to dress
elaborately; to dress up.

MEKATA weight; **mekata de uru** to sell by
weight; **mekata o hakáru** to weigh (a
thing).

mékimeki more and more; visibly; rapidly.
**Nihongo ga mékimeki jootatsu shite
imásu.** You are making rapid progress
in Japanese.

mekkíri considerably, noticeably.

mekúbase suru to wink meaningfully at.

mekura blindness; blind person; **mekura
méppoo ni** recklessly; **mekura ságuri
o suru** to fumble; to grope. **Mekura
hébi ni ojízu.** Fools rush in where
angels fear to tread.

memái dizziness; **memái ga suru** to be dizzy.

memeshíi effeminate, unmanly.

memori graduations (on a thermometer, etc.);
gradations; markings.

men face; mask; surface; facet, aspect, phase,
side; **men to mukatte** face to face;
men suru to face, front on; to border
on; to look out on. **Heyá wa toorí ni
men shimásu.** The room looks out on
the street; **menboku** face,
countenance; honor; **menboku o isshin
suru** to undergo a complete change.

mén cotton (fabric); **ménka** raw cotton;
ménshi cotton thread.

mendóo trouble, difficulty; troubles;
complications; **mendóo na**
complicated; troublesome; **mendóo o
kakéru** to give trouble; **mendóo o
míru** to take the trouble; to look after;
mendookusái troublesome. **Mattaku
mendookusái desu.** It's a great deal of
trouble.

men'eki immunity (to disease); **men'eki ni
nátte iru** to be immune to; **men'eki
chuusha** inoculation.

ménjo exemption; excuse; discharge; **ménjo
suru** to exempt (from a tax); to
release; to excuse, etc.

menjoo diploma.

menkai interview; **menkai suru** to have an
interview; **menkáibi** reception;
visitors' day; office day.

menkurau to be confused; to be upset; to be
at a loss.

menkyójoo license; certificate; **menkyóryoo**
license fee; **menkyójoo o mótte iru** to
hold a license.

menmitsu na detailed, minute; close; nice;
meticulous **menmitsu ní** minutely, etc.

menshiki acquaintance; **menshiki no áru hito**

acquaintance; **ichi ménshiki mo nái hito** complete stranger.

menshoku discharge, dismissal; **menshoku suru** to dismiss, discharge.

menuki no principal, main; **menuki no basho** busiest section; business center; **menuki no oodóori** main thoroughfare; busy street.

merikómu to cave in; to sink.

mesaki foresight; **mesaki ni** before one's eyes; under one's nose; **mesaki no miénai** stupid; **mesaki no** at hand; immediate.

meshí (*colloq.*) boiled rice; meal; food; **meshí o taku** to cook rice.

meshiagaru to eat; to drink (*pol.*)
Meshiagatte kudasái. Please help yourself.

meshita (*n.*) inferior, subordinate.

meshitsúkai servant; employee.

mesu female (animal); **mesu neko** a she-cat.

metsuboo downfall; ruin, destruction.

métsuki expression of the eyes; **kowái métsuki** menacing look.

métta na reckless; inconsiderate; **métta ni** rarely, seldom; recklessly; thoughtlessly.

meue superiors; seniors; **meue no hitó o uyamáu** to respect one's superiors.

mezaman dókei alarm clock.

mezamashíi remarkable; brilliant; admirable.

mezáwari eyesore; offense to the eye.

MEZURASHÍI rare, unusual; new; curious; **mezurashii mono** a novelty, curio.

mi body; person; self; oneself; heart; soul; seed; fruit; nut; berry; **mi mo kokoró mo** body and soul; **mi o ayamáru** to lead a dissipated life; **mi no ue** one's station in life; **mi no mawari no mono** personal belongings.

miageta admirable, praiseworthy; respectable.

miawaséru to exchange glances; to look at each other; to put off, postpone, defer; to abandon.

mibóojin widow.

míbun social position, social standing; identity; **mibun o akásu** to reveal one's identity.

míburi gesture, motion; **míburi o suru** to gesture, make a motion.

mibúrui shivering, trembling; shiver; shudder; **mibúrui suru** to shiver (with cold); to tremble (with fear); to shudder (with horror). **Omótta daké de mo mibúrui ga suru.** The mere thought of it makes me shudder.

MICHI way, road, route, course; highway; **kómichi** path, lane; **michi ni mayóu** to lose one's way; **michi o oshieru** to show the way; **michi o kiku** to ask directions; **michibata** roadside, wayside; **michibíku** to lead, guide; **michisuji** route, course.

michigáeru to mistake (by sight) one thing for another; **michigáeru hodo kawaru** to change beyond recognition.

michi no unknown, strange.

michinori distance, journey; **kishá de ichijíkan hódo no michinori** about an hour's ride by train.

michishírube guidepost; street sign.

michizure fellow traveler, companion on a trip.

mídara na indecent, obscene, lewd.

midare disorder; disturbance; irregularity; **midaréru** to be disordered; to go out of order; **midásu** to put out of order; to turn upside down; to agitate, disturb; to demoralize.

midashi index; title; headline; heading.

MÍDORI, MIDORIIRO green color; **midorigakátta** greenish; **mídore no** green, verdant.

mié appearance, show, display; **mie no tamé ni** for show; **mié ni suru** to do (something) for show or for the sake of appearances; **mié o haru** to show off.

MIÉRU to be visible; to see, catch sight of; to be in sight; to look like; to seem, appear; to be found; **miénaku náru** to disappear, become missing, become invisible. **Toshi no wari ni wákaku miéru.** He looks young for his age. **Mé ga miéru yóo ni nátta.** Now I can see things.

miesuita transparent; obvious, plain.

migaki polish; burnishing; **nihongo ni migaki o kakéru** to brush up one's Japanese; **MIGAKU** to polish; to rub; to brush; to improve; to refine; **kutsú o migaku** to polish shoes; **há o migaku** to brush one's teeth; **migakiagéru** to polish (silver, etc.).

migamae attitude (posture) of being ready for action; **migamae o suru** to stand ready; to brace oneself.

migawari substitute; scapegoat; stand-in; **migawari o tatéru** to put in one's place.

MIGI (*n.*) right, right hand side; **migi e magaru** to turn to the right; **migi ni déru** to surpass, outdo. **Migigawa kóotsuu.** Keep to the right.

migiwa waterside, water's edge.

MIGOTO NA beautiful; fine; pretty; brilliant; excellent; superb; **migoto ni** beautifully, etc. **Mígoto mígoto!** Well done!

migurushíi ugly, unsightly; dishonorable, disgraceful.

mihakarai choice (at one's discretion); **mihakaráu** to choose (at one's discretion); to select (something) on one's own. **Sore wa anata no omihakarai ni makasémasu.** I leave the choice to you.

mihárai outstanding (unpaid) account; **mihárai no** outstanding, unpaid, unsettled.

miharashi view, prospect, outlook; **miharashi ga yói** to have a fine view.

mihari watch, vigil, lookout, observation; **miháru** to watch, keep watch, stand guard; **mé o miháru** to open one's

eyes wide; **mé o mihátte** with
wide-open eyes.
mihon sample, swatch, specimen.
MIJIKAÍ short, brief; **mijikáku suru** to
curtail, shorten, abbreviate.
míjime misery; sadness; **míjime na** sad,
miserable, pitiful.
mijin atoms; particles; **mijin ni náru** to be
smashed to atoms.
MIJÍTAKU dress; equipment; preparation;
mijítaku o suru to dress, get dressed;
to equip; to prepare oneself.
mijuku immaturity, unripeness; **mijuku na**
unripe, green, immature,
inexperienced. **Watakushi no Eigo wa
mijuku desu.** My English is far from
perfect.
mikai no uncivilized, savage.
mikake dáoshi no deceptive. **Sore wa
mikake dáoshi desu.** It's not as good
as it looks.
mikaku sense of taste; palate; **mikaku o
sosoru** to tempt the taste; **mikaku ni
áu** to suit one's taste.
MÍKAN tangerine (popular fruit in Japan).
mikan no incomplete, unfinished.
mikáta way of looking at things; point of
view, viewpoint; **atarashíi mikáta o
suru** to look at something in a new
light; to see from a new point of view.
mikawásu to exchange looks.
mikazuki new, crescent moon.
miki trunk, stem.
mikiri abandonment; **mikiri o tsukéru** to
wash one's hands of; to have nothing to
do with; to give up; to desert; **mikíru**
to give up, abandon.
MIKKA three days; third day of the month;
mikkákan three days; **Sángatsu
mikka** March 3; **mikka ni agezu**
almost every other day.
mikkai secret meeting, rendezvous.
mikkoku suru to inform against, betray;
mikkókusha informer.
MIKOMI promise, hope, anticipation,
prospect; **mikomi no áru** promising;
mikomi ga hazureru to prove contrary
to expectations.
mikonsha unmarried person.
mikoshi anticipation, expectation;
speculation; **mikósu** to anticipate,
foresee; to speculate (financially).
mikubíru to make light of; to think meanly
of.
mikudasu to look down on; to despise.
mimai sympathy visit; **mimai ni iku** to visit a
sick person; **mimáu** to visit a sick
person.
míman under; below; less than; not more
than; **hyakuen míman** less than one
hundred yen; **jissai míman no** under
ten years of age; ten years and under.
mime features; face; looks; **mime yói**
good-looking; **mime uruwashíi**
beautiful, fair, pretty.
MIMÍ ear; hearing; **mimí ga yói** to have a
good ear; **mimí ni ireru** to inform;

mimí ni háiru to reach one's ears;
mimí o katamukéru to listen; **mimí o
sobatatéru** to strain one's ears; **mimí
ni táko ga dekíru** to din into one's
ears; **miminari** ringing in the ears;
mimi záwari no grating, jarring (to the
ears). **Miminari ga suru.** My ears are
ringing.
mimochi conduct, behavior; **mimochi ga yói**
well-behaved, of good conduct;
mimochi ga warúi to lead a fast life,
be of loose morals.
mimono sight, spectacle; attraction.
mimoto one's birth, parentage; identity;
history; career.
mimuki look; **mimúki mo sézu** without
looking around; without a look at;
straight ahead.
MINÁ, MINNA all; everyone; everything;
miná de in all; in a body; all told.
Miná de íkura desu ka? How much
for them all together? How much for
the lot?
minage suru to drown oneself.
minagoroshi massacre, extermination,
wholesale murder.
minakami source of a river or stream;
headwaters.
MINAMI south; **minami no** southerly;
southern; **minami ni** to the south; on
the south.
minamoto source, fountainhead, origin, root.
minaosu to look at again; to have another
look; to take a turn for the better,
improve, look up.
minarai apprenticeship; apprentice; **mináráu**
to receive training, practice as an
apprentice; to follow suit, copy; to
learn from another.
MÍNARI dress, attire; personal appearance.
minashigo orphan.
minásu to regard as; to consider, think of; to
suppose.
minato harbor, port.
mine peak, summit, top; back.
minikúi indistinct, obscure; illegible; difficult
to see.
mínji civil affairs; civil case; **minji saibansho**
civil court.
minogású to neglect; to overlook; to forgive.
minoo non-payment; default in payment;
minoo no unpaid; in arrears.
minóru to bear fruit; to ripen.
mínu furí o suru to pretend not to see; to
wink at; to connive.
min'yoo ballad, folksong, popular song.
MIOBOE recognition; remembrance; **mioboe
ga áru** to remember seeing before; to
recollect; to recognize.
MIOKÚRU seeing someone off; **hito o
miokuri ni iku** to go to see a person
off. **Hikoojoo e tomodachi o miokuri
ni ikimásu.** I am going to the airport to
see a friend off.
miosame last look, farewell look.
miotori unfavorable comparison; **miotori ga
suru** to compare unfavorably with; to

suffer by comparison; to be eclipsed by.

miotoshi oversight, omission.

MÍRAI (*n.*) future, time to come; future life; **mírai no** (*adj.*) future, prospective.

miren na unmanly; cowardly; lingering attachment; regret; **miren ga áru** to be still attached to.

MÍRU to see, look at, glance at, observe; to judge; to read; to look after, etc.; **yóku míru** to have a good look at; **chótto míru** to at first glance; **shinbun o míru** to read (look at) a newspaper. **Íma ni míró!** You'll soon see!

miryoku charm, fascination; (glamour) appeal; **miryoku ga nái** to have no appeal for; to have nothing attractive about; **miryoo suru** to fascinate, charm.

misadaméru to make sure of.

misageháteta mean, contemptible.

misaki cape, headland, promontory.

MISÉ store, shop; booth; **misé o hiráku** to open a store; to start a business.

misekake pretense, make-believe; appearance; **misekakéru** to pretend, make a show of.

MISÉRU to show, let see, exhibit, display; to make something look like; to give an air of; **isha ni miséru** to consult a doctor; to be examined. **Anáta no nóoto o mísete kudasái.** Please let me see your notebook.

miseshime lesson; object lesson, warning, example; **miseshime ni náru** to serve as a warning (lesson) to.

míshimishi iu to creak.

MÍSO soy bean paste (food used in daily diet); **míso o tsukéru** to make a mess of; to make a poor showing; **miso shiru** soybean soup. **Soko ga míso da.** That's the beauty of it.

misoka last day of the month; **oomísoka** New Year's Eve.

misokonai misjudgement, mistaken impression; **misokonáu** to misjudge, make a mistake, make a wrong estimation.

missetsu na close, intimate. **missetsu na kankei ga áru** to be closely related to; to be in close connection with.

misshíri = **mitchíri** severely, seriously; closely; diligently; in earnest.

misuboráshii shabby, ragged, seedy.

misumisu before one's very eyes; in full knowledge of the situation.

mitásu to fill, satisfy, appease, gratify; **kiboo o mitásu** to gratify a desire; **juyoo o mitásu** to meet a demand; to supply a need.

mitate diagnosis (medical); choice; **mitateru** to diagnose; to choose, select; **mitate chígai** wrong diagnosis; mistaken judgment.

mitchaku suru to stick, adhere to; to be close together; to be interlocked.

mitchíri see **misshiri.**

mitei no unsettled, undecided.

mitodokeru to verify, make sure of; to satisfy oneself that.

mitomein private seal.

MITOMERU to see, witness; to catch sight of; to observe; to recognize; to admit.

mitooshi perspective, outlook; prospect; unobstructed view; **mitoosu** to get an unobstructed view; to see through; to see into.

mítsu honey; **mitsúbachi** honeybee; **mitsúbachi no su** beehive; **mitsuzuki ryókoo** honeymoon.

mitsudan secret conversation, confidential talk; **mitsudan suru** to have a private (confidential) talk; **mitsugi** secret; closed conference.

MITSUKERU to find out, discover; to detect; to sight, locate. **Uwagi o mitsukeru kotó ga dekínai.** I can't find my coat.

mitsumeru to stare at, fix one's eyes on.

mitsumori estimate; assessment; evaluation; **mitsumóru** to estimate; calculate; evaluate.

mitsurin thick forest, dense woods.

mitsu yúnyuu smuggling; **mitsu yunyúusha** smuggler; **mitsu yúnyuu suru** to smuggle.

mittomonái indecent; disgraceful; unsightly; ugly; plain-looking; **mittomonái otoko** poorly dressed man. **Mittomonai kotó o shité wa ikemasén.** Don't behave so disgracefully.

MITTSU = **SAN** three. (See also **mikka**.)

miuchi relations; relative; friends; followers.

miwake discrimination; judgment; **miwakeru** to discriminate; to discern; to judge.

miwatasu to look over; to gaze out on; **miwatasu kágiri** as far as one can see.

miyage = **omiyage** souvenir; gift, present; **miyagebánashi** account of interesting or unusual things seen or heard on a trip.

miyako capital; metropolis.

miyasúi evident, easily seen, clear.

mizen ni beforehand; before something happens; **mizen ni fuségu** to prevent (keep from) occurring; to take preventive action prior to something.

mizo ditch, drain, gutter; groove.

mizore sleet. **Mizore ga furimásu.** It's sleeting.

mizou no unheard of; unprecedented.

MIZU water; cold water; **mizu no tooránai** waterproof; watertight; **mizu de yusugu** to rinse with water; **mizu o waru** to dilute; **mizuírazu de kurasu** to live alone (wihtout outsiders in the same house); **mizubúkure** water blister; **MIZUGI** swim suit; **mizugiwa** water's edge; **mizugiwadátte** splendidly; brilliantly; **mizugiwadátta** splendid; striking; beautiful; **mizugúruma** water-mill wheel; **mizugúsuri** liquid medicine; **mizuhake** drainage; drain; **MIZUKE** dampness; moisture; **mizuke no áru** juicy; watery; **mizuke no nái** dry; parched; **mizukémuri** spray; **mizukoshi** filter; strainer; **mizukasái** watery; **mizunomi** water glass, tumbler; **mizusáshi** water pitcher; **mizutame** reservoir; water tank; **mizutori** waterfowl; **mizuúmi** lake.

mizuhiki colored paper-cord used for tying up formal presents (red and white are chosen for ceremonious occasions).

mizuiro (*n.*) light blue; **muzuiro no** (*adj.*) light blue.

mizukakéron fruitless argument; endless dispute.

mizumizushii fresh-looking; ruddy.

mizusaki ánnai, mizusaki annainin pilot (of a boat).

MO particle denoting: as well as; too; also; as many (much) as; no less (fewer) than; neither . . . nor; even; even if; although; in spite of; **dónna ni áme ga hídokute mo** no matter how hard it may rain; **futté mo tétte mo** rain or shine. **Watakushi mo ikimásu.** I'll too. **Hitori mo imasén.** There isn't even one person.

mochi durability; wear; rice cake; **mochi ga yói** to wear well, be durable.

mochiagaru to be lifted, raised up; to arise; to take place; **MOCHIAGERU** to raise, lift up; to hold up; to praise; to flatter. **Kono hako wa omókute mochiageru kotó ga dekimasen.** This box is too heavy for me to lift up. **Mochiagenáide kudasái.** Please don't lift it up.

mochiáu to balance, keep balanced; to remain steady; to share; to pool (expenses).

mochiawase things on hand, in stock; **mochiawaséru** to have on hand; to have in stock. **Mochiawase ga nái.** There isn't any on hand.

mochibá post, station; duty; round, beat, route.

mochidásu to take out, bring out; to carry out; to carry away; to remove; to save; to propose; to introduce.

mochiíru to use; to make use of, employ; to adopt; to apply.

mochikáeru to pass from one (hand or person) to another.

mochikakéru to propose; to court.

mochikomi delivery to the door; cartage; **mochikomu** to carry in, bring in.

mochikotaéru to endure; to hold out; to stand.

mochimóno property, possessions, belongings. **Kono hón wa Tanaka-san no mochimóno desu.** This book is Mr. Tanaka's. This book belongs to Mr. Tanaka.

mochinaósu to improve; to pick up; to recover (usually used when speaking of illness).

mochinige suru to make off with, run away with.

mochínushi owner, proprietor, possessor.

MOCHÍRON = **muron** of course; naturally; to be sure; certainly; no doubt; needless to say. **Mochíron sukí desu.** Of course I like it! Certainly, I like it.

mochiyóru to contribute one's share; to bring one's quota.

modaéru to be in agony; to be worried; to suffer great agony.

modokashii irritating; slow; slow-moving; not quick enough; unsatisfactory; **modokashigáru** to lose patience.

modori return; temporary recovery; **modóru** to return, come back; to go back; to turn back; to recede; **MODÓSU** to return; to give; to send back; to throw up, vomit.

moeagaru to burst into flames, blaze up; **moegara** embers; cinders.

moekíru to burn out, be burned up.

MOERU to burn, blaze, be in flames; to sprout; to bud; **moetsúku** to catch fire; to ignite; **moesashi** embers; half-burnt stump; **moeyasúi** combustible, inflammable; **moenai** non-combustible; **moeru omói** burning passion. **Ié ga moeru.** The house is on fire. **Hí ga yóku moete imasu.** The fire is burning briskly. (See also **hí.**)

mofuku mourning clothes.

mogáku to struggle; to writhe; to wriggle.

mógu to break off; to tear off.

moguri diving; diver; unlicensed practitioner; **mogúru** to dive (into water); to dip; to creep (into bed); **toko ni mogúru** to get into bed; to crawl into bed.

móji letter, character, ideograph; **moji dóori no** literal; **móji no wakáru** literate, educated; **móji ni akarui** to be learned.

mójimoji suru to hesitate.

mojíru to twist, distort; to parody, mimic.

mokei model, pattern.

MÓKKA now, at present, for the present, currently; **mókka no** (*adj.*) present; existing; **mókka no tokoro** for the time being.

mókkyo tacit permission; **mókkyo suru** to give tacit permission.

mokugeki observation; **mokugeki suru** to observe, witness; **mokugékisha** eyewitness.

MOKUHYOO mark, sign; goal, target, objective;—**o mokuhyoo ni suru** to aim at; to have (something) as one's objective.

mokuji table of contents revelation.

mokumoku to silently, in silence; **mokumokutaru** silent, dumb; implicit.

mokunin tacit approval; passive consent; **mokunin suru** to tolerate; to give tacit approval; to connive.

mokurei nod; **mokurei suru** to nod; to greet with a nod.

mokuroku table of contents; list; catalogue.

mokuromi plan.

mokusan expectation; calculation; estimate; **mokusan ga hazureru** to be disappointed in one's expectations; to fail to come up to one's estimate.

mokushi suru to overlook; to pass unnoticed.

mokusoku suru to measure with the eye.

mokusoo meditation.

moku súru to regard, look upon as.

MOKUTEKI aim, purpose, intention; **mokutékichi** destination, end of the journey.

MOKUYÓOBI Thursday.

mokúzai wood, lumber, timber.

mokuzen before one's eyes; immediate; **mokuzen ni** before one's eyes; in the presence of; **mokuzen ni semáru** to be close at hand; to be right in front of one's eyes; to be imminent.

momareru to be tried; to be knocked around, tossed about.

momegoto trouble; dissension.

MOMEN cotton; cotton cloth; **momen íto** cotton thread; **momen mono** cotton goods; cotton clothes.

momeru to get into a dispute; to get into trouble; to have trouble; to feel discord; to be rumpled.

momiáu to shove and push, jostle; to struggle with a person.

momikésu to rub out; to crush out; to smother; to hush up; to stifle.

momiryóoji massage; **momiryóoji suru** to massage.

MOMO peach.

momohiki underwear (shorts), drawers, trunks.

MOMOIRO (*n.*) pink; **momoiro no** (*adj.*) pink, pinkish.

momu to rub, massage; to crumple up; to wrinkle.

MÓN gate; gateway; crest, coat of arms; **mon'ei** gatekeeper.

MONDAI question, problem; subject, topic; **mondai to náru** to give rise to discussion; to be criticized; **mondai ni naránai** to be out of the question; to be insignificant; **roodoo móndai** labor problem.

mondori útsu to turn a somersault.

mongen closing time, lockup time.

monjín pupil, disciple, follower(s).

mónku wording, words, terms, expression; complaint, grievance; objection; excuse; **mónku o iu** to make a complaint; to grumble; **mónku o iwazu ni** without question.

MONÓ thing, object; substance, matter; stuff, article; goods; possession; something; somebody; **mono ni suru** to secure; to take possession of; to make something of; **mono ni náru** to come to (anything) good; **mono ni naránai** to

come to nothing; to get nowhere; to end in failure.

monohoshiba place for drying clothes; **monohoshízao** clothes pole.

monomonoshíi showy, ostentatious; pretentious, pompous.

MONO NO though; although; only; but; about; some; **tó wa iu mono no** for all that; in spite of all that is said; **mono no nífun to tátánu uchi ni** in less than two minutes.

monookí storeroom, storehouse.

monosáshi ruler; footrule; yardstick.

monoshíri well-informed person; man of great knowledge; scholar.

monosugói dreary, dismal; ghastly, grim, gruesome, terrible; **monosugói arísama** horrible scene; **monosugoi hitode** a terribly large crowd of people.

MÓO already; not any longer; by now; now; soon, before long; presently; **moo sukóshi** a little more, few more; **moo ichido** once more. **Móo fuyú desu.** It's already winter. **Móo arimasén.** I haven't any more.

moo another. **Mizu o moo íppai kudasái.** May I have another cup of water?

moodéru to visit (a temple); to worship (at a temple or shrine).

móofu blanket.

moojuu wild beast; beast of prey.

móoka raging fire.

mookáru to be profitable; to make a profit; to pay; to be paying; **mooké** profit, gains, earnings; **mooké ni naránai** to be unprofitable; **mookéguchi** profitable job, work, undertaking; **mookéru** to make, earn profits; to make money; to prepare, make, make ready; to set up, establish; to frame.

moomoo dense, thick; dim; **moomoo to shite** thickly, in clouds.

mooretsu violence, fierceness; **mooretsu na** violent, fierce, furious, stormy; strong, intense; **mooretsu ni** violently, strongly, etc.; **mooretsu ni fúru** to rain hard (furiously).

mooshiawase agreement; understanding; appointment; **mooshiawáseta jikan ni** at the appointed (agreed upon) hour; **mooshiawaséru** to arrange; to agree upon; **mooshiawásete** by arrangement.

mooshidéru to make a proposal, make an offer; **mooshikomi** offer, proposal; **mooshikomi yóoshi** application form; **mooshikómu** to apply for; to propose.

mooshitate statement, declaration; allegation; testimony; plea; **mooshitatéru** to state, declare; to testify.

móoshon motion; **móoshon o kakéru** to motion for (a person to do something); to make eyes at; to encourage.

MÓOSU to say, tell (humble). **Hái, soo mooshimásu.** Yes, I'll tell him so. **Watakushi wa Yamada to mooshimásu.** My name is Yamada.

MOPPARA chiefly, mostly, principally; solely, exlcusively; entirely. **Káre wa moppara shigoto ni séidashite imasu.** He devotes himself to his business.
moraigo adopted child.
moraimono present, gift (that is received).
morásu to let leak; to reveal, disclose; to let out, omit, leave out.
MORAU to receive; to get, obtain; to be given; to be presented with; to get a person to do, have a person do (following a -te form). **Kono hón o morau kotó ga dekimasén ka?** Can't I get this book? Couldn't you give me this book? **Tanaka-san ni katte moraimashita.** I had Mr. Tanaka buy it.
moré leak, leakage, omission; oversight; **moréru** to leak; to escape; to come through; to get out; to get wind of; to be omitted; to be excluded; **morí** leak; **moré o fusagu** to stop a leak.
móri nursemaid; taking care of a baby.
mori forest; wood.
morikáesu to regain, recover.
MÓSHI MOSHI I say; say; if you please; please. **Móshi moshi.** Hello! Are you there (in a telephone conversation)?
MÓSHI MO in case of; if; provided that; **móshi mo no kotó ga áttara** if anything should happen; in case of emergency.
MÓSHIYA by any chance; by some possibility. **Móshiya kono kínjo ni shokudoo wa arimasén ka?** By any chance, is there a restaurant in this neighborhood?
mosu to burn.
mosurin muslin.
motaréru to lean on, lean against; to rest against; to recline on; to sit heavily on; to lie heavily on.
motaséru to let (someone) have, let (someone) take; to get (someone) to carry.
moteamasu to be embarrassed at, by; not to know what to do with.
motéru to be welcomed, made much of; to be popular; to receive attention.
MOTO origin, source, cause, root; investment price; cost price; **móto wa** originally, at first; **móto kara** from the beginning; **móto yori** from the first; originally; **motomoto** from the beginning, originally; **motone** original cost; cost price; **motone de uru** to sell at cost.
motó under; **oya no motó de** under parental supervision;—**no shusai no motó de** under the auspices of.
motode capital, funds; stock; **motode o orósu** to invest capital.
MOTOMÉRU to ask for, request, demand; to look for, search for.
MÓTSU to hold; to carry; to have in hand; to possess, own; **shíkkári to mótsu** to grasp firmly; to take firm hold of.

motsure tangle; entanglement; trouble; complications; **motsuréru** to get entangled, be in a knot; to become complicated.
mottai artificial importance; **mottai o tsukéru** to exaggerate the importance of; **mottaibúru** to put on airs.
mottaínái wasteful; extravagant; impious, sacrilegious; gracious; more than one deserves. **Máa, mottaínái!** What a waste! **Káre ni wa mottaínái hodo no chíi da.** The position is too good for him.
MÓTTE with; by means of; by, through, because, on account of; **tegami de motte toiawaseru** to inquire by letter.
motté kúru to bring; to fetch; to take along; **motte iku** to take, carry (away).
motte no hoka out of the question; outrageous; unpardonable.
MÓTTO more; much; still more. **Mótto kudasái.** Give me some more.
MOTTÓMO most, exceedingly, extremely. **Mottómo juuyoo desu.** It is most important.
MÓTTOMO indeed; it is true; but; **móttomo na** reasonable; right; rational; natural; **mottomorashíi** plausible.
móya haze, mist.
moyasu to burn.
moyoo pattern; design; appearance, aspect.
moyooshi meeting; gathering; **moyoósu** to organize, arrange; to hold (a meeting); to feel; to show signs of; to look like.
MOYORI NO nearest; adjacent, nearby. **Moyori no keisatsusho e shirasete kudasái.** Please notify any police station in your neighborhood.
mozoo imitation; **mozoo suru** to imitate, copy; **mozóohin** imitation, counterfeit.
muboo recklessness; thoughtlessness; **muboo na** reckless, rash; thoughtless, inconsiderate, ill-advised.
múcha nonsense; disorder; **múcha na** disorderly, confused; absurd, unreasonable; thoughtless; **múcha ni** recklessly; excessively, blindly; **muchakucha** unreasonable, absurd; mixed up, jumbled.
múchi ignorance; stupidity; **múchi na** ignorant, illiterate, etc.
muchuu unconsciousness; ecstasy; **muchuu ni náru** to become unconscious; to be carried away; to become ecstatic; **muchuu de** as in a dream; unknowingly; wildly, madly.
muda futility; uselessness; **muda na** fruitless, futile, no good, of no use; **muda ni náru** to go to waste; to be thrown away; to be in vain; **muda ni suru** to waste, throw away, etc.; **mudaashi o suru** to go for nothing; **mudaashi o suru** to go in vain; to go on a fool's errand.
mudabánashi idle talk, gossip.
mudan without warning; without permission.
muden wireless communication.

mueki no useless, futile.

MÚGI barley, oats, rye, wheat (general term for grain); **mugícha = mugiyu** barley tea; **mugiko** wheat flour; **mugimeshi** rice cooked with barley; **mugiwara bóoshi** straw hat; **mugíyu = mugícha** barley tea.

mugon silence, muteness; **mugon no** silent, speechless, dumb; **mugon de** silently, in silence.

múhi uniqueness; **múhi no** unequalled, matchless, unique.

muhon rebellion, revolt, insurrection; treason; **muhon suru** to rebel, revolt; **muhonnin** rebel, insurgent; traitor.

muhoo na unlawful, unjust, outrageous.

mushóoshuu without remuneration; **muhóoshuu no** free; **muhóoshuu de** free of charge, without recompense; **muhóoshuu de hataraku** to work without pay.

muígi = muimi senselessness; **muígi na** senseless, absurd, meaningless.

MUIKA sixth day of the month; six days.

muimi See **muígi.**

muíshiki unconsciousness; **muíshiki ni** unconsciously; mechanically, automatically.

mújaki innocence, naïveté; **mújaki na** naïve, innocent.

mujin See **mujinzoo.**

múji no plain, unfigured.

mujínzoo = mujin limitlessness.

mujoo heartlessness; **mujoo no** heartless, inhuman; highest; best; supreme.

mujóoken de unconditionally; **mujóoken no** unconditional; absolute.

mujun contradiction; inconsistency; **mujun no** contradictory; conflicting; inconsistent; **mujun suru** to be inconsistent.

mukae meeting (someone); **MUKAERU** to meet, go to meet; to greet, welcome, receive; to invite, call for, send for; **Tookyóo eki de hito o mukaeru** to meet a person at the Tokyo station.

mukaiáu to confront someone; to face each other.

mukaikaze head wind, adverse wind.

múkamuka suru to feel sick (nauseous); to feel offended; to get angry.

mukánkaku insensibility; unconsciousness; lack of feeling; **mukánkaku no** insensible; numb; unconscious.

mukánkei no unrelated; unconcerned, disinterested.

mukánshoo non-intervention.

mukashi ancient times, old days; long ago; remote antiquity; **mukashibánan** an old tale.

MUKAU to face, look out on; to be opposite; to meet, confront; to go toward; to turn toward; **kagamí ni mukau** to look in a mirror; **Beikoku ni mukau** to head for (leave for, go to) America.

mukéiken inexperience; **mukéiken no** green, inexperienced.

mukeru to point at; to turn; to face; to peel off; to come off; to face; to peel off; **mé ni mukeru** to turn one's eyes to.

muki direction; quarter; situation; aspect; exposure; suitability; **kaze no múki** direction of the wind.

múki without limit in time; **múki no** unlimited, indefinite (service); **múki enki** indefinite postponement.

mukidashi nakedness; **mukidashi no** naked, uncovered, bare; **mukidashi ni** frankly, openly; **mukidashi ni suru** to expose.

mukimi shellfish stripped of their shells; hulled shellfish.

múki ni náru to become spirited.

mukíryoku enervation, lethargy.

múkizu spotlessness; **múkizu no** blameless; flawless; spotless; sound, perfect.

MÚKO son-in-law; bridegroom.

MUKOO yonder; opposite direction; next to come; other party; ineffectiveness; **mukoo no** opposite, over there; invalid, ineffective; void; **mukoo ni** on the opposite side, across; **mukoo ni suru** to make void, invalidate, repeal; **mukoo ni náru** to become void, etc; **MUKOOGAWA** the opposite side.

mukóomizu recklessness; **mukóomizu no** reckless, foolhardy, rash; **mukóomizu ni** recklessly, head over heels.

muku to face; to turn (one's face to); to look, look out on; to point to; to tend toward; to suit, be fit for; to skin, peel, pare, strip.

múkuchi reticence; **múkuchi no** reticent, close-mouthed.

mukui retribution, punishment; reward, compensation.

mukuíru to reward, repay; to revenge; to retaliate.

mukúmu to swell; to become swollen.

mukyóka de without permission.

mukyóoiku illiteracy, lack of education; **mukyóoiku na** uneducated.

mukyuu without salary; without pay; **mukyuu de** gratuitously, freely, without pay, for nothing; **mukyuu no** unpaid, unsalaried.

muménkyo no unlicensed; without a license.

MUNÉ breast, chest; heart; mind; effect, purport, intention, principle; **mùné ni ukabu** to occur, come to mind; **muné o uchiakeru** to open one's heart (or mind); to unburden oneself. **Ashita kuru mune shirase ga arimashita.** There is a report to the effect that he should be arriving tomorrow.

munoo, munóoryoku incompetency, lack of ability; **munoo na** incapable, incompetent; **munoo na otoko** a good-for-nothing.

MURÁ village, hamlet, rural community; **mura yákuba** village (or municipal) office; **mura házure de** on the outskirts of the village.

mura unevenness, capriciousness; cluster, clump; **mura no áru** uneven, irregular, lacking in uniformity; capricious, fickle; **muragáru** to crowd, swarm, flock; **muragi** caprice; **muragi na hito** fickle person.

MURÁSAKI (*n.*) purple; **murásaki no** (*adj.*) purple.

murasu to steam; to cook by steam; **gohan o murásu** to steam boiled rice.

muré group; crowd; herd; flock.

murekusái stuffy, musty, moldy; **muréru** to be steamed; to be stuffy, to get musty, get moldy; **múreta** moldy, musty; stuffy.

MÚRI compulsion; coercion; unjustness, unreasonableness; **múri na** unreasonable, unjustifiable; unnatural; **múri ni** by force, forcibly; compulsorily; **muri yari ni** by force; **múri no nái** reasonable; natural; **múri na onegai** unreasonable request.

muríkai lack of understanding; **muríkai na** unsympathetic, unfeeling, heartless.

muríshi de without interest, interest free (money).

muron see **mochíron.**

murui matchlessness; **murui no** matchless, unique; unsurpassable.

múryoku weakness; debility, helplessness; **múryoku no** powerless, helpless, impotent; incompetent.

múryoo without charge; **múryoo no** free of charge, gratis; **muryoo de** free, for nothing, without charge; **muryoo shinryoojo** free clinic or infirmary.

musábetsu making no distinction; indifference; **musábetsu no** indiscriminate; equal; **musábetsu ni** indiscriminately; indifferently; equally.

musabóru to covet, be greedy for; **bóori o musabóru** to profiteer, make an excess profit.

musakurushíi filthy, dirty; shabby.

musan no having no property, unpropertied; **musánsha** a proletarian; person without property; the "have-nots"; **musan káikyuu** proletariat.

musebu to get choked.

muséifu anarchy; **museifu shúgi** anarchism; **museifu shugísha** anarchist.

muséigen limitlessness; boundlessness; **muséigen no** unlimited, limitless; free, unrestricted; **muséigen ni** freely.

musékinin irresponsibility; **musékinan na** irresponsible.

MUSENDÉNSHIN wireless telegraph; radiogram; **musendénshin de** by radiogram; **musendenshínkyoku** wireless telegraph office; wireless telegraph station; **musendénwa** radio-telephone.

museru to be choked (with).

muséssoo inconstancy; **muséssoo na** unprincipled; inconstant; unchaste.

mushaburitsúku to seize violently, pounce on; to grapple with.

múshakusha suru to be irritated; to be in an ugly mood; **múshakusha shita** irritated; shaggy, bushy; ragged.

músha musha munching, gobbling; **músha musha tabéru** to munch, to eat greedily.

múshi impartiality; disregard; **múshi suru** to disregard, ignore, take no account of, close one's eyes to;—o **múshi shite** in defiance of; disregarding.

MUSHI insect, bug; worm; moth, caterpillar; temper; feeling; **mushi no sukánu** disagreeable; **mushi o korosu** to keep one's temper; **mushi no shirase** hunch, premonition; **mushi ni sasaréru** to be bitten by an insect.

mushiatsúi to be hot and close, be sultry.

mushíkaku disqualification; incompetence; **mushíkaku no** disqualified; uncertified; unlicensed.

mushin innocence; request; **mushin no** innocent; involuntary; mechanical; **mushin suru** to make a request; to beg for.

mushínkei apathy; **mushínkei na** dull, apathetic; insensible; **mushínkei de aru** to be insensible to; to be apathetic.

múshiro rather (than); better (than); sooner (than).

mushiru to pull off; to take off; to pluck.

múshoku lack of color; **múshoku no** colorless; transparent; **múshoku no** unemployed, out of work.

mushózoku independence; being unattached; **mushózoku no** independent; unaffiliated, unattached; neutral.

mushuu odorless.

musoo dream; dreaming; daydream; **musoo suru** to dream of; to fancy.

músu to steam; to heat with steam; to be sultry.

musubi knot, tie; end, conclusion, close; **musubi no kotoba** closing remarks; **musubime** knot, tie; **MUSUBU** to tie, knot; to close (a bargain); to conclude; to enter into; to join, link; to form; **himo de musubu** to tie with a cord.

MUSUKO son.

MUSUME daughter; young woman; girl.

musúu countless number; **musúu no** numberless, countless, innumerable; **musúu ni** without number; innumerably.

mutéikoo non-resistance.

mutéppoo recklessness; **mutéppoo na** reckless, rash.

mutsumajíi harmonious; intimate, friendly, on good terms; **mutsumájiku** harmoniously; happily.

mutto suru to get offended, take offense; to be stuffy, muggy.

MUTTSÚ = rokú six.

muttsúri moodiness; moody person; **muttsúri shita** moody; sullen; grim.

muyámi na excessive; indiscreet, thoughtless; rash; unreasonable, etc.

múyoku generosity; **múyoku na** generous, unselfish.

muyoo no unnecessary, needless; useless.

múzai innocence (of a crime); **múzai hoomen** acquittal; **múzai no** guiltless, innocent; **múzai ni náru** to be found innocent; to be acquitted.

múzamuza helplessly; recklessly; without much fuss; without regret.

muzei no tax free, duty free, untaxed; **muzéihin** duty-free goods.

muzukáru to fret; to be peevish (said of an infant).

MUZUKASHÍI hard, difficult; troublesome; delicate; doubtful; **muzukashíi mondai** tough (touchy) question; hard problem; **muzukashíi byooki** illness difficult to cure; **muzukashíi tachiba** difficult situation.

múzumuzu suru to be itchy; to be irritated; to be impatient.

MYÓO strangeness; cleverness; **myóo na** strange, queer; curious; miraculous; mysterious; **myóo no hito** strange person; **myóo na kotó o iu** to say strange things; **myóo ni kikoeru** to sound funny.

MYÓOASA = **myoochoo** tomorrow morning. **Myooasa mairimasu.** I will come tomorrow morning.

MYÓOBAN tomorrow evening, tomorrow night.

MYOOGÓNICHI day after tomorrow.

myóoji surname, family name.

MYÓONICHI = **ashita** tomorrow.

N

NA = **namae** name, title; designation; surname; personal name; reputation, fame; pretext, pretense; **na bákari no** nominal, in name only; **na mo nái** nameless, unknown; **na no áru** famous, celebrated; **na wa** by name, in name; **na ga nái** to be nameless; **na ga shirete iru** to be well known, to be famous; to be popular; **na o kataru** to impersonate; **na o otósu** to lose one's reputation; **na o tsukéru** to name; **nadakái** famous, well-known; **nafuda** nameplate; name card.

ná green, leafy vegetables.

NÁBE pot, pan.

nadaméru to soothe, calm.

nadéru to pat; to smooth.

nadetsukéru to comb (hair); **kamí o nadetsukéru** to smooth down one's hair.

NÁDO and so forth; and the like, etc.; **watakushi nádo** the like of me; a person like myself.

náe seedling, shoot, sapling; **naedoko** seedbed; nursery.

nagabíku to be prolonged; to drag on. **Anó hito no byooki wa nagabíite iru.** His illness is dragging on.

nagagutsu high boots.

NAGÁI long, lengthy, **nagái aida ní wa** in the long run; **nagái aida** for a long time; **nágaku** for a long time; for many years; **nagáiki** longevity, long life; **nagáiki suru** to live to a great age.

nagamé view, scenery, landscape.

NAGAMÉRU to look at; to watch; **késhiki o nagaméru** to gaze at the landscape; **sóra o nagaméru** to look up at the sky; **hito no kao o nagaméru** to gaze into someone's face.

nagamochí oblong Japanese chest.

nagamóchi endurance, durability; **nagamóchi suru** to last long, endure.

naganága very long; **naganága to kataru** to speak at great length.

NAGANEN many years; **naganen no** long; long standing; **naganen no tomodaehi** a friend of long standing.

-NÁGARA suffix denoting: while; as; at the same time that; during. **Asagohan o tabenágara rajio o kiita.** I listened to the radio while eating breakfast. **Nenagara hón o yónde wa ikemasén.** Don't read books [while] in bed.

NAGÁRAKU for a long time.

nagaré stream, current; lineage; **nagarekómu** to flow into; **nagaréru** to flow; to run.

nágasa length; measure. **Nágasa wa nani hodo desu ka?** How long is it? What is its length?

nagasaréru to drift; to be swept away; **úmi e nagasaréru** to be washed out to sea.

nagashí kitchen sink; scrubbing by a bath attendant.

nagashíme sidelong glance; **nagashíme ni míru** to look askance at; to look at (someone) out of the corner of one's eyes.

NAGÁSU to let flow; to drain; to wash away; **mizu o nagásu** to pour water; to drain off; **se o nagásu** to wash one's back.

nagatarashíi lengthy; tedious.

nagawázurai lingering illness.

nagaya tenement house; block of houses.

nagedasu to throw out, discard; **ashí o nagedásu** to stretch one's legs.

nagekawashíi sad, lamentable.

nagekí grief, sorrow; **nagekí o kakéru** to be a source of constant trouble to others.

nagekomu to throw into.

nagéku to weep; to grieve.

NAGÉRU to throw, fling, toss; **nagetsukeru** to throw at.

nageyari neglect, negligence; **nageyari ni suru** to neglect; **shigoto o nageyari ni suru** to do sloppy work.

nagí lull, calm.

nagori traces, remains; parting; **mukashi no nagori** remains of the past; **nagori o oshímu** to grieve at parting.

naguriai fight, scuffle; **naguriai ni náru** to come to blows; **naguriai o suru** to fight; **naguriáu** to fight; **nagúru** to strike; to beat.

nagusame comfort, consolation; **nagusaméru** to comfort; **mízukara nagusaméru** to comfort oneself.

nagusami amusement, sport, diversion, recreation; **nagusami ni** for fun.

NÁI there is not; does not exist; be gone, missing; not to be found; have not (no); lack, be devoid of. **Nani mo nái.** There is nothing. **Okane ga nái.** I've no money.

-NAI suffix denoting: not; negative ending. **Shináide kudasái.** Please don't do it. **Kónaide kudasái.** Please don't come.

náibu (n.) inside, interior.

náichi homeland; mainland; interior; Japan proper (excluding Hokkaido).

NÁIFU knife; penknife.

náigai inside and outside; domestic and foreign; home and aborad.

naijoo internal conditions; real state of affairs. **Anohito wa sono kaisha no naijoo o yoku shitte imasu.** He knows the internal conditions of that company very well.

náika internal medicine; **naikái** physician.

náikaku cabinet; ministry; **Náikaku Sooridáijin** Premier; Prime Minister.

naimen (n.) inside, interior.

nainai de secretly; privately; **nainai no** secret; confidential; **nainai ni suru** to keep something secret.

náishi from . . . to; between . . . and . . . **Sore wa sen en naishi ni sen en shimasu.** It costs from one to two thousand yen.

naishin inner feelings; **naishin dé wa** at heart; inwardly. **Naishin wa góku íi hitó desu.** He is a good man at heart.

naishó secrecy; privacy; secret; **naishó de in** private; **naishobánashi** confidential talk; **naishoku** private occupation; outside work; side line.

naishúkketsu hemorrhage.

naitei unofficial decision; **naitei suru** to decide unofficially; to arrange tentatively.

naiyoo contents.

najimi familiarity; acquaintance; intimate friend; **najimi no** familiar; **najimi ni náru** to make friends with; **najímu** to become familiar with; to become attached to.

najíru to reprove, rebuke.

náka relations; relationship; **náka no íi** to be on good terms; to be friendly; **náka no waruí** to be on bad terms; to be unfriendly; **náka yoku suru** to keep on good terms with.

NÁKA interior; inside; center; **náka ni** within; **ie no náka ni** in the house, indoors; **hako no náka e ireru** to put in a box.

nakabá half; middle; **natsu no nakabá ni** in the middle of summer.

nakadachinin middleman; broker.

nakágai, nakagáigyoo brokerage;

nakagainin broker; commission merchant; **nakagáiten** brokerage house.

nakairi recess, intermission.

nakamá companion; member; (social) set; circle; **nakamá ni háiru** to take part (join) in.

nakamaházure ni sareru to be shunned, to be left out.

nakamí inside, interior; contents.

NAKANAKA very; considerably; rather, quite; easily; **nakanaka juudai na koto** (thing) of no small importance; **nakanaka dóoshite** on the contrary.

nakanáori reconciliation; **nakanáori o suru** to become reconciled; to settle differences; **kenka no nakanáori o saseru** to patch up a quarrel.

nakaniwa courtyard.

nakaore bóoshi man's felt hat.

nakaseru to move to tears; to make someone cry.

nakayásumi rest, respite (in the middle of work); **nakayásumi suru** to take a rest; to take a coffee break.

nákayoshi good friend, pal, chum; **náka-yoshi de áru** to be good friends with.

NAKÁYUBI middle finger.

nakenashi no small amount (of money) one has. **Nakenashi no kane o yarimáshita.** I gave him what little money I had.

náki deceased; late (lately deceased). **náki háha** my late mother; **íma wa náki Tanaká-shi** the late Mr. Tanaka; **nakigara** remains, corpse.

nakigóe cry; scream; **nakigóe de iu** to talk while sobbing.

nakigoto complaint; whimper; **nakigoto o iu** to grumble.

nakitsúku to implore, entreat.

nakóodo matchmaker.

NAKU to weep, cry; **nakunaku** tearfully; **naite mé o harasu** to cry one's eyes out; **nakitai dake naku** to have a good cry.

NAKUNARU to get used up; to run out of. **Moo kane ga nakunarimashita.** I am short of funds. My money ran out. **Watakushi no tokei ga nakunarimashita.** My watch is missing.

NÁMA fresh; raw; unripe; **namanamashíi** fresh; green; **namazákana** raw fish.

NAMAE = NA name. **Onamae wa?** What is your name?

namahánka incomplete; superficial; **namahánka no Eigo** superficial knowledge of English.

namahénji vague reply; **namahénji o suru** to give an evasive reply.

namaiki conceit; **namaiki na** conceited; affected.

namajii half-heartedly; indifferently; rashly; **namajii na** half-hearted.

namajikka ni thoughtlessly; rashly; half-heartedly; **namajikka na kotó o suru** to leave something half done.

namakemono lazy person; **NAMAKÉRU** to be lazy. **Kyóo wa ichinichi namákete shimátta.** I've loafed all day.

namákizu fresh bruise.

namamekashíi charming; coquettish.

namanurui lukewarm; **namanurui henji** half-hearted answer.

namari lead (metal); half-dried bonito; dialect; provincial speech.

NAMATÁMAGO raw egg.

NAMAUO raw fish.

NAMÉRAKA smoothness; **naméraka na** smooth, glassy; **naméraka ni** smoothly.

NAMÉRU to lick; to lap up; to experience; **naméru yoo ni kawaigáru** to dote on; **kúroo o naméru** to experience a hardship.

nami average; **nami no** average, common; **nami hazurete** out of the ordinary, uncommon.

NAMÍ wave; sea; **nami no oto** roar of the waves. **Namí ga takái.** The sea is rough.

námida tears; **námida o nagásu** to weep; **námida ni musebu** to be choked with tears; **namidagúmu** to be moved to tears.

namiútsu to undulate, wave.

nán difficulty; trouble; accident; defect; **nán naku** easily, without difficulty; **nan ni áu** to have difficulty.

NÁN- = **NANI** prefix denoting: what; which; how many. *Nan* is used only when the consonant which follows is *n, s, t, d, k,* or *g.* **Nannin imasu ka?** How many persons are there?

nanáme diagonal; **Nanáme ni** diagonally.

NANÁTSU = **SHICHI** seven.

NÁNBAN what number; what size. **Nánban desu ka?** What is your (telephone) number? **Nán ban?** Number, please (asked by a telephone operator).

NANBEN how often, how many times; **nánben mo** often; many times; over and over.

nanbutsu tough customer; difficult person.

NÁNDAKA somehow or other; somewhat. **Nandaka tsukáreta.** I don't know why, but I'm somewhat tired.

NÁN DE how; how; **nán de mo** any; whatever; anything, everything; by all means; probably; **náni ga nán de mo** at any rate; **nán de mooká de mo** anything and everything. **Nán de mo soo iu uwasa désu.** So they say. So I hear.

NÁNDO how many times; **nándo mo** many times, often.

NANDOKI = **ITSU** when; **nandoki démo** whenever.

NÁN GATSU what month.

nangí trouble; hardship; **nangí na** difficult;

troublesome; **nangí suru** to suffer hardship; **nangí o kakéru** to cause trouble.

NÁNI what?, why?, which, some, any, something; what!; well!; **náni wa tómo are** at all events, in any case; **náni ka ni tsukéte** in one way or another; **náni yori** more than anything else; **náni yori na** the most desirable; the nicest; **náni ka tabéru mono** something to eat. **Naní kuso.** Damn it! (See also **nán-**.)

nanige náku unintentionally; accidentally; **nanige náku yosoóu** to look innocent; to look unconcerned.

NÁNISHIRO anyhow; at any rate, for. **Nánishiro taihen isogashíi desu.** I am really very busy. (See also **NÁNSHIRO.**)

NANIGOTO what; something; everything; **nanigoto ní mo** in everything; **nanigoto ga aróo to** no matter what happens. **Nanigoto désu ka?** What's the matter? **Nanigoto mo nái** [Nothing has happened.] It's O.K.

nánitozo please (*formal*).

nán ji what time. **Nán ji desu ka?** What time is it?

nankínmame peanut.

nankuse fault; **nankuse o tsukéru** to find fault with.

nankyoku crisis, difficult situation; **nankyoku ni ataru** to face the music; to deal with the situation.

Nankyoku South Pole.

Nankyokúyoo Antarctic Ocean.

nanmon difficult problem; puzzle; ticklish question.

NÁNNEN what year; how many years. **Nán nen koko ni súnde imásu ka?** How many years have you lived here?

NÁNNICHI what day; how many days. **Kyoo wa nánnichi desu ka?** What date is it?

NAN NO what; what kind; no; not at all; **nan no tamé ni** why; **nán no yooji de** on what business. **Nán no kotó mo nákatta.** Nothing has happened.

nanoka See nanuka.

nanpa shipwreck.

nanpasen wrecked ship; **nansen** shipwreck; **nansen suru** to be shipwrecked.

NÁNSHIRO = **NÁNISHIRO** anyhow; at any rate; for.

NÁN TO how; what; **nán to itté mo** after all; when all is said and done; **nán to shité mo** at any cost; **Nán to máa!** What! **Nihongo de sore o nán to iimásu ka?** How do you say it in Japanese?

NANUKA = **NÁNOKA** seventh day of the month; seven days.

nanushi village head.

náo = **naosara** more; still; yet; all the more; less; **náo ichido** once again; **náo mata** furthermore; in addition. **Nao machigatte imasu.** It is still wrong.

NAÓRU to be repaired; to be corrected; to

recover, get well; **byooki ga naóru** to
recover from an illness. **Kono tokei wa
súgu naorimásu.** This watch can be
repaired easily.

NAOSARA more; still more; less; still less;
naosara fi to be so much better.

naoshí correction; mending, repair; **NAÓSU**
to repair, mend; to correct; to cure.
Kono kutsú o naóshite kudasái. I
want these shoes repaired.

nápukin napkin.

—NÁRA if; in case; provided. **Hitsuyoo nára
súgu mairimásu.** I will come if
necessary. **Hoshii nara agemasu.** If
you want it, I will give it to you.

NARABERU to arrange, put in order; to line
up; to compare with; **káta o naraberu**
to be (someone's) equal; **mihon o
naraberu** to show samples; **narabi**
row, line; equal; **narabi náki**
unequalled; **narabi ni** together with;
besides; **NARABU** to be in a row,
stand side by side; **itchókusen ni
narabu** to stand in a straight line.

naraí custom, habit; **naraí to náru** to form a
habit.

narasu to ring; to blow; to sound; to
complain; to be famous.

narásu to level; to smooth out; to tame; to
domesticate; to train; to get used to;
inú o narásu to train a dog; **kónnan ni
narásu** to inure (someone) to trouble.

NARÁU to learn; to take lessons; to imitate,
copy; **ikébana o naráu** to take lessons
in flower arrangement. **Anáta wa
okáasan ni narátte ryóori ga joozú
desu ne.** You are following in your
mother's steps as a good cook, aren't
you?

narazumono rascal.

NARÉRU to become familiar with; to get
used to; to become overly familiar; to
become tame; **náreta** domestic;
familiar. **Tookyoo no kúuki ni naréru
kotó wa muzukashíi.** It is hard for me
to adjust myself to the atmosphere of
Tokyo.

nari sound; ring; **nari o shizumeru** to be
silent; to watch breathlessly.

narí form, shape; size; personal appearance;
narí ga ookíi to be tall.

naritachi origin; organization.

naritátsu to consist of, be composed of.

nariyuki result, consequence; course (of
events); **nariyuki ni makaséru** to let
(something) take its own course; **koto
no nariyuki** course of events.

NÁRU to become; to make; to get; to grow; to
come; to set in; to pass; to attain; to
begin to; to come to; to get to; to
consist of; to be made of; to result in;
to turn out; to bear fruit; to grow (on a
tree); **byooki ga wáruku náru** to take
a turn for the worse (in an illness);
byooki ni náru to fall ill; **hontoo ni
náru** to come true; **sukí ni náru** to
begin to like; to develop a fondness

for; **toshi ni náru** to come of age.
Sámuku narimashita. It is getting
cold. **Ie no ringo ga yóku
narimashita.** My apple tree is laden
with apples. **Náru yoo ni shika
naránai yo.** Let things go their own
way. Take things as they come.

NARU to sound; to ring; to roar; to strike; to
resound; to be famous; **mimí ga naru**
to have a ringing in one's ears.

NARUBEKU = narutake as . . . as possible;
if possible; as . . . as one can,
narubeku háyaku as quickly as
possible; at the first opportunity.
Narubeku kúru yoo ni shimásu. I'll
try my best to come.

NARUHODO really; indeed; I see; certainly.
Naruhodo hontoo desu. I see it is
true. Indeed, you are right.

narutake See narubeku.

nasake sympathy; compassion; benevolence;
affection; **nasake áru hito** charitable
person; **nasaké o kakéru** to show
sympathy for; **nasakebukái**
compassionate; benevolent; charitable;
NASAKÉNAI unsympathetic;
heartless; cruel; miserable; pitiful;
shameful; deplorable; **nasakénai
arísama** a wretched condition. **Nán to
iu nasakénai kotó da!** What a shame!

násu to do, accomplish; to perform; to
achieve; to form; to constitute; to
make; to practice; to commit; **áku o
násu** to do wrong; **kokorozashi o násu**
to accomplish one's purpose; **en o
násu** to form a circle. (See also **suru**.)

nasúru to smear; to rub on; to blame.

nata hatchet.

NATSÚ summer; **natsubóoshi** summer hat;
natsufuku = natsumono summer
clothes; **natsuyásumi** summer
vacation.

natsukashigáru to long for; to pine for; to
languish; **mukashi o natsukashigáru**
to think fondly of the past; **natsukashíi**
dear; beloved; longed-for;
natsukáshiku longingly; fondly;
natsukashíi kókyoo one's beloved
home; one's dear native place;
natsukashíi omoide fond memories;
natsukashisóoni longingly;
yearningly. **Watakushi wa kókyoo ga
natsukashíi.** I long for home. I'm
homesick.

NATSUMÍKAN Chinese citron; bitter orange
(similar to grapefruit).

natsumono = natsufuku summer clothing.

nawá rope, cord; **nawá ni kakáru** to be
arrested; **nawabari** roping off;
nawabari o suru to rope off;
nawabari shita zaseki roped-off seats;
nawabari o arasu to trespass upon; to
encroach upon; **nawatóbi o suru** to
jump (skip) rope.

nawatsuki criminal.

náya outbuildings; shed; barn.

nayamí suffering, pain, anguish, distress; trouble; **nayamí ga áru** to have troubles; **nayamí ga nái** to have no troubles; to be carefree; **nayámu** to be worried about; to be troubled with; to suffer from; **nayánde iru** to be in pain; to be in distress.

nazashi designation; calling by name; **nazásu** to name; to call by name.

NÁZE why; for what reason; **náze da ka** somehow; without knowing why. **Náze sóo ka?** Why so? **Náze ka shiranai. I** don't know why.

nazo puzzle; riddle; **nazo o kakéru** to drop a hint; **nazo o satóru** to take a hint; **nazo o tóku** to solve a riddle.

nazukéru to name; to call; to tame; to domesticate; to win over; to gain the friendship of; **nazúku** to be tamed; to become attached to; to take kindly to.

NÉ root, origin, source, base, foundation; nature; **né mo nai uwasa** a groundless rumor; **né mo nái** groundless, false; **ne mo ha mo nái koto** a pure fabrication; **né ga tsuku** to take root; **né ni mótsu** to bear a grudge; **né o haru** to spread roots.

NE sound, tone; sleep; = **NEDAN** price, cost; value; **fue no ne** tone of a flute; **kane no ne** sound of a bell; **ne ga déru** to increase in price; **ne ga tarinai** to not get enough sleep; to sleep poorly; **ne o kiku** to ask the price; **ne o tsukéru** to set a price on. **Ne ga takái.** The price is high. It is high priced. **Ne ga yasúi.** The price is low. It is moderately priced.

neage price rise; price hike; **neage suru** to raise prices.

nébaneba suru sticky, gluey, gummy; clammy.

nebari stickiness, adhesiveness; perseverance; tenacity; **nebarizuyói** persistent; tenacious. **nebarizúyosa** perseverance, stick-to-itiveness; **nebáru** to be sticky, be adhesive; to persevere; to stick to a job. **Anó hito wa nebarí ga nái.** He lacks perseverance. He doesn't stick to it.

nebiraki spread; margin; difference in prices.

neboo oversleeping; late-riser, sleepyhead; **neboo suru** to oversleep; to get up late.

nebumi appraisal; estimation; **nebumi suru** to appraise, assess, value.

nedai bed, cot, couch.

NEDAN price, cost, terms. **Nedan wa íkura desu ka?** What is the price? (See also **NE.**)

nedaru to tease; to coax; to extort; to demand.

nedoko bed; **nedoko ni háiru** to go to bed; to get into bed; **nedoko o kosaeru** to make a bed.

néesan elder sister.

NEGÁI desire, wish; request; **negái ni yori** at one's request; **negái ga kanáu** to receive a wish; to have a desire fulfilled; **negáu** to petition; to beg; to wish; to hope for; **negawashíi** desirable. **Onegai shitái kotó ga áru. I** have a favor to ask of you. **Sore wa negátte mo nái kotó desu.** Nothing suits (pleases) me more than your proposal.

negaide application, petition; **negaidéru** to apply for; to send in (make) a petition; **negaisage** withdrawal (of a petition or application); **negaisage ni suru** to withdraw a petition or application.

négi onion, leek.

negiru to haggle; to beat down the price.

neiro tone; tone quality (of music).

néji screw; **néji de shíméru** to screw down.

nejiáu to contend; to struggle with someone.

nejifuseru to get (someone) down, to overpower (someone).

nejikéru to be crooked, twisted; to become perverse; **nejíketa** perverse, twisted; **nejikíru** to twist; to wrench off; **nejikómu** to screw in; to stuff into; to demand an apology; **NEJIMÁWASHI** screw driver; **nejiru** to twist; to screw; to distort.

nejitóru to wrench off; to twist (someone's) arm (and take something from him).

nekasu, nekaseru to put to sleep; to send to bed; to make (someone) lie down; to lay (something) on the side; to let (something) lie idle; to keep idle; **nekashimono** unsold goods; merchandise that does not sell.

nekkyoo enthusiasm; fanaticism, craze; rage; passion; **nekkyoo shite** frantically, mad with excitement; **nekkyoo saseru** to create excitement, stir up enthusiasm; to thrill; **nekkyoo suru** to go wild over, go crazy over; to grow excited; **nekkyóoteki** wild; enthusiastic; mad; hot-headed.

NÉKO cat, kitten; **neko zúki** cat lover; **néko mo shákushi mo** everyone; anybody and everybody.

nekóze hunchback; **nekóze no** stooping, hunchbacked.

NÉKUTAI necktie; **nékutai o shiméru** to tie a necktie; **nekútai o toku** to untie a necktie.

néma bedroom.

nemaki sleeping apparel, nightgown, pajamas, etc.; **NEMUI** sleepy, drowsy; **nemuku náru** to feel sleepy; to become sleepy; **nemuke** sleepiness, drowsiness; **nemuri** sleep, nap; **fukái nemuri** deep sleep; **NEMURU** to sleep; to fall asleep; **yóku nemutte iru** to be fast asleep; **nemutai** sleepy. **Taihen nemui.** I feel very sleepy. (See also **neru.**)

nén sense, feeling; idea; notion, thought; desire, wish; concern; **fuan no nén** feeling of uneasiness; **nén o irete** carefully; **nén o osu** to call one's attention to; to remind one of something.

NÉN year; **nén ni** yearly; per annum; **nén ni**

ichido once a year; **nén ni ichidó no** yearly, annual; **nénjuu** all year round, every day of the year; the whole year, the year through; **nenbyaku nénjuu** all year round; year after year; **néndo** business year, fiscal year; school year; **nenmatsu** at the end of the year; **nenpoo** annual salary.

nendaijun chronological order; **nendaijun no** chronological; **nendaijun ni** chronologically; **nenpyoo** chronology, chronological table.

nénga New Year's greetings; **nénga ni iku** to make a New Year's call; **nengájoo** New Year's card.

nen'iri carefulness; **nen'iri ni** carefully, scrupulously, minutely; **nen'iri na** careful, conscientious, attentive, etc.

nenryóo fuel; **ekitai nénryoo** liquid fuel.

nénshi New Year's Day; **nenshíkyaku** New Year's caller; **nenshi máwari** New Year's calls.

nenzúru to pray.

néon neon; **neonsáin** neon sign.

nerai aim, objective; **nerai o sadaméru** to take careful aim; **neraitokoro** one's objective, point aimed at; **nerau** to aim at; to watch for.

nerí (*n.*) kneading; **néru** to knead; to soften; to train.

NERU to sleep; to go to sleep, fall asleep; to take a nap; **nerarenai** to lie awake, to sleep poorly; **yóku neru** to sleep well. **Neru jikan da.** It's time to go to bed. It's time to go to sleep. (See also **nemuru.**)

nesage price reduction.

nesshín zeal, enthusiasm; **nesshín na** enthusiastic; **nesshín ni** eagerly, enthusiastically; earnestly. (See also **netchuu.**)

nessúru to heat, make hot; to ignite; to get excited.

netámu to be jealous; to be envious of.

netchuu = **nesshín** enthusiasm, zeal; **netchuu suru** to be enthusiastic about; **netchuu shite iru** to be devoted to, to be immersed in.

netsú heat; fever, temperature; craze, fad; enthusiasm; **netsú ga déru** to become feverish; **netsú ga áru** to be feverish; to be enthusiastic;—**ni netsú o ageru** to be deeply involved in; **netsuai** passionate love; **netsuai suru** to be madly in love; **netsujoo** fervor, zeal.

nettai tropics; **nettái koku** tropical country; **nettai no** tropical.

nétto (tennis) net.

nettoo boiling water; **nettoo o abiru** to be scalded.

NEUCHI value, worth; price; estimation; **neuchi no áru** valuable; **neuchi no nái** worthless; **neuchí ga agaru** to rise in value; to rise in one's estimation; **neuchi ga ochíru** to fall in value;

neuchi ga áru to be worthy of; to be worth.

nezumí rat; mouse; **nezumítori** mousetrap.

nezumízan geometrical progression. **Jinkoo ga nezumízan de fuéru.** The population increases by geometrical progression.

NEZUMIIRO (*n.*) gray; **nezumiiro no** (*adj.*) gray.

NI particle denoting: in; at; on; into; for; to; by; and; with; of; **ása ni** in the morning; **gózen sánji ni** at 3:00 A.M.; **hako ni ireru** to put into a box; **hito ni hanashikakéru** to speak to a person; **inú ni kamaréru** to be bitten by a dog; **mádo ni** at the window; in the window;—**ni chiyahoya suru** to make much of; **tana ni noseru** to put on the shelf; **Tookyoo ni iku** to go to Tokyo.

ní load, burden; package; luggage; freight; = **FUTATSU** two (See also **futsuka.**); **níban ní ni náru** to be a burden to; **ni o tsumi** to load; **ní o orósu** to unload; **ní o koshiraeru** to pack; **ní o tóku** to unpack.

niáu to suit; to become; to match; **niawánai** unsuitable, unbecoming. **Kono kimono wa kimi ni niáu.** This dress (suit) is becoming to you. **Sono tebúkuro wa booshi ni niáu.** Those gloves match the hat.

nibúi dull; dense; slow; thick-headed; **nibúru** to become dull, become blunt; to weaken; **késshin ga nibúru** to weaken in one's resolve.

níchanicha suru to be slimy; to be sticky; to be greasy.

nichibotsu sunset; **nichibotsu ni** at sunset; **nichibotsu no nochi** after sunset; after dark.

nichigen date; appointed day; time limit; term; **nichigen o sadaméru** to set a date; to appoint a day. **Nichigen ga kiréru** The term is expiring. Time is running out. **Kono shigoto ní wa betsu ni nichigen wa nái.** There is no time limit on this work. **Tegata no nichigen ga súgu kúru.** The bill is due. The payment will soon fall due.

NICHIJOO everyday; usually; always; **nichijoo no** daily; usual; ordinary; **nichijoo no koto** everyday occurrence; **nichijoo no shigoto** daily routine; everyday work; **nichijoo go** everyday speech; ordinary language.

NICHIYOO, NICHIYÓOBI Sunday; **Nichiyoo gákkoo** Sunday school.

nichiyóohin everyday necessity; articles used daily.

nidashi broth.

NIDÓ twice, two times; second time; **nidó to shinai** never again; **nidome** second time; **nidome no** second.

nieagáru well done (cooking).

niekiránai vague; undetermined; indecisive;

irresolute; **niekiránai henji** vague answer; noncommittal reply; **niekiránai hito** irresolute (undecided) person.

NIERU to boil; to cook; to be boiled; to be cooked. **Yóku niete imasu ka?** Is it well done? **Kono nikú wa yóku niete inai desu.** This meat is not well done. This meat is half cooked.

nietátsu to boil.

nieyu boiling water; **nieyu o nomaséru** to betray; to deceive; **nieyu o nomasaréru** to be betrayed.

NIGÁI bitter; **nigai keiken** bitter experience; **nigái keiken o shite mé ga saméru** to learn by bitter experience; to have one's eyes opened; **nigái kao o suru** to make a (sour) face; to frown; **nigami** bitterness; bitter taste; **niganigashíi** bitter; painful; unpleasant; disgusting; shameful. **Nigamí ga áru.** It is bitter. It tastes bitter. **Niganigashíi kotó da!** What a shame!

nigao portrait; likeness.

nigásu to release, set free; to let escape; to miss; **tomodachi o nigásu** to miss a friend. (See also **nigéru.**)

nigate tough customer; difficult person.

NIGATSU February.

nige escape; retreat; **nigé o útsu** to try to escape; to prepare an escape; to excuse oneself from; to shirk, evade; **nigéashi** flight; retreat; **nigéashi ni náru** to be ready to quit; to be inclined to run away; **NIGÉRU** to run away, flee; to escape; **mótte nigéru** to make off with something. **Anó hito wa ítsumo nigéashi ni nátte iru.** He is always ready to quit. **Nigé o útte mo damé desu.** Such an excuse is no good. (See also **nigasu.**)

nigiru to grasp, take hold of; to grip, seize.

nigiwai prosperity; bustle, activity, stir; **nigiwashíi** to be flourishing, prosperous; to be bustling; to be animated; **NIGIWÁU** to flourish, be prosperous; to be lively, be astir; to be crowded. **Tookyoo no machí wa nigiwátte iru.** The streets of Tokyo are crowded. **Misé wa minna nigiwátte iru.** All the stores are doing good business. All the stores are prospering.

NIGÍYAKA NA prosperous, flourishing; animated, lively; cheerful, gay; **nigíyaka no hito** happy fellow; **nigíyaka na basho** bustling section (place); **nigíyaka ni** gaily; animatedly; **nigíyaka ni asobu** to make merry.

nigori muddiness; impurity; voiced consonant; **nigorí mizu** muddy water; **nigóru** to become muddy; to become impure; **nigósu** to make muddy; to answer vaguely; to speak ambiguously; to equivocate; **kotobá o nigósu** to say something ambiguous; **nigótta** muddy;

cloudy; voiced. **Áme ga futtá no de iké ga nigorimashita.** The rain has made the pond muddy.

nigúruma cart, wagon.

Nihón Japan; **NIHÓNGO** Japanese (language). (See also **Nippon.**)

NÍISAN elder brother.

nijímu to blot; to run; to spread; to smudge; **ínki no nijínde iru** ink-stained. **Arau to iró ga nijímu.** If you wash it, the color will run.

nijínda blurred, smudged, smeared; stained.

NIJUU twenty. (See also **hatsuka.**)

nijuu duplication; **nijuu no** double, duplicate; **nijuu no ími** double meaning; **nijuu ni** doubly; twice; **nijuu ni sakusei suru** to make out in duplicate.

NIKAI second floor; twice, two times; **nikai ni agaru** to go upstairs; **nikai ni agaru** to go upstairs; **nikáiya** two-story house.

nikki diary, journal; **nikki ni tsukéru** to record in a diary, make an entry in a diary; **nikki o tsukéru** to keep a diary.

níkkoo sunshine, sunlight.

nikkyuu daily wage; **nikkyuu de hataraku** to work by the day; **nikkyuu de haráu** to pay by the day; **nikkyuu de haráu** to hire someone by the day.

NIKÚ meat; flesh; muscle; **niku no atsui** thick; **niku no usui** thin; **niku ga tsuku** to get fat; to gain weight; **nikú ga ochíru** to get thin; to lose weight; **nikú o kíru** to carve meat; **nikúya** butcher shop; **nikúrui** meat; **nikushoku** (n.) meat-eating; meat diet.

nikúi hateful, detestable; abominable; **nikúmu** to hate, abhor, detest; **nikumu béki** hateful, detestable.

-NIKÚI suffix denoting: difficult; troublesome; awkward. **Nihongo dé wa omóu kotó o iiarawashinikúi.** It is difficult to express my thought in Japanese.

NÍMOTSU baggage, luggage; load; belongings, personal effects; **nímotsu no mekata o hakáru** to weigh one's baggage; **nímotsu o azukéru** to check one's baggage.

nín duty; responsibility; task; office; post; kernel; **nín ni ataru** to undertake a responsibility; to take on a duty; **nín ni taénai** to be unequal to the task; to be incompetent; **nín ni tsuku** to assume one's post; take up one's duties; **nín o mattoo suru** to fulfil one's duty.

-NIN suffix used as a counter for people; **sanjúunin** thirty people.

NINGEN = HITO human being, man; mankind; **ningen íjoo no** superhuman; **ningen no** human, mortal.

ningyoo doll; puppet; **ningyoo no yóo ni** like a doll (charming, beautiful, handsome); **ningyooshíbai** puppet show; **ningyootsúkai** puppeteer.

NINJIN carrot.

nínjoo humanity; humaneness; kindness; sympathy; **nínjoo no áru hito** humane person, kind-hearted person; **nínjoo ga áru** to be humane; to be sympathetic; **nínjoo ga nái** to be inhuman, be heartless.

ninki popular feeling, popular sentiment; popularity; business (conditions); **ninki ni joojíru** to catch the popular fancy; **ninki no áru** popular; **ninki no nái** unpopular; **ninki o tóru** to win popularity; to gain favor. **Ninki ga yói** Business is brisk. **Ninki ga warúi.** Business is slack.

nínpu laborer; **ninpugáshira** foreman.

ninshiki recognition; **ninshiki suru** to recognize; to perceive.

níntai patience; endurance; perseverance; **níntai suru** to be patient; to persevere; **níntai ga dekínai** to have no patience with; to be impatient with; **níntai shite** patiently.

nintei recognition; conclusion; presumption; authorization, sanction; **nintei suru** to admit; to presume; to authorize.

nin'yoo appointment; employment; **nin'yoo suru** to appoint to a post.

nínzuu number of persons; **nínzuu no óoi ié** large family.

NIÓI smell, odor, scent; perfume, fragrance; **íi niói** sweet smell; fragrant odor; **niói ga íi** to be sweet smelling, be fragrant; **warúi niói** bad smell; foul odor; **niói ga warúi** to be foul smelling; **nióu** to smell; to be fragrant. **Gásu ga nióu.** I smell gas.

NIPPÓN Japan; **Nippón no** (*adj.*) Japanese; of Japan; **Nippongo** Japanese (language); **Nipponjín** Japanese (person). **Nippongo ga dekimásu ka?** Can you speak Japanese? (See also **Nihon.**)

niramí glare; sharp look; influence; authority; **niramí ga kiku** to have authority over; to have influence over; **niramí ga kikanai** to have no authority over; to have no influence over.

nirámu to glare at, scowl; **jitto nirámu** to stare fixedly.

NIRU to boil; to cook. **Watakushi wa nikú wa yóku nita hóo ga íi desu.** I like my meat well done.

niru resemble, be like, be similar to; **totemo yóku nite iru** to be very similar to; to resemble closely; **nite ínai** to have no resemblance to; to be dissimilar.

nise (*n.*) imitation, sham; counterfeit, forgery; **nise no** (*adj.*) counterfeit, forged, false; **nisemono** imitation, fake, counterfeit article.

NISHI west; **nishi no** western; **nishi ni** in the west; **nishi gawa ni** on the west (side).

nita like; similar.

—NI TSÚITE of; about; with; on; over; as to; concerning; regarding; on the subject of; in connection with; relating to; in the case of; **kono kotó ni tsúite** about

this; with regard to this matter; **kono tén ni tsúite** on this point; **—ni tsúite tekisetsu ni hiyoo suru** to express appropriate opinions of.

nittei daily routine; day's agenda.

NITTOO daily wages; **nittoo o haráu** to pay daily wages.

NIWA garden; yard; courtyard; **niwáshi** gardener.

níwaka abruptness, suddenness; **níwaka no** sudden; abrupt; unexpected; **níwaka ni** suddenly, abruptly; unexpectedly; all at once.

niwakaáme sudden shower, downpour.

NIWATORI chicken, hen; cock.

nizúkuri packing; crating; **nizúkuri suru** to pack; to crate; **nizúkuri ga yóku dekite iru** to be well packed; **nizúkuri ga fukánzen da** to be badly packed; **nizukurinín** packer.

nó field, plain.

NO particle denoting: pertaining to:—'s; of—;—'s own; in; at; on; for; by; **eigo no sensei** teacher of English; English teacher; **Góya no é** a painting by Goya; **ie no iriguchi** entrance to the house; **ishi no hashí** stone bridge; bridge made of stone; **kawa no hashi** bridge over the river; **kyóo no shinbun** today's newspaper; **mondai no hito** man in question; **otooto no hón** my brother's book; **yuki no hi** snowy day.

nobású to extend, lengthen, stretch, draw out, prolong; to postpone; to straighten; **issun dake nobású** to lengthen by one inch; **kanjóo o nobású** to defer (payment) on a bill.

noberu to express, state; to explain; **íken o nobéru** to express an opinion; **kansoo o nobéru** to give one's impression; **riyuu o nobéru** to state one's reason.

nóbetsu ni ceaselessly, perpetually, continuously.

nobí postponement; spread, growth; **nobí o suru** to stretch oneself; **nobíru** to extend, stretch; to be prolonged; to be deferred; to increase, grow, develop. **Watakushi no shuppatsu ga nóbita.** My departure has been delayed.

nobori rise, ascent; uphill road; streamer; **NOBORU** to climb; to go up, rise; to be prompted; **miyako ni noboru** to go to the capital; **yamá ni noboru** to climb a mountain. **Táiyoo ga noboru.** The sun rises.

nobose dizziness, vertigo; **noboseru** to be dizzy; to get excited; to be infatuated with; to be absorbed in; **nobosete iru** in the excitement. **Anó hito wa nobosete iru.** The blood has rushed to his head.

NOCHÍ future time; forthcoming time; **sono nochi** thereafter, since then; **mikka nochi** three days later; **nochi no** subsequent; future; **nochí ni** later on; afterwards.

—NÓ DE because of. **Kaze o hiitá no de
atamá ga itái desu.** My headache is
due to my cold. [I have a headache
because of a cold.]

NÓDO throat; voice; **nódo ga yói** to have a
sweet voice; **nódo o itaméru** to have a
sore throat. **Nódo ga kawakimáshita.**
I'm thirsty.

nódoka quiet, calm; peaceful; pleasant;
nódoka na quiet, calm; pleasant;
nódoka na ténki mild weather;
nódoka na kokoro peace of mind;
nódoka ni quietly; peacefully.

nogaréru to escape; flee, get away; to avoid,
evade; **abunai tokoró o nogaréru** to
have a narrow escape; **nogarerarénai**
unavoidable, inevitable. **Watakushi
wa nogaréru kotó ga dekínai.** I'm in
for it; it's inevitable.

nóhara field, plain.

nójuku camping outdoors; **nójuku suru** to
camp out.

noki eaves (of a house); **noki o naraberu**
to stand side by side; to stand in a row.

nokogíri saw; **nokogíri de hiku** to saw.

nokórazu all, entirely, wholly; without
exception; **issen mo nokórazu** to the
last cent.

NOKORÍ remainder, rest, balance; **nokori no**
remaining; **nokori náku** all; entirely;
nokorimono no remains, leavings,
leftovers, remnants, scraps (of food);
NOKÓRU to be left; to remain; to
linger. **Nokori no kane ga áru ka?** Is
there any money left? Have you any
money left? **Okane ga íkura ka
nokótte iru.** I have some money left.

NOKÓSU to leave behind; to keep in; to leave
over; to save; **kane o nokósu** to save
money; **shigoto o nokósu** to leave the
work (partly done).

nomaréru to be swallowed up; to be drunk
up; to be awed by; to cower.

nomaséru to give a drink, serve a drink; to let
(someone) drink; to treat (someone) to
a drink; **íppai nomaséru** to entertain
with liquor. **Dóozo mizu o íppai
nomásete kudasái.** Please give me a
drink of water.

nomikomu to swallow; to drink; to gulp; to
understand; to take in; to know. **Anáta
no iu kotó ga yóku nomikomenai.** I
can't grasp your meaning. I don't
follow what you say.

nomíkuchi faucet; **nomímizu** drinking water;
NOMÍMONO beverage; **tsumetai
nomímono** cold beverage; **nominikúi**
distasteful, disagreeable (to drink);
undrinkable; **NÓMU** to drink; to take
(in); to swallow; to smoke; **ocha o
nómu** to drink tea; **tabako o nómu** to
smoke.

NONBÍRI carefree; easily; **nonbíri to shita**
carefree; easy; quiet; **nonbíri to shita
seikatsu** carefree life; quiet life;
nonbíri suru to feel at leisure; to be at
ease.

—NÓNI particle denoting: although, though;
in spite of, despite. **Wakái noni yóku
hatarakimasu.** He works hard despite
his young age.

nónki light-heartedness; optimism; **nónki na**
carefree; easy-going; happy-go-lucky;
nónki ni leisurely; **nónki ni kurasu** to
take life easy.

nóo brain; talent; ability; skill; **Noh** play (also
spelled **No**); **nóo o itaméru** to rack
one's brains; **noo nashi no** good for
nothing.

nooen = **noojoo** farm; **nooen ni kurasu** to
live on a farm.

nooen na charming; engaging; bewitching;
voluptuous.

nóofu farmer; farm hand.

nóogu farm equipment.

nóogyoo farming, agriculture; **nóogyoo no**
agricultural.

nooíkketsu cerebral hemorrhage.

noojoo = **nooen** farm.

nóoka farmhouse; farmer.

nookoo density, thickness; **nookoo na** thick,
dense; heavy; rich; **nookoo ni** thickly,
densely; richly; **nookoo na tabémono**
rich food.

noómu dense fog.

nooritsu efficiency; capability; **nooritsu no
áru** efficient; capable; **nooritsu no
agaranai** inefficient; **nooritsu o ageru**
to increase efficiency, raise efficiency.

nóoryoku ability; facility; competency;
capability; faculty.

noosakúbutsu, noosánbutsu crops, farm
produce, agricultural products.

nooson rural area; farm village; agricultural
district; **nooson no** rural; agricultural.

nootan shading; tinting; light and shade.

nootén scalp; crown of the head.

noozei tax payment; **noozei suru** to pay taxes;
noozéisha taxpayer.

nori dried seaweed (a food).

norí paste; glue; starch; **norí de haru** to
paste; to glue; **norí o tsukéru** to
starch. **Kore ni norí o tsukéte hoshíi.**
I'd like this starched.

norikae transfer; change; changing;
norikaéeki junction, transfer point;
norikaeba transfer point;
norikaekíppu transfer ticket;
NORIKÁERU transfer; change (for a
train, car, ship, etc.). **Oosaka iki wa
koko de norikae désu.** You must
transfer here for Osaka. **Shinjuku de
básu ni norikáeru hóo ga yói deshóo.**
It will be better to transfer to a bus at
Shinjuku.

NORIMONO vehicle, conveyance.

noroí (n.) curse; (adj.) slow; lagging; tardy;
dull; dense; **norói kishá** slow train;
shigoto ga noróí to be slow at one's
work. **Anó hito wa bánji ni noróí
otokó da.** He is slow about
everything; **noróu** to curse; to wish
(someone) ill.

NORU to ride (in, on); to get (in, on); to go on board; to join; to take part in; to be taken in; to be recorded; **kishá ni notte iku** to go by train; **shínbun ni noru** to appear (be reported) in the newspaper; **soodan ni noru** to take part in a consultation; **umá ni noru** to mount a horse.

noseru to put on top of; to place on, set on; to carry; to load; to take on board; to impose upon; to publish; to record; **jidóosha ni hito o nosete yaru** to give (someone) a lift in a car; **jookyaku o noseru** to take on passengers.

nótto nautical mile, knot.

nottóru to follow; to conform to; to go by; to be in accord with.

NOZOITE except, excepting, with the exception of; but; **hitótsu nozoite minna** all but one; —**o nozoite** with the exception of; excluding; **shoosúu o nozoite** with a few exceptions. **Nichiyóobi o nozoite máinichi benkyoo suru.** I study every day-except Sunday.

nozoku to peep in, look in; to eliminate, remove, exclude; to abolish; to omit.

nozomí wish, desire, hope; expectation, aspiration, ambition; **nozomí o kakéru** to set one's heart on; **nozómu** to wish, desire, hope for, aspire to; to expect; to look out on, overlook; to front on, face; to meet; to attend; to be present; **shikí ni nozómu** to attend a ceremony. **Niwa wa yamá ni nozónde iru.** The garden faces the mountains.

nugéru to come off; to slip down.

NÚGU to take off; to pull off; to undress. **Kutsú o núgu no desu ka?** Shall I take off my shoes?

nuibari needle.

nuká rice bran; **nukamiso** salt and rice bran paste (for pickling).

nukaru to be muddy; to be slushy; to blunder, make a mistake; **nukarumi** mud; mud puddle.

nukasu to omit, exclude, leave out; to overlook.

nukedásu to get loose; to sneak out, steal out.

nuki gaki selection; excerpt.

nukitóru to pull out, extract; to abstract; to steal.

NUKU to pull out, take out, draw out; to extract (a tooth); to uncork; to unscrew; to select; to leave out, omit.

numá swamp, bog; **numachi** swampy place.

nurasu to wet; to dampen; to soak; to drench. **Ashí o nurasú na.** Don't get your feet wet!

NURERU to become wet, get wet. **Kao ga námida ni nurete iru.** His face is wet with tears.

nuri coating; varnishing; lacquering; painting; plastering.

NURU to apply; to spread on; to paint; to plaster; to coat; **pán ni báta o nuru** to spread butter on bread.

nurúi lukewarm; dull; sluggish; **nurumáyu** lukewarm water.

nusumaréru to be robbed; to be stolen; **nusumimíru** to steal looks at, look furtively at; **nusúmu** to steal; to rob; to snatch a minute's rest; to elude the eyes of others; **hitome o nusúnde áu** to meet (someone) secretly; **nusubito** thief. **Okane o nusumáreta.** My money has been stolen.

NÚU to sew; **hitogomi o núu** to go through a crowd; **kimono o núu** to sew clothes.

nyóoboo (*colloq.*) wife.

nyuubai rainy season.

nyuuden telegram (cable) received; —**no mune nyuuden ga átta.** A telegram has been received to the effect that.

nyuugaku (school) admission, matriculation; **nyuugaku suru** to enter school; to matriculate; **nyuugakushikén** entrance examination.

nyuugoku imprisonment.

nyuuhi cost; expenditure; expenses.

nyuuin suru to enter a hospital; to be hospitalized.

nyuujoo entrance; admission; **nyuujoo suru** to enter; to be admitted; **nyuujoo múryoo** free admission; **nyuujóoken** admission ticket; **nyuujóoryoo** admission fee.

nyuukai joining (an organization); admission; **nyuukai suru** to become a member (in an organization); **nyuukai o mooshikómu** to apply for membership.

nyuukoo entry (into port); docking; **nyuukoo suru** to enter port; to dock.

nyuumon (*n.*) entering private school; primer; **Nippongo nyúumon** Japanese (language) primer.

nyuusatsu bid; bidding; **nyuusatsu suru** to bid, make a bid. **nyuusen suru** to be selected; be accepted. **nyuusha suru** to enter a firm.

NYUÚSU news; **kaigai nyúusu** foreign news.

nyuutoo suru to join a political party.

nyuuwa gentleness; mildness; tenderness; **nyuuwa na** gentle; tender.

nyuuyoku bath; bathing; **nyuuyoku suru** to bathe.

nyuuyoo need, necessity; requirement; **nyuuyoo na** necessary; required; **nyuuyoo de áru** to be in need of; to want.

O

ó tail, brush; **ó o furu** to wag the tail; **ó hire o tsukéte hanásu** to exaggerate.

óashisu oasis.

OBÁ aunt; **obachan** auntie.

OBÁASAN grandmother; old woman.

ÓBI belt, sash (worn with a kimono); **óbi o shiméru** to do up a sash; **óbi o tóku** to take off an obi; **obiáge** sash-bustle; **obidóme** sashband.

obiéru to become frightened; to have a nightmare.

obikidásu to lure, entice.

obitadashíi immense, vast; **obitadáshiku** abundantly, profusely, in large numbers.

obiyakásu to threaten, intimidate; to scare.

oboé learning; memory; feeling; recollection; experience; **oboé ga yói** to have a good memory; to be quick to learn; **OBOÉRU** to remember; to keep in mind; to memorize; to learn; to recollect; **sámusa o oboéru** to feel chilly. **Yóku obóete imásu.** I remember it well.

oboreru to drown; to be drowned; to indulge in, to be addicted to.

obotsukanai uncertain, doubtful; almost hopeless; uneasy, weak.

obusáru to ride on someone's shoulders; to ride pickaback; to rely on; **obúu** to take (carry) on one's back; **kodomo o obúu** to carry a child on one's back.

OCHA = **CHA** tea (usually Japanese). (See also **koocha**.)

ochiáu to meet, rendezvous; to come (across) someone.

ochibureru to be ruined, be reduced to poverty.

óchido fault, error; blame; **óchido ga nái** to be blameless; **hito no óchido ni suru** to lay the blame on someone else.

ochiíru to fall; to be reduced; **kiken ni ochiíru** to be in danger; **kukyoo ni ochiíru** to get into trouble.

ochikomu to fall in, fall into. **Káre wa kawá ni ochikonda.** He fell into the river.

OCHÍRU to fall; to drop; to come down; to collapse; to be left out; to fall short of. **Yáne kara óchite ashí o ótta.** I fell from the roof and broke my leg. **Seiseki ga ochite kimashita.** My marks are going down.

ochitsuki composure, self-possession; **ochitsuki no áru** calm, self-composed; **ochitsuki no nái** fidgety, restless; **ochitsuki harátte** calmly; **ochitsuku** to settle down, become quiet; **ki ga ochitsuku** to feel relieved; to recover one's composure.

odáyaka na quiet, calm, peaceful, gentle; moderate; **odáyaka de nái** alarming, threatening; upsetting; serious; **odáyaka ni náru** to calm down, become calm.

odokashi threat, menace; **odokasu** to threaten, menace; to browbeat; to scare.

odori dance; dancing; **odoriagáru** to jump; to dance for joy.

odoróite in astonishment, in amazement.

odorokásu to astonish, surprise, amaze; to startle, frighten; **odoroki** amazement, wonder, surprise; **ODORÓKU** to be surprised, be amazed; to be frightened. **Káre wa odoróite tobiagátta.** He

jumped up in surprise. **Odoróku kotó wa nái.** Nothing is surprising about it. Don't be surprised.

odoru to dance; to step; **bando ni awásete odoru** to dance to a band.

odoshi threat, menace; **odosu** to frighten, intimidate; to browbeat.

oeru to end, conclude, finish; **kái o oeru** to bring a meeting to a close; **gyóo o oeru** to finish a course.

ogámu to worship, venerate; to pray for.

ogawa brook, stream.

ogináu to make good, make up for, supplement; **ketsuin o ogináu** to fill a vacancy; **sonshitsu o ogináu** to make up a loss.

ogósoka grave, solemn, austere; **ogósoka ni** with solemnity.

OHAYOO Good morning! **Ohayoo gozaimasu.** Good morning. (*pol.*).

OI nephew.

ÓI (*colloq.*) hello! hey! look here!

oichirásu to drive out; to scatter.

oidásu to drive out, expel, turn out, evict.

oihagi highway robber.

oiharáu to drive away; to send away.

OIKAKÉRU to chase, run after. **Inú ga néko o oikákete iru.** A dog is chasing a cat.

oikómu to corner; to drive in.

oikósu to outrun; to pass, to outdistance. **Hoka no kuruma o oikoshimashita.** He passed another car.

oimawású to run after; to chase around.

oioi gradually, little by little; step by step; eventually.

OISHII delicious, tasty, sweet. **Áa oishii!** It tastes good! **Góhan wa oishii deshita.** The meal was good.

oitatéru to evict; to urge; to drive away.

oitsúku to overtake, catch up with.

oitsuméru to corner, get into a corner.

OJI uncle.

ojigi bow (inclination of the head or body); **ojigi o suru** to bow.

OJÍISAN grandfather; old man.

ojike fear, fright; **ojiké ga tsuku** to be seized with fear, be frightened.

OJÓOSAN miss; daughter (*pol.*).

OKÁ hill, mound; land; shore.

OKÁASAN mother, mama.

OKAGE indebtedness, favor. **Okage sama de.** Thanks to your kindness.

okámi landlady; mistress; hostess (*at a restaurant*).

OKANE = **kane** money.

okáshi = **kashi** cake.

OKASHÍI amusing, laughable, funny; ridiculous; strange. **Nani mo okashíi kotó wa nái.** There is nothing funny. **Okashíi hanashí da.** The story is strange.

okashiya = **kashíya** cake shop, candy shop.

okasu to commit; to violate; to defy; to rape; to invade; to raid; to infringe on; to risk; to face; to visit; to damage; to desecrate; to assume; **kokuhoo o**

okasu to break the laws of the land.
Hidoi ame o okashite ikimashita. We
went despite the heavy rain.
okáwari second helping; another cup;
   okáwari suru to ask for a second
   helping.
óke tub, tank, pail; **óke íppai no mizu** pailful
   of water.
oki open sea.
okiagáru to get up; to sit up; **toko no ué ni
   okiagáru** to sit up in bed.
okidókei table clock.
okikáeru to rearrange; to displace.
okimono small, decorative ornament placed in
   the alcove of a guest room.
okinaóru to sit up, sit erect.
okinaósu to replace; to rearrange.
—ÓKI NI at intervals of; **gofun óki ni** at
   five-minute intervals; **ichinichi óki ni**
   every other day.
OKÍRU to get up; to rise; to raise oneself; **ása
   háyaku okíru** to get up early in the
   morning; **kan ga okíru** to have
   hysterics.
okite law, regulation, decree.
okizari desertion; **okizari ni suru** to desert; to
   leave behind.
okkúu na troublesome.
okonai act, deed; conduct; **okonai no yói**
   well-behaved; **okonáu** to act, perform;
   to carry out; to conduct. **Kekkonshiki
   wa mikka ni okonaimasu.** We will
   hold the wedding on the third.
okoraséru to offend; to anger; to irritate
   (someone).
okorí origin, source, cause, root.
okoríppói touchy, peevish, short-tempered.
OKÓRU to happen, occur, come about; to
   take place; to arise in; to originate; to
   get angry, lose one's temper; **okótte
   iru** to be angry. **Sensoo ga okóru ká
   mo shirenai.** A war may break out.
   **Tanaka-san wa sono hanashi o kiite
   taihen okorimashita.** Hearing that
   story, Mr. Tanaka got very mad (got
   very angry). **Yamada-san ga konai no
   de okótte imasu.** He is mad because
   Mr. Yamada hasn't come. **Sonnani
   okótte wa ikemasen.** Don't be angry
   so much.
OKÓSU to start, begin; to bring about; to
   establish; to promote; to improve, to
   awaken; to raise up, lift; to cause; to
   give rise to; **byooko o okósu** to fall ill;
   shíndai o okósu to make a fortune.
   Nánji ni anáta o okoshimashóo ka?
   When shall I wake you?
okotari negligence; **okotarigáchi no**
   negligent, neglectful; **okotari náku**
   diligently, carefully; **okotáru** to
   neglect; to fail to do.
OKU to put, place, lay, set; to keep; to
   establish, set up; to open; **fude o oku**
   to lay down a pen; **jochuu o hitóri oku**
   to hire a servant; **nokóshite oku** to
   leave; **sono mama ni shite oku** to

leave alone. **Kasa wa koko ni oite
   kudasai.** Please leave your umbrella
   here.
ÓKU one hundred million; (n.) back part;
   inner part; back; inner room; **óku e
   tóosu** to show a person to the guest
   room; **yamaóku** The heart of (that part
   deep inside) a mountain.
okubyóo cowardice, timidity; **okubyoomono**
   coward.
okufukai deep, profound; of great depth.
okúgai outdoors, in the open air.
okujoo rooftop.
okúnai interior of a house, indoors.
okurasu to delay; to put off.
okure lag; **okure o tóru** to be beaten; to be
   outstripped; **ki okure ga suru** to feel
   shy; to lose heart; **OKURERU** to be
   late for; to be behind time; to get (fall)
   behind; to be left behind; **kishá ni
   okureru** to miss a train.
okuridásu to send out; to forward; to see
   (someone) off; to show a person to the
   door.
okurikómu to see a person home; to escort
   (someone).
OKURIMONO present, gift; **okurimono o
   suru** to give (send) a gift.
OKURU to send; to see off; to send off; to
   escort; to spend, pass (time); to
   present; to make a present of; to
   bestow; **gákui o okuru** to confer an
   academic degree; **nímotsu o okuru** to
   send a package; **tanoshíi seikatsu o
   okuru** to live a happy life. **Éki made
   ookuri shimashóo.** I will escort you to
   the station. **Káre no sotsugyoóiwai ni
   mannénhitsu o okurimashóo.** Let's
   give him a fountain pen for a
   graduation gift.
ÓKUSAMA madam, Mrs.
okusoko depth, bottom; **kokoro no okusoko
   dé wa** in the back of one's mind; in the
   depths of one's heart.
okusoku guess, supposition; **okusoku suru** to
   guess, suppose.
okusúru to fear; to shrink; to hesitate; to be
   shy.
okuyukashíi graceful; refined.
okuyuki depth; length.
okuzáshiki inner room; back parlor.
omae you (*impolite: usually used in anger*).
omedeta happy event. **Omedetoo.**
   Congratulations! Happy Birthday!
omei slur; bad name; **omei o kiru** to get a bad
   name; to be dishonored; to have a bad
   heart.
omiyage = **miyage** souvenir; parting present;
   gift.
OMÓCHA toy; **omócha ni suru** to trifle
   with, toy with.
OMOI heavy; wealthy; serious, severe;
   important; **omoi byooki** serious
   illness; **ki ga omoi** to have a heavy
   heart.
OMOÍ thought, idea, mind; sense; heart;

feeling; love; care, worry; will, wish;
omoí o kakéru to take a fancy to;
omoí o kogásu to burn with love; **omoí
o korásu** to tax one's brain.
omoiatáru to occur to; to call to mind.
omoiawaséru to consider (together); put two
and two together. **Karekore
omoiawasete yamemashita.** Taking
everything into consideration, I gave
up the idea.
omoichigai misunderstanding; **omoichigai o
suru** to misunderstand.
OMOIDÁSU to recall, bring to mind,
remember. **Dóoshitemo omoidasénai.**
Try as I may, I can't recall it.
omoide recollections, memories.
omoigakenái unexpected, unforeseen; least
expected; chance, accidental;
omoigakenáku unexpectedly, etc.
omoikíru to resign oneself to; to give up;
omoikiri resolution; **omoikítte** boldly,
resolutely.
omoikítta radical, bold, daring.
omoikómu to be under the impression that; to
be possessed with (an idea).
omoinokósu to leave with regret.
omoíómoi each in his own way; as one
pleases.
omoishiraséru to teach someone (make
someone learn) a lesson.
omoitsuki plan, suggestion; **omoitsúku** to
recall; to think of, to hit on. **Yói
omoitsuki desu.** That's a great idea!
Umái shukoo o omoitsúita. I got a
brilliant idea.
omoitsuméru to brood over; to love
passionately.
omoiyari sympathy, consideration; **omoiyari
no áru** sympathetic; considerate, kind;
omoiyáru to sympathize with.
omokage features, looks; image, likeness.
omokurushíi heavy, ponderous; clumsy;
oppressed.
omomi weight, emphasis, importance.
omomuki effect; taste; elegance; air,
appearance; **omomuki no áru** refined,
elegant; **omomuki no nái** tasteless,
vulgar.
omomúku to go; to proceed to; to grow; to
get.
omomuro ni slowly; gently; softly.
ÓMO NA chief, major, leading; **ómo na
hitóbito** important persons; **ómo na
sangyoo** principal industries.
omoni heavy load.
omonjíru See **omonzúru.**
omonzúru = omonjíru to honor, respect,
think much of.
omoomoshíi serious; imposing; dignified;
omoomóshiku solemnly, seriously.
omori weight, plumb, sinker.
omosa weight, heaviness.
omoshi weight (heavy object used to put
pressure on something); paperweight;
omoshi o oku to place a weight on.
omoshirogáru to amuse oneself; to be
amused; to think (something) funny.

omoshirohánbun half in fun.
OMOSHIRÓI interesting; pleasant, diverting;
funny, odd; amusing; **omoshíroku**
pleasantly; interestingly, delightfully,
etc.; **omoshíroku nái** uninteresting,
dull, stupid; unpleasant;
omoshiromi interest; enjoyment; fun;
omoshirosóo ni with seeming
(apparent) interest, enjoyment; like
fun. **Kodomótachi wa omoshirosóo ni
asonde imasu.** The children are
playing, apparently enjoying
themselves.
OMOTE face; obverse; right side; exterior;
front; first half; **omoté ni** outdoors;
omote no to front door; **omoté o
dáshite** right side up; **Omote Nihón**
the Pacific side of Japan.
omotemon front gate.
omotemuki openly, publicly; officially;
omotemuki no public, open, etc.
omotezáshiki front parlor.
OMÓU to think; to consider; to believe; to
wish, desire; to yearn for; to feel; to
feel like; to regard (as); to expect; to
hope; to imagine; **yóku omóu** to think
well of. **Kimi ga koko ni irú to wa
omowánakkatta.** I had no idea you
were here. **Máa omótte mo minasái.**
Just think of it!
omowaréru to seem, appear; to look; to be
thought of (as). **Ame ga furisóo ni
omowaréru.** It looks like rain.
omowaseburi suggestive manner, coquetry;
omowaseburi na suggestive,
coquettish.
omowaséru to make (one) think; to remind
(one) of; to be suggestive of.
omowashíi satisfactory, desirable;
omowáshiku nái unsatisfactory.
omówazu unexpectedly; unconsciously,
unintentionally.
omoya main house.
ón kindness, goodness; favor; obligation; **ón
ni kanjiru** to feel indebted to; **ón ni
kiru** to be deeply grateful to; **ón o
káesu** to repay a kindness.
on sound; tone; voice.
onaídoshi same age; **onaídoshi de áru** to be
the same age.
ONAJI same, identical; equal, equivalent to,
similar, like; **onaji yóo na** of the same
kind; **onaji yóo ni** alike; **onaji ni**
equally, etc.
ONAKA stomach, belly, abdomen. **Onaka ga
suita.** I'm hungry. **Onaka ga itái.** I
have a stomach-ache.
ÓNDO temperature.
ongáeshi repayment of a favor; **ongáeshi o
suru** to repay a kindness (or favor).
óngaku (high frequency) music; **ongakuteki
no** musical; **óngaku no sensei** music
teacher; **ongakudoo** concert hall;
ongaku zúki music lover.

114

ongi favor, obligation.

oní fiend, devil; creditor; ghost; **oni no yóo na** fiendish, inhuman.

onjín patron, benefactor.

onjoo warm heart, warm feeling; **onjoo áru** warm-hearted.

onjooshúgi paternalism.

onjun na gentle, meek.

onkei favor.

onken moderation; **onken na** moderate, temperate; sensible; **onken na sétsu a** sensible opinion.

onkoo na gentle, courteous.

onkyoo sound, noise.

onkyuu pension; **onkyuu o ukéru** to receive a pension.

ONNA woman, female; female sex; mistress; **onna no ónna** woman's; feminine; **onnarashíí** womanly; ladylike; **ONNÁ NO KO** young girl; daughter; **onnashújin** landlady, mistress.

óno ax.

onóono each, everyone; all; respectively.

onsen, onsenba hot springs, spa; **onsényado** hot springs inn.

ónshi (highly respected) teacher (to whom a special indebtedness is felt).

onshin correspondence; **onshin suru** to correspond with.

onshírazu ingratitude; **onshírazu na** ungrateful.

onshitsu hothouse, greenhouse.

ónsu ounce.

ónwa na mild, gentle; genial.

oo oh! how!

ooame heavy rain, downpour.

ooárashi, ooare severe storm.

óobo subscription; application; **óobo suru** to sub....cribe to; to apply, make application; **oobósha** applicant; subsc...ber.

ooboo oppression, tyranny; **ooboo na** arbitrary; tyrannical; **ooboo o kíwaméru** to tyrannize; to be high-handed.

oobun English or any Occidental written language or alphabet; **oobundénpoo** telegram written in the English (or any Occidental) alphabet.

oobun no appropriate, suitable; reasonable.

ooburi heavy downpour.

oocháku dishonesty; cunning; laziness; **oocháku na** dishonest; cunning; selfish; lazy.

óoda assault and battery; **óoda suru** to assault.

oodan crossing, intersection; **oodan suru** to cross, run across.

oodeki triumph, great success.

ooen aid, assistance; **ooen suru** to aid, support.

OOFUKU (*n.*) going and returning, round-trip; **oofuku ryóko** round trip; **oofuku suru** to go and return; **oofukuhágaki** return (post) card; **oofukukíppu** round-trip ticket.

oogesa exaggeration; **oogesa na** exaggerated; **oogesa na hanashi** tall story,

exaggeration; **oogesa na kotó iu** to exaggerate.

oogí folding fan; **oogí o tsukau** to fan oneself.

oogóe loud voice; **oogóe de** in a loud voice, loudly.

óohei arrogance; **óohei na** arrogant; **óohei ni** arrogantly.

oohíroma large, grand hall.

ooi cover, covering; shade; screen; **ooí o suru** to cover, to wrap.

ÓOI there are lots of, heaps of, plenty, many, numerous, much. **Nihón ni wa yamá ga óoi.** There are many mountains in Japan. **Nihonjín ni wa Eigo o hanásu hitó ga óoi.** There are lots of Japanese who speak English. **Anó hito wa kodomo ga óoi.** He has many children.

óoi you hoo!, hello!

ooísogi urgency; **ooísogi de** in great haste, hurriedly; **ooísogi de iku** to hurry to, rush to.

oojíru see **oozúru**.

oojíkake large scale; **oojíkake de, oojíkake no** on a large scale.

oojíte in proportion to; according to; in reply to; **hitsuyoo ni oojíte** according to the need; according to the demand.

óojoo death; **óojoo suru** to die; to submit to, give in.

OOKATA probably, perhaps, maybe, almost, in general.

ÓOKEI O.K.

OOKÍI = **ÓOKINA** big, large, great; heavy; powerful; huge, massive; **hijoo ni ookíi** huge, of great proportions; **óokina kotó o iu** to talk big, brag.

óokiku big, large, on a large scale; **óokiku náru** to grow larger, be enlarged; **óokiku suru** to enlarge, make larger.

óokina see **ookíi**.

ookisa size, dimension, volume, bulk; **ookisa ga onaji** to be the same size; **ookisa ga chigau** to differ in size;—**kurai no ookisa de aru** to be about the size of.

ookoo (*n.*) being rampant; **ookoo suru** to overrun; to be rampant; to swagger; to go sideways.

óoku in many cases, in numerous cases; **óoku wa** mostly; for the most part; largely; **óoku no** a great many; plenty of, lots of; **óoku tomo** at most; generally.

Ookura Dáijin Finance Minister; **Ookuráshoo** Finance Ministry.

ookyuu emergency; first aid; **ookyuu téate** first-aid treatment; **ookyúusha** ambulance.

oomata big strides; **oomata ni arúku** to stride; to walk with long steps.

oome (*n.*) overlooking; **oome ni míru** to overlook; to close one's eyes to; to let (something) pass.

oomísoka New Year's Eve.

óomizu heavy flood.

oomúkashi remote antiquity; primitive ages; **oomúkashi kara** from time immemorial.

oonoo anguish, agony; worry; **oonoo suru** to suffer anguish; to be in agony.

oo-oo often, frequently; sometimes.

ooppira ni openly, publicly.

oorai (street) traffic, comings and goings; **oorai suru** to come and go; to rise and fall. **Oorai ga óoi.** Traffic is heavy.

ooryoo usurpation, embezzlement; **ooryoo suru** to appropriate unlawfully; **ooryóosha** embezzler; **ooryóozai** embezzlement.

oosen response; acceptance; **oosen suru** to accept the challenge.

oosetsu reception; **oosetsu suru** to receive, visitors; **oosetsuma** reception room, drawing room.

ooshin doctor's visit to a patient; house call.

ooshuu seizure, confiscation; **ooshuu suru** to seize.

ooshuu answer, reply; **ooshuu suru** to answer.

oosóoji general cleaning; **oosóoji o suru** to give a general cleaning.

ootai reception; **ootai suru** to receive; to wait on (a customer).

óoto vomiting; **óoto suru** to vomit.

ootóbai motorcycle.

ootome automation.

ootoo answer, reply.

oóu to cover; to veil; to wrap; to envelop; to hide, conceal; to shelter.

ooúridashi large bargain sale.

ooútsushi close up (in a movie).

ooyake (*n.*) public; government; **ooyake no** (*adj.*) public, open; official; **ooyake ni suru** to publish; to make known; **ooyake ni náru** to be made known.

ooyasúuri bargain sale.

óoyoo generosity; **óoyoo na** big-hearted, generous.

ooyoo practical application; **ooyoo dekíru** applicable; **ooyoo suru** to put into use; to apply; to put to practical use.

oozáppa na rough, loose; **oozáppa na hanashí** roughly outline a story.

OOZÉI crowd, large number of people; **oozéi de** in large numbers; **oozéi no** many; large crowd of; **oozéi no kázoku** large family.

oozóra sky; heavens.

oozúru = oojíru to respond, reply; to comply with; to apply for.

ópera opera.

Oranda Holland; **Orandago** Dutch (language); **Orandájin** Dutchman.

orei = rei salute, salutation; etiquette; thanks; appreciation; remuneration.

oréru to break, snap, give way, yield; to be folded; **órete déru** to meet halfway. **Tsúe ga óreta** The stick was broken.

orí cage, pen.

orígami paper-folding (popular Japanese pastime).

origamitsuki no certified, guaranteed.

oríibu olive.

orikasanáru to overlap; to lie one on another;

orikasanátte overlapped; (stacked) in piles.

orímono cloth, textile.

ORÍRU to go down; to come down; to get down, get off; to leave; to get out of; to alight, land; **dénsha o oríru** to get off a streetcar; **kaidan o oríru** to descend the staircase.

óroka not to mention; to say nothing of.

oroshí wholesale business; **oroshí de uru** to sell wholesale, at wholesale price; **oroshine** wholesale price(s).

orósoka careless, negligent; **orósoka ni suru** to neglect.

ORÓSU to take down; to lower; to bring down, to drop, let fall; to hand down; to unload; to let (someone) get off; to sell at wholesale. **Kodo de oróshite kudasai.** Please let me get off here.

ÓRU to break; to bend, fold; to pick; to weave; **haná o óru** to pick a flower.

orugan organ.

osáeru to stop; to curb, check, hold down, suppress.

osamáru to be at peace; to be calmed down, be pacified. **Kaze ga osamarimashita.** The wind has died down.

osaméru to govern, rule; **ié o osaméru** to manage a household.

osanái infant; young; childish; **osanái koro ni** in childhood.

osháberi chattering; gossip; gossiper; **osháberi na** gossipy, talkative; **osháberi suru** to chatter; to gossip.

oshi deaf and dumb person; deaf-mute.

oshi weight; influence; **oshi no tsuyói** overbearing, brazen; **oshi ga kiku** to have influence.

oshiagéru to push; to thrust up.

oshiáu to push, jostle.

oshidashi presence, appearance, look; **oshidashi no yói** of fine appearance.

oshidásu to push out; to press forward; to force out.

oshie teaching, instruction; lesson; **oshiégo** pupil; **oshiekómu** to instill, teach, train; **OSHIERU** to teach, give lessons; to show; to tell; **Nihongo o oshieru** to teach Japanese.

oshihiroméru to extend, expand, spread.

OSHÍI regrettable; precious, valuable; wasteful. **Sore wa oshíi kotó desu.** That's a pity! **Suterú no wa oshíi desu.** It's too good to throw away.

OSHIIRE closet.

oshikakéru to force oneself into; to go uninvited.

oshikoméru to force in; to stuff into; **oshikómu** to force something into.

oshimázu liberally, freely.

oshíme diaper.

oshímu to value, prize; to spare; to grudge; to be stingy of; to regret; **kane o oshímu** to be stingy with money; **wakaré o oshímu** to be reluctant to leave.

oshinábete generally, in general.

oshinokéru to push away, to push aside.

oshiroi face powder.
oshitaósu to fell; to push down.
oshitatéru to raise, set up, erect.
oshitóosu to push through; to persist to the end.
oshitsubúsu to crush, smash, squash.
oshitsukéru to press, push against; to compel.
ochitsumáru to be jammed; to get near the end of the year. **Kotoshi mo oshitsumátte mairimáshita.** It's getting near the end of the year.
oshiuri forcing a sale; **oshiuri suru** to force a person to buy.
oshiwakéru to push apart; to push through.
oshiyáru to push aside.
oshiyoséru to push to one side; to advance on.
OSOI late, tardy; behind time: slow: **ashí ga osoi** to walk slowly; **kaerí ga osoi** to be late in returning.
OSÓRAKU perhaps, maybe; in all probability; I'm afraid. **Osóraku moo Amerika e káetta no deshoo.** I suppose he has already returned to the United States.
osoré fear, terror; horror; awe, reverence; **osoré o idáku** to be afraid of; **osóreiru** to be overwhelmed, be awed; **osoreóoi** gracious, awe-inspiring; **osoreóoku mo** graciously. **Osóreirimasu.** I'm much obliged to you. **Osóreirimásu ga, kore o dóko ni okimashóo ka?** Excuse me—where shall I put this?
OSOROSHÍI fearful, awful, terrible, tremendous; **osoróshiku** terribly, etc; **osoróshiku atsúi** terribly hot; **osoróshisa** fear, terror, horror.
osóu to attack, assault.
osowaru to be taught.
OSU (*n.*) male (person), male (animal); **osu no** male (of a species); **osu neko, oneko** tomcat; (*v.*) to push, shove, press; to infer, deduce, guess; to recommend. **Yamada-san o oshimashita.** I recommended Mr. Yamada.
osui sewage; filthy water.
otafukúkaze mumps.
otaku See **taku.**
otearai See **teárai.**
oten stain; blot; blemish; **oten o tsukéru** to stain; to spot; **oten no nái** spotless.
OTÓ sound, noise; roar; tone, note; fame; **otó ni kikoeta** celebrated, noted; **otó o tátete** noisily; **otó o tatéru** to make a sound; to make noise.
OTOKO man; male; male adult; manly person; **otokorashíi** manly; **otokoráshiku** like a man; **otokó ni náru** to come of age; to become a man; **OTOKÓ NÓ KO** boy; **otokorashíi** manly; chivalrous; **otokoyámome** widower.
OTONA (male or female).
OTONASHÍI gentle, good, quiet; **otonáshiku suru** to keep quiet.
OTÓOSAN father (used as term of address by

the wife as well as children in the family).
OTOOTO younger brother.
otoroéru to decline; to fall.
otóru to be inferior; to fall behind.
otoshiiréru to trap, capture.
OTÓSU to drop, let fall; to lose; to dump; to remove; to take; to omit; to depreciate; **chikará o otósu** to lose strength, weaken. **Koppu o otóshite watta.** I dropped a cup and broke it.
OTOTOI day before yesterday.
OTÓTOSHI year before last.
otozuréru to call on, visit.
OTSURI = tsurisen small change (money).
otte later on; afterward.
OTTO husband.
OU to drive away, shoo; to pursue, to run after; **hi o otte day by day; jun o otte** gradually, in order; **hae o ou** to shoo flies.
óu to bear; to carry on one's back; to owe; to be due. **Watakushi wa ano hito ní óu tokoro ga óoi desu.** I owe him a lot. **Kodomo o senaka ni otte ikimashita.** She went there, carrying her child on her back.
OWARI end, termination, conclusion; **owari máde** to the last; **owari ni** in the end; **owari no** final, last; **owari o tsugeru** to come to an end; **OWARU** to end, come to an end, finish, complete. **Shigoto ga owatta.** The job is done.
owaseru to make carry; to lay a burden on.
OYÁ parent(s); dealer (of cards); **oyá no** parental; **oyá o uyamáu** to respect one's parents.
ÓYA oh!; oh dear!; my!
óyabun boss; master.
ÓYAJI old man; chap.
oyakáta boss, chief.
oyako parent and child.
oyáma female impersonator (actor).
oyáshiro Shinto shrine.
ÓYAYUBI thumb; big toe.
oyayúzuri inheritance; **oyayúzuri no** inherited (from one's parents).
oyobósu to influence, affect; exert; **kooéikyoo o oyobósu** to have a good influence on, to produce a good effect.
oyobu to reach; to amount to; to come up to; to extend; to cover; to match, equal; **oyobanai** to be no match (for); to be inferior (to); **oyobi mo tsukánai** not to begin to compare (to). **Sore ní wa oyobimasén.** Don't bother about that. **Watakushi wa káre ni oyobanai.** I'm no match for him.
oyogi (*n.*) swimming; swim; **oyógi ni iku** to go swimming; **OYÓGU** to swim; **yóku oyógu** to swim well. **Hitótsu oyogóo.** Let's go for a swim.
OYOSO about; roughly; as a rule; generally speaking; **oyoso gujúu yen** approximately 50 yen. **Óyoso káre hodo atama no yói monó wa nái.** It's

not too much to say that there is no one as sharp as he.

OYU = **YU** hot water; warm water; bath; **oyu ni háiru** to take a bath.

P

páatonaa partner.

PÁN bread; **pan ko** bread crumbs; **pán o éru** to earn one's living (bread); **pán o yaku** to bake bread; **pán'ya** bakery.

panamá boo panama hat.

panku puncture; **panku suru** to puncture.

panorama panorama.

párapara with a clatter; scattering as it falls; pitapat.

pásu pass, free ticket.

pátapata with a pattering sound; **pátapata suru** to patter; to flutter.

patchi Japanese-style close-fitting trousers (worn by workmen).

pachíri with a click.

pattári suddenly; all of a sudden; **pátto** suddenly; **pátto suru** to be gay; to be showy; **pátto moeru** to flare up.

pechánko flattened; crushed; **pechánako ni náru** to be flattened or crushed.

peeji page.

pékopeko cringing; hungry; **pékopeko suru** to cringe; to fawn upon. **Onaka ga pekopeko desu.** I'm awfully hungry.

PÉN fountainpen; pen; **penga** pen-and-ink drawing; **penjiku** penholder; **pensáki** pen point; **pen shúuji** penmanship.

penginchoo penguin.

penki paint; **penki o nuru** to paint; **penkiya** painter.

pérapera fluently, glibly; **pérapera hanásu** to speak fluently; **pérapera shabéru** to chatter, jabber.

perorí to with a quick motion of the tongue; **perorí to naméru** to lick; **shitá o perorí to dásu** to stick out the tongue; **perorí to tabéru** to eat rapidly; to make short work of a meal.

pésuto pest; black plague.

PIANO piano; **piano o hiku** to play the piano.

píipii whistling; piping; **piipii naku** to cheep, chirp (said of birds); **píípii shite iru** to be hard up (for money).

pikáichi number one; (*colloq.*) ace, star.

pikápika glitteringly; **pikápika suru** to glitter, sparkle, flash, twinkle.

PÍN pin; hairpin; **anzénpin** safety pin.

pínpin in a lively manner; **pínpin shite iru** to be full of life, to be in the pink, to be well and sound.

pinsétto tweezerrs.

pinto focus; **pinto o awaséru** to focus, adjust the focus (of a camera).

pírapira flapping.

píripiri smarting; **píripiri suru** to smart, sting, burn.

pisharí with a bang; **pisharí to o o shiméru** to slam the door shut.

pisutoru pistol, revolver.

pitarí, pittari suddenly, closely, flatly; **pittári**

góji ni at five (o'clock) sharp; **pittári to áu** to fit to a T; **pitarí to tomaru** to come to a dead stop, to stop suddenly.

pítchi pitch (vocal or in a game); **pítchaa** pitcher (in a ball game).

pointo point; decimal point; (railroad) switch.

pokan to vacantly; absent-mindedly; **pokan to shite iru** to look blank.

pókapoka growing warmer; **pókapoka shite kúru** to grow warmer; **pókapoka suru** to feel warm.

POKÉTTO pocket; **pocketto mánee** pocket money.

pónpu pump; **pónpu de mizu o kumiagéru** to pump up water (from a well).

ponchie cartoon; caricature.

póndo pound.

póoru pole.

póroporo in drops, tricklingly.

PÓSUTO postbox, mailbox; **pósuto ni ireru** to mail.

pótapota drop by drop; **pótapota to taréru** to fall in drops; to trickle; to drip.

potchíri just a little, a bit, a drop.

pótsupotsu little by little; in drops; bit by bit; **pótsupotsu kúru** to drop in (for a short visit).

pótto in a glow; **pótto kao o akaraméru** to blush.

púnpun piquantly; **púnpun nióu** to smell piquant; to smell fragrant; to stink, reek; **púnpun okóru** to be in a huff; to fume.

puremiamu premium; **puremiamu o tsukéru** to place a premium (on); **puremiamu ga tsúite iru** to be at a premium.

púro pro, professional athlete.

puropagánda propaganda; **puropagánda o suru** to publicize; to spread propaganda.

puropéra propeller.

puroretária proletariat; proletarians.

pyúu whizzing, whistling; **pyúu to fuku** to whistle; **pyúu to tobu** to whiz through the air.

R

-RA suffix denoting: and others; and the like, etc. **Kimíra ni wa ienai desu.** I can't tell it to you people.

ráchi picket-fence; limit; **ráchi mo nái** foolish, silly; **ráchi ga aku** to reach a settlement; **ráchi ga akanaí** to make little headway, remain unsettled; **rachígai ni déru** to go beyond bounds.

rágubii rugby.

-rai suffix denoting: since, the past; **sakunénrai** since last year.

raichoo suru to arrive in Japan.

RÁIGETSU next month; **saraigetsu** month after next.

raiharu = **raishun** next spring.

raihin guest; **raihínseki** visitor's seats.

raihoo visit, call; **raihoo suru** to visit.

raikai attendance; **raikai suru** to attend a

meeting; **raikáisha** audience; attendance; **raikyaku** visitor, guest.

raimei thunderclap.

RAINEN next year; **sarainen** year after next.

raion lion.

ráiraku frankness; **ráiraku na** frank; open-hearted; broad-minded.

raireki career, history, origin (personal); **raireki o tadásu** to inquire into one's past.

raishun = raiharu next spring.

RAISHUU next week; **saraishuu** week after next.

raisukáree curried rice.

ráiu thunderstorm. **Ráiu ga áru daroo.** There will be a thunderstorm.

raiyuu visit (from aborad); **raiyúusha** visitor; **raiyuu gáijin** foreign visitor.

RÁJIO radio; **rajio hóosoo** radio braodcasting; **rájio o kiku** to listen to the radio; **rájio o tomeru** to turn off the radio.

rakétto racket (tennis, etc.).

rakka (*n.*) falling; **rakka suru** to fall; to drop.

rakkan optimism; **rakkanteki** optimistic; **rakkan suru** to be optimistic.

rakkásan parachute.

rakkásei peanut.

RAKÚ comfort, ease; pleasure; **rakú na** comfortable, easy; **rakú o suru** to take it easy. **Oraku ni nasátte kudasái.** Make yourself comfortable.

rakuchaku settlement; **rakuchaku saseru** to settle, bring to a conclusion; **rakuchaku suru** to be settled.

rakudai rejection; failure in an exam; **rakudai suru** to fail (flunk) an exam; to be rejected.

rakuen paradise.

rakugaki scribbling.

rakugo comic story.

rakugósha straggler.

rakuséishiki inauguration ceremony; completion ceremony.

rakusen defeat in an election; failure; rejection; **rakusénsha** defeated candidate.

rakutan discouragement; despair; **rakutan saseru** to discourage; **rakutan suru** to be discouraged; to be disappointed.

rakutenka optimist; **rakutenshúgi** optimism.

ranboo volence, outrage; **ranboo na** violent; rude; rowdy; disorderly; **ranboo suru** to behave rudely; **ranboomono** ruffian, rowdy.

RÁNCHI lunch; **ránchi o tabéru** to have lunch.

randoku desultory reading.

rankan railing, handrail.

ránpu lamp.

ran'yoo abuse; misuse; **ran'yoo suru** to abuse.

ranzatsu disorder, confusion; **ranzatsu na** disorderly, untidy; **ranzatsu ni náru** to get confused; to be in disorder.

ranzoo overproduction; **ranzoo suru** to overproduce.

rappa trumpet, cornet, horn; **rappa o fuku** to blow a horn; **rappa nomi o yaru** to drink (something) directly from the bottle.

rasen screw; spiral spring; **rasenkei** spiral form; **rasenkei no** spiral-shaped.

rásha woolen cloth.

RASHÍI -like; becoming; looking (like); appear, seem; it seems to me; probably; **kodomorashíi** childish, childlike. **Soo rashíi.** I guess so. **Ame rashíi.** It looks like rain. **Kuru rashii desu.** It seems he is coming.

rashinban compass.

réesu lace; race.

RÉI custom, usage, habit, precedent; instance, case, example; zero; = **ORÉI** salute, salutation; etiquette; thanks, appreciation; remuneration; return; present; soul, spirit, memory; **reiteki na** spiritual; **réi ni yotte** as usual; **réi no** usual, customary; **réi o ageru** to for instance; **réi o ageru** to give an instance; **réi ni náru** to set a precedent; **réi o suru** to salute; to curtsy; to bow; **rei o nobéru** to express one's thanks.

reidai example; exercise.

réido zero; freezing point (Centigrade); **réido íka** below zero.

réifuku evening dress.

reigai exception; **reigai no** exceptional; **reigai ni suru** to except, make an exception of.

reigi courtesy, etiquette; **reigi tadashíi** courteous. **Káre wa reigí ga tadashíi.** He has good manners.

reihai worship; **reihai suru** to worship; **reihaidoo** chapel; church.

reijoo letter of thanks; **reijoo o dásu** to send a letter of thanks.

reikai regular meeting.

reikoku cruelty; **reikoku na** cruel; coldhearted.

reikoo strict enforcement; **reikoo suru** to enforce strictly.

reikyaku refrigeration; cooling; **reikyaku suru** to cool; to refrigerate; **reikyakúhin** refrigerator, freezer.

reiméiki dawn of a new age.

reinen ordinary year, average year; annually, every year; **reinen mátsuri** annual festival; **reinen no tóori** as usual; as every year.

reiraku ruin, downfall; **reiraku suru** to be ruined, go to ruin.

reisei coolness, calmness; **reisei na** cool, calm; **reisei na hitó** cold-hearted person; **reisei ni kangáeru** to think about something calmly.

reishoo cold smile, sneer; **reishoo suru** to sneer at; to mock; to give a mocking laugh.

reisoo formal wear; ceremonial dress.

reisui cold water; **reisuimásatsu** rubdown
with a cold wet towel; **reisúiyoku** cold
bath; **reisúiyoku suru** to take a cold
bath.

reitán indifference, coolness; **reitán na** cool;
cold; indifferent; **seiji ni reitán de áru**
to be indifferent to politics.

reitén zero, zero point; **reitén o tóru** to get a
zero.

reitóoniku frozen meat.

reizen offering to the spirits of the dead.

reizoo cold storage; refrigeration; **reizoo suru**
to refrigerate; **reizóoko** refrigerator;
reizóosha refrigerated freight car.

rekidai successive generations.

rekishi history; **Nippon rékishi** Japanese
history; **rekishijoo yuumei na tokoro**
place of historical interest; **rekishijoo
no jínbutsu** historical personage;
rekishika historian.

rekizen clear, obvious; **rekizen to** clearly,
plainly; **rekizen to shite akíraka
desu.** It's as plain as day.

rekkoku nations (of the world); (world)
powers.

rékkyo enumeration; **rékkyo suru** to
enumerate, list.

rekkyoo great (world) powers (countries).

rekóodo record; phonograph record; **rekoodo
yáburi no record-breaking; rekóodo o
tsukúru** to establish a record; to create
a new record; **rekoodo o yabúru** to
break a record; **rekóodo o kakéru** to
play a record (on a phonograph).

renmei joint signature; **renmei suru** to sign
jointly.

renpoo federation (of states); union;
commonwealth; **renpoo no** united,
federated, etc.

REN'AI love; **ren'ai jíken** love affair; **ren'ai
kánkei ni náru** to fall in love; to have
a love affair.

renchuu party; company.

rénga brick(s).

rengoo combination, union, confederation,
amalgamation; alliance, coalition;
rengoo suru to combine, etc.; **rengoo
no** allied; associated, etc.;
rengóokoku allied countries; **Kokusai
Rengoo** United Nations.

renketsu suru to couple, join, connect.

renraku connection; traffic; communication;
renraku suru to make contact;
renraku o tóru to get in touch with;
renraku o ushináu to lose touch, lose
contact; **renrakusen** ferryboat
(connected with a train).

renshuu practice, training, drill, rehearsal;
renshuu o tsunda well-trained;
renshuu suru to practice, etc.

rensoo association (of ideas); **rensoo suru** to
be reminded of; to associate (one) with
(another).

rentaisékinin joint responsibility.

Rentogen sen X-ray; **Rentogen sen ni kakáru**
to be X-rayed.

renzoku continuity; succession; **renzoku suru**

to continue; to last; **renzoku teki no**
continuous; consecutive; **renzokuteki
ni** continuously.

rénzu lens.

reppuu heavy wind, hurricane. **Reppuu ga
fúite iru.** There's a heavy wind
blowing.

resseki attendance;—**ni resseki suru** to
attend, be present at.

resseraréru to be ranked with.

réssha railway train.

ressúru to attend, be present; to rank with,
take one's place among.

rétsu row, rank, tier, column, line; **rétsu o
tsukúru** to form a row, line up.

rettoo archipelago, chain of islands;
Chishima réttoo the Kuriles.

rettoo inferiority; **rettoo na otoko** man of bad
moral character; **rettoo no** inferior, of
poor quality; **rettóohin** low-quality
goods.

rí advantage; benefit; interest; reason, right,
truth, principle; unit of measurement
equal to 2.44 miles; **rokúbu no ri** 6
per cent interest; **rí no áru**
advantageous, beneficial; reasonable;
justifiable; **rí ga áru** to be profitable;
rí o eru to profit from, gain by; **rí ni
somúku** to be against reason.

ríbon ribbon; **ríbon de musubu** to tie with a
ribbon.

ríchi intellect; **richiteki na** intellectual.

richigimono honest, upright man.

ríeki benefit, gain, profit; **ríeki no áru**
profitable, lucrative; **ríeki o hógo suru**
to protect one's interests; **riekíkin**
profits, proceeds.

rien = rikon divorce; **rien suru** to divorce.

rifújin unreasonableness; **rifújin na**
unreasonable, unjust.

rígai advantages and disadvantages; interests;
rígai ni kankei ga áru to have an
effect on one's interests; to have an
interest in.

rigaku hákushi Doctor of Science.

rigákushi Bachelor of Science.

rihatsu haircutting; hairdressing;
RIHATSUJO barber shop; **rihatsúshi**
barber.

ríido (n.) leading; **ríido suru** to lead.

ríji director; manager; **rijíchoo** chairman of a
board of directors; **rijíkai** board of
directors.

ríka science.

ríkai understanding, comprehension; **ríkai
dekiru** understandable,
comprehensible; **ríkai no nái** without
understanding; **ríkai no áru hitó**
sensible person; **ríkai suru** to
understand; to grasp; to appreciate;
rikáiryoku understanding,
comprehension.

rikímu to strain oneself; to brag; to swagger.

rikisaku masterpiece; elaborate work.

rikisetsu suru to emphasize, to lay stress on;
to be emphatic.

rikkóoho candidacy (for an election);

rikkóoho suru to run as a candidate; **rikkóoho o happyoo suru** to announce one's candidacy; **rikkoohósha** candidate.

rikoo cleverness, smartness; performance; **rikoo na** clever, shrewd, bright, intelligent; **rikoo soo na** bright-, intelligent looking; **rikoo suru** to carry out, to fulfill.

RIKON = **rien** divorce; **rikon suru** to divorce.

rikoshúgi egoism.

rikoteki egoistic, selfish.

riku, rikuchi land; **riku o iku** to go by land; **ríkuro** land journey, land road (route). (See also **rikujoo**.)

rikúgun army.

rikujoo land, ground; **rikujoo de** on land. (See also **riku**.)

rikutsu theory; argument; pretext; reason, logic; **rikutsu ni áu** to stand to reason; **rikutsu ga tatánai** to be unreasonable, be illogical; **rikutsuppói** argumentative; **rikutsuzeme** persuasive reasoning; **nán toka kán toka rikutsu o tsukéte** on one pretext or another; **rikutsuzeme ni suru** to persuade (someone) by reason.

rikuzoku in succession, one after another.

rímen back, reverse, other side; **rímen de** behind the scenes, in secret; **rímen de ayatsúru** to pull strings; **rímen o kansatsu suru** to look at the other side.

RINGO apple; **ringo no kí** apple tree.

ringoku neighboring country.

rinjin neighbor; **rinjin no yóshimi** neighborliness.

rinjuu one's last (deathbed) moment; **rinjuu no kotoba** dying words.

rínka neighboring house, house next door.

rinkaku contours, outline; **rinkaku o nobéru** to give an outline, sketch.

rínri ethics, morality.

rinyuu suru to wean.

RIPPA fineness, richness; **rippa na** fine, splendid, good, nice, excellent, stately; **rippa ni** superbly, admirably, sufficiently; **rippa ni seikatsu suru** to make a decent living. **Rippa desu.** It's splendid.

rippoo legislation; **rippoo no** legislative.

rippuku anger, rage; **rippuku suru** to get angry; **rippuku saseru** to make angry.

rirei relay race.

rireki personal history, career; **rireki ga yói** to have a good record of service; **rireki ga warúi** to have a poor record of service; **rirékisho** personal history, record of one's life.

ririku take-off; **ririku suru** to take off; to get afloat.

ririshíi imposing; majestic.

riron theory.

ríroseizen logical, valid.

risáichi stricken locality.

risáisha victim, sufferer.

risan dispersion; **risan suru** to be dispersed.

ríshi interest; **yasui ríshi** low interest; **takái ríshi** high interest; **ríshi o tóru** to charge interest.

risoo ideal; **takái risoo** high ideal; **risoo shúgi** idealism; **risooteki** ideal; idealistic.

risookyoo utopia.

risshoo proof; **risshoo suru** to prove, demonstrate, bear out.

risshun first day of spring.

risurin glycerine.

riteihyoo milestone; **ritei** mileage, distance.

rítsu rate, proportion; **rítsu o ageru** to raise the rate.

ritsuan plan, device; **ritsuan suru** to plan, design, devise.

riyoo utilization; **riyoo suru** to use; to make use of, utilize; to take advantage of; **kikái o riyoo suru** to take advantage of an opportunity.

riyuu reason, cause; **riyuu de** for reasons of; **riyuu náku** without cause, without provocation; **riyuu no áru** reasonable; **riyuu no nái** groundless; **riyuu o nobéru** to state one's reason.

rizai finance, economy.

ro hearth, fireplace; oar.

robata fireside.

roboo roadside, wayside; **roboo no chaya** wayside teahouse; **roboo no hitó** passerby; **roboo ni tátsu** to stand by the roadside.

rodai balcony (outdoor).

rohen fireside.

róji alley, lane.

roken discovery, exposure; **roken suru** to be found out; to be detected.

rokotsu frankness; **rokotsu na** frank, candid; plain; naked; **rokotsu na atekosuri** broad hint; **rokotsu ni iéba** frankly speaking.

ROKÚ six; **dái roku** the sixth; **ROKUJÚU** sixty; **rokumai byóobu** six-fold screen.

rokudenashi (n.) good-for-nothing.

ROKUGATSU June.

rokuon recording, transcription; **rokuónki** recorder (sound recording machine); **teepu shiki rokuónki** tape recorder; **rokuon suru** to record; to make a recording.

rón argument; discussion; essay; opinion; **rón o matánu** to be beyond argument; **ronbun** essay, article; thesis; **rongai** out of the question, irrelevant; **rónri** logic; **ronriteki** logical; **ronriteki ni** logically; **rónri ni awánai** to be illogical; **ronsetsu** essay; editorial, dissertation; **ronsetsu kisha** editorial writer; **ronzúru** to discuss; to argue.

ronkoku prosecution; **ronkoku suru** to prosecute.

róo wax; **róo o hiku** to wax; **roobiki** waxing; **roobiki no** waxed; **róogami** wax paper.

róoa deaf and dumb.

ROOBA old woman.

RÓOBO aged mother.

roobai confusion, panic; **roobai suru** to be confused; to be in a panic.

rooden short circuit.

roodoku recitation; **roodoku suru** to recite, read aloud.

roodoo manual labor, work; **jikangai róodoo** overtime work; **roodoo jíkan** working hours; **roodoo káikyuu** laboring class; **roodoo kúmiai** labor union; **roodoo kúmiai yakuin** labor leader; **roodoo móndai** labor problem; **roodósha** laborer; **roodoo sóogi** labor dispute; **roodoo úndoo** labor movement; **roodoo suru** to labor, work. (See also **róoryoku**.)

róogo old age.

roohi waste (of time, energy); extravagance; **roohi suru** to waste, squander; **jikan o roohi suru** to waste time.

ROOJIN old man; aged (person).

rooka corridor, passageway, hall.

ROOMAJI Roman letters; romanization (anglicization); **roomaji de tsuzuru** to spell in Roman letters.

róomansu romance.

ROOMA SÚUJI Roman numerals.

roonen old age.

roonin unemployed man; **roonin shite iru** to be out of work; to be studying for an entrance examination to a college.

rooren expert; **rooren na** experienced.

róoryoku labor, effort; **róoryoku fusoku** labor shortage. (See also **roodoo**.)

roosóku candle; **roosokútate** candlestick.

róosu sirloin.

rootai old person.

Rootari Kúrabu Rotary Club.

rooyá = keimusho prison, jail.

RÓSHIA = Soren Russia; U.S.S.R.; **Róshia no** (*adj.*) Russian; **Roshiago** Russian language; **Roshiájin** Russian (person).

roten open air; **roten no** outdoor.

rúi kind, sort, variety; description; similar case; parallel; **rúi no nái** unique; unparalleled; **ano rúi no hito** people of that sort.

ruibetsu classification; **ruibetsu suru** to classify.

ruiji resemblance, similarity, likeness; **ruiji no** similar, analogous; **ruijíten** point of resemblance; **—ni ruiji suru** to be like, be similar to.

ruikei total sum; **ruikei suru** to total.

ruirei similar case, analogy; **ruirei no nái** unique; exceptional.

rúnpen tramp, hobo.

RÚSU absence; **rusuchuu ni** during (one's) absence; **rúsu ni suru** to be out (not at home); **rúsu o tsukau** to pretend not to be in. **Sanpo ni itte rúsu desu.** He has gone out for a walk.

rusuban = rusui temporary caretaker (while a person is away from home).

rusui See **rusuban**.

ryáku abbreviation; abridgment; **ryaku sázu ni** in detail (without abbreviating); **ryakú shite** in short; **ryaku súru** to abridge; to abbreviate; **ryakugo** abbreviation; **ryakuji** simplified character; simpler substitute; abbreviation.

ryakudatsu suru to loot; to plunder.

ryakushiki informal way; **ryakushiki no** informal; **ryakushiki de, ryakushiki ni** informally.

ryakuzu rough sketch; **ryakuzu o tóru** to make a rough sketch of.

RYOKAKU traveler; passenger; tourist; **ryokaku annaijo** travelers' aid.

RYOKAN Japanese-style hotel or inn.

ryohi traveling expenses.

ryoken passport; **ryoken o káfu suru** to issue a passport; **ryoken o shinsei suru** to apply for a passport.

RYOKOO travel; trip; tour; **ryokoo suru** to travel; **ryokoo ni dekakeru** to start on a journey; **RYOKOO ÁNNAI** guidebook; **ryokoo annaisho** travel agency.

ryoo- prefix denoting: both, two; **ryooashi** both legs; both feet; **RYOOGAWA** both sides; **RYOOHOO** both; both sides; **ryoogan** both banks of a river; **ryoomen** both sides; **ryoomen o kansatsu suru** to examine both sides; **ryóoshin** both parents; **ryootan** both ends; **ryoote** both hands; **ryoote de mótsu** to hold in both hands. **Ryoohoo tomo shitte iru.** I know both of them.

ryóo quantity, volume; hunting; shooting; game; fishing; **ryóo ni iku** to go hunting; to go fishing.

ryóodo territory, possession.

ryoogae money-changing, exchange of money; **Béika o Nihon no okane ni ryoogae suru** to change American money into Japanese money.

ryoohoo remedy; method of treatment.

ryóoji consul; **ryoojíkan** consulate; **soo ryoojíkan** consulate general.

ryooji medical treatment.

ryookai comprehension; **ryookai suru** to comprehend, grasp; to see. **Sore wa watakushi ní wa ryookai dekínai.** It's beyond my comprehension.

ryóoken idea, thought, notion; intention; view; direction; **ryóoken o kiku** to ask (someone) his intention; **ryóoken o suéru** to make up one's mind. **Dóo iu ryóoken de sonna kotó o shitá no desu ka?** What made you do such a thing?

RYÓOKIN charge, fee; fare; **ryóokin o torázu ni** free of charge; **ryóokin o tóru** to charge.

ryookoo na successful; favorable.

ryoomáchisu = ryuumachi rheumatism.

RYÓORI cooking, cuisine; dish; food; **ryóori suru** to cook; to prepare food; **Nippon ryóori o tabéru** to have a Japanese meal.

ryooritsu compatibility; coexistence; **ryooritsu suru** to be compatible with; to be consistent with; **ryooritsu shigatái** to be incompatible with, to be inconsistent with.

ryooríya restaurant (Japanese-style).

ryóoshin both parents; conscience; **ryooshinteki** conscientious. **Ryóoshin ga togaméru.** My conscience bothers me.

ryooshuushoo receipt.

ryóoyoo convalescence; **ryooyoo suru** to convalesce.

ryúuchoo fluency; **ryúuchoo na** fluent; **ryúuchoo ni** fluently, eloquently; **ryúuchoo ni Nihongo o hanásu** to speak Japanese fluently.

ryuudóobutsu liquid diet.

ryuugaku suru to study aborad; **ryuugákusei** student studying abroad.

ryuugí style; method.

ryuukan influenza.

ryuukoo fashion, fad; popularity; **ryuukoo no** fashionable, in fashion; **ryuukoo suru** to be in fashion; to come into fashion; **ryuukoo ni okureru** to be out of fashion, out of style.

S

-SA suffix added to the stem of an adjective to make a noun (comparable to English -ty, -ness); **bakabakáshisa** stupidity, stupidness; **shitashísa** familiarity.

sa difference; margin. **Sa ga áru.** There is a difference.

SÁA come; now; well; let me see. **Sáa taihen na kotó o shita.** Oh, what have I done! **Sáa ikimashóo.** Let's go now.

sáabisu service (at a restaurant, store, etc.). **Sáabisu ga yói.** The service is good.

saachíráito searchlight.

sáakasu circus.

sabáketa sensible; frank; **sabáketa hito** man of the world.

sabaku desert.

sabáku to judge; to decide; to settle; to disentangle; to sell; **Hito o sabáku na.** Don't judge others.

sabasába shita refreshing; agreeable.

saaberu Occidental-style sword; saber.

sábetsu distinction; discrimination; differentiation; difference; **sábetsu no áru** discriminating; **sábetsu naku** without discrimination; **sábetsu o tsukéru** to discriminate.

sabí rust; patina; antique look; maturity; **sabí ga tsuku** to become rusty.

sabiréru to cease to flourish.

SABISHÍI lonely, lonesome; deserted, desolate.

sabóru to go slow; to sabotage; to cut classes.

sabotáaju sabotage; going slow.

sadamáru to fix; to become settled; to be determined; to be subjugated; **sadamátta** regular, fixed, definite;

sadaméru to establish; to lay down; decide; to settle. **Hi ga sadamarimáshita.** The date is fixed. **Sadamátta jikan ni kimásu.** He comes at a regular time. **Shuppatsu no hi o sadamemashita.** I decided on a date of departure.

sadámeshi surely; doubtlessly; no doubt; **sadámete** surely; to be sure.

—SÁE even; only. **Anó hito sae shitte imásu.** Even he knows it. **Okane sáe áreba kaimásu.** I'll buy it if only I have the money for it.

saegíru to cut off; to stop; to interrupt; to hinder, to obstruct, block; **mé o saegíru** to obstruct a view; **hito no hanashí o saegíru** to cut in; to interrupt (someone's) conversation.

saéru to be bright, be clear; to attain a rare skill; **mé ga saéru** to be wakeful. **Tsukí ga saéru.** The moon shines clearly. **Nakanaka sáeta ude desu.** He is quite expert in it.

saezúru to sing, warble (a bird).

safúran saffron.

sagaku balance; difference.

SAGÁRU to hang down; to fall; to go down (in price); to leave; to retire; **SAGÉRU** to hang down; to lower, let down; to clear away; to wear (a sword); **akari o sagéru** to lower a lamp; **nedan o sagéru** to lower a price; **ozen o sagéru** to clear a table. **Nichiyóohin no ne ga sagarimáshita.** The prices of ordinary commodities have come down.

sagashidásu to find out, discover.

SAGASU to seek, search for.

sági fraud; imposture; deceit, cheating; **sági o hataraku** to defraud; **sagíshi** swindler.

saguri probe; **saguri o ireru** to probe; **sagúru** to search for; to grope for; to probe; **íken o sagúru** to feel out (someone's) view; **pokétto o sagúru** to fumble in one's pocket.

ságyoo work, operation; **sagyoo chuu** while working; **ságyoo o hajimeru** to begin work; **sagyóoshitsu** workroom.

sáhai agency; management (of housing); **sáhai o suru** to act as an agent; **sahainin** agency.

sáhoo good manners; etiquette; **sáhoo o shiranai** ill-mannered.

sahodo so; so much; much (often used in the negative sense); **sahodo ni mo nái** not so much as you think.

SÁI talent; ability; difference; = **KÁNAI** (one's) wife; **sái no áru** talented; **gógaku no sái ga áru** to have an aptitude for languages; **sái o tanómu** to put too much confidence in one's own talents. **Sái ni kikimashóo.** I'll ask my wife.

sai year (as a counter for age); **sán sai** three years old; **juugó sai** fifteen years old.

saiai no dearest, beloved.

saibai cultivation (of plants); **saibai suru** to cultivate.

SÁIBAN judgment; trial; **saiban suru** to
    judge; **saibánchoo** chief judge;
    saibánkan judge, bench (legal);
    saibansho court of justice, law court;
    Saikoo Saibansho Supreme Court.
saiboo cell.
sáichi wit and intellect.
saijin sharp-witted person.
SÁICHUU in the midst of; in the course of; at
    the height of; **shokuji no sáichuu ni** in
    the middle of the meal. **Íma ga atsúi
    sáichuu da.** The summer heat is now
    at its height.
sáidaa soda pop, soda water.
saidai great and small; full particulars;
    greatest; maximum; **saidai morásazu**
    to the minutest details; **saidai no
    koofuku** the greatest happiness; **saidai
    sokúryoku** the maximum speed.
saidan altar.
saien talented girl; = **saikon** second
    marriage; **saien suru** to marry again.
SAIFU purse; wallet.
saigai calamity; **saigai o koomúru** to suffer a
    disaster.
saigen reappearance; **saigén suru** to reappear.
saigén limitation; **saigén ga nái** to be endless.
sáigetsu time; years. **Sáigetsu hito o mátazu.**
    Time and tide wait for no man.
SÁIGO (*n.*) one's last moment in life; (*adj.*)
    last; **hisan na sáigo o togéru** to die a
    sad death; **sáigo no** last, closing; **sáigo
    ni** lastly; **sáigo no toshi** the last year;
    saigo tsúuchoo an ultimatum.
saihai (baton of) command; direction,
    leadership; **saihai o furu** to command.
saihan reprinting; second edition; **saihan suru**
    to reprint; **saihan ni náru** to run into a
    second edition.
saihatsu reappearance; **saihatsu suru** to
    appear again; have a second attack (of
    a disease).
sáihi adoption or rejection; **sáihi o kimeru** to
    decide on the adoption or rejection.
saihoo sewing; needlework; **saihoo suru** to
    sew; **saihóoshi** tailor.
saijitsu national holiday.
SAIJOO (*n.*) best; highest; superlative; **saijoo
    no** (*adj.*) best; highest; **saijóohin**
    article of the best quality; **saijóokyuu**
    the superlative degree.
saikai meeting again; **saikai o yakusúru** to
    promise to meet again.
saikásoo lowest layer.
saiken debenture; **saikénsha** creditor.
saiketsu verdict, decision; **saiketsu suru** to
    bring in a verdict; to decide.
sáiki pressing creditor.
SAIKIN latest; **saikin no joohoo** latest
    information.
saikin bacterium.
saikon = **saien** second marriage; **saikon suru**
    to marry again.
saikoo maximum; revival; restoration;
    reconsideration; **saikoo suru** to

re-establish, renew; to reconsider;
    saikoo no ué de on reflection; **saikoo
    no** highest; supreme; **Saikoo
    Saibansho** Supreme Court.
saikóoten highest point.
saikóro dice.
saiku workmanship; **saiku o suru** to work; to
    make; to patch up; to manipulate.
sáikuru cycle.
saikutsu mining; **saikutsu suru** to work a
    mine.
saimatsu close of the year; **saimatsu no
    uridashi** year-end bargain.
saimin lower classes.
saimínjutsu hypnotism; **saiminjutsu o
    kakéru** to hypnotize (someone).
saimitsu smallness; minuteness; **saimitsu na**
    minute; detailed; **saimitsu ni** in detail.
saimoku details; items; **saimoku ni wataru** to
    go into detail.
sáimu debt; **sáimu o hatásu** to settle one's
    debts; **saimúsha** debtor.
sáin signature; **sain suru** to sign.
sainán misfortune, calamity, accident; **sainán
    ni áu** to meet with an accident
    (mishap); **sainán o manugaréru** to
    escape a disaster.
sainin reappointment.
sairai second coming; reincarnation.
sairei festival.
saisai again and again; **saisai no** repeated;
    frequent.
saisan over and over again.
saisei regeneration; resuscitation; **saisei suru**
    to come to life again.
saisen offertory; sacred pennies; **saisén bako**
    offertory box (at a Shinto shrine).
sáishi man of talent; one's wife and children.
saishiki coloring; painting; **saishiki shita**
    colored; **saishiki suru** to paint.
saishin rehearing; retrial; carefulness; latest;
    newest; **saishin suru** to rehear; to
    re-examine; **saishin no** careful,
    prudent; **saishin no chúui o mótte**
    most carefully; **saishinshiki** the latest
    type.
SAISHO beginning; **saisho no** first, original;
    saisho wa at first; **saisho ni** at the
    outset; in the first place; **saisho kara**
    from the very first.
saishoku (*n.*) living on vegetables only;
    vegetarian diet; **saishoku suru** to live
    on vegetables; **saishokushugísha**
    vegetarian.
saishoo (*n.*) minimum; smallest; **saishoo no**
    (*adj.*) smallest; least.
saishuu (*n.*) last, final; collection; **saishuu no**
    (*adj.*) last, final; **saishuu réssha** last
    train of a day; **saishuu suru** to collect;
    to gather samples.
sáisoku (*n.*) urging; calling upon; **sáisoku
    suru** to urge, press; **kane o sáisoku
    suru** to call upon a person in order to
    pay off one's debts.
saisoku detailed rules.
saitei no lowest, minimum.

saiten marking, scoring.

saiwai good fortune; happiness; **saiwai na** happy, fortunate; **saiwai ni** happily, fortunately.

saiyoo adoption; appointment; **saiyoo suru** to adopt; to use, employ.

saizen (*n.*) best; one's best; **saizen no** best; utmost; **saizen o tsukúsu** to do one's best.

SAJÍ spoon; **sají de sukuu** to spoon up; **sají o nagéru** to give up.

sajiki stand; gallery; upper boxes (in a theatre).

sáka tea and cake; **sáka o dásu** to serve refreshments.

SAKÁ sloping hill; slope; ascent; **saká ni náru** to slope; **saká o noboru** to go up a slope; **saká o kudaru** to go down a slope.

sakadachi o suru to stand on one's head.

sakaéru to prosper, flourish.

sakái boundary; border, frontier.

sakámichi a sloping way (road); sloping grade.

SAKAN prosperity; vigor; **sakan na** prosperous; splendid; vigorous; **sakan ni** actively; vigorously; **sakan ni náru** to become active.

SAKANA fish; **sakaná tsuri ni iku** to go fishing; **sakanaya** fishmonger; fish-dealer.

sakanobóru to go up; to go back, retrace.

sakarátte against; in the face of; **sakaráu** to oppose; to go against.

sakari height, climax; rut, heat; **sakari de áru** to be in full bloom; to be in the prime of.

sakasa, sakasama inversion, inverted order; **sakasa no** inverted; **sakasa ni** wrong side up; upside down; **sakasa ni náru** to be inverted.

sakasama See **sakasa**.

sakaya sake shop.

sakazúki cup; wine cup; **sakazúki o sásu** to offer a cup (of wine); **sakazúki o hósu** to drink up (a cup of wine or sake); **sakazúki o mawasu** to pass around a cup.

SAKE Japanese liquor, wine.

sáke salmon.

sakebi shout; cry; **sakébu** to shout; to cry.

sakei leaning toward the left; **sakei suru** to lean toward the left; to become communistic.

sakeme crack.

sakenómi drinker.

sakéru to avoid, to keep away from; to split; to be torn. **Kinomo ga sakemashita.** My dress was torn.

SAKI point; tip; future; destination; front; **saki e itte** later on; **saki no** (*adj.*) future; coming; former; **saki ni** beyond; previously; **saki ga nagái** to have a long future; **yubi no saki** tip of the finger. **Saki ni itte kudasái.** Please go ahead.

sakidátsu to precede.

sakigake pioneer; **sakigake no** the foremost; **sakigake o suru** to lead.

sakihodo kara for some time.

sakimáwari preoccupation, forestallment; **sakimáwari o suru** to get ahead of.

sakiototoi three days back, three days ago.

sakiotótoshi three years ago.

sakisóhon saxophone.

sakka writer, author; literary man.

sakkaku illusion.

sakki thirst for blood; menace; **sakki dátsu** to look menacing.

SÁKKI = SAKIHODO little while ago.

sákku sack; case.

sakkyoku musical composition, musical piece; **sakkyoku suru** to set to music.

sakkyokuka composer of music.

sáku device; plan; **sáku o megurasu** to devise a scheme; **sáku ga tsukíru** to be at wit's end.

saku to bloom.

SÁKU to rend, split, tear; **náka o sáku** to sever the two.

SAKÚBAN = YUUBE last evening, last night.

sakubun composition.

sakudoo maneuvers; artful management.

sakugen curtailment; retrenchment; **sakugen suru** to cut down.

sakuhin work (literary, musical, etc.).

sákui design; motif.

sakuin index; **sakuin o tsukúru** to provide with an index.

SAKÚJITSU = KINOO yesterday.

sákujo omission; **sákujo suru** to strike out; to omit.

SAKUNEN last year.

SAKURA cherry tree.

sakuranbo cherry (fruit).

sakurasoo Japanese primrose.

sakuryaku artifice; device; stratagem; scheme; **sakuryaku ní tómu** to be resourceful in scheming.

sakusei manufacture, production.

sakusen military or naval operation; strategy.

sákusha author; dramatist; poet; composer; maker.

SAKÚYA = YUUBE last night. (See also **sakúban**.)

sakyuu sandhill, dune.

-SAMA See **-SAN**.

samásu to wake up, awaken; to make sober; to cool; to bring down. **Kono ocha wa moo sukoshi samashite kara nomimashoo.** I will drink this tea after it has cooled a bit.

samatage disturbance; hindrance; **samatagéru** to obstruct, hinder.

samayóu to wander about; to stray.

samazáma various; **samazáma na hito** all sorts of people; **samazáma ni** in many ways.

SAMÉRU to wake up; to come to oneself; to become sober; to become cool; to be spoiled; to fade, discolor; **mé ga saméru** to be awakened; **yoí ga saméru** to become sober.

samezáme to bitterly; without restraint; **samezáme to naku** to weep bitterly.

SÁMO as though, as if; **sámo monzoku soo ni** with evident satisfaction. **Sámo ureshisóo desu.** He looks quite pleased.

samon inquisition, inquiry; **samon suru** to interrogate; **samón kai** court of inquiry.

samugári person who is oversensitive to cold; **samugáru** to complain of the cold; to be sensitive to the cold; **SAMÚI** cold; chilly; **samuke** chill; fit of cold; cold shiver; **samuke ga suru** to feel a chill; **SÁMUSA** coldness. **Samusa ga kibishiku narimashita.** The cold has become intense.

samurai knight.

SAN three.

—SAN Mr.; Mrs.; Miss; master. Yamada-san Mr. (Mrs., Miss) Yamada.

sanba midwife.

sanbashi landing pier.

sánbi praise; adoration; **sanbi suru** to praise.

sanbika hymn; **sanbika o utau** to sing a hymn.

sanbun prose.

sanbutsu product.

sánchi place of production; mountainous region; highlands.

sanchoo summit (peak) of a mountain.

sandán devising ways and means; **sandán suru** to find a means; **kane o sandán suru** to manage to raise money.

sandoítchi sandwiches.

sangaí three stories; third floor.

sangai damage; disaster; **sensoo no sangai** the evils of war.

SÁNGATSU March.

sangyoo (manufacturing) industry; **sangyoo no** industrial.

SÁNJUU thirty.

sanjuu no threefold, triple; **sanjuu no hako** nest (set) of three boxes.

sanjutsu arithmetic; **sanjutsu o suru** to do sums.

sanka participation;—**ni sanka suru** to take part in.

sankaku triangle; **sankaku no** triangular.

sankan visit; **sankan suru** to visit and see.

sankei visiting a temple; **sankei suru** to go and worship (at a Buddhist temple); **sankeinin** visitor to a temple, worshiper; pilgrim.

sankoo reference; comparison; **sankoo suru** to refer to; **sankoo ni náru** to serve as a reference; **sankoo no táme ni** for reference; **sankóonin** witness; **sankóosho** book of reference.

sánmai three sheets (of paper, or anything flat and thin); **sakana o sanmai no orósu** to fillet fish (to make three pieces, i.e., 2 pieces of fish and the bone).

sanmenkíji third-page items of a newspaper; general news.

sanmyaku mountain range.

sanpai worship; visit; **sanpai suru** to visit and worship (at a Shinto shrine).

SANPO a walk; **sanpo suru** to take a walk; **sanpo ni iku** to go for a walk.

sanpu scattering; **sanpu suru** to spread, scatter.

sanpuku side of a mountain.

sanretsu attendance; **sanretsu suru** to attend, be present at.

sanrin forest.

sanrísha tricycle.

sansei seconding, approval;—**ni sansei suru** to support; to approve of; **sanséiken** suffrage; political right; **sanséisha** supporter; seconder.

sanshoo comparison; reference; **sanshoo suru** to refer to.

sanshutsu production, output; **sanshutsu suru** to produce.

sánso oxygen.

sanson mountain village.

sansui hills and streams; landscape; landscape painting of mountains and rivers.

santan pitifulness; **santan táru** pitiful; tragic.

SANTÓO third class.

sán'yaku powdered medicine.

sanzai (n.) lying scattered; spending (money); squandering; **sanzai suru** to lie scattered; to spend money.

SANZÁN severely; terribly; **sanzan mátsu** to wait a long time; **sanzán na mé ni áu** to have a bitter experience.

saó pole, rod; **saodake** bamboo pole.

SAPPÁRI at all; quite; entirely; **sappári shita** refreshing. **Sappari wakarimasen.** I don't understand at all.

sappúukei tastelessness; **sappúukei na** tasteless; dry.

SARA dish, plate.

sárada salad; **saradáyu** salad oil.

SARAIGETSU month after next.

SARAINEN year after next.

SARAISHUU week after next.

sarakedásu to reveal; to bring shamelessly into view; to lay bare; **múchi o sarake dasu** to expose one's ignorance.

sára ni anew, afresh; once more, again; furthermore.

sárarii salary; **sararíman** salaried man.

sárasara in the least; smoothly; rustling; murmuring.

sarashi bleaching; refining; exposure; **sarashiko** bleaching powder; **sarashimómen** bleached cotton; **sarasu** to bleach; to expose; **hají o sarasu** to be put to shame.

sarau to kidnap, spirit away, snatch away; to dredge; to clean; to sweep away; **ninki o sarau** to win (popularity) by a clean sweep.

sarau (colloq.) to review; to repeat; to practice; **piano o sarau** to practice the piano.

sáru (n.) monkey; (v.), to go away, leave; to

126

take off; to divorce; **gakkoo o sáru** to leave school; **shoku o sáru** to retire from a post.

sarumata men's shorts (underwear).

sasaeru to support, maintain; **íkka o sasaeru** to support one's family.

sasageru to offer; to sacrifice; to lift up.

sásai na trifling; small; **sásai na koto** trivial matter.

sasayaki (*n.*) whispering; **sasayaku** to whisper.

sasen degradation; **sasen suru** to degrade; demote.

saseru to make; to let; to force; to cause; to get; **kodomo ni benkyoo o saseru** to make a child study.

-SASERU causative ending added to vowel verbs denoting: cause to, make to, force to, allow to, let; **koshikakesaseru** to make (someone) sit down; **tabesaséru** to make eat; to allow to eat; to let eat; to force to eat.

sashiageru to present, offer.

sashiatari for the present.

sashidashinin sender (of mail, etc.).

sashidásu to present, offer; to send.

sashidegamashíi impertinent.

sashie illustration; cut.

sashigane instigation; carpenter's square;—**no sashigane de** at the instigation of.

sashihiki deduction; balance; excess; ebb and flow; **sashihiki suru** to balance; to deduct; **sashihiku** to subtract, take away.

sashikakáru to come upon; to approach.

sashikómu to insert; to push in; to have a fit of acute pain. **Tsuki no hikarí ga mádo kara sashikomu.** The moonlight floods through the window.

SASHIMI sliced raw fish (popular Japanese food).

sashimukai face to face; facing each other; **sashimukai de** sitting face to face; **sashimukai ni náru** to sit face to face.

sashimukéru to send, dispatch.

sashióku to set aside; to leave; to leave out of consideration.

sashiosae attachment; seizure; **sashiosaéru** to seize; to attach. **Zaisan ga sashiosaerárete iru.** His property is under attachment.

sashisemátta pressing, urgent; imminent; **sashisemátta yooji ga áru** to have urgent business.

sashitoméru to prohibit; place a ban on.

sashitsukae engagement; hindrance; trouble; inconvenience; objection; **sashitsukae ga nákereba** if you have no objection; **sashitsukaéru** to be hindered; **sashitsukae ga nái** to be disengaged.

sashiwatashi diameter.

SÁSHIZU direction; instruction; **sáshizu suru** to direct; to instruct; **sáshizu no motó ni** under (someone's) direction.

sasoi invitation; temptation; **sasoi ni yoru** to call for; **sasoi o kakéru** to sound out (someone) on a subject.

SASOU to invite (someone) to call for; to tempt.

sássato quickly; promptly.

sasshi sympathy; consideration; **sasshi ga tsuku** to make out; to guess; **sasshi no áru** sympathetic.

SASSOKU immediately; directly; **sassoku no henji** quick answer.

sassúru to perceive; to surmise; to sympathize with.

SÁSU to point at; to pour in; to put in; to hold over one's head; to wear; to measure; to rise; to stream in; to play; to be tinged; to offer a cup (of sake); to stab; to stick; to put in; to sew; to stitch; to sting; **kitá o sásu** to point to the north; **kabin ni mizu o sásu** to pour water into a vase; **kabin ni haná o sásu** to put flowers in a vase; **higása o sásu** to hold a parasol over one's head; **kataná o sásu** to wear a sword; **sake o sásu** to offer a cup of sake; **kataná de sásu** to stab (someone) with a sword. **Hachi ga sashimashita.** A bee has stung me.

sasuga ni indeed; as one might have expected; true to one's reputation. **Ano hito wa sasuga ni erai desu.** He is indeed a great man.

sasuru to rub; to pat; to strike.

satá notice; news; report; instruction; order; **satá ga áru** to get news from; **satá o suru** to give notice.

sáte well; now; **sáte mata** again; **náni wa sate oki** first of all.

sato village; parent's home (of a married woman); **sato ni káeru** to come back to one's home village; to come back home.

SATÓO sugar (often used with a prefix o-); **satóo o ireru** to sugar; **satóo de katameta** candied. **Osatoo o kudasái.** Please give me some sugar.

satori comprehension; understanding; spiritual awakening (Buddhist term). **satori o hiráku** to be enlightened; **satóru** to comprehend; to perceive; **hí o satóru** to be convinced of one's error.

satósu to admonish; to counsel.

SATSU paper money.

-SATSU (counter for books) volume; copy.

satsubatsu na rough; warlike; violent; bloody.

satsuei (*n.*) taking a photograph; **satsuei suru** to take a photograph of.

sátsui murderous intent; **sátsui o okósu** to seek to kill a person.

satsujin homicide.

SATTO in a quick motion; **satto yuderu** to boil briefly in hot water.

sattoo pouring in; **sattoo suru** to rush in; **mooshikomi ga sattoo suru** to have a crowd of applicants.

sawagashíi noisy, unquiet; **séken ga sawagashíi** things look dark and ominous.

sawagásu to disturb, agitate.

sáwagi noise; shouts; **SAWÁGU** to get noisy;

to become agitated; **chiisái kotó ni
sawágu** to make a fuss over trifles.
sawari hindrance; impediment; affection;
harm; **SAWARU** to hinder; to be
injurious to; **jikoo ga sawaru** to be
affected by the weather; to touch; to
feel; **kenkoo ni sawaru** to affect one's
health; **hito no ki ni sawaru** to hurt
(someone's) feelings.
sawáyaka delightful; refreshing; clear; sweet;
fluent, eloquent; **sáyuu** to flow; **bénzetsu sawáyaka
na hito** a fluent speaker; **kíbun ga
sawáyaka ni náru** to feel refreshed.
sáyoku left wing.
SAYONÁRA, SAYOONÁRA good-by.
sayoo yes; just so; **sayoo no** such; of that sort;
sayoo ni so; in that manner.
sáyoo action, process, operation;—**ni sáyoo
suru** to act upon.
SAYOONÁRA See **sayonára.**
sáyuu (n.) right and left; **sáyuu suru** to
influence; **sáyuu ni** from side to side;
on the right and left.
SÁZO surely; indeed; how; **sázo otsukare
deshoo.** You must be tired.
sazukáru to receive; to be granted; to be
taught; **sazukéru** to grant; to confer
on; **hiden o sazukéru** to teach the
secrets.
SCHICHIGATSU July.
se current, rapid; shallows; back; ridge. **Se ni
hara wa kaerarenu.** Needs must when
the devil drives. Necessity is a hard
master.
sé, séi height (of the body). **Sé ga takái desu.**
He is tall.
sebaméru to narrow; to reduce; **séken o
sebaméru** to be humiliated.
sebiro man's suit.
sebíru to importune; to tease into.
sebone backbone, spine.
sechigarái, sechikarai stern; hard; **sechigarái
yonónaka** hard life.
seenen, seinen youth, young man.
séeto, seito pupil, student.
segámu to importune.
SÉGARE my son; our son.
sehyoo public opinion; popular judgment;
sehyoo ni noboru to be talked about.
SÉI family name; essence; spirit; vital power;
cause; effect; height; stature; life;
existence; nature; sex, gender; **sei ga
déru** to work hard; **sei o dásu** to work
hard;—**no séi de** owing to, because of;
séi no jun ni according to height. **Sei
ga tsukíru.** His energy is gone. **Séi ga
takái desu.** He is tall. **Séi ga hikúi
desu.** He is short.
-sei suffix denoting: student; **ichinénsei**
first-year student; **bunkásei** student of
literature.
seibo present given at the end of the year (as a
token of thanks for favors).
séibun ingredient; a component.
séibutsu living things.
seichoo growth; growing; **seichoo shita**

grown-up; **seichoo suru** to grow up; to
be brought up.
seidai splendor; prosperity; **seidai na**
prosperous; **seidai ni** splendidly; on a
grand scale.
séido system; institution; **séido no ué no**
institutional.
seien encouragement; **seien suru** to
encourage.
SÉIFU government.
seifuku conquest; uniform; **seifuku suru** to
subjugate.
seigaku vocal music; sacred music.
seigan petition; application.
seigén restriction; limit; **seigén suru** to
restrict; **seigén naku** without
limitations.
séigi righteousness; justice; **séigi no** righteous.
séigo correction of (typographical) errors in
printing.
séigyo control; **séigyo suru** to control.
seigyoo occupation; livelihood.
seihántai direct opposition; **seihántai no**
diametrically opposed; **seihántai ni** in
direct opposition; conversely.
seiheki predisposition; inclination.
seihen political change.
séihi success or failure; result.
seihin manufactured goods; products.
SEIHOKU northwest; **seihoku no**
northwesterly.
seihon bookbinding; **seihon suru** to bind a
book.
seihoo method of manufacture.
seihoo = nishi west; **seihoo no** western.
seihóokei (n.) square; **seihóokei no** (adj.)
square.
séii sincerity; faith; **seii áru** sincere; faithful.
seíppai to the best of one's ability; as hard as
possible.
séija right and wrong; good and evil; **séija o
wakéru** to discriminate between right
and wrong.
SEIJI government; politics; **seijígaku** politics;
the study of politics; **seijika** statesman;
politician.
seijin sage; saint; adult; attaining the age of
maturity; **seijin búru** to give oneself
sanctimonious airs; **séijin shita**
grown-up; **séijin suru** to grow up.
seijitsu sincerity; faithfulness; **seijitsu na**
sincere, honest; **seijitsu ni** sincerely.
seijuku ripeness; maturity; **seijuku shita** ripe;
mature; **seijuku suru** to ripen.
séika parental home.
seikai political world; **seikai ni háiru** to enter
upon a political career.
seikaku accuracy; character; **seikaku na**
correct, accurate.
SEIKATSU life; livelihood; **seikatsu ga
yútaka de áru** to be well off; **seikatsu
o tatéru** to earn one's living; **seikatsu
suru** to live; to support oneself.
seiken political power; political view; **seiken
o happyoo suru** to announce one's
political views; **seiken o nigiru** to take
the reins of government.

seiketsu cleanliness; purity; **seiketsu na** clean, pure; **seiketsu ni** cleanly; **seiketsu ni suru** to clean.

séiki vitality, vigor, life; **seiki ga míchite iru** to be full of life.

seiki century.

seikoo success; exquisiteness; **seikoo na** fine; ingenious; **seikoo shita** successful; prosperous; **seikoo suru** to succeed in.

seikyoo prosperity, boom.

seikyuu claim; demand; **seikyuu suru** to claim; to demand.

seimei declaration, statement; **seimei suru** to declare.

SÉIMEI name; full name; life; **seimei hóken** life insurance; **seimei hóken o kakéru** to insure one's life. **Kono byooki wa seimei ni kakawaru koto wa arimasen.** This disease will never prove fatal.

seimitsu precision; minuteness; **seimitsu na** minute, detailed; **seimitsu ni** minutely, in detail.

seimon front gate.

séimu government business; administration.

SEINAN southwest; **seinan no** southwestern.

seinen full age; youth, young man; young manhood; **seinen no** young, youthful; **seinen ni tassúru** to come of age.

seinengáppi date of one's birth.

séirai by birth, by nature; **séirai no** natural, innate.

seirei diligence; **seirei suru** to be diligent.

SEIREKI Christian era; year according to the Christian calender; A.D. **Kotoshi wa seireki sén kyúuhyaku rokujuu ichínen desu.** This year is 1961.

séiri adjustment; readjustment; putting things into order; **séiri suru** to adjust; to regulate.

seiritsu completion, conclusion; coming into existence; **seiritsu saseru** to bring into existence; **seiritsu suru** to come into being.

seiryaku policy; state policy.

seiryokka energetic person.

séiryoku energy, vigor; influence, power; **séiryoku no áru** influential, powerful; **séiryoku no nái** uninfluential, powerless; **séiryoku no oosei na** energetic, vigorous; **séiryoku o furuu** to wield power; **séiryoku o ushináu** to lose power.

seisai restraint; sanctions; **seisai o kuwaeru** to restrain, punish.

seisaku policy; fabrication, manufacture; **seisaku suru** to fabricate, manufacture, produce, make.

seisan feasible plan; liquidation; **seisan kajoo** overproduction; **juubun seisan ga áru** to be confident of success; **seisan suru** to liquidate; **seisánryoku** productive power.

seisei dóodoo with dignity and impartiality; fair and square.

seiséi suru to be refreshed; to feel revived.

seiseki results; marks; **seiseki ga yói** to be successful.

séishi life and death; life or death; **séishi fumei no** missing; **séishi no sakái ni áru** to hover between life and death.

seishi rest, repose; stillness; restraint; repression; paper manufacture; **seishi no** stationary, static, still; **seishi suru** to restrain; to check.

seishiki due form; formality; **seishiki no** formal; regular; **seishiki ni** formally; duly.

séishin soul, spirit; mind; will; **séishin shinkei antéizai** tranquilizer; **seishinbyoo** mental disease.

seishin séii with sincerity; with faithfulness.

seishitsu nature, character; property, quality.

seisho fair copy; **seisho suru** to make a fair copy of.

séisho Holy Bible.

seishuku silence, quiet; **seishuku na** silent; **seishuku ni** silently; in an orderly manner.

SEISHUN youth; **seishun jídai** youthful days.

seisoo formal dress; political strife; **seisoo suru** to dress up.

seisúru to control; to restrain.

seitai system of administration.

seitei enactment; establishment by law; **seitei suru** to pass a law; to establish.

sejten fine weather; clear sky.

SÉITO student, pupil.

seiton arrangement; regulation; **seiton shitá** orderly; well-organized; **seiton suru** to put in order; arrange; **seiton yóku shite iru** to be in good order.

seitoo polifical party; **seitoo bóoei** legal defense; reasonable self-defense; **seitoo na** proper; legal; fair and proper; **seitoo no** proper; legal; **seitoo ni** legally.

seitsuu suru to have a thorough knowledge of.

seiyaku oath; covenant; **seiyaku suru** to swear; **seiyakusho** written oath.

Séiyoo Western (Occidental) countries; **séiyoo no** occidental; **seiyóojin** (n.) Westerner; European; Occidental.

séizei to the best of one's power; at most.

seizen táru orderly; regular; well-organized; **seizen to** in good order.

seizon existence; **seizon suru** to exist.

seizoo manufacture, fabrication; **seizoo suru** to make, manufacture.

seizu drawing; cartography.

seji = oseji compliments; **seji no yói, oseji no yói,** affable.

SÉKAI world, earth; **sekaiteki** being worldwide, international.

sékaseka suru to bustle; to hustle.

séken public; people; world.

sekennami commonness; **sekennami no** common, ordinary; **sekennami ni** according to custom.

SÉKI seat; room; barrier; census register; domicile; dam, weir; **séki ni tsuku** to sit down, take a seat.

sekí cough; **sekí o suru,** to cough; **sekí ga déru** to suffer from a cough; **sekibárai** cough for clearing the throat; **sekibárai o suru** to clear one's throat.

sekidoo equator; **sekidoo no** equatorial.

sekihi tombstone; stone tablet.

sekihin extreme poverty; **sekihin ni** very poor.

sekiji seating order, seniority; precedence.

sekijitsu former days; old times.

sekikómu to be excited; to be agitated.

sekikónde impatiently; in haste.

sekimen blush (of embarrassment); **sekimen saseru** to make a person blush; **sekimen suru** to blush; to be ashamed.

sekinin responsibility; duty; obligation; **sekinin ga áru** to be responsible for; **sekinin o hatásu** to discharge one's duty; **sekinin o ou** to take the responsibility.

sekiryoo lonesomeness; desolation.

sekisetsu accumulated snow.

sekitán coal.

sekitatéru to hurry; to press.

sekitoméru to dam up; to check.

sekiyu petroleum; kerosene.

sekizui spine.

sekkai incision; operation; **sekkai suru** to incise.

sékkachi impetuosity; impetuousness; **sekkachi na** hasty; impetuous.

SEKKAKU with much trouble; with great pains; especially; kindly. **Sekkaku odaiji ni.** Please take special care of yourself.

sekkei plan, design; **sekkei suru** to plan, lay out; to draw up plans for the construction of a.

SEKKEN soap.

sekkin approach; proximity; **sekkin suru** to approach.

sekkyóo sermon; preaching; **sekkyóo suru** to preach; to admonish.

sekkyokuteki positive; **sekkyokuteki ni** positively.

SEMÁI narrow; limited.

semakurushíi narrow and close.

semáru to press; to urge.

semento cement.

seméru to attack; to torture; to call to account.

SÉMETE at least; at best. **Sémete moo ichinichi otomari kudasai.** Please stay at least one more day.

SÉN thousand; stopper; plug; choice; selection; line; route; **san zén** three thousand; **sén ni nátte** in a line; **Tookaidoosen** Tookaidoo Railroad (line); **sén ni háiru** to be selected; **sén ni moréru** to be left out; **sén o hiku** to draw a line; **sen o suru** to stop with a cork; **mimí ni sén o suru** to stuff cotton in one's ears.

SENAKA back (of the body).

senbai monopoly (of sales); **senbai suru** to monopolize (business).

senbatsu selection, choice; **senbatsu suru** to select; **senbatsu sareta** selected. (See also **sentei.**)

senbetsu parting present; farewell gift.

senboo envy; **senboo suru** to feel envy; **senboo no mató ni náru** to become the envy of.

SENCHA toasted tea (relatively inexpensive grade of Japanese tea).

senchaku first arrival.

senchi-méetoru centimeter.

sénchoo captain; master of a ship.

sendan arbitrary action; **sendan de** arbitrarily; at one's own discretion.

SENDEN publicity; propaganda; advertisement; **senden suru** to propagandize; to publicize.

sendoo guidance, leadership.

SENGETSU last month.

senkyooshi missionary.

SENMENJO washroom.

senmon no special; professional;**—o senmon ni atsukau** to specialize in.

sénmu torishimari yaku managing director.

sén no previous; **sén ni** previously.

senpai (*n.*) senior; superior.

senpatsu (*n.*) starting out in advance of someone else; **senpatsu suru** to start in advance; **senpatsutai** advance party.

senpoo other person; one's destination.

senpuku concealment; state of being latent; **senpuku suru** to lie hidden; to go into hiding. (See also **senzai.**)

senpukúki period of incubation; latent period.

senpuu whirlwind; cyclone, tornado; **senpúuki** electric fan.

senrei previous instance; precedence; **senrei no nái** unprecedented; baptism; christening; **senrei o hodokósu** to baptize; **senrei o ukéru** to be baptized.

senren polish; refinement; **senren sareta** refined; **senren suru** to refine.

senritsu melody; rhythm.

sénro railway line; railroad track.

senryaku strategy; **senryakuka** strategist.

senryoo capture; occupancy; **senryoo suru** to take a position; to occupy.

senryóo dyestuff, dye.

sensai one's former wife.

sensaku search; investigation; **sensaku suru** to search into.

sensei oath; **sensei suru** to swear; to take an oath.

SENSÉI teacher; an instructor; sir (in direct address); honorific for professional people (doctors, lawyers, etc.).

SENSÉNGETSU month before last.

sensen kyookyoo with great fear, with fear and trembling; **sensen kyookyoo to shite** living in constant fear.

SENSENSHUU week before last.

senshi death in military action; death on the battlefield.

senshínkoku advanced nation (in technology).

senshitsu cabin
sénshu champion; (sports) team.
senshutsu election; senshutsu suru to elect.
SENSHUU last week.
sensoo war; battle; sensoo ni iku to go to the
    front; sensoo ni kátsu to win; to win a
    battle; sensoo suru to make war; to
    fight.
sensu fan; folding fan.
sensui diving into water; submergence; sensui
    suru to dive; to submerge; sensúikan
    submarine.
SENTAKU wash, washing; laundry;
    selection; choice; sentaku suru to
    wash; to select; sentaku ni dásu to
    send to be washed; sentaku ga kíku to
    stand and wash; sentakuya laundry
    (shop); laundryman; sentaku ni
    makaséru to leave as a matter of choice.
sentan extreme point; extremity.
sente (n.)forestalling; the first move (in a
    game); sente o útsu to take the
    initiative; have the first move; You beat
    me to it.
sentei selection, choice; sentei suru to select,
    choose.
sententeki inherent, congenital.
sentoo head, lead; sentoo ni tátsu to head,
    lead.
SÉN'YA other night; few nights ago.
sen'yaku previous engagement; sen'yaku no
    táme owing to a previous engagement.
sen'yoo exclusive use, private use; sen'yoo no
    exclusive, private.
sen'yuu exclusive possession; sen'yuu suru
    to enjoy sole possession of.
senzai (n.) being latent; senzai íshiki
    subconscious; senzai no latent,
    dormant; senzai suru to be latent.
sénzo ancestor, forefather; sénzo no ancestral,
    hereditary.
senzoku specially attached;—ni senzoku suru
    to belong exclusively to.
seóu to carry on one's back; to bear; to
    shoulder; omoni o seóu to be burdened
    with a grave duty; sekinin o seóu to
    take a responsibility on one's own
    shoulders.
seppaku pressure; urgency; imminence;
    seppaku shita urgent, imminent;
    seppaku suru to draw near; to be
    pressed.
seppun kiss; kissing; seppun o nagéru to
    send a kiss; seppun suru to kiss, press
    one's lips upon.
serifu speech, dialogue (in a play).
séro cello, violincello.
sérori celery.
séru light serge.
serufutáimaa self-timer.
sessei temperance, moderation; sessei suru to
    be temperate.
sessen fighting at close quarters; sessen suru
    to fight hand to hand.
SÉSSEE TO as much as one can; diligently;
    sésse to hataraku to be busy at work.

sésshi Centigrade thermometer.
sesshoo negotiation; sesshoo suru to negotiate
    with.
SESSHOKU contact, touch; sesshoku suru to
    touch; to come in contact with;
    sesshoku o tamótsu to keep in touch
    with.
sessúru to touch; to receive; to get; to have an
    interview with.
SÉTAA sweater.
setchi establishment; setchi suru to establish.
setchuu compromise; setchuu suru to
    compromise.
SETOMONO porcelain; chinaware.
sétsu opinion, view; theory, doctrine; rumor.
sétsubi equipment, arrangement; sétsubi o
    suru to equip; to provide for.
setsudan cutting off, trimming; setsudan
    suru to cut off; to trim.
SETSUMEI explanation, elucidation;
    setsumei suru to explain; setsumeisho
    instruction booklet.
SÉTSUNA moment, instant; sétsuna no
    momentary; sono sétsuna at the very
    moment.
sétsu eagerly, earnestly.
setsuretsu poorness; clumsiness; setsuretsu
    na poor; clumsy; unskillful.
setsuritsu establishment, foundation;
    setsuritsu suru to establish, institute,
    found.
setsuyaku economy; saving; thrift; setsuyaku
    suru to save; to economize.
setsuyu admonition, reproof; setsuyu suru to
    admonish, warn, reprove.
setsuzoku connection, joining; setsuzoku
    suru to join, connect, link.
séttai reception; entertainment; séttai suru to
    receive; to entertain.
settei establishment, creation; settei suru to
    found, institute (a corporation, etc.).
sétto radio set, motion picture set.
settoku persuasion; settoku suru to persuade,
    convince.
settoo theft, larceny; settoo o hataraku to
    commit a theft.
SEWÁ help, aid, assistance; good offices;
    service; care; trouble; everyday life;
    sewá no yakeru troublesome;—no
    sewá ni náru to be under the care of;
    yokei na sewá o yaku to poke one's
    nose where one is not wanted; sewá
    suru to help, aid; to do a kind office;
    to take care of.
sewashíi busy; busily engaged.
shaba this world.
sháberu shovel.
shabéru to chatter; to prattle.
SHABON = SEKKEN soap.
shaburu to suck; to chew.
shachoo president of a company.
shadan interception; isolation; shadan suru
    to cut off from.
shadoo roadway.
shagamu to squat; to crouch.
shagareta hoarse (voice); grating (laugh).

shageki suru to shoot, fire at; **shagekijoo** rifle-range.

shain member of a company.

shajitsuteki realistic, true to life.

shákai society; **shákai no tamé ni** for the good of the public; **shakáigaku** sociology, social science; **shakai-shúgi** socialism; **shakai-shugísha** socialist.

shakkín debt; loan; **shakkin o káesu** to pay a debt; **shakkín o koshiraeru** to fall into debt; **shakkín suru** to borrow money; **shakkíntori** creditor.

shákkuri hiccup, hiccough; **shakkuri suru** to hiccup.

shakoo social life.

SHAKU Japanese foot; unit of measure corresponding to 3.30 cm. or 1.287 (American) foot.

shakuchi leased land; rented ground.

shákudo measure, gauge, scale.

shákushi wooden spoon.

shakuya rented house; **shakuya suru** to rent a house; **shakuyanin** tenant.

shámen slanting surface; slope.

shanpén champagne.

share play upon words, pun; joke; **share o iu** to crack jokes.

sharei remuneration, reward; thanks; **sharei suru** to reward; to remunerate.

shareru to adorn oneself; to try to look pretty.

shareta stylish, tasteful.

sharin wheel.

sharyoo vehicles, cars.

shasai debentures; bond.

shasei sketching; **shasei suru** to sketch; to make a sketch.

shasetsu editorial; leading article.

sháshi cross-eye.

SHASHIN photograph; photograph; **shashin no** photographic; **shashin ni tóru** to take a photograph of; **shashin o hikinobásu** to enlarge a photograph; **shashin o tóru** to have a photograph taken; to take a photograph; **shashin o yakitsukéru** to print a photograph; **SHASHÍNKI** camera.

SHASHOO conductor.

shatai body of a car.

SHÁTSU shirt, undershirt.

shattaa shutter.

shazai apology; **shazai suru** to acknowledge being at fault, apologize.

shazetsu refusal, denial; **shazetsu suru** to refuse, decline.

SHÍ four (see also **yo, yon, yottsu**); city, municipality; Mr. (*used mostly in writing*); teacher; master; death, decease; **shí no** city, municipal; **shiyákusho** municipal building; City Hall; **shí ni hín shite iru** to be at the point of death; **shí o osorénai** to face death with calmness.

—SHI particle denoting: in addition to it;—(n.) poetry, verse. **Kane mo áru shi chíi mo áru.** He has wealth and, in addition, high position.

shiage, shiageru finish, finishing; **shiage o suru** to give the finishing touches to; **shiagéru** to finish, complete.

shiai contest of skill, match; **shiai o suru** to play a match; **shiai o mooshikómu** to challenge to a game; **shiai o shoodaku suru** to accept a challenge (to a game).

shían meditation, consideration; **shían suru** to think; to consider.

SHIASÁTTE two days after tomorrow.

shiawase good fortune, happiness.

shibafu lawn; turf.

SHIBAI play, drama; theatre; **shibai ni iku** to go to the theatre; **shibai o útsu** to give a performance; to trick someone.

SHIBÁRAKU for a while, for some time; **shibáraku shite** after a while.

shibáru to bind; to tie up; **kizu o shibáru** to bind up a wound; **kisóku de shibáru** to restrict (someone) by a rule.

SHIBASHIBA often, many times, repeatedly.

shibatatáku to blink.

shibire numbness; insensibility; **shibiréru** to numb; to be numbed.

shibomu to fade, wither.

SHIBOO wish, desire; fat, grease, suet; death; **shiboo suru** to wish, desire; to die.

shibóosha applicant, candidate.

shibóru to press out, wring out, squeeze; **chié o shibóru** to rack one's brains; **námida ni sode o shibóru** to weep bitterly; **ushi no chichí o shibóru** to milk a cow.

shíbu branch; subdivision.

shibúi astringent; austere; glum; sullen; chaste; simple yet refined (in taste); quiet, sober; **shibúi kao** glum face; **shibúi konomi** quiet taste.

shibukí spray; **shibukí o tobasu** to spray, to splash.

shibúru to be reluctant, be unwilling; to become loose with griping pain (of bowels); not to go smoothly; **shibushibu** reluctantly, unwillingly.

shibutói churlish; stubborn.

shichí pawn;—**o shichí ni ireru o (shichí ni oku)** to pawn personal property.

SHICHÍ seven.

shichí fatal position; **schichí o dassúru** to have a hairbreadth escape.

SHICHIJÚU seventy.

shichíya pawnbroker, pawnshop.

shichóo mayor; city administration building; branch-office.

shichúu stew; support; stay; inside a city or town; **shichúu o neriarúku** to walk the streets in a procession.

shída fern.

SHIDAI order; the state of things; as soon as; **shidai ni** gradually; **shidai ni yotté wa** according to circumstances; **tsuki shídai ni** as soon as it comes. **Tenki shídai desu.** It depends upon the state of the weather.

shidoo guidance, leading; **shidoo suru** to guide; to lead.

shidóosha leader, director.

shiei private management; municipal management; **shiei no** private.

shíeki employment; service; **shíeki suru** to employ.

shifuku plain-clothes policeman.

shígai outskirts of a city, suburbs; streets.

shigai dead body, corpse.

shigaisen ultraviolet rays.

shigamitsúku to clasp, cling to.

shígan desire; application; volunteering; **shíganhei** volunteer; enlisted man; **shigánsha** applicant; **shígan suru** to apply for.

SHIGATSU April.

shigeki stimulus, stimulation; **shigeki suru** to stimulate.

shigemi thicket, bush.

shigéru to become dense; to grow thick and rank.

shígo after death.

SHIGOKU (adv.) very, extremely; **shigóku** (v.) to draw through the hand; to stroke (as a beard).

SHIGOTO work, task; job; **shigoto o suru** to work; **shigoto o tóru** to get a job; **shigotoba** workshop.

shigure wintertime rain; wintry shower.

shigusa manners, behaviors; gesture.

shíhai rule, control, management; **shíhai suru** to govern, rule, manage; **kanjoo ni shíhai sareru** to be influenced by personal feelings; **shihaikáikyuu** governing class; **shiháinin** manager, director.

SHIHARAI payment; **shiharai suru** to pay; **shiharai o seikyuu suru** to ask for payment; **shiharainin** payer (one who pays); **shiharaisaki** payee; **shiharáu** to pay; to discharge; **shiharau beki** payable.

shíhei paper currency.

shíhen volume of poems; Book of Psalms.

shihóo four sides, cardinal points; **shihóo ni** on all sides; **shihoo háppoo** all directions; **shihoo háppoo e** in all directions.

shihóoken jurisdiction; judicial authority.

shihon capital; fund; **shihon o too zúru** to invest one's capital in; **shihonka** capitalist; **shihónkin** capital; **shihonshúgi** capitalism.

shiin cause of death.

shíin scene.

shiire (n.) stocking; laying in, buying up (of goods); **shiire o suru** to stock goods; **shiiréru** to stock goods, lay in (goods), to buy up (goods).

shííru to compel; to force upon.

shiitagéru to oppress, tyrannize.

shíite against one's will, by force.

shíítsu bed sheets, linen.

shíji support, maintenance; **shíji suru** to support; to maintain.

shijin poet, poetess.

shijitsu historical facts.

shijoo market, fair; **shijoo ni déru** to appear in a market; **shijoo ni dásu** to bring to market.

shijuku private school.

SHIJÚU = YÓNJUU forty.

SHIJUU whole time, all the time, always.

shiká market price.

-SHÍKA only (used with a negative).

Osakana shíka arimasén. We have only fish. **Eigo shíka hanasemasén.** I can speak only English.

shikaeshi tit for tat; revenge; **shikaeshi o suru** to take revenge.

shikái municipal assembly; town assembly.

shikai chairmanship.

shikake device, mechanism.

shikakéru to begin; to set to work; to fasten upon; to make advances.

shikaku (sense of) sight, eyesight; assassin; **shikaku** qualification; capacity; **shikaku o áru** qualified;—**no shikaku de** in the capacity of; **shikaku o ushináu** to be disqualified for.

SHIKAKÚ (n.) square; **shikakú na** (adj.) square; **shikakúi hako** square box.

shikakubáru to be formal; to stand on ceremony.

SHIKÁMO moreover, furthermore.

shikaru to scold; to reprove.

shikáruni however, nevertheless, but, yet (formal); **shikáruni mata** on the other hand.

SHIKÁSHI however, nevertheless.

SHIKATA method, way, means; **shikata ga náku** (shikata náshi ni) having no other choice. **Shikata ga nái desu.** I cannot help it.

shiké stormy weather; scarcity of fish; **shiké o kúu** to be overtaken by a storm.

shikéi death penalty, capital punishment; **shikéi o senkoku suru** to pass sentence of death; **shikéi o shikkoo suru** to execute.

SHIKÉN examination, test; trial; **shikén ni tóoru** to pass the examination; **shikén o okonáu** to give an examination; **shikén suru** to examine, test; **shikén o ukéru** to take an examination.

shikí four seasons; command, order; ceremony; style, form; **shikí suru** to command, give an order;—**no shikí no motó ni** under the command of; **shikí o ageru** to celebrate.

-shiki suffix denoting: style; **seiyooshiki** Western style; Occidental style; **suisenshiki** flush style (toilet).

shikibetsu discrimination; discernment; **shikibetsu suru** to discern, distinguish.

shikibúton quiltlike mattress; bedding.

shikichi site, ground.

shikifu bed sheet.

shikii threshold, sill; **shikii o matágu** to cross the threshold.

shikiishi paving-stone; pavement.

shikíkan commander.

133

shikíkin deposit, key money (for renting a
house); shikíkin o íreru to make a
deposit on a house; to give key money.
shikimono matting; carpet; shikimono o
shiku to lay a carpet.
shikín fund.
shikiri partition; settlement of accounts.
SHIKIRI NI frequently; continually; eagerly.
shikisai color, tint.
shikísha intelligent people; persons of good
sense.
shikitsuméru to spread all over.
shikka at one's lap (honorific address to
parents, mostly used in letters);—no
shikka ni under the care of.
SHIKKÁRI firmly, tightly; strongly; exactly;
shikkári shita strong; substantial.
shikkéi disrespect; impoliteness; shikkéi na
impolite, rude; shikkéi suru to say
good-by. Shikkéi shimáshita. I beg
your pardon (in men's talk).
shikki lacquered-ware; damp; moisture;
shikki no áru wet, damp, moist.
shikkoo losing effect; invalidation; execution;
enforcement; celebration; shikkoo
suru to execute, carry out, enforce;
shikkoo yúuyo probation; a suspension
of execution; shikkoo yúuyo to náru
to be released on probation.
shikkui mortar; plaster; shikkui de nuru to
plaster.
shikomi training; teaching; shikómu to train;
to teach; to lay in; to buy.
shikoo enforcement; carrying out; taste;
shikoo sareru to take effect; shikoo
suru to enforce; shikoo ni teki suru to
suit one's taste.
shikóoryoku contemplative faculty; power to
think.
shikori stiffness; bump.
shiku to spread, lay; to pave; to issue; to
proclaim.
shikujíru to fail; to make a blunder; to be
cashiered.
SHIKYÓ death.
shikyoku branch office.
shikyoo bishop; condition of the market.
shikyuu supply, allowance; urgency; dispatch;
shikyuu no urgent, pressing; shikyuu
ni at once, promptly; shikyuu suru to
provide; to supply.
SHIMA island; stripes.
SHIMAI end, termination; shimai ni at last;
shimai ni náru to come to an end;
shimai ni suru to finish.
SHÍMAI sisters; informal No dance
(performed without wearing the formal
standard costume).
SHÍMARI tightness; locking, fastening;
prudence; shímari no áru firm;
locked; prudent; shímari no nái loose;
impudent; stupid; SHIMÁRU to shut,
to close; to grow tight; to tighten; to
sober down.
shímatsu management; circumstances; result;
economy; shímatsu no oenai

unmanageable; shímatsu suru to
manage; put in order.
shimátta compact; firm, well-set.
shimau to close; to finish; to put away.
shimedasu to shut out, exclude.
shimegane buckle; clasp; shimegane o
kakéru to buckle together.
SHÍMEI full name; naming; nomination;
shimei suru to name; to nominate.
shímei mission; errand; shímei o mattoo suru
to fulfil a duty.
shimekiri close; closed; deadline.
shimekomu to lock in, shut in.
shimekorósu to strangle to death.
shímen space (in a magazine or newspaper).
shimeppói damp; wet; shimeppói hanashi
tearful story.
SHIMÉRU to tie, bind; to close, shut; to let
down; to girdle; to take; to occupy;
jooseki o shiméru to occupy the top
seat.
shimeru to get damp; to get wet.
shimésu to point out; to show; to indicate.
shimesu to wet, moisten.
shímete altogether; in all.
shimi stain, blot; shimi no áru stained; shimi
dárake no spotty. Shimi ga
demashita. There is a stain.
shimijími carefully; fully; heartily; shimijími
kao o míru to look searchingly into
(someone's) face. shimijími kiku to
listen attentively to.
shímin citizen.
shimínken citizenship.
shimiru to penetrate; to soak into; to smart; to
be touched with; shínsetsu ga mi ni
shimiru to appreciate (someone's)
kindness fully. Kaze ga mi ni
shimiru. The wind is penetrating.
Kono kusuri wa shimiru. This lotion
smarts.
shimizu spring water.
SHIMÓ frost; lower part, foot, bottom.
shimó de kareru to be nipped by frost;
shimoyake frostbite.
shimon fingerprint; trial; inquiry;
examination; shimon o turu to take
(someone's) fingerpritns; shimon suru
to try (hear) a case.
shimuke one's behavior toward; one's
attitude; shimukéru to act toward; to
treat; to send.
SHÍN heart, mind; core; truth, reality; fact;
faith; fidelity; trust; shín kara heartily,
sincerely; shín made to the core; shín
ni truly; really; actually; shín no true;
real; veritable; shín ni semáru to be
true to one's nature; shín o oku to
trust, believe.
shína coquetry; shína o tsukúru to be
coquettish.
SHÍNA = CHÚUGOKU China; Shína no
(adj.) Chinese; Shinago Chinese
language; Shinájin Chinese (people).
shina article; goods, stuff.
shinabiru to wither; to droop.
shinagire out of stock; sold out.

shínai city; inside the city.

shin'ai affection, love; shin'ai náru dear, beloved.

shinamono article; goods.

shin'an new idea; new design.

shinario scenario.

shináyaka na pliant, flexible, supple.

shínboku friendship, intimacy; shinboku o hakáru to cultivate a friendship.

shínboo patience, endurance, forbearance; axle; shaft; shínboo no nái impatient; shínboo no yói patient; shínboo suru to endure; to be patient.

SHINBUN newspaper; journal; shinbundáne news matter; shinbun kisha journalist; pressman.

shinchiku new building; shinchiku no newly built; shinchiku suru to build, to rebuild.

shinchintáisha replacing the old with new; replacement; metabolism; shinchintáisha suru to be renewed, to be replaced.

shinchíshiki new knowledge; advanced idea.

shíncho books newly published.

shinchoo (n.) height, stature; care; prudence; (adj.) deep; profound; shinchoo ga takái to be tall; shinchoo na careful, cautious; ími shinchoo to have a deep meaning; to be of profound significance.

shinchuu brass.

shínchuu true motive; mind; shínchuu o sassuru to share (someone's) feelings.

SHINDAI bedstead; property; fortune; sleeper (on a train).

shindan diagnosis; shindan suru to diagnose.

shinden sanctuary (in a Shinto shrine).

shindoo tremor, shock, vibration; oscillation; shindoo suru to shake, vibrate (from an earthquake or collision); to swing, oscillate, move to and fro.

shingai infringement, encroachment; terror; horror; alarm; shingai suru to infringe; to make an attack upon; to stun with amazement.

shingaku theology.

shingari rear; rearguard; shingari o tsutomeru to bring up the rear.

shingata new style; new design.

shingénchi seismic center; center of disturbance.

shíngetsu new moon.

shíngi genuineness, authenticity; consideration; discussion; investigation; shíngi o tashikaméru to ascertain the truth; shingi suru to consider; investigate.

shingoo signal; kiken shíngoo danger signal; shingoo suru to signal, give a signal.

shíngu bedding and bedclothes.

shín'i real intentions; true meaning.

shinikakátta dying; at the point of death.

shinime moment of death.

shinimonogúrui death struggle; desperation; shinimonogúrui de desperately;

shinimonogúrui no desperate; shinimonogúrui ni náru to make a desperate effort.

shinin dead person.

shinitaéru to die out.

shiniwakaréru to be parted by death.

shínja believer; faithful (person).

shinjín divine worship; devotion; shinjin bukái pious, devout; shinjín suru to worship; to regard with adoration.

shínjitsu truth; reality; shínjitsu na true, real; shínjitsu ni truly, really.

shinjitsu sincerity; faithfulness; shinjitsu na sincere; faithful.

shinjoo article of faith; creed; (one's) true feelings.

shinju pearl.

shinjuu double suicide; suicide for love.

shínka evolution; real value, true worth; shínka o mítomeru to appreciate the true value; shínka suru to evolve.

shinkáichi newly developed district.

shinkan, shinkánsho new publication; new book.

shínkei nerves; shinkei kábin nervousness; being overly sensitive; shínkei no nervous; shinkéishitsu nervous temperament; shikeishitsu no nervous; shinkei súijaku nervous breakdown; shinkeitsuu neuralgia; shínkei séishin antéizai tranquilizer.

shinken na earnest; shinken ni náru to be earnest; to become earnest.

shinkíjiku new device; originality; shinkíjiku o dásu to introduce a new method.

shinkoku declaration; report (tax return, etc.); shinkoku suru to state; to report.

shínkoku na deep, serious.

shinkon new marriage; shinkon no newly married; shinkon ryokoo honeymoon; shinkon ryókoo o suru to go on a honeymoon.

shinkoo faith; belief; friendship; cordiality; advance, progress; march; shinkoo no jiyúu freedom of faith; shinkoo no nái unbelieving; shinkoo suru to believe in; to advance; to progress.

shínku hardship; tribulation; shínku suru to suffer hardship.

shinkuukan vacuum tube.

shinkyuu promotion; shinkyuu suru to win a promotion; to be promoted.

shinme sprout, shoot; shinme o dasu to bud, sprout.

shínmi blood relation; shínmi ni nátte sewá o suru to look after with great kindness.

shinmín subject.

shinmíri heart-to-heart; earnestly; shinmiri hanasu to have a heart-to-heart talk.

shinmitsu intimacy; familiarity; close friendship; shinmitsu na intimate, familiar; shinmitsu na aidagara de áru to have a strong friendship.

shinmotsu present, gift.

shinmyoo na fair; commendable, conscientious; docile; shinmyoo ni

commendably; quietly; meekly;
fairly.

shínnen faith, belief; deeply rooted
conviction; new year. **Shínnen
omedetoo.** I wish you a Happy New
Year.

shinnin confidence, trust; **shinnin suru** to
confide in, believe in.

shinnínjoo credentials.

shinnyuu invasion; inroad; trespass; intrusion;
shinnyuu suru to invade; to intrude
into; **shinnyúusha** invader; trespasser.

shinnyúusei new student; freshman.

shinobi stealthy movement; going in disguise.

shinóbi to bear, endure; to conceal; to hide
oneself; to steal along one's way;
fujíyuu o shinóbu to suffer privation;
hitome o shinóbu to elude
observation; **yó o shinóbu** to live in
concealment.

shinogiyói genial; nice; mild.

shinógu to endure, bear; to rise above.

shinónde patiently; meekly; secretly.

SHINPAI uneasiness; apprehension; anxiety;
worry, care; fear; **shinpai na koto**
trouble, difficulty; **shinpai no amari**
overcome with anxiety; **shinpai suru**
to fear; to be anxious.

shinpan new edition; new publication;
judgment; **shinpan no** newly edited;
newly published; **shinpan suru** to
judge; to umpire; **shinpánsha** umpire;
judge.

shínpi mystery; **shínpi no** mysterious, mystic.

shínpo progress, advance; improvement;
shínpo suru to make progress.

shínpu bride; catholic priest.

shinpuku admiration and devotion; honest
submission; **shinpuku suru** to
acknowledge another's superiority; to
obey faithfully.

shinrai trust, reliance, confidence; **shinrai
suru** to trust, to place confidence in.

shinratsu severity; poignance; **shinratsu na**
severe; poignant.

shinreki new calendar; Gregorian calendar;
solar calendar (*as distinguished from
the lunar calendar used in the past*).

shínri examination, trial; truth, truism;
psychology; psychic state; **shinrígaku**
psychology; **shínri o motoméru** to
seek truth; **shínri suru** to try; to
examine.

shinrin forest, wood.

shinroo bridegroom.

SHINRUI relation, relative.

shinryaku aggression; invasion; **shinryaku
suru** to invade.

shínryoku fresh green.

shínsa examination, investigation, inspection;
shínsa suru to examine; to inquire into;
shinsáin jury, committee of inquiry.

shinsai disaster caused by earthquake.

shinsatsu medical examination; **shinsatsu o
ukéru** to consult a physician;
shinsatsu suru to examine a patient.

shinsei sacredness, sanctity; application;
petition; **shinsei na** holy, sacred,
hallowed; **shinsei ni suru** to make
holy; **shinsei o kegasu** to defile the
sacredness; **shinsei suru** to apply;
shinseinin applicant; petitioner;
claimant.

shinseki relative.

shinsen na fresh, new.

SHINSETSU kindness; goodness;
friendliness; **shinsetsu na** kind, good,
cordial; **shinsetsu o suru** to do a
kindness.

shinsetsu new establishment; **shinsetsu no**
newly organized, newly formed;
shinsetsu suru to establish newly.

shínshaku consideration, allowance; **nán no
shinshaku mo náku** without any
consideration; **shínshaku suru** to take
into consideration.

shínshi gentleman; man of position; **shinshi
kyóoyaku** gentleman's agreement;
shinshirashíi gentleman-like.

shinshiki new style; new system; **shinshiki
no** of a new style; modern.

shinshin (*n.*) rising, promising; mind and
body; **shinshin no** (*adj.*) rising.

shinshitsu bedchamber, bedroom.

shínshoku food and sleep; **shínshoku o
wasurete** forgetful of sleep and other
comforts; regardless of oneself.

shinshoku erosion; **shinshoku suru** to erode.

shinshuku expansion and contraction;
elasticity; **shinshuku suru** to expand
and contract; **shinshuku jízai**
elasticity; **shinshuku jízai no** elastic.

shinshutsu (*n.*) marching out; emergence;
shinshutsu suru to march out; emerge.

shinsoo true state; **shinsoo o akíraka ni suru**
to disclose the real state of affairs;
shinsoo o kataru to lay bare the truth
of a matter.

shinsui fascination, infatuation; launching;
flooding, inundation; **shinsui suru** to
be fascinated; to launch; to be
launched; to be flooded; **shinsúishiki**
launching (ceremony).

shintai image of a god.

shíntai body; person; constitution; advance
and retreat; movement; **shintai kénsa**
physical examination; **shintai no**
bodily, corporal; **shintai suru** to move,
to act.

shintaku trust; **shintaku suru** to entrust with,
to leave in trust (property, etc.).

shintei presentation; **shintei suru** to present,
give.

shinten personal; confidential (written on the
envelope of a letter); **shinten no**
private, confidential; **shintensho**
confidential letter.

shínto believer (religious).

shin to shita silent, still; deserted.

shin to suru silence prevails.

shintsuu mental suffering; anxiety.

SHINU to die, pass away, expire; **shinu máde**

to the end; **shinu kákugo de** at the risk
of one's life.
shinwa myth, mythology.
shin'ya dead of night, midnight; **shínya ni**
late at night.
Shin'yaku Séisho New Testament.
shin'yoo confidence, trust; credit; **shin'yoo
ga áru** to be trusted by; **shin'yoo o éru**
to have credit with; **shin'yoo suru** to
trust; to credit; **shin'yóojoo** letter of
credit; **shin'yoo kúmiai** credit
association, credit union.
shin'yuu intimate friend.
shinzen amity, goodwill; **shinzen shísetsu**
goodwill mission.
shínzoku relation, relative.
SHINZOO heart; **shinzoobyoo** heart disease;
shinzoomáhi heart failure.
shinzui essence.
shinzúru to believe in; to accept (something)
as ture; to trust.
SHIÓ salt (often used with the prefix *o-*); tide;
current; opportunity; occasion;
shiokarái salty; **shió de aji o tsukeru**
to season with salt; **shió ni tsukeru** to
salt; to pickle in salt; **shió ga sásu** to
rise (*said of a tide*); **shió ga hiku** to
ebb.
shioki punishment; execution; **shioki o suru**
to punish; to execute.
shiokuri supply; allowance; **shiokuri o suru**
to furnish a person with money (for
living expenses, schooling, etc.).
shiorashíi moving, touching; plausible;
shiorashíi kotó o iu to say pretty
things.
shioreru to wither, droop; to be in low spirits.
shippai failure; defeat; **shippai suru** to fail; to
be unsuccessful.
shippi expenditure; useless expenses.
shippitsu writing; **shippitsu suru** to write.
shippó tail; **shippó o dásu** to give (someone)
away; to disclose (someone's) identity;
shippó o maku to acknowledge defeat;
shippó o osáeru to find fault (with
someone).
shippuu violent wind; gale.
shirabakkuréru (*colloq.*) to dissemble; to
pretend not to understand.
SHIRABÉRU to investigate; to examine; to
prepare a lesson for.
shírafu (*n.*) soberness; sobriety; state of not
being drunk.
shirákeru to become chilled; to be spoiled.
**Ano hito ga kuru to itsumo za ga
shírakemasu.** He is always a wet
blanket.
shiranu unknown, unfamiliar; **shiranu kao o
suru** to look on with indifference.
shirase information; news; sign; notice;
SHIRASERU to notify; to send a
notice; **kekkon o shiraseru** to send a
notice of marriage.
shirazu shírazu unawares; unconsciously.
shirei instructions; order, notice.
shíren trial, test; **shíren ni taéru** to stand the

test; **shíren o ukéru** to be tried, be
tested.
shireru to become known.
shíri private gain; self-interest; **shiri o
hakaru** to look to one's own interests.
shirí buttocks; rump; bottom; **shirí ga nagái**
to wear out one's welcome; **shirí ga
wareru** to be brought to light; to be
found out; **shirí o mukeru** to turn
one's back upon.
shirime contemptuous glance; **shirime ni
kakéru** to look disdainfully at.
shirioshi backing, support; **shirioshi o suru**
to back, support.
shíritsu private establishment (school, welfare
agency, etc.); municipal establishment;
shíritsu no (*adj.*) private; municipal,
city.
shirizokéru to refuse; to reject; to repel, to
drive back.
shirizóku to retreat, retire, withdraw; to leave;
íppo shirizóku to take a step
backward.
shiro fortress; castle.
shíro (*n.*) white; **SHIRÓI** (*adj.*) white;
shíroku suru to whiten.
shiróoto amateur.
shirozátoo white sugar, granulated sugar.
SHIRU to learn; to become acquainted with;
shitte iru to know. **Nihongo mo
Shinago mo shitte imasu.** He knows
both Japanese and Chinese.
shíru juice, sap; fluid; soup, broth; **shíru no
óoi** juicy, succulent.
shirushi sign, mark, symbol, badge; **shirushi
o tsukéru** to mark, to tick.
shirusu to write down; to describe.
shíryo consideration; thought; **shíryo no áru**
thoughtful; **shíryo no nái** thoughtless.
shíryoku desperate effort; funds, resources,
means; eyesight, sight, vision;
shíryoku o tsukúshite with desperate
courage.
shíryoo materials, data.
shiryuu branch stream.
shisai reason; circumstances; details,
particulars; **shisai no** minute, detailed;
shisai ni minutely, in detail.
shisaku speculation; meditation; trial
production; **shisaku ni fukéru** to be
engrossed in thought; **shisaku suru** to
think; to speculate; to manufacture on
a trial (experimental) basis.
shisan property; fortune; assets.
shisatsu inspection; examination; **shisatsu
shite aruku** to make a tour of
inspection; **shisatsu suru** to visit; to
inspect.
shisei carriage, posture, pose; municipal
organization; **shisei chóosa** municipal
census, **shisei o tadásu** to hold oneself
up.
shiséiji illegitimate child.
shiseki place of historical interest.
shisen line of vision (sight); branch line;
shisen o sakéru to avoid the public
gaze.

shisetsu institution; institute; **shisetsu suru** to institute; to equip.

shísetsu mission; envoy.

shísha dead person; branch office.

shisha preview; **shisha o okonáu** to hold a preview.

shishókan post-office box.

shíshoo teacher, master (of traditional arts and sports).

shishoo casualties; number of killed and wounded; **shishóosha** dead and injured.

shishúnki adolescence, puberty; **shishúnki no** adolescent.

shishutsu expenditure; payment; **shishutsu suru** to pay; to disburse.

shishuu collection of poems.

shishuu embroidery; **shishuu suru** to embroider.

shisoo thought, idea.

shissaku error, mistake; **shissaku suru** to do (anything) amiss; to make a mistake.

shisseki reproof, reprimand, **shisseki suru** to reprove.

shisshoku unemployment; **shisshoku suru** to become unemployed.

shísso simplicity, plainness, frugality; **shísso na** simple, plain; **shísso ni kurasu** to live a simple life; to live plainly.

shisshoo disappearance (of a person); running fast; going at full speed; **shissoo suru** to disappear; to run away; to run at full speed.

SHITÁ tongue; **shitá o dásu** to put out one's tongue; **shitá o maku** to be astonished.

SHITA foot; bottom; lower place;—**no shita de** under, below;—**no shita ni** under, below; **shita o down; downward; shita kara** from below, from the bottom; **shita no** lower; downward; subordinate; inferior.

shítabi burning with less intensity; **shitabi ni náru** to reach a low mark; to wane.

shitagáeru to be attended by; to bring under subjection.

shitagaki rough copy, draft; **shitagaki o suru** to draft; to make a rough copy.

SHITAGÁTTE accordingly; consequently; correspondingly; **shitagáu** to follow; to accompany; to obey.

shitagéiko preparation; rehearsal; **shitagéiko o suru** to prepare.

SHITAGI underwear, undergarment.

shitagókoro secret desire; intention; **shitagókoro ga áru** to have a secret desire.

shitagóshirae preparation; arrangement.

shitai dead body.

shitaji ground; groundwork; preparation.

shitakénsa previous examination.

SHITAKU preparation; arrangement; **shitaku o suru** to prepare.

shitamachi downtown.

shitami preliminary inspection.

shitamuki downward look; downward

tendency; **shitamuki no** downward; prone; **shitamuki ni náru** to look down.

shitanuri undercoating, prime; **shitanuri o suru** to put on the first coat (of paint).

SHITASHÍI intimate; familiar; **shitashíi aidagara de áru** to be on intimate terms; **shitáshiku** intimately; personally; **shitáshiku suru** to be great friends; **shitashimi** friendship, friendly feeling; **shitashimi no áru** familiar, close, affectionate; **shitashimi no nái** unfamiliar; strange; cold; **shitashímu** to become friendly with; to become a great friend of.

shitashírabe preliminary inquiry; preparation; doing homework; **shitashírabe o suru** to inquire beforehand.

shitatáru to drip; to drop.

shitate cut; tailoring; getting ready; culture; **shitate no yói** well-tailored; **shitate ni déru** to treat (someone) with deference; to behave humbly; **shitatemono** sewing; tailoring; **shitatéru** to make (clothes); to train for a trade; **shitateya** dressmaker; tailor.

shitatsúzumi (n.) smacking one's lips; **shitatsúzumi o útsu** to smack one's lips; **shitatsúzumi o útte tabéru** to eat with much relish.

shitau to yearn after; to long for.

shitauchi tut.

shitauke subcontract; **shitauke ni dásu** to sublet.

shitayaku subordinate official.

shitayomi preparation of one's lessons; rehearsal; **shitayomi o suru** to prepare one's lessons.

shitazumi (n.) being in the lower layer of something; **shitazumi ni náru** to be in the lower layer; to be placed under something; **shitazumi no seikatsu o suru** to be low in the social scale.

shitchi swampy land; damp ground.

shitei designation; private residence; **shitei no** recognized; appointed; **shitei suru** to designate; to name; to appoint.

shiteki (n.) being poetic, being poetical; pointing out; (adj.) private, personal; **shiteki suru** to point out; to show; to indicate.

shiten branch store.

shitogéru to bring about; to complete.

shitoo right and proper; fair; reasonable.

shitóshito gently; softly; damp; wet.

shitóyaka well-bred manners, gracefulness, gentleness; **shitóyaka na** gentle, graceful.

SHITSÚ nature, character; quality.

-shitsu suffix denoting: room, chamber; **kyooshitsu** classroom; **shinshitsu** bedroom.

shitsuboku simpleness, simplemindedness; **shitsuboku na** simpleminded.

shitsuboo disappointment; despair; **shitsuboo shite** disappointedly; **shitsuboo saseru**

to disappoint; **shitsuboo suru** to be
disappointed at.
shitsugen slip of the tongue; blunder in
speech.
shitsugyoo unemployment; **shitsugyoo suru**
to be thrown out of work.
shitsúji steward; manager.
shitsuke discipline; breeding; training;
shitsuke no yói disciplined, well-bred;
shitsukéru to train, bring up.
shitsukkói, shitsukói obstinate, persistent.
shitsumei loss of eyesight; **shitsumei suru** to
lose one's sight.
SHITSUMON question; interrogation;
shitsumon suru to question.
shitsúmu attending to one's business.
shitsúnai interior of a room; **shitsúnai de** in a
room; **shitsunai sóoshoku** interior
decoration.
SHITSÚREI breach of etiquette, discourtesy;
shitsúrei na impolite; **shitsúrei na
kotó o iu** to say rude things.
shitsuren broken heart; disappointment in
love; **shitsuren suru** to be crossed in
love; to become heartbroken.
shittakaburi pretension to knowledge;
shittakaburi o suru to pretend to
know.
SHITTE IRU See **shiru.**
shitto jealousy; **shitto suru** to be jealous.
shiwa wrinkles; lines on one's face; creases;
rumples; **shiwa ga yoru** to become
wrinkled; **shiwa ni náru** to be
crumpled; **shiwa o nobású** to smooth
the creases.
shiwaza act, action, deed.
shiyoo use, employ; private business, private
use; **shiyoo de** for private use; on
private business; **shiyoo suru** to use; to
make use of; to turn to private use;
shiyoohoo directions for use;
shiyoonin employee.
shízai private fortune, money; **shízai o toojite**
out of one's own purse, at one's own
expense.
shizen nature; **shizen no** natural, instinctive;
shizen ni naturally, spontaneously.
SHÍZUKA calmness, quietness, stillness,
peacefulness; **shízuka na** silent, quiet,
still, peaceful; **shízuka ni kurasu** to
live in peace; **shízuka ni náru** to
become still, get calm.
shizukú drop; **shízuku ga taréru** to drip.
shizumaru to become quiet; **shizumeru** to
quiet, calm, pacify; to quell; to
subdue; to sink, send to the bottom;
shizumu to sink; to go to the bottom;
to feel depressed.
sho writing; document; calligraphy,
penmanship; book.
-sho suffix denoting: public office;
keisatsusho police station; **Zeimusho**
Office of Internal Revenue.
shobatsu punishment; **shobatsu suru** to
punich; to impose a punishment.
shóbun disposition; management;

punishment; **shóbun suru** to dispose
of; to manage; to punish.
shóchi management, action; **shóchi suru** to
manage, to dispose of, to deal with.
shochuu kyúuka summer vacation.
shoen first public performance of a play.
shóga pictures and writings.
shogen preface, introduction.
shogéru to be dejected, cast down.
shohan first edition of a book.
shóho first step; elements; **shóho no**
elementary, rudimentary.
shohoo prescription.
shójo (*n.*) virgin, maiden; **shójo no** (*adj.*)
virgin.
shóka early summer.
shokan letter; **shokansen** letter paper.
shokatsu jurisdiction.
shokei punishment.
shóki heat, hot weather; expectation,
anticipation; first stage; beginning;
clerk; **shóki no** expected; **shóki ni
ataru** to be affected by the heat.
shokikán secretary.
shokken authority; official power; **shokken o
ran'yoo suru** to abuse one's official
authority.
shokki tableware.
shokkoo workman.
shoku office; situation, position; occupation,
employment, job; eating; food;
appetite; **shoku ga susumu** to have a
good appetite; **shoku ni tsuku** to take a
post; **shoku o motoméru** to look for
employment.
shokuátari attack of indigestion,
food-poisoning.
shokuba workshop; place of work.
shokúbutsu plant; **shokubutsúgaku** botany;
shokubutsúen botanical garden.
shokudai candle-stand.
SHOKUDOO dining room; **shokudóosha**
dining car.
SHOKÚEN table salt.
shokugo after a meal.
shokúgyoo occupation, employment.
shokugyoofújin working woman.
shokuhi charge for boarding; board.
shokúin staff; personnel.
SHOKUJI meal; diet; **shokuji o suru** to eat;
shokujidóki mealtime.
shokuji typesetting; typography; composition;
shokuji o suru to compose;
shokujikoo typesetter.
shokumin colonization, settlement; colonists;
shokumin suru to colonize; to found a
colony; **shokumínchi** colony;
shokumínchi no colonial.
shokúmotsu food.
shókumu duties, functions; **shókumu o
hatásu** to discharge a duty;
shokumujoo officially, in the line of
duty; **shokumujoo no** official.
shókun Gentlemen! (*used in a speech*).
shokunin workman; artisan.
shokupán bread; loaf of white bread.

shokuryóohin articles of food, foodstuffs.

shókushi = hitosashiyubi forefinger; index finger; **shókushi o ugokásu** to be desirous of.

shokutaku person with non-official status; person employed without tenure.

shokutaku dinner table; **shokutaku ni tsuku** to take one's seat at the table.

shokúyoku appetite; relish; **shokúyoku ga nái** to have no appetite; **shokúyoku o susumaseru** to stimulate one's appetite.

shokuyoo no used for food; **shokuyoo ni teki súru** to be fit for the table.

shomei signature; **shomei suru** to sign.

shómen document; letter.

shómotsu book.

shonbóri lonely, solitarily.

shonichi first day; opening day.

shóo chapter; section; mark; ministry; proof; evidence; trade; commerce; merchant; dealer; prize; reward; nature, disposition; character; quality; quotient (math.);—**no shóo to shite** in proof of; **shóo no yói** of good quality; **shóo ga áu** to be congenial; **shóo ga awánai** to be incompatible; **shóo o atáeru** to give a prize; **shóo o éru** to get a prize; **shóo suru** to praise; to admire.

SHÓOBAI trade, business; **shóobai ni naráni** not to be paying; **shóobai o suru** to do business; **shoobainin** merchant.

shóobatsu rewards (honors) and punishment. Gakkoo de shoobatsu o uketa koto wa arimasen. I have received no honors or punishment in my school days.

shoobén urine; **shoobén o suru** to urinate.

shóobi admiration; appreciation; **shóobi suru** to praise; to applaud.

shooboo prevention and extinction of fires; **shoobóofu** fireman; **shooboosho** firehouse; **shoobootai** fire company. (See also **hí**.)

shóobu match, contest; game; **shóobu o kimeru** to fight to a finish; **shóobu o suru** to have a match (game, sport).

shoobun innate disposition, temperament.

shoochi consent, acceptance; **shoochi no úe de** by mutual agreement; **shoochi suru** to consent; to agree to; to understand; to know.

shoochoo symbol; symbolism.

shóodai invitation; **shóodai o ukéru** to receive an invitation; **shóodai suru** to invite.

shoodaku consent, acceptance; **shoodaku suru** to consent to; to comply with.

shoodoku disinfection, sterilization; **shoodoku suru** to disinfect; **shoodokúzai** disinfectant; antidote.

shoodoo impulse; impetus.

shoofuda price tag; **shoofuda tsuki no** marked with a price tag; notorious; genuine.

shoogai injury, harm.

SHÓOGAI life; lifetime; all one's days; to the end of one's life; **shóogai no** lifelong; **shóogai o owaru** to end one's days.

shoogáibutsu obstacle.

shoogakkoo grade school, elementary school.

shoogaku small sum.

shoogakukin scholarship.

SHOOGATSU New Year; January.

shoogen testimony, evidence; **shoogen suru** to testify to.

shoogi game of Japanese chess; **shoogi o sasu** to play chess.

shoogidaoshi falling in rapid succession one after another; **shoogidaoshi ni naru** to fall forward, one upon another as when a train makes a sudden stop; to fall like ninepins.

SHÓOGO noon, midday.

shóogyoo commerce, trade; **shóogyoo no** commercial.

shoohai prize cup; medal; victory or defeat; **shoohai o arasou** to contend for victory.

shoohei engagement (for a position); employment; **shoohei suru** to engage; to employ.

shoohi consumption; spending; **shoohi suru** to consume; to spend.

shoohin short piece; sketch.

shóohin goods; commodity; **shoohínken** gift certificate (issued by retail stores); **shoohísha** consumer.

shoohyoo trade-mark.

shooji paper sliding-door.

shoojíki honesty, uprightness; **shoojíki na** honest, upright; **shoojíki ni** honestly, frankly.

shóojin devotion; aspiration; religious purification; abstinence from animal food; vegetable diet; **shóojin suru** to devote oneself to.

shóojo young girl; little girl.

shoojoo certificate of merit; honorary certificate.

shoojóo condition of illness; symptom.

shooka digestion; **shooka fúryoo** indigestion; **shooka suru** to digest; **shookáki** digestive organ.

shóoka singing; **shóoka o utau** to sing.

SHOOKAI introduction; recommendation; minute explanation; company, a firm; inquiry; reference, communication by letter; **shookai suru** to introduce, recommend; to inquire (of a person about a thing); to make reference to; **shookáijoo** a letter of introduction; **shookaisha** introducer.

shookáki fire extinguisher.

shookaku (n.) raising to a higher status; **shookaku suru** to be raised to higher ranks.

shookan summons; call to appear; **shookan suru** to summon; call up; **shookánjoo** summons; a written summons.

shookáryoku digestion.

shookasen fireplug, hydrant.

shooken securities; bond.

shooki soberness; **shooki ni káeru** to come to one's senses; **shooki o ushinau** to lose one's senses; to faint.

shookíbo small scale.

shookin prize (in money); **shookin o kakéru** to offer a cash prize.

shookizúku to come to one's senses.

shooko proof, evidence; **shookóbutsu** evidence (thing).

shookodatéru to prove; to testify.

shookoo brief tranquility; temporary ease.

shookóogyoo commerce and industry.

Shookoo Kaigisho Chamber of Commerce and Industry.

shookyokuteki negative; passive.

shookyuu raise in wages; promotion; **shookyuu suru** to be promoted.

shoomei illumination, lighting; proof; certification; **shoomei suru** to prove, to certify; **shoomeisho** certificate; **mimoto shoomeisho** identification card (or other document).

shoomén front; **shoomén kara míru** to take a front view; **shoomen shóototsu** head-on collision.

shoometsu extinction; disappearance; **shoometsu suru** to disappear; to be extinguished.

shóomi net; **shóomi gókiro áru** to weigh five kilograms net.

shoomon bond; deed; **shoomon o ireru** to give a bond; to sign a written agreement.

shoomoo consumption; waste; **shoomoo suru** to consume; to waste; to tire out (*colloq.*).

shoonen youth, boy; boyhood.

shoonéndan boy scout.

shóoni infant, baby; **shoonika** pediatrics.

shoonin recognition; acknowledgement; witness; surety; **shoonin suru** to recognize; to admit; **shoonin ni tátsu** to be a witness to.

shóonin merchant, trader; **shóonin ni náru** to become a merchant.

shóorai (*n.*) future; (*adj.*) **shóorai no** future; prospective.

shoorei encouragement; promotion; **shoorei suru** to encourage; to promote; to urge.

shóori victory, triumph; **shóori o éru** to win a victory.

shooryaku abbreviation, omission; **shooryaku suru** to eliminate; to omit.

shooryoo small quantity.

shoosai details, particulars; **shoosai ni** in detail; **shoosai no** minute, detailed.

shoosan praise; admiration; **shoosan suru** to praise; to admire.

shoosen merchant vessel.

shoosetsu fiction; romance; novel; **shoosetsuka** novelist, novel writer; **shoosetsuteki** fictitious, romantic.

shooshi death by fire.

shooshin promotion, advancement; prudence; caution; timidity; **shooshin na** timid; cautious; prudent; **shooshin suru** to rise in rank.

shoosho bond; document; certificate; diploma.

shooshoku light eating; **shooshokuka** light eater.

shóoshoo little, few; in a small degree.

shooshuu calling out; summons; convocation; draft (into military service); **shooshuu suru** to call out; to summon; to assemble.

shoosoku news; **shoosoku o kiku** to hear from; to have news of (someone); **shoosoku ni tsuujiru** to be well informed; **shoosókutsuu** well-informed person.

shoosoo irritation, fretfulness; impatience; **shoosoo suru** to fret; to fidget, be impatient.

shoosui emaciation, haggardness; **shoosui suru** to become emaciated.

shoo súru to call; to name.

shoosúu decimal, fraction; small number; minority; **shoosúu de aru** to be very few.

SHÓOTAI invitation; true character; **shóotai náku** out of one's senses; **shóotai o arawásu** to reveal one's true character; **shóotai o tsukámu** to get at the bottom of an affair; **shóotai suru** to invite.

shóoten shop, store; focus, burning point; **shóoten o awaséru** to focus; to bring in to focus.

shootoo (*n.*) putting out lights; **shootoo suru** to put out the light; **shootóorei** curfew.

shoototsu collision, crash; conflict; **íken no shoototsu** conflict of opinions; **shoototsu suru** to run into; to collide.

shóou slight rain, drizzle.

shoouíndoo show window.

Shóowa present era (counted from ascent of present emperor to throne in 1926); **Shoowa 36 nen** the year 1961.

shóoyo reward; giving a reward; **shóoyo o atáeru** to give a reward.

shooyoo commerce, business; **shooyoo no** commercial; pertaining to business.

SHOOYU soy sauce.

shoozen sadly, sorrowfully; **shoozen to** with a heavy heart, sadly.

shoozoo portrait; likeness; **shoozoo o kakaséru** to have one's portrait painted.

shoo zúru to produce; to yield; to grow; to arise; to spring up.

shóri management; transaction; treatment; **shóri suru** to manage; to treat.

shoron preface, introduction.

shorui documents, papers.

shosai study; library.

shóseki = hón books.

shosen in the end; after all.

shoshin belief, conviction; **shoshin o hireki suru** to express one's belief; **shoshínsha** beginner, novice.

shosúru to conduct oneself; to deal with; to condemn, sentence.

shotái household; **shotaidóogu** household necessities; **shotaijimíru** to be sobered down by household cares; **shotáimochi** family man; **shotáimochi ga íi** to be a good housekeeper; **shotáinushi** head of a household.

shotáimen first interview; **shotáimen no hito** a stranger.

SHÓTCHUU (*colloq.*) always; often; all the time; **Shótchuu kaze o hikimásu.** I catch cold often.

shóten bookshop.

shotoku income; earnings; **shotokúzei** income tax.

shotoo elementary.

shou to carry on the back.

shoyoo no necessary, requisite, needed.

shoyuu possession; **shoyuu suru** to have; to possess; **shoyúuchi** one's land; one's estate; **shoyúuhin** belongings; **shoyúuken** property; proprietorship, ownership; **shoyúusha** proprietor.

shozai whereabouts; site, position; situation; **shozai o hakken suru** to discover (someone's) whereabouts; **shozai o kuramásu** to conceal (one's own) whereabouts.

shozaíchi site, locality.

shozaifumei no missing.

shozoku one's post, one's detachment; **shozoku no** attached to, belonging to; **shozoku saseru** to attach; to put under the control of.

shozon opinion; view; intention; **shozon o akásu** to tell one's real intention; **shozon o tazunéru** to ask (someone's) opinion about.

shú lord; chief; principal; master; **shú to shite** mainly, chiefly.

shúbi course of an event; **shúbi yoku** successfully; luckily.

shuchoo assertion; maintenance; opinion; **shuchoo o tóosu** to impose one's opinion on someone else; **shuchoo suru** to assert, to maintain; to advocate; to insist upon.

shudai subject, theme.

SHUDAN means, way; measures, steps; **shudan o miídasu** to find the means to; **shudan o tóru** to take measures.

shuei guard; **shuei suru** to keep guard.

shuen feast, banquet; cocktail party; starring; playing the leading part; **shuen o moyoósu** to hold a cocktail party.

SHÚFU capital; metropolis; housewife.

shúgei manual arts; handicraft.

shúgi principle; ism; **shúgi o mamóru** to stick to one's principles.

shúgo protection, guard; **shúgo suru** to protect, watch over.

shuhitsu chief editor.

shúisho prospectus.

SHÚJIN master; employer; one's husband.

shujínkoo hero, heroine (in a novel).

shujín'yaku host, hostess.

shúju no various, several, sundry.

shújutsu surgical operation.

shukan subjectivity; subjective view; **shukanteki** subjective.

shukei paymaster; accountant.

shuken sovereignty; **shukénsha** supreme ruler; chief of state.

shukí memorandum, note; **shukí o káku** to make a memorandum of.

shukka outbreak of fire; **shukka suru** to start a fire.

shukke (Buddhist) priest.

shukketsu bleeding, hemorrhage; **shukketsu suru** to bleed; **shukketsu o tomeru** to stop bleeding.

shukkin attendance (at the office); **shukkin suru** to go to work; **shukkínbo** attendance record, time book; **shukkin jíkan** opening hour of an office.

shukkoo plan; idea; contrivance; handiwork, handicraft; manual work; departure of a ship from a port; **shukoo o korásu** to devise a plan; **shukkoo suru** to sail.

shukuboo cherished desire; **shukuboo o tassúru** to attain a cherished desire.

shukuchoku night duty; **shukuchoku suru** to keep night watch; to be on night duty; **shukuchokúin** person on night duty.

shukudai homework; **shukudai ni suru** to reserve for future discussion; to keep in abeyance.

shukuden congratulatory telegram.

shukufuku blessing; **shukufuku sareta** blessed, happy; **shukufuku suru** to bless.

shukuhai toast (congratulatory cup); **shukuhai o ageru** to drink a toast.

shukuhaku lodging, accommodation; **shukuhaku suru** to put up for the night; to lodge; **shukuhakunin** lodger; **shukuhakúryoo** room and board; lodging charge; hotel bill.

shukujitsu holiday.

shukumei fate, destiny; predestination; **shukumei no** predestined; **shukuméiron** fatalism; **shukumeirón sha** fatalist.

shukún distinguished service; meritorious deeds.

shukusatsuban pocket-sized edition of a book; monthly bound edition of newspapers.

shukúsha residence; lodging house; billet.

shukusha drawing on a small scale.

shukusho one's address; dwelling place, residence.

shukushoo reduction, curtailment; **shukushoo suru** to reduce; to retrench; to curtail.

shukusúru to congratulate.

shukuten celebration; commemoration; **shukuten o ageru** to celebrate.

shukutoo benediction.

shukuzu reduced drawing; reduced copy.

SHÚMI taste; interest; **shúmi no áru** tasteful; **shúmi no nái** tasteless, dull; **shúmi o mótsu** to have taste for; to like.

shumoku items; article.

shun season; **shun no yasai** vegetables in season.

shunin person in charge; responsible official.

shunkan moment, instant; **shunkan ni** in a moment; **shunkan no** momentary, instantaneous.

shunoo brains; soul; leader. **Tanaka-san wa sono jigyoo no shunoo to natte iru.** Mr. Tanaka is the driving force of that enterprise.

shunretsu na unrelenting; rigorous; drastic.

shuppan sailing; publication; **shuppan suru** to sail, set sail; to publish, issue; **shuppánsha** publisher.

shuppatsu departure; starting; **shuppatsu suru** to depart, to leave; to start; **shuppátsuten** starting point.

shuppei dispatch of troops.

shuren dexterity.

shúrui kind, sort, variety; **arayúru shúrui no** all kinds of; **onaji shúrui no** of the same kind.

shuryoku main force; main body.

shuryoo hunting; shooting; **shuryooka** hunter.

shusai sponsorship;—**no shusai de** under the auspices of.

SHUU week.

shuukyoku end, conclusion; **shuukyoku no** last, final; **shuukyoku o tsugeru** to come to an end.

shuunyuu income; receipts; revenue; **shuunyuu ga óoi** to enjoy a comfortable income.

shuuréssha last train.

shúuri repair; **shúuri suru** to repair, mend.

shuuryoo completion; **shuuryoo suru** to complete the course of.

shuusai genius; talented person.

shuusaku study.

shuusan gathering and dispersion.

shuusánchi distributing center.

shuusei amendment; revision; modification; **shuusei suru** to amend; to revise; to modify; **shuuséian** amendment (to a bill).

shuusen recommendation; mediation; end of a war; **shuusen suru** to recommend; to mediate; to come to the end of a war.

shuuséngyoo brokerage; commission agency; **shuusénryoo** commission; brokerage; **shuusenya** broker, commission agent; real estate agency; employment agency.

shuusennin go-between; middleman.

shuushi religion; sect, denomination.

shúushi income and expenditure; from beginning to end. **Shúushi ga tsugunawanai.** We cannot make ends meet.

shúushin morality, ethics.

shuushin lifetime; all one's life; **shuushin chóoeki** penal servitude for life; **shuushin káiin** life member.

shuushoku securing employment; installation; **shuushoku suru** to secure a position in an office; to enter into service.

shuushuku contraction, shrinking; **shuushuku suru** to contract; to shrink.

shuushuu collection; **shuushuu suru** to collect; to gather.

shuutai unseemly sight; shameful conduct; scandalous condition; **shuutai o enzúru** to behave disgracefully.

shuuten terminal point.

SHUUTO father-in-law; **SHUUTOME** mother-in-law.

shuutoo na cautious; scrupulous, thorough; **shuutoo na chúui** scrupulous (meticulous) care.

shúuu shower; **shúuu ni áu** to be caught in a shower.

shuuwai acceptance of a bribe; graft; **shuuwai suru** to take a bribe.

SHÚUYA all night; whole night through; **shuuya únten** all-night service (for trolley cars, buses).

shuuyoo culture; cultivation; accommodation; reception; **shuuyoo o tsumu** to make a constant effort to improve oneself; **shuuyoo suru** to cultivate; to take in; to quarter.

shuuyóoryoku capacity.

shuuzei collection of taxes; **shuuzei suru** to collect taxes; **shuuzéiri** tax collector.

shuuzen repair; mending; **shuuzen suru** to repair; to mend.

shuwan ability, skill, talent; **shuwan no áru** able, capable, talented.

shuyoo na chief; important; essential.

shúzoku race; family; class.

shuzooka sake-brewer.

soaku na crude, coarse; inferior.

SÓBA side; neighborhood; proximity; buckwheat; dark buckwheat noodles; **kake soba** buckwheat noodles served in soup; **mori soba** buckwheat noodles served with soup but in a separate container; **sóba ni** at hand, beside; **sóba no** neighboring.

sobadatéru to prick up one's ears; **mimí o sobadátete kiku** to strain one's ears to listen.

sobiéru to rise; to tower; to soar. **Yamá ga tákaku sobiéru.** The mountain towers.

SOBIÉTO = Sobiétto = Sóren U.S.S.R., Russia; **Sobietto séifu** Soviet Government.

SÓBO grandmother.

soboku simplicity, artlessness; **soboku na** simple, artless.

sóburi behavior; bearing; manner; **sóburi o suru** to behave oneself; to assume the air of.

sobyoo rough sketch.

sóchi management; disposal; dealing.

SOCHIRA = SOTCHI there; that way.
sodachi (*n.*) breeding, bringing up; **sodachi no warúi** ill-bred; of slow growth; **sodachi no yói** well-bred; of good social background.
SODATÉRU to bring up, raise; to train; **haná o sodatéru** to grow flowers; **kodomo o sodatéru** to bring up a child.
SODÁTSU to grow; to be brought up.
SODE sleeve; **sode ni sugáru** to hang on a person's sleeve; to beg for mercy; **sode o hiku** to pull (someone) by the sleeve.
soen long negligence; **soen ni náru** to neglect to visit.
soéru to add; to affix, attach; **chikará o soéru** to give a person assistance; **kyoo o soéru** to liven up the entertainment.
SÓFU grandfather; **SOFÚBO** grandparents.
sogai check; obstruction, impediment; **sogai suru** to check; to obstruct, impede.
sogeki (*n.*) sniping; **sogeki suru** to aim and shoot; to fire at; to snipe.
sógo discrepancy; disappointment, failure; **sógo suru** to go wrong, to be in disagreement.
sógu to chip; to cut aslant; to diminish, reduce; **kyóomi o sógu** to spoil the pleasure.
sokai settlement; concession.
sokkenái cold; blunt; dry; curt; **sokkenái áisatsu** curt salutation.
sokki shorthand, stenography; **sokkíroku** shorthand records; stenographic transcript; **sokkísha** stenographer.
sokkin spot cash; **sokkin de haráu** to pay cash.
sokkokan meteorological station, weather bureau.
SOKKÚRI (*n.*) whole; just as it is; altogether; **jitsubutsu sokkúri** to be true to life.
sokkyóokyoku improvisation (in music).
SOKO that place, there; bottom; depth; sole; **soko e** there, to that place; **soko kara** from there; **soko ni, soko de** there, in that place; **soko ni shiranai** bottomless, unpredictable; **kokoro no soko kara** from the bottom of one's heart.
sokode now; then; thereupon; accordingly.
sokói underlying motive; true intention.
sokoiji spite, malice; **sokoiji no warui** malicious, spiteful.
sokojíkara latent (potential) energy; reserve of force; **sokojíkara no áru** strong; energetic **sokojíkara no áru kóe** deep (tone of) voice.
sókoku fatherland, one's native land; **sokokúai** love of the fatherland.
sokonáu to harm, hurt, injure, damage, spoil, ruin.
sokonuke sáwagi boisterous merrymaking.
sokoo conduct, behavior; **sokoo ga osamaránai** to conduct oneself improperly.
SOKÓRA, SOKORA ÁTARI thereabouts; about there.

soko soko ni hastily, hurriedly.
sokotsu carelessness, heedlessness; **sokotsu na** careless, heedless.
-SOKU counter denoting: pair (for shoes, socks, and stockings); **kutsu issoku** one pair of shoes.
sokubai suru to sell on the spot.
sokubaku restriction, restraint; **sokubaku sareru** to be restricted; **sokubaku suru** to restrict.
sókudo speed, velocity.
sókui accession to the throne.
sókuji at once, immediately; **sokujitsu** same day; on the very same day.
sokumen side, flank; **sokumen no** lateral, flanking.
sokúryoku speed, velocity; **sokúryoku o choosetsu suru** to regulate the speed.
sokuryoo land survey; **sokuryoo suru** to measure; to survey; **sokuryóoshi** surveyor.
sokusei rapid completion; quick mastery; **sokusei kóoza** intensive course.
sokuseki footprint.
sokushi instantaneous death; **sokushi suru** to die instantly.
sokushin promotion; acceleration, hastening; **sokushin suru** to promote; to further; **shokúyoku o sokushin suru** to stimulate the appetite.
sokutatsu, sokutatsu yúubin special delivery; **sokutatsu de** by special delivery; **sokutatsu de dásu** to send by special delivery.
sokutei measurement; **sokutei suru** to measure.
sokutoo prompt answer, ready reply; **sokutoo suru** to reply at once.
SÓKUZA NI at once, immediately, instantly.
somaru to be dyed, to be colored; to be infected with.
SÓMATSU crudeness, coarseness; **sómatsu na** crude; coarse; poor; **sómatsu ni suru** to treat lightly; to handle roughly.
some dye; dyeing; **some ga yói** to be well dyed; **someko** household dyestuff, dye; **someru** to dye; to stain; **sometsuke** dyeing; printing; blue-and-white porcelain.
SÓMOSOMO in the first place.
somukéru to turn away, avert; **kao o somukéru** to turn one's face away.
SOMÚKU to revolt against; to rise against; to act contrary to; to disobey; to violate. **Ryóoshin ni somuku.** To go against one's principles.
són loss, damage; disadvantage; **són na** disadvantageous; **són ni náru** to be disadvantageous to; **són o suru** to suffer a loss.
sonaéru to prepare; to provide for; to offer; to dedicate; **denwa o sonaéru** to install a telephone; **igen o sonaéru** to possess great dignity; **man'ichi ni sonaéru** to prepare for the worst.

sonaetsukéru to provide with; to equip with.
sonawáru to be furnished with, be supplied with.
sonboo existence; life or death fate; **sonboo ni kansuru mondai** a question of life or death; **sonboo ni kansúru** to decide the fate.
sonchoo esteem, respect; appreciation; **sonchoo suru** to esteem, respect.
sónchoo village headman; mayor.
sondai haughtiness, arrogance; **sondai na** arrogant, haughty; **sondai ni kamaéru** to have a haughty bearing.
son'eki profit and loss; loss and gain; **son'eki o keisan suru** to calculate profit and loss.
sonemí jealousy, envy; **sonému** to be jealous of; to envy.
songai damage, injury; loss; **songai báishoo** compensation for damages; **songai báishoo o yookyuu suru** to sue for damages; **songai o ataéru** to do damage; **songai o koomúru** to suffer a loss.
sonkai village assembly.
SONKEI respect; high regard; honor; **sonkei suru** to respect, esteem, honor; **sonkei sareru** to be respected.
sonmin villagers.
SONNA that sort of, such; of the kind, of the sort; **sonna hito** such a person; a person like that; **sonna ni** so; in that way; so much; particularly.
SONNÁRA then; in that case; if so.
SONO that, those; **sono ba** that place; **sono ba de** then and there; on the spot; **sono go** after that, afterward; from that time on; **sono go no** later; **sono hen** about, thereabouts; **sonó hoka** besides, beyond, moreover; **sonó hoka no** other, another; **sonó hoka wa** the rest, the others; **sono kóro** around that time; in those days; **sono kóro no** of that time; **sono kuse** and yet, notwithstanding; **sono mama** as it is, in that condition; **sono mama ni shite oku** to leave as it is; **sonó ta** besides, moreover; beyond; **sono te** that trick [that hand]; that device; **sono tóori** just so; exactly in that way; **sono uchi ni** before long; by and by; in the meantime; **SONO UE** in addition; moreover. **Sono té wa kuwánu.** None of your games! I'm not so easily cheated. **Sono ue no kotó wa yakusoku dekimasén.** I can't promise any more than that.
sonryóo hire, rent (tools, articles); **sonryóo de kariru** to hire; **sonryóo de kasu** to hire out; to rent out.
sonshitsu loss, damage; disadvantage.
sonshoo injury, damage, casualty; **sonshoo o koomúru** to be damaged; **sonshoo suru** to injure, damage.
sonsúru to exist; to remain.

sóntoku loss and gain, profit and loss; **sóntoku no mondai de wa nái** not to be a question of money.
sonzai existence. **sonzai suru** to exist; to remain.
sonzoku continuance; **sonzoku suru** to continue; to last.
sonzúru to be worn out, be damaged.
SÓO that way; so; idea; thought, conception; bonze, priest, monk; layer, stratum; seam; **soo iu** that sort of; **soo iu wáke de** for that reason; **sóo o néru** to meditate; to work on a plan. **Sóo desu.** That is so. **Soo shite kudasái.** Please do so.
sooan draft; rough cast.
sooba current price; quotation; speculation; **sooba ni té o dásu** to engage in speculation; **soobáshi** speculator.
sooban sooner or later; by and by.
soobétsukai farewell meeting; farewell dinner.
sóochi arrangement, equipment; **sóochi suru** to equip with; to arrange.
sóochoo university president.
soochoo early morning; **soochoo ni** early in the morning.
soochoo na solemn; sublime.
sóoda soda; bicarbonate of soda.
soodai representative; deputy; **soodai ni náru** to represent.
soodan consultation, conference; **soodan no ue** after consultation; **soodan suru** to consult, confer; **soodan ni noru** to take part in a consultation.
soodásui soda water.
sóodoo confusion, disorder; disturbance. **sóodoo o okósu** to raise a disturbance.
soodóoin general mobilization.
soofu sending; **soofu suru** to send; to forward.
soogákari de full force; with a united force; everybody participating.
soogaku musical performance; music; total amount; sum total.
soogankyoo binoculars.
soogawa whole leather.
soogei sending off and welcoming (people).
soogi funeral service; **soogi o okonáu** to hold a funeral service; **soogísha, soogiya** undertaker.
sóogi dispute, quarrel; conflict; (labor) strike; **soogidan** strikers.
sóogo reciprocity; **sóogo no** mutual, reciprocal.
soogon grandeur; solemnity; **soogon no** magnificent; grand, solemn.
soogoo synthesis; putting together; looks, features; **soogoo o kuzúshite warau** to smile gleefully; to be radiant with joy; **soogoo suru** to put together.
soogoo dáigaku university.
soogyoo start of an enterprise.
soohaku paleness; **soohaku na** deadly pale.
soohígyoo general strike.
sóohoo both parties; both sides; each side; **sóohoo no** either; both; mutual.

sooi difference, disparity;—**ni sooi nái** must be, it is certain that; **sooi náku** certainly; without fail;—**to sooi suru** to differ; to disagree; to be contrary to.

sóoi new device; novel idea; originality.

SOOJI cleaning; sweeping; **sooji o suru** to clean; to sweep.

soojíshoku general resignation; **soojíshoku o suru** to resign in a body.

sóojite generally; in general; for the most part.

soojuku premature growth, precocity; **soojuku no** precocious.

soojuu management; control; manipulation; **soojuu suru** to manage; to handle; to control; **kikái o soojuu suru** to operate a machine; **otto o soojuu suru** to manage one's husband; **soojúushi** pilot; manipulator.

sookai freshness; exhilaration; **sookai na** refreshing, enlivening; **sookai ni suru** to refresh, to exhilarate, enliven; **sookai ni náru** to be refreshed.

sookai general meeting; general assembly.

sookan sending back; deportation; grand sight; first publication (of a new magazine, paper, etc.); **sookan suru** to send back, deport; **sookángoo** initial number (issue) of a magazine.

sookatsu summary; **sookatsu suru** to sum up; to summarize.

SOOKEI total; sum total; **sookei de** in all, as a total; **sookei suru** to sum up; to total.

sooken healthiness; **sooken na** healthy, sound; stout.

sookin remittance; **sookin suru** to remit money; to send money.

sóoko warehouse; **sóoko ni azukéru** to store in a warehouse; **sóoko ni hokan suru** to store.

sookon early marriage.

sookoo manuscript; copy; conduct, behavior; **sookoo o tsukúru** to draft; to make a draft.

SÓO KOO SURU UCHI NI in the meantime; meanwhile.

sookutsu den, lair; nest; **doroboo no sookutsu** den of thieves.

sookúzure collapse, complete rout; **sookúzure ni náru** to be routed.

sóokyo daring enterprise.

soomei wisdom, sagacity; **soomei na** wise; clear-headed.

sóomen Japanese noodle (popular in summer).

soomoku plants and trees.

soomókuroku general table of contents.

sóomu general affairs; director; manager.

soonan meeting with an accident; mishap; **soonan suru** to meet with an accident; **soonánsha** victim of an accident; **soonan shíngoo** signal of distress.

soonen manhood; prime of life.

soonyuu insertion; **soonyuu suru** to insert, put in.

sooon noise, hubbub.

soooo fitness, suitability; **soooo na** appropriate, adequate; **soooo suru** to be suitable, to be fitting.

sooran superintendence, control; **sooran suru** to superintend, manage.

soorei splendor, magnificence; **soorei na** magnificent, splendid.

sooretsu funeral procession.

sooretsu na heroic, tragic; **sooretsu na sáigo o togéru** to die a heroic death.

sooritsu establishment, foundation; institution; organization; **sooritsu suru** to establish, institute, found; **soorítsusha** a founder.

sooron introduction; general remarks; quarrel, dispute; **sooron suru** to quarrel; to argue.

sóoryo priest, monk, bonze.

sooryóoji consul-general; **sooryoojíkan** consulate-general.

sóosa search, investigation; process, operation; management; **soosa suru** to search, look for, hunt for.

soosai general manager; president; governor.

soosaku search, investigation; creation; organization; original work; **soosaku suru** to search, look for, hunt for; to create; to originate; to write an original work; **soosakuka** person of originality; fiction writer; **soosakutai** search party; **soosakuteki** creative, original.

soosénkyo general election.

sooshíháinin general manager.

sooshiki funeral; funeral services.

sooshin transmission of a message; telegraphic service.

sooshíngu personal ornaments, furnishings.

SOOSHITE = **soshite** and then; and in addition.

sooshitsu loss; forfeiture; **sooshitsu suru** to lose; to be lost.

soosho series (of books); collected works.

sooshoku ornamentation, decoration, adornment; **sooshoku no nái** plain, unadorned; **sooshoku suru** to ornament, adorn, decorate.

sooshúunyuu total income.

soosoo early; as soon as possible; without delay.

sóosu Worcestershire sauce.

soosúu total number.

sootaiteki relative; correlative.

sootatsu conveyance; delivery; **sootatsu suru** to send; to forward; to convey.

sootei binding; design; **sootei suru** to bind; to design.

sóoto daring enterprise.

sootoku governor-general; viceroy.

SOOTOO fitness, suitability; sweeping away; **sootoo na, sootoo no** suitable; respectable; reasonable; moderate; considerable; **sootoo ni kurashite iru** to be comfortably off; **sootoo suru** to be fit for; to sweep away.

soowa episode.

soozái plain, ordinary food.

soozen noisily; uproariously; **soozen to** in a noisy manner.

soozoku succession; inheritance; **soozoku suru** to inherit; to succeed; **katoku o soozoku suru** to inherit an estate.

soozokunin heir, successor.

soozoo creation; **soozoo suru** to create.

soozoo imagination, fancy; **soozoo ni tómu** imaginative; **soozoo suru** to imagine, fancy.

soozóoryoku power of imagination.

soozooshíi noisy, full of noise.

sopurano soprano.

SÓRA! there! **Sóra míro!** There! You see! I told you so (*colloq.*)!

SÓRA sky; air; heavens; **sóra de** by heart, by memory; **sóra tákaku** high up in the sky; **sóra de obóeru** to learn by heart; **sóra de yómu** to recite from memory.

soradánomi hoping against hope; vain hope.

sorairo sky-blue, azure.

soramóyoo look of the sky; weather; situation.

sorásu to bend, curve; to turn backward; to evade, elude, dodge; to turn aside; to draw off; **hanashí o wakí ni sorásu** to turn the talk away; **mé o sorásu** to look away; to avert one's eyes from; **shitsumon o sorásu** to parry a question.

sorazorashíi feigned; false; hypocritical; **sorazoráshiku** in obvious dissimulation, hypocritically.

SORE it, that; **sore dá kara** therefore, accordingly; **sore dake** that much, so much; **sore dá noni** yet, in spite of that; **sore démo** still, yet; **sore hodo** so much, so; **sore kara** and then, after that; **sore máde** till that time; **sore nára** then, if so; **sore ni** besides that; **sore tómo** or else.

SÓREN U.S.S.R., Russia

soréru to stray; to glance off.

sorí warp; curve; bend; **sorí ga áu** to get along (with each other) very well; **sorí ga awánai** not to be on good terms (with someone).

sorimí (*n.*) straightening oneself up; holding one's head high; **sorimí ni náru** to throw back one's head.

soroban abacus; finance; **soroban ga toréru** to pay; to be profitable; **soroban o hajíku** to move counters of an abacus; to calculate. **Soroban ga awánai.** The accounts do not square.

soroéru to put in order, arrange in order.

soroi set; suit; **sorói mo sorótte** without exception; **soroi no** of the same pattern, uniform.

SÓROSORO slowly, gradually; gently.

soróu to become complete; to be arranged in order; to gather, assemble; to agree, be in accord.

sóru to shave; to bend; to warp; to bend backward; **kao o sóru** to shave oneself. **Hi ni atatte ita ga sorimashita.** The sun has warped the board.

soryaku roughness; **soryaku no** rough, cursory; **soryaku ni** roughly.

sosei resuscitation; reanimation; revival; **sosei suru** to revive, come to life again; **sosei no omoí o suru** to feel revived, to feel a great relief.

soséihin article of inferior quality.

sósen ancestor.

soshaku chewing, mastication; **soshaku suru** to chew, masticate.

soshakúchi leased ground.

soshakúken lease.

sóshi obstruction; check, prevention; **sóshi suru** to check; to hold in check; to hinder, impede.

soshiki system; organization; formation; composition; **soshiki suru** to form; to organize; to constitute; **soshikiteki** systematic; methodical; **soshikiteki ni suru** to systematize.

soshíru to slander; to blame, speak ill of; *-te* form: **soshítte**

SOSHITE See **sooshite**.

soshitsu predisposition; nature; makings. **Ano hito ni wa shijin no soshitsu ga aru.** He is very poetic. (He has the poet in him.)

soshoku plain diet; **soshoku suru** to eat poorly (live on poor fare).

soshoo lawsuit; action; case; **soshoo o okósu** to sue; **soshoo suru** to sue; to start a lawsuit; to go to law; **soshoonin** plaintiff.

sosogu to pour into; to pour on; to water; to pour (itself) into.

sosokkashíi hasty; careless, heedless; **sosokkashíi kotó o suru** to act carelessly; to make a stupid mistake.

sosonokásu to tempt, entice; to stir up.

sosoru to incite, stir up, to excite.

sossen suru to take the lead; to take the initiative.

sosui drainage.

SOTCHI = SOCHIRA there; that way.

sotchinoke (*n.*) laying aside; neglecting; **sotchinoke ni suru** to neglect, to leave out in the cold.

sotchoku plainness, frankness, candidness; **sotchoku na** simple and honest; **sotchoku ni hanásu** to speak frankly.

SÓTO out-of-doors, outside; **sóto e iku** go outside.

sotobori outer moat (around Japanese castles).

sotogawa outer side; outside.

sotoúmi open sea.

sotsu waste; bungling; fault; **sotsu no nái** faultless, perfect; **sotsu ga nái** to be faultless.

sotsugyoo graduation; completion of a course of study; **sotsugyoo suru** to complete a course; to graduate from; **sotsugyóosei** graduate, alumnus; **sotsugyóo shiki** graduation ceremony; commencement; **sotsugyoo shóosho** certificate; diploma.

sotsuu drainage; understanding; **sotsuu suru** to drain; to draw off; to understand

(each other); **íshi ga sotsuu suru** to
come to a good mutual understanding.
SOTTO quietly; softly; gently; secretly; **sotto
shite oku** to leave it as it is.

sottoo (*n.*) fainting; **sottoo suru** to faint.

sówasowa nervously; restlessly; **sowasowa
suru** to be resless; to be nervous.

soyógu to rustle; to wave.

soyoo grounding; elementary knowledge;
culture; **soyoo ga áru** to be well
grounded in.

sóyosoyo to softly, gently (said only of the
blowing of the wind); **sóyosoyo fuku
kaze** gentle breeze.

sozei taxes; taxation.

sú vinegar; sandbank; shallow; **sú ni
noriagéru** to run aground.

su nest; den; **su ni tsúku** to brood, incubate;
su o tsukúru to build a nest.

suashi barefoot; naked; **suashi de**
barefoot(ed).

subarashíi splendid, magnificent.

subashikkói = subayái nimble; active;
smart; quick-witted.

subayái See **subashikkói.**

subekkói smooth; slippery; velvety.

suberikómu to slide into; to slip into.

subéru to slide; to slip; to glide.

súbesube shita smooth; velvety.

SÚBETE (*n.*) whole, all; altogether; **súbete
no all**; whole; every.

sudare bamboo blind; **sudare o kakéru** to
hang a bamboo blind; **sudare o maku**
to roll up a bamboo blind.

sude empty hand; hand; **sude de** unarmed,
empty-handed.

SÚDE NI already.

sudoori (*n.*) passing by without calling;
sudoorí suru to pass by without
calling (at someone's house).

SUE end; future; **sue ní wa** in the long run;
sue no last; final; youngest; **sue no
áru wakamono** a promising youth.

suekko youngest son, youngest daughter.

suéru to set, place, lay.

suetsuke fitting up; installation; **suetsuke no**
fixed, stationary; **suetsukéru** to fit up;
to set, place in position.

súgao unpainted face.

sugáru to cling to; to lean on.

súgata form, figure, shape; **súgata o kaeru** to
disguise oneself; **súgata o kakúsu** to
disappear.

suge náí cold; rough; flat; **suge náku** coldly;
roughly; flatly; **suge náku kotowáru**
to refuse flatly.

SUGI cryptomeria; Japanese cedar.

sugíru to pass by; to go too far.

-SUGÍRU suffix denoting: be excessively; do
(something) excessively; **omosugíru** to
be too heavy; **tabesugíru** to eat
excessively.

SUGÓI uncanny, weird; ghastly, lurid; **sugói
hikarí** lurid light.

sugósu to pass, spend (time); to take too
much.

súgosugo dejectedly; disconsolately; with a
heavy heart.

SÚGU soon; immediately; close by; near;
súgu hana no saki ni just under one's
nose; **súgu ni** immediately, instantly.

suguréru to surpass, excel; to be excellent; to
be strong.

sugúrete eminently; conspicuously; by far.

suhada bare skin; **suhada ni náru** to bare
oneself; **suhada ni kiru** to wear next to
the skin; **suhádaka** nudity; state of
being stark naked; **suhádaka de** stark
naked.

súi essence, pith; elegance; fashion; sour;
acid; **súi na** fashionable; refined,
tasteful; **súi mo amaí mo shirinúita
hitó** a person who has tasted the sweet
and bitter of life; **súi o kikasu** to
pardon (someone else's) folly.

suiagéru to suck up.

suichoku no perpendicular, vertical.

suichuu (*n.*) being in the water; **suichuu no**
(*adj.*) underwater; **suichuu ni** (*adv.*)
underwater.

suidásu to suck out.

suiden paddy field, rice field.

SUIDOO water service; waterworks; city
water; channel; **suidoo o hiku** to have
water pipes laid, to have water
supplied; **suidookan** water pipe.

suiei swimming; **suiéigi** bathing suit; **suieijoo**
swimming place.

súifu sailor, seaman; **súifu ni náru** to become
a sailor.

suigai damage by flood; flood-disaster;
suigáichi flooded district.

suigen, suigénchi source of a river;
fountainhead.

suihei water level; horizon; **suihei no** level,
horizontal; **suihei ni** horizontally.

SÚIHEI sailor (in the navy); **suihéifuku**
seaman's uniform.

suiheisen horizon; sealine; horizontal line.

suihen waterside.

suijaku emaciation, debility; **suijaku suru** to
be weakened; to grow weak.

suiji cooking, cookery; **suiji gákari** person in
charge of cooking, cook; **suiji suru** to
cook; **suijiba** kitchen.

suijóoki vapor, steam.

suijun water level.

suika watermelon.

suikan drunken fellow.

suiki moisture, humidity; dropsy; **suiki no
áru** moist, humid; **suiki ga kúru** to
become dropsical.

suikómu to inhale; to draw in; to absorb; to
suck in.

suikoo execution; **suikoo suru** to execute,
carry out.

suikuchi mouthpiece; cigarholder.

súikyo recommendation; **súikyo ni yotte**
through (someone's) recommendation.
súikyo suru to recommend.

súikyoo drunken frenzy; whim, vagary;

súikyoo de out of mere pique; just for kicks; **súikyoo na** frenzied with drink.

suimen water surface; **suimen kara ichi méetoru ue** one meter above the water; **suimen ni ukabu** to rise to the surface.

SUIMIN sleep; **suimin suru** to sleep; to go to sleep.

suimon floodgate.

SUIMÓNO soup (Japanese-style); **suimonó wan** soup bowl. (See also **súupu**.)

suinan calamity by water; casualty at sea.

súiri reasoning; induction; **súiri suru** to reason; to induce.

súiro waterway, watercourse.

suiron reasoning; **suiron suru** to reason; to deduce.

suiryoku hydraulic power; **suiryoku dénki** hydroelectricity.

suiryoo guess, conjecture; quantity of water; volume of water; **suiryoo suru** to guess; to presume; to consider.

suiryuu stream; watercurrent.

suisaiga water color painting; **suisaigáka** watercolor painter.

suisánbutsu marine products: fish, crabs, lobsters, clams, oysters, seaweeds.

suisángyoo fishery; marine-products industry. (See also **suisánbutsu.**)

suisatsu guess, conjecture; sympathy; **suisatsu suru** to conjecture, to guess, to infer from.

suisen bénjo flush toilet.

suisen recommendation; daffodil; **suisen suru** to recommend; **suisénjoo** letter of recommendation.

súisha water mill, water wheel.

suishin depth of water.

suishínki propeller; screw.

suishoo recommendation; approval; praise; **suishoo suru** to recommend; to praise.

súishoo crystal; **súishoo no yóo na** crystalline, crystal-like.

suisoku conjecture, supposition; inference; **suisoku suru** to conjecture, to suppose.

suisoo water tank, cistern.

Súisu Switzerland; **Súisu no** (adj.) Swiss; **Suisujin** Swiss (people).

suitai decline; decay; **suitai suru** to decline; to decay; to fall.

suítchi switch.

suitei presumption; conclusion; **suitei suru** to presume; to conclude.

suitoo canteen.

suitoo gákari cashier, teller.

suitorígami blotting paper, blotter.

suitóru to suck up; to absorb.

suitsúku to stick fast to, adhere.

suiun transportation by water; **suiun no bén** facilities for transportation by water. **Oosaka wa suiun no bén ga íi desu.** Osaka City has very good facilities for marine transportation.

súiyaku liquid medicine.

suiyoku cold-water bath; bathing.

SUIYÓOBI Wednesday.

sujzókukan aquarium.

SÚJI line; strips; muscle; sinew, tendon; fiber; plot; source, quarter.

sujigaki plot of a play.

sujimukai no See **sujimukoo no.**

sujimúkoo no diagonally opposite; **sujimúkoo no ié** a house diagonally across the street.

sujoo past career; one's past; birth; blood; origin; **sujoo no iyashíi** of low birth; **sujoo no shirenai** of unknown character; **sujoo no yói** of good family; of good birth.

sukáafu scarf.

sukáato skirt.

sukashi watermark; transparency; openwork; **sukashi no** watermarked.

sukasu to look through; to hold to the light; to thin out; to leave an opening.

SUKÉETO skating; pair of skates; **sukéeto o suru** to skate.

sukétchi sketch, sketching; **sukétchi ni iku** to go sketching; **sukétchi suru** to make a sketch.

SUKÍ fondness; love; fancy; taste; **suki na** favorite, pet; **sukí ni** as one pleases; at one's pleasure; **sukí ni náru** to become fond of; **sukí ni saseru** to let (someone) do as he pleases. **Sukí desu.** I like it.

suki opening; crack; chance, opportunity; leisure; unguarded point; spade, plow; **suki ga nái** to find no chance; **suki o nerau** to watch for a chance.

sukihara empty stomach.

sukíí ski.

sukikirai likes and dislikes; **sukikirai no óoi** squeamish; finical, finicky, too particular.

sukima space; crevice; intermission; **sukima náku** leaving no space; compactly.

sukitóoru to be transparent, be clear; **sukitóotta** clear, transparent.

SUKIYAKI Japanese dish of meat and vegetables usually cooked on the table.

sukízuki taste, liking, fondness; matter of taste; **sukízuki ga áru** each to his own taste. **Sore wa sukízuki desu.** It is a matter of taste.

SUKKÁRI completely, entirely.

sukobúru very, highly, extremely, awfully.

SUKÓSHI little, few, bit; **sukóshi demo** any, even a little; **sukóshi no** a little, a few, slight; **sukóshi mo** not in the least (used with a negative verb); **sukoshi zútsu** little by little.

Sukottorándo Scotland; **Sukottorando no** (adj.) Scots, of Scotland; **Sukottorandójin** Scot, Scotsman.

SUKU become empty; become sparse; **aida ga suku** to become separated; **té ga suku** to be disengaged. **Onaka ga sukimáshita.** I'm hungry. **Kono densha wa suite imásu.** This streetcar isn't crowded.

sukui help, rescue, relief, salvation; **sukui o**

motoméru to ask for help, call for help; to seek salvation; **sukuidásu** to help (someone) out of; to rescue; **sukuínushi** savior, deliverer.

sukumu to be cramped; to be paralyzed with fear.

SUKUNÁI to be few, little, scanty, scarce. **Shuunyuu ga sukunái desu.** His income is small.

sukunakaránu not a little; not small; considerable; much; **sukunakaránu méiwaku** considerable inconvenience; much trouble.

SUKUNÁKUTOMO at least, to say the least.

sukúramu scrimmage; **sukúramu o kúmu** to line up for a scrimmage.

sukurfín movie screen.

SUKUU to scoop, ladle; to trip up; to help, save, rescue; to relieve; **sukuu kotó no dekínai** hopeless.

súmai dwelling, residence, abode.

sumánai to be sorry for; to have no excuse for.

sumaséru to bring to an end.

sumáshita affected, stuck-up; indifferent.

SUMÁSU to finish, conclude, get through; to clear, clarify; to look demure; to be affected. **Góhan wa sumashimashita.** We have finished our meal.

sumáu to live, dwell.

SUMI corner, nook; India ink; ink-stick (cake of ink used to prepare ink for brush writing); **súmi kara súmai made** every nook and corner; **súmi ni oku** to put in the corner; **sumi o suru** to rub an ink-stick; **sumi o tsukeru** to dip in ink; to smear with ink.

SUMÍ charcoal; **sumíya** charcoal dealer.

sumika dwelling, residence.

sumikómu to live in an employer's house.

SUMIMASÉN pardon me; I'm sorry. **Sumimasen ga enpitsu o kashite kudasái?** Pardon me—may I borrow your pencil?

sumíyaka na quick, rapid, swift, speedy; prompt.

sumízumi all the corners; every nook and corner. **Kono hen wa sumizumi made shitte imasu.** I know every nook and corner of this neighborhood.

sumoo Japanese wrestling; wrestler; **sumoo o tóru** to wrestle.

SÚMU to reside, live; to end, come to an end; to become clear (said of a liquid); **Kono machi ni súnde imásu.** I live in this town. **Dóko ni súnde imásu ka?** Where do you live?

SÚN Japanese inch (corresponds to 1.193 American inches).

SUNÁ sand; **suna de migaku** to polish with sand; **suna o máku** to scatter sand.

súnao meekness, gentleness; **súnao ni** obediently, meekly; **súnao na** meek, gentle; **súnao ni suru** to obey; to be obedient.

SUNÁWACHI namely, that is to say; nothing but; neither more nor less; thereupon.

suné leg; shin; **suné ni kizu mótsu mi** someone having a guilty conscience; **óya no suné o kajíru** to sponge off one's parents.

sunéru to be peevish; to sulk; to be in a pet.

súnka moment's leisure; little time to spare; **súnka mo nái** to have no time to spare.

su nó mono vinegary dish; vegetables seasoned with vinegar.

sunpoo measure, dimensions; **sunpoo o tóru** to take measurements (for a new suit); **sunpoo no tóori ni** according to the measurements.

sunpoogaki measurement, specification.

Supéin Spain; **Supeingo** Spanish (language); **Supeinjín** Spaniard.

supóotsu sports; **supootsúman** sportsman.

suppádaka nudity, nakedness.

SUPPÁI sour, acid, tart. **Kono míruku wa suppaku natte imasu.** This milk has turned sour.

suppanúku to expose; to disclose.

suppokású to leave undone; to neglect.

suppon snapping turtle.

SUPÚUN spoon.

—súra particle denoting: even, so much as. **Kodomo sura shitte imasu.** Even a child knows it.

surarí to shita slender, graceful.

súrasura smoothly; without a hitch.

surechigau to pass by each other.

surekkarashi pert person.

suréru to rub; to graze; to be worn out; to grow vicious.

súri pickpocket, cutpurse.

suriherásu to wear down; to wear away.

surikiréru to get worn out; to become threadbare.

surikómu to rub in.

surímono printed matter; **surímono ni suru** to print.

surimúku to rub off; to chafe.

SURÍPPU slip (woman's undergarment).

súriru thrill.

suritsubúsu to grind down; to rub out of shape; to dissipate one's fortune.

SURU to do; to play; to practice; to make; to change one thing into another; to act as, officiate as. **Suru kotó ga nái desu.** I have nothing to do. **Nihongo no benkyoo o shimáshita.** I have studied Japanese. **Kyóoto e iku kotó ni shimáshita.** I have decided to go to Kyoto. **Anó hito wa kyóoshi o shite imásu.** He is a teacher. **Sore wa sen en shimásu.** It costs one thousand yen.

súru to pick (someone's) pocket; to grind; to bray; to print; to duplicate; to rub; to file; to lose one's fortune. **Kabu de okane o surimashita.** He lost his fortune through dabbling in speculation. **Meishi o sútte moratái desu.** I would like to have visiting cards printed.

surudói sharp, acute, keen, cutting.

SURUTO whereupon, just then; then, well. **Suruto minna de goman en desu ne?** Then the total will be fifty thousand yen, won't it?

susamají alarming, dreadful, fearful, terrible.

susamu to grow in intensity or violence; to go to ruin; to grow wild; to be addicted to.

susanda ruined, desolate, dreary. **Susanda seikatsu o shite imasu.** He is living a wild life.

suso skirt (of a dress); bottom (of a mountain); **zubon no suso** trouser cuff.

súsu soot; **susu dáreka no** sooty; **susukeru** to be stained with soot; **susubóketa, susúketa** smutty.

susugu to rinse; to wash.

susumeru to recommend; to advise, counsel; to encourage; to promote; to advance, put forward; to present, offer; to put on (a watch); **kooshoo o susúmeru** to proceed with the negotiations.

susumu to progress, advance, go forward.

susunde of one's own accord; willingly.

susurináku to sob; to whimper; **susurinaki** sobbing; **susurinaki o suru** to sob.

sutáa star (of movies or stage).

sutáato (n.) start (in a sport); **sutáato o kíru** to start.

sutajio studio (for movies, broadcasting).

sutánpu stamp; datemaker.

sutareru to fall into disuse; to go out of use or fashion.

SUTÁSUTA TO quickly, hurriedly.

sutebachi despair; self-abandonment; **sutebachi ni náru** to abandon oneself to despair.

sutebasho dumping ground.

sutéeshon railway station.

sutego deserted child; foundling.

SUTÉKI NA splendid, brilliant, fine, remarkable, superb; **SUTEKI NI** exceedingly, remarkably; **suteki na gochisoo** a fine dinner.

sutékki walking stick, cane.

sutemi disregard of one's life; desperation; **sutemi ni náru** to abandon oneself to despair.

sutene bargain price; **sutene no** ridiculously cheap; **sutene de uru** to sell at a sacrifice; to sell dirt cheap.

SUTERU to throw away, abandon; to give up.

suteuri sacrifice sale; a less-than-cost bargain; **suteuri ni suru** to sell at a sacrifice.

sutezérifu menace; parting shot; **sutezérifu o nokósu** to leave with a parting remark.

suto See **sutoráiki.**

sutóobu stove.

sutoráiki = suto strike (walkout of labor); strike (baseball).

sutóroo (beverage) straw.

SÚU (n.) number, figure; lot; (v.) to breathe; to inhale; to sip; to absorb; to smoke; **dai tasúu** majority; **iki o súu** to breathe the air; **tabako o súu** to smoke a cigarette.

SÚU- prefix denoting: several; **suujitsu** several days; **suunin** several persons.

suugaku mathematics; **suugaku no** mathematical; **suugákusha** mathematician.

suuhai worship; adoration; **suuhai suru** to worship, venerate.

SUUJI figure, numeral; **suuji no** numerical; **suujijoo** numerically.

suukoo loftiness, sublimity; **suukoo na** lofty, sublime.

SÚUPU soup (Occidental style); **suupu zara** soup plate. (See also **shiru** and **tsuyu.**)

suusei trend; drift; tendency; tide, current; **yó no suusei ni tomonátte** with the trend of the times.

suwari stability; **suwari ga yói** to sit well; to be stable; **SUWARU** to sit; to squat; to be set; **chan to suwaru** to sit straight; **rakú ni suwaru** to sit comfortably.

suyaki unglazed pottery; **suyaki no** unglazed.

súyasuya to quietly, gently, peacefully; **súyasuya to nemuru** to sleep quietly.

súzu tin.

suzu bell, handbell; **suzu no oto** tinkle of a bell; **suzu o narasu** to ring a bell.

suzume sparrow.

suzumí (n.) enjoying the cool air; **suzúmi ni iku** to go out to cool off; **suzúmu** to cool oneself; to enjoy the cool breeze.

suzunari cluster (of fruit); **suzunari ni nátte iru** to hang in clusters.

suzuri ink stone (used in preparing ink for brush-writing). (See also **sumí**); **suzuríbako** ink-stone case.

SUZUSHII cool, refreshing; **suzushíi kao o suru** to assume a nonchalant air; to appear calm and unconcerned.

T

tá (n.) others, rest; rice field, paddy field; (adj., adv.) many, much, plenty, ample; **tá no** other, another; **tá o tagayásu** to till a rice field; **tá ni mizu o hiku** to irrigate a rice field; **tá to suru** to appreciate highly; to be grateful.

TABAKO = SHIGARÉTTO cigarette; **tabakó ire** cigarette case; **tabako o súu** to smoke a cigarette; **tabakoya** cigar store (stand).

tabanéru to bundle; to tie up in a bundle.

tabeakíru to become tired of (a food).

tabehajiméru to begin to eat.

tabekáta how to eat. **Nihonshoku no tabekata o setsumei shite kudasai.** Please explain how to eat Japanese food.

TABEMÓNO food; provisions; edibles. **Nani ka tabemono wa arimasu ka?** Can we get something to eat? **Nihón de wa ómo na tabemóno wa okome desu.** In Japan, rice is the staple food.

TABÉRU to eat; to take; to live on; **gekkyuu de tabéru** to live on one's salary;

hitókuchi tabéru to have a mouthful (of food). **Yooshoku bakari tábete imasén.** I am eating only foreign (Occidental) food.

tabesugi overeating, surfeit; **tabesugíru** to overeat; **tabetsukéru** to be accustomed to eat. **Shina ryóori wa tabetsukéte imasén.** I am not accustomed to eat Chinese food.

tabezu gírai disliking (a food) without tasting; food prejudice.

tabí traveling; travel; journey; (Japanese) socks; **tábi issoku** pair of tabi; **tábi o haku** to put on socks; **tabí o suru** to travel; **tabibito** traveler; **tabihádashi** wearing socks but no shoes; **tabihádashi de** in one's socks.

-tabi times, occasion; **-tabi góto ni** whenever, every time when.

tabikóogyoo local performances (of a theatrical company); road performances.

tabisaki while on a journey. **Sono tegami wa tabisaki de uketorimáshita.** I received that letter while I was on a trip.

TABITABI often, many times, repeatedly. **Sono kotó wa tabitabi hanashi ni demáshita.** That subject came up often in our conversation.

taboo bright future; great promise; being fully occupied with; being busy; **zénto taboo no seinen** a promising young man; **taboo na** busy; **taboo ni torimagíre** on account of the pressure of business; **taboo de áru** to be busy.

TÁBUN perhaps, probably. **Kón'ya tábun kúru deshoo.** He will probably come this evening.

tabun (n.) reaching (others') ears; **tabun o habakáru** to be afraid of publicity.

tabyoo (n.) being sickly; being weak and feeble.

TÁCHI nature, character, quality, disposition; **táchi no yói** of good quality; **táchi no warúi** of bad quality.

tachiagáru to stand up, rise to one's feet.

tachiai presence, attendance;—**ni tachiai o motoméru** to request (someone's) presence as a witness; **tachiáu** to stand by; to fight with;—**ni tachiáu** to attend;—**to tachiáu** to fight with.

tachíban (n.) standing on sentry duty; **tachíban o suru** to stand watch; **tachíban o oku** to place a guard; **tachibánashi o suru** to talk standing; to stand chattering together.

tachidokoro ni on the spot, instantly. **Tachidokoro ni késshin shimashita.** He made up his mind in an instant.

tachidomáru to stop short; to halt, stand still; **kyuu ni tachidomáru** to come to a sudden halt.

tachidooshi (n.) standing the whole way; **Ueno máde tachidooshi deshita.** We had to stand the whole way to Ueno.

tachifusagáru to block (someone's) passage.

tachigie (n.) going out (said of a charcoal fire, etc.); being dropped (said of matters); **tachigie ga suru** to go out half-burned. **Sono keikaku wa tachigie ni narimashita.** The plan has fallen through.

tachigiki (n.) eavesdropping, overhearing; **tachigiki o suru** to eavesdrop.

tachigui (n.) eating while standing; **tachigui o suru** to eat standing.

tachigusare dilapidation (of a building); **tachigusare ni náru** to fall into ruin.

tachíru to enter; to penetrate; to interfere. **Shibafu ni tachíru bekárazu.** Keep off the grass. **Tachitta kotó o otazune shimásu ga . . .** It might be too personal, but may I ask . . .

tachiki standing tree.

tachikoméru to screen, envelop. **Kasumi ga tachikoméru.** The mist envelops all things.

TACHIMACHI at once; in an instant. **Nihon ni kuru to tachimachi yuumei ni narimashita.** As soon as he came to Japan, he became prominent.

tachimawáru to go round; to play one's part; to maneuver; **tachimawáru** to play one's part well; **zúruku tachimawáru** to act in a cunning way.

tachimi seeing a play from the gallery (from standing room).

tachimukáu to fight against.

tachinaóru to regain one's footing; to recover.

tachinoki removal; vacation; evacuation;—**ni tachinoki o meizúru** to order to vacate; **tachinoki méirei** order for removal; deportation order; an eviction order; **tachinokisaki** refuge; **tachinóku** to quit; to leave; to vacate.

tachiokure (n.) being late in getting started; **tachiokuréru** to be tardy, be behind time.

tachióojoo standstill, deadlock, being kept standing; **tachióojoo o suru** to come to a standstill; to be in a dilemma.

tachisukúmu to stand petrified with fear.

tachiyóru to call at;—**no uchí ni tachiyóru** to drop in.

tachizume (n.) being kept standing.

táda merely, only, simply; free of charge.

TÁDACHI NI at once, immediately, directly; without delay. **Tadachi ni kíte kudasai.** Please come immediately.

tadagoto trivial matter; commonplace (thing). **Tadagoto de nái.** It is no trivial matter.

TADÁIMA now, just now; **tadáima no tokoro** for the present; **tadáima de wa** now, nowadays.

tadai no heavy, great; serious; **tadai no songaí** heavy loss; **tadai no eikyoo o koomuru** to be seriously affected.

tadanori free ride; stealing a ride.

tadare sore; inflammation; **tadareru** to break out in sores; to be inflamed.

TÁDASHI however; provided that. **Tádashi**

kodomo wa hangaku desu. (But) children are (charged) half-price.
TADASHÍI right, proper.
tadásu to examine, investigate; to inquire into; to question.
todayóu to drift about; to wander; **kao ni ureí o tadayowásete** with a worried look; **namí ni tadayóu fúne** a boat drifting at the mercy of the waves.
tadóoshi transitive verb (one which can take the particle *o*).
tadóru to go on wearily.
taedáe brokenly; feebly, faintly.
taegatái intolerable, unbearable.
taemá break; gap; pause.
taéru to bear; to bear up; to become extinct; **kónku ni taéru** to bear up under privation; **nín ni taéru** to be equal to one's duty; **onshin ga taéru** hear nothing from (someone); **juunen no shiyoo ni taéru** to be good for ten years. **Kyookyuu ga taéru.** The supply is cut off.
táezu constantly; **táezu dóryoku suru** to make a constant effort.
tagá hoop; **tagá o hazushite sawaide iru** to go on a spree.
tagaéru to break; to violate; **yakusoku o tagaéru** to break a promise.
tagai with one another; with each other; mutually.
tagaku large sum.
tagayásu to till, plow, cultivate; **hatake o tagayásu** to farm; to work on a farm.
tagei varied accomplishments; **tagei na hito** a man of many talents; **tagei no omae** many-sided.
tagon (*n.*) telling others; **tagon suru** to tell others.
tagui kind, class, sort; **tagui náki** matchless, unique.
tagúru to haul in (hand over hand); to follow up; to trace to its source.
táhata farm; field; cultivated land.
tahóo another side; other side; **tahóo de wa** on the other side; **tahóomen** many directions; many sides; different subjects.
tái body; party; form; opposite; even, equal; versus, against;—**ni tai súru** versus, against, toward, to; **sán tai gó no seiseki** a score of 3 to 5; **tai Bei bóoeki** trade with the U.S.A.; **tái de** having no handicap; **tái o kawasu** to dodge; **tái o kúmu** to form in line; to form a party; **tái o nasánai** to be in bad form; **tái o tóku** to disband.
tai- prefix denoting: great, large, grand; general; main, principal; serious; **taínin** important mission; **taiyaku** important task.
-tái suffix denoting: be desirous of, want to do (something). **Tabetái desu.** I want to eat. **Mítai desu.** I want to see it.
taibetsu general classification; **taibetsu suru** to classify roughly.

táibu bulkiness; greater part; **táibu no** voluminous.
táibyoo serious illness.
táida idleness, laziness; **táida na** idle, lazy.
táido attitude; **táido o ippen suru** to change one's attitude completely.
taifúu gale, typhoon.
TAIGAI generally; almost; probably. **Doyoobi wa taigai uchi ni imasu.** I am usually at home on Saturdays.
taigaku = taikoo (*n.*) leaving school.
taigan opposite bank of a river.
taigen, taigen sóogo (*n.*) bragging, boasting; **taigen sóogo o suru** to boast.
táigi toil, exertion, labor; **taigi sóoni** languidly; **táigi desu** to feel tired.
táigo ranks; **táigo o midáshite** in confusion.
táigotettei spiritual awakening.
taigun large force; great army; large crowd (herd, flock, school, etc.); **kujira no taigun** large school of whales.
taiguu treatment; service; rating; **taiguu ga warúi** to treat coldly; to be paid poorly; **taiguu ga yói** to treat well, be hospitable, pay well.
taigyoo sit-down strike.
taihai crushing defeat; decay, corruption; **taihai suru** to be ruined; to meet with a crushing defeat.
taihan great part.
taihei peace, tranquility.
TAIHÉIYOO Pacific Ocean.
TAIHEN very, extremely, remarkably; **taihen na** serious, dreadful; innumerable; **taihen ni** very. **Áme ga taihen fútte imásu.** It is raining hard. **Taihen omoshiroi desu.** It is very interesting.
táiho deterioration; retrogression, going backward; arrest; apprehension; **taihójoo** warrant of arrest.
taihoo gun; cannon; **taihoo o útsu** to fire a gun.
táii general idea; résumé; outline; abdication.
táiiku physical education.
taiin suru to be released from (leave) a hospital.
taiji subjugation; wiping out; control.
taijoo (*n.*) leaving, exit;—**ni taijoo o meizúru** to order (a person) out of the room; **taijoo suru** to leave.
taijuu weight (of the body); **taijuu ga masu** to gain weight.
táika authority, distinguished person (in any circle; i.e., master painter, great musician, eminent scholar, etc.).
táika great fire; degeneration.
taika fireproof; **taika kénchiku** fireproof building.
taikai withdrawal of membership (from an association or society).
taikaku, taiku physique; **taikaku kénsa** physical examination.
taikan high official.
taikánshiki coronation.
taika rénga firebrick.
taikei system; **taikei o tatéru** to systematize.

taiken personal experience; **taiken suru** to experience.

taiketsu confrontation;—**to ... to o taiketsu saseru** to confront (someone) with (another).

táiki atmosphere; standing by; being ready; **táiki no shisei** in a position of readiness.

taikin large sum of money.

taiko drum.

taikobara potbelly, paunch, bay-window.

taikoo opposition; rivalry, confrontation; fundamental principle; code; withdrawal or expulsion from school; **taikoo úndoo** a countermovement; **taikoo suru** to oppose; to face; to counteract; to leave school; **taikóosaku** counterplan, countermeasures; **taikóosha** rival, antagonist.

táiku See **taikaku.**

taikutsu ennui; dullness;—**ni taikutsu suru** to be bored; to become weary of; **taikutsu saséru** to bore.

taikyaku retreat; **taikyaku suru** to retreat.

táikyo = taishutsu (*n.*) leaving, quitting; **táikyo suru** to leave, quit; **taikyo méirei o dásu** to issue an order for departure.

taikyoku general state; general situation; **taikyoku ni mé o tsukéru** to take a large view of things.

taikyoo leaving the capital.

taikyúuryoku durability; endurance.

taiman negligence.

taimen interview; meeting; dignity, honor, reputation;—**no taimen o sonjíru** to bring disgrace on; **taimen suru** to interview; to meet; **taimen o omonzúru** to have a sense of honor; to make much of one's dignity; **taimen o tamótsu** to keep one's reputation.

taimoo great ambition; **taimoo o idáku** to harbor an ambition.

tainin important mission; **tainin o hatásu** to carry out an important mission.

tainoo non-payment; **tainoo suru** to be delinquent in payment; **tainookin** arrears; **tainóosha** delinquent payer.

taion body temperature; **taion o hakáru** to take the (body) temperature; **taiónki** clinical thermometer.

taipísuto typist.

taipuráitaa typewriter.

taira evenness; level; flatness; **taira na** flat; **taira ni suru** to level, flatten.

tairagéru to subdue; to subjugate.

tairiku continent; **tairiku no** continental.

tairitsu opposition; rivalry.

tairyaku outline; summary; **tairyaku o nobéru** to give an outline.

tairyoo large quantity; big catch (of fish); **tairyoo séisan** mass production.

táisa great difference; **táisa o shoojíru** to make a great difference; **táisa ga áru** there is a great difference.

taisai grand festival; great fete.

taisan dispersion; **taisan saseru** to break up; **taisan suru** to take flight; to be dispersed.

taisei structure; system; organization; trend of affairs; general situation; completion, accomplishment; **sékai no taisei** international situation; **taisei ni tsuujíru** to be conversant with the trend; **taisei suru** to complete, accomplish.

TAISÉIYOO Atlantic Ocean.

taiseki accumulation; heap; **taiseki suru** to accumulate.

taisen great war; **Dai niji sekai táisen** World War II.

TAISETSU importance; **TAISETSU NA** important, precious. **Hakkíri kaku kotó ga taisetsu desu.** It is important to write clearly. **Taisetsu ni shite kudasái.** Please take good care of it.

taishaku loan; **taishakuhyoo** balance sheet.

taishíkan embassy; **taishikán'in** embassy attaché.

taishín'in Supreme Court (of the U.S.A.).

taishin kénchiku earthquake-proof building.

táishita great; important; remarkable; **táishite** very, greatly; importantly; remarkably.

taishitsu physical constitution.

taishoku gluttony; **taishoku no** gluttonous, greedy; **taishoku suru** to eat (too) much.

taishoku resignation; **taishoku téate** retirement allowance;—**o taishoku suru** to resign from an office; to retire from service.

taishoo object.

táishoo title of the highest officers of the army and navy; general, admiral; leader; head.

taishuka heavy drinker.

taishutsu (*n.*) leaving; **taishutsu suru** to leave, reitre from. (See also **táikyo.**)

TÁISOO very; exceedingly; many; much. **Taisoo omosiroi shibai desu.** It is an exceedingly enjoyable play.

taisoo physical exercise, gymnastics; **taisoo o suru** to exercise.

taisuru to front; to oppose; to be opposite to; to correspond to.

TAITEI generally; usually; mostly; **taitei no hitó** most people. **Taitei wa arukimásu.** Usually I walk. **Taitei oténki ni náru deshoo.** Probably the weather will become good.

taiteki powerful enemy. **Yudan taiteki.** False security is a great foe.

taitoku suru to master; to comprehend.

taitoo equality, equal footing; **taitoo ni** on equal terms; **taitoo no** equal.

táitoru title.

táiu heavy rain, downpour.

taiwa dialogue; conversation; **to taiwa suru** to talk with.

TAIWÁN Formosa; **Taiwán no** Formosan.

taiya tire.

taiyaku parallel translation; important task; heavy role.

taiyoo ocean; summary; general principle; résumé; **taiyoo no** oceanic.

TÁIYOO sun; **taiyóoreki** the solar calendar; Gregorian calendar.

taizai stay; **taizai suru** to stay.

taizen calmness, composure; **taizen to shite** calmly, composedly.

tájitsu one day in the future; some day.

tajoo na amorous; wanton; of loose morals.

takabúru to be proud; to be haughty; to hold up one's head.

takadai height; upland; **takadáka** at the height; **takadaka** to aloft, proudly.

takai another world; **takai suru** to die.

TAKÁI high, tall; **takái tatemóno** tall building; **takái yamá** tall mountain. **Nedan ga takái.** The price is high.

takaíbiki loud snore.

takamáru to rise; to swell; to be raised.

takara treasure.

takaru to swarm; to gather, assemble; to crowd.

tákasa height.

takatobi high jump; running away; **takatobi suru** to run away (to avoid).

takawárai loud laugh; ringing laughter.

take bamboo.

také length; measure; height; **také ga takái** to be tall.

takenawa (*n.*) being at its height, being in full swing.

taki waterfall.

takibi bonfire; wood fire; **takibi o suru** to make a fire.

takidashi boiling rice for sufferers in an emergency.

takimono fuel; firewood.

takitsuke kindling wood; **takitsukéru** to light, kindle; **kenka o takitsukéru** to fan a quarrel; to incite; **sutóobu ni hí o takitsukeru** to make a fire in the stove.

tákkuru tackle; **tákkuru suru** to tackle.

táko kite; **táko o ageru** to fly a kite.

takokujín foreigner.

TAKU (*n.*) house; husband; (*v.*) to burn; to make a fire; to boil rice; **taku** my house; my husband; **otaku** your house; your husband.

takuchi house lot; residential land.

takuetsu excellence; superiority; **takuetsu suru** to be distinguished, exceed in.

takuhatsu religious begging.

takujisho day nursery.

TAKUJOO DÉNWA desk telephone.

takumashíi robust, strong.

takumi skill, adroitness; cleverness; **takumi na** skillful, dexterous.

takurámu to scheme, plan; to play a trick; to design, devise; to invent; **muhon o takurámu** to conspire.

TAKUSAN much, many, a lot; **takusán no** numerous. **Moo takusán desu.** No, thank you (I've had enough). **Takusan tabemashita.** I ate a lot.

takusetsu excellent opinion; enlightened views.

TÁKUSHII = entaku taxicab.

takushoku colonization.

takusúru to trust; to entrust.

takuwae store, reserve, savings; **issen no takuwae mo nái** to have not a penny saved.

takuwaéru to save, amass, lay by, hoard; **hige o takuwaéru** to wear a mustache; **kane o takuwaéru** to save money.

tamá ball; globe; bead; jewel; **tama no áse** beads of perspiration; **mé no tama** eyeball; **teppoo no tamá** bullets; **tamá o nagéru** to throw a ball.

TAMA rare; seldom, not often; **tama ni** rarely, once in a while.

TAMÁGO egg; **tamágo no kimi** yolk of an egg; **tamágo no shiromi** white of an egg; **tamágo o káesu** to hatch an egg.

TAMANÉGI onion.

tamaranai to be unbearable; cannot help; be dying for.

tamari pool; waiting room.

tamarimizu stagnant water.

tamaru to collect, accumulate, gather; **haraí ga tamaru** to be in arrears; **shakkín ga tamaru** to run up debts.

támashii soul; spirit; **támashii o ubáu** to enchant.

tamatama by chance. **Tamatama káre wa byooki deshita.** It so happened that he was ill.

támátsuki billiards.

tamázan calculation on the **soroban** (an abacus).

TAME benefit; consequence; aim; reason; for the purpose of; for the sake of; because of; **hoomon shita táme ni** as a result of his visit; **tamé ni naránai** to be of no good; **tamé ni náru** to do good.

tameíke irrigation pond; reservoir.

tameíki sigh; **tameíki o tsuku** to heave a sigh.

tameráu to hesitate, waver.

tameru to save, put by, store; to accumulate, collect.

tameshi experiment; attempt; previous example; precedent. **tameshí ni** by way of experiment. **Sonna tameshí wa nái.** There is no precedent for this.

TAMÉSU to try, attempt; to make a trial of; to put to the test; **yúuki o tamésu** to put one's courage to test.

tamoto sleeve of Japanese dress; foot; **hashi no tamoto** foot of a bridge.

tan phlegm; **tan o háku** to expectorate; to spit out.

-tan measure of land (about .245 acres); roll of cloth (about 12 yards).

TANA shelf, rack; **jibun no kotó wa tana ni ageru** to criticize others without recognizing one's own defects; **tana ni ageru** to put up on a shelf.

TANAGÓKORO palm of the hand.

tanako tenant.

tanaoroshi inventory; stock-taking; fault-finding; **tanaoroshi suru** to take stock; to pick holes in (someone else's) character.

tanazarashi shop-worn merchandise; secondhand merchandise; **tanazarashi ni náru** to be shop-worn.

tanbo field, rice field.

tanchoo monotony, lack of variety; **tanchoo na** monotonous, dull.

tandoku (n.) being by oneself; **tandoku hikóo** solo flight.

táne seed; stone or pit of a fruit; breed; child; cause, sources; secret of a trick; **táne o máku, tanémaki o suru** to sow (seeds); **námida no táne** source of grief.

taneábura seed oil, rape-oil (used in cooking).

tanegire (n.) being incapable of supplying something, being exhausted;—**tanegire ni náru** to run short of (something).

tanen many years.

tangan entreaty, supplication, petition; **tangan suru** to entreat, supplicate, petition; appeal.

tán'i unit.

tani, tanima valley.

tanigawa stream running through a valley.

tanin stranger; (other) person.

tanin gyóogi (n.) standing on ceremony. **Tanin gyóogi ni naranaide kudasai.** Please don't stand on ceremony.

tanisoko bottom of a valley.

tan'itsu singleness; **tan'itsu no** single, sole, simple.

tan'itsuka unification.

TANJÓO birth; **tanjóo o iwáu** to celebrate a birth; **tanjóo suru** to be born; **TANJÓOBI** birthday.

tanjun simplicity, plainness; **tanjun na** simple, naïve, unsophisticated.

tanjuu pistol; revolver.

tánka = **wáka** Japanese verse of 31 syllables.

tanken exploration; expedition; **tanken suru** to explore; **tankenryókoo** an expedition.

tánki quick temper; **tánki na** irritable, quick tempered; **tánki o okósu** to become impatient.

tankoo coal mine; **tankóofu** coal-miner.

tankoobon separate volume; **tankoobon to shite shuppan suru** to publish in book form.

tánmei short life, early death.

tanmono cloth, piece goods; drapery.

tannin charge, duty; **tannin suru** to take charge of.

tanomí request; solicitation; reliance;—**o hito no tanomí de suru** to do something at the request of (someone else); **tánomi ni naranai** to be unreliable; **tanomoshíi** reliable, trusty; **sue tanomoshíi wakamono** a promising youngster.

TANÓMU to ask; to beg; to desire; to trust to;

to rely on (someone to do something); **isha o tanómu** to call a doctor; **kodomo o tanómu** to entrust someone with the care of a child. **Yamada-san ni tanónde kudasái.** Please ask Mr. Yamada to do it.

TANOSHÍI to be pleasant, delightful, enjoyable; **tanoshími** pleasure, enjoyment, amusement; **tanoshímu** to take pleasure in; to enjoy oneself; to amuse oneself with; **jínsei o tanoshímu** to enjoy life.

tánpaku quality of being simple; frankness; **tánpaku na** simple, unaffected, plain (as a diet).

tanpen short piece; **tanpen shóosetsu** short story.

tanrei na graceful.

tánren temper; forge; training; **seinen no íshi o tánren suru** to train the mind of a young man; **tetsu o tánren suru** to temper metal; **tánren suru** to temper; forge; to train.

tansei sigh; groan; lamentation; **tansei o morásu** to lament; to sigh deeply.

TANSHIN alone.

tánsho weak point or defect (in personality); **tánsho o ogináu** to remedy a defect;—**ga tánsho de áru**—is one's weak point.

tanshootoo searchlight.

tanshuku shortening, curtailment; **tanshuku suru** to shorten, cut off.

TANSU Japanese-style chest of drawers.

tantei detective, undercover man; **himitsu tántei** private detective; **tantei shóosetsu** detective story.

tantóo dagger.

tantoo suru to take charge of.

tanzúru to lament, deplore; to regret.

taoréru to fall; to fall down, tumble down; **taóreta ie** tumble-down house; **taorekakátta ginkoo** insecure financial institution.

TÁORU towel.

taósu to throw down; to bring down; to beat; **kí o kiritaósu** to fell a tree; **shakkín o taósu** to fail to pay a debt.

tappitsu elegant penmanship.

TAPPÚRI much, great deal, plentifully, full. **Go shaku tappúri aru.** It is a good five feet.

-tara suffix denoting: if, when, in case; **áme ga futtára** if (in case) it rains; **Yamada-san ga kitára** if Mr. Yamada should come.

tarásu to drop; to let drop; to dribble; to let fall; to hang down; to suspend; **makú o tarásu** to hang a curtain; **yodare o tarásu** to drool; **yuka e mizu o tarásu** to spill water on the floor.

tarazu not enough, insufficient; short of; **ni man en tárazu de** for less than 20,000 yen.

TÁRE = **DARE** who.

taréru to drip, trickle down, fall in drops.

Amadare ga nokí kara taréru. The rain drops from the eaves. **Kí no eda ga hikúku tárete iru.** The branches of the tree are drooping low.

tariru, taru to be enough, be sufficient; **shinrai surú ni tariru** to be worthy; to be trusted.

taru barrel, cask.

tarumu to become slack, loose, lax. **Nawá ga tarunde imasu.** The rope is slackening.

tasatsu murder, violence.

TASHIKA if I remember right; **táshika na** certain, sure. **Táshika desu.** It is certain. **Táshika soo iimáshita.** I think (I'm pretty sure) he said so.

tashikaméru to make certain, authenticate, verify.

tashimae supply, complement; supplement.

tashinami circumspection; self-control; accomplishments secretly enjoyed; **tashinami ga nái** lack of self-control. **Anó hito wa é no tashinami ga áru.** He can paint.

TASHOO more or less; in some measure, a little; somewhat. **Tashoo no chigai wa áru deshoo.** There will be some difference, but not much.

tasogare evening, twilight.

TASSHA healthiness; **tassha na** healthy, strong; **tassha ni kurasu** to enjoy vigorous health; **tassha ni náru** to get well. **Otassha desu ka?** Are you well?

tassúru to reach, arrive at, get to, attain; **mokutékichi ni tassúru** to arrive at a destination; **sen en ni tassúru** to run into 1000 yen.

TASU to add; **ní ni san o tasu** two plus three; **moo sukóshi mizu o tasu** to add a little more water.

tasukáru to be saved, be rescued; to be of help; **fushigi ni tasukáru** to have a miraculous escape; **taihen tasukáru** to be greatly relieved; **tasuke** salvation; preservation; deliverance; succor, help, aid, assistance; **kámi no tasuke** help from God; **tasuké bune** lifeboat; **TASUKÉRU** to help, aid, assist; to reinforce; **komátte iru hitó o tasukéru** to help a person in need.

tasúu large number, majority; **tasúu o shiméru** to command a majority; **tasúuketsu** decision by the majority.

tataeru to fill up to the brim; to be brimful; **mizu o óke ni tataeru** to fill the tub with water.

tatakau to fight with; to fight against; to fight a battle; **yuuwaku to tatakau** to struggle with temptation.

tataki (*n.*) striking, beating, pounding, chopping fine; concrete; **tataki no ike** concrete-lined pool.

tatakiáu to scuffle; **tatakifuséru** to knock down; **tatakikómu** to strike into; to train hard; **tatakikowásu** to knock to pieces; **tatakinomésu** to knock down.

tatakiotósu to strike (fruit) from a tree; to attack (someone) so violently that he is obliged to resign his post.

tatakitsukéru to throw a thing against something; to throw to.

tatáku to strike, beat, hit; to knock; **taiko o tatáku** to beat a drum; **to o tatáku** to tap at the door.

TATAMI floor mat made of rice straw tightly bound together and covered on the upper surface with matting; **tatami o shiku** to lay down a **tatami**.

tatamu to fold; to shut up; to wind up; to do away with; **ié o tatamu** to shut up one's house; **kamí o yottsú ni tatamu** to fold a paper into four.

tatari evil consequence; **tataru** to bring evil upon, to cast an evil spell on; to inflict a calamity on.

TÁTE length; height; shield; **táte no lengthwise;—ni táte o tsuku** to set oneself against, oppose, defy (someone).

-tate suffix denoting: just; fresh from; **takitate** just boiled; **kitate** just arrived; **dekitate** just completed.

tatéfuda sign, signboard.

tatégu furnishings (of a house); fixture. **tatégu o ireru** to furnish a house.

tateguya shop where house furnishings are made and sold.

tatekae (*n.*) defraying the expense for another person; **tatekaékin** the sum defrayed temporarily for another person; advance (payment).

tatekakeru to rest, stand, lean, set, place something against.

tatekomoru to shut oneself up, confine oneself, remain in seclusion.

tatekomu to be crowded (with people); to be pressed with business; to be crowded with buildings; **shigoto ga tatekónde iru** to be pressed (with business).

tatemae ceremony of putting the framework (in a Japanese house or other building).

tatemáe principle; policy; rule;—**o tatemáe to suru** to make a point of.

tatemashi extension of a building.

TATEMÓNO building, house; leading actor; leading figure. **Nihonshiki no tatemóno ni súnde imásu.** I live in a Japanese-style house.

tatenaosu to build again; to reconstruct.

TATÉRU to build, construct, erect, set up; to shut, close; **hatá o tatéru** to hoist a flag; **ié o tatéru** to build a house; **kinénhi o tatéru** to erect a monument; **to o tatéru** to shut the door.

tatétsubo floor space of a building. **Kono uchí wa tatétsubo ga hyakú tsubo áru.** The floor space of this house is 100 tsubo (tsubo: about 6 feet by 6 feet).

tatetsuke (*n.*) opening and shutting of doors and windows. **Kono uchí wa tatetsuke**

ga yói. The doors and windows of this
house open and shut smoothly.

táteyoko length and breadth; lengthwise and
crosswise.

TATOE even if, even though; simile,
metaphor, example; **tatoe dónna kotó
ga átte mo** whatever may happen;
tatóe ni iu yóo ni as the saying goes;
tatoe joodan ni mo séyo even in jest.

TATÓEBA for instance, for example.

tatoéru to compare; to give an example.

tatoogami folding paper-case; portfolio; tissue
handkerchief.

TÁTSU to sever, cut off; to chop off; to
break; to stand up, rise, get on one's
feet; to leave; **asu Tookyoo o tátsu** to
leave Tokyo tomorrow; **futatsú ni
tátsu** to cut in two; **sake o tátsu** to
abstain from sake; **séki o tátsu** to leave
one's seat. **Kemuri ga tátsu.** The
smoke is rising.

tatsujin master; expert; one who is adept;
yumi no tatsujin archery expert.

tatsumaki waterspout, sand pillar.

TATTA only, merely; **tatta íma** just now, a
moment ago.

tatte earnestly; **tatte no negái** earnest request.

tattóbu to value; to set a value on.

tattói noble, august, high (in rank); valuable.

taue rice transplantation; **taue doki** the
rice-planting season; **taué uta** the
rice-planting song; **taue o suru** to
transplant rice.

tawagoto silly talk, nonsense.

tawainái easy; innocent; droll.

tawamuréru to play; to frolic; to jest; to
dally; **onná ni tawamuréru** to flirt
with a woman.

tawara straw bag for rice; bale.

tawashi scrubbing brush.

tayásu to exterminate; to eradicate; to put an
end to.

TAYASÚI easy, simple. **Tayasui goyóo desu.**
It's an easy thing. I'll be glad to do it
for you.

tayoo pressure of business; many things to do.

táyori reliance, dependence; intelligence;
news, tidings; letter; **táyori to náru
hitó** one's second self; a reliable
person; **táyori ga nái** to hear nothing
from; **táyori o suru** to write a letter.

tayóru to rely on, depend on.

tayúmu to flag, slacken one's efforts, relax
one's attention.

tazei great number.

tazuna rein, bridle; **tazuna o shiméru** to
tighten the reins; **tazuna o yuruméru**
to slacken the reins.

TAZUNÉRU to look for, search for, hunt for;
ánpi o tazunéru to inquire after a
person; **michi o tazunéru** to ask the
way to.

TÉ hand; arm; paw; helping hand; possession;
handwriting; means, way; trick; hand
(in card-playing); **té ashi** hand and
foot; **téburi** gesture; **té ga aite iru** to

be free; to have no work on hand; **té ga
tarinai** to be short-handed.

-te suffix denoting: one who performs;
direction; **kamite** upper part; **shimote**
lower part; **yarite** clever fellow,
cunning fellow; **yomite** one who reads.

teaká dirt from the hands; **teaká ga tsuku** to
become soiled from handling.

tearai rough, violent; **tearai kotó o suru** to
act violently.

TEÁRAI = **oteárai** toilet, bathroom.

téashi hand and foot. **Watakushi no téashi ni
nátte hataraite kuremáshita.** He was
my right-hand man.

teatari shídai ni at random.

téate recompense; allowance; medical care;
rinji téate temporary allowance; **kizu
no téate o suru** to dress a wound;
téate o dásu to give an allowance.

teatsui hospitable; courteous.

tebánashi de with the hands free; openly;
broadly; **kodomo o tebánashi de
asobaseru** to leave children by
themselves; **tebánashi de jiténsha ni
noru** to ride a bicycle without using the
handle bars.

tebanásu to let go of, release.

tebáyaku quickly, rapidly.

tebikáe note, memo.

tebikaéru to withhold from, hold off (buying
goods, etc.).

tébiki leading another by the hand to show the
way; guidance; guidebook;
Yamada-san no tébiki de through Mr.
Yamada's good offices.

tebiroi wide, roomy; on a large scale;
tebiróku shóobai o suru to carry on a
large trade, do a big buisness.

tebúkuro gloves; **tebúkuro o hameru** to put
on gloves.

tebura empty hands; naked fist; **tebura de
hoomon suru** to call on (someone)
without bringing a present.

téburi gesture; customs.

tebúsoku to short of helping hands.

techígai something amiss, something wrong;
techígai ni náru to go wrong.

techoo notebook, memorandum-book.

tédashi meddling; interference; **tédashi o
suru** to poke one's nose into.

tedásuke aid, assistance; **tedásuke ni náru** to
be of help to.

tédate means, measures, steps; method.

tedori net receipts; **tedori hyaku en** to receive
100 yen net.

TEEBURU table (Occidental).

tefuki hand towel.

tegai no self-sustained, self-fed; **tegai no inú
ni té o kamaréru** to be bitten by a pet
dog; to be betrayed by a favorite
person.

tegákari hold; clue, trace; **tegákari o éru** to
find a clue to.

tegakéru to engage in; to have experience in;
to bring up.

TEGAMI letter, note, correspondence;

tegami o dásu to send a letter, write to; **tegami o morau** to receive a letter.

tegará merit; achievement, distinguished service.

tegaru na easy (not difficult) to do; **tegaru na shokují** light meal; **tegaru ni hoomon suru** to make an informal call.

tegata draft, bill, note; sign; **gohyáku en no tegata** draft for 500 yen; **yakusoku tégata** promissory note.

tegatái safe; steady and honest, reliable; prudent; of good reputation (said of a shop).

tegáwari substitute. **Watakushi wa tegáwari o sagashite imásu.** I am looking for someone to relieve me. I am looking for someone to take my place.

tegiwa workmanship, skill (in doing or making); **tegiwa yóku** cleverly, skillfully; **tegiwa ga warúi** unskillful.

tegókoro discretion, consideration; **tegókoro o kuwaeru** to use one's discretion.

tegoro handy; convenient; moderate (in price or size); just right. **Tegoro na uchí ga mitsukarimáshita.** We've found a house just right for us.

tegótae reaction, response; resistance; **tegótae ga áru** to be responsive; to be effective.

tegowái strong; handy.

tehái arrangement.

tehájime (n.) beginning; **tehájime ni** first, to begin with; **tehájime no** opening, first.

téhazu order, arrangement; plan; **téhazu o suru** to make arrangements.

tehódoki rudimentary lesson.

tehón model, pattern.

téi appearance, style; **téi yoku kotowáru** to decline politely.

teiboo dike; bank, embankment.

teichi lowland, low ground.

teiden power failure.

téido degree, standard, measúre, extent; **téido no takái** of high standard; **téido móndai** a question of degree.

TEIEN formal garden.

teigi definition.

téigi proposal; **téigi suru** to propose.

teihaku anchorage, mooring; **teihaku chuu no fúne** vessels in the harbor; **teihaku suru** to be at anchor.

teihyoo settled opinion; reputation;—**tó no teihyoo ga áru** to have the reputation of.

teiin regular staff; capacity (of a car); quorum.

teijuu suru to live (at a permanent address).

teika fixed price, list price; **teikahyóo** price list.

teika suru to grow worse, deteriorate.

teikei co-operation; **teikei suru** to join hands with; to act in concert with.

teiken definite view, fixed opinion.

teiketsu conclusion, contract; **shakkan o teiketsu suru** to arrange a loan.

téiki fixed (regular) time, definite period, time; speculation; **teiki joosháken** season ticket; commutation ticket; **teiki kankóobutsu** periodical; **téiki ni** periodically.

teikíatsu low atmospheric pressure.

teíkoku fixed time, appointed time.

téikoku empire; **téikoku no** imperial.

teikoo resistance, opposition;—**ni teikoo suru** to resist, oppose, fight.

teikyoo offer; **teikyoo suru** to offer; to put at (someone's) disposal.

teiyuu = **ténisu** tennis; **teikyuu o suru** to play tennis.

teikyuu na low; cheap; vulgar.

teikyúubi periodic holiday observed by stores.

TÉINEI NA polite, courteous; careful, scrupulous. **Teinei na taido de hanashimashita.** He spoke very courteously. **Teinei na shigoto o shimashita.** he did a very careful job.

teinen retirement age.

teinoo feeble-mindedness, imbecility; **teinóoji** imbecile child, idiot.

teíppai one's utmost.

teiraku fall; depression; **teiraku suru** to fall, go down.

teiré care; keeping; repairing; trimming (a garden); **teire no ikitodóíta uchi** carefully kept house; **teiré o suru** to repair, to renovate.

téiri low rate of interest.

teiryoo fixed quantity.

TEIRYUUJOO bus stop, streetcar stop.

teisai appearance, show; style; **teisai o tsukúru** to keep up appearances; **teisai ga yói** pleasing in appearance.

teisatsu reconnaissance.

teisei correction; revision; **teisei suru** to correct, revise.

teisetsu faithfulness, constancy, devotion.

teisha stopping a vehicle (car, train, etc.); **hijoo teisha** emergency stop; **teisha suru** to stop at; **teisha o meízuru** to order a vehicle to stop; **teishi** stop, stoppage, suspension; **shiharai o teishi suru** to suspend payment; to stop payment.

teishaba = **éki** railway station.

teishajoo railway station.

teishoku regular occupation.

teishoo discourse; lecture.

téishu head of a family; husband; innkeeper.

teishuku virtue; womanliness; **teishuku na** virtuous and refined (woman).

teishutsu presentation (in the formal, official sense); **teishutsúsha** introducer, presenter.

teishuu regular income; **teishuu ga nái** to have no regular income.

teisoo chastity, faithfulness.

teisúru to present, offer; to pass; **ikan o teisúru** to be a grand sight.

teitai accumulation, piling up; indigestion; **teitai suru** to accumulate, pile up.

teitaku mansion; residence.

teito metropolis; imperial capital.

teiton standstill; stagnation; **teiton suru** to come to a standstill.

teitoo mortgage, security;—**no teitoo ni tóru** to hold (something) as security.

TEIJIKA NA nearby; **teijika na tokoro** place near by.

téjina parlor tricks, conjuring tricks; **tejinashi** juggler.

tejoo handcuff.

tejun order; systematic plan; **tejun ga kurúu** to go out of order; **tejun o sadaméru** to arrange for.

tekágen discretion, consideration; **tekágen ga wakaránai** to be little used to; **tekágen o suru** to use one's discretion; to make allowances.

tékazu trouble;—**ni tékazu o kakéru** to give trouble.

teki enemy, opponent, antagonist; **teki mikata** friend and foe; **tekichi** enemy's land.

tekibishíi severe, strict, stern, rigorous, intense.

tekichuu hit, hitting the mark.

tekigáishin hostile feeling.

tékigi suitability for an occasion; **tékigi na** suitable; **tékigi ni** suitably; **tékigi no shóchi o suru** to act as one thinks fit.

tekigoo conformity, agreement; **tekigoo suru** to conform to.

tekihatsu disclosure, exposure; **tekihatsu suru** to disclose, expose; **fusei jíken o tekihatsu suru** expose.

tékihi fitness, suitability. **Tékihi wa wakarimasén.** I cannot tell whether it is suitable or not.

tekihoo proper method; legality.

tekihyoo apt remark; **tekihyoo o kudasu** to make a pertinent comment.

tekikaku = **tekkaku** exactness; acuteness; **tekikaku na** exact, acute.

TEKIMEN NI immediately.

tekin security (money), deposit; **tekin o útsu** to give a deposit.

tekinin competence, fitness.

tekioo fitness; adaptability.

tékipaki actively; briskly; promptly.

tekirei good example; conscription (draft) age.

tekiryoo proper quantity.

tekisei kénsa test for quality; aptitude test.

tekisetsu fitness, appropriateness; **tekisetsu na** appropriate.

tekishi = **tekitai** hostility, animosity.

tekishutsu extraction; quotation; **tekishutsu suru** to extract.

tekisúru to fit, suit, agree; **kenkoo ni tekisúru** to be good for one's health; **shokuyoo ni tekisúru** to be fit to eat.

tekisuto text, textbook.

tekitai (see **tekishi**)—**ni tekitai suru** to stand against.

TEKITŌO NA appropriate, suitable; **tekitoo ni** in an appropriate fashion. (See also **tekisetsu.**)

tekiyoo summary, résumé; application; **tekiyoo suru** to apply.

tekizai tékisho right person in the right place. **Kare wa tekizai tekisho desu.** He is the right man for that place.

tékizu wound; **tékizu o ou** to be wounded (in a fight).

tekkai withdrawal; **takkai suru** to withdraw.

tekkaku See **tekikaku.**

tekkan iron pipe.

tekken clenched fist.

tekkin konkuríito concrete reinforced with steel.

tekkíri surely, without doubt.

tekkoojo iron foundry, ironworks.

tekkotsu iron frame, steel skeleton.

tekkyoo iron bridge.

tekozúru to be at one's wit's end; to have much trouble with. **Ano hito ni wa zuibun tekozurimashita.** He was an awkward customer to deal with.

tekúbari preparation.

TÉKUBI wrist.

tékuchi way, means.

tekúru to go on foot.

tekuse no waruí light-fingered, thievish.

TEMÁ time; wages; **temáchin** wages, service charge. **Kono shigoto wa temá ga kakáru.** This job takes a lot of time. **Temá wa íkura desu ka?** How much do I owe you (for your services)?

temae this side.

temaegátte willfulness, selfishness; **temaegátte na yátsu** selfish fellow.

témane gesture; **témane o suru** to gesticulate.

temáneki beckoning.

temáwari one's personal effects.

temáwashi preparation, arrangement; **temáwashi ga yói** to be fully prepared in advance; **temáwashi suru** to get ready.

TEMIJIKA NI in short; **temijika ni iéba** to describe briefly.

temochibúsata feeling awkward, or ill at ease.

temotó money on hand; **temotó ga kurushíi** to be short of cash.

tempura See **tenpura.**

temúkai resistance.

ten dot; mark; point; **ten no uchidokoro no nai** faultless; **ookisa no ten de** in point of size.

tén heaven, sky.

tenami skill; **tenami o miséru** to show one's skill.

tenboo view, observation; **o tenboo suru** to view, look upon; **tenbookyoo** periscope; telescope; **tenbóosha** observation car; parlor car.

ténbun natural endowment; **ténbun no yútaka na** highly gifted.

tenchi change of air; **tenchi suru** to go (to another place) for a change of air.

ténchi heaven and earth; universe; sphere.

TENDE (*always used with a negative*) at all; altogether; **tende hanashi ni naránai** to leave no room for negotiation. **Tende yokunai.** It is no good at all.

téngoku heaven, paradise.

tenímotsu luggage, hand baggage; **tenímotsu toriatsukaijo** baggage room.

ten'in employee, shop-assistant.

tenioha grammatical particles such as *wa, ga, o, ni,* etc.

tenisu See teikyuu.

tenji Braille (dots).

tenjoo ceiling.

ténka entire country.

tenkai development, expansion; **tenkai suru** to develp, expand.

tenkan conversion; **tenkan suru** to convert, divert, turn.

tenkei model, specimen; **tenkeiteki Amerikájin** typical American.

tenken inspection; **tenken suru** to inspect.

TENKI, tenkoo weather; humor; **TENKI YÓHOO** weather forecast. **Kyóo wa ténki ga warúi.** The weather is bad today. He is ill-tempered today.

tenki turning point.

tenkin change of office;—**ni tenkin ni náru** to be transferred to.

ténko roll call.

tenkoo turn, shift; weather (see also **ténki**); **tenkoo fujun** unseasonable weather; **tenkoo suru** to turn, shift.

tenkyo change of residence;—**ni tenkyo suru** to move to.

ténmatsu details (of an event).

ténmei providence, fate; **ténmei o shiru** to resign oneself to fate.

tenmon astronomy; **tenmóndai** astronomical observatory; **tenmongákusha** astronomer.

tennen nature; **tennen no bi** natural beauty; **tennénshoku** natural color.

tennentoo smallpox.

tennin transfer; change of post.

tennóo emperor; **Tennoo Héika** His Majesty the Emperor.

ténnyo angel.

TENÓHIRA palm of the hand.

tenpen chfi natural disaster (earthquake, flood, typhoon, etc.).

TÉNPI oven.

tenpin gift of heaven; innate nature; **tenpin o hakki suru** to bring all one's talents into play.

tenpuku downfall; **tenpuku suru** to turn over, capsize.

TENPURA = TEMPURA deep fried fish, shrimps, and vegetables; gold-plating.

tenránkai exhibition.

tensai genius; natural gift; calamity; reproduction of something which was once published. **Tensái hada no hitó desu.** He is something of a genius.

tensaku correction (of a composition, poem, etc.).

ténsei nature; by nature. **Tensei shoojiki desu.** He is honest by nature.

tenseki suru to transfer one's legal domicile. (See also **tentaku.**)

tensen dotted line.

tensha transcription; **tensha suru** to copy, transcribe.

ténshi angel.

tenshin ranman naïvete; artlessness, innocence.

tensho letter of recommendation.

ténshu shopkeeper, storekeeper.

tenshúkaku castle tower.

tenshukyoo Roman Catholic Church.

tensoo transmission; forwarding; **yuubín-butsu o Kyóoto ni tensoo suru** to forward mail to Kyoto.

tensui óke rain-water tank.

tentai heavenly bodies.

tentak = tenseki change of residence.

tentan unselfishness.

tentekómai o suru to be in a business boom.

tentoo shop; overturning, fall; **tentoo ni dásu** to put something on sale; **ki ga tentoo suru** to lose one's presence of mind; **tentoo suru** to fall; to overturn.

tenugui Japanese towel; **tenuguí kake** towel-rack.

tenúkari fault; oversight.

tenurúi slow, dilatory.

tenzai suru to be dotted with.

teochí fault; slip; omission.

teoke wooden pail.

teókure ni náru to be too late.

teppén top, summit; **atama no teppén** crown (of the head).

teppitsu stylus (for handwritten mimeograph work).

tera Buddhist temple.

terasu = TÉRU to shine on, shed light on; to refer to; **jíjitsu ni terashite** in the light of the facts.

TEREBI, TEREBÍJON television.

terikaesu to reflect.

terikómu to shine into.

teritsukéru to shine down upon.

téro terrorism.

TÉRU to shine; to be fine; **tette mo futte mo** rain or shine. (See also terasu.)

teryóori homemade dish.

tesage handbag.

teságuri groping; **teságuri de iku** to grope (in the dark).

TESAKI hand; finger; agent; follower; tool; **tesaki no kíyoo na** dexterous.

tesei handmade; homemade.

teshita follower; agent, vassal. (See also **tesaki.**)

teshoku portable candlestick.

tesóo line in the palm; **tesóo o míru** to read a palm.

tessaku iron railing.

tessúru to pierce, penetrate.

tesuri handrail.

tesúu trouble, care; **tesúu ga kakáru** to require care, be troublesome.

tesúuryoo fee, commission.

tetsu iron; **tetsubin** iron kettle.

TETSUDÁI help, assistance; assistant, helper; **TETSUDÁU** to help, assist, lend a hand; **shigoto o tetsudáu** to help (someone) with work.

TETSUDOO railway, railroad.

tetsugaku philosophy; **tetsugaku joo** philosophically.

tetsujóomoo wire entanglements; barbed-wire entanglements.

tetsuke(kin) advance (money), deposit; **tetsukékin o útsu** to pay a deposit.

tetsuya all night through; **tetsuya suru** to be up all night.

tetsúzuki process, formalities, proceedings; **tetsúzuki o suru** to take steps.

tettei suru to get to the bottom; to be thorough.

tetteiteki na thoroughgoing.

tettoo tétsubi thoroughly (from beginning to end).

tettoribayái quick; rough and ready.

tewaké o suru to divide work.

tewátashi handing over personally.

tezáiku manual labor.

tezema narrowness; smallness. **Koko wa tezema de komárimasu.** We are cramped for space here.

tezúkami ni suru to take with the fingers.

tézuru connection; **tezuru o motoméru** to hunt up a connection.

tezuyói firm, resolute.

TO particle denoting: and; with; along with; if, when; as soon as. **Asoko wa háru ni náru to komimásu.** That place gets very crowded in spring. **Kyóoto e Yamada-san to ikimáshita.** I went to Kyoto with Mr. Yamada. **Tookyoo to Kyóoto e ikimáshita.** I went to Tokyo and Kyoto.

TO door; measure (about 3.97 gallons).

tobaku gambling.

tobasu to let fly; to omit; to hurry; **kaze ni booshí o tobasu** to have one's hat blown off by the wind.

tobiagáru to fly up; to take wing, take flight; to jump to one's feet.

tobiarúku to run about.

tobidásu to fly out; to take wing; to run out.

tobidóogu missile (weapon).

tobihi flying sparks; leap of flames; chicken pox.

tobiiri open contest.

tobikakáru to spring (leap, jump) upon.

tobikiri extra fine; best; choicest; **tobikiri jooto no shina** top-grade article.

tobikómu to jump (spring) into; to rush; **heyá ni tobikómu** to burst into the room; **mizu ni tobikómu** to dive into water.

tobikósu to jump over, leap over.

tobimawáru to fly about; to jump about.

tobinóku to jump back; to spring aside.

tobiokíru to jump out of bed; to start up; to jump for.

tobioríru to jump down, leap down.

tobira leaf of a gate (or door); title page of a book.

tobisáru to fly away.

TOBI TOBI NI here and there; at intervals; at random, without order; **tobi tobi no sporadic.**

tobitsúku to fly at, spring at, leap at.

tobokéru to pretend ignorance.

toboshíi to be scarce; to be short.

TOBU to fly; to jump, leap, bound.

tochi ground, land; **tochi no mono** a native, a villager.

TOCHUU on the way; halfway; **tochuu de yameru** to give up halfway; **tochuu de gésha suru** to stop over (on a train trip).

todaéru to cease, stop, end; to drop.

TODANA cupboard, closet.

TODOKÉRU to report; to send. **Okome o todókete kudasái.** Please send me the rice.

todokoori hitch, hindrance; being in arrears; **todokoori náku** duly, regularly; smoothly; **todokóoru** to be in arrears; to be left undone; to be stagnant. **Shigoto ga takusan todokóotte imasu.** There is a good deal of work left undone.

todóku to reach, get to; to attain; **mé no todóku kágiri** so far as (anyone) can see; **omói ga todóku** to realize one's objective.

todomáru to stop, halt, stand still.

todome finishing stroke, *coup de gráce.*

todoméru to stop, cease, put an end to; to censure, rebuke; to disapprove; **ki ga togaméru** to feel uneasy.

togarásu to sharpen; to point; to pout; **enpitsu o togarásu** to sharpen a pencil.

togáru to be pointed, come to a point; **togátta hana** hawk nose.

togé splinter; thorn; **togé ga áru kotoba** stinging words; **yubí ni togé o tatéru** to get a splinter in one's finger.

togéru to accomplish, achieve; to attain, gain, realize; to commit; **yakusoku o togéru** to fulfill one's promise.

togiréru to break; to pause; to be interrupted.

tógu to whet, grind, sharpen; **naifu o tógu** to sharpen a knife.

toguchi doorway.

tóho (*n.*) going on foot.

tohoo ni kureru to be bewildered; **tohoo mo nái** extraordinary; wild.

toiawaséru to inquire, to refer. **Taishikan de toiawasete kudasai.** Please inquire at the Embassy.

toitsuméru to press for an answer.

tojikómeru to confine, shut in; **áme ni tojikomeraréru** to be house-bound by rain; **tojikomóru** to confine oneself to; to shut oneself up.

tojimari o suru to lock a door.

TOJÍRU to bind; to file; to sew up.

TOJIRU to shut, close.

tokai city, town; **tokaijín** city people, townsfolk.

tokaku (to be) apt to; in one way or other; **tokaku suru uchi ni** in the meantime. **Wakái mono wa tokaku keisotsu de áru.** Young people are apt to act hastily.

tokásu to melt, liquefy; to fuse; **koori o**

tokásu to melt ice; **satóo o mizu ni tokásu** to dissolve sugar in water.

tokeáu to be melted together; to come to a mutual understanding.

TOKEI clock; watch; **oki dókei** clock; **ude dókei** wrist watch; **tokeiya** a watch-maker.

tokeru to melt; dissolve; **mizu ni tokéru** to be soluble in water; **netsú de tokéru** to melt by heat.

tokéru to get loose, come untied. **Musubime ga tokéta.** The knot has come untied.

TOKI time; hour; moment; time when; **tokí házure** no out of season; **tokí o éta** seasonable, timely. **Kyooto e itta tóki kaimáshita.** I bought it when I went to Kyoto.

TOKIDÓKI now and then; occasionally. **Tokidoki aimashita.** I met him occasionally.

tokifuseru to persuade; to convince; to argue down; to prevail upon.

tokitsukéru to persuade, prevail upon.

tokka special prices; **tokka hánbai** sale at reduced prices.

tokken exclusive right or privilege.

tokki projection; **tokki suru** to project.

tokkoo special virtue, efficacy.

tukkumiáu to grapple with each other.

tokku ni (adv.) long time ago.

tokku no (adj.) long time ago; **tokku no mukashi** long ago, ages ago.

tokkuri sake bottle.

tokkyuu special express (train).

TOKO alcove; floor; bed; bedding; **toko no ma** guest-room alcove in a Japanese house where hanging scrolls, flower arrangements, etc., are displayed; **toko o shiku** to spread out bedding, make a bed; **toko ni tsuite iru** to be in bed tokokázari alcove ornament.

tokoage (n.) leaving a sickbed.

tokoo voyage, passage; **tokoo ménjoo** passport; **—e tokoo suru** to make a voyage to; **tokóosha** passenger, emigrant.

TOKORO address, place; **tokoró de** then, well, now; **TOKORÓ GA** but, however, on the contrary; **tokoro o éru** to find a right place.

TOKOYA barbershop, barber.

toku profit, gain; virtue, morality; **toku na** profitable, advantageous; **toku o suru** to gain, profit, benefit.

tóku to untie, undo, unbind; to melt; to fuse; to smelt.

TOKUBETSU NO special, particular, exceptional; **TOKUBETSU NI** specially.

tokuchoo characteristic.

tokudane exclusive news, scoop (newspaper).

tokuden special telegram.

tókugi morality; **tokugijoo** morally; from the moral point of view.

tokuháin special representative, special correspondent (of a newspaper).

tokui pride, self-complacency; one's forte; customer, patron.

tokumei anonymity; **tokumei de** anonymously.

TÓKU NI especially. **Ashita wa tóku ni háyaku kite kudasai.** Please come especially early tomorrow.

tokusaku better way, wiser way.

tokusan speciality of a locality.

tokusei special make; de luxe.

tokusetsu specially set up, specially organized.

tokushi benevolence, charity; special envoy; **tokushi ka** charitable or self-sacrificing person.

tokushoku corruption, graft; special feature, speciality.

tokushu na special.

tokuten score (sports).

tóku to carefully, attentively.

tokutoku to proudly; with a triumphant air.

tokutóoseki special seat.

tokuyaku special contract.

tokuyuu no peculiar; characteristic.

tomádoi suru to go to a wrong house; to be bewildered on waking.

TOMARU to stop (at or in); to lodge; **hitóban tomaru** to stay overnight. **Itamí wa tomarimashita.** The pain is gone. **Kono kishá wa shinagawa de tomarimásu ka?** Does this train stop at Shinagawa Station?

tomásu to enrich, make wealthy.

TÓMATO tomato.

tomeru to stop, bring to stop; **gásu o tomeru** to turn off the gas; **kuruma o tomeru** to stop a car.

tomeru to give lodging (to a person), give shelter.

TOMO of course; even though; **dónna kotó ga okóru tomo** whatever may happen. **Ikimásu tomo.** Of course I will go.

tómo attendant; suite; **tómo ni** together with; including; **tómo o suru** to follow (someone). **Daika sóoryoo tomo ni sen en desu.** The price is 1000 yen, including postage.

TOMODACHI friend. **Tomodachi ni ái ni ikimasu.** I am going to see a friend.

tomodaore common ruin.

tómokaku at all events, at any rate.

tomokasegi suru to work (both husband and wife) for a living.

tomonáu to accompany, go with; **heigai ga tomonáu** to be attended with evil.

tomosu to burn, light, turn on (a lamp).

tómu to grow rich. **Ano hito wa keiken ni tónde imasu.** He has great experience.

tomurai funeral, burial; **tomuráu** to mourn for the dead; to hold a Buddhist mass for.

tón ton, tonnage.

tonaéru to recite; to repeat; to chant.

TONARI neighboring house; next-door neighbor; **tonari no** adjoining, next;

tonari átte iru to be next door to each other.

tonbo dragonfly.

tonda surprising; extraordinary; shocking, terrible; unexpected; **tonda mé ni áu** to meet with a misfortune.

tondemonái surprising; extraordinary; unexpected; awful; abused; **tondemonái kotó ni náru** to become serious; to take an unexpected turn.

TÓNIKAKU in any case.

tónjaku care, heed, regard; **jikan ni tónjaku náku** regardless of time.

tónkyoo ludicrousness; wild screech or act (to scare or make others laugh); **tónkyoo na** freakish.

tonneru tunnel.

TONNIKU pork.

TONOGATA men, gentlemen; **tonogata no** men's, gentlemen's.

tonshi sudden death.

tonsoo suru to run away.

TÓN TO not at all, not in the least; entirely. **Anó hito wa tón to kónai.** He does not come at all.

tonton byóoshi without a hitch. **Kotó ga tonton byóoshi ni hakonde imasu.** Things are going along swimmingly.

ton'ya wholesale shop, wholesale dealer.

TÓO ten; ten years old; counter for cattle (denoting: head); the said; rightness; propriety; justness; sword; knife; political party; tower, pagoda; **tóo no hónnin** man in question; **tóo o éta shikata** proper act; **Shakaitoo** Socialist Party; **tóogetsu** this month; **ushi háttoo** eight head of cows.

-too suffix denoting: grade, class; **ittóo** first class.

TÓOA East Asia.

tóoben answer; explanation; defense.

tooboe (*n.*) howling; **inu no tooboe** the howling of dogs; **tooboe suru** to howl.

tooboo flight, desertion; **tooboo suru** to run away; **tooбóosha** a fugitive.

TOOBUN for the time being. **Toobun áme wa furánai deshoo.** It won't rain for a while.

tóobun sugar content; **tóobun o fukúnda** sugary.

toochaku arrival; **toochaku jun ni** in order of arrival; **toochaku shídai** immediately on arrival; **toochaku suru** to arrive.

TÓOCHI this place, here.

toochoku (*n.*) being on duty; on watch.

toodal lighthouse.

toodori president, director.

tooen a distant (blood) relation.

toogé mountain pass, defile; crisis; **Hakone no toogé** Hakone Pass; **toogé o kosu** to pass the critical stage.

tóogi debate, discussion; **tóogi suru** to discuss, debate.

toogoku imprisonment.

Toogúu Crown Prince.

tóogyo rule, management.

tóoha party, faction; school; clique.

tóoha suru to traverse; to travel on foot; to tramp.

tooheki thievishness; kleptomania.

toohi escape, flight; **toohi suru** to escape, fly.

toohyoo (*n.*) voting; poll; **—ni toohyoo suru** to vote for; **toohyoo de kimeru** to decide by vote; **toohyoo ni iku** to go to the polls.

TOOI far; far away. **Tanaka-san no uchí wa koko kara tooi desu.** Mr. Tanaka's house is far from here.

tooin party member.

tooitsu unification, uniformity; **tooitsuteki** unifying.

tóoji at that time; at this time.

toojísha person concerned; **toojísha ni kakeáu** to negotiate with the persons concerned.

tóojitsu day in question; appointed day; day of issue (for a ticket, etc.).

toojoo suru to get on board a ship or plane.

toojoo stage entrance; **toojoo suru** to go on the stage.

TOOKA ten days; tenth day of the month.

tookan (*n.*) mailing, posting; **tegami o tookan suru** to mail a letter.

TOOKÁRAZU before long, in the near future.

tookei statistics; **tookei o tóru** to make a survey.

tóoki earthenware; registration; **tooki suru** to register.

tookoo suru to contribute to a periodical; to go to school; to surrender.

tooku a distant place; **ki ga tooku náru** to faint, swoon.

tookyókusha authorities concerned.

tookyóri equal distance.

tookyuu class, grade; **tookyuu o tsukéru** to grade.

toomáwari detour; roundabout way; **toomáwari o suru** to detour.

toomáwashi na roundabout, indirect; **toomáwashi ni** indirectly; in a roundabout way.

toome distant view; **toome ga kiku** to be able to see a long way off; **toomégane** telescope.

toomei na transparent.

toomen no present; urgent; immediate; **toomen no mondai** matter in hand.

toomichi long way, great distance.

toonan robbery, burglary.

TÓONI long ago; already.

tóonin person in question.

toonóku to recede; to get away. **Ashí ga toonóku.** His visits are becoming rarer.

toonori long ride, long drive; **toonori o suru** to take a long drive; **jiténsha no toonori o suru** to go on a long cycling excursion.

toorai suru to come, arrive; to occur; to come to hand. **Kikái ga toorai shita.** An opportunity presented itself.

164

toorei (*n.*) returning a salute; returning a call.

TOORÍ road, street; kind; traffic; **toorí o yoku suru** to clear a passage; **toori ippén no** casual; indifferent. **Iku toori mo áru.** There are many kinds.

TÓORI like, as; **watakushi no iu tóori** as I say.

toorigakari passing, chance; **toorigakari no hito** passers-by.

toorikakáru to happen to pass (come by).

toorikósu to go beyond; to walk past; to pass.

toorinuke passing through.

tooroku registration; **tooroku suru** to register.

tóoron, toorónkai debate, discussion; **tóoron suru** to debate.

tooroo fixed stone-lantern, dedicatory lantern.

TÓORU to go along; to pass; to go by the name of; to be admissible; to get through; **shikén ni tóoru** to pass an examination; **sujimichi ga tóotte iru** to be consistent; to be logical. **Kono básu wa Ginza o toorimásu.** This bus goes through Ginza.

tooryuu suru to stay at.

tóosa exploration; survey.

toosei management, control; regulation; **toosei suru** to bring under government control; to regulate, govern.

toosen (*n.*) winning a prize; success in a lottery; **toosen bángoo** winning numbers; **toosénsha** successful candidate.

tooshaban mimeograph, duplicator.

tooshi investment; **—ni tooshi suru** to invest in; **tooshisha** investor.

toosho contribution; **tooshóran** letters-to-the-editor column.

tóoshu present master; head of a family.

toosoo escape.

TÓOSU to let (someone) pass through; to admit; to carry; to realize; to make; to usher in; **mé o tóosu** to run over; glance over; **mon o toosu** to admit a person within the gates.

tóosutaa toaster; **tóosuto** toast (bread).

TOOTEI by no means (*used with a negative*); after all. **Sonna kotó wa tootei dekimasén.** I can't possibly do such a thing.

tootói precious, valuable; high; noble; sacred, holy. **Tootoi ojikan o sáite kudasaimashite arigatoo gozaimashita.** Thank you for spending your precious time on me.

TÓOTOO finally. **Tóotoo sono shigoto o shite shimaimáshita.** I've finally finished that work.

tootoo to flowing in torrents; eloquently; **tootoo to nagaréru** to flow majestically (as a river); **tootoo to nobéru** to speak fluently.

toowaku suru to be perplexed, be puzzled; to be embarrassed; to be at a loss.

tooyoo appointment, promotion; **tooyoo suru** to appoint, promote.

TÓOYOO Orient; **Tóoyoo no** (*adj.*) Oriental; **Tooyóojin** (*n.*) Oriental.

tooyoo kánji (ideographic) characters included in the official list of 1850 (**Tooyoo Kanji Hyoo**) designated by the Japanese Government as the basic symbols in writing.

tooza present time; current deposit; **tooza no kózukai** pocket money adequate for the present.

toozakáru to become more distant; to go away; **akuyuu ni toozakáru** to keep away from bad companions; **toozakéru** to keep clear of, away from; to keep at a distance.

toozen matter of course; naturally.

toozoku thief, robber, burglar.

toozúru to throw; to throw away, throw off; to abandon; **íppyoo o toozúru** to cast a vote.

toppatsu outbreak; **toppatsuteki** unexpected, sudden.

toppi na extravagant, fantastic, venturesome.

toppuu gust of wind.

tora tiger.

toraéru to catch, seize, take hold of; **eríkubi o toraéru** to seize (someone) by the neck.

torahóomu trachoma.

torai suru to come over the sea; to visit (a country).

TORÁKKU truck; track field.

toránpu playing cards; **toranpu o suru** to play cards.

TORI bird, fowl; **TORINIKU** chicken meat, poultry.

toriáezu in haste; for the time being.

toriageru to take up, take in one's hand; **fuhei o toriageru** to listen to a complaint.

toriatsukai (*n.*) handling (of a thing); arrangement (of a business); treatment (of a guest). **Toriatsukai chúui.** Handle with care.

toriáu to hold each other; to struggle for; to take notice of.

toriawase assortment; combination.

torichigaeru to mistake; to misunderstand; to misapprehend.

torichirasu to scatter about, put in disorder. **Heyá ga torichiráshite áru.** The room is untidy.

torié worth, merit, useful (strong) point; **torié no áru** useful, valuable, worthy; **torié no nái** worthless, good for nothing.

torihakaráu to manage; to arrange; to dispose of; to settle; to deal with.

toriharau to remove, take away, clear away; to clear by taking (things) away.

torihazusu to remove; to take to pieces.

toríhiki transaction, dealing; **toríhiki o suru** to do business with; **toríhiki o hajimeru** to open an account with; **torihikisaki** customer; business connection.

torii open front gate of a shrine, often painted red.

toriire harvest, crop; **toriire dóki** harvest-time; **toriireru** to take in; to harvest, gather in; to accept; to adopt.

toriisógi in a hurry; with dispatch.

torikaeru to change, exchange; to renew.

torikaeshi recovery, retrieval; **torikaeshi ga tsukánai** irrevocable.

torikáesu to get back; to regain, recover; to recall.

torikakaru to begin, commence; to set about.

torikawasu to exchange.

torikesu to cancel, revoke; **chuumon o torikesu** to cancel an order; **zenhánketsu o torikesu** to revoke a former decision.

torikimeru to arrange; to agree upon, settle, decide upon.

toriko captive, prisoner of war.

torikomu to take in; to bring over; to be in confusion; to get in favor with; **sentakumono o torikomu** to take in washing. **Kyóo wa sukóshi torikonde imásu.** This place is upset today.

torikoshigúroo unnecessary worry; **torikoshigúroo o suru** to run to meet trouble; to be overanxious.

torikowásu to pull down; to take down; to break down; to break up.

torikúmu to wrestle with; to grapple with; to be matched against.

torimagiréru to be in confusion; **zátsumu ni torimagiréru** to be under the pressure of routine business.

torimáku to surround, hem in, encircle, enclose; to fawn upon.

torimatomeru to gather all together; to collect; to pack; **kazai dóogu o torimatomeru** to collect one's household goods.

torimidásu to disturb; to lose one's composure. **Heyá wa torímidáshite atta.** The room was in disorder.

torimodósu to take back; to regain, recover; to resume.

torimótsu to treat; to receive; to entertain.

torinaósu to recover; to mend; to alter.

torinashi mediation, intercession; **torinásu** to plead for; to mediate; to recommend.

torinigásu to fail to catch; **kikái o torinigásu** to miss an opportunity.

torinokeru to remove, take away; to clear away, get rid of.

toriotósu to let fall, slip, drop; to miss one's hold.

torishimari management, supervision, control; **torishimaríyaku** manager, director; **torishimáru** to manage, control, superintend, oversee.

torisoroéru to put together; to gather; to assort.

toritate no fresh (from); **toritate no momo** fresh peaches; **toritate no sakana** fish fresh from the sea.

toritateru to collect; to promote; to patronize; **kashikín o toritateru** to collect loans;

yakunin ni toritateru to appoint (someone) to a post.

toritomeru to ascertain, make sure; to make definite; **ínochi o toritomeru** to have a narrow escape.

toritsugi intermediation; receiving a thing and handing it to another; agency; agent; answering a knock (or bell); usher; **toritsugi o suru** to act as an agent, to transmit; to convey.

toritsuke run on a bank.

toritsukeru to fit; to furnish; to install; to draw out (of the bank); **kikái o toritsukeru** to set up an apparatus.

toritsuku to hold fast to, cling to; to catch hold of; **toritsuku shima mo nai** to be left helpless.

toritsukuróu to mend, repair, patch; **teisai o toritsukuróu** to keep up appearances.

toriya bird-fancier; poultry dealer.

toriyoseru to get, obtain, procure.

tororo grated yam.

tórotoro suru to doze; to take a nap.

TÓRU to take; to take in one's hand, take hold of; to get; to fetch; to take; to pass; to receive; to gain; to accept; to adopt; to choose; to buy; to gather; to pick; to eat; to charge; to manage; to interpret; to take away; to catch; to deprive a person of; to possess; to take possession of; to need, require; to preserve; to engage; to subscribe to; to insist; **eiyóobutsu o tóru** to take nourishing food; **fude o tóru** to take a pen in hand; to write; **jikan o tóru** to take time; **jímu o tóru** to do business; **ichiban chiisái no o tóru** to pick the smallest one; **kane o toraréru** to have one's money stolen; **kí no mi o tóru** to pick fruit from trees; **kusá o tóru** to weed; **ni man en no gekkyuu o tóru** to receive a salary of 20,000 yen; **rishi o tóru** to charge interest; **sakana o tóru** to catch fish; **shashin o tóru** to have a picture taken; **shibai no séki o tótte oku** to reserve a seat at a theatre; **shinbun o tóru** to subscribe to a newspaper; **tsuyói taido o tóru** to assume a fair attitude toward; **wairo o toru** to accept a bribe; **wáruku tóru** to take amiss. **Heyá o tótte okimáshita.** I have engaged a room for you. **Káre wa kataku tótte ugokánai.** He tries to carry his point and won't yield. **Shió o tótte kudasái.** Will you pass me the salt? **Yasai wa ano misé kara torimásu.** We buy vegetables from that store.

Tóruko Turkey; **Torukogo** Turkish (language); **Torukójin** Turk.

tóryoo paints.

tóshi towns and cities; **toshi kéikaku** city planning.

TOSHI year; age; **toshí to tómo ni** with age; **toshí o mukaeru** to welcome the New Year; **toshí o okuru** to pass the years;

toshí o tóru to grow old; **toshigoro** age; marriageable age; **onaji toshigoro no** of about the same age; **toshigoro no musume** daughter of marriageable age; **toshishita** younger; junior; **toshiue** senior; older; **TOSHIYÓRI** old person. **Tanaka-san yóri mittsu toshishita desu.** He is three years younger than Mr. Tanaka. **Yamada-san yóri mittsu toshiue desu.** He is three years older than Mr. Yamada.

to shite as; for; in the capacity of; **orei to shite** as a token of thanks; **soodai to shite shusseki suru** to attend as a representative.

tósho books; **tosho gákari** librarian; **toshokan** library; **tósho etsuránshitsu** reading room.

toshikoshi New Year's Eve.

toshimawari luck attending one's age. **Kotoshi wa toshimawari ga warui.** This year is an unlucky one for me.

toshókan library.

TOSSA NO AÍDA NI in a moment; quick as thought; on the spur of the moment.

tosshin suru to rush; to dash; to charge.

totan zinc.

totan'ita galvanized iron sheets.

—totan ni just as; in the act of. **Watakushi ga hairu totan ni kare wa dete itta.** He went out just as I entered.

TOTEMO very, awfully; extraordinarily.

TÓOTOO at last, finally, at length.

totonoéru to prepare, get ready; to arrange.

totonóu to be prepared; to be arranged; to be in good order; to be ready, be settled.

totsúgu to marry; to be married.

TOTSUZEN suddenly, abruptly; all of a sudden; **totsuzen no** sudden, abrupt. **Totsuzen jishoku shimáshita.** He resigned without giving notice.

totté handle; knob; **totté o tsukéru** to fix a handle.

tottei jetty, breakwater.

TÓU to ask, question.

tózan mountain climbing.

tozetsu stoppage, cessation; interruption; **tozetsu suru** to be stopped; to be interrupted.

tsúba saliva; **tsuba o kakeru** to spit at.

tsubasa wings.

tsubo jar; land measure of six **shaku** (Japanese feet) square; **tsubo ni ireru** to pot (plant). **Kono niwa wa sanbyaku tsubo arimasu.** This garden has an area of three hundred **tsubo.**

tsubomeru to make narrow; to pucker up; **kasa o tsubomeru** to shut an umbrella; **kuchi o tsubomeru** to pucker up the lips.

tsubomi (flower bud).

tsubu grain; drop (of liquid).

tsubureru to be crushed; to be smashed, be broken; to break; **menboku ga tsubureru** to be put out of countenance; **tsubusu** to crush; to smash, break; **shindai o tsubusu** to dissipate one's fortune; **jikan o tsubusu** to kill time. **Ginkoo ga tsubureta.** The bank failed.

tsubuyáku to mutter, grumble; to murmur.

TSUCHÍ ground, earth; mud; clay.

tsuchikusái rustic; boorish.

tsúe cane, walking stick; **tsúe o tomeru** to make a stopover; **tsúe o tsuku** to walk with a walking-stick.

tsuge revelation, oracle.

tsugeguchi (n.) talebearing; **tsugeguchi suru** to carry tales.

tsugeru to tell; to inform; to bid; **itomá o tsugeru** to bid farewell.

TSUGÍ next, succeeding, adjacent; **tsugí no ma** next room. **Kono tsugi wa dáre desu ka?** Who comes next to him?

tsugi patch; **tsugi o ateru** to patch.

tsugime joint; seam; **tsugime náshi no** seamless.

tsugoo circumstances; **tsugoo ni yori** for certain reasons; **tsugoo yóku** fortunately. **tsugoo ga yói** to be convenient. **tsugoo suru** to arrange; to manage.

tsúgoo in all; together.

tsugu to pour out; to fill; to put; to join; to piece together; to rank next to; to be next to; to rank second to; to succeed; to accede, to inherit; **kí ni take o tsugu** to graft bamboo on a tree; to be incongruous; **ocha o íppai tsugu** to pour a cup of tea.

TSÚI unintentionally; by mistake.

tsui pair, couple.

tsuide order, sequence; **tsuide ni** by way of, incidentally, when, as; **tsuide no sétsu** at your convenience.

tsuihoo banishment, exile.

tsuika supplement, appendix; **tsuika suru** to add, supplement.

tsuikyuu investigation; **tsuikyuu suru** to inquire closely into (a matter).

TSÚI NI at last, finally; at length.

tsuiraku crash; fall; **tsuiraku suru** to fall; to crash.

tsuiseki pursuit, chase; **tsuiseki suru** to pursue.

TSUITACHI first day of the month.

tsuitate screen.

TSÚITE (always used following ni) of, about, concerning; **kono ten ni tsuite** on this point. **Kono mondai ni tsúite dóo omoimásu ka?** What do you think about this?

tsuitoo (n.) mourning; **tsuitoo suru** to mourn (a death); **tsuitoo no kotoba** memorial address; eulogy.

tsuitotsu (n.) bumping into the rear; **ni tsuitotsu suru** to collide (from behind).

tsuiyásu to spend, expend, lay out; **monó o mueki ni tsuiyásu** to be wasteful.

tsujitsuma consistency; **tsujitsuma no awánu** inconsistent.

tsukaéru to be clogged, be obstructed, be blocked; to be barred; to serve; to work under; **kotobá ga tsukaéru** to stammer, to stick in one's throat; **muné ga tsukaéru** to feel heavy in the stomach. **Kúda ga tsukáete iru.** The pipe is choked.

tsukai message; errand; messenger.

tsukaihatásu to squander, spend all (one's money).

tsukaikata usage, application. **Kono kikái no tsukaikata ga wakarimasén.** I don't know how to use this machine.

tsukaikómu to embezzle.

tsukaimichi employment, use.

tsukaimono present, gift; **tsukaimono o suru** to give a present; to send a gift.

tsukainaréru to be accustomed to using.

tsukaisugíru to use excessively; to spend too much.

tsukamaeru to catch; to seize; to take hold of; **tsukamaru** to be caught, be taken; to be arrested; **tsukámu** to seize, catch, grasp, hold.

tsukamaséru to let (someone) grasp; to bribe.

tsukamiai (n.) grappling, fighting (without a weapon).

tsukaré weariness, fatigue.

TSUKARÉRU to get tired, grow weary, become fatigued.

tsukaru to soak in; to be soaked in, be steeped in; **kaisui ni tsukaru** to take a dip in the sea).

tsukasadóru to rule, govern, administer; to take charge of.

TSUKAU to use, put to use, employ; to take; to spend; **atamá o tsukau** to use one's brain; **yú o tsukau** to take a hot bath. **Anó hito wa rippa na Nihongo o tsukaimásu.** He speaks good Japanese.

tsukeiru to take advantage of (someone); to presume on (someone's) good nature; to impose on (someone's) kindness.

tsukekomu to enter; to take advantage of another's weakness.

tsukemono pickles; pickled vegetables.

tsukenerau to prowl; to dog, shadow; to hang about.

tsukeru to soak in, steep in.

TSUKERU to attach one thing to another, to set one thing on another, to stick on, to sew on; to wear, to make an entry (in a book); **katá o tsukéru** to make an end (of something); **ki o tsukéru** to take care; **mikomi o tsukéru** to form a judgment; **kusuri o tsukéru** to apply a medicine; **na o tsukéru** to name; **pán ni báta o tsukéru** to spread butter on bread; **té o tsukéru** to put one's hand to a task; to eat.

tsuketodoke fee, payment of money, bribe; occasional presents.

TSUKÍ moon; month; **mikazuki** crescent;

tsukí ni nikai twice a month; **tsuki no de** rising of the moon.

-tsuki suffix denoting: assigned to; attached to; per. **Hitóri ni tsuki gosen en desu.** The charge is 5000 yen per person.

tsukiagéru to thrust up; to push up; to toss.

tsukiai keeping company; association; intercourse; **tsukiai no tamé ni** for the sake of friendship; **tsukiai nikúi** to be difficult to get along with; **tsukiai o suru** to keep company with; **tsukiáu** to keep company with, associate with.

tsukiatari dead end (street); collision, crash.

tsukidásu to thrust out, stick out, push out, stretch out.

tsukihájime beginning of a month.

tsukihi days and months; time; years; date.

tsukikáesu to thrust back.

tsukimatóu to follow, shadow (someone); to hang on; to pursue.

tsukímono accessory, adjunct, appendage; part; anything which is attached to or is an indispensable part of something.

tsukinami na monthly; commonplace; conventional.

tsukinúku to thrust through, pierce, penetrate.

tsukiókure no of the previous month; **tsukiókure no zasshi** back numbers of a magazine.

tsukiotósu = tsukitaósu to throw or push (someone) down or off.

tsukíru to become exhausted; to be used up, be consumed. **Okane ga tsukimáshita.** I ran out of money.

tsukisoi attendant; nurse; chaperon.

tsukisóu to attend (someone); to accompany.

tsukitaósu See tsukiotósu.

tsukitoméru to ascertain, make sure of; to assure, convince, satisfy oneself of.

tsukitóosu to thrust, pierce.

tsukitsukéru to thrust before; to put (place) under (someone's) nose; to point at.

tsukíyo moonlit night.

tsukízue end of a month.

tsukízuki no monthly; **tsukízuki no téate** monthly allowance.

tsukkakáru to fall on, pick a quarrel with (someone).

tsukkakéru to slip on.

tsukkíru to cross; to go (run) across; to go through.

tsukkómu to thrust in; to plunge in; to poke into.

TSUKU to arrive at; to come to hand; to thrust, pierce, stab; **tantó de tsuku** to stab (someone) with a dagger; to stick to, adhere to; to touch. **Fúne wa íma tsukimáshita.** The ship has just arrived. **Kóobe ni tsukimáshita.** He arrived at Kobe. **Té ni penki ga tsúite iru.** There is paint on his hand. **Té o tsukéte wa ikemasén.** Don't touch it.

TSUKUE table, desk.

TSUKÚRU to make, manufacture; to prepare, produce; to turn out; to frame; to

build, erect; to form; to raise; to
cultivate; to constitute; **ié o tsukúru**
build a house; **kane o tsukúru** to make
a fortune; **rájio o tsukúru** to make a
radio; **rétsu o tsukúru** to form in line.

tsukúsu to exhaust; to come to the end of; to
serve (someone); to make efforts.

tsukuzúku thoroughly, utterly, quite;
tsukuzúku iyá ni náru to become
utterly disgusted; **tsukuzúku
kangáeru** to reflect carefully.

TSÚMA wife, spouse; **TSÚMAKO** wife and
children, (one's) family.

tsumadátsu to stand on tiptoe.

tsumahájiki suru to flick; to disdain; to shun;
to scorn.

tsumamidásu to pick out, drag out, turn out.

tsumamu to pick, pinch, take a pinch of.

tsumaránai trifling, worthless, commonplace;
tsumaránai kotó matter of no
importance; **tsumaránai mono** trifling
thing; **tsumaránai yátsu** poor fellow.

TSÚMARI in the end; in the long run; finally;
in a word.

tsumáru to be blocked up; to be full, be
packed; to be shortened; **hentóo ni
tsumáru** to be at a loss for a reply;
kane ni tsumáru to be pressed for
money; **ki ga tsumáru** to be
oppressive.

tsumashíi frugal, thrifty, economical.

tsumazúku to take a false step; to lose one's
footing, stumble, fall.

TSUME nail; claw; hoof; hook; **tsume o kíru**
to cut one's nails.

tsumekakéru to crowd (a house); to throng to
(the door).

tsumekiri constant attendance; staying at
one's post without a break.

tsumekómu to cram; to stuff; to jam; to pack;
heyá ni hito o tsumekómu to crowd
people into a room.

tsumémono o suru to stuff, pack.

tsuméru to cram; to stuff; to fill; to pack; to
charge; **kaban ni tsuméru** to pack a
suitcase.

TSUMETAI cold (to the touch), chilly; icy;
tsumetai kokóro cold heart; **tsumetai
mizu** cold water.

tsúmi crime, offense; sin; fault; **tsúmi na**
sinful, cruel, inhuman.

tsumiagéru to heap up, make a pile; to
accumulate.

tsumidásu to send off, ship off.

tsumihóroboshi atonement of sins, expiation.

tsumikaéru to reship.

tsumikómu to load; to put on board; to take
in.

tsumini cargo, freight.

tsumitatéru to save up (money); to lay by; to
reserve, amass, accumulate.

TSUMORI intention; motive; expectation;
understanding. **Harátta tsumori desu.**
I believe I've paid for it. **Iku tsumori
desu.** I intend to go.

tsumorigaki written estimate; written
measurement.

tsumóru to accumulate; to be piled up; to
amount to. **Tsumóru hanashí ni yó o
fukáshita.** We had much to talk about
and sat up far into the night. **Yukí ga
tsumóru.** Snow is piled up on the
ground.

tsumu to pile up, heap up; to load; to
accumulate; to take on board; to pick;
to pluck; to pull out.

tsumujíkaze whirlwind, tornado.

tsuná cord, rope, line, **Tanomi no tsuná mo
kíreta.** The last ray of hope is gone.

tsunagi connection, link; **tsunagu** to tie,
fasten, chain, connect, join.

tsunami tidal waves.

tsúne usual state; **tsúne no** usual, ordinary,
common; **tsúne ni** always.

tsunéru to pinch.

tsunó horn; **tsunó o hayásu** to become
jealous.

tsunóru to solicit (a subscription); to collect;
to grow violent, severe, intense, fierce;
to become worse.

tsunzáku to rend, break; to pierce; to split.

tsuppáru to stretch (an arm or leg against
something); to plant one's feet on the
ground.

tsurai hard; painful; bitter; **tsuraku** bitterly,
harshly.

tsuranáru to range; to lie in a row; to be
present at. **Matsuda-san no
kekkónshiki ni tsuranátta.** I attended
Mr. Matsuda's wedding.

tsuranúku to pierce; to pass through.

tsurara icicle.

tsurasa pain, painfulness.

tsure companion.

tsuréai (*colloq.*) spouse, husband, wife.

tsuredátsu to go along with.

TSURERU to take (with). **Tomodachi o
tsurete ikimáshita.** I took a friend of
mine with me.

tsuresóu to be married, be man and wife.

tsuri (*n.*) fishing (with a hook and line);
change. **Gohyakú en no tsuri o
moraimáshita.** I received change of
500 yen. **Tsuri o shi ni ikimáshita.**
He went fishing.

tsuriai balance, equilibrium; harmony; **tsuriai
o tóru** to balance oneself.

tsurusu to hang, suspend; to swing.

tsutaeru to convey; to report; to deliver; to
communicate.

tsutawaru to be handed down; to be
transmitted.

tsuté intermediary; good offices; **tsuté o
motoméru** to hunt up connections.

tsutomáru to be fit for; to be equal to (a
position).

TSUTOME duty; service; **tsutomé o hatásu**
to discharge one's duties;
tsutoméguchi place of employment;
tsutomenin salaried person;
TSUTOMÉRU to serve, hold (fill) a

post; to exert oneself; to make an
effort; to endeavor; to labor, work;
tsutomesaki one's place of
employment. **Takagi-san wa ginkoo
ni tsutómete imásu.** Takagi works for
a bank.

tsutsu pipe, tube; gun barrel; gun.

tsutsúku to poke at; to pick at, to peck.

tsutsumashíi modest, reserved.

TSUTSUMÍ package, parcel; dike;
embankment; **tsutsumígami** wrapping
paper, a packing sheet; **TSUTSÚMU**
to wrap; to do up, to pack.

tsutsushimi prudence, discretion, caution;
tsutsushimi no nái immodest,
indiscreet; **tsutsushimi o wasureru** to
lose one's self-control; **tsutsushimu** to
be discreet; to be careful, be prudent;
to restrain oneself.

tsuttátsu to stand; to stand up straight.

tsúu connoisseur, authority, expert judge.

-tsuu counter for letters, telegrams; **tegami o
ittsuu dásu** to send a letter.

tsuuchi information; **tsuuchi suru** to inform;
tsuuchoo official communication,
notification.

tsuufuu ventilation.

tsuugaku suru to go to school.

tsuuji bowel movement; **tsuuji ga tomaru** to
become constipated; **tsuuji o tsukéru**
to loosen the bowels.

tsuujiru to pass; to run; to be opened (to
traffic); to be understood.

tsuujoo usually; ordinarily; as a rule.

tsuukai na extremely delightful; pleasant;
tsuukai na otoko a man of spirit. **Sore
wa tsuukai de átta.** It was a delightful
sensation.

tsuukan passing through customs.

tsuukan suru to feel keenly, feel acutely.

tsuukin suru to go to the office.

tsuukoku announcement, notice, information;
tsuukoku suru to notify.

tsuukoo passing; transit; **tsuukoodome no**
thoroughfare; **tsuukoodome ni suru** to
close a road; to stop traffic.

TSUUREI as a rule; commonly.

tsuusan sum total.

tsuusetsu na keen, acute.

tsuushin correspondence, communication;
tsuushínsha news agency.

tsuushoo common name.

tsuutatsu notification; **tsuutatsu suru** to
notify.

tsuuun transportation, moving van; **tsuuun
gáisha** a mover.

-TSUUWA suffix denoting: phone-call unit.
Ittsúuwa wa sánpun desu. One
telephone call unit is based on three
minutes' conversation.

tsuuwáryoo charge for a telephone call.

tsúuyaku interpretation, interpreter; **tsúuyaku
suru** to interpret.

tsuuyóomon public gate; side gate.

tsuuyoo suru to pass for; to circulate; to be
current; to hold good.

tsuya gloss, luster.

TSUYÓI strong, powerful, robust, healthy.

tsuyoki firmness; **tsuyoki o shimésu** to show
firmness.

tsuyoméru to strengthen; to invigorate; to
intensify; **ími o tsuyoméru** to
emphasize; **tsuyomí** strength, power;
strong point.

tsúyosa strength, power.

tsuyu rainy season (June-July); **tsuyu no iri**
start of the rainy season; **tsuyu no ake**
end of the rainy season.

tsúyu dew; dewdrop; = **otsuyu** soup, broth;
gravy (Japanese style). **Tsúyu ga
oríru.** The dew is falling.

TSUZUKERU to continue; to keep on.

tsuzuki continuation; connection; succession.

TSUZUKU to go on; to follow, go in
succession; to last. **Áme wa mikka
tsuzukimáshita.** The rain continued to
fall for three days.

tsuzumeru to contract; to condense; to
reduce, shorten, cut short.

tsuzuri spelling; **tsuzuru** to spell words; to
compose (a tune); **bún o tsuzuru** to
write.

U

úba matron; nurse; wet nurse.

ubagúruma baby carriage.

ubáu to take by force, snatch; to rob (someone
of something).

úbu naïveté; greenness.

UCHI house; home; inside, interior; **sono hí
no uchi ni** in the course of that day;
uchi no koto household matters; **uchi
de asobu** to play indoors.

uchiageru to shoot up; to send up; to set off.

uchiakeru to disclose, reveal; to confide (a
secret); **himitsu o uchiakeru** to give
secret information; to disclose secrets.

uchiáu to exchange blows.

uchiawase previous arrangement;
consultation; **uchiawase o suru** to
make arrangements for.

uchiwaséru to strike (one thing against
another); to make arrangements for
something.

uchidashi close; closing time (of a theatre);
embossment; **uchidásu** to begin to
beat; to strike out; to emboss; to close.
Uchidashi wa góji deshita. They
closed at five o'clock.

uchideshi apprentice; private pupil.

uchigawa inside.

uchikáesu to strike, beat, hit back, return a
blow.

uchikesu to deny; to negate; to contradict.

uchiki retiring disposition; shyness.

uchikiru to close; to discontinue; **kooshoo o
uchikiru** to drop negotiations.

uchikomu to drive in; to strike into; to shoot
into; to fall deeply in love with; to be
absorbed in; **kugí o uchikomu** to drive
a nail into; **tamá o uchikomu** to send
bullets into.

uchimaku real state of things; inside facts; **uchimaku o abáku** to see behind the scenes.

uchiotósu to strike down, knock down, floor; to shoot down.

uchitaósu to knock down, strike down, overthrow.

uchitokeru to open one's heart; to be frank, to be candid.

uchitomeru uchitóru to kill, slay, shoot dead.

uchiúmi inland sea.

uchiwa family circle; private circle (of friends); **uchiwa dóoshi** those who are of the same party (or family, etc.); member of the inner circle.

uchiwake item breakdown (of an account); details.

uchooten ni náru to be in ecstasy.

úchuu universe, cosmos.

UDÉ arm; ability; **udé o furuu** to exercise a talent; **udé o kasu** to lend a helping hand; **udé o tamésu** to test one's ability; **udekiki** able man; man of ability.

udon noodle; macaroni; **udonko** wheat flour; **udonya** restaurant where Japanese noodles are the specialty.

UE upper part, surface, topside; top, summit, head; after, on, upon; **ichiban ue no** uppermost; **shikén no ué de** on examination; **ue ni tátsu hitó** one who stands in authority over others; **ue no** higher; upper; superior.

ué hunger; starvation; **uejini** death by starvation; **uéru** to become hungry; to starve; to be famished; to hunger for.

uebóosoo vaccination; **uebóosoo o suru** to vaccinate.

uekáeru to transplant, replant; **hoka no hachí ni uekáeru** to transplant into another pot.

ueki plant; potted plant; **uekiya** nurseryman, gardener.

uekomi thicket, shrubbery.

ueru to plant.

uéshita up and down; shirts and trousers; **uéshita ni náru** to be upside down; **uéshita ni suru** to turn upside down.

netsuke (*n.*) planting; transplanting.

ugai gargling, rinsing the mouth; **ugai suru** to gargle; **ugaigúsuri** a gargle.

ugátsu to dig; to cut through; to pierce; **ugátta kotó o iu** to make a pointed remark.

UGOKÁSU to move; to shift; to remove, to set in motion; **chooshuu o ugokásu** to move an audience; **hito no kokoró o ugokásu** to touch the heart.

ugoki movement, motion; **UGÓKU** to move; to shift; to sway; to work; to be transferred to another position. **Ugóite wa ikemasén.** Don't move.

ugoméku to wriggle, squirm.

uisuki whiskey.

ukaberu to float, keep afloat.

ukabu to float; to come to the surface, appear. **Íi kangáe ga ukanda.** I hit upon a good idea.

UKAGAU to watch for, look for, be on the lookout for; to pay a visit; to inquire (*pol.*); **hito no kaoiro o ukagau** to study a person's face; **kikái o ukagau** to look for a chance. **Sono kotó wa Yamada-san ni ukagaimáshita.** I asked Mr. Yamada about it. **Yamada-san no otaku ni ukagaimáshita.** I visited Yamada's house.

ukareru to make merry; to be gay.

ukasareru to be carried away, be captivated; **netsú ni ukasareru** to be delirious with fever.

ukatsu carelessness, thoughtlessness; stupidity.

uke reputation, popularity; acceptance, assent, consent. **Anó hito wa uke ga íi.** He has a good reputation.

ukedásu = **ukemodósu** to redeem, take (something) out of pawn.

ukekotae reply, answer; **ukekotae o suru** to reply, answer.

ukemi acting on the defensive; passive (in grammar).

ukemochi charge.

ukemodósu See **ukedásu**.

ukenagasu to ward off, turn aside; **shitsumon o takumi ni ukenagasu** to ignore a question diplomatically.

ukeoi contract for work.

ukeóu to undertake; to take upon oneself; to assume.

ukéru to receive; to accept; to have, to obtain; to take; **hoomon o ukéru** to receive a visit; **shújutsu o ukéru** to have an operation (surgical). (See also **uketoru**.)

uketomeru to stop; to catch; to ward off. **tamá o uketomeru** to catch a ball.

uketori receipt; acceptance; **uketorinin** receiver, recipient.

UKETORU = **ukéru** to receive; to accept. **Tegami o uketorimáshita.** I received a letter.

uketsugi succession; inheritance.

uketsuke (*n.*) receiving; accepting; reception desk; **uketsuke gakari** receptionist.

ukewatashi delivery, transfer; **ukewatashi o suru** to deliver, transfer.

uki float, buoy; **ukiagáru** to rise to the surface; to float.

ukiashi unsteadiness; wavering, faltering; **ukiashi ni náru** to waver, become unsteady; **ukibúkuro** air bladder (of a fish), life buoy, life belt; **uku** to float; to come to the surface; to be left over; to be saved; **ki ga uku** to be gay, to be exhilarated.

UKKÁRI vacantly; carelessly; without attention.

UMÁ horse, mount; **umakata** driver of a pack horse; **umaya** stable.

umagóyashi clover; snail clover.

UMÁI good; nice; tasty; skillful; successful; profitable; **umái mono** delicious, dainty food.

umami deliciousness, flavor; **umami no áru hanashi** a nice speech.

umare birth, lineage; **umare no yói** to be well-born, be high-born; **UMARERU** to be born; **hínka ni umareru** to come from a poor family; **umareru to súgu** at birth.

umaretsuki by nature; by temperament.

umaru to be filled up; to be hurried.

umeawase amends, compensation; **sonshitsu no umeawase o suru** to make up for a loss.

umekí moan, groan; **uméku** to groan, moan.

umeru to bury; to reclaim; to fill up.

umetate reclamation; filling up; **umetatéchi** reclaimed land; **umetate kóoji** reclamation work.

ÚMI sea; ocean; **hí no umi** vast sheet of fire; sea of fire; **úmi de oyógu** to swim in the ocean; **umibe** beach, seashore.

umí pus; **umí o motsu** to form pus; **úmu** to form pus, fester.

umi no háha one's natural mother.

umitate fresh (said of an egg).

únmei destiny, fate, fortune; doom; **únmei no chóoji** fortune's favorite.

unpan transportation; **unpan suru** to transport.

UMU to bear, give birth to, be delivered of. **Anzúru yori umu ga yasúi.** Fear often exaggerates danger.

úmu existence, presence; yes or no; **úmu o iwasezu** forcibly; whether one will or not. **Ayamari no úmu o shirasete kudasái.** Let me know whether there is any mistake.

ún fortune, lot, destiny, fate; (*colloq.*) yes; h'm; well; sound uttered in groaning; **ún no warúi** unlucky; **ún no yói** lucky.

unadareru to hang one's head.

unagásu to urge, press, demand; to call upon; to stimulate.

unarí groan; roar; humming; **unáru** to groan; to roar; to howl; to hum.

unasaréru to have a nightmare, have bad dreams.

unazúku to nod, bow one's head in assent.

únchin freight; portage; shipping expenses.

undei no sá all the difference in the world.

UNDOO movement, motion; physical exercise; **undoo suru** to move; to exercise; to walk; to campaign; **undooka** athlete.

uné furrow.

unéru to wind; to undulate; **namí ga unéru** to swell.

únga canal; **ungáryoo** canal tools; **ungachitái** canal zone.

unomi ni suru to gulp down.

unsoo carrying, transport; **unsoo suru** to carry, transport; **unsooya** mover, forwarding agent.

UNTEN operation; driving; working; **unten suru** to drive, operate, work; **unténshu** engineer (operator of an engine); chauffeur; motorman (driver of streetcar or bus).

únto (*colloq.*) with great force; with all one's might; soundly; liberally; **kane ga únto áru** to have lots of money; **únto osu** to push with all one's might.

unubore self-conceit; **unubore ga tsuyói** to be full of conceit; **unuboreru** to be vain; to be conceited, to think highly of oneself.

ún'yu traffic; transport.

unzan operation, calculation; **unzan suru** to calculate.

unzári suru to be disgusted with.

UO fish; **uogashi** fish market.

uppun resentment, grudge, enmity.

URA reverse side; back, sole of the foot; lining of clothes; hidden meaning of an expression; second half of baseball inning.

uradana house in an alley.

uradóori back street.

uragaki endorsement; **uragaki suru** to endorse.

uragiri treachery, perfidy, **uragíru** to betray, turn traitor, go over to the enemy.

uraguchi back entrance.

uraji lining; cloth for lining.

urameshíi reproachful; resentful; hateful.

uramí resentment; grudge; hatred; malice; **uramí o idáku** to bear a grudge; **urámu** to bear a grudge; to feel bitter against; to think ill of.

urámichi byway; back road.

uramon back gate.

uranái fortunetelling; fortuneteller.

uranáu to divine; forecast; **minoue o uranáu** to tell (someone's) fortune.

uraniwa back yard; rear garden.

urate rear of a building.

URAYAMASHÍI enviable. **Anáta ga urayamashíi desu.** I envy you; **urayámu** to envy, be envious of, be jealous of; **hito no koofuku o urayamu** to envy a person his good luck.

urekko popular person; lion; **bundan no urekko** popular writer.

urekuchi market.

ureshigáru to be glad; to take delight in; to feel happy; **URESHÍI** glad, joyous, delighted, happy. **Ome ni kakárete ureshíi desu.** I'm glad to be able to see you.

uriage proceeds (returns) of a sale.

URIBA sales counter.

uribagákari counterman.

uridame receipts, cash in a money box.

uridashi bargain sale; opening sale; **uridásu** to offer for sale, place on the market, put on sale.

urikire sold out.

uriko salesgirl; salesman.

urimono for sale; **urimono ni dásu** to put up for sale.

URINE sale price.
urioshimi holding (hoarding) goods for future sale; **urioshimi o suru** to hoard goods for future sale.
urotáeru to be confused, be thrown into confusion; to be upset.
urotsuku to loiter, hang about; to wander about.
URU to sell; to deal in; to offer for sale. **Sore wa dóko de utte imásu ka?** Where is it sold?
úru to gain; to get.
urúmu to be wet; to be moist; to be blurred; to be dimmed.
uruoi moisture, damp; enrichment; grace, charm; **uruoi no áru** moist; profitable; tasteful.
uruósu to wet, moisten; to dip; to be moistened, be wet; to receive benefits.
URUSÁI annoying, tiresome, harassing, irksome.
urúudoshi leap year.
uruwashíi beautiful, pretty; fine; **gokigen uruwáshiku** in good humor; in excellent health.
úryoo rainfall; **uryookei** rain gauge.
usankusái suspicious-looking; uncanny.
USHI cattle; cow; bull; ox.
ushináu to lose; to miss; to part with; to be deprived of.
USHIRO (*n.*) back, rear; (*adj.*) **ushiro no** back, hind, rear; (*adv.*) **ushiroashi** hind legs; **ushiro ni** behind; **ushiro e mawaru** to get behind.
ushirogurái shady; not aboveboard; **ushirogurái kotó** underhanded, shady transaction.
ushiromuki standing with the back toward another.
ushiroyubi o sásu to point a finger of scorn at; **ushiroyubi o sasaréru** to be talked about as an object of scorn.
úso lie, falsehood; **makká na úso** a pack of lies; **úso no** false; **úso o tsuku** to lie; **úso happyaku o naraberu** to tell all sorts of lies.
usugurai gloomy, dim, dusky, dark.
USUI thin; light; weak; **nínjoo no usui hito** cold-hearted person.
usukimi warúi dismal; weird, eerie.
usuppera na thin; flimsy; superficial.
usurágu to thin; to fade, grow pale; to be toned down; to become dim.
usurasamúi chilly; rather cold.
utá ode, poem; song; **utá o utau** to sing a song; **utá o yómu** to compose a poem.
utagai doubt; **utagai náku** beyond doubt; **utagai o harásu** to clear away suspicion; **utagai o idáku** to harbor suspicion; **utagai o tóku** to clear up all doubts; **utagáu** to doubt; to be doubtful of. **Utagáu yóchi ga nái.** There is no room for doubt.
UTAU to sing, chant, carol; to recite; **hanauta o utau** to hum a song.

úten rainy weather; rainy day.
útouto suru to doze off, to slumber.
ÚTSU to strike, hit, beat; to fire, shoot; to drive in; to give a performance; to attack, assault; to send a telegram; **denpoo o útsu** to send a telegram; **fui o útsu** to make a sudden attack; **kugi o útsu** to drive in a nail; **pisutoru de útsu** to shoot with a revolver; **shibai o útsu** to give a play; to play a trick. **Tokei ga niji o útta.** The clock struck two.
Utsubushi ni on one's face.
UTSUKUSHÍI beautiful, fair; **utsukushíi hanashi** a beautiful story; **utsukushíi késhiki** beautiful scenery.
utsumúku to look down; to stoop; **utsumúite arúku** to walk with one's head bent.
utsurígi caprice, whim; **utsurígi no** capricious, changeable.
utsúru to be reflected; to fall upon; to be becoming; to be taken; **kagamí ni utsúru** to be reflected in a mirror; **shashin ni utsúru** to be photographed. **Ano káta ni wa ano kimono ga yóku utsúru.** That dress is very becoming to her.
utsúru to remove; to change, shift; to be infectious.
utsushí copy.
UTSÚSU to remove; to transfer; to pour; to carry; to turn; to direct; to copy, transcribe; to describe, picture; **jimúsho o utsúsu** to move the office; **miruku o hoka no bín ni utsúsu** to pour milk from one bottle into another.
utsuwa vessel; implement; caliber; sono **utsuwa de nái** to be by no means qualified.
uttae accusation, charge; lawsuit; complaint; petition; **uttae o kiku** to hear a case; **uttáeru** to sue; to complain to; **hootei ni uttáeru** to take legal proceedings against someone; **rísei ni uttáeru** to appeal to reason; **yóron ni uttáeru** to appeal to public opinion.
uttooshíi depressing, oppressive, gloomy.
uwabe surface, exterior.
UWAGI upper or outer garment; coat; man's jacket.
uwagoto o iu to be delirious.
uwaki fickleness, inconstancy; flirtation; **uwaki na** fickle, flirtatious; **uwakimono** licentious man, wanton woman.
uwame upward glance; **uwamuki** upward trend; **uwamúku** to look up, turn one's face upwards. **Sooba ga uwamuki de áru.** Prices show an upward trend.
uwanosora absentmindedness; **uwanosóra de kiku** to listen absently.
uwanuri final coating (of plaster or paint); **són no uwanuri o suru** to add to one's loss; to suffer loss upon loss.
uwasa rumor, report, talk; **uwasa o suru** to spread a rumor.

uwate better hand; **uwate ni déru** to get the upper hand.
uwayaku superior official.
uyamáu to respect; to honor.
uyamuya ambiguity; vagueness; **uyamuya ni suru** to obscure an issue; **uyamuya ni hoomúru** to suppress a matter.
uyauyáshiku respectfully.
úyoku right wing; right field (in baseball).
úyo kyokusetsu much meandering; **úyo kyokusetsu o héte** after aimless wandering.
uzoo múzoo rabble; all sorts and conditions of men.
uzukumáru to crouch, squat down.
uzúmaki eddy, whirlpool; **uzumáku** to whirl, swirl; to flow in whirls; to curl.
uzumaru to be filled up; to be buried; **uzumeru** to bury.
uzumoreru to be covered with; to live in obscurity.

V

vaiorin violin.
véeru veil.
viníiru plastic, vinyl.

W

WA particle denoting: sentence topic; = **as for. Doitsugo wa benkyoo shimáshita.** [As far as German is concerned] I studied German (but not French). **Kinóo wa ikimáshita.** I went yesterday (but not today). **Watakushi wa ikimasén.** As for me, I'm not going.
wá circle; ring; wheel; **wá ni wá o kakéru** to exaggerate.
wabiru to apologize for; to make an excuse; to beg pardon.
wabishíi miserable, poor, wretched; **wabishíi kurashi o suru** to lead a lonely life.
wabun text in Japanese; **wabun éiyaku** translating into English from Japanese; **wabun dénpoo** telegram in Japanese.
wadachi rut, wheel track.
wadai topic, subject; **wadai ni noboru** to be talked about.
wadakamari ill feeling; reserve; **wadakamari ga áru** to be vexed at something.
wadakamáru to be coiled up (as a snake); to be rooted; to be harbored.
Wa-Ei jísho, Wa-Ei jiten Japanese-English dictionary.
wafuku Japanese clothes; kimono.
wagamáma willfulness; waywardness; **wagamáma na** willful, wayward; **wagamáma o suru** to have one's own way; **wagamamamono** wayward person.
wagoo suru to harmonize with; to agree with each other.
wáiro bribery, bribe; **wáiro o tsukau** to bribe,

corrupt; **wáiro o tóru** to be bribed; to take a bribe.
waishatsu man's dress shirt.
wáiwai noisily, clamorously.
wáka = **tánka** Japanese verse of 31 syllables.
wakagaeri rejuvenation.
wakage youthful spirit.
WAKAI young, youthful; **wakái hito** young person; **wakákatta toki** when he was young; **wakamono** young man.
wakai suru to make up, settle amicably; to accommodate with.
wakarazuya blockhead; incorrigible person.
WAKARÉ farewell, parting; division; branch; **wakaré no sakazúki** a parting cup; **wakaré o oshímu** to be reluctant to part; **wakaré o tsugeru** to say good-by.
WAKARÉRU to branch off, split, part; to break up, be divided; to get separated; **eikyuu ni wakaréru** to part forever.
wakarí understanding; **wakari kítta** well-known; obvious; **wakarí nikui** hard to understand; **wakarí no yói** intelligent, sensible; **wakarí no warúi** slow to understand; **WAKÁRU** to understand, realize, comprehend.
wakasu to boil; to heat; **cha o wakasu** to make tea; **yú o wakasu** to boil water.
WÁKE reason; ground; meaning; circumstance; **wáke no wakaránai hanashi** a strange story; senseless talk; **wáke no wakátta hitó** a person amenable to reason; **wáke o tazunéru** to ask the reason. **Sore wa doo iu wáke desu ka.** What do you mean by that?
wakehedate partiality, favoritism; **wakehedate no nái** impartial, fair; **wakehedate o suru** to be partial, to discriminate.
wakemáe share, portion.
wakemé dividing line, decisive event; **WAKÉRU** to divide, separate; to distribute; to distinguish; **itsútsu ni wakéru** to divide into five parts. **Tochi o kodomo ni wákemashita.** He divided his estate among his children.
wakí (n.) side; other way; supporting role; **wakí no** (adj.) other, another; side, lateral; **waki ni yoru** to step aside; **wakí e oku** to lay aside; **wakí o tsutoméru** to support the leading actor (in a No play).
wakimáe discernment, discrimination; judgment; understanding; **wakimáe no nái** thoughtless, indiscreet; **wakimaéru** to discern, discriminate; to know; to understand.
wakimé sidelong glance; **wakimé mo furazu** without looking aside, devoting oneself entirely to; **wakimí o suru** to look aside; to look off.
WAKU (n.) frame, tambour; (v.) to boil; to gush out; to spring; to grow. **Furó ga wakimáshita.** The bath is ready. **Yú ga waite imasu.** The water is boiling.

waméku to cry; to scream, yell, shriek.

wán bay; inlet; gulf.

wanpaku kozoo spoiled child; naughty boy; **wánpaku na** willful; naughty.

wánryoku physical strength.

warai laughter; smile; ridicule; **waraigao** smiling face; smile; **waraigusa** laughing-stock, butt of ridicule; **warai jóogo** ticklish person; **WARAU** to laugh; to smile; to chuckle; to deride, jeer.

waraji sandals for traveling, straw sandals; **waraji o haku** to put on straw sandals; to fly from (official) pursuit; **waraji o núgu** to take off straw sandals; to settle down.

wareme crack, crevice, fissure.

wari rate, proportion, percentage; allotment; **wari no yói** profitable; **wari ni** comparatively; **nén ichíwari no risoku** interest of 10 per cent annually.

wariai rate, proportion; **wariai ni** comparatively.

waribiki discount, price reduction; **waribiki suru** to allow a discount.

waridásu to calculate, compute; to deduce from, conclude from.

warikiréru to be divisible. **Sanjuukú wa júusan de warikiréru.** Thirty-nine can be divided by 13.

WARU to split; to crush; to divide; to get lower than; to dilute; to open one's heart: to cut; to halve; to cleave; to rend; **juuní o rokú de waru** to divide 12 by 6; **maki o waru** to split wood for fuel. **Kono sake wa mízu o watte áru.** This sake is mixed with water.

warubiréru to act timidly; to fear; **warubírezu** with good grace; without fear.

warudákumi evil design, machination; **warudákumi o suru** to conspire.

warugashikói cunning, artful.

warugí ill will; **warugí no nái** without malice; **warugí no nái hito** good-natured person. **Watashi wa warugí de shitá no de wa arimasén.** I meant no offense at all.

WARÚI bad, ill, evil; unlucky; wormy, rotten; wrong; defective; detrimental, slanderous; **wáruku nátta tabemóno** spoiled food; **warúi kotó o suru** to do wrong; to commit a sin, commit a crime; **karada ni warúi** to be injurious to the health; **wáruku suru** to make a thing worse; **wáruku suru to** if things go wrong; **wáruku tóru** to take amiss. **Anó hito wa mé ga warui.** He has poor eyesight.

warujie (*n.*) craftiness, cunning; **warujie no áru** (*adj.*) cunning; **hito ni warujie o tsukéru** to put a person up to mischief.

warúkuchi abuse, abusive language; **káge de warúkuchi o iu** to backbite; **warúkuchi o iu** to speak ill of.

warumono bad fellow; rogue.

wárusa mischief; trick.

wasei of Japanese make.

wasen Japanese rowboat.

washizúkami grasping, clutching; **washizúkami ni suru** to grasp, clutch.

wasuregachi na forgetful.

wasuremono thing left behind; **wasuremono o suru** to leave (something) behind.

wasureppói to have a poor memory.

WASURERU to forget; to lose sight of; to leave behind; **shinshoku o wasureru** to forget sleep and food, be devoted to.

WATÁ cotton; cotton wool; **wata íre** padded clothes; **wata no ki** a cotton plant; **wata no yóo ni tsukaréru** to get dog-tired.

WATAKUSHI I; secrecy; privacy; **watakushi no** my; private; personal; **watakushi no nái** disinterested, unselfish; **watakushítachi** we.

watari passing; crossing; **watari ni fúne** opportune rescue; **watari o tsukéru** to pave the way; to establish some connection.

watariáu to cross swords with; to quarrel with.

wataru to go over; to go; **Chúugoku kara Nippón ni wataru** to come from China to Japan; **hashí o wataru** to cross a bridge; **úmi o wataru** to sail across the sea.

watashi ferry; place where passengers take a ferryboat; toll charged for ferrying; **watashibúne** ferryboat.

WATASU to pass (a man) over; to carry across; to take over; to ferry over; to hand deliver; to transfer; to make over; to pay; **kyúuryoo o watasu** to pay wages; **mukoogawa ni watasu** to take over to the other side (of the river).

wátto with a sudden outcry; **wátto nakidásu** to burst into tears.

wayaku suru to translate into Japanese.

wáza to purposely, on purpose; **wazatorashíi** artificial, unnatural; studied; **wazatoráshiku** artificially.

wazawai misfortune, adversity, calamity.

WAZAWAZA intentionally, on purpose; **wázawaza iku** to take the trouble to go.

WÁZUKA NA small (quantity); few (in number); slight.

wazurawashíi vexacious, troublesome, wearisome; **yonónaka ga wazurawashíi** to be weary of life.

wazurawasu to trouble; to keep a person busy; to exercise; to cause inconvenience.

Y

—YA particle denoting: and (*used when a list is incomplete*): or; as soon as; **are ya kóre ya de** with one thing or another; **tori ya kemono** birds and beasts; **Tookyoo ni tsukú ya** as soon as I got to Tokyo.

-ya suffix denoting: store; **sakanaya** fish market; fishmonger.

yáa oh; hallo.

yáado yard.

yábo boorishness; want of taste; **yábo na** uncouth, vulgar, unrefined; senseless; rusty; **yábo na otoko** boor, silly fellow.

yabuisha quack doctor.

yábun evening, nighttime. **Yábun ni demáshite osóreirimasu.** I must apologize for calling on you so late at night.

yabunirami squint; cross-eye; **yabunirami no** cross-eyed.

yabure rupture, breach; rent, tear; **kimono no yabure** rent in a garment; **yabure kábure** desperation, self-abandonment; **yaburéru** to be torn, be rent; to be broken; to be beaten; to fail in one's design; **YABURU** to tear, rend; to break, destroy, crush; **heiwa o yabúru** to disturb the peace; **kamí o yabúru** to tear a sheet of paper. **Káre no keikaku wa yabúreta.** His attempt had failed. **Kimono ga yabúrete iru.** The clothes are torn.

yáchin house rent; **yáchin no todokoori** rent arrears. **Yáchin ga agarimashita.** The rent has been raised.

YÁDO = **yadoya** hotel, inn, lodging; **ichíya no yádo o kasu** to give a night's lodging; **yádo o kóu** to ask for lodging; **yádo o tóru** to stay at an inn for the night.

yadonashi homelessness; homeless person, vagrant.

YADOYA = **yádo** inn, hotel; **yadoya ni tomaru** to stay at an inn; **yadoya no híyoo** hotel expenses.

yagai field; **yagai kóoen** outdoor exercise; **yagai no** open air, outdoors.

yagaku night study; evening school; **yagákkoo** night school.

yagate presently, soon; before long.

yágoo shop name; firm name.

yágu bedclothes, bedding.

yagura tower, turret; **hinomiyágura** fire tower.

yagyoo night work; **yagyoo téate** overtime (for night work); **yagyoo o suru** to work at night.

YAHÁRI too, also; as well; still; all the same. **Démo yahári yamemashóo.** I won't do it, notwithstanding your persuasion. **Yahári damé desu.** That won't do, either.

yáiyai hey!; hard; pressingly; **yáiyai itte sáisoku suru** to press (someone) for.

yáji heckling; cheering; rooting; **yajfru** to cheer; to support; to disturb; to heckle; to interrupt; to obstruct. **Bénshi o yajiritaóshita.** The speaker was hissed down.

yajiuma mob, busybodies, bystanders.

yakai evening party; ball; **yakai o moyaósu** to give a party.

YAKAMASHÍÍ noisy, uproarious; rigorous, strict. **Ano heyá wa taihen yakamashíí desu.** That room is very noisy.

yákan night, nighttime.

yakan kettle.

yáke despair, desperation.

yakeato ruins left after a fire.

yakedo scald, burn.

yakei night watch, night view; **Kóobe no yakei** the view by night of Kobe.

YAKERU to burn; to be destroyed; to be roasted; to be broiled; to be scorched; **hi ni yaketa kao** sunburnt face; **yakeru yóo na átsusa** burning heat of day; **muné ga yakeru** to have heartburn.

yakeshínu to perish by fire.

yaketsúku to scorch, burn; **yaketsúku yoo na táiyoo** burning sun.

yaki baking, roasting; firing of porcelain; tempering of a sword; vigor of a person. **Kono tóoki wa yaki ga íi desu.** This porcelain is well fired.

yakimashi further copies (prints) of a photograph.

yakimóchi toasted *mochi* (rice cake); jealousy; **yakimochi yáki** jealous person; **yakimóchi o yaku** to be jealous.

yákimoki suru to be impatient; to be nervous.

yakimono ceramic-ware, pottery; roast meat; steak.

yakin night duty, night work; **yakin o suru** to be on night duty.

yakinaoshi warming (of cooked food); literary rehash, adaptation; **yakinaoshi suru** to adapt from; to rehash. **Kore wa furui Nihon no shoosetsu no yakinaoshi desu.** This is an adaptation from an old Japanese story.

yakinaósu to bake for the second time; to roast again; to imitate.

yakiniku roast meat.

yakipan toast (bread).

yakitori roast fowl.

yakizákana broiled fish.

yákkai trouble; support; dependence; **yákkai o kakéru** to give trouble; to be under the care of; to be welcomed by; **yákkai na** troublesome, difficult, annoying; **yakkaimono** burden, drag, nuisance. **Yakkaibárai.** Good riddance to bad rubbish.

yakki to náru to get warm; to become excited.

YAKKYOKU pharmacy; dispensary.

yakoo réssha night train.

YAKU to burn; to set something on fire; to broil; to roast; to bake; to bake potatoes; **nikú o yaku** to roast meat; **sakana o yaku** to broil fish; **sumí o yaku** to make charcoal; **té o yaku** to burn one's fingers or hand.

YÁKU about, approximately; = **yakubun** translation, version; **yákusha** translator; **yakúsu, yaku suru** to translate.

yakú office; duty; part in a drama; **yakuba** office, public office; **yakumé** (official) duty; business; mission; **yakumé o hatásu** to discharge one's duties; **yakunin** government official; **yakusha** actor, actress; **yakusho** public office. **Yakú ni tátsu** to be of use; **yakú o tsutoméru** to play the part of.

yakuhin drugs, chemicals.

yakusoku promise; engagement; appointment; **yakusoku suru** to promise.

yakyuu baseball; **yakyuu o suru** to play baseball.

YAMÁ mountain; hill; mine; crown (of a hat); pile; speculation; climax (of a drama); **yama no yóo na** mountainous; **yamakúzure** landslide; **yamámichi** mountain road; **yamanóbori** mountain climbing; **yamabíraki** the opening of a mountain to pilgrims or climbers for the year; **yamadera** temple in the mountains; **yamáguri** mountainous country. **Koko ga kono shoosetsu no yamá desu.** Here is the climax of this novel. **Yamá ga atatta.** The speculation has turned out well.

yamadashi bumpkin, rustic.

yámai illness; **yámai ni kakáru** to become ill.

yamakaji forest fire.

yamamori heap; heaping up anything in measuring; heaping full. **Yamamori ni suru** to heap up; to fill to overflowing.

yamashíi to feel ashamed; to have qualms of conscience.

yamawake ni suru to divide equally into two parts.

yame end, conclusion, finish; abolition, stop, discontinuance; **yame ni suru** to be discontinued; **YAMERU** to stop; to break; to give up, abandon; to resign; to discontinue; **gakkoo o yameru** to leave school; **hanashí o yameru** to cease talking; **shoku o yameru** to retire from office; **toríhiki o yameru** to close an account.

yamiagari convalescence; **yamiagari no** convalescent.

yamitsuki infatuation; feeling ill; **yamitsuki ni náru** (*colloq.*) to develop into a passion; to be wholly given up to; **yamitsúku** (*colloq.*) to be taken ill; to be wholly given up to; to run madly after.

yamíyo dark night.

yamome widow.

YAMU to stop, cease, abate; to clamp down; to drop down; **yamu o énai** unavoidable; necessary; **yamu o ézu** unavoidably. **Áme ga yamimashita.** The rain has stopped.

yanami row of houses.

yáne roof; **yaneura** attic.

yánushi owner of a house; landlord.

yanwári softly; gently.

YAOYA fruit and vegetable market; greengrocer.

—YARA and so on; and the like; **náni yara káni yara** de with one thing or another.

yariba disposal place. **yariba ga nái** to be at a loss as to where to put (something); **yariba ni komáru** to be at a loss as to what to do with (something).

yaridásu to begin to do.

yarikake half-done, half-finished; **yarikakéru** to begin; to set about; to proceed to make; **yarikanéru** to hesitate to do (something). **Áno hito wa dónna kotó demo yarikanénai otokó da.** He is up to all sorts of things. He will go to any extreme; **yarikata** manner of doing; **yarikata ga íi** to go about one's task in the right way. **Sore wa yarikata shidai desu.** It depends on how you do it.

yarikoméru to silence; to snub; to put down; to argue down.

yarikuchi manner of acting; policy. **Yarikuchi ga shaku da.** I am displeased with his way of doing things.

yarikuri to make shift; **yarikuri o suru** to live by one's wits.

yarinaósu to do over again; to try again; to start over again; to resume.

yarippanashi ni suru to neglect; to leave in disorder.

yarisokonai failure.

yarisugíru to overdo; to go too far; to do too much.

yarisugósu to go past.

yaritogéru to accomplish, perform, achieve; to finish.

yarítori exchange; **yarítori suru** to exchange.

YARU to give, present (something to someone); to send, dispatch; to do; to undertake; **Kaneko-san ni hón o katte yaru** to buy a book for Kaneko; **tegami o yaru** to write a letter.

YASAI vegetables.

YASASHII gentle, tender; easy, simple; **yasashii mondai** easy question; **yasashii kotobá o kakéru** to speak kindly (words) to (someone).

yasegáman suru to endure (anything) because of pride.

yasei wildness; **yasei suru** to grow wild (without being cultivated).

YASERU to become lean (thin); to lose freshness.

yashiki mansion; premises; grounds; home site.

yashin ambition, aspiration; schemes; **yashin manman** highly ambitious; **yashin o idáku** to be ambitious; **yashinka** ambitious person.

yashinai nutrition; bringing up; **karada no yashinai ni náru** to be nutritious;

yashináu to bring up; to support; to subsist; to maintain; to feed.

yashináigo foster child.

yashinaioya foster father; foster mother.

yáshiro = **oyáshiro** Shinto shrine.

yasuágari (n.) being inexpensive, being cheap, being economic.

yasubúshin flimsily constructed building.

YASÚI cheap, inexpensive; **yasúi hon** cheap book; **yasumono** low priced (cheaply made) article. **Bukka ga yásuku nárimashita.** Prices have come down. **Yasumonókai no zeni úshinai.** Penny-wise and pound-foolish.

-YASÚI suffix denoting: easy to, simple to; **kowareyasúi** to be easy to break; **yomiyasúi** to be easy to read.

yasumáru to be rested; to feel at rest; **karada no yasumáru tokí ga nái** to be too busy to relax for a moment; **yasuméru** to rest (oneself); to give rest; to ease; **kadara o yasuméru** to rest from work; **ki o yasuméru** to set (one's mind) at ease.

YASUMI rest; recess; holiday; vacation; **natsuyásumi** summer vacation; **YASÚMU** to rest; to go to bed; to take a vacation; **gakkoo o yasúmu** to be absent from school; **yóru háyaku yasúmu** to go to bed early in the evening.

yasunzúru to be content (with); to rest satisfied; to be at ease; **í o yasunzúru** to set (someone's) mind at ease.

yasuppói cheap, flashy; mean; **yasuppóku miéru** to look cheap.

yasúraka na peaceful, calm; **yasúraka ni** peacefully, at rest.

yasuri file, rasp; **yasuri o kakéru** to file.

yasuúkeai ready promise; irresponsible promise; **yasuúkeai o suru** to promise readily; to promise without due consideration.

yasuuri bargain sale; **yasuuri o suru** to sell at a bargain price.

yasuyado lodging house; cheap inn.

yasuyásu easily, with ease.

yátai (n.) float (in a festival); one's fortune; **yátai mise** open-air stall (or booth).

yatara na careless; indiscriminate.

YATOI employment; employee; **yatoi gaikokújin** foreign employees; **yatoiire** employment, hire; **yatoiire kookokúran** want-ad column; **yatoinin** employee; servant; **yatóinushi** employer; **yatóu** to engage, employ, hire.

yatsuátari ni indiscriminately, recklessly.

yatsugibaya ni in rapid succession.

yatsuréru to get thin; to be worn out, to waste away; **míru kage mo náku yatsúrete iru** to be a mere shadow of one's former self.

yattee miru to try, attempt.

YATTO at last; with difficulty; **yatto kurashito iku** to have great difficulty making both ends meet; **Yatto kippu ga kaeta.** I could buy a ticket only with difficulty.

yattoko pincers, nippers; wrench.

YATTSU = HACHI eight. (See also **yooka, hachigatsu.**)

yattsukeru to attack.

yawarageru to soften, lessen, lighten; to moderate; to relax; **koe o yawarageru** to speak softly. **kotoba o yawarageru** to speak gently (with soft words); **yawaragu** to soften; to be softened; to become mild, become moderate; **YAWARAKAI** soft, gentle, tender, mild; **yawarakai niku** tender meat. **Arashi ga yawaragimashita.** The storm has abated.

yáya to some degree, somewhat. **Yáya shina ga ochiru.** It is somewhat inferior in quality.

YAYAKKOSHII difficult, complicated, intricate. **Yayakkoshii hanashi desu.** It is a complicated story.

yayamo sureba to be apt to, be liable to.

YŌ night, evening; world; age; times; *(when preceded by something)* above, over; more, than; **san mairu yo** over three miles; three miles plus; **yo o akasu** to pass a night without sleep; **yo ni deru** to see the light; to rise in the world; **yo o itou** to be weary of life; **yo o saru** to depart this life; to die. **Yo ga akeru.** The day is breaking.

yoakashi (n.) sitting up all night.

YOAKE dawn, daybreak; **yoake ni** at dawn, at daybreak.

yobawari (n.) calling (someone) by name; **dorobóo yobawari suru** to brand as a thief.

yóbi reserve; preparation; **yóbi no reserve**, spare; **yobíhin** spare store, reserve supply; **yobíkin** reserve fund, emergency fund.

yobiageru to call out, call up; **namae o yobiageru** to call out (someone's) **name.**

yobiatsuméru to call together, assemble, summon.

yobidashi subpoena; calling out; summoning; **yobidásu** to call out; to call up.

yobigoe cry; cry of street hucksters.

yobiiréru to call (someone) in; to hale (someone) into.

yobikakéru to call (out) to; to speak to, address.

yobiko whistle; birdcall; **yobikóbue** (police) whistle.

yobikomu to call a person in.

yobiokosu to wake, rouse; to call; **kioku o yobiokosu** to call to mind.

yobimono chief attraction; feature attraction; **kyoogi chuu no yobimono** feature attraction of the tournament.

yobirin (call) bell; buzzer.

yobitateru to call out; to call to; to ask to come.

yobitomeru to call and stop; to call to (someone) to stop; to call (someone) back.

yobiuri hawking.

yobiyoseru to call, summon, send for; to call together, assemble.

yoboo prevention, precaution; **yoboo chuusa** preventive injection, inoculation; **yoboo suru** to prevent; to keep as a precaution against.

yoboyobo tottering.

YOBU to call; to call out to; to nail; to call after; to send for; to invite; **isha o yobu** to send for a doctor.

yobun (n.) surplus, extra; **yobun no** (adj.) surplus, extra, remaining.

yobyoo complication.

yochi room, space; foresight; **yochi suru** to know beforehand.

yodan digression; **yodan ni wataru** to digress; **yodan wa shibaraku oki** to return to the main subject.

yodare saliva; **yodare o tarasu** to slobber.

yodooshi all night, all night through.

yofukashi o suru to keep late hours; to sit up late at night; **yofuke late hours; yofuke ni** late at night.

yogen prediction, prophecy; **yogen suru** to foretell, predict.

yogi bedcover.

yogi nai unavoidable.

yógisha night train.

yogore dirt, filth, soil; **yogoreme** visible stain; **yogoreru** to become dirty, become filthy; to be stained; **yogoreppói** easily soiled; liable to be soiled.

YOGOSU to make unclean; to stain; to soil, foul.

yóha aftermath; tail end; **taifuu no yóha** the end of a typhoon.

yohaku space; margin.

YOHODO to a great degree; very greatly; for a good while; **yohodo mae** quite a while ago; **yohodo no** large number of, great deal of.

yohoo forecast, prediction; **tenki yohoo** weather forecast; **yohoo suru** to forecast, predict.

yoi evening; **yoi no kuchi ni** in the early evening; **yoi no myoojoo** evening star; Venus.

YÓI = íi good, right, fine; **yói kangae** a good idea. **Sore de yói.** That will do. **Itte yói.** You may go.

yoí intoxication; **yoí ga deru** to become intoxicated; **yoí ga mawaru** to get tipsy; **yoí ga sameru** to sober up; **yoidore** drunkard; **yoidore ni naru** to be drunk.

yoigoshi overnight.

yoin trailing note, reverberation; agreeable aftertaste; suggestion; **yoin no aru** trailing; suggestive; pregnant.

yoippari (n.) sitting (staying) up very late; **yoippari no asaneboo** late to bed and late to rise.

yoizame (n.) sobering up.

yojiréru to be twisted, be contorted; **yojíru** to twist.

yóka spare time; **yóka ni** in spare time; **yóka ga aru** to have leisure; **yóka o riyoo suru** to take advantage of spare time.

yokan presentiment, premonition; chill in the air (early spring); **yokan ga suru** to have a premonition.

yokare ashikare right or wrong; rightly or wrongly.

yókaze night wind.

-yoke suffix denoting: shelter, screen; **hiyoke** sunshade.

YOKEI NA extra; unnecessary; enough and to spare; superfluous; **yokei na mono** unnecessary (thing); **yokei na hiyoo** extra expenses. **Yokei na osewa desu.** Mind your own business.

yokéru to avoid, shun; to keep off from; to keep aloof.

yoki expectation, anticipation; **yoki ni hanshite** contrary to expectation.

yoki shinai unexpected; unlooked for; **yoki suru** to expect, anticipate.

yokin money deposited; **yokin suru** to deposit money in the bank.

YOKKA four days, fourth day of the month.

yokkaku bathers; visitors at a spa (or hot spring).

yokkyuu craving, desire.

YOKO width; side; flank; **yoko no** sidelong; horizontal; **yoko ni** across, crossways; **yoko kara kuchi o dasu** to cut in; to put in a word; **yoko ni naru** to be down; **yokobai ni naru** to lie on one's side.

yokochoo lane; side street.

yokodori suru to snatch.

yokogiru to cross, traverse; to sail across; **toori o mukoo e yokogiru** to go across the street.

yokoku notice, announcement; **yokoku nashi ni** without warning; **yokoku no toori** as previously announced; **yokoku suru** to give notice in advance.

yokome sidelong glance; **yokome de miru** to look askance at; **yokome o tsukau** to cast a sidelong glance.

yokomichi byroad; wrong direction; digression; **yokomichi ni hairu** to deviate from.

yokomoji Occidental script or letters.

yokoo rehearsal; preliminary exercise.

yokoppara side (of the body).

yokoshima wickedness; **yokoshima na** wicked.

YOKOSU to send; to forward; to hand over, give over, deliver.

yokotaéru to lay down (something); **mi o byooshoo ni yokotaeru** to become ill; to lie down in a sickbed.

yokotaoshi ni náru to fall sideways.

yokotate length and breadth; **yokotate ni** lengthwise and breadthwise.

yokotawáru to lie down; to lie across; **nagaisu ni yokotawaru** to lie on a sofa.

yokoyari interruption (of conversation); **—ni yokoyari o ireru** to break in; to cut in.

yokozuke ni suru to bring alongside (a pier, etc.).

YÓKU well; finely; often; thoroughly. **Kono hon wa yoku kakete iru.** This book is written well.

yoku greed, desire;

yoku ni fukai avaricious, greedy; **yoku o hanarete** without ulterior motive; **yoku toku zuku de** for gain; for self-interest; **yokubari** greedy person; **yokubáru** to be avaricious, be greedy.

YOKUÁSA following (next) morning.

YOKUBAN following (next) evening.

yokuboo desire, ambition.

YOKUCHOO next morning.

YOKUGETSU next month.

YOKUJITSU next day.

yokujoo public bath.

yokume partiality, prejudice; **yokume de miru** to show prejudice. **Ikura yokume de mite mo.** Even if I give it the benefit of the doubt.

YOKUNEN next year.

yokusei control, suppression; **yokusei dekinai** uncontrollable; **yokusei suru** to control; to suppress.

YOKUSHITSU bathroom.

YOKUSOO bathtub.

yokusúru to bathe; to take a bath; **onkei ni yokusuru** to be favored with; **onten ni yokusuru** to receive a special favor.

yokutoku zuku self-interest; mercenariness; **yokutoku zuku de** from a selfish motive.

YOKUYOKU very, extremely; carefully; **yokuyoku iya ni natta** being quite sick of; **yokuyoku no koto de nakereba** unless driven to extremes; **yokuyoku no riyuu** a very strong reason.

YOKUYOKUJITSU next day but one; two days later.

YOKUYOKUNEN next year but one; two years later.

yokuyoo intonation, modulation; **yokuyoo no áru** modulated; **yokuyoo no nái** monotonous; **yokuyoo o tsukéru** to modulate.

yokyoo entertainment; extra show, side show.

yomáwari night watch; night watchmen.

yómei remainder of one's life; **yómei ikubaku mo nái** to have only a few years left (to live).

yoméru to be able to read; to read well; to see; to understand; to see through. **Kono shoosetsu wa chótto yoméru.** This novel is rather interesting (reading).

yomí reading; Japanese reading of a Chinese character (**kun** reading); **yomiagéru** to read out, read aloud; to finish reading, read through; **hón o yomiagéru** to read

through a book; **yomiayamari** misreading; mispronunciation; **yomiayamáru** to misread; to mispronounce; **yómikaki** (*n.*) reading and writing; **yómikaki ga dekíru** to be able to read and write; **yomikáta** reading, pronunciation; reading lesson; **yomikikaséru** to read (a book) to (someone); **yomikonásu** to digest what one reads; **yomímono** reading, reading matter; **kodomo no yomímono** children's books; juvenile literature; **yominaósu** to reread; **yominikúi** illegible; difficult to read; **yominikui jí** illegible handwriting; **yomiotósu** to overlook (miss) in reading; to skip (over); **yomiowaru** to read through; to finish reading; **yomité** poet; reader; **yomiyói** easy to read; legible; **yomiyói jí** legible handwriting; **YOMU** to read; to recite; to understand; to see; **hito no kaoiro o yómu** to read (someone's) face; **hito no shínchuu o yómu** to guess what a person means; **musabori yómu** to devour (a book); **utá o yómu** to recite a poem; to compose a poem; **zatto yómu** to run one's eyes over; to scan.

yómichi night journey; **yómichi o suru** to go by night.

yomigáeru to come to one's senses; to be freshened; to be brought to life; to rise from the dead. **Yomigáetta yóo na kokochi ga suru.** I feel myself again (a new man).

YÓN = YOTTSÚ = SHÍ four; **juuyón** fourteen; **yónjuu** forty.

yonabe night work; **yonabe o suru** to do night work.

YONAKA midnight; **yonaká ni** in the dead of night; in the middle of the night.

yonareru to get used to the world; to grow accustomed to the ways of the world; to grow worldly; **yonarénu** inexperienced; green; **yonáreta hito** man of the world. **Káre wa máda yonarenai.** He has seen little of life.

yondokoronái unavoidable; urgent; pressing; necessary; **yondokoronáku** unavoidably; out of necessity; unwillingly.

yonen nái wholly engrossed; earnest; eager; **kenkyuu ni yonen nái** to be absorbed in study.

yonjuu See **shijúu.**

yonónaka world; public; times; **yonónaka e déru** to start life; **yonónaka ga iyá ni náru** to be sick of the world.

—YÓO manner, style, way, appearance; main point, essence; business, task; use; service. **—no yóo na** of the manner of, like; **—no yóo ni** in the manner of; **yóo wa** in brief, in short; **yóo ga áru** to have business on hand; **yóo o tasu** to go to the toilet; **—no yóo desu** it's like. **Kúru yoo desu.** It appears that he is coming.

180

yóobo foster mother.

yooboo expectation; urgent request; look, countenance; **yooboo suru** to demand.

yoochíen kindergarten.

yoodan business talk.

yoodatéru to lend, advance (money); to accommodate.

yóodo iodine.

yoofúbo foster parents.

YOOFUKU Occidental clothes.

yoogísha suspect, suspected person.

yóogo protection, safeguard; **yóogo suru** to protect, defend.

yoogo wording; terms.

yóogu tools, implements.

yoogúruto yogurt.

yoohínten imported goods shop.

yoohoo direction for use; uses.

yóoi preparation, provision; prudence; **mán'ichi no yóoi o suru** to prepare for an emergency; **yóoi suru** to get ready.

YOOI easiness, simplicity; **yooi de nái** difficult; **yooi na** easy, simple.

yooiku suru to bring up; to rear.

yooikúin orphanage.

YOOJI = YÓO business (See also **yookén.**); toothbrush; toothpick.

yóoji infant; baby; childhood, early years.

yóoka adoptive family.

yóojin care, prudence; **yoojin bukái** careful; **yóojin no tame** as a precaution; **yóojin suru** to be careful; **yoojínboo** bodyguard.

yoojin high official.

yóojo adopted daughter.

yoojóo suru to take care of one's health.

YOOKA eight days; eighth day of the month.

yookai dissolution; melting, smelting, fusion; **yookai suru** to dissolve; melt; to smelt; to fuse.

yóokan Occidental-style building.

yóokan bitter-sweet jelly of beans (*popular snack or dessert item*).

yookén, yooji business; matter of business. **Náni ka goyooken ga arimásu ka?** Have you any business to transact?

yooki weather; gaiety; receptacle; vessel; **yooki na** bright; cheerful (of disposition); **yooki ni atarareru** to be affected by the weather; **yooki ni náru** to be merry, become lively.

yookoo traveling abroad; essential point; essentials; **yookoo suru** to go abroad.

yookyuu claim; demand; request; **yookyuu suru** to claim; to demand; **yookyúusha** claimant.

yóomu important mission.

yoomuki business; mission; errand; **yoomuki o tazunéru** to inquire into (someone's) business; to ask (someone) his business.

yoorei example.

yóoro important position; high office; **yóoro ni tátsu** to occupy an important position.

yooróoin old-age home, nursing home; **yooróokin** old-age pension.

YOORÓPPA Europe; **Yooroppajín** European.

yoosen letter paper.

yoosha náku without ceremony; mercilessly.

yóoshi point, gist; essential (important) points; summary; blank printed forms; **denpoo yóoshi** telegraph form.

yooshi adopted son; **yooshi o suru** to adopt a child.

yooshiki mode; form; style.

yoosho Occidental books.

yooshoku Occidental food; **yooshokuya** restaurant serving Occidental food.

yooshoku shínju cultured pearl.

yooshu (Occidental) wine.

yóoso essential element; important factor.

yoosoo Occidental-style books, clothes, dress; **yoosoo suru** to be dressed in European style.

YOOSU condition; circumstances; appearance; **—no yoosu o suru** to show signs of; **yoosu o ukagau** to observe; to see how things stand.

yoosúru to embrace, hug, take into one's arms; to have, possess.

yootáshi transacting business; government contractor; **yootáshi ni iku** to go out on an errand.

yootén gist; main point.

yóoto use; **yóoto ga hirói** to have various (many) uses.

YOOYAKU at last; at length; gradually; narrowly; **yooyaku ma ni áu** to be barely on time. **Yooyaku áme ga yanda.** At last the rain stopped.

yopparai drunkard, drunk.

yoréru to be twisted, get twisted; **yoreyore no** worn out; seedy; threadbare.

—YORI from; out of; at; in; since; than; before; **úmi no kánata yori** from beyond the sea. **A wa B yori sé ga takái.** A is taller than B. **Kái wa gógo yóji yori hajimaru.** The party is to begin at four in the afternoon.

yorí twist, ply; **yori ito** twisted thread; **yorí o kakéru** to give a twist.

yoriai meeting; gathering.

yoridásu to pick out, single out; to sort out.

yoridokoro ground; source; authority; reliance; **yoridokoro no áru** sure, reliable, authentic; **yoridokoro no nái** groundless, unfounded, unreliable.

yorikakáru to lean (stand) against.

yorimichi stop (on the way); **yorimichi o suru** to visit on the way; to break a journey.

yorinúku to choose, select, pick out; **yorinuki no** choice, select; **tasúu no uchi kara yorinúku** to pick (a few) out of a large number.

yorisóu to draw close, draw near; to nestle.

yoritóru to choose.

yoriwakéru to sort out, assort, classify; to pick out; to separate.

yorokeru to totter; to stagger.
YOROKÓBI joy, delight; congratulations; **yorokobi o noberu** to congratulate; **yorokobashíi** glad, joyous, delighted; **yorokobásu** to delight, rejoice; to bring joy, gladden; **YOROKÓBU** to be glad; to rejoice; to be delighted (at). **Konna yorokobashii koto wa arimasen.** Nothing gives me as much pleasure. **Yorokonde.** Gladly. With pleasure.
yóron public opinion.
YOROSHÍI = YÓI = ÍI to be good; to be permissible; to be acceptable.
YOROSHIKU well; properly; in an appropriate way; best regards. **Aoki-san ni yoroshiku.** Please remember me to Aoki.
yóroyoro unsteadily; **yóroyoro to arúku** to walk unsteadily (feebly or drunkenly).
yorozuya general store.
YÓRU evening, night.
yoru to depend on; to hang on; to be based upon, be founded on; **goirai ni yori** at your request; **saikin no chóosa ni yoréba** according to the latest information.
yoseru to let approach, let come near; to bring near; to draw near; to add; **isu o yoseru** to draw up one's chair; **—ni mi o yoseru** to become dependent on.
yóshi all right; well; good; now; even if, though; reason, significance, cause, means, effect; **yóshi naki** silly; **yóshi nanigoto ga okoróo tomo** whatever may happen. **—no yóshi** They say that . . . **Yóshi bóku ga yatte miyóo.** Now I'll try.
yoshin preliminary tremors; preliminary examination.
yoshuu preparation; rehearsal; **yoshuu suru** to prepare lessons; to rehearse.
YOSÓ somewhere else; another place; **yosó de** elsewhere, somewhere else; **yoso goto** another's affair; **yosó mi** looking off, aside, away.
yosoku estimation; estimate; forecast; **yosoku suru** to estimate, to forecast, predict.
yosoo anticipation; expectation; **yosoo suru** to expect, anticipate; **yosóogai ni** unexpectedly; **yosóogai no** unexpected.
yosoóu to dress (attire, equip) oneself in.
YÓSU to stop; to drop; to leave off; to give up; to cut off; **tabako o yósu** to stop smoking. **Joodan wa yóse.** None of your jokes.
yosutébito hermit; monk.
yótayota unsteadily.
yotei plan; schedule; **yotei no tóori** as prearranged.
yótsugi heir; heiress.
yotsukado crossroads; corner of the street.
YOTTE and so, consequently, therefore.
yótto a yacht.
YOTTSÚ = YÓN = SHÍ four. **Yottsu kaimáshita.** I bought four of them.

yóu to get drunk; to feel sick (from motion); **fúne ni yóu** to get seasick; **hikooki ni yóu** to get airsick; **sake ni yóu** to get drunk.
YOWAI weak; feeble (in body); poor-spirited; delicate (things); mild, gentle; **ki no yowái** faint-hearted; softhearted, limited; **karada ga yowái** to have a weak constitution; to be in poor health; **yowamí** weakness, feebleness; **yowamí ni tsukekómu** to take advantage of (someone's) weak point; **yowamí o miséru** to display cowardice; **yowámushi** weak person; crybaby; **yowané** weakness; confession of weakness; **yowané o fuku** to betray weakness; to complain.
yowaki (stock-market term) bears; shorts; selling spirit.
yowátari (n.) going through the world; living; **yowátari no hetá na** dull-witted, shiftless; **yowátari no joozú na** shrewd, hard-headed.
yoyaku reservation; advance booking; **yoyaku suru** to book in advance; to subscribe to; **yoyaku mooshikomíkin** subscription (money); initial installment; **yoyákusha** subscriber.
yoyuu spare, reserve (money, time, etc.); **yoyuu shakushaku** to have a good deal in reserve.
YÚ = OYU hot water; **yú ni háiru** to take a bath; **yú o tsukawaseru** to bathe (a child or invalid); **yú o sásu** to pour hot water; **yú o wakasu** to boil water.
YUBÍ finger, toe; **yubí o kuwaeru** to look with envy; **yubiwa o yubí ni hameru** to put a ring on a finger.
YÚBUNE bathtub.
yudan negligence; inattention; carelessness; imprudence; unguarded moment; **sukoshi mo yudan ga nái** to be always on one's guard; **yudan suru** to be negligent. **Yudan taiteki.** Danger comes soonest when it is despised.
YUDAYÁJIN Jew, Jewish.
yudéru to boil; to seethe.
YUDONO bathroom (for bathing only).
yuen lampsoot, lampblack; **yuen ga tátsu** to smoke.
yugaméru to distort; to contort; to crook, bend; to curve; to warp; **kao o yugaméru** to make a wry face; **yugámu** to warp; to swerve, deflect; to be crooked or distorted.
yúge jet of steam, vapor; **yúge o tátete okóru** to fume (with anger).
yuigon testament, will; one's dying wish. **yuigon o káku** to make a will; **yuigon o sézu ni shinu** to die intestate; **yuigon suru** to leave a will.
yúiitsu only, sole; unique.
yuisho lineage, blood; history.
YUKA floor; **yuka o háku** to sweep the floor; **yukaita** floor board.

yúkai pleasure; happiness; merriment; **yúkai na** pleasant, happy, merry, joyful.

yukashíi attractive; amiable; winning, engaging.

yukata light, unlined cotton garment worn in summer.

yuketsu blood transfusion.

YUKI = IKI going; bound for; **Oosaka yuki no kishá** the Osaka train.

YUKÍ snow; **yukí o itadaku** snow-capped; **yukí o káku** to shovel away the snow; **yukidoke** thawing (of ice and snow); **yukidoke ga suru** to thaw; **yukí ga fúru** to snow. **Yukí ga tsumóru.** The snow covers the ground.

yukiatari báttari rashly; impetuously; on the spur of the moment; **yukiatari báttari ni yaru** to take chances, to act impetuously.

yukichigai (n.) crossing. **Kimi no tegami wa bóku no to yukichigai ni nátta.** Your letter crossed mine.

yukidomari blind alley; dead end (of a street); impasse.

yukigakari circumstances; convention.

yukigake ni on one's way to.

yukiki going and coming; traffic; **yukiki no hito** passers-by; acquaintances; **yukiki suru** to come and go; to associate.

yukisaki one's destination.

yukitodóku to be scrupulous; to be prudent, be careful; to be attentive.

yukitsuke no favorite; regular; **yukitsuke no mise** one's favorite shop.

yukiwatáru to extend; to prevail; to spread; to penetrate; to pervade.

yukizumáru to stand still; to arrive at a deadlock; **kotobá ga yukizumáru** to be at a loss for words.

YUKKÚRI slowly, at leisure, leisurely; **yukkúri suru** to enjoy one's free time. **Yukkúri nasái.** Stay as long as you can.

YUKU = IKU to go, proceed; to travel; **kishá de yuku** to go by train; **úmaku yuku** to go well; to be successful. **Ashitá wa ikanai.** I'm not going tomorrow. **Háyaku itte kudasái.** Please go early.

yukue (n.) whereabouts; **yukue fúmei** missing; **yukue o kuramasu** to conceal oneself; **yukue o sagasu** to trace (someone).

yukusaki destination; future.

yukusue (n.) future.

yukute way; path; **yukute o saegíru** to stand in the way; **yukute o terasu** to light the way.

yukuyuku on the way; **yukuyuku wa in the end, in the course of time.**

yumé dream; **yume no yó dream world; —o yumé ni míru** to see in a dream; **yumé kara saméru** to wake from a dream; to be disillusioned; **yumé o míru** to dream.

YUNOMI mug, cup.

YUNYUUHIN imports, imported goods.

yurai origin; history; **yurai suru** to originate.

yure shake, sway, rock, jolt, roll, pitch; **yureru** to shake, rock, pitch; to tremble; **yuriokósu** to shake up; to wake up by shaking; **yuru** to shake; to swing; to joggle.

yurúi (adj.) relaxed, loosening, slack; **yuruméru** to loosen, unloose; to unbend, relax; **té o yuruméru** to loosen one's hold of; **yurúmu** to loosen, become (get) loose; to abate. **Ki ga yurunde iru.** His attention is wandering.

yurushí permission, leave; license; initiation; pardon, forgiveness; **yurushí o éte** with permission; **yurushí o kóu** to ask permission; **YURÚSU** to permit, allow; to approve; **jikan no yurúsu kágiri** so far as time permits.

yurúyaka na lenient; mild; **yurúyaka na saká** a gentle slope.

yúruyuru slowly, leisurely.

YUSHUTSU export, exportation; **yushutsu suru** to export; **yushutsúhin** exports.

yusoo transportation, conveyance; **yusoo suru** to convey, transport.

yusuburu to shake; to swing.

YUSUGU to wash out; to rinse.

yusuri extortion, blackmail; blackmailer; **yusuru** to extort (money), blackmail; to squeeze.

yútaka na abundant, plentiful, copious. **Rokushaku yútaka na ooótoko desu.** He measures a full six feet.

yutánpo hot-watter bottle. **Yutánpo o irete oyasuminasái.** Get into bed with a hot-water bottle.

yutori (n.) room, margin; elbow room; spare (money, time); **yutori o tóru** to leave some room for.

yuttári shita easy; composed; **yuttári shita kimochi ni náru** to feel easy; to feel at home.

YUU = IU to speak, talk; to mention.

YUU to tie; to dress; to arrange; **kamí o yuu** to dress one's hair.

YUUBE last night; yesterday evening. (See also **sakúban.**)

yuuben eloquence; **yuuben na** eloquent, fluent; **yuuben o furuu** to speak eloquently; **yuubenka** eloquent speaker.

yúubi grace, elegance; refinement; **yúubi na** graceful, elegant.

YUUBIN mail, post; **gaikoku yúubin** foreign mail; **yuubin chókin** postal savings; **yuubin haitatsufu** mailman; **yuubin káwase** money order; **YUUBÍN KÍTTE** postage stamp; **sokutatsu yúubin** special delivery; **yuubin o dásu** to send a letter by mail; **YUUBÍNBAKO** mailbox, letter box; **yuubínbutsu** mail, postal matter; **dái ísshu yuubínbutsu** first-class mail; **dái níshu yuubínbutsu** second-class mail;

YUUBÍNKYOKU post office. (See also **yuusóoryoo**.)

yuuboo hopefulness; **yuuboo na** hopeful, promising; **zénto yuuboo na seinen** a promising youth.

yúuchoo na sedate, calm, composed; tedious, wearisome, slow.

YUUDACHI shower; **yuudachi ga kúru** to have a shower; **yuudachi ni áu** to be caught in a shower.

yuudai na magnificent, imposing.

yuudoku na poisonous, venomous.

yuudoo inducement; **—o yuudoo suru** to draw, lure, lead.

yuueki usefulness; benefit, advantage; instructiveness; **yuueki na** useful, advantageous; **yuueki désu** to be useful; to be beneficial; **yuueki ni tsukau** to make the best use of.

yuuénchi recreation ground; public playground.

yuuetsu superiority, supremacy; **yuuetsu suru** to be superior to, to surpass; **yuuétsukan** sense of superiority.

yuugai bad, harmful, injurious; **kenkoo ni yuugai de áru** to be bad for the health.

YUUGATA evening.

yúugi play, game, amusement; **yúugi o suru** to play a game.

yuugoo melting, fusion, union; harmony; **yuugoo suru** to melt down; to harmonize; to fuse, unite.

yuuguu warm treatment; **—ni yuuguu sareru** to be received cordially by; **—o yuuguu suru** to give a warm reception to.

YUUHAN supper, evening meal.

yuuhi setting sun.

yúui na capable, able, efficient; **shóorai yúui na** promising.

YUUJIN friend, companion.

yuujoo friendliness; friendly feelings.

yuujuufudan irresolution, indecision; **yuujuufudan no** irresolute.

yuukai abduction, kidnaping; **yuukai suru** to kidnap; **yuukáisha** kidnaper.

yuukan evening issue, evening paper.

yuukan na brave, courageous, daring; **yuukan ni** courageously.

yuukénsha elector, voter.

yúuki courage, valor; **yúuki rinrin** spiritedly; bravely; **yúuki o dásu** to gather one's courage; **yúuki o ushináu** to lose courage.

yuukoo na efficient; meritorious; **yuukoo de áru** to be effective, to hold good; **yuukoo ni tsukau** to make good use of.

yuukyuu salaried.

yuumei na famous, noted, celebrated; **yúumei ni náru** to become famous.

yúumoa humor; **yúumoa ni tómu** to have a sense of humor.

yunyúu import, importation; **yunyúu suru** to import; be introduced.

YUURANBÁSU sight-seeing bus.

yúuretsu superiority; inferiority; merits; difference; **yúuretsu ga nái** to be equal; **yúuretsu o arasóu** to strive for superiority.

yúuri being profitable.

yúuryo anxiety, concern; **yúuryo subéki** serious, grave; **yúuryo suru** to become anxious about, become troubled.

yuuryokka influential person; **yuuryoku na** powerful, influential; controlling.

yuuryoo na superior, excellent, choice; **yuuryoo na seiseki** excellent result.

YUUSÉN DÉNWA telephone.

yuusénken priority, first claim.

yúushi volunteer; supporter; interested person.

yuushoo victory; superiority.

yuushuu superiority; sublimity, excellence; **yuushuu na** superior, best, excellent.

yuusóoryoo postage. (See also **yuubin, yuuzei**.)

yuutai generous treatment; hospitality, welcome; voluntary resignation; voluntary retirement; **yuutai o ukéru** to be welcomed at; **—o yuutai suru** to resign or retire voluntarily.

yuutoo superiority; excellency; top grade; **yuutoo no** high-grade, superior, excellent, first-rate; **yuutoo de sotsugyoo suru** to graduate with honors.

yuuutsu na melancholy, cheerless, gloomy.

yuuwa suru to melt; to soften; to soothe; to conciliate, placate, propitiate; to be reconciled with.

yuuwaku temptation, enticement; **yuuwaku suru** to tempt, entice; **yuuwaku to tatakau** to resist temptation.

yuuyake evening glow; afterglow.

yuuyami twilight, dusk; **yuuyami semáru kóro** in the gathering dusk.

yúuyo delay; hesitation; extension of time, grace, reprieve; **yúuyo náku** without delay; without allowing an extension; **yúuyo o atáeru** to give an extension; **yúuyo suru** to hesitate, give time.

yuuyoo usefulness; **yuuyoo na** useful, serviceable; **yuuyoo ni** usefully, effectively.

yuuyúu leisurely; deliberately; serenely, placidly, calmly.

yuuzai guiltiness; conviction; culpability; **yuuzai no** guilty.

yuuzei postage. (See also **yuubin, yuusóoryoo**.)

yuuzuu circulation (of a bill or note); accommodation; versatility; adaptability; **yuuzuu o kikasu** to adapt oneself; **—o yuuzuu suru** to advance money.

YÚYA = FURÓYA public bath; bathhouse.

yuzuriáu to compromise, concede mutually, meet halfway.

yuzuriukéru to obtain by transfer; to take over; to inherit.

yuzuriwatashi alienation; conveyance; transfer.

yuzuru to make over; to hand over; to transfer; to part with; **hito ni séki o yuzuru** to make room for; **ippo mo yuzuranai** not to yield a step.

Z

záazaa plenty, freely, profusely (said of rain or water); **záazaa mizu o nagásu** to let water run freely. **Áme ga záazaa fútte iru.** It is pouring.

ZABÚTON cushion to sit on; **zabúton o shiku** to seat oneself on a cushion.

zadan familiar conversation, table talk; **zadánkai** (discussion) meeting.

záiaku sin, transgression, offense, crime; **záiaku o okasu** to commit a sin; to commit a crime.

zaibatsu powerful financial group.

zaichuu containing. **"Insatsúbutsu zaichuu." "**Printed matter only."

zaidan foundation; financial group.

zaigai abroad, overseas; **zaigai nipponjín** Japanese residents abroad.

zaigaku in school; **zaigaku chuu** while in school; **zaigaku suru** to be in school, at school.

zaigen source of revenue; resources; **zaigen ni toboshíi** to lack financial resources.

zaigoo sins, sinful acts; **zaigoo no fukái** sinful.

ZAIJUU residence; **Nyuuyóoku zaijuu no Nipponjín** Japanese residents in New York.

zaikyoo (*n.*) being in the capital; staying in Tokyo; **zaikyoo no yuujin** a friend in the capital (in Tokyo).

zaimoku wood, timber, lumber.

záinin criminal, offender, malefactor.

záirai existing hitherto; **záirai no** usual, ordinary, conventional.

záiryoku financial status.

zairyóo raw material; data.

zairyuu residing, dwelling; **—ni zairyuu suru** to reside in.

zaisan property; fortune; **zaisan o tsukúru** to make a fortune; **zaisanka** man of fortune.

zaisei finance; financial affairs; **zaisei joo** financially, from a financial point of view; **zaisei joo no fiscal.**

zaishoku service; tenure (of office); **zaishoku chuu** during one's term of office.

ZAITAKU being at home. **Myóonichi wa gozaitaku deshóo ka?** Will you be at home tomorrow?

zakka miscellaneous goods; **zakkashoo** grocer; drygoods store.

zákkubaran na frank, plain, outspoken; **zákkubaran ni** frankly, plainly; **zákkubaran ni hanásu** to speak plainly.

zánbu remainder, rest, balance.

zanbú to with a great splash.

zangé repentance; penitence; confession of sins; **zangé suru** to repent, be penitent.

zangén slander; false charge.

zankoku cruelty, brutality; harshness, cold-heartedness; inhumanity; **zankoku na** cruel, brutal, merciless, harsh; **zankoku ni atsukau** to treat cruelly.

zánmu remaining business; **zánmu o séiri suru** to wind up affairs.

zannén regret, chagrin; mortification; **zannén na** regrettable; mortifying; **zannén ni omóu** to regret; to be sorry for.

zannin brutality, cruelty; cold-heartedness; **zannin na** brutal, cruel; **zannin ní mo** brutally, cruelly; **zanninsei** cruel nature.

zanpai rout, crushing defeat; **zanpai suru** to be routed, be beaten to the ground.

zanshi suru to be killed in an accident.

zánsho heat of late summer, lingering summer, Indian summer.

zansónsha survival; **zanson suru** to survive; to subsist; to remain, be left.

zappaku na loose; unsystematic, incoherent; crude; **zappaku na gíron** poor argument.

zappi miscellaneous expense; incidental expense.

zappoo general news; **zappóoran** news columns.

ZARA NI in plenty; plentifully; everywhere; **zara ni áru** to be very common; to be found everywhere.

zárazara rough feeling; **zárazara suru** to feel rough.

zaseki seat; room.

zasetsu breakdown; setback; collapse; discouragement; **zasetsu suru** to break down, receive a setback; to become discouraged; to collapse. **Keikaku wa chuuto de zasetsu shita.** The plan collapsed before it was completed.

ZASHIKÍ room; living room in a Japanese house; **kyaku o zashikí e tóosu** to show a visitor into the living room.

zashoo suru to run ashore, run aground; to be stranded.

ZASSHI magazine, periodical, journal; **zasshi o tóru** to subscribe to a magazine.

zasshu crossbreed, hybrid; variety; various kinds; **zasshu no** mixed, crossbred, hybrid; **zasshu o tsukúru** to cross, interbreed.

zatsudan chatting, gossiping; **zatsudan suru** to gossip, chat.

zatsuji miscellaneous affairs.

zátsumu routine work; miscellaneous business; **zátsumu ni owareru** to be kept busy with miscellaneous business.

zatsu na rough, coarse; miscellaneous; **zatsu ni káku** to write carelessly, scribble; to draw roughly; **zatsu na kotobá o tsukau** to speak roughly; **zatsu na tatekáta** crude (flimsy) construction.

zatsuon hubbub; murmur; static (on the radio).

zatsuyoo miscellaneous business.

zatsuzen disorder, confusion; indiscriminately, desultorily; **zatsuzen to shita** disorderly; desultory; indiscriminate. **Zatsuzen to tsumikasánete áru.** They are heaped in disorderly fashion.

zatta no sundry, miscellaneous, various, diverse; all sorts of; **zatta no mono** all sorts of things.

ZATTO roughly; hastily; briefly; approximately; **zatto shita** rough, cursory, coarse; **zatto shita mitsumori** rough estimate; **zatto mé o tóosu** to glance cursorily through (a book); **zatto setsumei suru** to explain briefly.

zattoo bustle; congestion; confusion; **zattoo shita machi** busy street; **zattoo suru** to bustle; to be crowded (with).

zawameki to be noisy; to rustle.

zawatsuku to be noisy; to rustle; to murmur; to be agitated.

záwazawa murmuringly, rustlingly; noisily; **záwazawa suru** to be noisy; to be agitated.

zé ga hi demo whether right or wrong; by hook or by crook; by all means. **Zé ga hi demo sore o té ni irenákereba naránai.** By hook or by crook, I must get it.

ZÉHI by all means; under any circumstance.

ZÉI tax, duty; rate; **zéi o chooshuu suru** to collect taxes; **zéi o kasúru** to impose a tax (on); to levy a tax; **zéi o osaméru** to pay taxes; **zeikan** customs; customhouse.

zeitáku, zeitakúhin luxury; extravagance; **zeitáku na** luxuriant, extravagant; **zeitáku ni** luxuriantly, extravagantly; **zeitáku ni kurasu** to live in luxury; **zeitáku o iu** to ask too much; **zeitáku o suru** to indulge in luxury.

zekkoo severance of a friendship or acquaintanceship.

zekkoo no finest, best; capital, splendid; **zekkoo no kikái** splendid opportunity; golden opportunity.

zekkyoo exclamation, ejaculation; **zekkyoo suru** to exclaim; to shout, yell.

zen Buddhist sect emphasizing religious meditation.

zén'aku good and bad; right and wrong.

zenbu first part; front; forepart.

ZÉNBU (*n., adv.*) all parts, whole, entire lot; **zenbu de** altogether; in all.

zenbun complete sentence; full text.

zénchi complete recovery; perfect cure; **zénchi suru** to be completely cured or recovered.

zenchoo presage, omen; sign, symptom.

zéndai mimon no unprecedented, unheard-of; record-breaking.

ZENGAKU total amount, sum total.

ZÉNGO before and after; order; thereabouts; somewhere about; **zengo no kankei** context (of a sentence); **zéngo o tsuujite** from the first to the last.

zéngo fukaku (*n.*) being unconscious; **zéngo fukaku ni** quite unconsciously.

zengósaku remedial measures; **zengósaku o koozúru** to consider the remedies.

zén'i good intention; good faith; **zén'i no** well-meant, well-intentioned, in good faith.

zenin approval; **zenin suru** to approve.

zen'in whole House (Diet); everybody present; all members.

ZENJITSU previous day, day before.

zenjutsu no previously mentioned, above-mentioned.

zénka previous criminal record; **zenkamono** ex-convict.

zenkai complete recovery of health.

zénkai last occasion; previous installment; **zénkai ni** last time, previously; **zénkai no** last, previous.

zénkan whole volume, entire book.

zenkei whole view; panoramic view; bird's-eye view.

zenken full power; full authority; **zenken o inin suru** to entrust a person with full power (or authority).

zénki previous period; first term; first half of the year; **zénki no** afore-mentioned, above-mentioned; **zénki no tóori** as mentioned above.

zénkoku whole country, whole land; **zénkoku ni** throughout the country; **zenkokuteki no** national, country-wide.

zenkoo good conduct, good deed.

zénkoo whole school; **zenkoo seito** the whole student body.

zenmai flowering fern; spring (of clocks, etc.).

zenmetsu annihilation, extermination; **—o zenmetsu saseru** to annihilate.

zennan zénnyo pious men and women, pious people.

zennín virtuous person.

zennoo advance payment; **zennoo suru** to pay in advance.

zenpai total abolition; complete defeat, crushing defeat; **zenpai suru** to abolish, make a clean sweep of; to suffer a crushing defeat.

zenpan first half.

ZENPOO front; **zenpoo ni** ahead, in front; **zenpoo no** front, forward.

zenpuku no utmost, greatest; whole-hearted; **zenpuku no dóryoku o suru** to exert oneself to the utmost.

zenrei precedent; previous example; **zenrei no nái** unprecedented.

zénretsu front rank.

zénryoku all one's energy (strength, power); **zénryoku o tsukúsu** to do one's best.

zenryoo goodness, integrity; **zenryoo na** good, virtuous, honest.

zensei height of prosperity; zenith of power; **zensei jídai** golden age; age of prosperity; **zensei o kiwaméru** to be at the height of prosperity.

zensékai whole world; world at large; zensekai ni all over the world.

zénsha former, prior.

zenshaku (*n.*) advance.

zénshi whole city; all over the city; zénshi itáru tokoró ni everywhere in the city; zenshímin all the citizens; all the residents of the city.

zenshin advance, progress; gradual (slow but steady) advance; whole body; full-length photo (of the body); all over the body; antecedents; (one's) past; good sense; conscience; zenshin fuzui total paralysis; zenshin fuzui ni naru to become paralyzed; zenshin ni tachikaeru to come to one's senses; to see the error of one's ways; zenshin suru to advance, press forward, advance gradually, move step by step.

zénsho taking proper measures; zénsho suru to manage tactfully.

zenshoo complete victory; unbroken series of victories; complete destruction by fire; zenshoo suru to be entirely destroyed by fire; to win a victory.

zenshóogai one's whole life; zenshóogai o tsuujíte throughout one's life.

ZENSHUU last week; preceding week; week before; complete works; complete collection; zenshuu no kyóo just a week ago.

zensokúryoku full speed, top speed; zensokúryoku o dásu to go at full speed.

ZENTAI whole body; entirety; naturally; as a matter of course; on earth; zentai de in all, altogether; zentai to shite in general; zentai ni wholly, entirely, generally; zentai no whole, entire, complete.

zénto future; prospect; future career; zénto ni nozomi o kakéru to pin one's hopes on one's future; zénto ryooen the goal is a long way off.

ZÉN'YA previous night; sono zén'ya night before.

zen'yaku complete translation; previous engagement.

ZENZEN entirely, completely, wholly; thoroughly; exactly; at all. Zenzen shiranai. I don't know at all.

zeppan out of print.

zeppeki precipice, cliff.

zéro zero, nought, nothing.

zessei matchless, peerless.

zesshoku fasting, abstention from food; zesshoku suru to go without food.

zessoku cessation of breathing; expiration; zessoku suru to die, expire.

zessúru to go out of existence, become extinct; to exceed, be beyond (something).

zetchoo highest point, summit, zenith; zetchoo ni tassúru to reach the summit.

zetsuboo despair, hopelessness; zetsubooteki no hopeless, desperate; mattaku zetsuboo de áru to be utterly hopeless; zetsuboo suru to despair, give up hope.

zetsudai no gigantic, colossal, enormous; zetsudai no dóryoku o suru to make a supreme effort.

zetsuen isolation; insulation; zetsuen suru to sever connections with; to insulate; zetsuen'sen insulated wire.

zetsumei death; zetsumei suru to die, expire.

zetsumetsu extermination; extinction; zetsumetsu suru to exterminate, stamp out; to die out.

zétsumu nil, nought, nothing; —wa zétsumu de áru there can be no such.

ZETTAI absoluteness, positiveness; zettai ni decidedly, absolutely; zettai no absolute, positive; zettai zetsumei desperation, last extremity.

zokkai = zoku world; life; laity; zokkai no worldly, mundane.

zokkoo continuation; zokkoo suru to continue, proceed with.

zokkoku dependency; subject state, tributary.

zoku world, people; laity; zoku na worldly; popular; common; vulgar; zoku ni commonly, popularly; zokuaku being coarse, vulgar, gross, unrefined.

zokuhatsu, zokushutsu successive occurence; zokuhatsu suru to occur in succession.

zokuhen sequel.

zokusetsu common saying; popular view; tradition.

zokushoo popular designation; popular name.

zoku súru to belong to; to pertain to; to come under. Beikoku ni zoku súru. It belongs to the United States.

zókuzoku successively, in rapid succession; zókuzoku suru to feel chilly; to shiver; to thrill.

zonbun to the full; to one's heart's content; omóu zonbun naku to cry to one's heart's content.

zonmei living, being alive; existence; zonmei chuu ni during one's lifetime; zonméisha survivor.

zonzái na careless, inattentive; rough; rude; zonzái ni roughly, crudely, carelessly; zonzái na mono no iikata o suru to be rough spoken; zonzái ni káku to write carelessly.

zonzúru to know; to be aware of, be conscious of; to think; to be acquainted with. Kono fukín wa yóku zonjíte imásu. I know this neighborhood well. Sonó hito o go-zónji desu ká? Are you acquainted with him?

zóo image, statue, statuette; figure; elephant.

zoochiku extension; addition; zoochiku suru to enlarge; to build an extension.

zoochoo presumption; zoochoo suru to become arrogant.

zooen reinforcements; zooen suru to reinforce.

zoogaku increase, augmentation; zoogaku o

suru to increase, raise (money, salary, etc.).

zoogen increase and/or decrease.

zóoho supplement, enlargement;—o zóoho suru to enlarge, supplement.

zoohoo salary increases; zoohoo suru to give a raise (in salary);—ga zoohoo ni natta. He got a raise.

zooin increase in personnel; increased staff.

zooka increase, augmentation; zooka suru to increase, augment; zookáritsu the rate of increase.

zoohéikyoku mint (for money).

zookin cleaning rag; mop.

zookyuu wage increase, pay increase; zookyuu suru to increase wages.

zóoo hatred, spite, antipathy.

ZOORI sandals; zoori o haku to wear sandals.

zoosaku fittings; furniture; alterations; features; zoosaku no sorótta kao regular features, comely face; zoosaku o suru to make alterations in a house. Zoosakuzuki kashiya. Furnished house to let.

ZOOSA NÁI not difficult, easy, simple; zoosa náku easily, without difficulty.

zoosen shipbuilding; zoosenjo shipyard, dockyard.

zooshi increase in capital; —ni zooshi suru to increase the capital . . .

zooshin promotion; betterment; increase; zooshin suru to promote; to increase; to be conducive to; nooritsu o zooshin suru to increase efficiency.

zoosho collection of books.

zooshuu additional income; increase of receipts.

zoosui rise (swelling) of a river; zoosui suru to rise, swell.

zootei presentation, offer; zootei suru to present; to give a present; zootéihin gift, present; zootéisha giver.

zootoo exchange of presents; zootoo suru to exchange presents; zootóohin presents, gifts.

zoowai bribery, corruption; zoowai suru to bribe; to offer a bribe; zoowai jíken bribery case; zoowáisha briber.

zóoyo presentation; donation; present; zóoyo suru to present; to donate; zooyósha donor.

zoozei increase in taxation, tax increase; zoozéi an bill for an increase in taxation; ichíwari no zoozei a 10 per cent increase in taxation; zoozei suru to increase taxes.

zórozoro dragging along, trailing along; going with many followers. Minná ga zórozoro tsúite arúku. They follow at his heels.

zotto suru to shudder, shiver; to feel shocked. hito o zotto saseru to make (someone) shudder; kángáete mo zotto suru to shudder at the thought of.

zu drawing, picture; diagram; map; zu de setsumei suru to illustrate by a diagram; zu ni noru to be puffed up; zu o hiku to draw a diagram.

-zu a negative-ending denoting: not, without. Góban o tabézu ni ikimáshita. He went there without eating.

zuan plan, design; sketch; zuan o tsukúru to prepare a design; zuanka designer, draftsman.

zúbazuba (colloq.) frankly, candidly; zubazuba itte shimau to speak frankly.

ZUBÓN trousers, pants.

zubora negligence; nonchalance; slovenliness; zubora na negligent, slovenly; zubora ni negligently; with nonchalance; zubora ni náru to become negligent.

zuboshi bull's eye, mark; zuboshi o sasaréru to hit the mark.

zubunure ni náru to become soaked (drenched) to the skin.

zubutói bold, daring, audacious; impudent; zubutói yátsu bold fellow; zubutói kotó o suru to do a bold thing.

zudón to with a bang, with a thud. Zudón to teppoo no otó ga shita. Bang! went the gun.

zugayóoshi drawing paper.

ZUIBUN fairly, pretty, tolerably; extremely; zúibun na awful, nasty, very disagreeable; zúibun samúi very cold.

zuihitsu stray notes; essay; jottings; miscellaneous writings.

ZUII liberty, freedom; absence of restraint; zuii ni freely, voluntarily; zuii no free, voluntary, optional. Gozuii ni meshiagatte kudasái. Please help yourself.

zúiichi (n.) best; foremost; Nippon zúiichi no sakura no meisho the most famous place for cherry-blossoms in Japan. Sékai zúiichi desu. It is the largest in the world.

zuiji at any time; as occasion demands.

zuikoo accompanying; attendance on a journey; zuikoo suru to accompany (someone).

zuikóoin staff (personnel), attendants.

zujoo overhead; over one's head; zujoo ni óchite kuru to fall on one's head; zujoo o tobu to fly overhead.

zukai illustration, graphic representation; zukai suru to illustrate; zukai shite setsumei suru to illustrate with a diagram.

zúkazuka straightly, directly.

zúkizuki itámu = zúkizuki suru to throb with pain.

zumen drawing, plan, map.

-zumi suffix denoting: maximum weight capacity of; shipment by; kisenzumi shipment by freight; kyuutonzumi kásha nine-ton freight car.

zungari shita dumpy, stocky.

ZÚNOO head; brains; zúnoo meiseki no

clear-headed; **zúnoo o yoosúru
shigoto** brain work.

zunúkete exceptionally, extraordinarily; far
above the average; **zunúkete sé no
takái kodomo** an exceptionally tall
child.

zúnzun rapidly; apace; in leaps and bounds;
zúnzun saki e iku to go ahead at a
rapid pace; **zúnzun susumu** to proceed
rapidly.

zurarí to all in a row; in a long row; **zurarí to
narabu** to stand in a long row; to sit in
a long row.

zuréru to slip down; to slip off.

zúru (*n.*) cheating; (*v.*) to slip down. **Zubón
ga zúru.** His trousers are slipping.

zurúi sly, crafty; unfair; **zurúi otoko** foxy
fellow; **zurúi kotó o suru** to do a
tricky thing.

zurukéru to shirk (neglect) one's duty; to be
tardy; to be idle; **gakkoo o zurukéru**
to play truant from school.

zushín to with a thud; with a heavy sound.

zutazuta pieces; **zutazuta ni** in pieces, into
stripes; **zutazuta ni hikisáku** to tear to
shreds; **zutazuta ni kiru** to cut to
pieces.

ZÚTSU each, apiece; **hí ni sankai zútsu** three
times a day; **hitóri ni mittsu zútsu**
three pieces to each person; **ni sannin
zútsu** by twos and threes; **sukoshi
zútsu** little by little, bit by bit.

ZUTSUU headache; **wareru yóo na zutsuu** a
splitting headache; **zutsuu no táne** a
cause of worry; **zutsuu ga suru** to
have a headache.

ZUTTO directly to the point; straight to the
spot; very much; by far; all the time;
zutto íi very much better; **zutto ízen**
long time ago; **zutto tsuzuite** all the
time. **Zutto massúgu ni oidenasái.**
Keep straight on.

zúutai body, frame, physique.

zuuzuuben dialect spoken in the northeastern
part of Japan.

zuuzuushíi impudent, audacious; shameless;
zuuzúushiku impudently, audaciously,
shamelessly; **zuuzúushiku náru** to
become impudent; **zuuzuushísa**
impudence, audacity, effrontery;
shamelessness. **Zuuzuushíi otokó da.**
He is impudent.

ENGLISH-JAPANESE

A

a (an) hitótsu, ichí (but no word is usually used for this).
　There is a man. Hito ga imásu.
　He is a policeman. Júnsa desu.
abandon (to) suteru (*give up*); misuteru (*forsake, desert*); yameru (*relinquish*).
abbreviate (to) ryaku suru (*simplify*); shooryaku suru (*omit, cut out*).
abbreviation ryáku, ryakugoo.
ability shúwan (*capacity*); gíryoo (*skill*).
able dekíru; binwan na.
able (to be) dekíru.
abolish (to) haishi suru.
about góro (*point in time*); kúrai, gúrai, hodo, bákari (*quantity*); mawari (*nearness of a place*).
above —no ué (*higher than, over*); —íjoo (*more than*).
abroad gaikoku (*foreign country*); káigai (*overseas*).
absence rúsu (*from home, from the office*); kesseki (*from school, from a meeting*).
absent (to be) rúsu desu; kesseki desu.
absolute zettaiteki.
absorb (to) suiagéru (*suck up*); suitóru (*take in*).
abstain (to) kiken suru (*from voting*).
abstract chuushooteki na.
absurd okashii, báka na.
abundant takusán no.
abuse akuyoo.
abuse (to) akuyoo suru.
academy akádemii, gakkai.
accent ákusento.
accent (to) kyoochoo suru (*emphasize*).
accept (to) ukéru, osaméru (*take in*); shoodaku suru (*agree to*).
acceptance shoodaku.
accident jíko.
　by accident guuzen ni.
accidental guuzen no.
accidentally guuzen ni; omoi gake náku (*unexpectedly*).
accommodate (to) tekioo saseru (*adapt, adjust*).
accommodation tekioo (*adaptation*); shisetsu (*facilities*).
accompany (to) isshoni, tsuite iku.
accomplish (to) shitogéru, kansei suru.
accord itchi, choowa (*harmony*); íshi (*choice, will*).
according to —ni yoréba; —ni yotte (*depending on*).
account kanjoo (*statement of money*); hanashí (*narration*).
accuracy seikaku sa.
accurate seikaku na.
accuse (to) hínan suru.
accustom (to) narásu; shuukan o tsukéru (*habituate*).
ache itami.
ache (to) itámu.
achieve (to) shitogéru (*accomplish*).
achievement kooseki.

acid *adj.* suppái.—*n.* sán.
acknowledge (to) mitoméru.
acknowledgment uketorí (*receipt*).
acquaintance shiriai.
acquire (to) éru (*gain*); té ni ireru (*acquire property or rights*).
across mukoogawa (*across the street*).
　Go across. Yokogíru.
　come across—miataru (*happen to find*).
act makú (*of a play*); okonai (*deed*).
act (to) suru (*do*); furumau (*behave*).
active katsudooteki, sakan na.
activity katsudoo.
actor yakushá; eiga háiyuu (*movie actor*).
actress joyuu.
actual hontoo no.
actually hontoo ni.
acute surudoi (*sharp*); kyuusei no (*opp. of chronic*).
adapt (to) tekigoo saseru (*make fit*).
add (to) kuwaéru.
addition tashizan (*math.*); kuwáeta nomo (*thing added*).
address júusho (*of a place*); hanashi (*speech*).
address (to) hanashikakéru (*speak to*).
　to address a letter tegami ni atena o káku.
adequate tekitoo na.
adjective keiyóoshi.
adjoining tonari no.
administer (to) kánri suru.
admiral kaigun táishoo.
admiration kanpuku, kanshin.
admire (to) kanshin suru, uyamáu.
admission nyuujóoryoo (*charge*).
admit (to) mitoméru (*recognize*); irerú (*let in*).
admittance nyuujoo (*entrance*).
　No admittance. Nyuujoo shazetsu.
adopt (to) toriiréru.
adult otona.
advance (to) susumeru.
advantage ríeki (*benefit*).
adventure booken.
adverb fukushi.
advertise (to) kookoku suru.
advertisement kookoku.
advice chuukoku.
advise (to) chuukoku suru.
affair koto, kotogara.
affect (to) eikyoo suru (*influence*).
affected kidotta (*in manner*).
affection aijoo.
affectionate aijoo no áru.
affirm (to) dangen suru (*state as a fact*).
affirmation dangen.
afloat ukabiagáru.
afraid kowái.
after áto de (*later*); áto (*next to*); sorekara (*and then*).
afternoon gógo.
afterward sono go.
again mata, moo ichido.
against —ni táishite.
age (to) toshí o toru (*said of a person*); furuku naru (*said of a thing*).
agency dairíten (*office of an agent*).

agent dairínin (*person*).
aggravate (to) motto waruku suru (*make worse*).
ago máe.
agree (to) sansei suru.
agreeable kokoroyói (*pleasing*).
agreement keiyaku, kyootei, dooi.
agricultural nóogyoo no.
agriculture nóogyoo.
ahead máe ni (*in front of*); saki ni (*of time or place*).
aid énjo.
   first aid ookyuu téate.
   first-aid station ookyuu teatesho.
aid (to) énjo suru.
aim mokuteki (*purpose*).
aim at (to) neráu.
air kúuki.
airfield hikoojoo.
air force kuugun.
airmail kookuubin.
airplane kikóoki.
airport kuukoo.
aisle toorímichi.
alarm odoroki (*sudden fear*); keihoo (*warning*).
   alarm clock mezamashi-dókei.
alcohol arukooru.
alike onaji yóo ni (*in a similar way*).
all minná, súbete, zenbu.
alliance doomei.
allow (to) yurúsu (*permit*); ataeru (*give*).
ally mikata.
almost taitéi, hotóndo.
alone hitóri de.
along —ni sotte (*parallel to*); issho ni (*together with*).
already súde ni, móo.
also yahári, matá,—mo.
altar saidan.
alter (to) kaeru.
alternate *adj.* hitotsu oki no.—*n.* kawari no hito (*person*); kawari no mono (*thing*).
alternate (to) hitotsu oki ni suru.
although kéredomo.
altitude tákasa.
altogether miná de (*in all*); mattaku (*completely*).
   It's five hundred yen altogether. Mina de gohyaku en desu.
always itsu mo (*at all times*); ítsu demo (*at any time*).
amaze (to) odorokaséru.
amazement odoroki.
ambassador táishi.
ambitious haki no aru, yashin no aru.
amend (to) teisei suru.
America Beikoku, Amerika.
   American Beikokújin, Amerikájin (*person*); Amerika no (*pertaining to the U.S.A.*).
among —no náka no,—no naku ni,—no naka de.
amount gáku (*partial*); soogaku (*total*).
ample juubun na.
amuse (to) tanoshimaséru, omoshirogaraséru.

amusement goraku.
amusing omoshirói.
analyze (to) bunseki suru, kentoo suru.
ancestor sósen.
anchor ikari.
ancient furúi, mukashi no.
and to, ya, soshite.
anecdote itsuwa.
angel ténshi.
anger ikari.
anger (to) okóru.
angry (to be) okótte iru.
   to get angry okóru.
animal doobutsu.
animate (to) kappatsú ni suru.
annex bekkan (*building*).
annihilate (to) zenmetsu saséru.
anniversary kinénbi.
announce (to) koohyoo suru (*publish*); seimei suru (*declare*).
annoy (to) komaraséru.
annual maitoshi no.
annul (to) torikesu.
anonymous tokumei no.
another hoká no.
answer henjí, kotáe.
answer (to) kotáeru, henjí o suru.
anticipate (to) yosoo suru.
antique kottoohin.
anxiety shinpai.
anxious (to get) shinpai suru.
any nani ka, dare ka; sukóshi mo (*not even a little*).
anybody dáre ka, dáre demo.
anyhow tómo kaku.
anything náni ka, nan demo.
anywhere dóko demo.
apart betsu betsu ni.
apartment apáato.
apiece —zutsu.
apologize (to) ayamáru.
apparent akíraka na (*obvious*).
appeal (to) uttaéru.
appear (to) arawaréru (*make an appearance*).
appearance mikake (*mien*).
appease (to) nadameru.
appendix furoku (*of a book*); móochoo (*of the body*).
appetite shokuyoku.
applaud (to) hákushu kassai suru.
applause kássai.
apple ringo.
application mooshikomi (*request*).
apply (to) mooshikómu.
appoint (to) ninmei suru.
appointment ninmei (*assignment to office*); yakusoku (*engagement*).
appreciate (to) kánsha suru (*thank*); arigataku omou (*feel gratified*).
appreciation kansha.
appropriate tekitoo na.
approve (to) sansei suru (*agree*); yói to omou (*think well of*).
April Shigatsu.
apron épuron, maekake.
arbitrary dokudanteki na.

arcade nakamisedóori, aakéedo.
architect kenchikuka.
architecture kenchiku.
ardent nésshin na.
area akichí (*open space*); chíiki (*region*).
argue (to) iiarasóu.
argument iiarasói, ronsoo.
arise (to) okóru (*start, originate*).
arithmetic sanjutsu.
arm udé (*of the body*); búki (*weapon*).
arm (to) v.t. busoo saseru; v.i. busoo suru.
army rikúgun.
around —no mawari ni.
arouse (to) me o samasaséru (*awaken*);
    sawagaseru (*stir up*).
arrange (to) seitón suru (*set in order*);
    uchiawáseru (*make an arrangement*).
arrangement uchiawase (*plan*).
arrest kensoku.
arrest (to) kensoku suru, tsukamaéru.
arrival toochaku.
arrive (to) toochaku suru, tsúku.
art geijutsu (*art in general*); bíjutsu (*fine
    arts*).
article shinamono (*commodity*); kiji (*writing*).
artificial jinzoo no (*not natural*).
artist geijutsuka, geinóojin (*performing
    artist*); bijutsuka (*person skilled in one
    of the fine arts*).
artistic geijutsuteki no.
as —to shite (*in the capacity of*);—no yoo ni
    (*in such a manner*);—hodo (*as . . . as*).
ascertain (to) tashikaméru, kakutéi suru
    (*determine*).
ash hai.
ashamed (to feel) hazukáshiku omou.
aside sóba ni; wakí e (*nearby*).
ask (to) kiku, tazuneru.
asleep (to be) nemutte iru.
aspire (to) netsuboo suru.
aspirin asupírin.
assault shuugeki, bookoo.
assemble (to) atsumeru (*bring together*);
    atsumaru (*come together*).
assembly shuukai.
assign (to) ategau (*allot*); shitei suru
    (*designate*).
assist (to) tetsudáu, tasukéru.
assistant tetsudái, joshu.
associate (to) koosai suru (*mingle with*);
    rensoo suru (*relate in thinking*).
assume (to) hikiukeru (*undertake*).
assurance hoshoo, ukeai.
assure (to) hoshoo suru.
astonish (to) odorokásu, bikkúri saseru.
astound (to) bikkúri gyooten saseru.
asylum seishin byóoin.
at ni, de.
athlete undooka.
athletics undoo.
atmosphere fun'iki.
attach (to) tsukéru.
attack (to) koogeki suru, seméru, osou.
attain (to) tassúru (*gain*); toochaku suru
    (*reach*).
attempt (to) kokoromíru.

attend (to) —ni shusseki suru (*be present at*).
attention chúui.
attic yane ura.
attitude táido.
attorney bengóshi (*lawyer*).
    power of attorney dairinin.
attract (to) chuui o hiku (*draw attention*);
    miwakú suru (*entice*).
attraction miwaku.
attractive miwaku ga aru, aikyoo ga aru.
audience chooshuu.
August Hachigatsu.
aunt oba, obasan.
author chósha (*writer of a book, composer*).
authority táika (*great expert*); tookyokusha
    (*government*).
authorize (to) kengén o ataeru.
automatic jidooteki.
automobile jidóosha.
autumn áki.
average heikin.
avoid (to) sakéru.
awake (to be) me ga sámete iru.
awaken (to) okósu (*arouse*).
award shoohin, shóoyo.
award (to) shóoyo o dásu.
aware (to be) shoochi shite iru.
away achira ni, atchi ni.
    Go away. Atchi e ike.
awful osoroshíi, taihen na.
awkward fúben na, bukíyoo na.

B

baby akanboo.
back senaka (*of the body*); urá (*of a house,
    etc.*).
background haikei.
backward ushiro ni (*toward the back*); gyaku
    ni (*in a reverse direction*).
bacon beekon.
bad waníi.
badge kishoo.
bag fukuro.
baggage nímotsu (*heavy, such as trunks*);
    tenímotsu (*hand luggage*).
bake (to) yaku.
baker pán'ya.
bakery pán'ya.
balance hakari (*scale*); nokori (*remainder*).
balcony barukoni, rodai.
ball tama (*sphere*); mari, booru (*for a game*).
balloon keikikyuu (*lighter-than-air-craft*);
    fuusen (*toy*).
banana banana.
band bando, gakudan.
bandage hootai.
banister tesuri.
bank ginkoo (*financial institution*); dote (*of a
    river*).
bank note satsu.
bankruptcy hasan.
banquet enkai.
bar baa (*for drinks*); kanaboo (*rod*).
barber rihátsushi, tokoya.
barbershop rihatsuya.

bare hadaka no.
barefoot suashi no.
barge tenmasen.
barn ushigoya.
barrel taru.
barren ko o umanai *(sterile);* fumoo no *(land).*
basin tarai.
basis kiso, kónkyo.
basket kago.
    waste-paper basket kuzu-kago.
bath o-fúro *(hot);* mizu-buro *(cold).*
    to take a bath huro ni hairu.
bathe (to) kaisuiyoku o suru *(in the sea);* mizu o abiru *(in running water).*
bathroom furoba, yudono *(bath);* benjo *(toilet).*
battle ikusa, sensoo.
bay wan.
be (to) iru, óru *(there is: animate);* áru *(there is: inanimate);* désu *(it is—).*
beach umibe, kaigan.
bean mamé.
bear kumá.
bear (to) gáman suru *(endure);* úmu *(give birth to).*
beard hige.
beat (to) útsu.
beautiful utsukushíi, kírei na.
beauty utsukushísa; bijin *(beautiful woman).*
beauty parlor biyóoin.
because kara, node *(used after a sentence or clause).*
become (to) —ni naru.
becoming (be) niáu *(befitting).*
bed nedoko, bétto; shindai *(berth).*
beef gyuuniku.
beer bíiru.
beet bíitsu, kabu.
before máe, máe ni.
beg (to) tanómu.
beggar kojiki.
begin (to) *v.t.* hajimeru; *v.i.* hajimaru.
beginning hajime.
behave (to) furumau.
behavior furumai.
behind ushiro ni, áto ni.
belief kakushin *(conviction);* shinkoo *(faith);* íken *(opinion).*
believe (to) shinjiru.
bell kane, beru.
belong (to) —ni zokusuru.
below shita ni.
belt beruto; óbi *(sash);* kawa-óbi *(leather).*
bench bénchi, shoogi.
bend (to) *v.t.* mageru; *v.i.* magaru.
beneath shita ni.
benefit ríeki *(good advantage);* onkei *(favor).*
beside —no sóba ni, —no sóba de.
besides —no hoka ni, sono ue *(moreover).*
best ichiban ii.
bet kake.
bet (to) kakéru.
betray (to) uragíru *(act treacherously);* azamuku *(deceive).*
better motto ii.

between —no aida ni.
beware (to) yoojin suru.
beyond —no mukoo ni.
bicycle jiténsha.
bid (to) ne o tsurkéru *(offer a price);* nyuusatsu suru *(make a bid).*
big ookíi.
bill kanjoogaki *(grocer's bill, restaurant bill of fare).*
billion júu-oku.
bind (to) yuwaéru, shibáru *(tie).*
bird tori.
birth tanjoo.
    to give birth úmu.
birthday tanjóobi.
biscuit bisuketto *(tea biscuit, cookie).*
bishop kantoku *(Protestant);* shikyoo *(Catholic).*
bit sukoshi.
bite kamikizu *(dog bite),* sashikizu *(mosquito bite).*
bite (to) kámu *(chew);* kúu *(said of insects).*
bitter nigái.
bitterness nigami.
black kurói.
blade ha.
blame seme *(censure);* tsumi *(crime, sin).*
blame (to) seméru; hihan suru *(criticize).*
blank hakushi *(blank sheet of paper);*
    fill in a blank form yooshi.
blanket kettoo, móofu.
bleed (to) shukketsu suru.
bless (to) kiyoméru *(consecrate);* agameru *(praise, glorify).*
blessing shukufuku *(benediction);* kami no megumi *(God's blessing).*
blind *adj.* mekura no.
blindness moomoku.
block katamari *(bulky piece);* kukaku *(row of houses).*
block (to) fusagu, samatagéru.
blood chi.
bloom (to) haná ga saku *(flowers).*
blossom haná.
blotter suitórigami.
blouse burausu.
blow (to) fúku *(wind).*
blue aói.
blush (to) sekimen suru, akaku náru.
board ita *(plank);* makanai *(food).*
boardinghouse geshukuya.
boast (to) jiman suru.
boat bóoto *(rowboat);* fúne *(powered by motor).*
body karada *(living or dead person);* shigai *(corpse).*
boil (to) wakasu *(water);* yudéru *(cook in water).*
boiler bóiraa.
bold daitan na.
bomb bakudan.
bomb (to) bakugeki suru.
bond shooken *(document).*
bone honé.
book hón.
    textbook kyookásho.

bookseller hón'ya.
bookstore hón'ya.
border kokkyoo *(frontier of a country)*;
    kyookai *(boundary, limit)*.
boring omoshirokunai *(uninteresting)*.
born (to be) umareru.
borrow (to) kariru.
both futari tomo *(people)*; ryoohoo *(things)*.
bother (to) nayamásu *(annoy)*; jama suru
    (trouble).
bottle bín.
bottom soko.
bounce (to) hanekáeru.
bowl donburi.
box hako.
boy shoonen, otoko no ko.
bracelet udewa.
braid uchihimo.
brain atama *(intellectual ability)*.
brake buréeki.
branch eda *(of tree)*; shiten *(office, etc.)*.
brave yuukan na.
brassière burájaa.
bread pán.
break (to) kowásu *(destroy)*; yabúru *(tear, rip)*.
breakfast asahan.
breast mune *(human)*.
breath íki.
breathe (to) iki o suru.
breeze soyokaze.
bribe wairo
    to take a bribe wairo o toru.
brick rénga.
bride hanayome.
bridegroom hanamuko.
bridge hashi.
brief mijikái *(short)*.
bright akarui *(with light)*; hade na *(of color)*.
brighten (to) akaruku suru *(with light)*.
brilliant migoto na.
bring (to) motte kuru.
    to bring up sodatéru *(a child)*; mochidasu
    (for discussion).
Britain Eikoku. See also English.
    British Eikoku no.
broad hiroi.
broadcast hoosoo.
broadcast (to) hoosoo suru.
broil (to) yaku.
broken kowáreta.
brook ogawa.
broom hooki.
brother níisan *(elder)*; otooto *(younger)*.
brother-in-law gi-kei, giri no áni *(elder)*;
    gitei, giri no otooto *(younger)*.
brown chairo.
bruise uchikizu.
bruise (to) *v.t.* uchikizu o ukeru.
brush fude *(for writing)*; hake, burashi *(for sweeping)*.
bubble awa.
buckle bakkuru, bijoo.
bud tsubomi.
Buddha Hotoke.
    a statue of Buddha Butsuzoo.
    Buddhism Búkkyoo.

budget yosan.
build (to) tatéru.
building tatémono.
bulletin keiji *(pinned on a board)*; kaihoo
    (publication).
    bulletin board keijiban.
bundle tsutsumi.
burn (to) yaku; moyasu *(throw into a fire)*.
burst (to) sakeru *(pipes, etc.)*.
bus basu.
bush shigemi.
business yooji *(errand)*; shigoto *(work)*;
    shóobai *(profession)*.
businessman kaishain.
busy isogashii.
but ga, shikashi, keredomo *(however)*.
butcher nikúya.
    butcher shop nikúya.
butter báta.
button bótan.
buy (to) kau.
buyer kaite, baíyaa.
by sóba ni *(nearby)*; de *(by means of)*.

C

cab takushii *(taxi)*.
cabbage kyabetsu.
cable keeburu *(rope, wire)*; kaigai denshin
    (cablegram).
cage tori kago *(for birds)*; orí *(for animals)*.
cake kéeki.
calendar karendaa, koyomi.
calf koushi.
call (to) hoomon suru *(to make a call, visit)*.
call (to) yobu.
calm shízuka na, odáyaka na.
calm (to) shizuka ni suru.
camera kámera, shashínki.
camp kyánpu.
camp (to) kyánpu suru.
can kan.
can (be able) dekíru *(can do)*; —koto ga
    dekíru *(can—)*.
can opener kan-kiri.
cancel (to) torikesu *(revoke)*; sákujo suru
    (delete).
candidate koohósha.
candle roosoku.
candy kyandee, ame.
cap booshi *(hat)*; futa *(lid)*.
capital shúfu *(city)*; shihon *(money)*.
capricious kimagure na.
captain rikugun táii *(army)*; sénchoo
    (merchant ship); kaigun táisa *(navy)*.
captive toriko.
capture (to) toriko ni suru, tsukamaeru.
car kuruma *(vehicle)*; jidóosha *(automobile)*;
    dénsha *(streetcar)*.
carbon paper kaabon péepaa.
card hagaki *(post card)*; e-hagaki *(illustrated
    post card)*; toranpu *(playing card)*.
care (to) kamau *(be concerned)*; sewa o suru
    (care for a child).
    to take care daiji ni suru.
careful chuuibukái.

careless fuchúui na.
caress aibu; hooyoo.
carpenter dáiku.
carpet júutan.
carry (to) motte iku *(take to)*; hakobu *(transport)*.
carve (to) kíru *(meat)*; chookoku suru *(sculpture)*.
case hako *(box)*; jíken *(matter)*.
cash genkin.
    to cash a check kogitte o genkin ni kaeru.
cashier genkin gákari, genkin suitoo gákari.
castle shiro.
cat néko.
catch (to) toraeru.
    I have caught a cold. Kaze o hikimashita.
    I could not catch the train. Kisha ni ma ni aimasen deshita.
category shúrui *(kind)*; búrui *(class)*.
cathedral jiin, hóngam.
Catholic Kyúukyoo, Katoríkku.
cattle ushi *(cow)*; kachiku *(live-stock)*.
cause gen'in.
    without cause gen'in nashi ni.
cause (to) gen'in to naru *(bring about)*; —sa seru *(cause a person to do . . .)*.
cease (to) yamu, owaru *(come to an end)*.
ceiling tenjóo.
celebrate (to) iwáu.
cellar chikáshitsu.
cement semento.
cemetery bóchi, hakaba.
center chuushin *(of a circle)*.
central chuushin no, chuuoo no.
    central heating danboo-soochi *(heating system)*.
century séiki.
ceremony shiki.
certain táshika na *(without doubt)*; áru *(a certain)*.
certainty tashika na koto.
certificate shoomeisho.
chain kusari.
chair isu, koshikake.
chairman gíchoo.
chalk hakuboku, chóoku.
challenge choosen.
challenge (to) choosen suru.
champion chanpion, sénshu *(athletic)*; tooshi *(fighter)*; yoogosha *(defendant)*.
chance chansu *(opportunity)*; guuzen *(coincidence)*; unmei *(luck, fortune)*.
    to take a chance chansu o tóru.
change henka, hawari *(alteration)*; komakai okane *(small change)*; otsuri *(money returned as change)*.
change (to) kaeru *(make different)*; kawaru *(become different)*.
chapel reihaidoo *(place of worship)*.
chapter shóo.
character tokuchoo *(unique feature, distinctive mark)*; seishitsu *(disposition)*.
characteristic *adj.* dokutoku no.
charge (to) komeru *(load)*; kokuhatsu suru *(accuse)*; tsuke ni suru *(charge to an account)*.

charitable omoiyari no aru *(sympathetic)*.
charity jízen.
charming miwakuteki na *(fascinating)*; taihen utsukushii *(very attractive)*; aikyoo no aru *(engaging)*.
chase (to) oikakéru.
chat (to) shabéru, uchikutsuroide hanásu.
cheap yasúi.
cheat (to) damásu.
check kogitte *(bank check)*.
check (to) kuitoméru *(hold back, hamper)*.
check hóo.
cheer (to) nagusameru *(comfort)*; genkizukéru *(enliven)*.
cheerful akarui *(disposition)*; génki na *(lively)*.
cheese chíizu.
chemical *n.* kagaku séihin. —*adj.* kágaku no.
chemistry kágaku.
cherish (to) daijí ni suru.
cherry sakura no haná *(blossom)*; sakura no kí *(tree)*; sakuranboo *(fruit)*.
chest muné *(of the body)*; hako *(box)*.
chestnut kuri.
chew (to) kámu.
chicken niwatori, chíkin.
chief *n.* shunin *(head person)*. —*adj.* ómo na.
chimney entotsu.
chin agó.
China Chúugoku, Shína.
    Communist China Chuukyoo.
    Chinese Shinájin, Chuugokújin *(person)*; Shína no *(pertaining to the country)*.
chip kirehashi, kake.
chocolate chokoréeto.
choice sentaku *(selection)*; yorigonomi *(preference)*.
choke (to) *v.t.* chissoku saseru *(suffocate)*; *v.i.* chissoku suru.
choose (to) erábu *(make a choice of)*; yóru *(pick out)*.
chop (to) kizamu *(mince)*.
chopsticks háshi.
Christian Kirisutokyoo-shínja.
    Christianity Kirisutokyoo.
Christmas Kurisúmasu.
church kyookai.
cigar hamaki, shígaa.
    cigar store tabakoya.
cigarette makitábako, shigarétto.
circle maru *(circumference)*.
circular *adj.* marui. —*n.* kaijoo.
circulate (to) kubáru *(distribute)*.
circumstances jijoo *(conditions)*; baai *(case)*.
citizen shímin.
city shí.
city hall kookaidoo.
civilization bunmei.
civilize (to) bunmei ni michibíku.
claim seikyuu *(demand)*; yookyuu *(request)*; shuchoo *(insistence)*.
claim (to) seikyuu suru *(demand)*; shuchoo suru *(maintain)*.
clamor sáwagi *(loud noise)*.
clap (to) hákushu suru *(applaud)*.

class shúrui *(kind)*; kaikyuu *(social status)*; kúrasu *(school)*.
  first class ittoo *(in plane, etc.)*.
classic koten.
classify (to) bunrui suru.
clause jookoo.
clean kírei na.
clean (to) sooji suru *(rooms, etc.)*.
  to make clean kírei ni suru.
cleaners kuriininguya.
cleanliness seiketsu sa.
clear kírei na.
  The sky is clear today. Kyoo wa sóra ga hárete imásu.
  This is clear. Kore wa kirei desu.
  clear soup osúmashi.
clerk jimúin *(office)*; ginkóoin *(bank)*.
clever rikoo na *(intelligent)*; joozu na *(dexterous)*; kíyoo na *(skillful)*.
climate kikoo.
climb (to) noboru.
clip kuríppu.
clip (to) karu.
clock tokei.
  alarm clock mezamashi dókei.
close —no sóba ni *(nearby)*; no chikáku ni *(close to)*; kínjo ni *(in the neighborhood)*.
close (to) v.t. shiméru; v.i. shimáru.
closed kyuugyoo *(business)*.
closet todana *(cupboard)*; oshiire *(for storage)*.
cloth kiré, nuno *(general term)*.
  cotton cloth momen mono.
  silk cloth kinú mono.
clothes kimono *(Japanese)*; yoofuku *(occidental)*.
cloud kúmo.
cloudy kumótte iru.
clover kuróobaa.
club boo *(heavy stick)*; kúrabu *(association)*.
coal sekitán.
coarse arai, sómatsu na *(roughly made)*; katoo na *(rude)*.
coast kaigan *(beach)*; engan *(shore)*.
coat haori *(Japanese)*; uwagi *(occidental-style jacket)*.
cocktail kákuteru.
code kisóku *(set of rules)*.
coffee koohíi.
coffin hitsugi, kan'oke.
coin káhei.
cold samúi *(weather)*; tsúmetai *(to the touch)*.
  to catch a cold kaze o hiku.
  It is cold. Samúi desu.
  I am cold. Watashi wa samúi desu.
coldness sámusa.
collaborate (to) kyoodoo de hataraku *(work together)*.
collar káraa *(for men)*; kubiwa *(for animals)*.
collect (to) v.t. atsuméru *(gather, get together)*; v.i. atsumáru *(come together)*.
collection shuushuu *(of stamps, etc.)*; kashikin chóoshuu *(of debts)*.
college daigaku *(university)*.

colonial shokumínchi no.
colony shokumínchi.
color iró.
color (to) iró o tsukéru *(add color)*.
column enchuu *(pillar)*; rán *(newspaper)*.
comb kushí.
comb (to) kushí de tokásu, kushí o kakéru *(one's hair)*.
combination kumiawase.
combine (to) kumiawaséru *(join together)*.
come (to) kúru.
  to come around yatte kúru.
  to come back káette kuru.
  to come in háiru.
comedy kígeki.
comet suisei.
comfort nagusame *(consolation)*.
comfort (to) nagusameru *(console)*.
comfortable kokochi yói, rakú na.
comma kónma, kuten.
command shikí *(military direction)*; meirei *(order)*.
command (to) meizúru *(direct)*; shíhai suru *(control)*; meirei suru *(give orders)*.
commander shikísha.
commercial shóobai no, shóogyoo no.
commission nínmu *(charge, duty)*; toritsugi *(agency)*; tesúuryoo *(for service)*.
commit (to) okasu *(a crime)*.
common futsuu no *(ordinary)*; atarimae no *(usual)*.
  common sense jooshiki.
communicate (to) renraku suru *(contact)*; tsuushin suru *(correspond with)*.
communication renraku, tsuushin; shomen *(written message)*.
  mass communication masukomi.
community shákai *(society)*.
companion nakama *(comrade)*; aite *(partner)*; tsure *(traveling)*.
company kyaku *(social)*; kaisha *(firm)*.
compare (to) hikaku suru, kuraberu.
comparison hikaku.
compete (to) kyoosoo suru, kisóu.
competition kyoosoo *(rivalry)*; shiai *(contest)*.
complain (to) fuhei o iu *(make a complaint)*.
complaint fuhei, kujoo.
complete zénbu no *(entire)*; kanzen na *(perfect)*.
complex fukuzatsu na *(complicated)*.
complexion kaoiro.
complicate (to) fukuzatsu ni suru.
  to get complicated fukuzatsu ni náru.
compliment sánji *(praise)*; oseji *(flattering speech)*.
compose (to) sakkyoku suru *(music)*; shi o tsukúru *(poetry)*.
composer sakkyokuka *(of music)*.
composition sakubun *(as a school subject)*; sakuhin *(prose or poetry)*; sakkyoku *(musical)*; haigoo *(arrangement)*.
comprise jóoho *(concession)*; dakyoo *(agreement)*.
compromise (to) dakyoo suru.
conceit unubore *(overweening, excessive self-importance)*.

conceited unuboreta.
conceive (to) jutai suru *(become pregnant)*; kokoró ni idáku *(form a conception of, imagine)*.
concentrate (to) shuuchuu suru.
concern jígyoo *(enterprise)*; shinpai *(anxiety)*.
    a matter of great concern juudai na mondai.
    to be concerned shinpai suru.
concerning —ni tsuite.
concert ongákukai.
concrete konkuríito *(for building)*.
condemn (to) hínan suru *(censure)*; senkoku suru *(sentence)*.
condense (to) asshuku suru *(compress)*; mijikáku suru *(shorten)*.
condition jootai *(aspect)*; jooken *(terms)*.
    critical condition kiken jóotai.
    on condition that —no jooken de.
conduct furumai *(behavior)*; okonai *(deed)*.
    bad conduct warúi okonai.
    good conduct yói okonai.
conduct (to) okonáu *(perform)*.
    to conduct a business shóobai o keiei suru.
    to conduct an orchestra ookésutora o shikí suru.
conductor shashoo *(of trains, etc.)*; shikísha *(of an orchestra)*.
confess (to) jinin suru *(acknowledge)*; mitomeru *(admit)*; hákujoo suru *(make a confession)*.
confession kokuhaku, hákujoo.
confidence shin'yoo, shinrai *(trust)*; jishin *(self-confidence)*.
confident jishin no áru.
confidential himitsu no.
confirm (to) tashikaméru *(establish firmly)*; kakushoo suru *(verify)*.
confirmation kakunin *(corroboration)*; kakushoo *(proof)*.
congratulate (to) iwáu, shukúsu.
congratulations omedetoo gozaimásu.
connect (to) tsunagu *(join)*.
connection kankei *(relation)*; tsunagari *(link)*.
conquer (to) seifuku suru.
conquest seifuku.
conscience ryóoshin.
conscientious ryooshinteki na.
conscious kizúite iru *(aware)*.
consent dooi *(assent)*; itchi *(unanimity)*.
conservative hoshuteki na.
consider (to) yóku kangáete míru *(contemplate)*; kóoryo ni ireru *(to take into account)*; kangáeru *(think)*.
considerable kánari no *(much)*.
consideration kóoryo *(careful thought)*; omoiyari *(thoughtful regard)*.
consist of (to) —kara náru *(be composed of)*.
consistent shubi ikkan shita.
constant kawaranai *(unchanging)*; chuujitsu na *(faithful)*.
constitution kénpoo *(of a state)*; taikaku *(of the body)*.
constitutional kenpoojoo no.
consul ryóoji.
consulate ryoojíkan.

contagious densensei no.
    a contagious disease densenbyoo.
contain (to) ireru *(include)*; háitte iru *(have within)*.
container iremono.
contemporary géndai no *(of the day)*; doojídai no *(existing at the same time)*.
contented manzoku shita.
    to be contented manzoku shite iru.
contentment manzoku *(satisfaction)*.
contents naiyoo.
continent *n.* táiriku.
continual taema no nái *(unceasing)*.
continue (to) *v.t.* tsuzukeru; *v.i.* tsuzuku.
contract keiyaku *(agreement)*; keiyakusho *(written document of an agreement)*.
contractor keiyakunin, ukeoinin.
contradict (to) hanbaku suru *(rebut)*; mujun suru *(conflict with)*.
contradiction hanbaku *(rebuttal)*; mujun *(inconsistency)*.
contradictory mujun shite iru.
contrary hantai no.
    on the contrary hantai ni, kaette.
contrast taishoo.
contrast (to) taishoo suru.
contribute (to) kífu suru *(money, etc.)*; kikoo suru *(to a publication)*.
contribution kífu *(donation)*; kikoo *(something written for a publication)*.
control toosei *(government)*; yokusei *(restraint)*.
    birth control sanji seigen.
control (to) tóogyo suru *(govern)*; toosei suru *(regulate)*.
controversy ronsoo, gíron *(dispute)*.
convenience bénri, tsugoo.
convenient tsugoo no yói, bénri na.
convent shuudóoin.
convention kyoogíkai, káigi, shuukai.
conversation kaiwa *(dialogue)*; hanashi *(talk)*.
converse (to) hanásu.
convert (to) kaeru *(change into)*; kaishuu saseru *(to a religion)*.
convict (to) yuuzai to senkoku suru *(declare guilty)*.
conviction kakushin *(firm belief)*; yuuzai hánketsu *(verdict of guilty)*.
cook ryoorínin *(of Japanese or any other kind of food)*; kókku *(for other than Japanese food)*.
cook (to) ryóori suru, ryóori o tsukúru.
cool suzushíi *(temperature)*; tsumetai *(to the touch)*; reisei na *(unexcited)*; reitán na *(lacking in zeal)*.
cool (to) tsumetaku suru.
copy utsushi *(of a letter, etc.)*; mosha *(of a picture)*.
corporation kaisha *(firm)*; shadan-hóojin *(corporate body)*.
correct tadashíi *(right)*; táshika na *(sure)*; seikaku na *(accurate)*; machigai no nái *(without error)*.
correct (to) naósu; koosei suru *(proofread)*; tensaku suru *(school papers)*.
correction teisei *(of an error)*; koosei *(in*

proofreading); tensaku *(of a school composition)*.
correspond (to) buntsuu suru, tsuushin suru *(exchange letters)*; itchi suru *(agree)*.
correspondence tsuushin; buntsuu.
correspondent tsuushin'in *(of a periodical)*.
corrupt (to) fuhai suru *(rot)*; daraku suru *(morally)*.
corruption daraku *(moral deterioration)*.
cost nedan *(price)*; híyoo *(expense)*.
costume fukusoo, kimono; yoofuku *(occidental)*; ishoo *(fancy dress)*.
cotton watá *(raw)*; momen *(woven)*.
cough sekí.
count keisan *(reckoning)*.
count (to) kazóeru.
counter kauntaa *(restaurant, etc.)*; chooba *(in Japanese-style hotel)*.
countless kazoekirénai.
country inaka *(rural region)*; kuni *(nation)*.
countryman inaka mono *(a rustic)*; dookokújin *(compatriot)*.
couple futatsú *(of things)*; futarí *(of people)*; futsuka *(of days)*; fúufu *(man and wife)*.
courage yúuki.
  to have courage yúuki ga áru.
course kamoku, katéi *(of study)*; kóosu, michi *(road followed)*; yarikatá *(line of conduct or action)*.
court saibanshó *(tribunal)*.
  law court hootei.
courteous téinei na; teichoo na *(polite)*.
courtesy téinei *(politeness)*; kóoi *(favor)*; reigi *(civility)*.
courtyard nakaniwa.
cousin itóko
  second cousin mata ítoko.
cover futa, kábaa.
cow meushi.
crack wareme *(split)*; sukimá *(chink)*; hibí *(flaw)*.
crack (to) *v.t.* waru, *v.i.* wareru; hibí ga háiru *(break without separating)*.
  to crack a nut kurumí o waru.
  to crack a joke joodán o tobasu.
  a hard nut to crack nan móndai.
cradle yurikago.
crash shoototsu *(collision)*.
crash (to) shoototsu suru.
crazy kichigai jímita *(half-crazed)*.
  crazy about muchuu ni nátta.
cream kuríimu.
create (to) tsukúru *(bring into being)*; soosaku suru *(produce)*.
creature ikímono *(living thing)*.
credit kuréjitto, shin'yoo *(trust)*.
creditor kashi nushi, saikénsha.
crime tsúmi.
  to commit a crime hanzai o okasu.
crisis kikí *(crucial time)*; tooge *(of a sickness, etc.)*.
  political crisis seiji no kikí.
  financial crisis kéizai no kikí.
critic hihyooka *(reviewer)*.

critical hihyooteki no *(inclined to criticize)*; kikí no *(serious)*.
criticism hihyoo, hihan.
criticize (to) hihyoo suru *(discuss critically)*; hinan suru *(find fault with)*.
crooked magatte iru *(bent)*; nejíreta *(twisted)*; fushóojiki na *(dishonest)*.
crop shuukaku *(yield)*; toriire *(harvest)*.
cross juuji *(lines that intersect)*; juujika *(religious symbol)*.
crossing tokoo *(ocean)*; koosáten *(intersection)*.
crossroads koosáten; yotsukado.
crouch (to) kagamu.
crow kárasu.
crowd hito gomi.
  to be crowded kónde iru.
crown kanmuri.
crown (to) eikan o sazukéru *(reward or honor)*.
cruel zankoku na.
cruelty zangyaku.
crumb pan kúzu.
crumble (to) kuzuréru *(collapse)*; mú ni kisúru *(come to nothing)*; koná ni suru *(break into crumbs)*.
crust pán no kawá.
crutch matsubázue.
cry sakebi góe *(shout)*; naki góe *(crying)*.
cry (to) sakébu *(shout)*; naku *(weep)*.
cunning warugashikói *(sly)*; kosúi *(crafty)*.
cup chawan *(teacup)*; koppu *(glass)*; káppu *(trophy)*.
  a cup of coffee koohíi íppai.
  a cup of tea o-cha íppai.
cure (to) naósu;
  to be cured of naóru.
curiosity kookíshin.
curious kookíshin ga tsuyói *(inquisitive)*; kímyoo na *(strange)*.
curl káaru *(of hair)*.
current *adj.* génzai no *(present)*; ryuutsuu shite iru *(in general circulation)*. —*n.* nagaré *(stream)*.
curtain madó kake, káaten *(for a window)*; makú *(theatre)*.
curve yumi nari *(arched shape)*; kyokusen *(curved line)*.
curve (to) *v.t.* mageru; *v.i.* magaru.
cushion kússhon; zabúton *(for sitting)*.
custom shuukan *(habit)*; fúuzoku *(convention)*.
customhouse zeikan.
customs official zeikánri.
customary futsuu no *(ordinary)*.
customer kyaku.
cut kiríkizu *(wound)*; kirehashi *(a piece of something)*.
cut (to) *v.t.* kíru; *v.i.* kiréru.

D

dagger tantóo.
daily máinichi no.
  daily newspaper nikkán shínbun.
dainty kyasha na.

201

dam dámu, séki.
damage songai *(loss)*; hígai *(injury, harm)*.
damage (to) damé ni suru.
damp shimeppói *(of things)*; shikki no óoi *(of atmosphere)*.
dance dánsu *(foreign)*; odori *(Japanese)*.
dance (to) odoru.
danger kiken.
dangerous abunái.
dark kurai *(little light)*; kói *(color)*; kurói *(person)*.
dash (to) tosshin suru *(rush)*.
date yakusoku *(appointment)*; hizuke *(on a letter)*.
daughter musume *(plain form)*, ojóosan *(pol.)*.
dawn yoake.
day hi, hirú *(daytime)*.
  day after tomorrow asátte.
  day before yesterday ototoi.
  yesterday kinóo.
  today kyóo.
dazzle (to) me o kuramasu.
dead shinda *(lacking life)*.
  dead leaves kareha.
deaf tsúnbo.
deal torihiki *(business)*.
  a great deal hijoo ni takusán.
deal (to) torihiki suru *(trade)*; tsukiáu *(associate with)*.
dealer shóonin.
dear takái *(price)*; kawaí *(beloved)*.
death shí *(loss of life)*; shiboo *(act or fact of dying)*.
debate ronsoo.
debt shakkín *(sum due)*; sáimu *(liability)*.
debtor karinushi.
decanter tokkuri.
decay fuhai *(rot)*.
decay (to) kusáru *(rot)*; otoroéru *(decline)*; táika suru *(deteriorate)*.
deceased shiboo.
deceit azamuki.
deceive (to) damásu *(cheat)*; azamúku *(delude)*.
December Juunigatsu.
decent óntoo na *(proper)*; joohín na *(modest)*; kánari rippa na *(respectable)*.
decide (to) kiméru.
decision kettei.
decisive ketteiteki.
deck kanpan, dékki *(of a ship)*; hitó kumi *(of playing cards)*.
declare (to) shinkoku suru *(report)*; mooshitatéru *(state)*.
decline jítai *(refuse)*.
decline (to) jítai suru.
decrease genshoo.
decrease (to) v.t. herasu, sukunáku suru; v.i. heru.
decree hanketsu *(judicial decision)*; hoorei *(ordinance)*.
dedicate (to) sasageru *(consecrate)*; yudanéru *(give oneself to one's work)*.
deed kóoi *(action)*; jikkoo *(performance)*; okonai *(act)*; shoosho *(document)*.

deep fukái *(opp. of shallow)*; kói *(color)*.
deer shiká.
defeat haisen *(military)*; shippai *(failure)*.
defeat (to) v.t. makasu;
  to be defeated v.i. makeru.
defect kettén.
defend (to) mamóru.
defense booei.
defiance choosen *(challenge)*; múshi *(setting at naught)*.
define (to) téigi suru.
definite hakkíri shita.
defy (to) choosen suru *(challenge)*; múshi suru *(set at naught)*.
degree do *(on a thermometer, etc.)*; gákui *(diploma)*.
  by degrees dandan.
delay chien.
delay (to) v.i. okureru.
delegate daihyoo *(representative)*.
delegate (to) haken suru *(depute)*; inin suru *(entrust)*; daihyoo suru *(represent)*.
deliberate (to) shían suru *(consider)*; shíngi suru *(discuss)*.
deliberately shinchoo ni, yuuyuu to.
delicacy bimyoosa *(of coloring, etc.)*.
delicate yowái *(in health)*; kowareyasúi *(fragile)*.
  a delicate situation muzukashíi tachiba.
delicious oishii.
delight ureshisa.
deliver (to) todokéru *(goods)*; watasu *(hand over)*.
deliverance kyuushutsu *(from bondage, etc.)* sukui dásu kotó.
delivery haitatsu *(forwarding)*.
demand yookyuu, motomé *(request)*; juyoo *(for goods)*.
  to be in demand juyoo ga áru.
democracy minshushúgi, demokurashii.
demonstrate (to) jitsuen suru.
demonstration jitsuen *(exhibition)*; jíi úndoo, démo *(mass meeting, protest parade)*.
denial hitei *(negation)*; hinín *(disavowal)*; kyóhi *(refusal)*.
denounce (to) kokuhatsu suru *(inform against)*; háki suru *(repudiate)*.
dense fukái *(as fog)*; oishigétta *(as forest)*; konda *(crowded)*.
density mítsudo.
dentist háisha.
deny (to) uchikesu.
depart (to) déru.
department bumon *(section)*; depáato *(department store)*.
departure shuppatsu.
depend (to) tayóru *(for support)*; tánomi ni suru *(rely on)*.
dependent tayótte iru *(on one's parents, etc.)*.
deplore (to) nagéku *(lament)*.
deposit tekin *(as a binder)*; yokin *(in a bank)*.
depress (to) kiochi suru.
depression fukéiki *(in business)*; yuuutsu *(of mind)*.
deprive (to) ubaitóru.
depth fukása.

deride (to) azakéru.

descend (to) kudaru *(go down)*; oríru *(alight from)*; kudari ni náru *(slope down)*.

descendant shíson.

describe (to) setsumei suru, nobéru *(give an account of)*.

description setsumei, jojutsu *(of a person)*.

desert sabaku.

desert (to) suteru *(one's family or friend)*; dassoo suru *(from the army)*.

deserve (to) shikaku ga áru *(be entitled to)*; shoosan o ukéru shikaku ga áru *(be worthy of)*.

design zuan *(sketch)*; kooan *(idea, scheme)*; dezáin *(dress, etc.)*.

designer zuanka *(of patterns)*; kooánsha *(of ideas)*; dezáinaa *(of dresses)*.

desirable nozomashíi.

desire yokuboo *(craving)*; nozomi *(wish, hope)*.

desire (to) nozómu *(long for)*; kiboo suru *(wish)*.

desk tsukue, désuku.

desolate wabishíi, sabishíi.

despair zetsuboo, rakutan *(despondency)*.

despair (to) zetsuboo suru *(lose hope)*; rakutan suru *(be disappointed)*.

desperate zetsuboo teki na *(beyond hope)*; kiken na *(dangerous)*; hisshi no *(frantic)*; mukóomizu no *(reckless)*.

despise (to) misageru.

despite ákui *(malice)*; bujoku *(insult)*; keibetsu *(scorn)*.

    despite —ni mo kakawárazu.

dessert dezáato.

destiny únmei.

destroy (to) kowásu; hakai suru *(demolish)*; dainashi ni suru *(ruin)*; zenmetsu saseru *(annihilate)*.

destruction hakai.

detach (to) hikihanásu *(unfasten, separate)*.

detail saimoku *(item)*; kuwashíi koto, shoosai *(particulars)*.

    in detail kuwáshiku.

detain (to) hikitoméru.

detect (to) tantei suru.

detective tantei.

    detective story tantei shóosetsu.

determination saiketsu *(decision)*; késshin *(resolution)*; ketsudán ryoku *(firmness of purpose)*.

determine (to) kakutei suru *(ascertain)*; kimeru *(decide)*.

detest (to) kirau.

detour mawari michi.

detrimental furíeki na, yóku nái.

develop (to) hatten saseru *(cause to grow)*; keihatsu suru *(unfold)*; genzoo suru *(photo negatives)*.

development seichoo *(growth)*; hatten *(gradual progress)*; kakuchoo *(expansion)*.

device kufuu.

devil oní, ákuma.

devise (to) kufuu suru.

devoid kakete iru *(lacking in)*.

devote (to) sasageru *(give up, direct)*.

devour gátsugatsu tabéru *(eat hungrily and greedily)*; horobósu *(destroy)*.

    devour a book musabori yómu.

dew tsúyu.

dial daiyaru, mojiban.

    telephone dial daiyaru.

dial (to) diayaru o mawasu.

dialect hoogen.

dialogue kaiwa.

diameter chokkei.

diamond daiyamóndo, kongóosekí.

diary nikki.

    to keep a diary nikkí o tsukéru.

dictate (to) kakitoraséru *(a letter)*.

dictation kakitori *(practice in spelling)*; koojutsu *(business)*.

dictionary jísho, jíten, jíbiki *(lexicon)*.

    English-Japanese dictionary Ei-Wa jíten. **Japanese-English dictionary** Wa-Ei jíten.

die (to) shinu.

diet shokuji ryóohoo *(prescribed allowance of food)*.

Diet gíkai *(Japanese Congress)*.

differ from (to) chigau.

difference chigai *(dissimilarity)*; sábetsu *(distinction)*; iken no sooi *(disagreement)*.

different (be) chigau.

difficult mu zukashíi.

difficulty kónnan, mendoo.

dig (to) hóru.

digest (to) shooka suru *(food)*; kanryaku ni suru *(abbreviate)*.

dignity igen *(of bearing)*.

dim usugurai.

dimension ménseki *(area)*; ookisa *(size)*.

diminish (to) v.i. chiisáku náru *(in size)*; sukunáku náru *(in number)*.

dine (to) shokuji o suru.

dining room shokudoo.

dinner hirú no shokuji, hiruhan *(noon meal)*; ban no shokuji, yuuhan *(evening meal)*.

dip (to) tsukeru, hitasu.

diplomacy gaikoo *(between nations)*; kakehiki *(tactful dealing)*.

diplomat gaikóokan.

direct massúgu na *(straight)*; jíka no *(direct rays, etc.)*.

direct (to) shíiji suru *(point the way)*; sáshizu suru *(order)*.

direction hoogaku *(way)*; shidoo suru *(guidance)*; kánri *(control)*; sáshizu *(instruction)*.

director shiháinin *(manager)*; juuyaku *(of a company)*; shunin *(chief)*.

directory juushóroku.

    telephone directory denwachoo.

dirt óbutsu *(filth)*; doró *(mud)*; hokori *(dust)*.

dirty kitanái.

disability múryoku.

disabled múryoku ni nátta.

disadvantage fúri.

disagree (to) itchi shinai.

disagreeable fuyúkai na.

disagreement fuítchi *(discord)*; fuchóowa *(disharmony)*; iken no sooi *(dissent)*; fúwa *(quarrel)*.

disappear (to) miénaku náru.

disappearance miénaku náru kotó, shooshitsu.

disappoint (to) shitsuboo saseru.

disapprove (to) sansei shinai.

disaster tensai *(calamity)*.

disastrous hisan na, saigai no ookíi *(flood, etc.)*.

discharge káiko *(release from duty)*; jotai *(army)*.

discharge (to) funaoroshi o suru *(cargo)*; hassha suru *(a gun)*; hima o dásu *(dismiss)*.

discipline kúnren *(drill)*, kiritsu *(order)*.

disclaim (to) hóoki suru.

disclose (to) arawásu *(expose)*; abáku *(reveal)*; happyoo suru *(make known)*.

disclosure bákuro.

discomfort fukái.

disconnect (to) kíru *(sever a connection)*.

discontent fumánzoku na.

discontinue (to) chuushi suru.

discord fúwa.

discount waribiki.

discount (to) waribíki suru.

discourage (to) rakutan saseru.
　to be discouraged gakkári suru.

discouragement rakutan.

discover (to) mitsukeru *(find small things)*; hakken suru *(find more important things)*.

discovery hakken.

discreet shíryo no áru *(judicious)*; shinchoo na *(prudent)*; yoojinbukái *(wary)*.

discretion shíryo *(prudence)*.

discuss (to) tóogi suru *(talk over)*; tóoron suru *(argue)*.

discussion tóogi *(debate)*; tóoron *(argument)*.

disdain keibetsu.

disdain (to) keibetsu suru.

disease byooki.

disgrace fuméiyo *(dishonor)*; hají *(shame)*.

disguise hensoo.
　in disguise hensoo shite.

disguise (to) hensoo suru.

disgust iyaki.

disgust (to) muné o wáruku suru *(nauseate)*; kimochi wáruku saseru *(create an aversion)*.
　be disgusted unzári suru.

dish sara.

dishonest fushóojiki na.

disk enban.

dislike kirai.

dislike (to) kirau.

dismiss (to) ikaseru *(allow to go)*; menshoku suru *(expel)*; hima o dásu *(discharge)*.

dismissal hima.

disobey (to) somúku.

disorder ranzatsu *(lack of order)*; kónzatsu *(confusion)*.

dispense with (to) shóbun suru *(dispose of)*.

display chinretsu *(show)*; hyoogen *(manifestation)*; misebirakashi *(ostentation)*.

displease (to) ki ni sawaraseru *(offend)*.

displeasure fuman *(dissatisfaction)*.

disposal shóbun.

dispose (to) naraberu *(arrange)*; —ki ni náru *(be inclined to)*.
　to dispose of shóbun suru.

dispute kóoron *(debate)*; sóogi *(controversy)*; kenka *(altercation)*.

dispute (to) tóogi suru *(argue about)*; hanbaku suru *(contest)*; teikoo suru *(oppose)*.

dissolve (to) tokásu *(melt)*; torikesu *(annul)*.

distance kyóri.

distant tooi *(far off)*.

distinct hakkíri shita *(clear)*; tokushu na *(different)*.

distinction tokuchoo *(individuality)*.

distinguish (to) miwakéru *(through sight)*; kikiwakéru *(through sound)*.

distort (to) yugaméru *(twist)*; kojitsukéru *(pervert)*.

distract (to) ki o toraréru.

distress nayami *(worry)*; nageki *(grief)*; kutsuu *(pain)*.

distribute (to) wariatéru *(allot)*; makichirásu *(spread out)*; bunpai suru *(apportion)*; kubáru *(deal out)*.

district chihóo *(region)*; kú *(city ward)*.

distrust fushín'yoo.

distrust (to) shinjínai.

disturb (to) jama suru.

disturbance jama.

ditch mizo, horiwari *(trench)*.

dive (to) tobikómu.

divide (to) wakéru *(separate, part)*; waru *(by cutting)*; shikíru *(by partition)*.

divine shinsei na.
　divine being kámi.
　divine service reiháishiki.

division warízan *(math.)*; bunkatsu *(separation)*.

divorce (to) rikon suru.
　divorced rikon shita hito.

dizziness memái.

dizzy memái ga suru.

do (to) suru *(act)*; tsukúru *(make)*.

dock hatoba, dókku.

doctor isha *(medical)*; hákase *(academic)*.

doctrine shúgi.

document shórui *(papers)*; shoosho *(deed)*; búnsho *(official letter)*.

dog inú.

doll ningyoo.

dome maru ténjoo.

domestic katei no *(household)*; kainarasareta *(domesticated, tame)*; kokúnai no *(native, pertaining to one's country)*.
　domestic affairs káji *(of a household)*.
　domestic animal kachiku.

dominate (to) shihai suru *(govern)*.

door to, dóa *(occidental style)*.
　Japanese sliding door shooji.
　entrance door genkan.
　back door uraguchi.

dose tekiryoo.

dot ten.

double nibai.

double (to) nibai ni suru.

doubt utagai *(lack of certainty)*; fushin *(misgiving)*.

doubt (to) utagáu *(disbelieve)*; fushin ni omóu *(question)*.

doubtful táshika de nái *(uncertain)*; hakkíri shinai *(ambiguous)*; utagawashíi *(questionable)*.

doubtless utagai nai.

down shita.

dozen dáassu.

draft kawase tegata *(bank order)*; shitae *(sketch)*; shitagaki *(of a plan)*.

   draft (draught) of wind sukimá kaze.

drag (to) hiku *(draw forcibly)*; hikizuru *(pull)*.

drain (to) haisui suru *(carry away water)*; nomihosu *(drink up)*.

drama engeki, dórama *(a play)*; gekiteki jíken *(event)*.

draw (to) káku *(pictures)*; sagéru *(money from the bank)*; hiku *(pull)*.

   to draw back shirizóku.

drawer hikidashi *(of a table, etc.)*.

drawing room zashiki.

dread osore.

dread (to) osoréru.

dreadful osoroshíi.

dream yumé.

dream (to) yumé o míru.

dreamer kuusooka, musooka.

dress kimono *(Japanese)*; dóresu, yoofuku *(occidental)*.

dress (to) *v.t.* kimono o kiseru; *v.i.* kimono o kiru.

dressmaker yoofukuya *(of occidental clothes)*; shitateya *(of Japanese clothes)*.

drink nomímono.

   drinking water nomímizu.

drink (to) nómu.

drip (to) shitatáru.

drive (to) unten suru.

driver unténshu.

drop itteki *(of liquid)*.

drop (to) *v.t.* otóso *(let fall)*; *v.i.* ochíru *(from a height)*.

drown (to) oboreru.

drug kusuri *(medicine)*; masúiyaku *(narcotics)*.

drugstore kusuriya.

drum taiko; dóramu *(occidental style)*.

drunk yótte iru.

   a drunken person yopparai.

dry kawáita *(of things)*; kansoo shita *(of climate)*.

dry (to) kawakásu *(make dry)*; nugúu *(wipe one's eyes, etc.)*; kawáku *(become dry)*.

dryness kawaki *(thirst)*.

duck ahiru *(domestic)*; kámo *(wild)*.

due manki *(payable)*; toozen no *(fit, proper)*.

   due to —no tamé ni.

dull nibúi *(blunt)*; bonyári shita *(stupid)*; omoshiróku nái *(uninteresting)*.

dumb oshi.

during —no aida, —kan, —chuu (juu).

   during ten years juunen kan.

   during one's absence rúsu no aida, rusu chuu.

dust chiri; hokori *(a finer dust than chiri)*.

dust (to) sooji suru, hokori o haráu.

dusty hokori no óoi.

Dutch Oranda no.

duty tsutome *(work to be done)*; gímu *(moral or legal obligation)*; kanzei *(on imported goods)*.

dwarf kobito *(person)*; kogata no *(undersized)*.

   dwarf trees bonsai no ki.

dwell (to) súmu.

dye senryóo.

dye (to) someru.

E

each káku *(prefix)* —zútsu.

   each person méi mei.

   each person or thing sorézore *(of several)*.

   each other otagai ni.

   each time —tabí ni.

eager nésshin na *(ardent)*.

eagle washi.

ear mimí.

early *adj.* hayái. —*adv.* háyaku.

earn (to) kaségu *(by labor)*.

earnest majime na *(serious)*, nésshin na *(intense)*.

earth tsuchí *(soil)*; chikyuu *(world)*.

ease rakú, kiraku.

ease (to) rakú ni seru.

easily yasashíku; tegaru ni *(readily)*; súrasura to *(smoothly)*.

east higashi.

   the East Tóoyoo.

   East Asia Tóoa.

Easter fukkátsusai.

eastern higashi no.

easy yasashíi.

eat (to) tabéru *(plain)*; meshiagaru *(pol.)*.

echo yamabiko *(as phenomenon of nature)*; hankyoo *(in other cases)*.

echo (to) hankyoo suru.

economical keizaijoo no, keizaiteki na.

economize (to) setsuyaku suru *(use economically)*.

edge há *(of blade)*; hashi *(of cloth)*; kishí *(of cliff, etc.)*.

edition han.

   first edition shohan.

   new edition shinpan.

   revised edition kaiteiban.

editor henshúusha *(of books or magazines)*; shuhitsu *(of newspaper)*.

editorial shasetsu.

education kyooiku.

   to receive an education kyooiku o ukéru.

effect kekka *(consequence)*.

effective yuukoo na *(operative)*; yuunoo na *(efficient)*.

efficiency nooritsu.

effort dóryoku *(strenuous attempt)*; honeori *(exertion)*; róoku *(strain)*.

with an effort hone ótte.
without any effort dóryoku sézu ni.
egg tamago.
egoism jiko chuushin shúgi.
eight yattsú, hachí.
eighteen juuhachí.
eighteenth juuhachí ban.
eighth dái hachí.
eightieth hachijúu ban.
eighty hachijúu.
either dóchiraka no (one of the two); dóchira mo (each of two).
　　either . . . or —ka . . . ka, —ka arúiwa . . . ka.
elastic shinshukusei no áru, shináyaka na (flexible).
elbow hijí.
elder toshiue no.
　　elder brother níisan.
　　elder sister néesan.
elderly nenpai no.
eldest ichiban toshi ue no.
　　eldest son chóonan.
　　eldest daughter chóojo.
elect (to) erábu (choose); sénkyo suru (by vote).
election sénkyo.
electric dénki no.
electrical dénki no.
electricity dénki.
elegant yúuga na (graceful); joohín na (tasteful).
element yóoso (component part).
elementary shotoo no.
elephant zóo.
elevator erebéetaa.
eleven juuichí.
eleventh dái juuichí.
eliminate (to) nozoku (exclude); sákujo suru (get rid of); habúku (omit).
eloquence yuuben.
eloquent yuuben na.
else hoka ni.
　　something else hoka ni náni ka.
　　anyone else hoka ni dáre ka.
elsewhere hoka ni dóko ka.
elude (to) nogaréru (evade); sakéru (escape adroitly from).
embark (to) joosen suru (board a ship); shuppan suru (depart).
embarrass (to) komaraséru.
　　I was embarrassed. Komarimáshita.
embarrassing toowaku saseru.
embarrassment toowaku (perplexity).
embassy taishikan.
embody gutaika suru (make concrete).
embrace (to) daku, (a person); torimáku (encircle); hoogan suru (contain).
embroidery nuitori.
emerge (to) arawaréru (come out into view).
emergency hijóoji.
eminent kéncho na (distinguished).
emotion kanjoo (feeling).
　　with emotion kandoo shite.
　　appeal to the emotions kanjoo ni uttaéru.
emperor tennóo.
emphasis kyoochoo.

emphasize (to) kyoochoo suru.
emphatic tsuyoi.
empire téikoku.
employee yatoinin, shiyoonin.
employer yatóinushi.
employment shokúgyoo (occupation); shigoto (work).
empty kara no.
enable (to) —ga dekíru.
enamel enameru.
enclose (to) kakomu (surround); kakou (shut in).
enclosure kakoi (fence); doofúubutsu (enclosed materials).
encourage (to) genki zukéru (hearten); yuuki zukéru (put courage into).
encouragement hagemashi.
end sue (latter part); owari (the close); ketsumatsu (conclusion); shimai (finish).
end (to) owaru, shimau.
endeavor jinryoku, dóryoku.
endeavor (to) dóryoku suru (try hard); kokoromíru (attempt).
endorse (to) uragaki suru.
endure (to) gáman suru (bear bravely); mochikotáeru (hold out).
enemy teki.
energy chikara (power); génki (vigor).
　　mental energy seishin nóoryoku.
　　atomic energy genshíryoku.
enforce (to) shiiru (press).
engage (to) yatóu (hire).
engaged isogashíi (busy); kon'yaku shite iru (betrothed).
engagement yakusoku (formal promise); kon'yaku (betrothal); yooji (business).
engine kikái (machine); kikán (boiler).
engineer gíshi (of factory).
English eigo no (pertaining to the language); Eikoku no (pertaining to the country); Eikokujin (pertaining to people).
engrave (to) hóru; insatsu suru (print).
enjoy (to) tanoshímu.
enjoyment tanoshimi.
enlarge (to) ookíku suru (make bigger); hikinobásu (a photograph, etc.).
enlist (to) gúntai ni háiru (in the army); hito no shíji o éru (secure one's support).
enormous kyodai na.
enough juubun.
enter (to) háiru.
entertain (to) tanoshimaséru (amuse); motenasu (guests).
entertainment goraku (amusement); yokyoo (public show).
enthusiasm nésshin.
enthusiastic nésshin na.
entire kanzen na (complete); zentai no (whole).
entitle (to) na o tsukéru.
entrance iriguchi.
entrust (to) makaséru (a duty, etc.); azukéru (a thing to another person).
enumerate (to) kazoéru (count).
envelope fuutoo (for letters).

envious urayamashíi.

envy urayami, sonemi *(jealousy)*.

envy (to) urayámu *(feel envy of)*; sonému *(begrudge)*.

episode soowa, episóodo.

equal onaji *(the same)*; byoodoo no *(equable)*.

equal (to) —ni hitoshíi.
    A equals B. A wa B desu.

equality byoodoo.

equator sekidoo.

equilibrium tsuriai.

equip (to) yóoi o suru *(supply)*; sóobi suru *(fit)*; mijítaku suru *(array)*.

equipment shitaku, júnbi.

era jidai.

erase (to) kesu nuguikésu *(wipe out)*.

eraser keshi gomu.

erect (to) tatéru *(set up)*.

err (to) machigáeru.

errand tsukai.

error machigái.

escalator esukaréetaa.

escape toosoo *(running away)*; datsugoku *(from prison)*.

escape (to) nigéru *(get free)*; nogaréru *(get off safely)*.

escort (to) goei suru *(with military)*; tsukisóu *(accompany)*.

especially tóku ni.

essay ronbun.

essence yootén *(main points)*; hóntai *(a thing in itself)*; yóoso *(element)*.

essential kanarazu iru, nákute wa naránai *(necessary)*; honshitsuteki no *(of essential character)*.

establish tatéru, setsuritsu suru *(found)*; kakutei suru *(ascertain)*; seitei suru *(prove)*.

establishment setsuritsu *(business firm)*.

estate shoyúuchi *(property)*; jísho *(ground)*.

esteem sonkei *(respect)*.

esteem (to) sonkei suru.

esthetic fúuryuu na, biteki na.

estimate mitsumori *(of the cost)*; hyóoka *(of the value)*.

estimate (to) hyóoka suru *(appraise)*; mitsumóru *(compute)*; hándan suru *(judge)*.

estimation mitsumori, hyóoka.

eternal eikyuu no *(everlasting)*; huhen no *(immutable)*.

eternity eikyuu, eien *(infinite time)*; fumetsu *(immortality)*.

ether eeteru.

European Yooroppájin *(people)*; Yooróppa no *(pertaining to Europe)*.

evade sakéru.

evasion káihi.

eve yuugata *(evening)*; zénya *(the evening or day before a festival)*.

even mo, démo *(also)*; taira na *(level)*; choodo *(just)*.

evening ban, yóru, yuugata.
    Good evening! Konban wa.
    yesterday evening sakúban, yuube.
    tomorrow evening myóoban, ashita no ban.

event dekígoto, jíken.

ever ítsu demo *(always)*; táezu *(incessantly)*; ima máde ni *(up to now)*; itsu ka *(on any occasion)*.

every mai-, dónna —démo; zénbu *(all)*.
    everyday máinichi.
    every year maitoshi.

everybody dáre mo *(referring to members of a group)*; dáre demo *(no matter who)*; minna *(all)*.

everything nán demo *(no matter what)*; zénbu, minna *(all things)*.

everywhere dóko de mo *(no matter where)*; hóoboo *(all over)*.

evidence shooko *(proof)*.

evident akíraka na *(obvious)*.

evil *adj.* warúi, akushitsu na *(wicked)*; fukitsu na *(unlucky)*. —*n.* áku *(vice)*; jáaku *(wickedness)*; warúi koto *(bad thing)*.

evoke (to) hikiokósu *(draw forth)*.

evolve (to) tenkai suru *(unfold, unroll)*; hatten suru *(develop)*.

exact seikaku na *(accurate)*; genmitsu na *(precise)*; genkaku na *(rigorous)*.

exaggerate (to) kochoo suru, oogesa ni iu.

exaggeration kochoo, oogesa.

exalt (to) takaméru *(raise high)*; homesoyásu *(extol)*.

exaltation takaméru koto.

examination kénsa *(inspection)*; chóosa *(investigation)*; koosatsu *(consideration)*; shikén *(test)*.

examine (to) shirabéru *(inspect)*; shikén suru *(give a test)*.

example réi *(illustration)*; tehón *(model, pattern)*.

exceed sugíru, kosu *(go over)*.

excel (to) sugúreru.
    He excels in English. Eigo ni sugúrete iru.

excellence subaráshisa, kesshutsu *(superiority)*; chóosho *(great merit)*.

excellent sugúreta.

except —no hoka wa.

except (to) nozoku *(omit)*; koshoo o iu *(take exception)*.

exception reigai.

exceptional reigaiteki na.

exceptionally reigaiteki ni *(unusually)*; hijoo ni *(very)*.

excess yobun.

excessive yobun no *(surplus)*; hoogai na *(exorbitant)*.

exchange kookan *(of things in general)*; ryoogae *(of coins only)*.

exchange (to) torikaeru, kookan suru *(barter)*.

excite (to) *v.i.* sawágu *(a body of people)*, *v.t.* ugokásu *(arouse a feeling)*.
    to get excited koofun suru.

excitement koofun.

exclaim sakebu *(cry out)*; zekkyoo suru *(speak vehemently)*.

exclamation zekkyoo *(outcry)*; kantánshi *(an interjection)*.
    exclamation mark kantánfu.

exclude (to) nozoku.

exclusive dokusenteki *(monopolistic)*; —o nozoite *(not including)*.

excursion ensoku *(picnic)*; yuuran ryókoo *(pleasure tour)*.

excuse koojitsu *(bad)*; iiwake *(apology)*.

excuse (to) yurúsu *(forgive)*; benkai suru *(vindicate)*.

  Excuse me. Gomen nasái.

execute (to) jikkoo suru *(carry out)*; suikoo suru *(perform)*.

execution shikkoo, suikoo.

exempt (to) menzúru *(free)*.

exercise undoo *(of the body)*; renshuu *(lesson)*.

exercise (to) undoo suru *(engage in athletics)*; renshuu suru *(practice)*.

exert (to) tsukúsu *(put forth)*; mochiíru *(use)*.

exertion dóryoku, jínryoku *(vigorous effort)*.

exhaust (to) kará ni suru *(empty)*; tsukai tsukúsu *(use up)*; tsukarehatesaséru *(tire out)*.

exhaustion hiroo *(extreme fatigue)*.

exhibit (to) tenji suru *(show publicly)*.

exhibition hakuránkai *(exposition)*; tenjíkai *(show)*.

exile tsuihoo *(banishment)*; tsuihoonin *(person in exile)*.

exile (to) tsuihoo suru.

exist sonzai suru, áru *(be)*.

existence sonzai *(being)*; seizon *(life)*.

exit déguchi.

expand hirogeru *(spread out)*; kakuchoo suru *(extend)*; kakudai saseru *(amplify)*.

expansion kakuchoo *(dilation)*; hirogari *(expanse)*.

expansive koodai na *(extensive)*; kokoro no hirói *(comprehensive)*.

expect (to) kitai suru *(look forward to)*; —to omóu *(suppose)*.

expectation kitai *(anticipation)*; yosoo *(probability)*.

expedition tanken *(for exploration)*.

expel (to) oiharáu *(drive out)*; menshoku suru *(dismiss)*.

expense híyoo.

expensive takái, kóoka na *(costly)*.

experience keiken *(personal observation)*.

experience (to) keiken suru *(undergo)*.

experiment (to) shikén suru *(test)*; tamésu *(try out)*.

expert *adj.* kuróoto *(in doing something)*. —*n.* senmonka *(specialist)*.

expire (to) kikan ga kireru *(come to an end)*; íki o hikitóru *(breathe one's last)*; kieru *(die out)*; shoometsu suru *(become extinct)*.

explain (to) setsumei suru *(give an explanation)*; káishaku suru *(interpret)*; benmei suru *(justify by an explanation)*.

explanation setsumei.

explanatory setsumeiteki, setsumei no.

explode (to) bakuhatsu suru.

exploit tegara *(brilliant achievement)*.

exploit (to) kuimono ni suru *(take advantage of for one's own ends)*.

explore (to) tanken suru *(search through)*; chóosa suru *(inquire into)*.

explosion bakuhatsu.

export yushutsu.

export (to) yushutsu suru.

expose (to) sarasu *(leave unprotected)*; chinretsu suru *(exhibit)*; roshutsu suru *(in photography)*; abáku *(disclose, reveal)*.

express sokutatsu *(special delivery)*; kyuukoo *(train)*.

express (to) iiarawásu *(state)*.

expression hyoojoo *(facial)*; hyoogen *(verbal)*.

expressive hyoojoo ni tómu.

expulsion hoochiku.

exquisite sensai na *(delicate)*.

extend (to) nobásu *(in length or term)*; hirogeru *(in breadth)*; okuru *(an invitation, greetings)*.

extensive koodai na *(far-reaching)*.

extent han'i *(space, scope, degree)*.

  to some extent áru ten máde wa.

exterior sóto, hyoomen *(surface)*.

exterminate (to) tayásu.

external gáibu no *(outside)*.

extinct horóbite shimatta.

extinction shoometsu.

extinguish kesu *(put out)*; tayásu *(put an end to)*.

extra betsu no.

  an extra googai *(edition of a newspaper)*.

extract bassui *(excerpt)*.

extract (to) nuku *(pull out)*; nuki-tóru *(pull out with difficulty)*; tekishutsu suru *(draw forth)*.

extraordinary futsuu de nái *(exceptional)*; hibon na *(uncommon)*; ichijirushíi *(remarkable)*.

extravagance zeitaku *(lavish wastefulness)*; hoojuu *(unrestrained excess)*.

extravagant zeitaku na *(profuse, wasteful)*; múcha na *(unreasonable)*; hóogai na *(exorbitant, excessive)*.

extreme kyokután na *(utmost)*; ichiban tooi *(outermost)*.

extremely taihen, hijoo ni.

extremity hashi *(extreme point)*.

eye mé.

eyebrow máyuge.

eyeglasses mégane.

eyelid mábuta.

F

fable otogibánashi, guuwa.

face kao.

face (to) mukau.

facilitate yasashiku suru.

facility yooi *(ease)*; béngi *(convenience)*.

fact kotó *(of an occurrence)*; jikoo *(particulars)*.

  in fact jitsú wa.

factory kooba, koojoo.

faculty shuwan *(aptitude)*; gakubu *(of a university)*.

fade iró ga saméru.
fail (to) shippai suru *(be unsuccessful)*; hasan suru *(become bankrupt)*.
  without fail machigái naku, kitto, zéhi.
faint usui *(of color)*; yowái *(wanting in courage)*; kásuka na *(of sound, etc.)*.
faint (to) kizetsu suru.
fair *adj.* kírei na *(pretty)*; iro no shirói *(of complexion)*; koohei na *(impartial)*. —*n.* ichi *(market)*; jizen íchi *(bazaar)*.
faith shinkoo *(belief)*; shinjoo *(creed)*; kyóogi *(religious doctrine)*; shinrai *(trust)*.
faithful chuujitsu na.
fall tsuiraku *(drop)*; taki *(cascade)*; áki *(autumn)*; kanraku *(surrender)*; gakai *(of a government)*.
fall (to) ochíru *(drop)*; fúru *(rain, snow)*; sagáru *(prices)*.
  fall down korobu.
false úso no, hontoo de nái *(not true)*; fujitsu na *(not faithful)*; sorazorashíi *(feigned)*; nise *(counterfeit)*.
fame meisei.
familiar yóku shirarete iru *(well known)*; kikináreta *(to the ear)*; minareta *(to the eye)*; arifureta *(common)*; shitashíi *(intimate)*.
family kázoku.
  family name myóoji.
famine bússhi no ketsuboo *(scarcity of food)*; kikín *(failure of crops)*; kíga *(starvation)*.
famous yuumei na.
fan sensu *(folding)*; uchíwa *(non-folding)*.
  electric fan senpúuki.
fancy soozóoryoku *(imagination)*; kangáe *(idea)*.
fantastic kuusootéki na *(extravagant)*; iyoo na *(grotesque)*; soozoojoo no *(imaginary)*.
far tooi.
  as fas as máde.
  so far ima máde *(up to now)*.
  one-way fare katamichi.
fare ryóokin *(cost of transportation)*.
farm hatake *(field)*; noojoo *(ranch)*.
farmer nóofu, hyakushoo.
farming nóogyoo *(agriculture)*.
farther mótto tooku.
farthest ichiban tooi.
fashion tsukuri káta *(shape)*; ryuukoo, fásshon *(style)*.
fashionable (to become) ryuukoo suru.
fast hayái.
fasten (to) shikkári tomeru *(make fast)*; kukuri tsukéru *(attach securely)*.
fat *adj.* futótta. —*n.* abura.
fatal inochi ni kakawáru.
  fatal wound chiméishoo.
  fatal accident chimeitéki jíko.
  fatal disease fúji no yámai.
fate únmei *(destiny)*; ún *(appointed lot)*.
father otóosan *(pol.)*; chichi *(plain)*.
faucet jáguchi.
fault kettén *(defect)*; tánsho *(weak point)*; machigái *(mistake)*.
favor onegai *(request)*.

Could [will] you do me a favor? Onegai dekimásu ka?
favor (to) ekohíiki o suru *(be partial to)*; shíji suru *(support)*.
favorable kooi aru *(well disposed)*; shoodaku no *(consenting)*.
favorite *adj.* ki ni iri no *(preferred)*; dáisuki na *(liked greatly)*. —*n.* ninkimonó *(person)*.
fear osore *(dread)*; shinpai *(anxiety)*.
fear (to) osoréru.
fearless daitán na.
feather hane.
feature tokuchoo *(characteristic)*; yootén *(striking point)*; kaodachi *(appearance)*.
February Nigatsu.
federal chuuoo seifu no *(pertaining to the central government)*.
fee gessha *(monthly)*; shinsatsúryoo *(doctor's)*.
feeble yowái *(weak)*; bonyári shita *(indistinct)*.
feed (to) tabesaséru.
feel (to) sawaru *(touch)*; kanjiru *(perceive a sensation)*.
feeling kankaku *(sense)*; kimochi *(sensation)*; kanjoo *(emotion)*.
fellow *adj.* nakama no. —*n.* nakama *(associate)*.
fellowship shoogákukin *(grant)*; shinboku *(friendliness)*.
fellow worker shigoto nákama.
female onna *(woman)*.
  female sex josei.
feminine onna no.
fence kakíne *(enclosure for garden)*; kakoi *(for other purposes)*.
fencing kéndoo *(Japanese-style)*; fénshingu *(foreign)*.
ferocious kyooboo na *(fierce)*; yaban na *(savage)*.
ferry watashibúne *(ferryboat)*; renrakusén *(connected with trains)*.
fertile kóeta *(productive)*.
fertilize (to) híryoo o hodokósu.
fertilizer híryoo *(manure)*; kagaku híryoo *(chemical)*.
fervent netsuretsu na *(ardent)*.
fervor netsuretsu *(ardor)*.
festival saijitsu *(feast day)*; omatsuri, matsuri *(of shrine or temple)*.
fetch motte kúru.
fever netsú.
few ní san *(two or three)*; sukóshi *(not many)*.
fiber sén'i.
fiction shoosetsu.
field nóhara *(open country)*; bokusóochi *(meadow)*.
  rice field tá.
fierce araarashíi *(ferocious)*; mooretsu na *(violent)*; hageshíi *(furious)*.
fiery hí no yoo na *(glowing)*.
fifteen júugo.
fifteenth dái júugo; júugo nichi *(of the month)*; júugo ban.
fifth dái go.
fiftieth dai gojúu.

fifty gojúu.

fig ichíjiku.

fight kenka *(brawl)*; sensoo *(battle)*.

fight (to) sensoo suru *(wage war)*; dóryoku suru *(struggle for)*; kenka suru *(quarrel)*.

figure suuji *(number)*; katachí *(form)*; súgata *(body)*; moyoo *(design, pattern)*.

file yasuri *(tool)*; rétsu *(row)*; fáiru *(official file)*; tojikomi *(for letters)*.

fill (to) *v.t.* ippai ni suru; *v.i.* ippai ni náru *(become full)*.

film fuirumu *(for camera)*; éiga *(motion picture)*.

filthy kitanái *(unclean)*; gehín na *(obscene)*.

final sáigo no *(last)*; shuukyoku no *(conclusive)*.

    finally tóotoo.

finance zaisei.

finance (to) kane o dasu.

financial zaiseijoo no.

find (to) mitsukeru.

fine *adj.* komakái *(small)*; hosóoi *(slender)*; usui *(thin)*; utsukushíi *(beautiful)*; ii *(good)*.

fine *n.* bakkín *(penalty)*.

finger yubi.

finish (to) shimau, oeru; dekiagaru *(complete a piece of work)*; shiagéru *(get a thing done)*.

fire hí; kájí *(conflagration)*.

fireworks hánabi.

firm *adj.* katai *(compact)*; shikkári shita *(rigid)*.

firm shóokai, kaisha *(commercial)*.

first *adj.* dái ichí no, ichí ban no *(ordinal number)*. —*adv.* hajíme.

    at first hajíme wa.

    for the first time hajímete.

fish sakana, uo; sashimi *(name of a dish)*.

    raw fish namazákana.

fish (to) tsuri o suru.

    go out fishing tsuri ni iku.

fisherman ryóoshi.

fist nigiri kóbushi.

fit *adj.* tekitoo na *(appropriate)*; datoo na *(proper, right)*. —*n.* hossa *(convulsion)*.

fit (to) tekitoo suru *(be proper for)*; tekigoo suru *(be fit for)*; awaséru *(make to suit)*; júnbi suru *(qualify)*; áu *(be adjusted to fit)*.

fitness tekitoo.

five itsútsu, go.

fix (to) kimeru *(determine)*; toritsukéru *(arrange)*; naósu *(mend)*.

flag hatá.

flame honoo.

flank sokumen *(side)*.

flank (to) sokumen o mamóru.

flash hirameki *(lightning)*.

flat hiratai *(level)*; kin'itsu no *(unvarying)*; ki no nuketa *(stale)*.

flatter oseji o iu.

flattery oseji *(insincere compliment)*.

flavor aji *(taste)*; kaori *(smell)*.

fleet kantai *(navy)*.

flesh nikú *(meat for eating)*; nikutai *(of the human body)*.

flexibility shináyakasa.

flexible shináyaka *(pliable)*.

flight hikoo *(trip by air)*; tooboo *(a fleeing)*; kaidan *(of stairs)*.

fling (to) tosshin suru *(dash, rush)*; nagetsukéru *(hurl, toss)*.

flint hiuchí ishi.

float (to) uku *(on water)*; ukabu *(on water or in air)*.

flood oomizu.

flood (to) shinsui saseru *(inundate)*; shinsui suru *(be inundated)*; hanran suru *(overflow)*.

floor yuka *(of a room)*.

flourish (to) sakaeru *(thrive)*.

flow nagaréru.

flower haná.

    flower arrangement ikébana, kádoo.

fluid ekitai.

fly haí.

fly (to) tobu.

foam awá.

foam (to) awá ga tátsu.

fog kiri *(mist)*; móya *(haze)*.

    thick fog nóomu.

fold hída *(in a garment)*.

fold (to) tatamu.

foliage ha.

follow (to) —ni shitagáu *(go or come after)*; —ni tsúite kúru *(come traveling with someone)*; —ni tsúite iku *(go accompanying someone)*; issho ni iku *(accompany)*.

following sono tsugí no *(next)*.

    the following day akuru hi.

fond (be) konómu.

fondness sukí.

food tabemóno.

fool báka.

foolish báka na *(silly)*; bakarashíi *(non sensical)*; bakágeta *(ridiculous)*.

foot ashí *(of the body)*; shaku *(Japanese measure)*; fíito *(American measure)*.

football futtobóoru, shuukyuu.

footstep ashidori *(tread)*; ashiáto *(footprint)*.

for —no kawari ni *(in place of)*; —o daihyoo shite *(representing)*; —ni táishite *(in return for, in contrast with)*; —no tsugunai ni *(in compensation for)*; —no tamé ni *(on behalf of, in support of, for the purpose of, because of)*; —ni mukatte *(in the direction of)*; —no wari ní wa *(in respect of)*.

    for example tatóeba.

    for the first time hajímete.

    for the most part daibúbun.

    for the present ina no tokoro.

forbid kinjíru.

force chikara *(strength)*; gúntai *(troops)*.

    by force múri ni.

force (to) bookoo suru *(use force upon)*; kojiakéru *(break open)*; oshíyaru *(impel)*; múri ni, shíite *(when followed by a causative verb)*.

    I forced him to go. Muri ni ikaseta.

ford (to) asase o wataru *(wade across)*.
foreground zenkei.
forehead hitai.
foreign gaikoku no *(pertaining to foreign countries in general)*; séiyoo no *(of the Occident)*.
foreigner gaikokújin, gaijin *(foreigners in general)*; oobéijin *(Occidental)*.
forest mori *(grove)*; shinrin *(dense growth)*.
forget (to) wasureru.
forgetfulness wasureppói kotó.
forgive yurúsu.
forgiveness yurushi.
fork hooku *(for eating)*; wakarémichi *(parting of the ways)*; shiryuu *(of a river)*; matá *(of a tree)*.
form katachi *(shape)*; keishiki *(formality)*; yóoshi *(blank)*.
form (to) katachizukúru *(shape)*; tsukúru *(organize)*; —ni náru *(constitute)*; tsukuriagéru *(build up)*.
formal seishiki no.
formation sóshiki.
former máe no, saki no *(previous)*.
formerly máe ni *(previously)*; móto *(originally)*.
formula hooshiki, yarikata *(method)*.
forsake (to) misuteru *(abandon)*.
fort yoosai.
fortieth shijuu ban mé no; dái yónjuu.
fortunate ún ga íi.
fortunately ún yoku, shiawase ní mo *(luckily)*; orí yoku *(opportunely)*.
fortune shiawase *(good luck)*; zaisan *(wealth)*; únsei *(fate)*.
forty shijúu, yónjuu.
forward zenpoo e *(onward)*.
 move forward zenshin suru.
forward (to) okuru *(goods)*; kaisoo suru, tensoo suru *(letters)*.
foster yoo—.
 foster daughter yóojo.
 foster mother yóobo.
 foster father yóofu.
 foster son yooshi.
found (to) setsuritsu suru *(establish, start)*; kisó o okú *(lay the base of)*.
foundation dodai *(groundwork)*; kónkyo *(basis)*; shuppátsuten *(beginning)*; zaiden *(endowed institution)*.
founder soorítsusha *(one who establishes or lays a foundation)*.
fountain funsúi.
four yottsú, shí, yón.
fourteen juushí, juuyón.
fourteenth juuyon ban mé no *(place)*; júuyokká *(of the month)*.
fourth yottsu me, dái shí, dái yón; yokka *(of the month)*.
fowl torí *(bird)*.
fox kitsuné.
fragment kakera, kirehashi.
fragrance yói níói.
fragrant nioi no íi.
frail yowayowashíi.
frame gakubuchi.

frame (to) é o gakú ni ireru *(a picture)*.
frank sotchoku na *(open-hearted)*; koozen no, akarasama na *(without guile)*.
frankness sotchoku.
free táda *(gratis)*; jiyúu na *(liberated)*; múzei *(without tax)*.
free (to) v.t. hanásu *(let go free)*; v.i. jiyúu ni náru *(be set free)*.
freedom jiyúu *(liberty)*; dokuritsu *(independence)*.
freeze (to) v.t. kooraseru; v.i. kooru.
freight kámotsu *(goods)*.
French furansu no *(pertaining to France)*; furansugo *(language)*; furansújin *(people)*.
frequent tabitabi no *(recurring often)*.
frequent (to) yóku iku *(visit often)*.
frequently tabitabi *(often)*; yóku *(at short intervals)*.
fresh mizumizushíi *(newly grown)*; dekitaté no *(just made)*; shinsen na, atarashíi *(said of foods)*.
friction masatsu, atsureki.
Friday Kin'yóobi.
friend tomodachi; yuujin *(used among men only)*.
friendly yuujoo no aru.
friendship yuujoo *(friendly attachment)*; yúugi *(intimacy)*.
frighten (to) odorokásu;
 be frightened bikkúri suru, odoróku.
frightening kowái.
fringe fusá *(tuft)*; herí *(border)*.
frivolity fumájime.
frivolous fumájime na.
frog kaeru.
from —kara.
 from now on íma kara.
front máe, zenmén *(forward part)*; zenpoo *(forward place)*; shoomen *(of a building)*; sensen *(line of battle)*.
frost shimó.
fruit kudámoto.
fry (to) furai suru, ageru.
frying pan furái pan, age nábe.
fuel nenryóo.
fugitive n. toosóosha *(runaway)*; booméisha *(political refugee)*.
fulfill (to) hatásu *(perform)*; jikkoo suru *(execute)*.
full ippai no *(filled to capacity)*.
fully mattaku.
fun tanoshimi *(amusement)*.
function hataraki.
function (to) hataraku.
fund kikín.
fundamental kisoteki na.
funds shikín *(sum of money)*.
funny kokkei na.
fur kegawa.
furious okótte iru *(angry)*.
furnace ro.
furnish (to) kyookyuu suru *(provide)*; sonaéru *(equip)*.
furniture kágu.
furrow áto *(track)*; wadachi *(rut)*; fukái shiwá *(deep wrinkle)*.

furrow (to) kao o shikameru *(make a wrinkle in the face).*
further sonó ue *(besides).*
  further away mótto saki.
  further on mótto saki e.
fury gékido *(wild anger);* kyooboo *(violence).*
future *adj.* mírai no. —*n.* mírai *(time to come);* shóorai *(prospect).*
  in the future mírai ni, shoorai.

G

gaiety nigiyákasa *(mirth).*
gain ríeki *(opposite of loss);* mooke *(earnings);* zooka *(increase).*
gain (to) te ni ireru, éru *(obtain);* masu *(increase).*
gallant isamashíi.
gallery gyáraii *(of fine arts);* tachimí-seki *(standing room in a theatre).*
gamble (to) kakegoto o suru, kakéru.
game yúugi *(amusement);* kyóogi *(sporting contest);* shoobugoto *(of chance).*
garage garéeji.
garden niwa.
  public garden kooen.
gardener uekiya, niwáshi.
garlic ninniku.
gas gásu.
gasoline gasorin.
gate món.
gather *v.t.* yoseatsuméru *(bring together);* atsuméru *(collect);* saishuu suru *(pick up);* tsumu *(as flowers); v.i.* atsumáru *(assemble).*
gay yooki na *(said of people);* hadé na *(said of colors).*
gem hooseki *(jewel).*
gender séi.
general *adj.* ippan no, ippanteki no *(belonging to the whole);* taitei no *(common to many).*
  in general, generally ippan ni.
general táishoo *(military).*
generalize (to) ippanka shite kangáeru.
generation sédai *(used when referring to people, as in "young generation");* jidai *(period of time).*
generosity kandaisa, kimae no yósa.
generous ki no ookíi.
genius tensai.
gentle otonashíi *(said of people);* yasashíi *(said of manners);* odáyaka na *(quiet).*
gentleman shínshi.
genuine honmono no *(authentic);* seijitsu na *(sincere).*
geographical chiriteki no.
geography chíri.
germ baikin.
German dóitsu no *(pertaining to Germany);* doitsugo no *(language);* doitsújin no *(people).*
gesture mĭburi.
get (to) náru *(become, turn);* té ni ireru *(get hold of).*
ghastly zotto suru.

giant *adj.* óoki na. —*n.* ooótoko *(big man).*
gift miyage *(souvenir);* okurimono, purézento *(present);* sainoo *(talent).*
gifted sainoo no áru *(talented).*
girl onná no ko.
give (to) ageru *(to others: pol.);* yaru *(to others: fam.);* watasu *(hand over);* kudasáru *(from others: pol.);* kureru *(from others: fam.).*
  give back káesu.
glad ureshíi *(delighted, happy).*
  be glad yorokóbu.
gladly yorokónde.
glance hitóme.
  at a glance hitóme de.
glance (to) chirátto míru *(look rapidly);* zatto mé o tóosu *(read rapidly).*
glass garasu *(material).*
  looking glass kagami.
  drinking glass koppu.
gleam kagayaki *(shine);* hirameki *(of intelligence).*
gleam (to) kagayaku.
glitter kagayaki.
glitter (to) pikápika hikaru.
globe tamá *(round object);* chikyuu *(the earth).*
gloomy kurai *(dark);* usugurai *(somber);* inki na *(depressed).*
glorious kooei áru *(illustrious);* soogon na *(majestic);* subarashíi *(delightful).*
glory kooei *(honor);* sookan *(splendor).*
glove tebúkuro.
  a pair of gloves tebúkuro hitókumi.
go (to) yuku, iku *(plain);* máiru *(humble);* irassháru *(pol.).*
  to go away itte shimau.
  to go back káeru.
  to go down oríru *(stairs, etc.).*
  to go down kudaru *(to a train).*
  to go into hairu.
  to go out déru.
  to go up noboru.
god kámi *(deity);* guuzoo *(idol).*
gold kín.
golden kin'iro no.
good íi, yói.
  Good afternoon! Konnichi wa.
  Good evening! Konban wa.
  Good morning! Ohayoo gozaimásu.
  Good night! Oyasumi nasái *(said when going to bed).*
good-by sayonara.
goods shinamono.
goodwill kóoi.
goose gachoo.
gossip goshíppu, uwasabanashi.
gossip (to) uwasabanashi o suru, hito no uwasa o suru.
govern (to) osaméru *(rule);* kánri suru *(control).*
government seiji *(politics);* seitai *(form of government);* kánri *(management);* toochi kikán *(governing body).*
grace shitoyákasa.

graceful shitóyaka na.
grain kokúmotsu.
grammar bunpoo.
grand subarashíi *(magnificent)*; rippa na *(splendid)*.
  Grand! mígoto desu.
grandchild magó.
granddaughter mago músume.
grandfather ojíisan, sófu.
grandmother obáasan, sóbo.
grandson mago músuko.
grant kyóka *(permission)*; joseikin *(funds)*.
grant (to) kikitodokéru *(consent to)*; ataeru *(give)*; júyo suru *(bestow)*; yurúsu *(allow, permit)*.
grape budoo.
grapefruit gureepu furúutsu.
grasp (to) nigiru *(in the hand)*; tsukámu *(with the hand or mind)*.
grass kusá.
grasshopper inago.
grateful arigatái.
gratitude kánsha.
grave *adj.* juudai na *(serious)*.
grave haká *(place of burial)*.
gravel jari.
gray nezumi iro, hai iro.
grease abura.
great ookíi *(large)*; idai na *(much above the average)*.
greatness idaisa.
greedy kuiíji hatta *(for food)*; yokufukái *(for gain)*.
green mídori.
greet (to) áisatsu suru.
greeting áisatsu.
grief fukái kanashimi *(deep sorrow)*; hunoo *(distress)*.
grieve (to) *v.t.* fukáku kanashimaséru *(cause grief to)*; kurushimaséru *(distress)*; *v.i.* fukáku kanashímu *(feel grief)*; nagéku *(lament)*.
grin (to) niyátto warau.
grind surikudáku.
groan unari góe.
groan (to) unáru, uméku.
grocer shokuryoohin'ya.
grocery store shokuryoohin'ya.
grope teságuri suru.
gross juuni dáasu *(12 doz.)*.
ground jímen *(surface of earth)*; dodai *(foundation)*.
group gurúupu; shuudan *(assemblage)*.
group (to) matomeru.
grow (to) hattatsu suru *(develop)*; seichoo suru *(said of animate things)*; haéru *(flourish in earth)*.
growth seichoo.
grudge urami.
  hold a grudge against uramu.
gruff bukkiráboo na.
guard hoshoo *(sentry)*; shashoo *(of a train)*; bannín *(watchman)*.
guard (to) mamóru.
guardian kookennin *(legal)*; hogósha *(keeper)*.

guess suiryoo, ate zuiryoo.
guess (to) soozoo suru.
  guess right iiatéru.
guide annáisha *(tourist)*; michi annaisha *(one who shows the way)*; shidóosha *(leader)*.
guide (to) annái suru *(lead the way)*.
guilt tsúmi.
gum norí, gómu.
  chewing gum chuuíngamu.
gun júu *(firearm)*; teppoo *(rifle, shotgun)*; kenjuu *(revolver)*.
gush (to) fukidéru.

H

habit shuukan.
habitual shuukanteki na *(customary)*; jooshuuteki *(regular)*.
hail arare *(small hailstone)*; hyóo *(large hailstone)*.
hail (to) arare ga fúru.
hair ke *(in general)*; kamí *(of the head)*.
hairdo heya sutáiru.
hairdresser biyóoshi.
half hanbún.
  half-hour hanjíkan, sanjippun.
hall hiroma, hóoru.
ham hámu.
hammer kanazúchi.
hand té.
hand (to) watasu *(hand over)*.
handbag handobákku, tesage.
handful te ippái.
handkerchief hankachi.
handle té, hikite *(of a door)*; e, té *(of a tool)*.
handle (to) atsukau.
handsome tanrei na *(good looking)*; yooboo no utsukushíi *(beautiful)*.
handy kíyoo na *(said of persons)*; chóohoo na, bénri na *(said of things)*.
hang *v.t.* kakéru *(something)*; kubi o kukuru *(a person)*; *v.i.* sagáru *(hang down)*.
happen (to) furikakáru *(befall)*; okóru *(occur)*.
happening dekígoto *(event)*; jíken *(incident)*.
happiness koofuku *(well being)*; shiawase *(fortune, luck)*.
happy ureshíi, koofuku na *(felicitous, joyous)*; shiawase na *(favored by luck)*.
harbor minato.
hard katai *(solid, as opposed to soft)*; muzukashíi *(difficult)*.
harden (to) katameru, kataku suru *(solidify)*; katamaru *(become solid)*.
hardly hotóndo *(used with a negative expression)*.
hardness kenroo.
hardship kónnan.
hardware kanamono.
  hardware store kanamonoya.
hardy joobu na.
hare no-úsagi.
harm gái *(damage)*, songai *(loss)*; sonshoo *(injury)*.

harm (to) gai suru.
harmful warúi.
harmless gái no nái.
harmonious tsuriai no tóreta *(balanced)*.
harmony chooshi *(musical)*; haigoo *(of colors)*; enman, choowa *(between persons)*.
harsh soaku na *(coarse)*; fuchóowa na *(discordant)*; kibishíi *(stern)*.
harvest shuukaku.
haste isogi.
hasten (to) isógu *(hurry)*; isogaséru *(hurry a person)*; hayaméru *(a result)*; isóide iku *(hurry to)*.
hat booshi.
hate nikumi.
hate (to) nikúmu, kirau.
hateful nikurashíi.
hatred nikushimi.
haughty gooman na.
have (to) mótsu *(possess, hold)*; nómu *(drink)*; tabéru *(eat)*; uketoru *(receive)*.
haven minato.
hay karekusa.
he káre, anó hito.
head atama *(of the body)*; kashira *(leader)*; shunin *(chief)*.
headache zutsuu.
heal *v.t.* naósu *(mend)*; *v.i.* naóru *(be mended)*.
health kenkoo.
healthy kenkoo na, joobu na.
heap yamá.
head up tsumu.
hear (to) kiku.
hearing kiku chikara.
    hard of hearing mimí ga tooi.
heart shinzoo *(organ of the body)*; kokoro *(as seat of the emotions)*.
heat (to) atataméru, átsuku suru.
heaven téngoku *(Christian)*; gokuraku *(Buddhist)*.
    Heavens! óya máa!
heavy omoi.
hedge iké gaki.
heed (to) shitagáu.
heel kakato.
height tákasa.
heir soozokunin.
heiress soozokunin.
helm káji.
help tetsudái.
help (to) tetsudáu *(give a helping hand)*; sewá o suru *(take care of)*; tasukéru *(rescue)*.
helper tetsudái.
helpful yaku ni tátsu.
hem fuchi *(margin)*; herí *(edge)*; sakái *(border)*.
hen mendori.
henceforth kore kara.
her, hers kánojo no.
herb yakusoo *(medical)*.
herd muré.
here kokó *(this place)*; kotchí, kochira *(this side)*.
herewith koko ni.

hero eiyuu *(of a battle)*; shujínkoo *(of a novel)*.
heroic eiyuuteki.
heroine jojóofu *(person of great deeds)*; onna shujínkoo *(of a novel)*.
herring níshin.
herself jibun *(self, same word is used for both male and female)*.
    by herself hitóri de, jibun de.
hesitate (to) tameráu, chúucho suru.
hide (to) kakúsu *(conceal)*; himitsu ni suru *(keep secret)*; kakuréru *(conceal oneself)*.
hideous zotto suru yóo na.
high takái.
higher —yóri mo takái.
hill oka *(small mountain)*; saká *(on a road)*.
him ano káta ni, anó hito ni *(to him)*; ano káta o, anó hito o *(as object of sentence)*.
himself jibun. *(Same word used also for "herself".)*
    by himself jibun de.
hind ushiro no.
hinder (to) jama suru, samatogéru.
hinge chootsúgai.
hint hinto, honomekashi *(allusion)*; atekosuri *(insinuation)*.
hint (to) honomekású *(allude to)*; atekosúru *(insinuate)*.
hip oshiri, koshi.
hire (to) yatóu *(servants, etc.)*; kariru *(cars)*.
his anó hito no, káre no.
historian rekishika.
historic rekishijoo no, rekishiteki no.
history rekishi.
hit (to) útsu, tatáku, nagúru.
    to hit against butsukeru.
hoarse shagare góe.
hoe kuwa.
hold (to) mótsu *(have)*; okonáu *(a ceremony)*; kaisai suru *(an exhibition or conference)*; tamótsu *(maintain)*.
hole aná.
holiday yasumi *(period of recreation or rest)*; matsuri *(festival)*; saijitsu *(national holiday)*.
hollow *adj.* kara no *(empty)*. —*n.* kubomi *(cavity)*.
holy shinsei na *(sacred)*; koogooshíi *(divine)*; shinkóoshin no fukái *(deeply pious)*.
homage kéii *(respect)*.
home uchi, taku *(one's abode)*; katei *(family)*.
    home town kókyoo, kuni.
honest shoojíki na *(truthful)*; seijitsu na *(sincere)*; sotchoku na *(frank)*.
honesty seijitsu.
honey hachi mitsu.
honor méiyo *(fame)*; shin'yoo *(credit)*; sonkei *(esteem)*.
honor (to) meiyo o ataeru *(exalt)*; hijoo ni sonkei suru *(venerate)*.
honorable tootói, sonkei subéki.
hood zukín *(garment)*.
hoof hizume.
hook kugi *(to hang things on)*.

hope kiboo *(opp. of despair)*; kitai *(confident anticipation)*; mikomi *(probability)*.
hope (to) nozomi o kakéru *(count on)*; nozomu *(desire)*.
hopeful kiboo ni míchite iru, ate ni shite iru.
hopeless nozomi no nái.
horizon chiheisen *(of land)*; suiheisen *(of sea)*.
horizontal yoko no.
horn tsunó *(of animals)*; tsuno bue *(wind instrument)*, horun *(English horn)*.
horrible osoroshíi *(terrible)*; monosugói *(ghastly)*.
horror kyoofu.
horse umá.
horseback (on) umá ni notte iru.
hosiery kutsushita.
hospitable motenashi no yói.
hospital byooin.
host shújin *(one who entertains another, hotel-keeper)*.
hostess hósutesu, onna shújin *(in a hotel or restaurant)*; okámi *(in an inn)*; shújin *(at home)*.
hostile tékii no áru.
hot atsúi.
hotel hóteru *(occidental-style)*; yadoya, ryokan *(Japanese-style)*.
hot spring onsen.
hour jikan.
    two hours ni jíkan.
house ié *(the structure)*; uchi *(home, one's abode)*.
household shotai, katei *(home)*.
housekeeper kaséifu.
how dóo, dónna ni.
    how much íkura.
    how many dono kurai, íkutsu.
    how long dono kurai, nágaku.
    how often nando kúrai.
    How beautiful! Máa kírei desu ne.
    How are you? Ogénki desu ka?
however ga, keredomo; dónna ni —mo, íkura —mo *(in whatever way, to whatever degree)*.
howl (to) hoéru *(said of animals)*; unáru *(said of the wind)*.
human *adj.* ningen no *(characteristic of man)*. —*n.* ningen, hito.
    human being ningen.
    human race jínrui.
    human nature ningensei.
humane nínjoo no áru *(compassionate)*; jihibukái *(merciful)*.
humanity jíndoo.
humble kenson na *(modest)*; hikaeme na *(not pretentious)*.
humid shimeppói *(damp)*; shikki no takái *(of high humidity)*.
humiliate jisónshin o kizutsukéru, hají o kakaséru *(mortify)*.
humility kenson *(humbleness)*.
humor kishitsu *(disposition)*; kíbun *(mood)*; kimagure *(caprice)*; kokkei *(jocularity)*.
    in good humor jookígen.
hundred hyaku.

hundredth hyakubanme no.
hunger ue *(famine)*; kuufuku *(craving for food)*.
hungry (be) onaka ga suku.
hunt kári *(hunting)*, ryóo.
hunt (to) kari o suru *(shoot animals)*; sagasu *(look for)*.
hunter ryóoshi.
hurry n. isógu kotó, isogi.
    be in a hurry isóide iru.
hurry (to) isógu.
hurt (to) *v.i.* itámu; *v.t.* itaméru.
husband otto, shújin.
hush (to) shízuka ni saseru *(quiet)*; damaraséru *(silence)*; osaéru *(restrain)*.
hyphen háifun.
hypocrisy gizen.
hypocrite gizénsha.
hypothesis kasetsu.

I

I watakushi, watashi, bóku *(used by men among friends)*.
ice koori.
icy koori de tsúrutsuru shita.
idea kangáe *(thought)*; chíshiki *(knowledge)*; inshoo *(impression)*; shínnen *(belief)*; omoitsuki *(intention)*.
ideal *n.* risoo. —*adj.* risooteki na.
idealism kannénron.
idealist risooka.
identical dooitsu no.
idiot hakuchi.
idle shigoto no nái *(unemployed)*; hima de áru *(not active)*; namakéru *(lazy)*.
idleness namakeru kotó.
if móshi.
ignoble iyashíi, gehín na.
ignorance múgaku *(lack of education)*; múchi *(lack of knowledge)*.
ignorant múgaku na *(without education)*; múchi na *(unthinking, uninformed)*; fuánnai no *(unaware)*.
ignore (to) múshi suru.
ill kagen ga warúi, byooki no *(sick, unwell)*; warúi *(bad, evil)*.
illness byooki.
illusion sakkaku *(optical)*; moosoo *(delusion)*.
illustrate (to) sashie o ireru *(pictures and diagrams)*; rei o shimesu *(give examples)*.
illustration sashie *(picture)*; rei, tatoe *(example)*.
image súgata *(form)*; chookokúzoo *(carved statue)*; guuzoo *(idol)*.
imaginary soozoo no.
imagination soozoo.
imagine (to) soozoo suru *(form a mental picture)*; omóu, kangáeru *(suppose)*.
imitate (to) maneru, mane o suru.
imitation *n.* mane *(copy)*; magaimono, nisemono *(fake)*.
immediate súgu no, chokusetsu no.
immediately súgu ni.
imminent sashisemmátta *(impending)*.

immobility fudoosei.
immoral fudóotoku na.
immorality fudóotoku.
immortal fújimi no, shinu koto no nái.
immortality fúshi, fukutsusei.
impartial koohei na.
impatience tánki na kotó.
impatient (be) ki ga hayái *(of character)*;
      tánki na *(quick tempered)*.
imperfect fukánzen na *(incomplete)*; kekkán
      no áru *(faulty)*.
impertinence shitsúrei.
impertinent shitsúrei na *(rude)*; namaiki na
      (insolent).
impetuosity sékkachi.
impetuous gekiretsu na, nesshín na.
impious fushínjin na.
import yunyuuhin *(goods)*.
import (to) yunyuu suru.
importance juuyoosei.
important daiji na *(of consequence)*; kan'yoo
      na *(essential)*; chomei na *(eminent)*.
impossible fukánoo na.
impress (to) osu *(imprint)*; inshoo zukéru
      (produce a vivid impression); kandoo
      saseru *(move deeply)*.
impression inshoo.
      be under the impression that—to omótte
      iru, ki ga suru.
imprison (to) keimusho ni ireru.
improve (to) *v.t.* jootatsu saseru *(ameliorate)*;
      yóku suru *(better)*; kairyoo suru
      (reform); *v.i.* jootatsu suru *(become
      better)*.
improvement kairyoo *(reform)*.
improvise (to) kufuu suru.
imprudence fukínshin.
imprudent fukínshin na.
impulse shoodoo *(propulsion)*; shigeki
      (impetus).
impure fujun na *(adulterated)*.
in ni, de; tame ni *(in order to)*—*no naka ni
      (inside)*,—*no uchi ni (within)*.
inadequate fujúubun na.
inaugurate *v.t.* hajimeru *(begin)*; *v.i.* hajimaru
      (be inaugurated).
incapable —ga dekínai, múryoku na.
incapacity munoo, futékitoo.
inch ínchi *(American measure)*.
incident dekígoto *(occurrence)*.
include *v.i.* fukúmu; *v.t.* fukuméru.
      to be included háitte iru.
income shuunyuu *(earnings)*.
incomparable hikaru no dekínai.
incompatible ki no awánai *(inharmonious)*;
      itchi shinai *(inconsistent)*; ryooritsu
      shinai *(not able to coexist)*.
incompetent chikara no nái, munoo na.
incomplete fukánzen na.
incomprehensible ryookai dekínai.
inconvenience fúben.
inconvenient fúben na *(not suitable)*; tsugoo
      ga warúi *(troublesome)*.
incorrect machigátte iru *(inaccurate)*; datoo
      de nái *(improper)*.
increase zooka.

increase (to) *v.t.* fuyásu *(quantity)*; ookíku
      suru *(size)*; ageru *(price)*; fuéru *(in
      quantity)*; *v.i.* ookíku náru *(in size)*;
      tákaku náru *(in price)*.
incredible shinjirarénai.
incur ukéru *(meet with)*; áu *(run into)*.
indebted kari no áru *(owing money)*; sewa ni
      natte iru *(obliged)*.
indecision fukétsudan.
indecisive niekiránai.
indeed hontoo ni *(in fact)*.
independence dokuritsu *(self-government)*.
independent dokuritsu no.
index sakuin *(of books)*.
index finger hitosashí yubi.
indicate (to) shimésu.
indicative —o shimésu *(giving an indication
      of)*; —o honomekásu *(giving a hint)*.
indifference mukánshin.
indifferent reitán na *(pertaining to feelings)*;
      mutónjaku na *(pertaining to
      appearance)*.
indignant fungai shita *(angered)*.
indignation fungai.
indirect toomáwashi no *(devious)*; kansetsu no
      (not straightforward).
      indirect answer kansetsu no henji.
indirectly kansetsu ni.
indiscretion shiryo no nái kotó *(imprudence)*.
indispensable zettai hitsuyoo na *(absolutely
      necessary)*; sakerarénai *(unavoidable)*.
individual *adj.* kóko no *(separate)*; dokutoku
      no *(peculiar)*. —*n.* kójin.
indivisible wakéru koto no dekínai *(entity)*.
indolence bushoo *(sloth, idleness)*.
indolent bushóo na *(idle, lazy, slothful)*;
      mukátsudoo no *(inactive)*.
indoors okúnai.
      to go indoors naka e háiru.
induce (to) sasoikomu *(attract)*.
induct (to) hikiiréru *(introduce into a place)*.
indulge (in) —ni fukéru.
indulgence kimama, wagamáma.
indulgent tenurui *(not severe)*.
      indulgent parent yasashii.
industrial sangyoo no.
industrious kinben na *(hard-working)*.
industry sangyoo.
inexhaustible tsukínai *(limitless)*; taénai
      (unfailing); tsukarénai *(unwearied)*.
inexplicable fukákai na *(incomprehensible)*.
inexpressible iiarawasénai *(indescribable)*.
infallible zenzen ayamari no nái *(free from
      error)*; kesshite machigawánai *(never
      mistaken)*.
infamous hyooban no warúi *(notorious)*;
      fuménboku na *(shameful)*.
infancy akanboo no toki *(babyhood)*; shóki
      (beginning of existence).
infant *n.* akanboo, chiisái kodomo *(very
      young baby)*. —*adj.* akanboo no
      (pertaining to a baby).
infantry hohei.
infection kansen *(contagion)*.
infer (to) súiri suru *(conclude by reasoning)*;
      ketsuron o hikidású *(draw
      conclusions)*.

inference ketsuron *(conclusion)*, suiron *(deduction)*.
inferior shita no *(less important)*; shita no kaikyuu *(lower in rank)*; sómatsu na *(poor quality)*.
infernal myoodo no, jigoku no *(hellish)*; hidoo no *(inhuman, devilish)*.
infinite kagiri no nái *(endless)* hijoo na *(very great)*.
infinity mugen *(boundlessness)*.
inflict (to) ataeru *(impose)*.
influence eikyoo *(effect)*, séiryoku *(personal)*.
influence (to) eikyoo suru.
inform (to) shiraseru.
information shirase *(news)*; hoochi *(report)* chíshiki *(knowledge)*.
ingenious rikoo na *(clever)*; kíyoo na *(skillful)*; koomyoo na *(cleverly contrived)*.
ingenuity rikoosa *(cleverness)*.
ingratitude onshirazu.
inhabit kyojuu suru *(reside)*; súmu, yadóru *(live in)*.
inhabitant kyojúusha.
inherit (to) soozoku suru.
inheritance isan *(thing inherited)*; soozoku *(an inheriting)*.
inhuman zannin na.
initial *adj.* hajime no *(beginning)*. —*n.* kashira ji *(letter)*.
   initial stage shóki.
initiate (to) hajimeru *(begin)*; seishiki ni kanyuu saseru *(admit)*.
initiative dokusóoryoku *(originality)*.
injurious yuugai na *(harmful, hurtful)*.
injury kegá *(wound)*; songai *(damage)*.
injustice fuhoo, fusei *(iniquity)*, fukóohei *(unjust act)*.
ink sumí *(Japanese only)*; ínki, ínku *(other)*.
inkwell inki tsubo.
inland kokúnai no *(domestic)*.
inn yadoya, ryokan.
innate umaretsuki no *(inborn)*.
innkeeper ryokan no shújin, yadoya no shújin.
innocence mújaki *(freedom from wrong)*.
innocent múzai no *(not guilty)*; mújaki na *(guileless)*.
inquire tazunéru.
inquiry toiawase.
inscription káite aru kotó.
insect mushi.
insensible mukánkaku na *(not able to feel)*; heiki na *(callous)*.
inseparable hanasu koto ga dekínai.
inside náka.
insight kenshiki.
   man of insight kenshiki áru hito.
insignificant tsumaránai *(unimportant)*; muími na *(meaningless)*.
insincere séii no nái.
insinuate (to) sore to náku iu *(hint)*.
insist (to) kyoochoo suru; ii háru.
   He insisted on this point. Káre wa kono ten o kyoochoo shita.
insistence kyoochoo; shuchoo.

inspect (to) shirabéru *(examine)*; ken'etsu suru *(view officially)*.
inspection ken'etsu *(official viewing)*; chóosa *(critical examination)*.
install (to) ninmei suru *(place a person in office)*; sóochi suru, toritsukéru *(put in position for use)*.
installment nashikuzushi *(a portion of money paid at stated times)*.
instance réi *(example)*; baai *(occasion)*.
instant *adj.* kyuu na. —*n.* sókuji *(precise moment)*; shunkan *(moment)*.
instantaneous sókuza no.
   instantaneous death sokushi.
instantly sókuza ni, súgu.
instead (of) kawari ni.
instigate (to) sosonokásu *(incite)*.
instinct hónnoo.
instinctive honnooteki no.
institute kyookai, gakkai *(institution, society)*.
institute (to) setsuritsu suru *(establish)*.
institution setsuritsu *(establishment)*; seitei *(of law)*; séido *(system)*; kanrei *(custom)*; gakkai *(learned society)*.
instruct (to) oshieru *(teach)*; kyóoju suru *(educate)*.
instruction júgyoo *(a lesson)*; yoohoo *(a teaching or precept)*.
instructor kyóoshi.
instrument doogu *(for work or means)*; gakki *(musical)*.
insufficiency fujúubun *(inadequacy)*; futékitoo *(incompetency)*.
insufficient fujúubun na *(not sufficient)*; futékitoo na *(inadequate)*.
insult bujoku *(insolence)*; buréi *(impoliteness)*.
insult (to) bujoku suru.
insuperable nozokinikúi *(insurmountable)*.
insurance hoken.
   life insurance seimei hóken.
insure (to) hoken o tsukéru.
integral kanzen na.
intellect chíshiki.
intellectual *adj.* chíshiki no. —*n.* chishikíjin.
intelligence chíryoku *(mental ability)*; chisei *(mentality)*; joohoo *(information)*.
intelligent kashikói.
intend (to)—tsumori.
   I intend to marry her. Anó hito to kekkon suru tsumori désu.
intense nesshín na.
intensity kyóodo.
intention kangáe.
interest kyóomi *(pleasurable concern)*; kanshin *(intellectual curiosity)*; riken *(pecuniary concern)*; ríshi *(rate)*.
   have an interest in kyóomi o mótsu.
interest (to) kyóomi o okosaséru *(attract attention)*; kookíshin o hiku *(excite the curiosity of)*; doojoo o hiku *(excite sympathy)*.
interesting omoshirói.
interfere (to) kanshoo suru *(meddle)*; chootei suru *(mediate)*; jama suru *(interrupt)*.
interference boogai, jama.

217

interior náka, náibu.
intermediate chuukan no.
international kokusaiteki, kokusai.
  international relations kokusai kánkei.
interpose (to)—no aida ni ireru.
interpret (to) káishaku suru, hándan suru
  (construe).
interpretation káishaku, setsumei
  (explanation); hándan *(judgment)*;
  tsúuyaku *(translation)*.
interpreter tsúuyaku.
interrupt (to) saegíru *(break in upon)*; jama o
  suru *(hinder)*; chuushi saseru *(break
  the continuity of)*.
interruption chuushi, jama.
interval kankaku.
interview menkai *(meeting)*; mensetsu, kaiken
  (with reporters).
interview (to) menkai suru.
intimacy shinmitsu.
intimate shinmitsu na *(very friendly)*;
  kojinteki no *(personal)*; shitashíi
  (friendly).
intimidate (to) obiyakásu.
into ni, no naka e.
intolerable gáman no dekínai.
intolerance kyooryoo.
intolerant kyooryoo na *(bigoted)*.
intonation kóe no táka hiku, intonéeshon.
introduce (to) shookai suru *(a person)*.
introduction shookai *(of a person)*; jobun *(of
  a book)*.
intuition chokkan.
invade (to) shinnyuu suru *(overrun)*;
  shinryaku suru *(aggress)*; oshiyoséru
  (rush into).
invariable kawaranai.
invasion shinryaku.
invent (to) hatsumei suru *(method, etc.)*;
  kangaedásu *(a story)*.
invention hatsumei *(something discovered
  after experimentation)*; tsukurigoto *(a
  falsehood)*.
inventor hatsumeika.
invert (to) hantai ni suru *(reverse)*.
invest (to) tooshi suru.
investment tooshi.
invisible mé ni tsukánai.
invitation shootai.
invite (to) shóotai suru, manéku.
invoice okurijoo, inbóisu.
invoke (to) kámi ni inóru.
involuntary muíshiki no.
involve (to) hikikómu.
iron tetsu *(metal)*; airon *(for pressing)*.
iron (to) airon o kakeru *(clothes)*.
irony hiniku.
irregular fukísoku na.
irreparable torikaeshi ga tsukánai.
irresistible tomeru koto no dekinai.
irritate (to) iraira saseru.
irritation shigeki *(medical term)*; okoraséru
  kotó *(exasperation, annoyance)*.
island shimá.
isolate (to) kákuri suru.

issue hakkoo *(of a newspaper or other
  publication)*; mondái ten *(problem)*.
issue (to) hakkoo suru.
it sore *(often omitted in Japanese)*.
  It's late. Osoi desu.
  It's here. Koko ni arimásu.
Italian *adj.* Itárii no,—*n.* Itaríijin *(people)*.
item koomoku.
its sono.
itself hitoride ni *(by, of itself)*.
ivy tsuta.

J

jacket uwagi; jáketsu *(sweater)*.
jam jámu.
January Ichigatsu.
Japan Nippón, Nihón.
Japanese *adj.*—Nippón no, Nihón no.
  Nipponjín *(person)*; Nippongo,
  Nihongo *(language)*.
jar tsubo, kamé.
jaw agó.
jealous shittobukai.
jealousy yakimóchi, shitto.
jelly jérii.
jewel hooseki.
job shigoto *(work)*; shokúgyoo *(occupation)*;
  chíi *(position)*.
join (to) awaséru *(put together)*; kuttsukéru
  (fasten); renketsu saseru *(connect,
  link)*; issho ni náru *(become united)*.
joint *n.* kansetsu *(of the body)*; awaseme
  (seam); tsugime *(junction)*. *adj.*
  kyoodoo no *(common)*.
joke joodán.
joke (to) joodán o iu *(jest)*; fuzakéru *(be
  humorous)*.
jolly yúkai na.
journal nikki *(diary)*; nikkan shínbun *(daily
  newspaper)*; zasshi *(magazine)*.
journalism jaanarízumu *(practice of)*;
  shinbúngaku *(study of)*.
journalist jaanarísuto, shinbunkisha
  (reporter).
journey ryokoo.
joy yorokobi.
joyous ureshíi.
judge saibánkan *(public officer in a court of
  justice)*; shinpánkan *(umpire)*; kanteika
  (connoisseur).
judge (to) hándan suru *(estimate, conclude)*;
  sáiban suru *(at court)*.
judgment hándan *(adjudication)*; hanketsu
  (court decision); hihan *(criticism)*;
  handánryoku *(powers of
  discrimination)*.
judicial saibanjoo no.
juice shíru, júusu.
July Shichigátsu.
jump tobiagari.
jump (to) tobu.
June Rokugatsu.
junior *adj.* toshishita no. *(opp. to senior)*.
just *adj.* tadashíi *(upright)*; koosei na
  (impartial); seitoo na *(lawful)*; tekitoo

na *(proper)*; jissai no *(actual)*.—*adv.*
choodo *(exactly)*; hon no *(only)*; yatto
(hardly).
justice séigi *(righteousness)*; kooketsu
(integrity); koosei *(fairness)*.
justify seitooka suru.

K

keen eibin na *(acute)*.
keep káu *(animals)*; mótsu *(hold)*; tótte oku
(hold on to).
  keep quiet shízuka ni suru.
  keep in mind obóete oku.
  Keep still! Oshizuka ni.
kettle yakan.
key kagí.
kick (to) kéru.
kill (to) korosu.
kin miyóri.
kind *adj.* shínsetsu na *(gentle)*.
kind shúrui *(class, variety, sort)*.
kindly *adv.* shínsetsu ni.
kindness shinsetsu *(benevolence)*; aijoo
(love); kóoi *(good will)*.
king oo.
kingdom ookoku *(monarchical state)*; kuni
(realm).
kiss seppun, kíssu.
kiss (to) kíssu suru, seppun suru.
kitchen daidokoro, katte.
kite táko.
knee hiza.
kneel (to) hizamazúku.
knife náifu.
knit (to) ámu.
  knitting amímono.
knock (to) tatáku.
  knock at the door to o tatáku.
  knock against—ni butsukáru.
knot musubime.
know (to) shitte iru *(plain)*, zonjíte iru *(pol.)*.
knowledge chíshiki *(information)*; gakúmon
(learning).
known yuumei na.
  make known shiraseru.
Korean *adj.* Kánkoku no, Choosén no.—*n.*
Choosenjín *(people)*; Choosengo
(language).

L

label fuda; ráberu, retteru.
labor *n.* roodoo, shigoto.
laboratory jikkenjo.
lace réesu *(fabric)*; himo *(of shoe)*.
lack (to) fusoku suru.
lacquer urushi.
  lacquer ware nuri mono.
lady kifújin.
  Ladies Fujin bénjo *(toilet)*.
lake mizuúmi; -ko *(in compound names)*.
  Lake Biwa Biwako.
lamb kohitsúji.
lame bíkko.
lamp dentoo *(electric)*.

land riku *(solid part of the earth's surface)*;
jímen *(ground)*.
land (to) jooriku saseru, jooriku suru
(disembark); oríru *(alight)*.
landscape késhiki.
language kotoba, géngo; -go (in compounds).
  Japanese language Nihongo.
lantern choochín *(paper)*; tooroo *(metal)*; ishi
dóoroo *(stone)*.
large ookíi, ookína.
last *n.* ichiban áto *(end of something)*;—*adj.*
saikin no *(most recent)*; sáigo no
(final), owari ni *(after all others)*;
saikin no *(most lately)*.
  last night yuube, sakúban.
last (to) tsuzuku *(continue)*; mochi kotáeru
(endure); nagamóchi suru *(wear well)*.
lasting eizoku suru *(durable)*; fuhen no,
eikyuu no *(permanent)*.
latch kannuki.
late osoi *(opp. to early)*; ko- *(prefixed to the
name of someone deceased)*.
lately saikin ni.
latter áto no, kóosha no.
laugh warai.
laugh (to) warau.
laughter oowárai.
lavish kimae no yói.
law hooritsu.
lawful hooritsu ni kanátta.
lawn shibafu.
lay (to) oku *(put)*; umu *(eggs)*.
layer sóo.
lazy namakéru; bushóo na.
lead namari *(mineral)*; shidoo *(guidance)*.
lead (to) annái suru *(guide)*.
leader shidóosha *(guide)*.
leadership shidóoryoku.
leaf ha.
leak (to) móru.
lean (to) katamúku *(incline)*; yorikakáru *(lean
against)*.
leap hiyaku.
leap (to) tobikoéru *(pass over)*; tobu *(jump)*.
learn naráu, benkyoo suru *(study)*; kioku suru
(memorize).
learned hakugaku na, gakumon no aru.
learning gakúmon *(knowledge)*; hakushiki
(erudition).
least ichiban chiisái *(in size)*; ichiban sukunái
(in number).
  at least sukunáku tomo.
leather kawá.
leave yasumi *(holiday)*.
leave (to) déru *(depart)*; tátsu *(depart for a
long trip)*; azukéru *(on deposit)*.
lecture koogi *(in classroom)*; kooen *(in
public)*; setsuyu *(admonition)*.
left *n.* hidari.
leg ashí.
legal hooritsujoo no.
legend densetsu.
legislation hooritsu seitei *(enacting of laws)*;
hooritsu *(laws)*.
legislator rippóosha.
legislature rippóobu.

legitimate goohoo no *(lawful)*.
   doori ni kanátta *(reasonable)*.
leisure hima.
lemon remon.
   lemonade remonéedo.
lend (to) kasu.
length nágasa.
lengthen (to) nágaku suru *(make longer)*;
   nobásu *(prolong)*.
less chiisái *(in size)*; sukóshi no, sukunái *(in
   quantity)*.
   less—yori chiisái *(smaller than)*.
   less—yóri sukunái *(fewer than)*.
lesson júgyoo *(schoolwork)*; gakka *(subject)*;
   ka *(chapter)*.
let (to) saseru *(allow)*; kasu *(loan)*.
   house for let kashiya.
letter tegami *(epistle)*; jí *(in alphabet)*.
level *n.* heimen *(flat surface)*; heichi *(flat
   ground)*.—*adj.* taira na *(even)*; suihei
   no *(horizontal)*.
   (at) the same level onaji tákasa *(said of
   height)*; onaji teido *(said of degree)*.
liable seme o oubéki *(responsible)*; fukusubéki
   (subject to); kakari yasúi *(exposed to)*.
liar usótsuki.
liberal hoofu na, takusan no *(abundant)*; kéchi
   kechi shinai *(not sparing)*; kimae ga íi
   (generous); shinpoteki na
   (progressive).
liberty jiyúu.
library toshókan *(public)*; shosai, toshóshitsu
   (private, home).
license kyóka *(permission)*; ninka
   (authorization); kyokásho, menjoo
   (certification).
lick (to) naméru.
lie uso.
   tell a lie uso o tsuku.
lie (to) yoko ni náru *(rest)*.
lieutenant rikugun chúui *(army)*; kaigun táii
   (navy).
life ínochi *(animate existence)*; génki *(energy)*.
lift (to) ageru *(raise)*; mochiageru *(hold up)*.
light *adj.* karui *(weight)*; usui *(color)*; yasashii
   (work).—*n.* hikari *(beam)*; akari *(of
   lamp, flame)*; kootaku *(brightness)*.
   sunlight hí no hikari.
light (to) hí o tsukéru.
   light the lamp akari o tsukéru.
   light the fire hí o tsukéru.
   light up terasu.
lighten (to) akaruku suru *(make bright)*;
   karuku suru *(diminish in weight)*.
lighthouse toodai.
lighting shoomei *(illumination)*.
lightning inabíkari *(from cloud to cloud)*.
   flash of lightning hirameki.
like *adj.* onajiyóo na *(similar)*; nite iru *(alike)*.
like (to) konómu, suku.
   Would you like to go? Ikitái desu ka?
likely tábun *(probably)*; tekitoo na *(suitable)*;
   tanomoshíi *(promising)*; mottomo
   rashíi *(creditable)*.
likewise dooyoo ni *(similarly)*; mata *(too,
   also)*; náo mata *(moreover)*.

liking n. konomi.
limb té ashi *(hand or foot)*; eda *(branch)*.
limit seigén *(in the abstract sense)*; kyookai,
   sakái *(boundary)*.
limit (to) seigén suru.
limp bíkko o hiku.
line kei, sén *(made with pencil)*; íto *(thread)*;
   rétsu *(row)*; kakei *(lineage)*; iegara
   (family); michi *(course, route)*;—sen
   (suffixed to name of railroad), shóobai
   (trade).
   Tokaido Line Tookaidoosen *(The Tokaido
   Railroad)*.
line (to) sén o hiku *(mark with lines)*; rinkaku
   o tóru *(outline)*; ichirétsu ni suru
   (align); urá o tsukéru *(cover with
   lining)*; rétsu o tsukúru *(line up)*.
   lining urá *(of dresses)*.
linen asa.
linger (to) úrouro suru; nagabíku.
link tsunagime.
link (to) tsunagu.
lion raion, shíshi.
lip kuchibiru.
liquid ekitai.
liquor sake *(Japanese rice wine)*; yooshu
   (foreign).
list mokuroku *(catalogue)*; kakakuhyoo
   (price).
list (to) kakinaraberu.
listen kiku.
literary búngaku no.
literature búngaku.
little chiisái *(not big)*; sukóshi *(quantity)*;
   tsumaránai *(trivial)*; kéchi na *(mean,
   petty)*.
live *adj.* íkite iru.
live (to) súmu *(dwell)*; ikíru *(exist)*; íkite iru
   (be living); ikinagaráeru *(remain
   alive)*; kurasu *(spend the days)*.
lively génki no yói *(spirited)*; yooki na
   (cheerful); kappatsu na *(brisk)*.
liver kanzoo *(organ of body)*; kimó, rébaa
   (food).
load omoni *(burden)*; nímotsu *(on a cart)*.
load (to) tsumu.
loan kashikin *(money that is lent)*; shakkín
   (borrowed money).
loan (to) kasu *(lend)*; kariru *(borrow)*.
local chihooteki no, chíhoo no.
locate (to) mitsukeru.
location basho.
lock kagí.
lock (to) kagí o kakéru.
locomotive kikánsha.
log maruta.
logic rónri.
logical ronriteki na.
loneliness sabishísa.
lonely kódoku no *(isolated)*; sabishíi
   (lonesome).
long nagái *(lengthy)*; hosonagái *(elongated)*;
   takái *(tall)*.
   a long time nagái aida.
   before long ma mó naku.
   long ago mukashi.

longing akogare.
look ichi moku *(glance)*; yooboo *(aspect)*; yoosu *(deportment)*; kaotsuki *(countenance)*.
look (to) míru *(oneself)*; goran nasáru *(pol.: used in speaking of another person)*; miéru *(have the appearance, seem)*.
    Look out! Abunái.
loose yurúi *(not tight)*; darashi no nái *(lax)*; fumímochi na *(wanton)*; fuséikaku na *(inexact)*.
loosen (to) tóku *(undo)*; yuruméru *(slacken)*.
lord shiháisha *(ruler)*; shújin *(master)*; shú *(Christ)*.
lose (to) nakusu *(cease to have)*; otósu *(by dropping)*; makeru *(be beaten)*.
loss són, sonshitsu.
lost nakushita *(gone out of one's possession)*; yukue fúmei no *(missing)*.
lot (a) takusan *(great deal)*; oozéi *(multitude)*.
    a lot of people oozéi no hito.
loud *adj.* oogóe no, óokina kóe no *(said of a voice)*; óokina otó *(said of a sound)*; soozooshíi *(noisy)*; kebakebashíi *(gaudy)*.
love ái *(parental, fraternal)*; ren'ai *(between man and woman)*.
love (to) aisúru *(as a parent)*; koi súru, ren'ai suru *(one of the opp. sex)*.
    fall in love kói ni ochíru.
lovely utsukushíi *(beautiful)*; kawairashíi *(charming)*; subarashíi *(wonderful)*.
low hikúi *(not high)*; yowái *(weak)*; iyashíi *(in society)*.
lower (to) sagéru, orósu *(haul down)*; ichidan to sagéru *(make less elevated)*.
loyal chuujitsu na; chúugi na.
loyalty chuusetsu; chúugi.
luck ún, kooun.
    good luck ún ga íi.
    bad luck ún ga warúi.
lucky ún ga íi, kooun na.
luggage nímotsu.
luminous hikáru.
lump katamari.
lunch híru, ohíru, hiruhan, ránchi.
lung hai.
luxurious zeitáku na.
luxury zeitáku.

M

machine kikái.
mad ki no kurútta, kichigái *(insane)*; muchuu no *(infatuated)*.
madam ókusama.
madness kichigái.
magazine zasshi.
magistrate hánji.
magnificent rippa na *(grand, stately)*; subarashíi *(splendid)*.
maid musume *(girl)*; jochuu *(servant)*.
mail yuubin.
main ómo na.
    mainland hóndo.

main road hondoo.
main street hondóori.
maintain (to) tamótsu, íji suru.
majesty igen *(dignity)*.
    His Majesty héika.
major *adj.* ómo na
majority daibúbun *(opp. to minority)*; kahansúu *(plurality)*; daitasúu *(most of, greater part)*.
make (to) tsukúru; koshiraeru *(construct, manufacture)*.
male osu *(animal)*; otoko *(human)*.
malice tékii
man ningen *(human race)*; otoko *(male human)*.
manage (to) keiei suru *(a business)*.
management toriatsukai *(handling)*; soojuu, tóogyo *(control)*; keiei *(direction)*.
manager shiháinin, manéejaa.
mankind jínrui *(human race)*.
manner gyoogi *(deportment)*; táido *(attitude)*; yarikata *(method)*.
manners sáhoo.
manufacture seizoo.
manufacture (to) seizoo suru.
manufacturer seizóosha; seisakuka, seizoogyóosha.
manuscript genkoo.
many *adj.* takusán no, oozéi no.
map chízu.
maple mómiji.
March Sángatsu.
march kooshín *(parade)*; kooshín kyoku *(music)*.
march (to) kooshin suru *(in a parade)*; susumu *(proceed)*.
marine úmi no *(oceanic)*; kookaijoo no *(nautical)*.
mark shirushi, máaku; áto *(impression)*; shimi *(stain)*; kizuato *(scar)*; kizu *(scratch)*.
mark (to) máaku o útsu.
    to make a mark shirushi o tsukéru.
market ichiba, maakétto.
marriage kekkon.
marry (to) kekkon suru.
marvel fushigi.
marvelous fushigi na.
masculine otoko no.
mask men, másuku.
mask (to) men o kabúru.
mass *n.* taishuu.
    mass communication masukomi.
    mass production tairyoo seisan.
mast masuto, hobashira.
master shújin *(of the house)*; shújin *(employer)*; senséi *(teacher)*.
master (to) joozu ni náru *(become skillful)*; yóku oboeru *(learn well)*.
masterpiece meisaku, kessaku.
mat tatami *(for floor of Japanese house)*.
match mátchi *(for fire)*; shiai *(contest)*; kyóogi *(game)*.
match (to) niau *(be suitably associated, fit together)*.

material *n.* zairyóo *(cloth, etc).*
maternal haha kata no.
mathematics suugaku.
matter mondai *(problem);* jíken *(event);* koto *(thing).*
matter (to) kamau, mondai ni suru.
matress matoresu.
mature (to) otona ni náru *(reach adulthood);* jukusuru *(as a fruit).*
maximum saidaigen.
May Gógatsu.
may —ká mo shiremasen.
  have my permission to—té mo ii desu.
  It may rain. Ame ga furu ka mo shiremasen.
mayor shíchoo.
me watashi ni *(to me);* watashi o *(as obj. of verb).*
meadow bokujoo.
meal shokuji, góhan.
mean *adj.* iji no warúi, hiretsu na *(base).*
mean (to) imi suru.
  What does it mean? Sore no imi wa nan desu ka?
meaning ími.
meantime, meanwhile sono aida ni.
  in the meantime soo shite iru uchi ni.
measure sunpoo *(dimension);* monosashi *(yardstick).*
measure (to) sunpoo o tóru *(length);* hakáru *(reckon).*
meat nikú.
mechanic shokkoo *(worker in a factory).*
mechanical kikaiteki no; kikai no.
mechanically kikaiteki ni.
medal metaru, kunshoo *(military).*
meddle (to) kanshoo suru *(interfere).*
mediate (to) chootei suru *(arbitrate);* chuukai suru *(act as an intermediary);* torinásu *(intercede).*
medical igakuteki no.
medicine kusuri *(a drug);* ígaku *(the science).*
mediocre nami no, taishita koto no nai.
mediocrity heibon.
meditate (to) mokusoo suru.
meditation mokusoo *(contemplation).*
medium *adj.* chuu kurai no.—*n.* chuu kurai.
meet (to) au, o me ni kakaru *(pol.).*
meeting kai *(assembly).*
melt (to) *v.t.* tokásu; *v.i.* tokéru.
member kaiin *(of an association).*
memorize (to) obóéru.
memory kioku.
mend (to) naósu *(repair);* tsugu *(darn);* tsukuróu *(patch up).*
mental seishin no.
mention genkyuu.
  honorable mention hoojoo.
mention (to) iu, hanásu *(in speaking);* káku *(in writing).*
  Don't mention it. Doo itashimáshite.
merchandise shóohin.
merchant shóonin.
merciful jihibukái *(compassionate).*
merciless mújihi na.
mercury suigin.

mercy jihi *(compassion).*
merit *n.* káchi *(worth);* tegara *(deed).*
merry yukai na; tanoshíi *(joyous).*
message kotozuke *(verbal).*
messenger tsukai.
metal kane.
metallic kane no, kanamono no.
method hoohoo.
metropolis shufu *(capital);* chuushin-chi *(central place).*
microphone maikurohon, maiku.
midday hiru.
middle naka no, chuukan no *(intermediate);* chúui no *(medium).*
  in the middle of mannaka ni.
  Middle Ages Chúusei.
  middle class chuusan kaikyuu.
midnight mayónaka.
might *n.* chikara *(strength).*
mighty chikara no tsuyói, taishita.
mild otonashíi *(gentle);* kandai na *(not severe).*
mildness odayakasa.
military rikúgun no.
milk gyuunyuu, míruku *(cow's).*
milkman gyuunyuu ya.
mill mizu-guruma *(water);* kazaguruma *(wind);* seifunjóo *(flour).*
million hyaku man.
  one hundred million ichioku.
millionaire hyakuman chooja.
mind kokóro *(intention);* kangae *(thought);* atama *(brain, head).*
  frame of mind kimochi.
mind (to) ki ni kakéru *(bear in mind);* sewá o suru *(take care of).*
mine *pron.* watashi no, watashi no mono.
mine *n.* kóozan *(for mineral).*
miner kóofu.
mineral *n.* koobutsu.—*adj.* koobutsu no.
minimum saishoogen no.
minister dáijin *(of state);* kóoshi *(diplomatic);* bokushi *(of religion).*
ministry -shoo *(suffix);* seishoku *(of church).*
  Ministry of Foreign Affairs Gaimushoo.
mink tén, mínku.
minor miseinensha *(legal: less than 20 years old).*
minority shoosuu *(smaller number);* shoosuu too *(opp. to majority);* miséinen *(legal infancy).*
minute fun *(time).*
  Wait a minute! Chótto mátte kudasai.
  Any minute now. Moo sugu desu.
miracle kiseki *(religious).*
mirror kagami.
miscellaneous iroiro na.
mischief itazura.
mischievous itazurazuki na.
misdemeanor fugyóoseki.
miser kechinboo.
miserable fukóo na *(unfortunate);* hisan na *(wretched);* áware na *(pitiable).*
miserably míjime ni.
misery komatte iru koto *(a state of being in distress).*

misfortune fukoo *(unhappiness)*; sainan *(calamity)*.
mishap omoigakenai dekígoto.
misprint insatsu chígai, misupurínto.
Miss -san *(same suffix as for Mr. and Mrs.)*.
   Miss Yamada. Yamada-san.
miss (to) ma ni awánai *(fail to get on time)*; nakusuru *(lose)*; kizukánai *(fail to perceive)*.
mission dendóo kai, mísshon *(religious)*; shísetsu *(official)*.
missionary senkyóoshi, dendóoshi.
mist kasumi.
mistake machigái.
mistake (to) machigáu.
Mister -san. *See* Miss.
   Mr. Yamada. Yamada-san.
mistrust fushín'yoo.
mistrust (to) shinyoo shinai, ayashímu.
mistrustful utagaibukái.
misunderstand (to) gokai suru.
misunderstanding gokai *(mistake)*; íken no sooi *(disagreement)*.
misuse machigátte tsukau koto.
misuse (to) machigátte tsukau.
mix (to) *v.t.* mazéru *(put together)*; *v.i.* mazáru, majiwáru *(associate)*.
mixture mázeta mono.
mob gunshuu *(crowd)*.
mobilization dooin.
mobilize (to) dooin suru.
mock (to) baka ni suru *(ridicule)*; maneru *(mimic)*.
mockery baka ni suru koto.
mode ryuukoo, móodo.
model móderu *(photography, fashion)*; mokei *(copy)*; tehon *(example)*; hinágata *(miniature)*.
model (to) katadoru *(to copy)*.
moderate onken na *(temperate)*; tegoro no *(medium)*.
moderate (to) sétsudo o mamóru *(keep within bounds)*; yawaragéru *(one's temper)*.
moderation tékido, sessei.
modern kíndai no; kindaiteki *(of the present time)*; géndai no *(contemporary)*; modan na *(new in fashion)*.
modest kenson no *(unassuming)*; shitoyaka na *(moderate, unaggressive)*.
modesty kenson.
modification henkoo.
modify (to) arataméru *(alter)*; kanwa suru *(lessen)*; keigen suru *(tone down)*.
moist *adj.* shikkéta, shiméppoi.—*n.* shikke.
moisten (to) shimesu *(dampen)*; shimeru *(become moist)*.
moment shunkan.
   Just a moment! Chótto mátte kudasái.
   Any moment now. Moo súgu desu.
monarchy kunshu séitai *(system)*; kunshúkoku *(nation)*.
monastery shuudóoin.
Monday Getsuyóobi.
money kane, okane.
   paper money satsu.
monk shuudóosoo.

monkey sáru.
monologue hitorigóto.
   to talk to oneself hitorigóto o iu.
monopoly dokusen; senbai.
monotonous tanchoo na.
monotony tanchoo.
monster kaibutsu *(dragon, etc.)*.
monstrosity kikái na kotó.
monstrous kikái na.
month tsukí.
   this month kongetsu.
   last month séngetsu.
   next month ráigetsu.
monthly *adj.* maigetsu no.—*adv.* maigetsu.—*n.* gekkanzásshi.
monument kinénhi.
monumental kinen no.
mood kibun *(feeling)*; kigen *(temper)*.
moody muttsúri shita.
moon tsukí.
   full moon mángetsu.
moonlight tsuki no hikari.
mop móppu.
moral *adj.* dootokuteki na *(virtuous)*.—*n.* kyookun *(maxim)*.
morale shiki.
moralist dootoku shugísha.
morality dootoku.
more mótto.
morning ása.
morsel hitó kire *(a little piece)*.
mortal *adj.* kanarazu shinu *(subject to death)*.
mortgage teitoo.
mortgage (to) teitoo ni suru.
mosquito ka.
most *adj.* taitei no *(greatest number)*; daitai *(the majority of)*; ichíban *(used for the superlative)*.
   most numerous ichiban óoi.
mostly taitei.
moth ga.
mother okáasan, okáasama *(polite)*; háha *(plain)*.
motion undoo *(opp. to rest)*; téburi, míburi *(gesture)*.
motionless ugokánai.
motive dooki.
motor hatsudóoki, móotaa.
motor (to) unten suru *(drive a car)*.
mount yama *(mountain)*.
mount (to) daishi ni haru *(pictures)*; noboru *(ascend)*.
   mount a horse umá ni noru.
mountain yama.
mountainous yama no óoi.
mourn (to) nagéku, kanashímu *(lament)*.
mournful kanashimi ni shizunda.
mourning mo.
mouse nezumi.
mouth kuchi.
movable ugokasu koto no dekíru.
move ungoki, idoo.
move (to) *v.t.,* ugokásu; *v.i.* ugóku, kosu *(change one's dwelling)*.
   move back hikkoméru, hikkómu.
   move forward *v.t.* máe e dásu; *v.i.* máe e déru.

movement koodoo *(action)*.
movies éiga.
moving ugókasu, kandoo saseru *(touching to the emotion)*; hikkoshi *(changing one's dwelling)*.
much takusan, takusán no.
  much better mótto íi.
mud doró.
muddy doró no óoi; doro dárake no *(covered with mud)*.
mule rába.
multiple tasúu no.
multiply kakéru; masu *(increase)*.
multitude oozei, gunshuu.
mumble (to) bútsu butsu iu.
municipal shí no, tóshi no.
municipality jichíku, shi tóokyoku.
munitions gunjúhin.
murder hitogoroshi, satsujin.
  to commit a murder hitogoroshi o suru.
murder (to) hito o korosu.
murmur zawameki, sasayaki.
murmur (to) sasayaku.
muscle kínniku.
museum hakubútsukan.
  art museum bijútsukan.
mushroom kínoko.
music óngaku.
musical *adj.* óngaku no.
musician ongakuka.
must —nákereba naránai,—nakereba ikenai *(have to)*;—ni chigai nái *(in the sense of an obvious inference)*.
  I must go. Ikanákereba naránai. Ikanákereba ikenai.
  You must have said so. Soo itta ni chigai nái.
mustard karashi.
mute oshi no *(dumb)*.
mutter (to) bútsu butsu iu *(mumble)*; sasayaku *(murmur)*.
mutton hitsuji no nikú.
my watashi no *(of or relating to me)*; uchi no *(pertaining to things or persons of one's home)*.
myself jibun, watakushi júshin.
mysterious fushigi na *(strange)*; fukákai na *(inexplicable)*.
mystery shínpi; fukákai na koto.
myth shinwa.

N

nail tsume *(of a finger or toe)*; kugi *(instrument)*.
nail (to) kugi o útsu.
naïve mújaki na *(innocent)*; adoke nai *(unsophisticated)*.
naked hadaka no.
name namae *(designation)*; hyooban *(fame)*.
  first name namae.
  last name myóoji.
  My name is . . . Namae wa . . . to iimásu.
  What is your name? Onamae wa?
name (to) namae o tsukéru.
nameless na no nái.

namely sunáwachi.
nap keba *(of wool)*; hirune *(short sleep)*.
napkin nafukún.
narrow semái.
narrow (to) *v.t.* sebaméru; *v.i.* semáku náru.
nasty iji no warúi.
nation kokumin *(people)*; kuni *(country)*.
national kokumin no, kuni no.
nationality kokuseki.
nationalization kokkateki ni suru kotó, kokueika.
nationalize (to) kokuei ni suru *(to have the state operate)*.
native *adj.* naikoku no *(opp. to foreign)*; dochaku no *(aboriginal)*.—*n.* naikokújin *(opp. to foreigner)*; dojin *(aborigine)*.
natural shizen no, shizen no mama no *(nonartificial)*; mikáikon no *(uncultivated)*.
naturalness kazarike no nái kotó.
nature seishitsu *(character)*; shizen *(the physical universe)*.
naughty itazura na.
naval káigun no.
navy káigun.
near sóba no, chikái *(not far)*; kínjo no *(around the corner)*.
nearly hotóndo *(almost)*; káre kore *(about)*.
neat kichínto shita *(tidy, orderly)*; kozappári shita *(smart, dapper)*; shúmi no íi *(trim)*; seizen to shita *(orderly)*.
neatness sappári shite iru kotó.
necessarily yamú naku, hitsuyoo ni kararete.
necessary hitsuyoo na.
necessity hitsuyoo.
neck kubi.
necklace kubi kázari.
necktie nékutai.
need iriyoo *(want)*; hitsuyoo *(necessity)*; nyuuyoo *(demand)*; kyuuboo *(destitution)*.
  be in need of iriyoo desu.
need (to) iru *(want)*; hoshíi desu *(wish to have)*.
needle hári.
needless fuhitsúyoo na.
needy konkyuu shite iru.
negative *n.* uchikeshi *(expression)*; néga *(photograph)*.—*adj.* insei no *(opp. to positive)*; hantai no *(contrary)*.
neglect kamawánai kotó *(want of attention)*; múshi *(disregard)*.
neglect (to) namakéru, múshi suru.
negotiate kooshoo suru, dánpan suru.
negotiation kooshoo, dánpan.
Negro Kokujin, Níguro.
neighbor tonari.
neighborhood kínjo.
neither dóchira mo . . . de nái.
  neither one dóchira mo.
  neither . . . nor—démo náku . . . démo nái.
nephew oi.
nerve shínkei *(in anatomy)*; daitán *(pluck)*; yúuki *(courage)*.
nervous shinkéishitsu no *(behavior)*; shínkei

no *(pertaining to nerves)*; kuróoshoo no *(apprehensive)*.
nest su.
net amí.
neutral chuuritsu no *(not involved in hostilities)*; kooheimúshi no *(impartial)*.
neuter chuusei.
never kesshite *(with a negative verb)*.
nevertheless —ni mo kakawárazu.
new kóndo no *(recently appointed)*; atarashíi *(recently acquired)*.
news táyori *(tidings)*; nyúusu, hoodoo *(newspaper news)*.
newspaper shinbun.
next tsugí no, ichiban chikái *(nearest)*; tonari no *(neighboring)*; kóndo *(after this)*.
nice íi, yói *(agreeable)*; shínsetsu na *(kind)*.
nickname adana.
niece méi.
night yóru.
nightmare warúi yume.
nine kokónotsu, kú, kyúu.
no iie.
> *Note that when answering a question in the negative, the usage of yes and no in Japanese is opposite to their usage in English.*

Didn't you see it?
No, I didn't. Hai, mimasén deshita.
Yes, I did. Iie, mimáshita.
nobility kázoku, kízoku *(titled group)*.
noble *adj.* kooketsu na *(high minded)*; yuudai na *(imposing)*; kedakái *(dignified)*; mibun no takái *(aristocratic)*.
nobody dáre mo, dónata mo *(followed by a negative verb)*.
noise otó *(sound)*; urusái otó *(unpleasant sound)*.
noisy soozooshíi.
nominate (to) shimei suru.
nomination shimei.
none dáre mo, dónata mo *(of persons)*; dóre mo *(of things)* *(followed by a negative verb)*.
nonsense bakágeta kotó, bakarashíi kotó.
noon hirú, shóogo.
normal *adj.* atarimae no *(not strange)*; hyoojunteki na *(standard)*; futsuu no *(regular)*; heikin no *(average)*.
north kitá.
northern kita no.
northwest nishi kita, seihoku.
nose hana.
nostril hana no aná.
not -nai, -masén.
  I do not go. Ikimasén *(polite)*.
  I do not go. Ikanai *(plain)*.
  It is not expensive. Tákaku arimasen.
  It is not a station. Eki de wa arimasén *(ja arimasen)*.
note tegami *(a letter)*; kiroku *(for later reference)*; satsu *(paper money)*.
note (to) shirusu *(mark down)*; hikki suru *(take note of)*.
  note down kakitomeru.

nothing nani mo *(with a negative verb)*.
notice shirase, kokuchi *(public notice)*; chuumoku *(observation)*.
notice (to) ki o tsukéru, chúui suru *(pay attention to)*.
notify (to) tsuuchi suru *(inform)*; happyoo suru *(announce)*.
notion ippanteki gáinen *(general conception)*; kangáe *(idea)*, iken *(opinion)*; ikoo *(intention)*.
noun meishi *(substantive)*.
nourish jiyoo ga áru.
nourishment jiyoo, jiyóobutsu *(nutriment)*; shokúmotsu *(food)*.
novel *adj.* atarashíi *(new)*; kawatta *(strange)*.—n. shoosetsu.
novelty kawatta mono *(thing)*; kawatta kotó *(event)*.
November Juuichigatsu.
now íma.
  now and then toki doki.
nowadays konogoro; chikágoro.
nowhere doko ni mo *(with a negative verb)*.
nude *adj.* hadaka no *(naked)*.—n. núudo, rataiga *(in art)*.
nuisance méiwaku *(action)*; yákkai na hito *(person)*.
nullify (to) mukoo ni suru *(make invalid)*; yaméru *(cancel)*; damé ni suru *(make useless)*.
numb (to become) kogoeru *(from cold)*; shibiréru *(from pressure)*.
number suuji *(numeral)*; banchi *(indicating location)*; ban, bangoo *(for telephone or room)*;-goo *(issue of a periodical)*.
number (to) kazoéru *(count)*.
numerous takusán no.
nun áma.
nurse kangófu.
nursery kodomo beya *(for children)*; uekiya *(for plants)*.
nut kurumi.

O

oak káshi.
oar kái.
oat karasu múgi.
oath chikai.
  to take an oath chikai o tatéru.
obedience fukujuu *(submission)*; juujun *(dutifulness)*.
obedient juujun na, súnao na.
obey shitagáu, iu koto o kiku.
object monó *(article)*; mokuteki *(aim)*.
object (to) hantai suru.
objection hantai *(adverse reason)*.
  I have no objection to it. Hantai shimasén.
objectionable iyána *(offensive)*; mónku no desóo na *(open to objection)*; omoshirokunái *(unpleasant)*.
objective *n.* mokuteki *(purpose)*.—adj. kyakkanteki no.
objectively kyakkanteki ni.
objectivity kyakkansei.

obligation gímu *(duty)*; ón *(debt of gratitude)*; girí *(sense of duty)*.
obligatory gimuteki, hitsuyoo na.
oblige (to) múri ni saseru *(compel)*.
    be much obliged arígatoo zonjimásu.
obliging shínsetsu na.
oblique katamúita, naname ni, aimai na.
obscure *adj.* bonyári shita.
obscurity aimaisa.
observation kansatsu *(notice)*; kanshi *(watching)*.
observatory tenmondai *(astronomical)*; sokkoojo *(meteorological)*.
observe (to) mokugeki suru *(catch sight of)*; míru *(see)*; ki ga tsúku *(notice)*.
observer bookánsha; óbuzáabaa *(at a conference)*.
obstacle shoogai *(hindrance)*; jama *(impediment)*.
obstinacy goojoo *(stubbornness)*; gankyoo *(persistence)*.
obstinate gánko na *(stubborn)*; gankyoo na *(persistent)*.
obvious akíraka na.
obviously akíraka ni.
occasion orí, kikái.
occasionally toki *(on occasion)*; tama ni *(at times)*.
occupation shigoto *(employment)*; shokúgyoo *(calling)*; gyóomu *(business)*; shóobai *(trade)*; senryoo *(military)*.
occupy (to) senryoo suru *(by force of arms)*; súmu *(live in)*; te ga fusagaru *(take up space)*.
    to be occupied fusagatte iru.
occur (to) okóru.
occurrence dekígoto.
ocean úmi.
    Indian Ocean Indóyoo.
October Juugatsu.
odd hén na *(strange)*; hanpa no *(not paired)*.
    odd number kisúu.
odor kaori *(fragrance)*; niói *(smell)*.
of no
    roof of the house ie no yáne.
off *(usually expressed by verbs)*.
    The button is off. Botan ga hazurete imásu.
    He cut it off. Kirihanáshite shimaimáshita.
    The train is off. Kishá wa déte shimaimáshita.
offend (to) *v.i.* ki ni sawaru *(displease)*; *v.t.* okoraséru *(make angry)*.
offense hansoku *(transgression)*; tsúmi *(crime)*; bujoku *(insult)*.
offensive *adj.* fuyúkai na *(unpleasant)*; buréi na *(insolent)*; iyána *(disgusting)*; kooseiteki *(aggressive)*.—*n.* koogeki.
offer mooshikomi, mooshiide.
offer (to) sonaéru *(as act of worship)*; sashiageru *(as a present)*; mooshidéru *(make an offer)*; teikyoo suru *(propose to give)*; susumeru *(proffer)*.
offering sonaemono *(to a deity)*; kenkin *(gift of money to a church)*.
office jimúsho *(in general)*; yakusho *(of govt.)*.

head office hónsha, hontsen.
branch office shiten.
officer yakunin *(civil)*; shóokoo *(military)*.
official *adj.* seishiki no *(formal)*; omote muki no *(public)*.—*n.* yakunin.
often tabi tabi, yóku.
oil abura.
old furúi *(of things)*; toshiyori *(of persons)*.
old age roonen.
old man toshiyori, ojíisan.
olive oríibu.
    olive oil oriibu óiru.
ominous fukitsu na *(inauspicious)*; yóchi suru *(prognostic)*; ken'aku na *(threatening)*.
on —no ué ni, —no ué de, —no ué no.
    on the desk tsukeu no ué ni.
once ichi do *(one time)*; móto *(formerly)*; máe ni *(before)*.
    at once súgu ni.
    all at once kyuu ni, totsuzen.
    once in a while tokidoki.
    once a year ichínen ni ichido.
    once more moo ichido.
one hitótsu, ichí *(a single person or thing)*; katáhoo *(one of a pair)*; kata *(in compounds, as:* kata me = *one eye)*.
one *pron.* hito, jibun.
oneself jíshin, jibun.
onion tamanégi.
only táda *(merely, but)*; tatta *(emphatic)*; honno *(nothing but)*.
open *adj.* hiráita, hirobíro shita.
open (to) *v.t.* akeru; *v.i.* aku.
opening kuchi *(gap)*; aná *(hole)*; hajime *(beginning)*; kuchi, kikái, chánsu *(opporunity)*.
opera ópera, kágeki.
operate *v.i.* ugóku *(function)*; *v.t.* soojuu suru *(work)*; kánri suru *(superintend)*.
operation shújutsu *(surgical)*; ságyoo *(working)*; unten *(of a mechanism)*.
opinion kangáe, kenkai *(notion)*.
opponent hantáisha *(in debate)*; aite *(in sport)*; kyoosóosha *(in business)*.
opportune kootsúgoo no.
opportunity kikái.
oppose (to) hantai suru.
opposite *adj.* no mukoo no, no mukai no *(facing)*.—*n.* mukoogawa *(the other side)*.
opposition hantai.
oppress (to) shiitagéru. osaéru.
oppression appaku *(tyranny)*; kónnan *(hardship)*.
optimism rakutenshúgi.
optimistic rakutenteki.
oral kootoo no, kuchi de iu, kuchi no. **oral examination** kootoo shikén.
orange *n.* múkan *(tangerine)*, orénji.
orator enzétsusha.
oratory yuuben, enzetsu.
orchard kudamono bátake, kajúen.
orchestra kangéngaku, ookésutora.
ordeal shíren *(severe trial)*.
order iitsuke, meirei *(injunction)*; kunrei *(instruction)*; jun *(regular*

arrangement); chuumon _(commission to supply)._
in order to —táme ni.
put in order séiri suru.
order (to) iitsukéru _(command)_; chuumon suru _(give an order for)._
ordinary futsuu no _(common)_; atarimae no _(not special)._
organ orugan _(musical instrument)._
organization koosei _(formation)_; soshiki _(system)_; dantai _(body)._
organize (to) soshiki suru _(to form)_; sooritsu suru _(to institute)._
Orient Tóoyoo.
oriental _adj._ tóoyoo no.—_n._ Tooyoójin.
origin moto, kígen.
originality dokusoosei.
originate (to) hajimeru, soosaku suru _(invent)._
ornament kazari.
orphan kóji.
other hoka no _(not the same)_; moo hitótsu no _(additional)._
ought —béki desu _(obligation)._
You ought to go to a doctor. Isha e iku beki desu.
ounce ónsu.
our, ours watashítachi no, watashídómo no.
out sóto e _(outside)._
outcome kekka.
outdo (to) dashinúku.
outer soto no, sotogawa no.
outlast (to)—yóri mochi ga íi.
This outlasts that one. Kore wa sore yori mochi ga ii desu.
outlay kéihi _(expenses)_; shuppi _(expenditure)._
outlet déguchi.
outline rinkaku _(contour)_; aramashi _(essential points)._
outline (to) aramashi o nobéru _(state the gist)_; autorain o kaku _(write)._
outlook mikomi.
output sangaku _(product, yield)._
outrage ranboo.
outrageous ranboo na, hidói.
outside sóto, omote.
oval daen no, daenkei no.
oven ténpi, óbun.
overcoat gaitoo, óobaa, oobaakóoto.
overcome (to) —ni uchikátsu; —ni makeru _(be overcome)._
overflow (to) hanran suru _(said of a river)_; koboréru _(water in a vessel)._
overlook (to) miotósu _(omit seeing)_; miwatásu _(view from a high place)_; minogásu _(refrain from seeing)._
overpower (to) makasu, attoo suru.
overrule (to) iatsu suru, kyakka suru _(reject, decide against)._
overrun (to) habikóru, afuréru.
overseas káigai no.
oversight miotoshi _(failure to notice)_; shissaku _(mistake)._
overtake (to) oitsúku.
overthrow (to) hikkurikáesu _(upset)_; uchitaósu _(knock down)_; seifuku suru _(vanquish)_; kutsugáesu _(subvert)._

overwhelm (to) attoo suru _(crush)_; seifuku suru _(defeat)._
owe (to) —ni kari ga áru _(be financially indebted to a person)._
own _adj._ jibun no.
own (to) mótsu.
owner mochínushi _(proprietor)_; ninushi _(of goods)._
ox ushi.
oxygen sanso.
oyster káki.

P

pace -ho, -po _(suffix: step)._
He took two paces. Ního arukimashita.
pace (to) arúite hakáru.
pacific odáyaka na _(quiet, calm)_; shízuka na _(still, as water; placid, as the sea; serene, as the mind; peaceful, as sleep)_; heiwateki no _(not warlike)._
Pacific Ocean Taihéiyoo.
pack (to) tsutsúmu, nizúkuri suru.
page _n._ peeji.
pagoda tóo.
pain kurushimi _(distress)_; nayami _(suffering)_; itami _(ache)_; fuan _(uneasiness)._
pain (to) _v.t._ kurushiméru _(cause pain to)_; _v.i._ itámu _(ache, smart)._
painful itái.
paint penki.
paint (to) penki o nuru _(a house, etc)_; e o káku _(a picture)._
painter penkiya _(for houses)_; ekaki _(artist)._
painting e o kaku koto _(art, hobby, vocation)_; e _(that which is painted)._
pair ittsui _(of objects)_; fúufu _(married couple)_; hitókumi _(a set)._
pair (to) kumiawáseru.
pale usui _(of color)_; aói _(of the face)._
palm te nohira _(of the hand)._
pamphlet panfurétto.
pan nábe.
pancake pankéeki.
pane garasu íta.
window pane mádo no garasu íta.
pang sashikomi _(sudden sharp pain)_; uzuki _(twinge)._
panic kyookoo.
panorama panorama.
pants zubón.
paper kamí.
parachute parashúuto, rakkásan.
parade kanpéishiki _(military)_; paréedo, gyooretsu, kooshin _(for popular celebrations)._
parade (to) kooshin suru.
paragraph páragurafu.
parallel _adj._ heikoo no.
parallel (to) heikoo suru.
paralysis mahi.
paralyze mahi suru.
parcel tsutsumi _(package)_; kozútsumi _(for mail)._
parcel post kozutsumi yúubin.
pardon yarushi.

pardon (to) yóosha suru *(forgive)*; yurúsu *(excuse)*.
  Pardon me! Shitsúrei.
parent ryóoshin.
parenthesis kákko.
park kooen.
park (to) chuusha suru.
parliament gíkai.
part bún, búbun *(portion, piece)*; bu *(of a book)*; hen *(district)*.
  the greater part daibúbun.
part (to) wareru *(separate, divide, split)*; kiréru *(as a cable)*; wakaréru *(take leave)*.
  to part with tebanásu.
  to part from hanaréru.
partial hiiki na *(biased, not fair)*; ichi búbun no *(not total)*.
partially ichibúbun.
particular *adj.* soré zore no, mei mei no *(individual)*; betsudan no, tokubetsu no *(special)*; kichoomen na *(precise)*.—*n.* kuwashíi kotó *(a detail)*.
particularly tóku ni, tokubetsu ni.
party seitoo *(political)*; enkai *(entertainment)*.
pass tooge *(over a mountain)*; pásu, kippu *(ticket)*; nyuujóken *(of admission)*.
pass (to) tóoru *(go beyond)*; tátsu *(time)*.
passage fúne no ryokoo *(on a ship)*; watashi *(across a river)*; rooka *(corridor)*.
passenger jookyaku *(train, etc.)*; senkyaku *(ship)*.
passing *adj.* ichijiteki no *(temporary)*.—*n.* tsuuka *(passage)*.
passion joonetsu *(emotion)*; netsujoo *(intense emotion)*; nekkyoo *(fervid devotion)*; kanshaku *(fury)*.
passive *adj.* ukemi no.—*n.* ukemi *(grammatical verb form)*.
past *n,* káko *(time gone by)*; rireki *(past life or career)*.
  half-past seven shichiji hán.
past *adj.* káko no *(gone by)*; súgita bákari no *(just passed)*; ízen no *(ago)*.
  the past year sakunen.
paste *n.* norí.
patch tsugi.
patch (to) tsugu.
patent tokkyo.
paternal chichi no, chichikata no.
path kómichi.
pathetic kanashíi.
patience gáman *(forbearance)*; shínboo *(perseverance)*.
patient *adj.* gaman zuyói, shinboo zuyói.
patient kanja *(sick person)*.
patriot aikókusha.
patriotism aikókushin *(nationalism)*.
patron hogósha *(protector)*; kooénsha, patoron *(backer)*; hiikí kyaku *(regular customer)*.
patronize (to) híiki ni suru.
pattern gara, moyoo *(of fabric)*; tehón *(model)*; mihon *(sample)*.
pause kyuushi *(short stop)*.
pause (to) *v.i.* tomaru.

pave (to) hosoo suru.
pavement hodoo.
pay kyúuryoo *(salary)*; chíngin *(wages)*.
pay (to) haráu.
payment shiharai *(paying)*; shiharaikin *(sum paid)*.
pea endóomame *(any dried variety)*.
  green peas guriin píisu.
peace heiwa *(opp. to war)*.
peaceful heiwa na.
peach momo.
peak itadaki.
pear nashí.
pearl shinju.
peasant hyákushoo *(farmer)*; inakamono *(rustic)*.
pebble jari.
peculiar tokushu no *(characteristic)*; hén na *(strange)*.
pecuniary kinsenjoo no.
pedal petaru.
pedal (to) petaru o fumu.
pedestrian hokóo sha.
peel kawa.
peel (to) kawá o muku.
pen pén *(for writing)*; orí *(sty)*.
  fountain pen mannénhitsu.
penalty bakkin *(fine)*; kéi *(punishment)*.
pencil enpitsu.
penetrate (to) *v.t.* hairikómu *v.i.* tsukíiru.
peninsula hantoo.
penitence kóokai *(repentance)*.
pension onkyuu *(government)*; nenkin *(annuity)*.
people hitóbito, hito, hitótachi *(individuals collectively)*; kokumin *(a nation)*.
pepper koshóo.
perceive (to) ryookai suru *(apprehend)*; shikibetsu suru *(discern)*; wakáru *(grasp)*.
percentage hyakubún ritsu, paasentéeji.
perfect kanzen na.
perfect (to) kansei suru.
perfection kansei *(completion)*; kanzen *(being unblemished)*; jukutatsu *(proficiency)*.
perfectly kanzen ni.
perform (to) suru *(do)*; nashitogéru *(accomplish)*; enjíru *(act, as in a play)*.
performance suru koto *(doing)*; jikkoo *(execution)*; engeki *(of a drama)*; yokyoo *(entertainment)*.
perfume koosui.
perfume (to) koosui o tsukéru.
perhaps tábun *(probably)*; hyotto suru to *(maybe)*.
peril kiken.
period jidai *(era)*; shuushífu *(in punctuation)*.
periodical zasshi *(magazine)*.
perish (to) horobíru *(suffer destruction)*; kusáru *(spoil, decay)*; sinu *(die)*.
permanent eikyuu no *(lasting)*; eikyuuteki na *(perpetual)*; fuhen no *(unchanging)*.
permission yurushi *(permitting)*; ménkyo *(license)*; dooi *(consent)*.
permit ménkyo *(license)*; menkyójoo *(written permission)*.

permit (to) kyóka suru *(allow)*.
perplex (to) *v.t.* komaraséru *(throw into confusion)*; *v.i.* komáru *(be perplexed)*.
persecute (to) hakugai suru.
persecution hakugai.
perseverance níntai.
persist (to) ganbáru *(insist on)*; jizoku suru *(last)*.
person hito; -nin *(suffix)*.
   three persons sannín.
personal kójin no *(individual)*; jibun no *(one's own)*; shiyoo no *(private)*.
personality jinkaku *(character)*; kósei *(distinctive personal quality)*.
perspective mikomi *(prospect)*.
persuade (to) tokifuséru.
pertaining to —ni kán shite.
petty chiisái *(small in size)*; sásai na *(trifling)*; kéchi na *(mean)*.
pharmacist kusuriya.
pharmacy kusuriya.
phenomenon genshoo.
phenomenal hijoo na.
philosopher tetsugákusha.
philosophical tetsugakuteki.
philosophy tetsugaku.
photograph shashin.
   take a photograph shashin o tóru.
photograph (to) utsusu.
phrase kú.
physical shizen no *(natural)*; nikutai no *(bodily)*.
physician isha.
physics butsurigaku.
piano piano.
pick (to) tsumu *(flowers, grass)*; erábu *(select)*.
   to pick up hirou.
picnic pikuníkku, ensoku.
picture shashin *(photo)*; é *(painting)*.
picture (to) egaku.
picturesque é no yoo na.
pie pái.
piece kire *(obtained by cutting)*; kakera *(broken piece)*.
pig buta.
pigeon háto.
pile yamá *(heap)*.
pile (to) tsumu.
   to pile up tsumiagéru.
pill gan'yaku.
pillar hashira.
pillow mákura.
pilot mizusaki ánnai *(of a ship)*; soojúushi *(of a plane)*.
pin pín.
pin (to) pin o sasu.
pinch (to) tsunéru.
pine mátsu.
pink pínku, momoiro *(color)*.
pious keiken na *(devout)*; shinjinbukái *(religious)*.
pipe kiseru, páipu *(for smoking)*; tekkan *(of iron)*.
pitiful kawaisóo na *(touching)*; míjime na *(miserable)*.

pity doojoo.
pity (to) doojoo suru.
place tokoro.
place (to) oku.
   to take place okoru.
plain *adj.* akíraka na *(evident)*; karui *(said of food)*; jimí na *(unadorned)*; futsuu no *(ordinary)*.
plain heichi *(level ground)*.
plan zumen *(drawing)*; keikaku *(project)*.
plan (to) keikaku suru *(devise a method or course)*.
plane hikóoki *(airplane)*; heimen *(level surface)*.
plant shokúbutsu.
plant (to) ueru.
plaster kooyaku *(medical)*; kabe *(mud)*; shikkui *(sand and lime)*.
plate sara *(for eating)*; íta *(of metal)*.
platform purattohóomu, hóomu *(for trains)*; endan *(stage)*.
platter oozara.
play asobi *(children's play)*; shibai, engeki *(dramatic performance)*.
play (to) asobu *(for amusement)*; hiku *(a string or keyboard instrument)*; fuku *(a wind instrument)*.
plea negai.
plead (to) uttaeru.
pleasant kokoromochi no yói *(giving pleasure)*; yúkai na *(cheerful)*.
please (to) yorokobásu *(delight)*; tanoshimaséru *(give pleasure to)*.
   Please. Dóozo.
pleasure tanoshími *(delight)*; yorokobi *(enjoyment)*.
pledge yakusoku *(promise)*; shirushi *(guarantee)*.
pledge (to) teitoo ni ireru *(give as a pledge)*; yakusoku suru *(promise)*.
plenty takusan *(much)*; juubún *(enough)*.
plot jísho *(land)*; inboo *(conspiracy)*.
plot (to) takurámu *(scheme secretly)*; inboo o megurásu *(conspire)*.
plow suki.
plow (to) tagayásu.
plum ume.
plunder (to) ryakudatsu suru.
plural fukusúu.
plus púrasu, tasu.
pocket pokétto.
   pocket money kozukai.
poem shi, utá.
poet shijin.
poetic shiteki no.
poetry shi, utá.
point saki *(tapering end)*; kangáe *(opinion)*; ten *(dot, stage, step)*; pointo *(prominent feature)*.
point (to) togarásu.
   to point out yubi sásu *(with the hand)*; chúui o hiku *(draw attention)*.
pointed togátta.
poison dokú.
poison (to) dokú o ireru *(infect with poison)*; dokusatsu suru *(kill with poison)*.

poisoning chúudoku.
polar kyokuchi no.
pole sao.
policeman júnsa.
policy shudan *(method)*; hooshin *(guiding principle)*; seisaku *(course of action in govt.)*.
   insurance policy hoken shoosho.
polish tsuya.
   shoe polish kutsúzumi.
Polish Poorandozín *(people)*; Poorando no *(country)*.
polish (to) migaku.
polite téinei na.
politeness téinei.
political seijijoo no, seíjiteki no.
   political party seitoo.
politics seiji.
pond iké.
poor bínboo na *(opp. to rich)*; warúi *(in quality)*; kawaisóo na *(worthy of pity)*.
popular ninki no áru *(liked)*; hyooban no íi *(famous, talked of)*; taishuuteki ni *(in general favor)*.
population jinkoo.
pork butaniku.
port minato.
porter mónban *(gatekeeper)*; akaboo *(at railway stations)*; booi *(at hotels)*.
portrait shoozooga.
position tsutoméguchi *(employment)*; tachiba *(circumstances)*; oki dokoro *(place)*.
positive *adj.* táshika na *(sure)*; meikaku na *(definite)*; utagai no nái *(unquestionable)*; jishin no áru *(convinced)*.—*n.* póji *(in photography)*.
possess (to) mótsu.
possession mochímono *(thing held)*.
possibility kanoosei.
possible dekíru.
post hashira *(pillar)*; kúi *(a stake)*; yuubínbutsu *(mail)*; pósuto *(mailbox)*.
post card hagaki *(plain)*; ehagaki *(picture)*.
postage yuubínryoo.
   postage stamp kitte.
poster pósutaa.
posterity shíson.
post office yuubínkyoku.
pot nábe *(pan)*; tsubo *(jar)*; hachí *(bowl)*.
potato jagaimo.
pound póndo.
pour (to) tsugu *(into glass)*; hídoku fúru *(of rain)*.
poverty bínboo.
powder kona.
power chikara.
powerful tsuyói *(strong)*; yuuryoku na *(influential)*.
practical jissaiteki na *(opp. to theoretical)*; jitsuyoóteki na *(useful)*.
practice jitsuyoo *(opp. to theory)*; kéiko *(exercise)*.
practice (to) jikkoo suru *(carry out)*; kéiko suru *(exercise)*.
praise shoosan *(commendation)*.
praise (to) homéru.

prank itazura.
pray (to) inóru.
prayer inori.
preach (to) sekkyoo suru.
precaution yóojin.
precede (to) sakidátsu.
preceding máe no.
precept kyookun.
precious kóoka na *(costly)*; taisetsu na *(highly esteemed)*.
precise seikaku na *(exact)*; kuwashíi *(detailed)*; kichoomen na *(regular)*.
precision seikaku *(accuracy)*; seimitsu *(exactitutde)*.
predecessor zennínsha.
preface jobun.
prefer —hóo ga sukí desu *(one thing to another)*.
   I prefer this. Kono hóo ga sukí desu.
pregnant ninshin shite iru.
prejudice henken *(bias)*.
prejudice (to) henken o ataeru.
preliminary kari no, yobiteki no.
prepare (to) shitaku o suru, júnbi o suru.
prescribe (to) sáshizu suru *(dictate)*; shohoo o káku *(medicine)*.
presence shusseki *(at a meeting, etc.)*.
present *adj.* shusseki shite iru *(opp. to absent)*; íma no, génzai no *(now existing)*.—*n.* génzai *(the present time)*; íma *(now)*; okuri mono, purézento *(gift)*.
   to make a present okurimono o suru.
   for the present toobun.
present (to) ageru, sashiageru *(a gift)*; shookai suru *(introduce a person)*; miséru *(exhibit)*; teishutsu suru *(offer)*; nobéru *(state)*.
preserve (to) hozon suru *(maintain)*; satoozuke ni suru *(in sugar)*; suzuke ni suru *(in vinegar)*.
preside (to) shikai suru.
president shachoo *(of a company)*; toodori *(of a bank)*; daitóoryoo *(of a country)*; gakuchoo *(university)*.
press shinbun *(newspaper)*; assákuki *(machine)*.
press (to) susumeru *(urge)*; shiméru *(squeeze)*; purésu suru *(iron)*; osu *(push)*.
pressing purésu.
pressure atsúryoku *(compulsion)*.
prestige meisei *(fame)*; ishin *(dignity)*.
presume (to) suitei suru *(assume)*; katei suru *(suppose)*; omóu *(guess)*.
pretend (to) misekakéru *(lay claim)*;—furí o suru *(make believe)*.
pretext koojitsu *(pretense)*; benkai *(excuse)*.
pretty *adj.* kírei na *(beautiful)*.—*adv.* kánari *(fairly)*.
prevail (to) kátsu *(be victorious)*; yuusei de áru *(be predominant)*; ryuukoo suru *(be prevalent)*.
prevent (to) samatagéru *(hinder)*; mamóru *(guard against)*; jama o suru *(stand in one's way)*.

prevention booshi, yoboo.
previous saki no *(former)*; máe no *(prior to)*.
  the previous year máe no toshi.
prey gisei *(victim)*.
price nedan *(charge)*; daika *(cost)*.
pride hokori *(in something or someone)*;
  unubore *(self-conceit)*; kooman
  (haughtiness).
priest sóoryo *(Buddhist)*; kánnushi *(Shinto)*;
  bokushi *(Protestant)*; shínpu
  (Catholic).
principal *adj.* dái ichí no *(first)*; ómo na
  (main, most important).—*n.* genkin
  (money); koochoo *(of a school)*.
principle gensoku *(fundamental rule)*; shúgi
  (doctrine, an -ism).
print *(to)* shuppan suru *(publish)*; insatsu suru
  (to put into print).
prison keimúsho.
prisoner shuujin *(criminal)*; hóryo *(of war)*.
private *adj.* watakushi no, shiyoo no *(opp. to
  public)*; shiei no *(privately operated)*;
  kójin no *(personal)*.
privilege tokken *(prerogative)*; tokuten
  (peculiar right).
prize shoohin.
prize *(to)* omonjíru *(esteem)*; daijí ni suru
  (value highly).
probable arisóo na *(likely to be)*; yuuboo na
  (promising).
probably tábun *(perhaps)*; taitei *(most likely)*.
problem mondai.
procedure tetsúzuki *(steps)*; júnjo *(way of
  proceeding)*.
proceed *(to)* susumu *(move on)*; hajimeru
  (begin); tsuzukeru *(continue)*.
process hoohoo *(method)*; katei *(course)*.
procession gyooretsu.
proclaim *(to)* koohyoo suru *(publish)*; fukoku
  suru *(promulgate)*; sengén suru
  (declare officially).
produce *(to)* san súru *(yield)*; enshutsu suru
  (as plays).
product sanbutsu *(agricultural produce)*;
  seisakúhin *(of industrial manufacture)*.
production seisaku *(through manufacture)*.
productive hoofu na *(producing abundantly)*;
  yóku tsukuridásu *(bring forth)*.
profess to hakujoo suru.
profession shokúgyoo *(a calling)*; koogen
  (avowal); sengén *(declaration)*.
professional shokugyoo joo no *(pertaining to
  work)*; senmonteki *(technical)*.
professor kyooju *(of a university)*.
profile yokogao.
profit ríeki *(pecuniary gain)*; éki *(advantage)*.
profit *(to)* éki o éru, toku o suru.
profits ríeki.
program puroguramu *(theatrical, concert,
  etc.)*; keikaku *(plan)*.
progress zenshin *(movement forward)*.
progress *(to)* shinpo suru *(improve)*; zenshin
  suru *(advance)*; tsugoo yóku iku *(get
  on well)*; hattatsu suru *(develop)*.
prohibit kinjíru *(forbid)*.
prohibition kinshi *(a forbidding)*.

project keikaku *(plan)*; kigyoo *(industrial)*.
project *(to)* keikaku suru *(devise)*; tsukidásu
  (protrude).
promise yakusoku *(engagement)*; keiyaku
  (contract); mikomi *(hope)*.
promise *(to)* yakusoku o suru.
  to keep a promise yakusoku o mamóru.
prompt hayái, subayai *(quick)*; sumíyaka na
  (speedy); sassoku no *(done quickly)*.
prompt *(to)* unagasu.
promptness binsoku.
pronounce *(to)* hatsuon suru *(aticulate)*;
  senkoku suru *(announce formally)*;
  sengén suru *(declare)*.
proof shoomei *(demonstration)*; shooko
  (evidence); insatsu suru *(printing)*.
proper tekitoo na *(appropriate)*; joohin na
  (respectable); dokutoku no
  (particular); tadashíi *(correct)*.
property zaisan *(assets)*; jísho *(land)*.
proportion wari, wariai *(ratio)*; warimae
  (share); tsuriai *(balance)*.
proposal mooshikomi.
propose *(to)* teian suru *(propound)*;
  mooshikómu *(offer)*.
prosaic sanbun no *(of prose)*; omoshirokunái
  (dull, commonplace).
prose sanbun.
prospect mikomi *(outlook)*; nagame *(view)*;
  mitooshi *(mental view)*; yosoo
  (expectation).
prosper *(to)* sakaéru, han'ei suru.
prosperity hánjoo *(of a business)*; ryuusei *(a
  thriving)*; kooseizuri *(success)*.
prosperous sakan na *(thriving)*; ríeki no áru
  (profitable).
protect *(to)* hógo suru *(keep safe)*; fuségu
  (defend).
protection hógo *(a protecting)*; kooen
  (patronage).
protector hogósha.
protest kóogi *(dissent)*; fufuku *(disapproval)*.
protest *(to)* kóogi suru *(make a protest)*;
  hantai suru *(oppose)*; genmei suru
  (declare formally).
Protestant Purotésutanto, Shinkyoo.
proud tokui na.
prove *(to)* shoomei suru *(demonstrate)*;
  tashikaméru *(make certain)*; jikken
  suru *(experiment)*.
proverb kotowaza.
provide yóoi suru *(supply)*.
  provide with kyookyuu suru.
province chihóo *(place at a distance from the
  capital)*; hán'i *(sphere or scope)*.
provision chozóohin *(of food, etc.)*;
  shokuryóohin *(supplies)*; kitei
  (stipulation); júnbi *(preparation)*; yóbi
  (reserve).
provoke *(to)* kanjoo o okosaséru *(call forth)*;
  okoraséru *(rouse to anger)*; fungai
  saseru *(exasperate)*; okósu *(stimulate)*.
proximity chikái koto.
prudence yóojin, shinchoo na koto.
prune sumomo.
psychological shinrigaku joo no.

psychology shinrígaku.
public *adj.* ooyake no *(opp. to personal)*;
    kookai no *(open to all)*.—*n.* kokumin
    (the people).
  to make public koohyoo suru.
publication happyoo *(public notification)*,
    shuppan *(publishing)*; shuppanbutsu
    (published materials).
publish (to) shuppan suru *(books, etc.)*;
    happyoo suru *(make known)*.
publisher shuppánsha.
pull (to) hiku.
pulpit koodan.
pulse myakú.
pump pónpu.
punish (to) bassúru.
punishment bátsu *(act of punishing)*; keibatsu
    (penalty imposed by court).
pull séito *(scholar)*; deshí *(disciple)*; hitomi
    (of the eye).
purchase kaimono *(that which is bought)*;
    torihiki *(act of buying)*.
purchase (to) kaú, koonyuu suru.
pure junsui no *(unmixed)*; seijun na
    (uncontaminated); kírei na *(unsullied)*;
    junketsu na *(chaste)*; keppaku na
    (guiltless).
purity junketsu *(chastity)*.
purpose mokuteki *(object)*;—tsumori
    (intention).
  I intend to go. Iku tsumóri desu.
purse saifu.
pursue (to) oikakéru *(chase)*; tsukimatóu
    (follow closely); jikkoo suru *(carry
    on)*.
pursuit tsuiseki *(chase)*.
push (to) osu *(opp. to pull)*; oshiugokasu
    (move by pushing); tsukidásu *(thrust)*;
    shíiru *(force)*.
put *v.t.* oku.
  put away shimau.
  put off nobásu, enki suru.
  put on kabúru *(a hat)*; kiru *(a dress)*; haku
    (shoes); tsukéru *(a light)*.
puzzle nazó *(enigma)*; kangae móno *(quiz)*;
    nandai *(difficult problem)*.
puzzle (to) toowaku saseru *(perplex)*.
  be puzzled toowaku suru.

Q

quaint fuugáwari na.
qualify (to) tekioo saseru *(fit)*; shikaku o éru
    (have the qualifications for).
  be qualified for shikaku ga áru.
quality hinshitsu *(degree of excellence)*;
    seishitsu *(property)*.
quantity ryoo, bunryóo *(amount)*; suuryoo
    (numbers).
quarrel (to) kenka suru.
quarter yon bun no ichí *(one-fourth part)*; hen
    (district).
queen jooo.
queer hén na, myóo na *(strange)*; okashii
    (funny); okáshi na *(unusual)*.

quench (to) iyásu *(one's thirst)*; kesu
    (extinguish).
question shitsumon *(interrogation)*; koto
    (matter); mondai *(problem)*.
question (to) shitsumon suru, tazuneru
    (inquire); tóu *(ask)*; gimon o okósu
    (raise a doubt); utagáu *(doubt)*.
quick hayái.
quickly háyaku.
  Come quickly! Háyaku kite kudasái.
quiet *adj.* shizuka na *(calm)*; otonashíi *(of
    character)*; ochitsuita *(not showy)*.—*n.*
    shizukésa *(stillness)*; kyuusoku
    (repose); ochitsuki *(peace of mind)*.
  Keep quiet! Shizuka ni shite kudasai!
quiet (to) *v.t.* shízuka ni saseru; *v.i.* shízuka ni
    náru.
quit (to) hanásu *(let go)*; hooki suru
    (abandon); yameru *(cease)*.
quite sukkári *(completely)*; jijitsujoo
    (actually); kánari *(somewhat)*; tashoo
    wa *(to a certain extent)*; taihen *(very)*.
  quite good totem yoroshii.
quote (to) in'yoo suru *(cite)*; hikiai ni dásu
    (refer to); mitsumóru *(estimate)*.

R

rabbit usagi.
race kyoosoo *(contest)*; jinshu *(of human
    beings)*.
race (to) kyoosoo suru.
radio rájio.
rag bóro.
rage ikari.
ragged boro boro no.
rail réeru *(of railway)*; tesuri *(of a fence)*.
railroad tetsudoo.
  railroad staton éki, sutéeshon.
  railroad train kishá.
rain áme.
rain (to) áme ga fúru.
rainbow niji.
rainy ame fúri no.
  rainy season nyuubai.
  rainy weather úten.
raise (to) ageru *(move upward)*; mochiageru
    (lift up); kakageru *(hoist)*; saibai suru
    (grow).
raisin hoshibudoo.
rake kumade.
range hán'i *(scope)*; narabi *(row)*; dennétsuki
    (electric cookstove); gasu kónro *(gas
    stove)*.
range (to) *v.t.* naraberu.
rank rétsu *(row)*; kaikyuu *(military)*.
ransom minoshirókin *(money demanded)*;
    kaihoo *(release from captivity)*.
rapid *adj.* hayai.—*n.* kyuuuryuu *(swift
    current)*.
rapidity sókudo.
rapidly kyuu ni, háyaku.
rapture uchooten.
rash sékkachi na.
rat nezumi.

rate wariai *(proportion)*; sooba *(of exchange)*; sókudo *(speed)*.

rate (to) nedan o tsukéru, mitsumóru *(estimate)*.

rather *(tolerably, fairly)*; múshiro *(instead of)*; sukóshi *(somewhat)*.

   rather than—yóri mo.

   rather good kánari yói.

   I'd rather go. Watakushi wa dóchira ka to ieba ikitái desu.

ration haikyuu shokuryóohin.

rational rikutsu no áru.

rave (to) tawagoto o iu *(talk wildly)*; donáru *(talk furiously)*.

raw náma no *(uncooked)*.

ray koosen, hikari.

reach (to) todóku *(come to)*; oitsuku *(overtake)*;—ni tassúru *(attain to)*.

react (to) *v.i.* hannoo suru *(act in response)*.

reaction handoo *(against)*; hanpatsu *(repulsion)*.

read (to) yómu.

reading dokusho.

ready yóoi no totonótta *(completely prepared)*; yorokónde . . . suru *(willing)*; kákugo no tsúita *(mentally prepared for)*; tejika no *(handy)*.

real hontoo no *(true)*; jitsuzai suru *(actually existing)*; jissai no *(opp. to imaginary)*; honmono no *(genuine)*.

reality shinjitsu *(opp. to fancy)*; genjitsu *(actuality)*.

realization jitsugen.

realize (to) jitsugen suru *(effectuate)*; ki ga tsuku, omóu *(come to understand)*.

really hontoo ni.

   Really! Sóo nan desu ka!

rear ushiro.

rear (to) *v.t.* sodáteru *(bring up)*.

reason riséi ryoku *(intellectual faculty)*; doori *(explanation)*; riyuu *(cause)*; dooki *(motive)*; wáke *(ground)*; iiwake *(excuse)*.

reason (to) súiri suru *(draw a conclusion)*; hándan o kudasu *(form a judgment)*; kentoo suru *(examine critically)*.

   by reason of —no tame ni.

reasonable riséi no aru *(endowed with reason)*; múri ga nai *(justifiable)*; koohei na *(fair minded)*; goori teki na *(rational)*.

reasoning riron, ronkyuu.

reassure (to) anshin saseru.

rebel muhonnin *(person)*.

rebel (to) boodoo o okósu *(take up arms against)*; shitagawanai *(disobey)*; somúku *(act against)*.

rebellion hanran *(revolt)*; boodoo *(riot)*; hankoo *(resistance)*; múshi *(defiance)*.

recall torikeshi *(act of revoking)*; kaisoo *(recollection)*.

recall (to) omoidásu *(recollect)*; torikésu *(revoke)*; yobikáesu *(call back)*.

receipt uketori.

receive (to) uketoru.

receiver reshíibaa *(radio)*; uketorinin *(person)*.

recent chikágoro no *(modern)*; atarashíi *(new)*; saikin no *(the latest)*.

reception kangei *(welcoming)*; kangéikai *(social entertainment)*.

recess kyuuka *(vacation)*; yasumi jíkan *(school)*; kyuukei *(conference)*.

reciprocal soogo no *(mutual)*; okaeshi no *(done in return)*.

recite (to) anshoo suru *(repeat from memory)*; roogin suru *(as a poem, etc.)*; monogatáru *(recount)*.

recognize (to) wakáru, mitomeru.

recoil (to) handoo *(as a gun)*; hanekaeri *(spring back)*.

recollect (to) omoidásu.

recollection oboe *(reminiscence)*; kaisoo *(remembrance)*; tsuioku *(retrospection)*; omoide *(that which is recollected)*.

recommend (to) suisen suru.

recommendation suisen.

reconcile (to) wakai saseru.

record kiroku *(written note)*; rireki *(career)*; rekóodo *(phonograph)*.

record (to) kiroku suru *(in writing)*; rokuon suru *(in sound)*.

recover (to) torimodósu *(get back)*; zenkai suru *(from sickness)*.

recruit shinpei.

rectangle kukei.

red *adj.* akai.—*n.* áka.

redeem (to) shookan suru.

redouble (to) issoo tsuyoméru.

reduce (to) *v.t.*—ni suru *(convert)*; herasu *(make small)*.

reduction waribiki *(discount)*.

reed áshi.

refer (to) sankoo ni suru *(consult)*; makaséru *(a matter to a person)*.

reference mimoto shoomeísho *(a statement of qualifications for someone)*; kikiawase *(inquiry)*; kankei *(relation)*.

refine (to) seisei suru *(oil, etc.)*.

refinement seisei *(of oil, etc.)*; joohinsa *(elegance)*.

reflect (to) hansha suru *(throw back light, etc.)*; arawásu *(show)*; kangáeru *(ponder)*.

reflection hansha.

reform kaikaku *(political)*; kanka *(of persons)*.

reform (to) kaizen suru *(amend)*; arataméru *(make better)*; kaikaku suru *(renovate)*.

refrain orikaeshi.

refrain (to) sashihikáeru *(abstain from)*; gáman suru *(forbear)*.

refresh (to) árata ni suru *(make new)*.

refreshment tabemóno *(food)*; karui nomímono *(drink)*; sáka *(tea and cake)*.

refuge hínan *(shelter)*; hinanjo *(place of retreat)*; hógo *(protection)*.

   to take refuge hínan suru.

refund harai modoshi.
refund (to) harai modósu.
refusal kotowari.
refuse kotowáru (*decline*); jítai suru (*decline to receive*); shoodaku shinai (*reject*).
refute (to) hanbaku suru.
regard kóoryo (*consideration*); sonkei (*respect*).
  in regard to—ni tsúite.
regime tóochi (*administration*); kánri (*control*); genseifu (*government in power*).
regiment rentai.
register choomén (*record book*); meibo (*of names*).
register (to) káku (*a name*); kakitome ni suru (*a letter*).
  registered letter kakitome.
regret kóokai (*repentance*); shitsuboo (*disappointment*); zánnen (*remorse*).
regret (to) zánnen ni omóu (*be sorry for*); ki no dóku ni omóu (*deplore*); ikan ni omóu (*lament*); kóokai suru (*repent*); óshiku omóu (*be sorry for the loss of*).
regular kimatta (*according to rule*); futsuu no (*usual*); téiki no (*at intervals*).
regulate (to) choosetsu suru.
regulation kisóku.
rehearsal shitagéiko, renshuu.
rehearse (to) shitagéiko suru, renshuu suru.
reign jidai (*period*).
reign (to) osaméru.
reinforce (to) hokyóo suru.
reject (to) kotowáru.
rejoice (to) yorokóbu.
relapse burikaeshi (*recurrence of illness*).
relate (to) hanásu (*narrate*); kankei o tsukéru (*connect*).
relation kankei (*connection*); shinrui (*kinsman*).
relationship kankei.
relative *adj.* hikakuteki, kankei áru.—*n.* shinrui, shinseki (*kinsman*).
relax (to) kutsurógu (*take one's ease*); yurúmu (*become lax*); yawarágu (*become less strict*).
relaxation kibarashi (*recreation*); kyuuyoo (*rest*); yurumi (*of muscles*); tegókoro (*of regulations*).
release (to) hanásu (*let go free*); tóoka suru (*let fall from*); happyoo suru (*make public*).
relent (to) yawarágu, kandai ni náru.
relentless mújihi na.
relevant kankei no áru.
reliable táshika na.
reliance shinrai (*trust*); shin'yoo (*confidence*).
relic ibutsu.
relief kyuujo (*help*); keigen (*alleviation*); ánraku (*comfort*).
relieve (to) tasukéte yaru (*aid*); rakú ni suru (*give comfort*).
religion shuukyoo (*of religion*);
  Buddhist religion Bukkyóo.
  Shintoism Shintoo.
religious shuukyóoteki na (*of religion*);

shinkoo no (*devout*); shinjin bukái (*godly*); keikan na (*pious*).
relinquish (to) suteru, hóoki suru.
relish aji (*taste*); kaori (*flavor*); fuumí (*good taste*).
relish (to) ajiwátte míru (*savor*); oishiku tabéru (*eat with pleasure*); tanoshímu (*enjoy*).
reluctance chúucho.
reluctant iyagáru, fushoo bushoo no.
rely upon tayóru (*depend upon*).
remain todomáru, taizai suru (*stay*).
remainder nokori (*remaining part*); zanryúusha (*remaining person*).
remark itta kotoba (*anything said*); fken (*comment*).
remark (to) —ni chuumoku suru (*take notice of*); hihyoo suru (*comment*).
remarkable chuumoku subéki (*noteworthy*); sugúreta (*exceptional*); subarashii (*striking*).
remedy kusuri (*medicine*); chiryoo (*treatment*).
remember (to) oboéru; omoi dásu (*recollect*).
remembrance omoide (*recollection*); kiokúryoku (*memory*); kinen (*commemoration*).
remind (to) omoidasaseru (*bring something to mind*).
remorse kóokai (*regret*); ryóoshin no togamé (*pangs of conscience*).
remote tooi, hanáreta.
removal iten (*of or from house*); kaishoku (*position*).
remove (to) dokeru, torinozoku.
renew atarashiku suru (*make new again*); irekáeru (*replace*); kurikaesu (*repeat*).
rent yáchin (*for a house*).
rent (to) kasu (*to somebody*); kariru (*from somebody*).
repair shuuzen (*act of repairing*); kaifuku (*restoration to a sound state*).
repair (to) naósu (*mend*); kaifuku suru (*restore*); teisei suru (*remedy*).
repeat (to) kurikáesu (*do once more*); sono mama tsutaeru (*tell to another*); kurikáeshite okonáu (*do over again*).
repent (to) kuíru, kóokai suru.
repetition kurikaeshi, hanpuku.
reply henji.
reply (to) henji suru.
report hookoku; shirase (*account*).
report (to) hookoku suru.
represent (to) dairi suru (*persons, etc.*); arawásu (*as a symbol*); egaki dásu (*portray*).
representation daihyoo (*delegate*); mooshitate (*petition*).
representative dairinin; daihyoo (*delegate*).
repress (to) yokuatsu suru (*suppress*); yokusei suru (*keep uder control*).
reprimand shikari.
reprimand (to) shikaru, hínan suru.
reprisal shikaeshi, fukushuu.
reproach shikari (*upbraiding*); to game (*censure*).

reproach (to) shikaru.
reproduce (to) fukusha suru *(make a copy)*; saisei suru *(remake)*.
reputation hyooban, meisei.
request negái, seikyuu.
request (to) negáu *(beg)*; tanómu *(ask)*.
require (to) iru *(need)*.
rescue sukuidashi, kyúujo.
rescue (to) sukuidásu *(deliver from)*; káihoo suru *(set free)*.
research (to) kenkyuu suru, shirabéru.
resent (to) okóru, hankan o mótsu.
resentment urami *(animosity)*; fungai *(indignation)*.
reservation yoyaku *(at a hotel)*.
reserve júnbi *(readiness)*; yobíhin *(stock)*.
  without reserve fukuzoonáku *(freely)*.
reserve (to) tótte oku *(set apart, keep in store)*.
reside (to) súmu.
residence súmai; júusho.
resign (to) yameru *(relinquish)*; dannén suru *(abandon)*; jishoku suru *(give up office)*; taishoku suru *(retire)*.
  to resign oneself shitagáu, akiraméru *(accept one's fate)*.
resignation jishoku.
resist (to) teikoo suru *(withstand)*; gekitai suru *(repel)*; hantai suru *(oppose)*.
resistance teikoo, hantai.
resolute shikkári shita.
resolution ketsudan *(firmness)*; késshin *(formed purpose)*.
resolve (to) késshin suru *(determine)*; kaiketsu suru *(settle)*.
resort hoyóochi *(for health)*.
  summer resort hishóchi.
resort (to) —ni uttáeru.
resources shígen.
respect sonkei *(esteem)*; kankei *(relation)*.
  in respect to —ni kanshite.
respect (to) kooryo suru *(heed)*; sonchoo suru *(treat with deference)*; uyamáu *(revere)*.
respectful téinei na, reigi tadashíi *(well mannered)*.
respective kákuji no, sorézore no.
respite yúuyo *(delay)*; shikéi no shikkoo yúuyo *(reprieve)*; ichijiteki chuushi *(temporary cessation)*.
responsibility sekinin.
responsible sekinin ga áru.
rest nokori *(remainder)*; yasumi *(repose)*; suimin *(sleep)*; teishi *(cessation of motion)*.
rest (to) yasúmu; suimin o tóru *(take repose)*.
restaurant ryooríya *(Japanese)*; résutoranto *(Occidental-style)*.
restless ochitsukanai.
restoration fukkoo *(revival)*; kaifuku *(recovery)*.
restore (to) móto ni modósu *(bring back)*; káesu *(give back)*; fukushoku saseru *(reinstate)*; fukkoo suru *(reestablish)*; naósu *(reconstruct)*.
restrain (to) yokusei suru.

restraint yokusei.
  without restraint enryo náku.
restrict seigén suru, kagíru.
restriction seigén *(limitation)*.
result kekka.
result (to) —ni owaru *(end up in)*.
resume (to) futatabi hajimeru.
retail kouri.
retail (to) kouri suru.
retain (to) hóji suru *(keep)*; kioku suru *(memorize)*.
retaliate (to) shikaeshi suru.
retaliation shikaeshi, fukushuu.
retire (to) intai suru *(from work)*; yasúmu *(rest)*.
retirement intai.
retract torikesu.
retreat taikyaku *(military)*.
retreat (to) taikyaku suru.
retrieve (to) torimodósu *(recover)*; sukuidásu *(rescue)*.
return (to) káeru *(come back)*; káesu *(give back)*.
reveal (to) shimésu *(disclose)*; shiraseru *(make known)*; bákuro suru *(divulge)*.
revelation happyoo *(disclosure)*; Mokushíroku *(Book of the Bible)*.
revenge fukushuu.
revenue shotoku *(income of an individual)*; sainyuu *(of the state)*.
reverence suuhai *(veneration)*; sonkei *(esteem)*.
reverend bokushi *(Protestant clergyman)*; shínpu *(Catholic clergyman)*.
reverse abekobe, hantai.
reverse (to) abekobe ni suru.
revert (to) móto ni modóru.
review hihyoo *(critical)*; fukushuu *(study)*.
review (to) saichóosa suru *(view again)*; kansatsu suru *(survey)*; kaisoo suru *(reconsider)*; hihyoo o káku *(books)*.
revise (to) teisei suru *(correct)*.
revision kaisei, kaitei.
revive (to) fukkatsu suru.
revoke (to) torikesu *(annul)*; haishi suru *(abolish)*.
revolt hanran.
revolt (to) hanran o okósu *(rebel)*.
revolve (to) mawaru, kaiten suru.
revolution kakumei.
reward hoobi, hooshuu.
reward (to) —ni mukuíru *(repay)*; hoobi o ataeru *(give a reward to)*.
  be rewarded mukuiraréru.
rhyme in.
rib abara bone.
ribbon ríbon.
rice íne *(plant)*; komé *(raw grain)*; góhan *(cooked)*.
rich kanemóchi no *(wealthy)*; yútaka na *(abundant)*.
richness yuufukui.
rid (get) torinozoku.
riddle nazo.
ride noru kotó.
ride (to) —ni noru.

ridiculous bakarashíi.
rifle shoojuu.
right *adj.* tadashíi *(correct)*; mottómo na
    (reasonable); máchigai no nái *(not
    wrong)*; migi no *(direction)*. —*n.* kénri
    (privilege); migi *(direction)*.
    have a right to kénri ga aru.
    to the right migigawa ni.
righteous koohei na, tadashíi.
righteousness séigi, koohei.
rightful tadashíi.
rigid kyúukutsu na *(not flexible)*; genkaku na
    (strict).
rigor genkaku.
rigorous genkaku na.
ring wá *(circle, link, wheel)*; yubiwa *(for
    finger)*.
ring (to) *v.t.* narasu; *v.i.* naru.
rinse (to) yusugu.
riot sóodoo, boodoo.
riot (to) soodoo o okósu.
ripe jukúshita.
ripen (to) jukúsu *(become ripe)*; jukusaséru
    (make ripe).
rise agari, shusse.
rise (to) agaru *(go up)*; okíru *(from bed, etc.)*;
    déru *(said of the sun)*.
risk booken *(hazard)*; kiken *(peril)*.
    run a risk booken o suru, chansu o toru.
risk (to) kiken ni sarasu *(expose to peril)*;
    kakéru *(venture)*; ichí ka bachí ka yatte
    míru *(take the chance of)*.
rite gíshiki.
ritual gíshiki *(rite)*; shikiten *(ceremony)*.
rival kyoosóosha *(competitor)*; teki *(enemy)*;
    aite *(in sport)*.
rivalry kyoosoo.
river kawá.
road michi, dóoro.
    main road oo dóori.
    middle of the road michi no mannaka.
roar unari *(of an animal)*; todoroki *(of waves,
    etc.)*.
roar (to) unáru *(of animals)*; todoróku *(of
    waves, etc.)*; donáru *(vociferate)*.
roast róosuto.
roast (to) róosuto ni suru.
    roast beef roosuto bíifu.
rob (to) nusúmu.
robber doroboo.
robbery nusumi.
robe koromo.
robust ganjoo na.
rock iwá.
rock (to) *v.t.* yusuru; *v.i.* yureru.
rocky iwa no óoi.
rod boo, saó.
roll maki gami *(of paper)*; roorú pan *(bread)*.
roll (to) korobasu *(roll over)*; maku *(wind)*;
    tsutsúmu *(enwrap)*; sáyuu ni yusuru
    (shake from side to side); korobu
    (tumble down).
romantic romanchíkku na.
romanticism roomanshúgi.
roof yáne.
room heyá *(of a house)*; basho *(space)*.

There's no room. Basho ga arimasén.
    make room for basho o tsukúru.
root né.
rope nawá, tsuná.
rose bara.
rot (to) kusáru *(decay)*.
rough zára zara shita *(opp. to smooth)*; deko
    boko no *(opp. to level)*; arai *(of the
    sea)*; ranboo na *(riotous)*; gekiretsu na
    (violent); arappói *(rude)*.
round *adj.* marui. —*adv.* maruku. —*n.* maru,
    én *(circle)*.
round off (to) shiagéru.
rouse mé o samásu.
rout (to) haisoo suru.
route tsúuro, rúuto.
routine kimatta júnjo *(fixed procedure)*.
rove (to) urotsuku.
row narabi *(line)*; sáwagi *(disturbance)*.
    be in a row narande iru.
    place in a row ichirétsu ni oku.
row (to) kógu *(a boat)*.
royal kooshitsu no.
rubber gómu.
rub (to) kosúru *(any object)*; sasuru *(the
    body)*.
rubbish garakuta, gomí.
rude busáhoo no *(unmannerly)*; sóya na
    (uncivil); shitsúrei na, buréi na
    (impolite); ranboo na *(rough)*.
ruin háikyo *(remains)*; koseki *(historical site)*;
    hakai *(destruction)*; metsuboo *(decay)*.
ruin (to) wáruku suru *(damage)*; damé ni suru
    (make useless).
rule monosáshi *(measure)*; jóogi *(ruler for
    lines)*; kisóku *(principle)*.
    as a rule ippan ni.
rule (to) súji o hiku *(mark with lines)*;
    osaméru *(govern)*.
ruler shiháisha *(sovereign)*; jóogi *(for drawing
    lines)*.
rumor uwasa.
run (to) hashíru, kakéru.
    run away nigéru.
rural inaka no.
rush ooisógi *(great haste)*; kyuugeki na zooka
    (sudden increase).
rush (to) isógu.
    rush into tobikómu.
    rush out tobidásu.
    rush toward hashítte iku.
Russia Soren, Roshiya.
Russian Róshiya no *(pertaining to Russia)*;
    Roshiyájin *(person)*; Roshiyago
    (language).
rust sabí.
rust (to) *v.t.* sabisaséru; *v.i.* sabíru.
rustic inaka no; inaka mono no *(person)*.
rusty sábita.
rye raimugi.

S

sacred shinsei na *(hallowed)*.
sacrifice gisei *(surrender of a desirable
    thing)*.

sacrifice (to) gisei ni suru *(renounce something).*
sacrilege bootoku.
sad kanashii.
sadden (to) kanashimaséru.
saddle kurá.
sadness kanashimi.
safe *adj.* buji na, anzen na *(free from danger)*; táshika na *(reliable).* —*n.* kínko *(strongbox).*
safe (be) buji na, anzen na.
safely buji ni.
safety buji, anzen.
sail ho.
sail (to) shuppan suru *(depart)*; fúne de iku *(go by boat)*; kóokai suru *(navigate).*
saint séija, seijin.
sake tame; mokuteki *(purpose).*
  for the sake of —no tamé ni.
salad sárada.
salary gekkyuu *(monthly)*; hookyuu *(annual).*
sale uridashi *(bargain)*; hanbai *(selling).*
salt shio, shokúen *(for the table).*
salt (to) shió de aji o tsukéru.
salute éshaku *(nod)*; áisatsu *(greeting)*; keirei *(military).*
salute (to) áisatsu suru.
salvation sukui.
same onaji.
  all the same mattaku onaji.
sample mihon, sánpuru.
sanctuary reihaidoo *(in a church)*; shinden *(Shinto shrine).*
sand suna.
sandal sándaru *(Occidental-style)*; zoori *(Japanese-style).*
sandwich sandoítchi.
sandy suna no *(pertaining to sand)*; sunachi no *(land)*; usuchairo no *(in color).*
sane shooki no.
sanitary eiseiteki na.
sap jueki *(of trees)*; génki *(vitality).*
sap (to) yowaraseru.
sarcasm hiniku, fuushi.
sarcastic hiniku na.
sardine iwashi.
sash óbi.
satiate (to) akitaranai.
satin shúsu.
satisfaction mánzoku.
satisfactory mánzoku na *(contented)*; juubún na *(sufficient)*; yói *(adequate, good).*
satisfy (to) mánzoku saseru *(gratify)*; zénbu hensai suru *(discharge)*; baishoo suru *(recompense).*
saturate (to) hitasu.
Saturday Doyóobi.
sauce sóosu *(Worcestershire)*; shooyu *(Japanese).*
saucer koohíi zara *(for coffee cup)*; chataku *(for Japanese teacups).*
sausage sooséeji.
savage *adj.* yaban na. —*n.* yabanjín.
save (to) sukuu *(rescue)*; takuwaéru *(hoard)*; setsuyaku suru *(economize)*; tasukéru *(from injury)*; tameru *(put by).*

be saved tasukáru.
  to save time jikan o setsuyaku suru.
savings chokin, ginkoo yókin *(bank).*
savior sukuínushi.
say (to) iu *(plain)*, ossháru *(pol.).*
  Say! Chótto!
scales hakari *(weighing instrument)*; uroko *(of fish).*
scan (to) kuwashíku shiraberu.
scandal shuubun, gigoku, oshoku.
scanty sukunái, tomoshíi.
scar kizu ato.
scarce sukunái, fusoku na; mare na.
scarcely karóojite *(with difficulty)*; yatto *(barely)*; hotóndo *(with a negative verb; almost, not).*
  scarcely know hotóndo zonjimasén.
scare (to) *v.t.* odokasu.
  get scared odoróku.
scarf sukáafu, erímaki.
scatter *v.t.* makichirásu *(strew)*; oichirásu *(disperse).*
scene késhiki *(landscape)*; bamen *(movie, etc.).*
scenery késhiki; kookei *(sight, spectacle).*
sceptic utagai bukái hito.
schedule jikanhyoo *(time-table)*; ichiranhyoo *(catalogue).*
scheme keikaku *(in a good sense)*; takurami *(in a bad sense).*
scholar séito *(student)*; gakusha *(learned man).*
school gakkoo.
  primary school shoogákkoo.
  junior high school chuugákkoo.
  senior high school kootoogákkoo.
  go to school tsuugaku suru.
  leave school taigaku suru.
science kágaku.
scientific kagakuteki.
scientist kagakúsha.
scissors hasami.
scold (to) shikaru.
scope hán'i.
scorn keibetsu.
scorn (to) keibetsu suru.
scornful keibetsuteki na.
scrape (to) kezuru, káku.
scratch tsume kizu *(made by nail or claw)*; kasuríkizu *(wound).*
scratch (to) káku *(an itchy place)*; hikkáku *(cause a wound).*
scream sakebigóe.
scream (to) sakébu *(cry out).*
screen shikiri *(partition)*; makú *(curtain).*
  folding screen byoobu.
  paper screen shooji *(in a Japanese house).*
scribble (to) nagurigaki suru.
screw néji.
  screw driver nejimáwashi.
scroll makimono.
scruple chúucho, tamerai.
scrupulous ryooshin teki na.
scrutinize (to) sensaku suru.
sculpture chookoku.
sea úmi.

seal hán, ín, fuuin *(impression)*; azárashi *(animal)*.

seal (to) hán o osu; fuujíru *(close up)*.

seam nuime.

search soosaku *(quest)*; sensaku *(inquiry)*; tsuikyuu *(close inquiry)*; ginmi *(scrutiny)*.

search (to) sagasu *(explore)*; jitto mitsuméru *(scrutinize carefully)*; saguru *(probe)*; shirabéru *(examine)*.

seashore kaigan.

seasickness funayoi.

season kisétsu.

rainy season báiu.

season (to) aji o tsukéru.

seat koshikáke *(anything to sit on)*; isu *(chair)*; bénchi *(bench)*; séki *(place where one sits)*.

seat (to) koshikakéru.

second *n.* dái ni *(in succession)*; byóo *(in time)*; futsuka *(of the month)*; —*adj.* ni banmé no.

second (to) sansei suru *(support)*.

secondary dái ní no.

secret *adj.* himitsu na. —*n.* himitsu.

secretary hishó *(in a business office)*; shoki *(recording officer; as a title)*.

sect shuuha, há.

section bun *(part)*; kúiki *(area, zone)*.

secure anshin na *(free from care)*; buji na *(safe)*; daijóobu na *(sure)*.

secure (to) shikkári to suru *(make fast)*; éru *(obtain)*; hoshoo suru *(guarantee)*.

security tánpo *(for debts)*; teitoo *(deposited as a pledge)*; anzen *(safety)*.

see míru *(look at)*; miséru *(show)*; —ni áu *(meet face to face)*; wakáru *(comprehend)*; tamésu *(try out)*.

I see. Wakarimáshita.

seed táne.

seek (to) sagasu *(look for)*; sagashimotoméru *(try to obtain)*.

seem (to) miéru.

He seems not to know it. Shiranai rashii.

seize (to) tsukamaeru.

seldom métta ni, amari, soo *(with negative)*.

I seldom go. Soo ikimasén.

select (to) erábu.

selection sentei.

self jibun, jíshin.

myself watashi jíshin de, watashi mo.

by itself shizen ni.

by oneself hitóri de.

selfish migátte na *(concerned unduly with oneself)*; rikoteki na *(egoistic)*.

selfishness wagamáma na.

sell (to) uru.

semicolon semikóron.

senate jooin *(U.S.)*; sangín *(Japan)*.

senator jooingín *(U.S.)*; sangiingín *(Japanese)*.

send (to) okuru *(to a distant place)*; todokéru *(nearby)*; dásu *(by mail)*.

senior toshiue *(in age)*; senpai *(in rank)*.

sensation kankaku *(perception by the senses)*; kimochi *(feeling)*; kandoo *(excited feeling)*; koofun *(excitement)*; hyooban *(of gossip, etc.)*.

sense chikaku *(perception)*; íshiki *(consciousness)*; kanji *(sensation)*; kánnen *(mental discernment)*; funbetsu *(practical judgment)*; ími *(meaning)*.

senseless mukánkaku na *(thoughtless)*; bakágeta *(foolish)*.

sensibility kankaku.

sensible kenmei na *(wise)*; kashikói *(sagacious)*; shiryo no aru *(thoughtful)*.

sensitive kanjiyasúi *(delicate)*; shinkei kabin na *(overly sensitive)*; súgu ki ni suru *(touchy)*.

sensitiveness shinkei kabin.

sentence búnshoo *(in writing)*; bún *(gram.)*; senkoku *(judgment)*.

sentiment kanji, joosoo.

sentimental senchiméntaru na; kanshooteki na.

separate wakáreta *(disconnected)*; betsu no *(distinct)*; kóko no *(individual)*; hitori hitóri no *(single)*; kakuri shita *(isolated)*.

separate (to) hanásu *(animate things)*; wakéru *(inanimate things)*; setsudan suru *(sever)*; hikihanásu *(disconnect)*; hanaréru *(disunite)*; bekkyo suru *(live apart, part company)*.

separately betsu betsu ni, tandoku ni.

separation bunri, dátsuri.

September Kúgatsu.

serene ochitsuita *(tranquil)*; háreta *(unclouded)*; uráraka na *(bright and clear)*; odáyaka na *(placid)*.

sergeant gúnsoo *(army)*; keíbu *(in a police force)*.

series shirízu, renzoku.

serious majime na *(solemn)*; juudai na *(important)*; kitoku na *(dying, critically ill)*.

seriously majime ni.

sermon sékkyoo.

servant meshitsúkai.

maidservant jochuu.

serve (to) hóokoo suru *(act as a servant)*; kyúuji o suru *(wait on table)*; yakú ni tátsu *(be of use)*; tsugoo ga yói *(be suitable)*; —no tamé ni hataraku *(give service to)*.

service sewá *(assistance rendered)*; hóokoo *(servant's occupation)*; sáabisu *(treatment in hotels, etc.)*; reihai *(religious)*.

session káiki *(period)*; kaitei *(sitting of law court)*; gakki *(school term)*.

set *adj.* kimatta, kitei no. —*n.* kumi *(things of the same kind)*.

complete set hitó kumi.

set (to) *v.t.* oku *(place)*; tatéru *(erect)*; hajimeru *(begin)*; totonoeru kimeru *(fix)*; *v.i.* háiru *(as the sun)*.

settle (to) kimeru *(fix)*; kaiketsu suru *(solve)*; ochitsuku *(settle down)*; imin suru *(colonize)*.

settlement kaiketsu *(of an affair)*; jídan

(*agreement*); seisan (*liquidation*);
rinpókan (*social service*).
seven nanátsu, shichí.
seventeen juunána, juushichí.
seventeenth dái juunána; juushichi nichi (*of
the month*).
seventh dái shichí; nanoka (*of the month*).
seventieth dái nanájuu no.
seventy nanájuu, shichijuu.
several iro iro no (*diverse*); súuko no
(*various*).
  several times suukai.
severe hidói (*harsh*); kibishíi (*strict*); genkaku
na (*stern*); gensei na (*rigidly accurate*);
mooretsu na (*intense*); hijoo ni (*very*).
severity gekiretsu (*harshness*); genkaku
(*strictness*).
sew (to) núu.
sewer gesui.
sex séi.
  female sex mesú (*animals*); josei (*humans*).
  male sex osú (*animals*); dansei (*humans*).
sexual seiteki no.
shabby misuborashíi.
shade hikage (*of sun*); káge (*of trees, etc.*).
shade (to) káge ni suru (*cast shade upon*);
hikarí ga ataranai yóo ni suru (*protect
from light*); kakúsu (*screen from view*).
shadow káge.
shady káge no óoi.
shake (to) v.t. yusuru (*rock, swing*); furu (*by
holding*); v.i. furueru (*tremble*).
shallow asai.
sham adj. nise no. —n. nise.
sham (to) —no furí o suru.
shame hají (*disgrace*); hazukáshisa
(*consciousness of shortcoming*);
fuménboku (*ignominy*); fuméiyo
(*dishonor*).
shame (to) hají saséru.
shameful hazukashíi.
shameless haji shírazu no.
shape katachi (*form*); keijoo (*configuration*);
súgata (*guise*).
shape (to) katachi o tsukéru.
shapeless katachi no nái.
share bún (*part*); wakemáe (*portion*); kabu
(*finance*).
share (to) wakéru (*divide*); buntan suru
(*partake*).
shareholder kabúnushi.
sharp adj. surudói (*as blades, needles*); yóku
kiréru (*as edge for cutting*); saki no
togátta (*pointed*); nukeme no nái
(*shrewd*).
sharpen (to) tógu (*an edge*); togarásu (*a
point*); kezuru (*a pencil*).
shatter (to) konagona ni kowásu (*break in
pieces*); kujíku (*hope*).
shave (to) hige o sóru (*in popular speech*);
kezuru (*plane*).
she ano onna no hito, kánojo.
shed koya.
shed (to) namida o nagásu (*tears*).
sheep hitsuji.
sheer kewashíi (*steep*); mattaku (*utter*).

sheet shikifu (*for a bed*); ichí mai no kamí (*of
paper*).
shelf tana.
shell kará (*of mollusks*); kóo (*of lobster, crab,
etc.*).
shelter hinanjo (*refuge*); hinangoya (*shed*);
hógo (*protection*).
shelter (to) v.t. hógo suru (*protect*); yadorásu
(*lodge*); kakumáu (*give refuge*); v.i.
hínan suru (*take refuge*).
shepherd hitsujíkai.
shield táte.
shield (to) hógo suru.
shift kootai (*act of taking a turn*).
shift (to) v.t. utsúsu, kaeru.
shine (to) hikáru (*glitter*); téru (*as sun or
moon*); kagayaku (*sun*).
ship fúne.
  steamship kisen.
ship (to) fúne de okuru (*send by ship*); okuru
(*send by any means*).
shipment funazumi (*ship's load*); ní (*cargo*);
tsumini (*the goods shipped*).
shirt shátsu, waishatsu (*occidental style*);
juban (*Japanese*).
shiver mibúrui.
shiver (to) furueru, mibúrui suru.
shock shókku, shoogeki (*impact*); shoototsu
(*collision*); shindoo (*by earthquake*);
kandoo (*of the mind*).
  have a shock bikkúri suru.
shock (to) odorokásu (*with fear*); odoróku (*be
shocked*).
shoe kutsú.
shoemaker kutsúya.
shoot útsu (*as a gun*).
shooting shageki.
shop mise; -ya (*in compounds*).
  butcher shop nikúya.
shopping kaimono.
shore kaigan.
short mijikái (*not long*); hikúi (*not tall*).
  short distance shookyóri.
shorten (to) v.t. mijikáku suru (*make shorter*);
tsuméru (*curtail*); v.i. mijikáku náru
(*become shorter*); tsumáru (*be
curtailed*).
shorthand sokki.
shot happoo (*of a gun*); chuusha (*injection*).
shoulder káta.
shout oogóe (*loud voice*).
shout (to) oogóe de yobu (*call out*); oogóe o
dásu (*utter a loud cry*); sakébu, donáru
(*utter with a shout*).
  to shout at donari tsukéru.
shove (to) oshiwakéru.
shovel sháberu.
show shibai, misemóno (*public show*).
show (to) miséru (*let see*); oshieru (*point out*).
shower niwaka áme (*of rain*); yuudachi (*in
summer*).
shrill kandakái.
shrimp ebi.
shrine jínja (*Shinto*).
shrink (to) chijimu.
shrub kanboku.

shun (to) sakéru.
shut *adj.* shimátta, tójita.
shut (to) *v.t.* shiméru *(a door, etc.)*; tojíru *(things with lids)*; *v.i.* shimáru *(be shut)*.
shy hazukashíi *(bashful)*; uchiki na *(timid)*; kimari ga warúi *(embarrassed)*.
sick (be) kagen ga warúi *(unwell)*.
  He got sick. Byooki ni narimáshita.
sickness byooki.
side kawa (gawa).
sidewalk hodoo, jindoo.
siege kakomi.
sigh tameíki.
sigh (to) tameíki o tsuku.
sight shíryoku *(power of seeing)*; nagame *(view, scene)*; késhiki *(scenery)*.
  out of sight miénai.
sign sáin *(signature)*; shirushi *(indication)*; chookoo *(symptom)*; zenchoo *(omen)*; fugoo *(mark)*; kanban *(signboard)*; miburi *(gesture)*.
sign (to) shomei suru *(one's name)*.
signal shingoo, keihoo.
signal (to) shingoo o okuru.
signature shomei.
significance ími *(meaning)*; juuyoo *(importance)*.
significant juuyoo na.
signify (to) —o ími suru.
silence seishuku, chinmoku.
silence (to) kuchi o tsugúmu *(to keep silent)*.
silent shízuka na.
silk kínu.
  silk cloth kénpu.
silken kínu no.
silkworm káiko.
silly baka na.
silver gín.
silvery gin'iro no.
similar nite iru *(resembling)*; onaji yóo na *(same kind)*; ruiji shita *(alike)*.
similarity ruiji.
simple kantan na *(not complicated)*; tanjun na *(not combined)*; wake no nái, yasashíi *(easy)*.
simplicity tanjun, kantan.
simply tán ni.
simulate (to) —no mane o suru.
simultaneous dooji no.
sin tsúmi.
sin (to) tsúmi o okasu.
since —kara *(because)*; —te kara *(after)*.
sincere seijitsu na.
sincerely hontoo ni *(truly)*; seijitsu ni.
sincerity seijitsu.
sinew súji.
sing utau; naku *(birds)*.
  sing a song utá o utau.
singer káshu; utaite.
single táda hitótsu no *(one only)*; kóko no *(individual)*.
  bachelor hitorimono.
singular mezurashíi *(uncommon, rare)*; hén na *(strange)*; fushigi na *(wondrous)*.
sinister nínsoo no warúi.

sink nagashi *(in a kitchen)*.
sink (to) *v.i.* shizumu *(be submerged)*; *v.t.* shizumeru *(submerge, go down)*.
sinner tsumibito.
sip (to) susuru.
sir senséi *(teacher, lawyer, title of respect)*.
  Thank you, sir. Arígatoo gozaimásu.
sister imooto *(younger)*; ane *(elder)*.
sister-in-law giri no ane *(older)*; giri no imooto *(younger)*.
sit (to) koshikakéru *(on a chair)*; suwaru *(on the floor, Japanese style)*.
site basho *(place)*; shikichi *(for a building)*.
situation tsutomé guchi *(employment)*; jijoo *(circumstance)*.
six muttsú, rokú.
sixteen juurokú.
sixteenth dái juurokú, juurokunichi *(of the month)*.
sixth dái rokú; muika *(the sixth of the month)*.
sixtieth dái rokujúu.
sixty rokujúu.
size ookisa, sáizu *(dimension)*; sunpoo *(measure)*.
skate (to) sukéeto o suru.
skates sukéeto.
skeleton gáikotsu.
sketch sukétchi *(rough drawing)*; shitagaki *(rough draft)*; gaiyoo *(outline)*; shasei *(from nature)*.
ski (skiing) sukíi.
  a pair of skis sukíi hitókumi.
skill gíjutsu.
skillful joozú na.
skin hifu *(human, animal)*; kawá *(of animals or fruit)*.
skirt sukáato *(occidental dress)*; suso, hakama *(Japanese kimono)*.
skull zugáikotsu.
sky sóra.
  blue sky aozóra.
slander (to) wáruku iu; chuushoo suru.
slap hirate uchi.
  to slap (someone's) face kao o hirate de útsu.
slate *n.* sekiban.
slaughter tosatsu *(butchering)*; gyakusatsu *(massacre)*.
slave dorei.
slavery dorei séido.
sled sori.
sleep nemuri.
sleep (to) nemuru *(slumber)*; yasúmu *(rest, doze)*.
sleeve sode.
slender hossóri shita *(slim, opp. to stout)*; kabosói *(slight)*; yowái *(weak, feeble)*; hinjaku na *(meager)*.
slice kire.
slice (to) usuku kíru.
slide (to) subéru.
slight kyasha na *(slender)*; karui *(not severe)*; sukóshi no *(small, not great)*.
slight (to) keibetsu suru.
slip suríppu *(article of woman's clothing)*.
slip (to) subette korobu *(trip)*; tsumazúku

(stumble); fumihazúsu *(miss one's footing)*.
slipper suríppa.
slippery subekkói, tsúru tsuru shita.
slope keisha *(slant)*; koobai *(incline)*; saká *(hill)*; shamen *(inclined plane)*; keisháchi *(sloping ground)*.
slot kuchi.
slovenly bushóo ni.
slow osoi.
slow (to be) okureru *(get behind time)*.
slowly yukkúri.
slowness osoi kotó.
slumber karui nemuri, madoromi.
slumber (to) *v.i.* útouto suru *(sleep lightly)*; nemuru *(sleep)*; utatane suru *(doze)*; inémuri suru *(drowse)*.
sly zurúi.
small chiisái *(not big)*; hosói *(slender)*.
smart subashikói *(clever)*; haikara na, sumáato na *(elegant in dress)*.
smash (to) kowásu.
    to be smashed kowaréru.
smear (to) nasuritsukéru.
smell n`iói *(odor)*; kaori *(scent)*; akushuu *(stink)*.
smell (to) kagu *(get the odor of, exercise the sense of smell)*; nói ga suru *(emit an odor)*; wanúi nioi ga áru *(be rank)*; hijoo ni kusái *(stink)*.
smile bishoo, hohoemi.
smile (to) n`íko niko suru, hohoému.
smoke kemuri.
smoke (to) kemuri o háku *(emit smoke)*; tabako o nómu *(use tobacco)*.
smooth súbe sube shita *(not rough)*; taira na *(level, even)*; odáyaka na *(not ruffled)*; dekoboko no nái *(not jagged)*.
smooth (to) nobasu, nadaraka ni suru.
smother (to) chissoku saseru *(choke)*; akubi o kamikorosu *(a yawn)*; kanjoo o osaéru *(an emotion)*; kakúsu *(conceal)*; momikésu *(stifle)*.
smuggle (to) mitsuyúnyuu suru.
snake hébi.
snapshot sunappu sháshin.
snatch (to) hittakúru *(grab)*; nusumu *(steal)*.
sneer (to) reishoo suru.
sneeze (to) kushámi o suru.
snore (to) ibiki o káku.
snow yukí.
    snowfall yukifuri.
snow (to) yukí ga fúru.
snowstorm fúbuki.
so (thus) désu kara.
    and so on —nádo, —too.
    It is so. Sóo desu.
    I think so. Soo omoimásu.
soak (to) shimitóoru *(permeate)*; nurasu *(drench)*.
soap sekken, shabon.
sob susuri naki.
sob (to) susuri náku.
sober yótte inai *(not intoxicated)*; majime na *(serious)*.

sociable shakooteki na *(fond of company)*; koosai jóozu na *(companionable)*.
social shákai no, shakaiteki na.
society shákai *(community)*; jooryuu shákai *(upper class)*; tsukiai *(companionship)*; dooseki *(company)*; kái *(association)*.
sock(s) kutsushita *(occidental)*; tábi *(Japanese)*.
socket sokétto *(electric)*.
soft yawarakái *(not hard)*; yasashii *(not harsh)*.
soften (to) yawarakáku suru *(as an object)*; yawaragéru *(in feeling)*.
soil tsuchí *(earth)*; tochi *(ground)*.
soil (to) yogosu.
soldier heitai.
sole *adj.* tatta hitóri no *(one and only: pertaining to persons)*; tatta hitótsu no *(pertaining to inanimate things)*; tandoku no *(exclusive to one)*; dokutoku no *(unique)*. —*n.* soko *(of a shoe)*; ashi nó ura *(of the foot)*.
solemn genshuku na.
solemnity genshuku, soogon.
solicit segámu *(ask earnestly of)*; kongan suru *(importune)*; konsei suru *(entreat)*.
solid joobu na *(strong)*; katai *(hard)*.
solitary hitóri de kurasu *(living alone)*; tsure nashi no *(without companions)*; sabishíi *(lonely)*; hitodoori no mare na *(unfrequented)*.
solitude kodoku *(being alone)*; sabishísa *(loneliness)*.
soluble tokéru.
solution káishaku *(a solving)*; setsumei *(explanation)*; kaiketsu *(settlement)*.
solve (to) kaiketsu suru *(clear up)*; setsumei suru *(explain)*; kaitoo suru *(find an answer)*; tóku *(a problem)*.
some ikuraka no *(an indefinite quantity)*; sukóshi *(a little, a few)*; ní-san *(two or three)*; san-shi *(three or four; often omitted in Japanese)*.
    Give me some water, please. Mizu o kudasái.
somebody dónata ka *(polite)*; dáre ka *(plain)*.
somehow dóo ni ka *(in some way or other)*; nán to ka shite *(in one way or another)*; dóomo *(for some reason or other)*.
someone dáre ka.
something náni ka.
sometime ítsuka *(at an indefinite time)*; sono uchi ni *(at a time hereafter)*; shibáraku *(for a certain period)*.
sometimes tokí ni wa *(at times)*; toki doki *(occasionally)*; tama ni *(now and then)*.
somewhat íkuraka *(in some measure)*; sukóshi *(a little)*; ikubun *(to some extent)*.
somewhere dóko ka ni, dóko ka de *(in or at someplace)*; dóko ka e *(to someplace)*; áru tokoro *(a certain place)*.
son musuko.
song utá.
    popular song ryuukóoka.
soon súgu.
soot súsu.

soothe (to) nadaméru *(calm down)*; nagusaméru *(comfort)*; shizumeru *(assuage)*.

sore *adj.* tadareta *(inflamed)*; itámu *(painful to the touch)*. —*n.* odéki *(boil)*; tadare *(a festering)*.

sorrow kanashími, nageki.

sorry (be) ki no doku ni omou.
  I am sorry Sumimasen. Gomen nasái.
  Excuse me. Oki no doku desu *(I am sorry for you)*.

sort shúrui *(kind, class)*; hinshitsu *(character, nature)*.

sort out (to) yoriwakéru.

soul támashii.

sound *adj.* kenkoo na, kenzen na *(of healthy mind)*; itande inai *(undamaged)*; táshika na *(reliable)*; ronriteki na *(logical)*. —*n.* otó *(that which is heard)*; hibikí *(reverberation)*.

sound (to) fukú *(a wind instrument)*; narasu *(another musical instrument)*; áizu suru *(give a signal)*; otó o saseru *(make a sound)*.

soup súupu *(occidental style)*; suimono *(Japanese)*.

sour suppái.

source moto *(origin)*; minamoto *(of a river)*.

south minami.

southeast toonan.
  Southeast Asia Toonan Ájia.

southern minami no.

southwest seinan.

sovereign kúnshu.

sow (to) máku *(scatter)*; makichírasu *(disseminate)*; hiroméru *(propagate)*.

space aita basho *(room)*; supéesu; tokoró *(place)*; kankaku *(interval)*; kyóri *(distance)*.

space (to) kankaku o oku.

spacious hirobíro to shita *(vast, broad)*; óokii *(large)*.

spade sháberu *(occidental)*; suki *(Japanese)*.

spare (to) tebanásu.

spare *adj.* yóbi no *(held in reserve)*; yobun no *(superfluous)*; fuyoo no *(not required)*; hinjaku na *(scanty)*; kiritsúmeta *(stinted)*. —*n.* yóbi *(reserve)*.

spare (to) oshímu *(use grudgingly)*; ken'yaku suru *(economize)*; yurúsu *(forebear)*; sashi hikaeru *(refrain from)*.

spark hí no ko, híbana *(of fire)*; kirameki *(gleam)*; kakki *(animating principle)*.

sparkle (to) kagayáku.

sparrow suzume.

speak (to) hanásu *(narrate)*; iu *(mention)*.

speaker hanáshite, enzétsusha *(one who delivers a speech)*; kooénsha, kooshi *(lecturer)*; supíikaa *(radio loudspeaker)*.

special tokubetsu no *(of a particular kind)*; sen'yoo no *(private)*; tokutei no *(definite)*; namihazure no *(extraordinary)*; tokushu no *(particular)*.

specialty tokusánhin *(special product)*; meisan *(famous product)*; tokushoku *(special feature)*.

specific tokushu na, tokutei na.

specify (to) shitei suru.

spectacle kookei *(sight)*; sookan *(noteworthy scene)*; misemóno *(public show)*.

spectator kenbutsunin *(onlooker)*; bookánsha *(bystander)*.

speculate (to) kangáeru *(consider)*; shisaku suru *(meditate)*; suisoku o suru *(conjecture)*; tooshi suru *(invest)*.

speech hanashí *(talk)*; hanásu nóoryoku *(faculty of speaking)*; kotoba *(language)*; enzetsu *(public address)*.

speed sokúryoku *(velocity)*; háyasa *(swiftness)*.

speedy sokúryoku no hayái.

spell majinai *(charm)*.

spell (to) tsuzuru.

spelling tsuzuri.

spend (to) tsukau *(pay out)*; kurasu *(time)*.

sphere tamá *(globe)*; kyuumen *(spherical surface)*; tenatai *(heavenly body)*.

spice yakumi *(condiment)*; kaori *(fragrance)*; kóoryoo *(aromatic vegetable flavoring)*.

spider kúmo.

spill (to) kobósu.
  to get spilled koboréru.

spin (to) tsumúgu *(yarn)*; kakéru *(a web)*; mawasu *(a top)*; máyu o tsukúru *(silk: by a silkworm)*.

spirit támashii *(as distinct from matter)*; séishin *(disposition of mind)*; kakki *(vigor)*; nétsui *(ardor)*.

spiritual seishinteki na *(concerned with things of the mind or soul)*; kámi no *(divine)*; shinsei na *(sacred)*; shuukyoojoo no *(religious)*.

spit (to) tsúba o háku.

spite ijiwáru *(malice)*; urami *(grudge)*.
  in spite of —ní mo kakawárazu.

spite (to) ijiwaru o suru.

spiteful ijiwarúi.

splash (to) hanekakéru, haneagéru.

splendid rippa na *(imposing)*; subarashíi *(magnificent)*; mígoto na *(admirable)*.

splendor kagayaki, mígoto.

split (to) *v.t.* saku *(crack)*; waru *(divide)*; sógu *(cleave)*; *v.i.* wareru.

spoil (to) itaméru *(damage)*; damé ni suru *(render useless by injury)*; wáruku suru *(make bad)*.

sponge *n.* kaimen, suponji.

spontaneous shizen no *(natural)*; jihatsuteki no *(voluntary)*; jidooteki na *(self-acting)*.

spoon sají.

spoonful saji ippai no.

sport undoo, supóotsu *(recreation)*; tanoshími *(pastime)*; joodán *(jest)*.

spot tokoro *(place)*; ten *(speck)*; shimi *(stain)*.

spread (to) *v.t.* hirogeru *(in length and breadth)*; nuru *(butter)*; hiromáru *(news)*; *v.i.* hirogaru *(to be disseminated)*.

spring háru *(season)*; báne *(of machinery)*; onsen *(of hot water)*; izumi *(of cold water)*.

spring (to) tobu *(leap)*; shoojíru *(proceed, originate)*.

sprinkle (to) maku *(with water)* furikakéru (with powder, etc.).

sprout (to) mé o fuku *(put forth shoots)*; háete kuru *(spring up)*.

spry subashikói.

spur (to) hakusha o kakéru *(a horse)*.

spurn (to) hanetsukéru.

spy supái, kanchoo.

spy (to) sagúru.

squadron kantai.

squander (to) mudazúkai suru.

square seihóokei *(geom.)*; hiroba *(in a town)*.

squeeze (to) hasámu *(between two things)*; nigiri shiméru *(in one's hand)*; shibóru *(press out liquids)*.

squirrel rísu.

stable *n.* umagoya. —*adj.* shikkári shita *(firm)*; antei shita *(steady)*; kyóoko na *(steadfast)*.

stack inamura.

stack (to) tsumi kasanéru.

stadium kyoogijoo, sutajíamu.

staff saó *(pole)*; boo *(rod)*; shokúin *(of a business)*.

staff (to) shokuin o soróeru.

stage bútai, sutéeji *(theatrical)*; endan *(elevated platform)*.

stain shimi, yogore.

stain (to) *v.t.* yogosu; *v.i.* yogoreru *(get stained)*.

stair(s) dán, kaidan.

stammer (to) domóru.

stamp kitte *(for postage stamps)*; hán *(rubber stamp, etc.)*; ingyoo *(personal seal)*; keshiin *(postmark)*.

stamp (to) sutanpu o osu.

stand dái *(to set things on)*; hankoo *(resistance)*; bóogyo *(defense)*; uriba *(booth)*.

stand (to) tátsu *(get up)*; tachitsuzukeru *(remain standing)*; tátte iru *(be in a standing position)*; oite áru *(be placed: speaking of an inanimate thing)*; áru *(be located)*; tachiagaru *(stand up)*; tatéru *(erect)*.

star hoshi *(celestial)*; sutáa, hanágata *(theatrical)*.

stare (to) —o mitsuméru.

start hajime *(beginning)*; shuppátsuten *(starting point)*; odoroki *(shock)*.

start (to) *v.t.* hajimeru *(begin)*; *v.i.* hajimaru *(begin)*; shuppatsu suru *(depart)*; déru *(of trains, etc.)*.

starve (to) uéru.

state kókka *(political body)*; jootai *(condition)*.

state (to) iu *(say)*; hanásu *(tell)*; nobéru *(express in speech)*; chinjutsu suru *(express in writing)*.

stately doodóo to shita.

statement seimei.

station éki, sutéeshon *(railway)*.

statistic tookei.

statue zóo.
   bronze statue doozoo.

statute kisóku *(rule, regulation)*.

stay taizai.

stay (to) *v.t.* tomaru *(stop)*; *v.i.* okuraseru *(delay)*.

steady shikkári shita.

steak bifuteki.

steal nusúmu.

steam jóoki, suchíimu.

steam (to) musu.

steamer kisen *(steamship)*.

steel hagane.

steep *adj.* kyuu na, kewashíi *(precipitous)*; kyuukóobai no *(high-pitched)*.

steer (to) káji o tóru.

stem kukí.

stenographer sokkísha.

stenography sokki.

step dán *(of a staircase)*; ashi oto *(sound of a footstep)*; ashi áto *(footprint)*; dankai *(successive stage)*.

step (to) arúku *(walk)*; fumu *(tread on)*.

sterile ko o umanai *(barren)*; fumoo no *(not fertile)*; minori no nái *(unproductive)*.

stern *adj.* genkaku na *(severe)*; kakoku na *(harsh)*.

stew shichuu.

stew (to) torobi de niru.

stick boo.

stick (to) sásu *(pierce)*; tsuku *(adhere)*.

stiff kowabátta *(rigid)*; katai *(hard)*; súra sura to ugokánai *(not moving freely)*.

stiffen (to) kowabáru.

still *adj.* shízuka na *(quiet)*. —*adv.* máda *(more)*; yahári *(after all)*; sore démo *(nevertheless)*; ima máde *(yet)*.
   Keep still! Jittó shite! Ugokánaide!

stimulate (to) shigeki suru.

stimulus shigeki.

sting hári *(of an animal)*; tógé *(of a plant)*.

sting (to) sásu, píri piri suru.

stinginess kéchi.

stingy kéchi na.

stir (to) ugokásu *(move, shake)*; kakimawasu *(liquids)*.

stitch (to) núu *(sew)*; kagaru *(darn)*.

stock zaikohin *(goods)*; shihon *(capital)*; kabuken *(shares)*.

stock (to) takuwáeru.

stocking kutsushita.

stomach hará.

stone ishí.

stool koshikake.

stop teiryuujo *(stopping place for buses, etc.)*; shuushi *(end)*.

stop (to) yameru *(discontinue)*; tomeru *(cause to cease)*; teishi suru *(suspend)*; jama suru *(interrupt)*; yokusei suru *(restrain)*; sóshi suru *(prevent)*; owaraséru *(put an end to)*; fusagu *(block)*; tomaru *(come to rest)*.

store misé.
   department store depáato.

stork tsúru.

storm árashi *(speech)*; uwasa *(gossip)*;

story hanashi *(speech)*; uwasa *(gossip)*; monogátari *(tale)*; itsuwa *(anecdote)*; densetsu *(legend)*.

stove sutóobu.

straight massúgu na *(opp. to crooked)*; itchókusen no *(in a straight line)*.

straighten (to) massúgu ni suru.

strain kinchoo *(tension)*; hijoo na dóryoku *(excessive effort)*; karoo *(overexertion)*.

strain (to) muri o suru.

strange mezurashíi *(rare)*; fushigi na *(wondrous)*; kímyoo na *(odd)*.

stranger shiranai hito *(unknown person)*; yosó no hito *(outsider)*.

strap himo.

straw wára.

strawberry ichigo.

stream nagare *(current)*; ogawa *(small river)*.

stream (to) nagaréru.

street machí *(with houses, etc.)*; michi *(road, way)*.

strength tsúyosa *(vigor)*; táiryoku *(bodily)*.

strengthen (to) tsúyoku suru *(make stronger)*; zookyoo suru *(reinforce)*; tsúyoku náru *(become stronger)*.

strenuous hone no oréru.

stress kyoochoo *(emphasis)*; appaku *(pressure)*; kinpaku *(strain)*.

stress (to) kyoochoo suru.

stretch (to) nobásu *(extend in length)*; hirogeru *(extend in breadth)*; dásu *(reach out)*; nobíru *(lengthen)*.

strict kibishíi.

stride káppo.

stride (to) káppo suru.

strife arasoi *(conflict)*.

strike sutoráiki, hígyoo.

strike (to) bútsu *(beat)*; tatáku *(rap, knock)*; shoototsu suru *(collide)*; sutoráiki o suru, hígyoo suru *(quit work)*; kokoró o útsu *(impress)*.

string himo.

strip (to) hadaka ni suru *(lay bare)*; toriharáu *(divest)*; kimono o núgu *(undress)*.

stripe shimá.

strive (to) honeóru *(try hard)*; dóryoku suru *(endeavor)*; funtoo suru *(struggle vigorously)*.

stroke dageki, súji *(line)*; káku *(of a Japanese character)*.

stroll sanpo.

stroll (to) sanpo suru.

strong tsuyói *(having strength)*; joobu na *(not easily broken)*; kenkoo na *(healthy)*; daijóobu na *(reliable)*.

structure koosei *(construction)*; kumitate *(framework)*; kenchiku *(building)*; soshiki *(organization)*.

struggle kumiuchi *(body to body)*; arasoi *(strife)*; honeori *(violent effort)*.

struggle (to) dóryoku suru *(make great efforts)*; mogáku *(writhe)*; tatakau *(fight)*; arasóu *(contend)*.

stubborn gánko na *(hardheaded)*; goojoo na *(obstinate)*; shibutói *(perverse)*; te ni oenai *(intractable)*; fukutsu no *(unyielding)*.

student séito, gakusei.

studious yóku benkyoo suru *(assiduous in study)*; gakumonzúki no *(given to study)*; nesshín na *(zealous)*.

study benkyoo *(application of the mind)*; kenkyuu *(research, investigation, etc.)*.

study (to) benkyoo suru; naráu *(learn)*.

stuff shina *(material, goods)*; mono *(substance, matter)*; garakuta *(rubbish)*; tawagoto *(nonsense)*.

stuff (to) tsumekomu *(fill with something)*; tsumemóno o suru *(cooking)*.

stumble (to) tsumazúku *(trip up)*; yoroméku *(miss one's footing)*; yóro yoro arúku *(walk unsteadily)*.

stump kirikabu.

stun (to) mé o mawasaseru.

stunt kyokugei *(tricks)*.

stupendous tohoo mo nái.

stupid óroka na.

stupidity baka sa, oroka sa.

stupor mahi.

sturdy shikkári shita.

stutter (to) domóru.

style ryuukoo, sutáiru *(mode of fashion)*; hanashiburi *(mode of speaking)*.

subdue seifuku suru *(conquer)*; uchikátsu *(overcome)*; iatsu suru *(render submissive)*; yokusei suru *(repress)*.

subject shinmin *(of a country)*; mondai *(theme of discussion)*; gakka *(of study)*.

subject (to) shitagáeru *(subdue)*.

subjective shukanteki.

subjugate (to) seifuku suru *(subdue)*.

sublime suukoo na.

submission fukujuu *(subjection)*; koofuku *(surrender)*.

submissive juujun na.

submit (to) teishutsu suru *(turn in)*; shitagawaséru *(yield)*.

subordinate búka, háika.

subordinate (to) shita ni oku.

subscribe (to) yoyaku suru *(to newspapers, etc.)*; sansei suru *(give assent)*.

subscription yoyaku.

subside (to) shizumaru *(become tranquil)*; hekomu *(dent)*.

subsidy hojókin *(grant of money)*.

subsist (to) kurashite iku.

substance honshitsu, hóntai.

substantial jitsuzai suru *(actual)*; hontoo no *(real)*.

substantiate (to) shoomei suru.

substitute kawari *(a person)*; daiyóohin *(a thing representing another)*.

substitute (to) dairi suru *(person)*; daiyoo suru *(thing)*.

substitution daiyoo.

subtle bimyoo na.

subtract (to) hiku *(take out or away)*.

subtraction hikízan.

suburb kóogai.
succeed (to) áto o tsugu *(be a successor to)*; seikoo suru *(effect one's purpose)*.
success seikoo *(favorable termination)*; kooun *(good fortune)*.
successful seikoo suru.
succession renzoku *(sequence)*; keishoo *(to a position, throne, etc.)*.
successor soozókusha.
such konna *(like this, of this sort)*; sonna *(like that, of that sort)*.
sudden kyuu na.
suddenly kyuu ni *(abruptly)*; fui ni *(unexpectedly)*.
sue (to) uttáeru, soshoo o okósu *(take legal action)*; uttáeru *(bring suit)*.
suffer (to) kurushímu *(be in pain)*; gáman suru *(endure patiently)*; songai o koomúru *(a loss)*.
suffering kurushimi *(pain)*; songai *(loss)*.
sufficient takusan *(plenty)*; juubún na *(enough)*.
sugar satóo, osatoo.
suggest (to) omoi dasaséru *(hint)*; ii dásu *(propose)*.
suggestion kangáe; anji, hínto *(hint)*; teigi *(proposal)*.
suicide jisatsu.
    to commit suicide jisatsu suru.
suit yoofuku, súutsu *(of clothes)*; kokuso *(legal proceedings)*.
suit (to) niáu *(fit)*; tsugoo ga íi *(be convenient)*.
suitable choodo íi *(fitting, proper)*; niáu *(becoming)*.
sulk (to) mutto suru *(be offended)*; sunéru *(pout)*.
sullen fukígen na *(in a bad mood)*; inki na *(gloomy)*.
sum gáku *(quantity)*; gookei *(total amount)*; kingaku *(amount of money)*.
summary tekiyoo sho *(brief account)*; gaiyoo *(synopsis)*.
summer natsú.
summit choojóo *(top)*.
summon (to) shookan suru.
summons shookanjoo.
sumptuous zeitaku na.
sum up (to) gaikatsu suru.
sun hi, táiyoo.
    rising sun ásahi.
    setting sun yuuhi.
sunbeam níkkoo.
sunburn hiyake.
Sunday Nichiyóobi.
sundry iroiro no.
    sundry expenses zappi.
    sundry goods zakka.
sunny urárakana.
sunrise hi no de.
sunset hi no iri.
sunshine hinata.
superb subarashíi.
superficial uwabe daké no *(outward)*; senpaku na *(shallow; said of persons)*.
superfluous yokei na.

superintendent kantoku *(supervisor)*; kanrísha *(manager)*; koochoo *(of school)*.
superior sugúreta *(better)*; jootoo no *(of great excellence)*; yuusei na *(larger)*; kookyuu no *(of higher rank)*.
    to be superior sugurete iru.
superiority yuushuu.
superstition meishin.
supervise (to) kantoku suru.
supper yuuhan.
supplement bessatsu *(of a book)*; furoku *(of a magazine)*.
supplement (to) oginau.
supplementary furoku no.
supply kyookyuu *(a supplying)*; kyookyuuhin *(thing supplied)*.
supply (to) kyookyuu suru.
support sasaemono *(prop)*; shíji *(moral support)*; fuyoo *(maintenance)*.
support (to) shíji suru *(hold up)*; motaseru *(maintain)*; genkizukéru *(encourage)*; tasukéru *(assist)*.
suppose (to) soozoo suru *(imagine)*; omóu *(think)*; katei suru *(assume tentatively)*; suitei suru *(presume)*.
suppress shizumeru *(subdue)*; kinshi suru *(stop)*; osaéru *(restrain)*; kamikorosu *(smother)*.
supreme saikoo no.
sure táshika na *(certain)*; ate ni náru *(reliable)*; hontoo no *(true)*; joobu na *(stable)*.
surely táshika ni.
surety tánpo *(pledge)*; hoshoonin *(sponsor)*.
surf yose nami *(on the shore)*; uchinami *(on rocks)*.
surface hyoomén.
surgeon geká i.
surgery geka *(treatment)*; shújutsu *(operation)*.
surmount (to) noboru *(climb)*; uchikátsu *(overcome)*.
surname myóoji.
surpass (to) suguréru *(be better than)*; shinógu *(outdo)*; sugíru *(exceed)*; amáru *(be beyond)*.
surplus yojoo *(the remainder)*; amari *(the rest)*.
surprise bikkúri *(amazement)*; omoigakenai kotó *(something unexpected)*.
surprise (to) bikkúri saseru *(strike with wonder)*; odorokásu *(cause surprise)*; fui uchi suru *(take unawares)*.
surrender hikiwatashi *(of a thing)*; koosan *(of person)*; koofuku *(of an army)*.
surrender (to) tewatásu *(hand over)*; hooki suru *(give up something)*; koofuku suru *(submit)*.
surround (to) torimáku.
surroundings kankyoo.
survey sokuryoo *(land measurement)*; kenchi *(land surveying)*; tsuuran *(comprehensive view)*.
survey (to) miwatásu *(look over)*; ippanteki ni míru *(take a general view)*; kenbun suru *(inspect)*; choosa suru *(examine)*.

survive (to) iki nokóru *(pertaining to people)*; nokóru *(pertaining to other cases)*.
susceptibility kanjusei.
susceptible takan na, kanjooteki na.
suspect utagawashíi hito *(suspected person)*.
suspect (to) kanzúku *(have an inkling)*; —de wa nai ka to omóu *(half-believe)*; soozoo suru *(surmise)*; utagáu *(doubt)*.
suspense fuan *(feeling of)*; mitei.
suspension chuuburarin.
suspicion kéngi *(distrust)*; utagai *(doubt)*.
suspicious utagai bukái *(distrustful)*; ayashíi *(doubtful)*.
sustain (to) saseru.
swallow tsubame *(bird)*.
swallow (to) nomikomu.
swamp numa.
swan hakuchoo, suwan.
sway (to) yureru
swear (to) háku *(with a broom)*; akutai o tsuku *(curse)*.
sweat áse.
sweat (to) áse ga déru.
sweep (to) háku *(with a broom)*; sooji suru *(clean up)*.
sweet amai *(of taste)*; kawairashíi *(of face)*; yasashii *(of disposition)*.
sweetness aíráshisa *(of person)*; amasa *(of food)*.
swell (to) fukureru *(bulge out)*; hareru *(become swollen)*; ookíku naru *(expand)*.
swift hayái.
swim (to) oyógu.
swindler sagíshi.
swing (to) yureru, búra bura ugóku *(as a pendulum)*; fureru *(use as a swing)*.
switch *n.* suítchi *(elec.)*.
   to switch on suítchi o ireru.
   to switch off suítchi o kíru.
sword katana.
syllable onsetsu.
symbol shoochoo *(emblem)*; fugoo *(mark, sign)*.
symbolic shoochooteki.
symbolize (to) shoochoo suru *(be a symbol of)*; fugoo de arawásu *(represent by symbols)*.
symmetrical tsuriai no tóreta.
symmetry tsuriai, kinsei.
sympathetic omoiyari no áru *(compassionate)*; ki no átta *(congenial)*.
sympathize (to) ki no dóku ni omóu *(feel sympathy)*; sansei suru *(agree with)*; nagusameru *(condole)*.
sympathy doojoo.
symptom chookoo.
syrup shíróppu.
system shoshiki *(organization)*; hoohoo *(method)*; chitsújo *(order)*.

T

table teeburu *(European)*; chabudai, taku *(Japanese low table)*.
tablecloth teeburu kuroosu, teeburúkake.

tablespoon teeburu supúun.
tacit anmoku no
tacitly soreto náku, anmoku ni.
taciturn múkuchi na.
tack (to) byóo de tomeru.
tact josai nása, kiten.
tactfully josai naku, úmaku.
tag fuda.
tail o, shippo.
tailor yoofukuya *(for occidental clothes)*; shitateya *(for Japanese clothes)*.
take (to) tóru *(get, lay hold of)*; motte iku *(carry or take to)*; tsukámu *(grasp)*; uketoru *(receive)*; tsurete iku *(take to, lead to)*.
tale hanashi, monogátari *(old story)*.
talent sainoo *(special faculty)*; shuwan *(natural ability)*.
talk hanashi; osháberi *(a chattering)*; danwa *(conversation)*.
talk (to) hanásu.
talkative osháberi na.
tall takái.
   He is tall. Sé ga takái desu.
tame náreta *(domesticated)*; súnaona *(docile)*; juujun na *(submissive)*; mukíryoku no *(dull)*.
tangerine míkan
tangle (to) kogurakasu *(entangle)*; karamaséru *(confuse)*.
tank mizuoke, tánku *(for water, etc.)*; tánku, sénsha *(vehicle of war)*.
tar koorutaa.
tardy gúzuguzu shita, jikan ni okureru.
target mato.
tarnish henshoku.
   to be tarnished kumótte iru.
tarry (to) nagái suru.
task shigoto *(piece of work)*; hone no oréru shigoto *(toil)*; tsutome *(duty)*.
taste aji *(of food)*; shúmi *(for art)*.
taste (to) aji o míru.
tax zei, zeikin.
taxi tákushíi.
tea ocha *(Japanese)*; koocha *(black tea)*.
teach oshieru *(give instruction)*; shitsukéru *(train)*.
teacher senséi.
team chíimu.
tear námida *(teardrop)*; kagizaki *(a rent in clothing)*.
tear (to) yabúru *(rend)*; mushiri tóru *(pull violently away)*; yaburéru *(become torn)*; hagásu *(tear off)*.
tease (to) nayamasu *(annoy)*; ijimeru *(torment)*.
teaspoon cha saji.
technical gijitsuteki no.
technique gíjutsu
tedious kudói, nagatarashíi.
telegram denpoo.
telegraph denshin.
telegraph (to) denpoo o útsu.
telephone denwa.
telephone (to) denwa o kakéru.

tell (to) hanásu *(relate)*; iu *(say)*; oshieru *(instruct)*.

temper umare tsuki *(disposition)*; seishitsu *(temperament)*; kidate *(personality)*; kigen *(mood)*.

temperance sessei, kinshu *(moderation)*.

temperate odáyaka na *(mild)*; tékido no *(moderate)*.

temperature óndo *(of the air)*; taion *(of the body)*.

tempest ooárashi.

temple (o) miya *(Shinto)*; (o) tera *(Buddhist)*; komekami *(of the forehead)*.

temporary hakanái *(transient)*; kari no.

tempt (to) yuuwaku suru *(seduce)*; sosoru *(incite)*; izanáu *(induce)*; unagásu *(persuade)*.

temptation yuuwaku *(seduction)*; tameshi *(trial)*.

ten tóo, júu.
 ten days tooka.
 ten o'clock júuji.

tenacious shinboo zuyói *(unyielding)*; nebari zuyói *(tough)*.

tenacity kyoojin-sei, gankyoo.

tenant tanako, shakkanin *(of a house)*; shakuchinin *(of land)*.

tend (to) mukau *(be directed toward)*; keikoo ga áru *(have a tendency)*; kooken suru *(serve)*; ki o tsukéru *(attend to)*; káihoo suru *(watch over)*.

tendency keikoo *(trend)*; seiheki *(inclination)*; fuuchoo *(drift)*.

tender *adj.* yawarakái.

tennis ténisu, teikyuu.

tense tokí *(of a verb)*.
 present tense génzai.
 past tense káko.
 future tense mírai.

tense katakurushíi *(stiff)*.

tension kinchoo.

tent ténto, ténmaku.

tenth dái júu, juu banme, júu ban.
 tenth of the month tooka.

tepid nurúi.

term kígen *(limited period)*; jooken *(condition)*; gakki *(of school)*.

terrace takadai, térasu.

terrible osoroshíi *(dreadful)*; hidói *(awful)*; hisan na *(wretched)*.

terrify (to) odorokásu.
 be terrified at —ni odoróku.

territory ryóodo *(as a colony)*; ryóochi *(possession of a state or individual)*.

terror kyoofu.

test tameshi *(experiment)*; shikén *(probe)*; shikínseki *(touchstone)*.

test (to) kénsa suru.

testify (to) shoogen suru *(give evidence)*; shooko dateru *(attest)*.

testimony shoomei *(law)*; shooko *(evidence)*.

text shudai; tékisuto *(of a document)*.

textbook kyookásho.

than yóri, yórimo.
 less than íka.
 more than íjoo.

thank (to) rei o iu.
 Thank you. Arígatoo.
 Thank you very much. Doomo arígatoo gozaimásu.

thanks kánsha *(gratitude)*.

that *adj.* sono —*pron.* sore, are.
 that man anó hito.
 That's it! Sóo da!

thaw yukidoke.

theatre gekijoo.

their (theirs) ano katágata no, ano kátatachi no, anó hitotachi no.

theme daimoku, shudai *(subject)*; wadai *(topic)*.

themselves ano katágata jíshin.

then sono tóki, sono tóki ni *(at that time)*; sore kara *(after that)*; sore de *(at that point)*; sono baai *(in that case)*.

theoretical rironteki.

theoretically rironjoo.

theory gákuri *(scientific principle)*; riron *(opp. to practice)*; gakusetsu *(doctrine)*.

there asoko, achira *(places outside of immediate reach)*; soko, sochira *(places nearby)*.
 there is (are) orimásu, imásu *(for animate beings)*; arimásu *(for inanimate beings)*.

thereafter sore írai.

therefore sore désu kara.

thereupon sokode.

thermometer kandankei *(weather)*; taiónkei *(clinical)*.

these kono.

thesis ronbun.

they ano katagata, ano katátachi, ano hitotachi *(pertaining to people)*; are *(pertaining to things)*.

thick atsui *(flat things)*; futói *(round things)*; koí *(liquids, hair, etc.)*.

thicken (to) atsuku suru, kóku suru.

thickness atsusa; kósa.

thief doroboo.

thigh mómo.

thimble yubinúki.

thin usui *(flat things, liquids)*; hosói *(round things)*; yaseta *(persons)*.

thing monó *(in concrete sense)*; kotó *(abstract)*.

think kangáeru *(conceive)*; omóu *(suppose)*; jukkoo suru *(ponder)*; soozoo suru *(imagine)*; shían suru *(meditate)*.

third *n.* dái san, sanbanme. —*adj.* dái san no, sanbanmé no.
 third of the month mikka.

thirst nódo no kawakí.
 to quench one's thirst nódo no kawakí o iyású.

thirsty (be) nodo ga kawaite iru.

thirteen júusan.

thirty sánjuu.

this *adj.* konó —*pron.* kore.
 this one kore.

thorn togé.

thorough kanzen na *(complete)*; tetteiteki na *(utter)*; mattakú no *(out and out)*.

though ga *(but, however)*.
  Though it was raining ... Áme ga futte itá ga ...

thought kangáe, shisoo *(that which is thought)*; shisaku *(cogitation)*; shían *(meditation)*; án *(idea)*.

thoughtful shínsetsu na *(kind)*.

thoughtless karuhazumi na *(careless)*; fushínsetsu na *(inconsiderate)*.

thousand sén.
  three thousand sanzén.
  ten thousand mán, ichimán.

thrash (to) muchiútsu.

thread íto.

thread (to) ito o tóosu.
  thread a needle hári ni íto o tóosu.

threat kyoohaku.

threaten (to) kyohaku suru.

three mittsú, san.

threshold iriguchi *(entrance)*; shikii *(door-sill)*.

thrift ken'yaku.

thrifty ken'yaku na.

thrill súriru, senritsu.

thrill (to) kandoo suru; súriru o kanjiru.

thrilling wákuwaku saseru yóo na.

thrive (to) hánjoo suru.

thriving hánjoo suru.

throat nódo.

throb (to) dooki ga suru, dóki doki suru.

throne gyókuza.

throng gunshuu.

through *prep.* —o tooshite *(by the medium of)*; tsuranúite *(across)*; —no naka ni *(in the midst of)*; —juu *(during the whole period)*. —*adv.* hajime kara owari made *(from beginning to end)*; zutto *(all the way)*.

throughout *prep.* —juu *(periods of time)*. —*adv.* sukkári, dóko mo ka mo *(everywhere)*.

ton tón.

throw (to) nagéru *(fling)*; hooru *(hurl)*.

thumb oyayubi.

thunder (to) kaminari ga naru.

thunderbolt kaminari.

Thursday Mokuyóobi.

thus kono yóo ní, koo iu fúu ni *(in this manner)*; désu kara *(so, therefore)*; shitagátte *(accordingly)*.

thwart (to) jama suru.

ticket kippu, -ken *(in compounds)*.
  ticket of admission nyuujooken.
  ticket window kippu úriba.

tickle (to) kusuguru.

ticklish kusuguttái.

tide shío, chooryuu.

tidy kichín to shita *(arranged in good order)*; kogírei na *(neat)*.

tie musubime *(knot)*; tsunagari *(connection)*.

tie (to) shibáru *(tie roughly)*; iwaéru *(tie up)*.
  tie a knot musubu.

tiger tora.

tight katai *(close)*; kataku musunda *(compact)*;

harikítta *(taut)*; kitchíri átta *(close fitting)*.

tile kawara, táiru.

till máde.
  till now ima máde.
  till then sono tóki made.

tilt (to) katamúku.

timber zaimoku.

time tokí; jíki *(opportunity)*; jikan *(hour)*; kikán *(period)*; jidai *(era)*.
  from time to time tokidoki.
  in time ma ni áu yóo ni.
  What time is it? Nánji desu ka?

timid uchiki na.

timidity uchiki.

tin súzu.
  tin can kán, kanzume no kán.

tinkle (to) chirín chirin naru.

tiny chísana.

tip saki *(end)*; kokorozuke, chíppu *(gratuity)*; chadai *(gratuity given in Japanese inns)*.
  tip over (to) hikkurikáesu.

tire taiya *(for wheels)*.

tire (to) *v.t.* tsukaresaséru; *v.i.* tsukaréru *(get tired)*.

tired tsukáreta.

tireless tsukaré o shiranai.

tiresome taikutsu na.

title daimoku, shomei *(of a book)*; katagaki *(rank)*.

to e *(toward)*; máde *(until, up to)*.
  Tell him to come. Kúru yoo ni itte kudasái.
  I went to buy. Kai ni ikimáshita.
  to him sonó hito ni.

toad hikigáeru.

toast yaki pan, tóosuto *(bread)*; kanpai *(proposing a health)*.

toast (to) *(bread)* pán o yaku.

tobacco tabako.

today kyóo.

toe ashi no yubi.

together issho ni, mínna de *(all together)*.

toil honeori.

toil (to) roodoo suru; kúroo suru.

toilet habakari, gofujoo, tóire, oteárai, benjo *(washroom)*.

token shirushi *(sign)*; kinenhin *(souvenir)*; katami *(keepsake)*.

tolerable gáman dekíru.

tolerance kandai.

tolerant kandai na.

tolerate (to) oome ni míru *(permit)*; gáman suru *(endure)*; kandai ni toriatsukáu *(be broadminded)*.

toll zeikin *(tax)*; tsuukóoryoo *(passage money)*; shishóosha no kazu *(casualties)*.

tomato tomato.

tomb haká *(grave)*; nookotsujoo *(vault)*.

tomorrow ashita, myóonichi.

tone otó; kuchoo *(of speech)*; iroai *(color)*.

tongs híbashi.

tongue shitá.

tonight kón'ya, kónban.

too mo *(also)*; amari, anmari *(excessively)*.
　It's too expensive. Anmari takái desu.
tool doogu.
tooth há.
toothache há no itami.
toothbrush ha búrashi.
toothpaste neri hamígaki.
toothpick tsuma yóoji.
tooth powder hamigakíko.
top ue *(summit)*; kóma *(toy)*.
top (to) ue ni naru.
topic topíkku; shudai *(subject)*; wadai *(of conversation)*.
torch táimatsu.
torment kashaku *(torture)*.
torment (to) kurushiméru.
torture *n.* goomon, kurushimi *(anguish)*.
toss (to) nagéru.
total *adj.* sookei no *(entire)*; kanzen na *(complete)*. —*n.* gookei *(total amount)*.
totally kanzen ni.
touch (to) sawaru.
touching áware na.
touchy shínkei kabin na.
tough tsuyói *(strong)*; ganjoo na *(robust)*; goojoo na *(stubborn)*; hidói *(laborious)*; katai *(hard)*.
tour ryokoo, tabí *(travel)*; man'yuu *(pleasure trip)*.
tour (to) ryokoo suru.
tourist kankóokyaku, yuuránsha, tsúurisuto; santóo *(third class)*.
　Tourist Agency Tsuurisuto Byúuroo.
tournament shiai.
toward —no hóo e *(direction)*; góro *(about: in point of time)*.
towel tenugui *(Japanese)*; táoru *(occidental)*.
tower tóo.
town machí, tokai *(city)*.
toy omócha.
trace áto *(remains)*; keiseki *(vestige)*; kekka *(evidence)*.
trace (to) toosha suru *(through paper)*; tsuiseki suru *(track down)*.
track sénro *(railroad)*.
trade shóobai *(domestic)*; booeki *(with foreign countries)*.
　trade union roodoo kúmiai.
tradition shikitari.
traditional dentooteki no.
traffic torihiki *(commerce)*; kootsuu *(movement of people, vehicles, etc.)*.
tragedy higeki *(opp. to comedy)*; kanashii dekígoto *(sad event)*.
tragic higekiteki no.
trail kómichi *(mountain path)*; áto *(trace)*.
trail (to) áto o tsukéru *(pursue)*.
train kishá *(steam- or diesel-engine powered)*; densha *(electric)*.
train (to) kyooiku suru *(educate)*; shikómu *(animals)*.
training kúnren.
traitor uragirimono *(betrayer)*; kokuzoku *(rebel)*.
trample (to) fumiarásu.
tranquil shízuka na.

tranquility heian.
tranquilizer chinséizai shinkei seishin anteizai, torankiraizaa.
transaction torihiki.
　business transaction shoogyoo tórihiki.
transfer norikae kíppu *(ticket)*.
transfer (to) norikáeru *(change cars)*; utsúsu *(shift)*; ugokásu *(move)*; yuzuru *(hand over)*.
transistor toranjísutaa;
　portable transistor radio keitai yoo toranjisutaa rájio.
transition hensen, súii *(change)*.
translate (to) hon'yaku suru.
translation hon'yaku, yáku.
translator hon'yákusha.
　interpreter tsúuyaku.
transmission dentatsu.
transmit (to) watasu *(hand over)*; tsutaeru *(pass on)*.
transparent sukitóotta.
transport *n.* unsoo.
transport (to) unpan suru *(carry)*; unsoo suru *(by ship or railroad)*.
transportation yusoo *(conveyance)*; unsoo *(shipping)*; kootsuu no ben *(means of travel)*.
trap wána.
trap (to) wána de tóru.
trash gomí, kúzu *(rubbish)*; garakuta *(odds and ends)*.
travel ryokoo, tabí.
travel (to) ryokoo suru.
traveler ryokóosha.
tray bon.
treacherous uragíru yoo na, fuchúujitsu no *(disloyal)*.
treachery uragiri.
treason muhon.
treasure takara.
treasure (to) daijí ni suru.
treasurer kaikéiyaku.
treasury kaikei.
treat gochisoo.
treat (to) motenasu *(entertain)*; atsukau *(deal with)*; chiryoo suru *(give medical treatment)*; ogoru *(treat a person to)*.
treatment toriatsukai *(conduct toward)*; chiryoo *(medical)*.
treaty jooyaku.
　commercial treaty tsuushoo jóoyaku.
tree kí.
　evergreen tokiwági.
tremble (to) furueru.
trembling *adj.* furete iru. —*n.* mibúrui.
tremendous taihen na.
trench mizo *(ditch)*; zangoo *(military)*.
trend keikoo *(general tendency)*; hookoo, múki *(general direction)*.
trial sáiban *(law)*; shiren *(hardship)*; kokoromi *(experiment)*.
triangle sánkaku.
tribe shúzoku.
tribulation kánnan.
tribunal saibansho *(a court of justice)*; sáiban *(that which judges)*.

trick itazura, toríkku *(mischief)*; shikata *(stratagem)*.

trick (to) damásu.

trifle tsumaránai mono *(negligible thing)*; kudaranai koto *(insignificant matter)*.

trifle (to) tsumaranái koto ni jíkan o tsubúsu.

trifling tsumaranai *(uninteresting)*; kudaranai *(trivial)*.

trim (to) karikómu.

trimming kazari.

trip ryokoo.

  to take a trip ryokoo ni iku.

trip (to) tsumazúku *(take a false step)*; tsumazukaséru *(trip up)*.

triple sanbai no.

triumph shóori *(victory)*; daiséikoo *(signal success)*.

triumph (to) shóori o éru.

triumphant shóori o éta.

trivial kudaranai.

troop gúntai.

trophy káppu, tórohii.

trot (to) hayáashi de kakéru.

trouble kónnan *(difficulty)*; mendóo *(bother)*; shinpai *(anxiety)*; nangi *(distress)*.

trouble (to) mendóo o kakéru *(put to inconvenience)*; komaraséru *(perplex)*; jama suru *(disturb)*.

  Don't trouble yourself! Shinpai shinái de kudasái.

trousers zubón.

truck torákku.

true hontoo no *(opp. to false)*; makoto no *(true-hearted)*; shín no *(real)*; jíjitsu no *(actual)*; seikaku na *(exact)*.

truly hontoo ni *(correctly)*; chuujitsu ni *(faithfully)*; jitsú ni *(really)*; mattaku *(indeed)*.

trump toránpu.

trumpet toránpetto.

trunk mikí *(of tree)*; toránku *(baggage)*.

trust shin'yoo *(faith)*; gímu *(responsibility)*; shinrai *(reliance)*; kakushin *(confidence)*.

trust (to) shin'yoo suru *(give credit to)*; shinrai suru *(rely on)*.

trusting shinzúru.

trustworthy ate ni náru.

truth hontoo no koto *(correspondence to reality)*; jíjitsu *(fact)*.

truthful shoojíki na *(veracious)*; jitchoku na *(upright)*.

truthfully shoojíki ni.

truthfulness seijitsu, seikakusa.

try (to) tamésu, kokoromíru *(prove by experiment)*; yatte míru *(attempt)*.

  to try to go ikoo to suru.

tube kúda, chúubu.

Tuesday Kayóobi.

tumble (to) korobu *(of persons)*; taoréru *(of things)*; ochíru *(roll over)*.

tumult oosáwagi *(uproar)*.

tune senritsu, shirabe *(melody)*; fushí *(air)*.

tune (to) chooshi o awaséru *(adjust)*; choowa suru *(be in harmony)*.

tunnel tonneru.

turf shiba, shibafu.

turkey shichimenchoo.

turmoil sóodoo.

turn junban *(order)*; kaiten *(turning)*; magarime *(curve)*; hookoo ténkan *(in direction)*.

turn (to) mawasu *(cause to revolve)*; mawaru *(revolve)*; magaru *(swerve)*.

  Turn left. Hidari e magatte kudasái.

turnip kabu, kabura.

twelfth dái juuní;

  twelfth of the month juuninichi.

twelve juuní.

twentieth dái níjuu;

  twentieth of the month hatsuka.

twenty níjuu.

twice ni dó.

twilight yuukata, tasogare *(poetic)*.

twin futago.

twist (to) nejíru *(distort)*; yoriawaséru *(intertwine)*; orikómu *(interweave)*.

two futatsu, ní.

type katá *(specimen)*; móderu *(model)*; tenkei *(pattern)*; táipu, katsuji *(printing)*.

type (to) táipu suru.

typewriter taipuráitaa.

tyranny ooboo, gyakusei.

tyrant bóokun.

U

ugliness migurushíi koto.

ugly mittomonái.

ulcer kaiyoo.

ulterior hyoomén no, sotogawa no.

ultimate sáigo no.

ultimately sáigo no.

umbrella karakása *(of paper)*; koomorigása *(occidental-style).*

umpire shinpánkan, anpaiya.

umpire (to) shinpan suru.

unable dekínai.

  I'm unable to do it. Suru kóto ga dekimasén.

unanimity manjoo itchi.

unanimous onaji kangáe no *(agreeing in opinion)*; manjoo itchi no *(consent of all)*.

unanimously íku dooon ni *(with one voice)*; manjoo itchi de *(with a unanimous vote)*.

unaware kizukánai.

unbearable tamaranai *(unendurable)*; gaman dekínai *(not able to be borne)*.

unbelievable shinjirarénai.

unbutton botan o hazusu.

uncertain fukákutei na *(undecided)*; gúra gura shita *(unsteady)*; táshika de nái *(not sure)*; abunai *(risky)*; hakkíri shinai *(not settled)*.

uncertainty hakkíri shinai koto.

unchangeable fuhen no.

uncle oji, ojisan.

uncomfortable kokoromochi no warúi, rakú de nai.

uncommon métta ni nai *(infrequent)*; hijoo na

(extraordinary); mezurashíi *(rare)*;
fushigi na *(strange)*.
unconscious kizetsu shita *(having lost
consciousness)*; kizukánai *(unaware)*.
unconsciously shirazu ni.
uncover (to) futa o tóru *(take off a lid)*; ooí o
tóru *(take off a covering)*.
undecided kimatte inai.
undeniable hitei dekínai, mooshíbun no nái.
under —no shita ni, —no shite de, —no shita
no.
undergo ukéru; shújutsu o ukéru *(undergo an
operation)*.
underground chiká *(subterranean)*; himitsu
no *(secret)*.
underline (to) shita ni sén o hiku
(underscore); kyoochoo suru
(emphasize).
underneath —no shita ni, —no shita de, —no
shita no.
understand (to) wakáru; rikaisuru.
understanding adj. wakari no yói. —n. ríkai.
undertake (to) hikiukéru *(take upon oneself)*;
kuwadatéru *(attempt)*.
undertaking shigoto *(task)*; jígyoo
(enterprise).
undesirable nozomáshikunái.
undignified omomi no nái, hin no nái,
fukínshin na.
undo (to) móto ni káesu *(reverse)*; torikesu
(annul); hazusu *(unfasten)*; tóku *(a
knot)*; akeru *(open, as a parcel)*; núgu
(take off); muda ni suru *(bring to
naught)*; tokéru *(come undone)*.
undress (to) kimono o núgu *(oneself)*; kimono
o nugaséru *(make someone else
undress)*.
uneasiness fuan.
uneasy fuan na; ochitsukanai *(restless)*.
unemployed shigoto no nái *(out of work)*;
shiyoo shinai *(unused)*.
unequal fukóohei na, fubyóodoo na.
uneven fusóroi na *(not in line)*; deko boko na
(rough).
uneventful buji heion na.
unexpected omoigakenái *(not expected)*; yóki
shinai *(unforeseen)*; totsuzen na
(sudden); igai na *(surprising)*.
unexpectedly igai ni, fui ni *(abruptly)*.
unfailing tsukínai *(inexhaustible)*; shinrai no
dekíru *(sure)*.
unfair fukóohei na *(biased)*; tadashikunái *(not
right)*.
unfaithful fuchúujitsu na.
unfamiliar yóku shiranai *(not well known)*;
shirarenai *(unknown)*; keiken ga nái
(inexperienced).
unfavorable yókunai *(not good)*; fúri na *(not
satisfactory)*; tsugoo no warúi
(inconvenient).
unfit tekishínai *(unsuitable)*; funíai na
(unbecoming).
unfold (to) hirogeru.
unforeseen fui no, omoigakenai.
unforgettable wasurerarenai.
unfortunate fukóo na.

unfortunately ainiku *(unluckily)*; zannen
nagara *(regrettably)*.
ungrateful arigatáku omótte inai.
unhappily fushiáwase ni.
unhappiness fushiáwase.
unhappy fushiáwase na.
unharmed buji na.
unhealthy karada no yowái *(sickly)*; dokú ni
náru *(harmful to the health)*.
unheard of máda kiitá koto no nái.
unhesitatingly chúucho sezu ni.
unhoped for boogai no, kitai shinákatta.
unhurt kega no nái.
uniform adj. onaji yóo na *(about the same)*;
soroi no *(of the same pattern)*. —n.
yunifoomu, seifuku.
uniformity kin'itsu, kakuitsu.
uniformly dooyoo ni.
unify (to) tooitsu suru.
unimportant daijí de nái, tsumaránai
(worthless).
unintentional kói de nái.
unintentionally kói de náku, shiyoo to
shináide.
uninviting ki no susumanai.
union kumiai *(association)*; gappei
(combination); engumi *(marriage)*.
  labor union roodoo kúmiai.
unique hitotsu kirí no *(single, sole)*; dokutoku
no *(peerless)*; subarashíi *(wonderful)*.
unison itchi, kyoodoo.
unit tán'i.
unite (to) awaséru *(join into one)*; ketsugoo
suru *(combine)*; gappei suru
(amalgamate); gattai suru *(coalesce)*.
united rengoo shita.
United Nations Kokuren.
United States Amerika Gasshúukoku.
unity tooitsu, itchi.
universal zen sékai no *(covering all the
world)*; ippan ni okonawaréru *(widely
practiced)*.
universe úchuu.
university daigaku.
unjust fukóohei na.
unjustifiable iiwake no tatánai, too o énai.
unkempt darashí no nái.
unkind fushínsetsu na.
unknown shirarete inai.
unlawful fuhoo no, hooritsu ni han súru.
unless —nákereba *(if not)*.
  Unless you come . . . Anáta ga
  kónakerebe . . .
unlikely arisóo de nái, hontooráshiku nái.
unlimited saigen no nái, seigén no nái.
unload (to) tsumini o ageru *(a ship's cargo)*;
ní o orósu *(take down from a truck or
train)*.
unlucky ún no warui.
unmask (to) bákuro suru.
unmistakably machigai náku.
unnecessary yokei na *(superfluous)*; mueki na
(useless); muda na *(of no use)*;
fuhitsúyoo na *(not necessary)*.
unoccupied asite iru *(untenanted)*; yooji ga
nái *(disengaged)*.

unofficial hikóoshiki no *(informal)*.
unpack (to) ní o tóku, nímotsu o hiráku.
unpleasant fuyúkai na *(disagreeable)*; iyá na
(offensive).
unpublished shuppan sarete inai.
unquestionably táshika ni.
unravel (to) tóku, hodóku *(disentangle)*;
kaiketsu suru *(solve)*.
unreal hi-genjitsuteki no.
unreasonable wáke no wakaránai *(not
governed by reason)*; hoogai na
(exorbitant).
unrecognizable wakari kanéru, mitomegatái.
unreliable ate ni naránai.
unrest fuon, fuan jóotai.
unrestrained kimama na, yokusei no nái.
unrestricted seigen nai.
unroll (to) tóku, hirogeru.
unsafe abunai *(dangerous)*; anzen de nái *(not
safe)*.
unsatisfactory fumánzoku na *(not
satisfactory)*; fujúubun na
(inadequate).
unsatisfied fumánzoku na, manzoku shite
inai.
unscrupulous buénryo na, mukóo mizu no.
unseemly mittomonái.
unseen kakúrete iru, miénai.
unselfish rikoteki de nái, jibun o wasureta.
unspeakable iiyoo no nái.
unstabe fuántei na.
unsteady shikkári shinái.
unsuccessful seikoo shinái, fuséikoo no.
unsuitable futekítoo na *(inappropriate)*;
niawánai *(not becoming)*.
unthinkable kangaerarénai.
untidy darashi ga nái.
untie (to) hodóku.
until máde.
  until now ima máde.
untiring tsukarénai.
untrue úso no, hontoo de nái.
untrustworthy ate ni naránai.
untruth úso.
unusual ijoo na *(uncommon)*; mare na *(rare)*;
métta ni nái *(not frequent)*; nárete inái
(unfamiliar); mezurashíi *(strange)*;
reigai no *(exceptional)*.
unwarranted hoshoo no nái, fukakújitsu na.
unwell guai ga warúi.
unwholesome kenkoo ni yókunai, kenzen de
nái.
unwilling fuhón'i no *(disinclined)*; ki ga
susumanai *(reluctant)*.
unwise óroka na, kashikókunai.
unworthy kudaranai *(wanting merit)*;
fusawashíku nái *(unsuitable)*.
unyielding gánko na.
up ue, ue ni.
  eat up tábete shimau.
  give up akiraméru.
upheaval dooran.
uphold (to) saseru, shíji suru *(support)*;
kakunin suru *(court decision)*.
upkeep ijíhi *(expense)*; íji *(maintenance)*.
upon —no ue ni, —no ue de, —no ue no.

upper ue no.
upright tátte iru *(erect)*; shoojíki na *(honest)*.
uprising boodoo *(revolt)*; íkki *(riot)*.
uproar oosáwagi *(disturbance)*; soozooshíi
kóe *(clamor)*.
upset (to) kutsugáesu *(overturn)*; taósu
(overthrow); shippai saseru *(frustrate)*;
awatesaseru *(make nervous)*.
  to be upset roobai suru.
upside down sakasama *(topsy turvy)*; abekobe
(reverse).
upstairs nikai.
upward uwamuki no.
uranium uranyúumu.
urge (to) susumeru *(incite)*; isogaséru
(hasten); karitatéru *(press)*; hagemásu
(exhort).
urgency seppaku shita koto, kinkyuu no koto.
urgent isogi no, kinkyuu no.
urinate (to) shooyoo o suru, shoobén suru.
us watashítachi.
U.S.A. Amerika Gasshúukoku.
use tsukaikata *(manner of using)*.
  to be of use yakú ni tátsu.
use (to) tsukau.
used to —ni naréru *(accustomed)*.
  he used to go iku kóto ni nárete imásu.
  He used to go there every day. Máinichi
itta monó desu.
useful yakú ni tátsu *(serviceable)*; chóochoo
na *(handy)*; yuuyoo na *(good for
something)*.
useless muyoo na *(of no service)*; damé na
(fruitless); muda na *(futile)*.
usher annái.
usher (to) annái suru.
usual futsuu no *(commonplace)*; ítsu mo no
(habitual).
usually ítsu mo, taitei.
usurp (to) ooryoo suru, shingai suru.
utensil doogu.
utility jitsuyoo, yuuyoo *(usefulness)*; kooeki
jígyoo *(public utility)*.
  The rent includes utilities. Yáchin ni wa
suidoo-gasu-denki ga haitte imasu.
utilize riyoo suru.
utmost kyókudo no, seizei no, sei íppai no
(maximum effort).
utter tetteiteki no *(total)*; kanzen na
(complete); mattaku *(entirely)*;
mujóoken no *(unconditional)*.
utter (to) iu *(say)*; hanásu *(speak)*; ii arawásu
(express).
utterly zenzen *(absolutely)*; mattaku *(totally)*;
sukkári *(completely)*.

V

vacant kara no *(empty)*; aite iru *(unoccupied)*;
karite no nái *(untenanted)*.
vacation yasumi.
vague hakkíri shinái *(indefinite)*; aimai na
(ambiguous).
vain yakú ni tatánai *(useless)*; muda na
(fruitless); unubore no tsuyói,
kyoéishin no tsuyói *(conceited)*; muda
ni *(in vain)*.

valiant isamashíi *(brave)*; yúuki no áru *(courageous)*.

valid táshika na *(well founded)*; yuukoo na *(effective)*.

validity seitoo sa, kakujitsu sa.

valley tani.

valuable kóoka na *(precious)*; neuchi no áru *(in terms of money, materially)*.
  valuables kichoohin.

value neuchi *(worth)*; atai *(cost)*.

value (to) nebumi suru *(appraise)*; sonchoo suru *(rate highly)*; daijí ni suru *(think important)*.

valued kichoo na.

valve bén, bárubu.

vanilla bánira.

vanish (to) kieuséru *(disappear)*; usuréru *(fade away)*; nakunaru *(cease to exist)*.

vanquish seifuku suru *(conquer)*; makasu *(defeat)*.

vapor yúge *(of water)*; kitai *(gaseous state of liquid or solid)*.

variable kawariyasúi, kawaru.

variance fúwa *(antagonism)*; hendoo *(deviation, discord)*; fuítchi, chigai *(divergence)*.

vanity kyoéishin, unubore *(conceit)*.

variation hénka, chigai *(modification, change)*.

varied sama záma no.

variety hénka ni tómu koto *(diversity)*; kuichigai *(difference)*; shúrui *(kinds)*.

various iroiro no.

varnish (to) urushi o nuru.

vary (to) kaeru, chigaeru *(alter)*; hénka o soéru *(diversify)*.

vase tsubo.
  flower vase kabin.

vast hirói.

vault kínko *(safe)*.

veal ko ushi no nikú.

vegetable yasai.

vehemence hageshísa.

vehement hageshíi, nesshín na.

vehicle norimono.

veil makú *(curtain)*; béeru *(for face)*.

veil (to) béeru o kakeru.

vein joomyaku *(blood vessel)*.

velocity sokúryoku, háyasa *(speed)*.

velvet biroodo, berubétto.

venerable sonkei subéki, rippa na *(respected)*.

venerate (to) uyamáu.

veneration sonkei.

vengeance fukushuu.

venom dokú *(poison)*; urami *(ill will)*.

venomous doku no aru.

ventilation kazetooshi, tsuufuu.

ventilator tsuufúu ki.

venture kiken na kuwadate.

venture (to) kiken ni sarasu *(risk)*; omoikítte yaru *(brave danger)*.

verb dooshi.

verdict hyooketsu *(of law)*; hándan *(judgment)*; kettei *(decision)*.

verge hashi *(edge)*; herí *(brink)*; kyookai *(border-line)*.
  on the verge of —ni hínsuru.

verge (to) chikazuku.

verification kakunin.

verify (to) shoomei suru *(prove)*; tashikaméru *(ascertain)*.

versatile tagei no, bannoo no.

verse shi *(poem)*; ku *(line of a poem)*.

version hanashi *(of a story)*; hon'yaku *(translation)*; íken *(opinion)*.

vertical suichoku no, táte no *(perpendicular)*.

very taihen, táisoo, hijoo ni, hanahadáshiku.

vessel fúne *(ship)*; iremono *(receptacle)*.

vest chokki.

vex (to) urusagaraséru *(annoy)*; okoraséru *(provoke)*; nayamásu *(distress)*.

via —keiyu.

vibrate (to) yureru *(oscillate)*; furueru *(quiver)*.

vice n. fudótoku *(depravity)*; akuheki *(evil habit)*.—*adj.* fuku.

vice-president fuku daitóoryoo *(of a country)*; fuku káichoo *(of a society)*; fuku sháchoo *(of a firm)*.

vice versa abekobe, hantai.

vicinity kínjo *(neighborhood)*; chikái koto *(nearness)*.

victim higáisha *(injured one)*; soonánsha *(sufferer)*; giséisha *(one who is a sacrifice)*.

victor shoorísha.

victorious shoori o éta, kátta.

victory shóori.

view késhiki *(prospect)*; íken *(opinion)*.

view (to) míru; yuuran suru *(sightseeing)*.

vie (with) (to) kisóu.

vigor séiryoku *(vitality)*; génki *(energy)*.

vigorous génki na *(energetic)*; tsuyói *(strong)*; kappatsu na *(active)*.

vile katoo na.

village mura.

villain warumono.

vindicate (to) béngo suru.

vindictive shuunen bukái.

vine tsúru.

vinegar sú.

violence bookoo *(outrage)*; bóoryoku *(exertion of physical force)*.

violent hageshíi, hidói *(wild)*.

violet n. sumire *(flower)*; murasaki iro *(color)*.

violin baiorin, teikin.

virtue toku *(moral excellence)*; zenkoo *(opp. to vice)*; misao *(chastity)*; kooketsu *(uprightness)*.

virtuous dootoku no takái *(morally good)*; kooketsu na *(honorable)*; dootokuteki na *(moral)*.

visibility shikái.

visible me ni miéru.

visibly me ni míete.

vision shíryoku *(actual sight)*.

visit hoomon *(call on someone)*; omimai *(to sick people)*.

visit (to) otazune suru, hoomon suru *(a person)*; kenbutsu suru *(museums, etc.)*.

visitor okyakusáma *(guest)*.

visual shikaku no.
  visual education shikaku kyóoiku.

visualize (to) kokoró ni egáku.
vital séimei no *(of life)*; hijoo ni juudai na *(very important)*; kan'yoo na *(indispensable)*.
vitality táiryoku.
vivacious kaikatsu na *(jovial)*; yooki na *(lively)*; génki na *(spirited)*.
vivid hakkíri shita.
vocabulary tango *(individual words)*; goi *(list of words)*.
vocal kóe no.
vocation shokúgyoo *(profession)*; shóobai *(business)*; teigyoo *(regular employment)*; ténshoku *(calling)*.
vogue hayari.
voice kóe.
voice (to) kóe o dasu *(utter)*; íken o haku *(give expression to)*.
void kóoryoku no nái *(not binding)*; mukoo *(nullified)*.
void (to) dásu *(throw, send out, empty)*.
volume yóoseki *(of a solid)*; ryóo *(quantity)*; -kán, -satsu *(counter for books and magazines)*.
  one volume issatsu.
voluminous kasabáru.
voluntary jihatsuteki.
volunteer shibóosha.
vomit (to) háku.
vote hyoo.
vote (to) toohyoo suru.
vouch for (to) hoshoo suru *(guarantee)*; hoshóonin ni náru *(stand sponsor for)*.
voucher uketori *(receipt)*.
vow seiyaku *(promise)*; chikai *(oath)*.
vow (to) seiyaku suru *(promise)*; dangén suru *(assert)*; chikau *(pledge)*.
vowel boin.
voyage kóokai.
vulgar gehín na.
vulnerable yowami no áru.

W

wade (to) wataru.
waffle wáffuru.
wag (to) furu.
wage chíngin.
wager kakégoto *(act of betting)*; kaké *(bet)*.
wager (to) kakégoto o suru.
wages chíngin *(pay)*; kyúuryoo *(salary, payroll)*.
wagon kuruma.
waist koshi.
wait mátsu koto *(act of waiting)*.
wait (to) mátsu.
waiter booisan, kyúuji, wéetaa.
wake (to) okósu.
  be awakened okosaréru.
walk sanpo.
  Go for a walk (take a walk). Sanpo suru.
walk (to) arúku.
wall kabe.
wallet saifu *(purse)*; satsu-íre *(for paper money)*.
walnut kurumi.

waltz wárutsu.
wander (to) aruki mawáru.
want ketsuboo.
want (to) iru *(need)*; hoshíi desu *(want to have a thing)*.
  want to go ikitai.
war sensoo.
war (to) sensoo o suru.
warble (to) saezúru.
ward bóogo *(guard)*; mihari *(watch)*; kyoodoo byóoshitsu *(in a hospital)*; ku *(division of a city, borough)*.
wardrobe tansu.
ware, wares saikumono *(handicraft)*; toojíki *(chinaware)*.
warehouse sóoko.
warfare sensoo *(war)*.
warm atatakái.
warm (to) atatakaku suru *(keep warm)*.
warmth atatákasa.
warn (to) chúui suru *(caution)*; imashiméru *(admonish)*.
warning chúui, kunkai *(admonition)*; yokoku *(notice)*.
warrant hoshoo *(guarantee)*; shooméisho *(certificate)*.
warrant (to) hoshoo suru.
warrior héishi *(soldier)*; yúushi *(distinguished soldier)*.
wary yoojin bukái.
wash sentaku *(washing)*.
wash (to) arau.
washroom benjo, ote árai, habakari, tóire.
waste amarimono *(waste material)*; kúzu *(refuse)*.
  wastepaper kamikúzu.
waste (to) muda ni suru.
watch tokei *(timepiece)*.
  wrist watch ude dókei.
watch (to) bán o suru *(guard)*; ki o tsukéru *(pay attention)*.
watchful yoojin bukái *(cautious)*.
water mizu.
water (to) mizu o yaru *(plants)*.
waterfall taki.
waterproof *adj.* mizu no tooránai.—*n.* boosui, taisui.
watt wátto.
wave namí.
wave (to) yureru *(sway)*; hirugáeru *(flutter)*; furimawásu *(brandish)*.
waver (to) tameráu *(hesitate)*.
wax róo, wákkusu.
way michi *(road)*; toori *(street)*; hoohoo *(method)*.
we watashítashi, watakushidómo.
weak yowái.
weaken (to) yówaku suru *(make weak)*; yówaku náru *(get weak)*.
weakly yowayowashíi, byóoshin na *(sickly)*.
weakness kettén *(weak points)*.
wealth zaisan *(riches)*; tómi *(fortune)*.
wealthy kanemóchi no *(rich)*; yútaka na *(well off)*.
weapon búki.
wear (to) kiru *(coat, dress)*; haku *(pants,*

shoes); shiméru (*girdle*); kabúru (*hat*); hameru (*ring, gloves*); kakéru (*spectacles*).
weariness hiroo (*fatigue*); taikutsu (*tedium*).
weary tsukáreta (*tired*); ákita (*bored*); taikutsu na (*tedious*).
weather ténki.
  rainy weather áme, áme no hi.
  cloudy weather kumótta hi.
weave (to) óru.
wedding kekkónshiki (*ceremony*).
wedge kusabi.
Wednesday Suiyóobi.
weed zassoo.
weed (to) zassoo o nuku.
week shúu (*counter for weeks*).
  this week konshuu.
  next week raishuu.
  two weeks ni shúukan.
week end *n.* shuumatsu, wiikuéndo.
weekly shuukan zásshi (*periodical*).
weep (to) naku.
weigh (to) mekata o hakáru.
weight mekata.
welcome kangei.
  You're welcome. Yóku irassahimáshita. (*Glad that you've come.*) Dóo itashimáshite. (*Nothing at all. Don't mention it.*)
welfare fukúshi (*well-being*); han'ei (*prosperity*).
well ído (*for water*).
west nishi.
western nishi no.
wet nureta, nurete iru.
wet (to) nurasu.
  be wet nurete iru.
whale kujira.
what *pron.* nán, náni. —*adj.* dóno (*which*)
  What is it? Nán desu ka?
  what he said itta koto (*that which he said*).
whatever nán de mo.
  whatever he saw nán de mo míta mono.
  whatever he heard nán de mo kiita koto.
wheat ko mugi.
wheel kuruma, wá.
when ítsu (*interrogative*);—tokí, tokí ni (*at the particular time that*);—tára (*if, when*);—to (*whenever*).
  When I went to Kyoto . . . Kyóoto e itta tóki . . .
  When I asked Mr. Yamada . . . Yamada-san ni kiitára . . .
  When I have a headache . . . Atamá ga itái to . . .
whenever —to, tabí ni (*every time*); ítsu mo (*always*); ítsu de mo (*at all times*).
where dóko ni dóko de, dóko e (*in what place*); dóchira (*pol, used like dóko*); dóko e (*whither*).
wherever dóko . . . de mo; dóko . . . té mo.
whether ka, ka dóo ka,—mo—mo.
which *pron.* dóre (*of several*); dóchira (*of two*).—*adj.* dóno.
while —uchi ni;—aida ni.
  Wait a while. Chótto mátte kudasaí.

whim kimagure.
whimper (to) shikushiku naku.
whine (to) nakigoe o dásu.
whip múchi.
whip (to) múchi de útsu (*lash*); sékkan suru (*flog*).
whisper sasayaki.
whisper (to) sasayáku (*speak softly or under the breath*); naisho bánashi o suru (*speak in secret*).
whistle fue (*instrument*); kuchi bue (*made with the mouth*).
whistle (to) kuchibue o fuku.
white *adj.* shirói.—*n.* shíro.
who *n.* dónata, dáre (*interrogative*).
whoever dáre de mo.
whole *adj.* zen- (*prefix*); -juu (*suffix*); zénbu no.—*n.* zénbu.
wholesale oroshi, oroshi úri.
wholesome kenkoo ni yói (*salubrious*); kenzen na (*sound*).
whom dáre ni, dónata ni (*as indirect object*); dáre o, dónata o (*as direct object*).
whose dónata no, dáre no.
why náze, dóo shite.
wicked warúi (*bad*); yokoshima na (*sinful*); ijiwáru na (*ill-tempered*).
wide hirói.
widen *v.t.* hirogeru; *v.i.* hirogaru.
widow mibóojin.
widower otoko yámome.
width haba.
wife tsúma; ókusama (*your wife*); kánai (*my wife*).
wig katsura.
wild yasei no (*opp. to domestic*); areháteta (*uncultivated*); arai (*untamed*); ranboo na (*lawless*); kyóoki no (*frantic*).
wilderness arano.
wildness ranboo sa.
will íshi (*the faculty*); íshi no chikara (*will power*); kétsui (*determination*); negai (*wish*); kiboo (*desire*); yuigónjoo (*testament*).
will (to) yuigon o nokósu (*bequeath*).
willful kói no.
willing yorokónde . . . suru.
  I'm willing to go. Yorokónde ikimásu.
willingly yorokónde.
win shóori, kachí.
win (to) tóru (*prizes*); kátsu (*races*); hakusúru (*fame, etc.*).
wind kaze.
wind (to) makú.
window mádo.
windy kaze ga fuku.
wine budóoshu (*grape*); sake (*Japanese: made from rice*).
wing hane (*of birds*); yóku (*airplane*).
wink mekúbase, mabátaki (*blink*); isshúnkan (*instant*).
winner shoorísha (*victory*); jushóosha (*recipient of an award*).
winter fuyu.
wipe (to) fuku.
wire harigane (*metal*); denpoo (*telegram*).

wire (to) denpoo o útsu *(send a telegram)*.
wisdom fúnbetsu *(prudence)*; chié *(intelligence)*.
wise kashikói *(sagacious)*; shíryo no aru *(sensible)*; hakushiki na *(learned)*.
wish negai *(longing)*; nozomi *(hope)*.
wish (to) —ga hoshíi *(wish for something)*; nozómu *(hope)*.
wit kichí *(smart utterance)*; ríchi *(intelligence)*; fúnbetsu *(sense)*.
witch miko, májo.
with —to, —to issho ni *(together with)*; de *(by means of)*.
withdraw (to) hikisagéru *(take back)*; sáru *(remove)*; hikiagéru *(evacuate)*.
withdrawal hikisage, tekkai.
wither (to) kareru.
within —no uchi ni, náka ni *(internally)*; ie no náka ni *(in the house)*; okúnai ni *(indoors)*.
without —náshi de *(not with)*; —no sóto de *(outside)*.
witness shooko *(testimony)*; shoogen *(verbal evidence)*; mokugékisha *(eyewitness)*; shoonin *(legal)*.
witness (to) mokugeki suru *(be a spectator)*; shimésu *(show)*; shoonin to shite shomei suru *(sign as a witness)*.
witty ki no kiita, kashikói *(clever)*.
woe kunoo *(affliction)*.
wolf óokami.
woman onna, onna no hito, fujin *(lady)*.
  women fujin bénjo *(toilet)*.
wonder odoroki *(feeling)*; fushigi *(cause of)*; kiseki *(miracle)*.
wonder (to) odoróku *(be surprised)*; fushigi ni omóu *(take as strange)*.
wonderful fushigi na *(strange)*; subarashíi *(splendid)*.
wood kí; zaimoku *(lumber)*.
woods hayashi.
woodwork ki záiku.
wool yoomoo *(coat of sheep)*; ke ito *(yarn)*; ke *(material)*.
woolen keori no.
word kotoba *(speech)*; yakusoku *(promise)*; táyori *(news)*.
  word for word ichiji ichíji.
work roodoo *(manual labor)*; shigoto *(mission, job)*; shoku *(employment, occupation)*; chosaku *(literary work)*.
work (to) shigoto o suru *(manually or mentally)*; hataraku *(manual labor)*.
worker roodóosha *(wage earner)*; shokunin *(craftsman)*.
work of art geijutsu sákuhin.
workshop shigotoba, seisakujo.
world sékai *(earth)*; chikyuu *(the globe)*; séken *(society)*.
worldliness zokushuu.
worldly kono yo teki no.
worm mushi.
worry shinpai *(care)*; kúroo *(trouble)*; mendoo *(difficulty)*.
worry (to) *v.i.* shinpai suru; *v.t.* shinpai saseru *(make one worry)*.

Don't worry! Shinpai shináide kudasái.
worse —yóri mo warúi, sára ni warúi.
worship reihai *(religion)*; suuhai *(admiration)*.
worship (to) reihai suru, ogámu.
worst ichiban warúi.
worth *adj.* neuchi ga aru, kai ga aru *(worthwhile)*. —*n.* kachi, neuchi.
worthless neuchi no nai.
worthy kachi no aru *(good enough for)*;—ni fusawashii *(deserving)*.
wound kega *(injury)*; kizu *(scratch)*.
wound (to) kizu tsukéru *(injure)*; kegá o saseru *(hurt)*.
  get wounded kegá o suru.
  wounded kegá o shita.
wrap (to) tsutsúmu.
wrathful ikidóotte iru.
wreath hanawa.
wreck nansen *(of a ship)*.
  a wrecked ship nanpasen.
wreck (to) hakai suru *(demolish)*; kowásu *(bring disaster on)*.
  to be shipwrecked nansen suru.
wrestle (to) sumoo o tóru *(Japanese-style)*; résuringu o suru *(occidental-style)*; kutoo suru *(struggle with)*.
wrestler sumóotori *(Japanese-style)*; résuraa *(occidental-style)*.
wrestling sumóo *(Japanese-style)*; résuringu *(occidental-style)*.
wretched míjime na.
wring shibóru.
wrinkle shiwa.
wrinkle (to) hitai ni shiwa o yoseru *(one's forehead)*.
  to wrinkle with age toshi o tótte shiwa ga yoru.
wrist tékubi.
  wristband udewa.
write (to) káku.
writer chósha *(author)*; sakka *(novelist)*; shoki *(clerk)*; káita hito *(one who writes)*.
writing hisseki *(handwriting)*; káita mono *(that which is written)*.
  in writing káita mono de.
  to put in writing shomen ni suru.
written kaite áru, kakáreta.
wrong *adj.* warúi, yóku nai *(bad)*; ayamátta, machigátta *(mistaken)*; fusei na *(not moral)*. —*n.* fusei, fúgi.
wrong (to) fusei o okonáu.

Y

yacht yotto.
Yankee yánkii.
yard nakaniwa *(garden)*; yáado, yáaru *(measure)*.
yarn íto.
  wool yarn keito.
yawn akubi.
yawn (to) akubi o suru.
year toshí, —nen.
  this year kónnen, kotoshi.
  ten years júunen.
  per year nén ni.

yearly mainen no *(every year)*; nén ni ichidó no *(once a year)*.
yearn for (to) —ni kogaréru.
yearning akogare.
yeast íisuto, kooji.
yell sakebigóe.
yell (to) sakébu.
yellow *n.* kiiro,—*adj.* kiiroi.
yen én *(Japanese currency)*.
yes hai, ee, sayoo de gozaimásu *(extra pol.)*.
yesterday kinóo, sakújitsu.
yet máda *(still)*;—ga kéredomo *(nevertheless)*. **and yet** sore ná noni.
yield (to) sansúru *(produce)*; yurúsu *(grant)*; ataéru *(give over)*; shitagáu *(follow)*.
yielding juujun na *(compliant)*.
yoke kubiki.
yolk tamágo no kimi.
you anáta *(sing.)* anatagata *(pl.)*; kimi *(used by men to close men friends)*.
young wakái.
your anáta no *(sing.)*; anatagáta no *(pl.)*.
yours anáta no, anáta no monó *(sing.)*, anatátachi no, anatátachi no monó *(pl.)*.
yourself jíshin, jibun.
youth wakái toki *(the period)*; wakái otoko *(young man)*.
youthful wakawakashíi.
youthfulness wakawakáshisa.

Z

zeal nésshin.
zealous nésshin na.
zero zéro, réi.
zipper zíppaa.
zone chitái, chíiki *(area)*;—tai *(in compounds)*.
 temperate zone ontai.
 safety zone anzen chitái.
zone (to) chíiki o kugíru.
zoo doobútsuen.
zoology doobutsú gaku.

GLOSSARY OF GEOGRAPHICAL NAMES

Africa Afuríka.
Algeria Arujeria.
Alaska Arasuka.
Alps Árupusu.
America Amerika, Beikoku.
 North America Kita Amérika, Hokubei.
 Central America Chuuoo Amérika, Chuubei.
 South America Minami Amérika, Nanbei.
Argentina Aruzénchin.
Asia Ajiya.
Atlantic Ocean Taiséiyoo.
Australia Oosutorária.
Bombay Bónbei.
Brazil Buraziru.
Burma Bíruma.

Canada Kánada.
Ceylon Seiron.
Chile Chírii.
China Chúugoku, Shína.
Cuba Kyúuba.
Czechoslovakia Chékkosurobakiya.
Denmark Denmáaku.
Egypt Ejiputo.
England Eikoku.
Europe Yooróppa, Óoshuu.
Geneva Juneebu.
Germany Dóitsu.
 Western Germany Seidoku, Nishi Dóitsu.
 Eastern Germany Toodoku, Higashi Dóitsu.
Greece Gírisha.
Hawaii Háwai.
Hokkaido Hokkáidoo.
Holland Oranda.
Hong Kong Hónkon.
Hungary Hangárii.
Iceland Aisurándo.
India Índo.
Indo-china Indo shína.
Indonesia Indonéshia.
Iran Íran.
Ireland Airurándo.
Italy Itárii.
Japan Nippón, Nihón.
 Japan Sea Nihónkai.
Kobe Kóobe.
Korea Kánkoku *(South)*; Choosén *(North)*.
Kyoto Kyóoto.
Kyushu Kyúushuu.
London Róndon.
Malaya Maree.
Manila Mánira.
Mexico Mekíshiko.
Moscow Mósukoo.
New York Nyuu Yóoku.
New Zealand Nyuu Jiirándo.
Norway Noruee.
Osaka Oosaka.
Pacific Taihéiyoo.
Pakistan Pakísutan.
Peiping Pékin.
Persia Íran.
Philippines Fuiríppin, Hiríppin.
Poland Poorándo.
Russia Róshiya, Sóren, Sobiétto.
San Francisco San Furanshísuko.
Siberia Shiberiya.
Singapore Shingapóoru.
Southeast Asia Toonan-Ajiya.
Spain Supéin.
Sweden Suéeden.
Switzerland Súisu.
Taipei Taihoku.
Taiwan Taiwán.
Thailand Tái.
Tokyo Tookyoo.
Turkey Tóruko.
United States Gasshúukoku.
 U.S.A Amerika Gasshúukoku, Beikoku.
Washington, D.C. Washínton.